LINUX
DEVICE
DRIVERS

THIRD EDITION

D0701813

Jonathan Corbet, Alessandro
Rubini, and Greg Kroah-Hartman

O'REILLY®

Beijing · Cambridge · Farnham · Köln · Paris · Sebastopol · Taipei · Tokyo

Linux Device Drivers, Third Edition

by Jonathan Corbet, Alessandro Rubini, and Greg Kroah-Hartman

Published by O'Reilly Media, Inc., 1005 Gravenstein Highway North, Sebastopol, CA 95472.

O'Reilly books may be purchased for educational, business, or sales promotional use. Online editions are also available for most titles (*safari.oreilly.com*). For more information, contact our corporate/institutional sales department: (800) 998-9938 or *corporate@oreilly.com*.

Editor:	Andy Oram
Production Editor:	Matt Hutchinson
Production Services:	Octal Publishing, Inc.
Cover Designer:	Edie Freedman
Interior Designer:	Melanie Wang

Printing History:

February 1998:	First Edition.
June 2001:	Second Edition.
February 2005:	Third Edition.

 This book uses RepKover,™ a durable and flexible lay-flat binding.

ISBN: 0-596-00590-3

[M]

LINUX
DEVICE
DRIVERS

Other Linux resources from O'Reilly

Related titles	Understanding the Linux Kernel	Linux Pocket Guide
	Linux in a Nutshell	Building Embedded Linux Systems
	Running Linux	Designing Embedded Hardware
	Linux Network Administrator's Guide	

Linux Books Resource Center

linux.oreilly.com is a complete catalog of O'Reilly's books on Linux and Unix and related technologies, including sample chapters and code examples.

ONLamp.com is the premier site for the open source web platform: Linux, Apache, MySQL, and either Perl, Python, or PHP.

Conferences

O'Reilly brings diverse innovators together to nurture the ideas that spark revolutionary industries. We specialize in documenting the latest tools and systems, translating the innovator's knowledge into useful skills for those in the trenches. Visit *conferences.oreilly.com* for our upcoming events.

Safari Bookshelf (*safari.oreilly.com*) is the premier online reference library for programmers and IT professionals. Conduct searches across more than 1,000 books. Subscribers can zero in on answers to time-critical questions in a matter of seconds. Read the books on your Bookshelf from cover to cover or simply flip to the page you need. Try it today with a free trial.

Table of Contents

Preface

This is, on the surface, a book about writing device drivers for the Linux system. That is a worthy goal, of course; the flow of new hardware products is not likely to slow down anytime soon, and somebody is going to have to make all those new gadgets work with Linux. But this book is also about how the Linux kernel works and how to adapt its workings to your needs or interests. Linux is an open system; with this book, we hope, it is more open and accessible to a larger community of developers.

This is the third edition of *Linux Device Drivers*. The kernel has changed greatly since this book was first published, and we have tried to evolve the text to match. This edition covers the 2.6.10 kernel as completely as we are able. We have, this time around, elected to omit the discussion of backward compatibility with previous kernel versions. The changes from 2.4 are simply too large, and the 2.4 interface remains well documented in the (freely available) second edition.

This edition contains quite a bit of new material relevant to the 2.6 kernel. The discussion of locking and concurrency has been expanded and moved into its own chapter. The Linux device model, which is new in 2.6, is covered in detail. There are new chapters on the USB bus and the serial driver subsystem; the chapter on PCI has also been enhanced. While the organization of the rest of the book resembles that of the earlier editions, every chapter has been thoroughly updated.

We hope you enjoy reading this book as much as we have enjoyed writing it.

Jon's Introduction

The publication of this edition coincides with my twelfth year of working with Linux and, shockingly, my twenty-fifth year in the computing field. Computing seemed like a fast-moving field back in 1980, but things have sped up a lot since then. Keeping *Linux Device Drivers* up to date is increasingly a challenge; the Linux kernel hackers continue to improve their code, and they have little patience for documentation that fails to keep up.

Linux continues to succeed in the market and, more importantly, in the hearts and minds of developers worldwide. The success of Linux is clearly a testament to its technical quality and to the numerous benefits of free software in general. But the true key to its success, in my opinion, lies in the fact that it has brought the fun back to computing. With Linux, anybody can get their hands into the system and play in a sandbox where contributions from any direction are welcome, but where technical excellence is valued above all else. Linux not only provides us with a top-quality operating system; it gives us the opportunity to be part of its future development and to have fun while we're at it.

In my 25 years in the field, I have had many interesting opportunities, from programming the first Cray computers (in Fortran, on punch cards) to seeing the minicomputer and Unix workstation waves, through to the current, microprocessor-dominated era. Never, though, have I seen the field more full of life, opportunity, and fun. Never have we had such control over our own tools and their evolution. Linux, and free software in general, is clearly the driving force behind those changes.

My hope is that this edition helps to bring that fun and opportunity to a new set of Linux developers. Whether your interests are in the kernel or in user space, I hope you find this book to be a useful and interesting guide to just how the kernel works with the hardware. I hope it helps and inspires you to fire up your editor and to make our shared, free operating system even better. Linux has come a long way, but it is also just beginning; it will be more than interesting to watch—and participate in—what happens from here.

Alessandro's Introduction

I've always enjoyed computers because they can talk to external hardware. So, after soldering my devices for the Apple II and the ZX Spectrum, backed with the Unix and free software expertise the university gave me, I could escape the DOS trap by installing GNU/Linux on a fresh new 386 and by turning on the soldering iron once again.

Back then, the community was a small one, and there wasn't much documentation about writing drivers around, so I started writing for Linux Journal. That's how things started: when I later discovered I didn't like writing papers, I left the univeristy and found myself with an O'Reilly contract in my hands.

That was in 1996. Ages ago.

The computing world is different now: free software looks like a viable solution, both technically and politically, but there's a lot of work to do in both realms. I hope this book furthers two aims: spreading technical knowledge and raising awareness about the need to spread knowledge. That's why, after the first edition proved interesting to the public, the two authors of the second edition switched to a free license, supported by our editor and our publisher. I'm betting this is the right approach to information, and it's great to team up with other people sharing this vision.

I'm excited by what I witness in the embedded arena, and I hope this text helps by doing more; but ideas are moving fast these days, and it's already time to plan for the fourth edition, and look for a fourth author to help.

Greg's Introduction

It seems like a long time ago that I picked up the first edition of this *Linux Device Drivers* book in order to figure out how to write a real Linux driver. That first edition was a great guide to helping me understand the internals of this operating system that I had already been using for a number of years but whose kernel had never taken the time to look into. With the knowledge gained from that book, and by reading other programmers' code already present in the kernel, my first horribly buggy, broken, and very SMP-unsafe driver was accepted by the kernel community into the main kernel tree. Despite receiving my first bug report five minutes later, I was hooked on wanting to do as much as I could to make this operating system the best it could possibly be.

I am honored that I've had the ability to contribute to this book. I hope that it enables others to learn the details about the kernel, discover that driver development is not a scary or forbidding place, and possibly encourage others to join in and help in the collective effort of making this operating system work on every computing platform with every type of device available. The development procedure is fun, the community is rewarding, and everyone benefits from the effort involved.

Now it's back to making this edition obsolete by fixing current bugs, changing APIs to work better and be simpler to understand for everyone, and adding new features. Come along; we can always use the help.

Audience for This Book

This book should be an interesting source of information both for people who want to experiment with their computer and for technical programmers who face the need to deal with the inner levels of a Linux box. Note that "a Linux box" is a wider concept than "a PC running Linux," as many platforms are supported by our operating system, and kernel programming is by no means bound to a specific platform. We hope this book is useful as a starting point for people who want to become kernel hackers but don't know where to start.

On the technical side, this text should offer a hands-on approach to understanding the kernel internals and some of the design choices made by the Linux developers. Although the main, official target of the book is teaching how to write device drivers, the material should give an interesting overview of the kernel implementation as well.

Although real hackers can find all the necessary information in the official kernel sources, usually a written text can be helpful in developing programming skills. The text you are approaching is the result of hours of patient grepping through the kernel sources, and we hope the final result is worth the effort it took.

The Linux enthusiast should find in this book enough food for her mind to start playing with the code base and should be able to join the group of developers that is continuously working on new capabilities and performance enhancements. This book does not cover the Linux kernel in its entirety, of course, but Linux device driver authors need to know how to work with many of the kernel's subsystems. Therefore, it makes a good introduction to kernel programming in general. Linux is still a work in progress, and there's always a place for new programmers to jump into the game.

If, on the other hand, you are just trying to write a device driver for your own device, and you don't want to muck with the kernel internals, the text should be modularized enough to fit your needs as well. If you don't want to go deep into the details, you can just skip the most technical sections, and stick to the standard API used by device drivers to seamlessly integrate with the rest of the kernel.

Organization of the Material

The book introduces its topics in ascending order of complexity and is divided into two parts. The first part (Chapters 1–11) begins with the proper setup of kernel modules and goes on to describe the various aspects of programming that you'll need in order to write a full-featured driver for a char-oriented device. Every chapter covers a distinct problem and includes a quick summary at the end, which can be used as a reference during actual development.

Throughout the first part of the book, the organization of the material moves roughly from the software-oriented concepts to the hardware-related ones. This organization is meant to allow you to test the software on your own computer as far as possible without the need to plug external hardware into the machine. Every chapter includes source code and points to sample drivers that you can run on any Linux computer. In Chapters 1 and 1, however, we ask you to connect an inch of wire to the parallel port in order to test out hardware handling, but this requirement should be manageable by everyone.

The second half of the book (Chapters 12–18) describes block drivers and network interfaces and goes deeper into more advanced topics, such as working with the virtual memory subsystem and with the PCI and USB buses. Many driver authors do not need all of this material, but we encourage you to go on reading anyway. Much of the material found there is interesting as a view into how the Linux kernel works, even if you do not need it for a specific project.

Background Information

In order to be able to use this book, you need to be confident with C programming. Some Unix expertise is needed as well, as we often refer to Unix semantics about system calls, commands, and pipelines.

At the hardware level, no previous expertise is required to understand the material in this book, as long as the general concepts are clear in advance. The text isn't based on specific PC hardware, and we provide all the needed information when we do refer to specific hardware.

Several free software tools are needed to build the kernel, and you often need specific versions of these tools. Those that are too old can lack needed features, while those that are too new can occasionally generate broken kernels. Usually, the tools provided with any current distribution work just fine. Tool version requirements vary from one kernel to the next; consult *Documentation/Changes* in the source tree of the kernel you are using for exact requirements.

Online Version and License

The authors have chosen to make this book freely available under the Creative Commons "Attribution-ShareAlike" license, Version 2.0:

http://www.oreilly.com/catalog/linuxdrive3

Conventions Used in This Book

The following is a list of the typographical conventions used in this book:

Italic
> Used for file and directory names, program and command names, command-line options, URLs, and new terms

Constant Width
> Used in examples to show the contents of files or the output from commands, and in the text to indicate words that appear in C code or other literal strings

Constant Width Italic
> Used to indicate text within commands that the user replaces with an actual value

Constant Width Bold
> Used in examples to show commands or other text that should be typed literally by the user

Pay special attention to notes set apart from the text with the following icons:

This is a tip. It contains useful supplementary information about the topic at hand.

This is a warning. It helps you solve and avoid annoying problems.

Using Code Examples

This book is here to help you get your job done. In general, you may use the code in this book in your programs and documentation. The code samples are covered by a dual BSD/GPL license.

We appreciate, but do not require, attribution. An attribution usually includes the title, author, publisher, and ISBN. For example: "*Linux Device Drivers*, Third Edition, by Jonathan Corbet, Alessandro Rubini, and Greg Kroah-Hartman. Copyright 2005 O'Reilly Media, Inc., 0-596-00590-3."

We'd Like to Hear from You

Please address comments and questions concerning this book to the publisher:

O'Reilly Media, Inc.
1005 Gravenstein Highway North
Sebastopol, CA 95472
(800) 998-9938 (in the United States or Canada)
(707) 829-0515 (international or local)
(707) 829-0104 (fax)

We have a web page for this book, where we list errata, examples, and any additional information. You can access this page at:

http://www.oreilly.com/catalog/linuxdrive3

To comment or ask technical questions about this book, send email to:

bookquestions@oreilly.com

For more information about our books, conferences, Resource Centers, and the O'Reilly Network, see our web site at:

http://www.oreilly.com

Safari Enabled

 When you see a Safari® Enabled icon on the cover of your favorite technology book, that means the book is available online through the O'Reilly Network Safari Bookshelf.

Safari offers a solution that's better than e-books. It's a virtual library that lets you easily search thousands of top tech books, cut and paste code samples, download chapters, and find quick answers when you need the most accurate, current information. Try it for free at *http://safari.oreilly.com*.

Acknowledgments

This book, of course, was not written in a vacuum; we would like to thank the many people who have helped to make it possible.

Thanks to our editor, Andy Oram; this book is a vastly better product as a result of his efforts. And obviously we owe a lot to the smart people who have laid the philosophical and practical foundations of the current free software renaissance.

The first edition was technically reviewed by Alan Cox, Greg Hankins, Hans Lermen, Heiko Eissfeldt, and Miguel de Icaza (in alphabetic order by first name). The technical reviewers for the second edition were Allan B. Cruse, Christian Morgner, Jake Edge, Jeff Garzik, Jens Axboe, Jerry Cooperstein, Jerome Peter Lynch, Michael Kerrisk, Paul Kinzelman, and Raph Levien. Reviewers for the third edition were Allan B. Cruse, Christian Morgner, James Bottomley, Jerry Cooperstein, Patrick Mochel, Paul Kinzelman, and Robert Love. Together, these people have put a vast amount of effort into finding problems and pointing out possible improvements to our writing.

Last but certainly not least, we thank the Linux developers for their relentless work. This includes both the kernel programmers and the user-space people, who often get forgotten. In this book, we chose never to call them by name in order to avoid being unfair to someone we might forget. We sometimes made an exception to this rule and called Linus by name; we hope he doesn't mind.

Jon

I must begin by thanking my wife Laura and my children Michele and Giulia for filling my life with joy and patiently putting up with my distraction while working on this edition. The subscribers of LWN.net have, through their generosity, enabled much of this work to happen. The Linux kernel developers have done me a great service by letting me be a part of their community, answering my questions, and setting me straight when I got confused. Thanks are due to readers of the second edition of this book whose comments, offered at Linux gatherings over much of the world, have been gratifying and inspiring. And I would especially like to thank Alessandro Rubini for starting this whole exercise with the first edition (and staying with it through the current edition); and Greg Kroah-Hartman, who has brought his considerable skills to bear on several chapters, with great results.

Alessandro

I would like to thank the people that made this work possible. First of all, the incredible patience of Federica, who went as far as letting me review the first edition during our honeymoon, with a laptop in the tent. I want to thank Giorgio and Giulia, who have been involved in later editions of the book and happily accepted to be sons of "a gnu" who often works late in the night. I owe a lot to all the free-software authors who actually taught me how to program by making their work available for anyone to study. But for this edition, I'm mostly grateful to Jon and Greg, who have been great mates in this work; it couldn't have existed without each and both of them, as the code base is bigger and tougher, while my time is a scarcer resource, always contended for by clients, free software issues, and expired deadlines. Jon has been a great leader for this edition; both have been very productive and technically invaluable in supplementing my small-scale and embedded view toward programming with their expertise about SMP and number crunchers.

Greg

I would like to thank my wife Shannon and my children Madeline and Griffin for their understanding and patience while I took the time to work on this book. If it were not for their support of my original Linux development efforts, I would not be able to do this book at all. Thanks also to Alessandro and Jon for offering to let me work on this book; I am honored that they let me participate in it. Much gratitude is given to all of the Linux kernel programmers, who were unselfish enough to write code in the public view, so that I and others could learn so much from just reading it. Also, for everyone who has ever sent me bug reports, critiqued my code, and flamed me for doing stupid things, you have all taught me so much about how to be a better programmer and, throughout it all, made me feel very welcome to be part of this community. Thank you.

## CHAPTER 1

An Introduction to Device Drivers

One of the many advantages of free operating systems, as typified by Linux, is that their internals are open for all to view. The operating system, once a dark and mysterious area whose code was restricted to a small number of programmers, can now be readily examined, understood, and modified by anybody with the requisite skills. Linux has helped to democratize operating systems. The Linux kernel remains a large and complex body of code, however, and would-be kernel hackers need an entry point where they can approach the code without being overwhelmed by complexity. Often, device drivers provide that gateway.

Device drivers take on a special role in the Linux kernel. They are distinct "black boxes" that make a particular piece of hardware respond to a well-defined internal programming interface; they hide completely the details of how the device works. User activities are performed by means of a set of standardized calls that are independent of the specific driver; mapping those calls to device-specific operations that act on real hardware is then the role of the device driver. This programming interface is such that drivers can be built separately from the rest of the kernel and "plugged in" at runtime when needed. This modularity makes Linux drivers easy to write, to the point that there are now hundreds of them available.

There are a number of reasons to be interested in the writing of Linux device drivers. The rate at which new hardware becomes available (and obsolete!) alone guarantees that driver writers will be busy for the foreseeable future. Individuals may need to know about drivers in order to gain access to a particular device that is of interest to them. Hardware vendors, by making a Linux driver available for their products, can add the large and growing Linux user base to their potential markets. And the open source nature of the Linux system means that if the driver writer wishes, the source to a driver can be quickly disseminated to millions of users.

This book teaches you how to write your own drivers and how to hack around in related parts of the kernel. We have taken a device-independent approach; the programming techniques and interfaces are presented, whenever possible, without being tied to any specific device. Each driver is different; as a driver writer, you need to understand your specific device well. But most of the principles and basic techniques are the same for all drivers. This book cannot teach you about your device, but it gives you a handle on the background you need to make your device work.

As you learn to write drivers, you find out a lot about the Linux kernel in general; this may help you understand how your machine works and why things aren't always as fast as you expect or don't do quite what you want. We introduce new ideas gradually, starting off with very simple drivers and building on them; every new concept is accompanied by sample code that doesn't need special hardware to be tested.

This chapter doesn't actually get into writing code. However, we introduce some background concepts about the Linux kernel that you'll be glad you know later, when we do launch into programming.

The Role of the Device Driver

As a programmer, you are able to make your own choices about your driver, and choose an acceptable trade-off between the programming time required and the flexibility of the result. Though it may appear strange to say that a driver is "flexible," we like this word because it emphasizes that the role of a device driver is providing *mechanism*, not *policy*.

The distinction between mechanism and policy is one of the best ideas behind the Unix design. Most programming problems can indeed be split into two parts: "what capabilities are to be provided" (the mechanism) and "how those capabilities can be used" (the policy). If the two issues are addressed by different parts of the program, or even by different programs altogether, the software package is much easier to develop and to adapt to particular needs.

For example, Unix management of the graphic display is split between the X server, which knows the hardware and offers a unified interface to user programs, and the window and session managers, which implement a particular policy without knowing anything about the hardware. People can use the same window manager on different hardware, and different users can run different configurations on the same workstation. Even completely different desktop environments, such as KDE and GNOME, can coexist on the same system. Another example is the layered structure of TCP/IP networking: the operating system offers the socket abstraction, which implements no policy regarding the data to be transferred, while different servers are in charge of the services (and their associated policies). Moreover, a server like *ftpd* provides the file transfer mechanism, while users can use whatever client they prefer; both command-line and graphic clients exist, and anyone can write a new user interface to transfer files.

Where drivers are concerned, the same separation of mechanism and policy applies. The floppy driver is policy free—its role is only to show the diskette as a continuous array of data blocks. Higher levels of the system provide policies, such as who may access the floppy drive, whether the drive is accessed directly or via a filesystem, and whether users may mount filesystems on the drive. Since different environments usually need to use hardware in different ways, it's important to be as policy free as possible.

When writing drivers, a programmer should pay particular attention to this fundamental concept: write kernel code to access the hardware, but don't force particular policies on the user, since different users have different needs. The driver should deal with making the hardware available, leaving all the issues about *how* to use the hardware to the applications. A driver, then, is flexible if it offers access to the hardware capabilities without adding constraints. Sometimes, however, some policy decisions must be made. For example, a digital I/O driver may only offer byte-wide access to the hardware in order to avoid the extra code needed to handle individual bits.

You can also look at your driver from a different perspective: it is a software layer that lies between the applications and the actual device. This privileged role of the driver allows the driver programmer to choose exactly how the device should appear: different drivers can offer different capabilities, even for the same device. The actual driver design should be a balance between many different considerations. For instance, a single device may be used concurrently by different programs, and the driver programmer has complete freedom to determine how to handle concurrency. You could implement memory mapping on the device independently of its hardware capabilities, or you could provide a user library to help application programmers implement new policies on top of the available primitives, and so forth. One major consideration is the trade-off between the desire to present the user with as many options as possible and the time you have to write the driver, as well as the need to keep things simple so that errors don't creep in.

Policy-free drivers have a number of typical characteristics. These include support for both synchronous and asynchronous operation, the ability to be opened multiple times, the ability to exploit the full capabilities of the hardware, and the lack of software layers to "simplify things" or provide policy-related operations. Drivers of this sort not only work better for their end users, but also turn out to be easier to write and maintain as well. Being policy-free is actually a common target for software designers.

Many device drivers, indeed, are released together with user programs to help with configuration and access to the target device. Those programs can range from simple utilities to complete graphical applications. Examples include the *tunelp* program, which adjusts how the parallel port printer driver operates, and the graphical *cardctl* utility that is part of the PCMCIA driver package. Often a client library is provided as well, which provides capabilities that do not need to be implemented as part of the driver itself.

The scope of this book is the kernel, so we try not to deal with policy issues or with application programs or support libraries. Sometimes we talk about different policies and how to support them, but we won't go into much detail about programs using the device or the policies they enforce. You should understand, however, that user programs are an integral part of a software package and that even policy-free packages are distributed with configuration files that apply a default behavior to the underlying mechanisms.

Splitting the Kernel

In a Unix system, several concurrent *processes* attend to different tasks. Each process asks for system resources, be it computing power, memory, network connectivity, or some other resource. The *kernel* is the big chunk of executable code in charge of handling all such requests. Although the distinction between the different kernel tasks isn't always clearly marked, the kernel's role can be split (as shown in Figure 1-1) into the following parts:

Process management
> The kernel is in charge of creating and destroying processes and handling their connection to the outside world (input and output). Communication among different processes (through signals, pipes, or interprocess communication primitives) is basic to the overall system functionality and is also handled by the kernel. In addition, the scheduler, which controls how processes share the CPU, is part of process management. More generally, the kernel's process management activity implements the abstraction of several processes on top of a single CPU or a few of them.

Memory management
> The computer's memory is a major resource, and the policy used to deal with it is a critical one for system performance. The kernel builds up a virtual addressing space for any and all processes on top of the limited available resources. The different parts of the kernel interact with the memory-management subsystem through a set of function calls, ranging from the simple *malloc/free* pair to much more complex functionalities.

Filesystems
> Unix is heavily based on the filesystem concept; almost everything in Unix can be treated as a file. The kernel builds a structured filesystem on top of unstructured hardware, and the resulting file abstraction is heavily used throughout the whole system. In addition, Linux supports multiple filesystem types, that is, different ways of organizing data on the physical medium. For example, disks may be formatted with the Linux-standard ext3 filesystem, the commonly used FAT filesystem or several others.

Device control

Almost every system operation eventually maps to a physical device. With the exception of the processor, memory, and a very few other entities, any and all device control operations are performed by code that is specific to the device being addressed. That code is called a *device driver*. The kernel must have embedded in it a device driver for every peripheral present on a system, from the hard drive to the keyboard and the tape drive. This aspect of the kernel's functions is our primary interest in this book.

Networking

Networking must be managed by the operating system, because most network operations are not specific to a process: incoming packets are asynchronous events. The packets must be collected, identified, and dispatched before a process takes care of them. The system is in charge of delivering data packets across program and network interfaces, and it must control the execution of programs according to their network activity. Additionally, all the routing and address resolution issues are implemented within the kernel.

Loadable Modules

One of the good features of Linux is the ability to extend at runtime the set of features offered by the kernel. This means that you can add functionality to the kernel (and remove functionality as well) while the system is up and running.

Each piece of code that can be added to the kernel at runtime is called a *module*. The Linux kernel offers support for quite a few different types (or classes) of modules, including, but not limited to, device drivers. Each module is made up of object code (not linked into a complete executable) that can be dynamically linked to the running kernel by the *insmod* program and can be unlinked by the *rmmod* program.

Figure 1-1 identifies different classes of modules in charge of specific tasks—a module is said to belong to a specific class according to the functionality it offers. The placement of modules in Figure 1-1 covers the most important classes, but is far from complete because more and more functionality in Linux is being modularized.

Classes of Devices and Modules

The Linux way of looking at devices distinguishes between three fundamental device types. Each module usually implements one of these types, and thus is classifiable as a *char module*, a *block module*, or a *network module*. This division of modules into different types, or classes, is not a rigid one; the programmer can choose to build huge modules implementing different drivers in a single chunk of code. Good programmers, nonetheless, usually create a different module for each new functionality they implement, because decomposition is a key element of scalability and extendability.

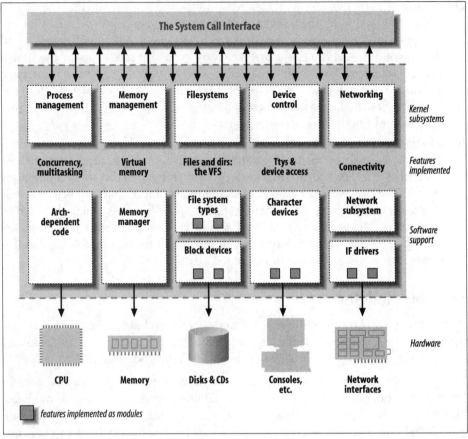

Figure 1-1. *A split view of the kernel*

The three classes are:

Character devices

A character (char) device is one that can be accessed as a stream of bytes (like a file); a char driver is in charge of implementing this behavior. Such a driver usually implements at least the *open*, *close*, *read*, and *write* system calls. The text console (*/dev/console*) and the serial ports (*/dev/ttyS0* and friends) are examples of char devices, as they are well represented by the stream abstraction. Char devices are accessed by means of filesystem nodes, such as */dev/tty1* and */dev/lp0*. The only relevant difference between a char device and a regular file is that you can always move back and forth in the regular file, whereas most char devices are just data channels, which you can only access sequentially. There exist, nonetheless, char devices that look like data areas, and you can move back and forth in them; for instance, this usually applies to frame grabbers, where the applications can access the whole acquired image using *mmap* or *lseek*.

Block devices

> Like char devices, block devices are accessed by filesystem nodes in the */dev* directory. A block device is a device (e.g., a disk) that can host a filesystem. In most Unix systems, a block device can only handle I/O operations that transfer one or more whole blocks, which are usually 512 bytes (or a larger power of two) bytes in length. Linux, instead, allows the application to read and write a block device like a char device—it permits the transfer of any number of bytes at a time. As a result, block and char devices differ only in the way data is managed internally by the kernel, and thus in the kernel/driver software interface. Like a char device, each block device is accessed through a filesystem node, and the difference between them is transparent to the user. Block drivers have a completely different interface to the kernel than char drivers.

Network interfaces

> Any network transaction is made through an interface, that is, a device that is able to exchange data with other hosts. Usually, an *interface* is a hardware device, but it might also be a pure software device, like the loopback interface. A network interface is in charge of sending and receiving data packets, driven by the network subsystem of the kernel, without knowing how individual transactions map to the actual packets being transmitted. Many network connections (especially those using TCP) are stream-oriented, but network devices are, usually, designed around the transmission and receipt of packets. A network driver knows nothing about individual connections; it only handles packets.

> Not being a stream-oriented device, a network interface isn't easily mapped to a node in the filesystem, as */dev/tty1* is. The Unix way to provide access to interfaces is still by assigning a unique name to them (such as eth0), but that name doesn't have a corresponding entry in the filesystem. Communication between the kernel and a network device driver is completely different from that used with char and block drivers. Instead of *read* and *write*, the kernel calls functions related to packet transmission.

There are other ways of classifying driver modules that are orthogonal to the above device types. In general, some types of drivers work with additional layers of kernel support functions for a given type of device. For example, one can talk of universal serial bus (USB) modules, serial modules, SCSI modules, and so on. Every USB device is driven by a USB module that works with the USB subsystem, but the device itself shows up in the system as a char device (a USB serial port, say), a block device (a USB memory card reader), or a network device (a USB Ethernet interface).

Other classes of device drivers have been added to the kernel in recent times, including FireWire drivers and I2O drivers. In the same way that they handled USB and SCSI drivers, kernel developers collected class-wide features and exported them to driver implementers to avoid duplicating work and bugs, thus simplifying and strengthening the process of writing such drivers.

In addition to device drivers, other functionalities, both hardware and software, are modularized in the kernel. One common example is filesystems. A filesystem type determines how information is organized on a block device in order to represent a tree of directories and files. Such an entity is not a device driver, in that there's no explicit device associated with the way the information is laid down; the filesystem type is instead a software driver, because it maps the low-level data structures to high-level data structures. It is the filesystem that determines how long a filename can be and what information about each file is stored in a directory entry. The file-system module must implement the lowest level of the system calls that access directories and files, by mapping filenames and paths (as well as other information, such as access modes) to data structures stored in data blocks. Such an interface is completely independent of the actual data transfer to and from the disk (or other medium), which is accomplished by a block device driver.

If you think of how strongly a Unix system depends on the underlying filesystem, you'll realize that such a software concept is vital to system operation. The ability to decode filesystem information stays at the lowest level of the kernel hierarchy and is of utmost importance; even if you write a block driver for your new CD-ROM, it is useless if you are not able to run *ls* or *cp* on the data it hosts. Linux supports the concept of a filesystem module, whose software interface declares the different operations that can be performed on a filesystem inode, directory, file, and superblock. It's quite unusual for a programmer to actually need to write a filesystem module, because the official kernel already includes code for the most important filesystem types.

Security Issues

Security is an increasingly important concern in modern times. We will discuss security-related issues as they come up throughout the book. There are a few general concepts, however, that are worth mentioning now.

Any security check in the system is enforced by kernel code. If the kernel has security holes, then the system as a whole has holes. In the official kernel distribution, only an authorized user can load modules; the system call *init_module* checks if the invoking process is authorized to load a module into the kernel. Thus, when running an official kernel, only the superuser,* or an intruder who has succeeded in becoming privileged, can exploit the power of privileged code.

When possible, driver writers should avoid encoding security policy in their code. Security is a policy issue that is often best handled at higher levels within the kernel, under the control of the system administrator. There are always exceptions, however.

---

* Technically, only somebody with the CAP_SYS_MODULE capability can perform this operation. We discuss capabilities in Chapter 6.

As a device driver writer, you should be aware of situations in which some types of device access could adversely affect the system as a whole and should provide adequate controls. For example, device operations that affect global resources (such as setting an interrupt line), which could damage the hardware (loading firmware, for example), or that could affect other users (such as setting a default block size on a tape drive), are usually only available to sufficiently privileged users, and this check must be made in the driver itself.

Driver writers must also be careful, of course, to avoid introducing security bugs. The C programming language makes it easy to make several types of errors. Many current security problems are created, for example, by *buffer overrun* errors, in which the programmer forgets to check how much data is written to a buffer, and data ends up written beyond the end of the buffer, thus overwriting unrelated data. Such errors can compromise the entire system and must be avoided. Fortunately, avoiding these errors is usually relatively easy in the device driver context, in which the interface to the user is narrowly defined and highly controlled.

Some other general security ideas are worth keeping in mind. Any input received from user processes should be treated with great suspicion; never trust it unless you can verify it. Be careful with uninitialized memory; any memory obtained from the kernel should be zeroed or otherwise initialized before being made available to a user process or device. Otherwise, information leakage (disclosure of data, passwords, etc.) could result. If your device interprets data sent to it, be sure the user cannot send anything that could compromise the system. Finally, think about the possible effect of device operations; if there are specific operations (e.g., reloading the firmware on an adapter board or formatting a disk) that could affect the system, those operations should almost certainly be restricted to privileged users.

Be careful, also, when receiving software from third parties, especially when the kernel is concerned: because everybody has access to the source code, everybody can break and recompile things. Although you can usually trust precompiled kernels found in your distribution, you should avoid running kernels compiled by an untrusted friend—if you wouldn't run a precompiled binary as root, then you'd better not run a precompiled kernel. For example, a maliciously modified kernel could allow anyone to load a module, thus opening an unexpected back door via *init_module*.

Note that the Linux kernel can be compiled to have no module support whatsoever, thus closing any module-related security holes. In this case, of course, all needed drivers must be built directly into the kernel itself. It is also possible, with 2.2 and later kernels, to disable the loading of kernel modules after system boot via the capability mechanism.

Version Numbering

Before digging into programming, we should comment on the version numbering scheme used in Linux and which versions are covered by this book.

First of all, note that *every* software package used in a Linux system has its own release number, and there are often interdependencies across them: you need a particular version of one package to run a particular version of another package. The creators of Linux distributions usually handle the messy problem of matching packages, and the user who installs from a prepackaged distribution doesn't need to deal with version numbers. Those who replace and upgrade system software, on the other hand, are on their own in this regard. Fortunately, almost all modern distributions support the upgrade of single packages by checking interpackage dependencies; the distribution's package manager generally does not allow an upgrade until the dependencies are satisfied.

To run the examples we introduce during the discussion, you won't need particular versions of any tool beyond what the 2.6 kernel requires; any recent Linux distribution can be used to run our examples. We won't detail specific requirements, because the file *Documentation/Changes* in your kernel sources is the best source of such information if you experience any problems.

As far as the kernel is concerned, the even-numbered kernel versions (i.e., 2.6.*x*) are the stable ones that are intended for general distribution. The odd versions (such as 2.7.*x*), on the contrary, are development snapshots and are quite ephemeral; the latest of them represents the current status of development, but becomes obsolete in a few days or so.

This book covers Version 2.6 of the kernel. Our focus has been to show all the features available to device driver writers in 2.6.10, the current version at the time we are writing. This edition of the book does not cover prior versions of the kernel. For those of you who are interested, the second edition covered Versions 2.0 through 2.4 in detail. That edition is still available online at *http://lwn.net/Kernel/LDD2/*.

Kernel programmers should be aware that the development process changed with 2.6. The 2.6 series is now accepting changes that previously would have been considered too large for a "stable" kernel. Among other things, that means that internal kernel programming interfaces can change, thus potentially obsoleting parts of this book; for this reason, the sample code accompanying the text is known to work with 2.6.10, but some modules don't compile under earlier versions. Programmers wanting to keep up with kernel programming changes are encouraged to join the mailing lists and to make use of the web sites listed in the bibliography. There is also a web page maintained at *http://lwn.net/Articles/2.6-kernel-api/*, which contains information about API changes that have happened since this book was published.

This text doesn't talk specifically about odd-numbered kernel versions. General users never have a reason to run development kernels. Developers experimenting with new features, however, want to be running the latest development release. They usually keep upgrading to the most recent version to pick up bug fixes and new implementations of features. Note, however, that there's no guarantee on experimental kernels,* and nobody helps you if you have problems due to a bug in a noncurrent odd-numbered kernel. Those who run odd-numbered versions of the kernel are usually skilled enough to dig in the code without the need for a textbook, which is another reason why we don't talk about development kernels here.

Another feature of Linux is that it is a platform-independent operating system, not just "a Unix clone for PC clones" anymore: it currently supports some 20 architectures. This book is platform independent as far as possible, and all the code samples have been tested on at least the x86 and x86-64 platforms. Because the code has been tested on both 32-bit and 64-bit processors, it should compile and run on all other platforms. As you might expect, the code samples that rely on particular hardware don't work on all the supported platforms, but this is always stated in the source code.

License Terms

Linux is licensed under Version 2 of the GNU General Public License (GPL), a document devised for the GNU project by the Free Software Foundation. The GPL allows anybody to redistribute, and even sell, a product covered by the GPL, as long as the recipient has access to the source and is able to exercise the same rights. Additionally, any software product derived from a product covered by the GPL must, if it is redistributed at all, be released under the GPL.

The main goal of such a license is to allow the growth of knowledge by permitting everybody to modify programs at will; at the same time, people selling software to the public can still do their job. Despite this simple objective, there's a never-ending discussion about the GPL and its use. If you want to read the license, you can find it in several places in your system, including the top directory of your kernel source tree in the *COPYING* file.

Vendors often ask whether they can distribute kernel modules in binary form only. The answer to that question has been deliberately left ambiguous. Distribution of binary modules—as long as they adhere to the published kernel interface—has been tolerated so far. But the copyrights on the kernel are held by many developers, and not all of them agree that kernel modules are not derived products. If you or your employer wish to distribute kernel modules under a nonfree license, you really need

---

* Note that there's no guarantee on even-numbered kernels as well, unless you rely on a commercial provider that grants its own warranty.

to discuss the situation with your legal counsel. Please note also that the kernel developers have no qualms against breaking binary modules between kernel releases, even in the middle of a stable kernel series. If it is at all possible, both you and your users are better off if you release your module as free software.

If you want your code to go into the mainline kernel, or if your code requires patches to the kernel, you *must* use a GPL-compatible license as soon as you release the code. Although personal use of your changes doesn't force the GPL on you, if you distribute your code, you must include the source code in the distribution—people acquiring your package must be allowed to rebuild the binary at will.

As far as this book is concerned, most of the code is freely redistributable, either in source or binary form, and neither we nor O'Reilly retain any right on any derived works. All the programs are available at *ftp://ftp.ora.com/pub/examples/linux/drivers/*, and the exact license terms are stated in the *LICENSE* file in the same directory.

Joining the Kernel Development Community

As you begin writing modules for the Linux kernel, you become part of a larger community of developers. Within that community, you can find not only people engaged in similar work, but also a group of highly committed engineers working toward making Linux a better system. These people can be a source of help, ideas, and critical review as well—they will be the first people you will likely turn to when you are looking for testers for a new driver.

The central gathering point for Linux kernel developers is the *linux-kernel* mailing list. All major kernel developers, from Linus Torvalds on down, subscribe to this list. Please note that the list is not for the faint of heart: traffic as of this writing can run up to 200 messages per day or more. Nonetheless, following this list is essential for those who are interested in kernel development; it also can be a top-quality resource for those in need of kernel development help.

To join the linux-kernel list, follow the instructions found in the linux-kernel mailing list FAQ: *http://www.tux.org/lkml*. Read the rest of the FAQ while you are at it; there is a great deal of useful information there. Linux kernel developers are busy people, and they are much more inclined to help people who have clearly done their homework first.

Overview of the Book

From here on, we enter the world of kernel programming. Chapter 2 introduces modularization, explaining the secrets of the art and showing the code for running modules. Chapter 3 talks about char drivers and shows the complete code for a memory-based device driver that can be read and written for fun. Using memory as the hardware base for the device allows anyone to run the sample code without the need to acquire special hardware.

Debugging techniques are vital tools for the programmer and are introduced in Chapter 4. Equally important for those who would hack on contemporary kernels is the management of concurrency and race conditions. Chapter 5 concerns itself with the problems posed by concurrent access to resources and introduces the Linux mechanisms for controlling concurrency.

With debugging and concurrency management skills in place, we move to advanced features of char drivers, such as blocking operations, the use of *select*, and the important *ioctl* call; these topics are the subject of Chapter 6.

Before dealing with hardware management, we dissect a few more of the kernel's software interfaces: Chapter 7 shows how time is managed in the kernel, and Chapter 8 explains memory allocation.

Next we focus on hardware. Chapter 9 describes the management of I/O ports and memory buffers that live on the device; after that comes interrupt handling, in Chapter 10. Unfortunately, not everyone is able to run the sample code for these chapters, because some hardware support *is* actually needed to test the software interface interrupts. We've tried our best to keep required hardware support to a minimum, but you still need some simple hardware, such as a standard parallel port, to work with the sample code for these chapters.

Chapter 11 covers the use of data types in the kernel and the writing of portable code.

The second half of the book is dedicated to more advanced topics. We start by getting deeper into the hardware and, in particular, the functioning of specific peripheral buses. Chapter 12 covers the details of writing drivers for PCI devices, and Chapter 13 examines the API for working with USB devices.

With an understanding of peripheral buses in place, we can take a detailed look at the Linux device model, which is the abstraction layer used by the kernel to describe the hardware and software resources it is managing. Chapter 14 is a bottom-up look at the device model infrastructure, starting with the kobject type and working up from there. It covers the integration of the device model with real hardware; it then uses that knowledge to cover topics like hot-pluggable devices and power management.

In Chapter 15, we take a diversion into Linux memory management. This chapter shows how to map kernel memory into user space (the *mmap* system call), map user memory into kernel space (with *get_user_pages*), and how to map either kind of memory into device space (to perform direct memory access [DMA] operations).

Our understanding of memory will be useful for the following two chapters, which cover the other major driver classes. Chapter 16 introduces block drivers and shows how they are different from the char drivers we have worked with so far. Then Chapter 17 gets into the writing of network drivers. We finish up with a discussion of serial drivers (Chapter 18) and a bibliography.

## CHAPTER 2

Building and Running Modules

It's almost time to begin programming. This chapter introduces all the essential concepts about modules and kernel programming. In these few pages, we build and run a complete (if relatively useless) module, and look at some of the basic code shared by all modules. Developing such expertise is an essential foundation for any kind of modularized driver. To avoid throwing in too many concepts at once, this chapter talks only about modules, without referring to any specific device class.

All the kernel items (functions, variables, header files, and macros) that are introduced here are described in a reference section at the end of the chapter.

Setting Up Your Test System

Starting with this chapter, we present example modules to demonstrate programming concepts. (All of these examples are available on O'Reilly's FTP site, as explained in Chapter 1.) Building, loading, and modifying these examples are a good way to improve your understanding of how drivers work and interact with the kernel.

The example modules should work with almost any 2.6.x kernel, including those provided by distribution vendors. However, we recommend that you obtain a "mainline" kernel directly from the *kernel.org* mirror network, and install it on your system. Vendor kernels can be heavily patched and divergent from the mainline; at times, vendor patches can change the kernel API as seen by device drivers. If you are writing a driver that must work on a particular distribution, you will certainly want to build and test against the relevant kernels. But, for the purpose of learning about driver writing, a standard kernel is best.

Regardless of the origin of your kernel, building modules for 2.6.x requires that you have a configured and built kernel tree on your system. This requirement is a change from previous versions of the kernel, where a current set of header files was sufficient. 2.6 modules are linked against object files found in the kernel source tree; the result is a more robust module loader, but also the requirement that those object files be available. So your first order of business is to come up with a kernel source tree (either from the *kernel.org* network or your distributor's kernel source package), build a new kernel, and install it on your system. For reasons we'll see later, life is generally easiest if you are actually running the target kernel when you build your modules, though this is not required.

 You should also give some thought to where you do your module experimentation, development, and testing. We have done our best to make our example modules safe and correct, but the possibility of bugs is always present. Faults in kernel code can bring about the demise of a user process or, occasionally, the entire system. They do not normally create more serious problems, such as disk corruption. Nonetheless, it is advisable to do your kernel experimentation on a system that does not contain data that you cannot afford to lose, and that does not perform essential services. Kernel hackers typically keep a "sacrificial" system around for the purpose of testing new code.

So, if you do not yet have a suitable system with a configured and built kernel source tree on disk, now would be a good time to set that up. We'll wait. Once that task is taken care of, you'll be ready to start playing with kernel modules.

The Hello World Module

Many programming books begin with a "hello world" example as a way of showing the simplest possible program. This book deals in kernel modules rather than programs; so, for the impatient reader, the following code is a complete "hello world" module:

```
#include <linux/init.h>
#include <linux/module.h>
MODULE_LICENSE("Dual BSD/GPL");

static int hello_init(void)
{
    printk(KERN_ALERT "Hello, world\n");
    return 0;
}

static void hello_exit(void)
{
    printk(KERN_ALERT "Goodbye, cruel world\n");
}

module_init(hello_init);
module_exit(hello_exit);
```

This module defines two functions, one to be invoked when the module is loaded into the kernel (*hello_init*) and one for when the module is removed (*hello_exit*). The *module_init* and *module_exit* lines use special kernel macros to indicate the role of these two functions. Another special macro (*MODULE_LICENSE*) is used to tell the kernel that this module bears a free license; without such a declaration, the kernel complains when the module is loaded.

The *printk* function is defined in the Linux kernel and made available to modules; it behaves similarly to the standard C library function *printf*. The kernel needs its own printing function because it runs by itself, without the help of the C library. The module can call *printk* because, after *insmod* has loaded it, the module is linked to the kernel and can access the kernel's public symbols (functions and variables, as detailed in the next section). The string KERN_ALERT is the priority of the message.* We've specified a high priority in this module, because a message with the default priority might not show up anywhere useful, depending on the kernel version you are running, the version of the *klogd* daemon, and your configuration. You can ignore this issue for now; we explain it in Chapter 4.

You can test the module with the *insmod* and *rmmod* utilities, as shown below. Note that only the superuser can load and unload a module.

```
% make
make[1]: Entering directory `/usr/src/linux-2.6.10'
  CC [M]  /home/ldd3/src/misc-modules/hello.o
  Building modules, stage 2.
  MODPOST
  CC       /home/ldd3/src/misc-modules/hello.mod.o
  LD [M]   /home/ldd3/src/misc-modules/hello.ko
make[1]: Leaving directory `/usr/src/linux-2.6.10'
% su
root# insmod ./hello.ko
Hello, world
root# rmmod hello
Goodbye cruel world
root#
```

Please note once again that, for the above sequence of commands to work, you must have a properly configured and built kernel tree in a place where the makefile is able to find it (*/usr/src/linux-2.6.10* in the example shown). We get into the details of how modules are built in the section "Compiling and Loading."

According to the mechanism your system uses to deliver the message lines, your output may be different. In particular, the previous screen dump was taken from a text console; if you are running *insmod* and *rmmod* from a terminal emulator running under the window system, you won't see anything on your screen. The message goes to one of the system log files, such as */var/log/messages* (the name of the actual file

---

* The priority is just a string, such as <1>, which is prepended to the *printk* format string. Note the lack of a comma after KERN_ALERT; adding a comma there is a common and annoying typo (which, fortunately, is caught by the compiler).

varies between Linux distributions). The mechanism used to deliver kernel messages is described in Chapter 4.

As you can see, writing a module is not as difficult as you might expect—at least, as long as the module is not required to do anything worthwhile. The hard part is understanding your device and how to maximize performance. We go deeper into modularization throughout this chapter and leave device-specific issues for later chapters.

Kernel Modules Versus Applications

Before we go further, it's worth underlining the various differences between a kernel module and an application.

While most small and medium-sized applications perform a single task from beginning to end, every kernel module just registers itself in order to serve future requests, and its initialization function terminates immediately. In other words, the task of the module's initialization function is to prepare for later invocation of the module's functions; it's as though the module were saying, "Here I am, and this is what I can do." The module's exit function (*hello_exit* in the example) gets invoked just before the module is unloaded. It should tell the kernel, "I'm not there anymore; don't ask me to do anything else." This kind of approach to programming is similar to event-driven programming, but while not all applications are event-driven, each and every kernel module is. Another major difference between event-driven applications and kernel code is in the exit function: whereas an application that terminates can be lazy in releasing resources or avoids clean up altogether, the exit function of a module must carefully undo everything the *init* function built up, or the pieces remain around until the system is rebooted.

Incidentally, the ability to unload a module is one of the features of modularization that you'll most appreciate, because it helps cut down development time; you can test successive versions of your new driver without going through the lengthy shutdown/reboot cycle each time.

As a programmer, you know that an application can call functions it doesn't define: the linking stage resolves external references using the appropriate library of functions. *printf* is one of those callable functions and is defined in *libc*. A module, on the other hand, is linked only to the kernel, and the only functions it can call are the ones exported by the kernel; there are no libraries to link to. The *printk* function used in *hello.c* earlier, for example, is the version of *printf* defined within the kernel and exported to modules. It behaves similarly to the original function, with a few minor differences, the main one being lack of floating-point support.

Figure 2-1 shows how function calls and function pointers are used in a module to add new functionality to a running kernel.

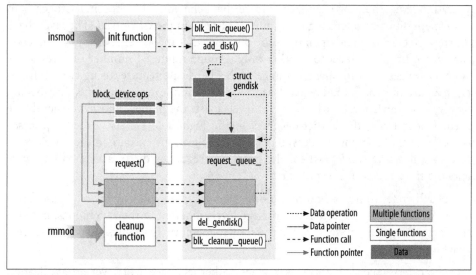

Figure 2-1. Linking a module to the kernel

Because no library is linked to modules, source files should never include the usual header files, *<stdarg.h>* and very special situations being the only exceptions. Only functions that are actually part of the kernel itself may be used in kernel modules. Anything related to the kernel is declared in headers found in the kernel source tree you have set up and configured; most of the relevant headers live in *include/linux* and *include/asm*, but other subdirectories of *include* have been added to host material associated to specific kernel subsystems.

The role of individual kernel headers is introduced throughout the book as each of them is needed.

Another important difference between kernel programming and application programming is in how each environment handles faults: whereas a segmentation fault is harmless during application development and a debugger can always be used to trace the error to the problem in the source code, a kernel fault kills the current process at least, if not the whole system. We see how to trace kernel errors in Chapter 4.

User Space and Kernel Space

A module runs in *kernel space*, whereas applications run in *user space*. This concept is at the base of operating systems theory.

The role of the operating system, in practice, is to provide programs with a consistent view of the computer's hardware. In addition, the operating system must account for independent operation of programs and protection against unauthorized access to resources. This nontrivial task is possible only if the CPU enforces protection of system software from the applications.

Every modern processor is able to enforce this behavior. The chosen approach is to implement different operating modalities (or levels) in the CPU itself. The levels have different roles, and some operations are disallowed at the lower levels; program code can switch from one level to another only through a limited number of gates. Unix systems are designed to take advantage of this hardware feature, using two such levels. All current processors have at least two protection levels, and some, like the x86 family, have more levels; when several levels exist, the highest and lowest levels are used. Under Unix, the kernel executes in the highest level (also called *supervisor mode*), where everything is allowed, whereas applications execute in the lowest level (the so-called *user mode*), where the processor regulates direct access to hardware and unauthorized access to memory.

We usually refer to the execution modes as *kernel space* and *user space*. These terms encompass not only the different privilege levels inherent in the two modes, but also the fact that each mode can have its own memory mapping—its own address space—as well.

Unix transfers execution from user space to kernel space whenever an application issues a system call or is suspended by a hardware interrupt. Kernel code executing a system call is working in the context of a process—it operates on behalf of the calling process and is able to access data in the process's address space. Code that handles interrupts, on the other hand, is asynchronous with respect to processes and is not related to any particular process.

The role of a module is to extend kernel functionality; modularized code runs in kernel space. Usually a driver performs both the tasks outlined previously: some functions in the module are executed as part of system calls, and some are in charge of interrupt handling.

Concurrency in the Kernel

One way in which kernel programming differs greatly from conventional application programming is the issue of concurrency. Most applications, with the notable exception of multithreading applications, typically run sequentially, from the beginning to the end, without any need to worry about what else might be happening to change their environment. Kernel code does not run in such a simple world, and even the simplest kernel modules must be written with the idea that many things can be happening at once.

There are a few sources of concurrency in kernel programming. Naturally, Linux systems run multiple processes, more than one of which can be trying to use your driver at the same time. Most devices are capable of interrupting the processor; interrupt handlers run asynchronously and can be invoked at the same time that your driver is trying to do something else. Several software abstractions (such as kernel timers, introduced in Chapter 7) run asynchronously as well. Moreover, of course, Linux can run on symmetric multiprocessor (SMP) systems, with the result that your driver could be executing concurrently on more than one CPU. Finally, in 2.6, kernel code has been made preemptible; this change causes even uniprocessor systems to have many of the same concurrency issues as multiprocessor systems.

As a result, Linux kernel code, including driver code, must be *reentrant*—it must be capable of running in more than one context at the same time. Data structures must be carefully designed to keep multiple threads of execution separate, and the code must take care to access shared data in ways that prevent corruption of the data. Writing code that handles concurrency and avoids race conditions (situations in which an unfortunate order of execution causes undesirable behavior) requires thought and can be tricky. Proper management of concurrency is required to write correct kernel code; for that reason, every sample driver in this book has been written with concurrency in mind. The techniques used are explained as we come to them; Chapter 5 has also been dedicated to this issue and the kernel primitives available for concurrency management.

A common mistake made by driver programmers is to assume that concurrency is not a problem as long as a particular segment of code does not go to sleep (or "block"). Even in previous kernels (which were not preemptive), this assumption was not valid on multiprocessor systems. In 2.6, kernel code can (almost) never assume that it can hold the processor over a given stretch of code. If you do not write your code with concurrency in mind, it will be subject to catastrophic failures that can be exceedingly difficult to debug.

The Current Process

Although kernel modules don't execute sequentially as applications do, most actions performed by the kernel are done on behalf of a specific process. Kernel code can refer to the current process by accessing the global item current, defined in *<asm/ current.h>*, which yields a pointer to struct task_struct, defined by *<linux/sched.h>*. The current pointer refers to the process that is currently executing. During the execution of a system call, such as *open* or *read*, the current process is the one that invoked the call. Kernel code can use process-specific information by using current, if it needs to do so. An example of this technique is presented in Chapter 6.

Actually, current is not truly a global variable. The need to support SMP systems forced the kernel developers to develop a mechanism that finds the current process on the relevant CPU. This mechanism must also be fast, since references to current happen frequently. The result is an architecture-dependent mechanism that, usually, hides a pointer to the task_struct structure on the kernel stack. The details of the implementation remain hidden to other kernel subsystems though, and a device driver can just include *<linux/sched.h>* and refer to the current process. For example, the following statement prints the process ID and the command name of the current process by accessing certain fields in struct `task_struct`:

```
printk(KERN_INFO "The process is \"%s\" (pid %i)\n",
        current->comm, current->pid);
```

The command name stored in `current->comm` is the base name of the program file (trimmed to 15 characters if need be) that is being executed by the current process.

A Few Other Details

Kernel programming differs from user-space programming in many ways. We'll point things out as we get to them over the course of the book, but there are a few fundamental issues which, while not warranting a section of their own, are worth a mention. So, as you dig into the kernel, the following issues should be kept in mind.

Applications are laid out in virtual memory with a very large stack area. The stack, of course, is used to hold the function call history and all automatic variables created by currently active functions. The kernel, instead, has a very small stack; it can be as small as a single, 4096-byte page. Your functions must share that stack with the entire kernel-space call chain. Thus, it is never a good idea to declare large automatic variables; if you need larger structures, you should allocate them dynamically at call time.

Often, as you look at the kernel API, you will encounter function names starting with a double underscore (_). Functions so marked are generally a low-level component of the interface and should be used with caution. Essentially, the double underscore says to the programmer: "If you call this function, be sure you know what you are doing."

Kernel code cannot do floating point arithmetic. Enabling floating point would require that the kernel save and restore the floating point processor's state on each entry to, and exit from, kernel space—at least, on some architectures. Given that there really is no need for floating point in kernel code, the extra overhead is not worthwhile.

Compiling and Loading

The "hello world" example at the beginning of this chapter included a brief demonstration of building a module and loading it into the system. There is, of course, a lot more to that whole process than we have seen so far. This section provides more detail on how a module author turns source code into an executing subsystem within the kernel.

Compiling Modules

As the first step, we need to look a bit at how modules must be built. The build process for modules differs significantly from that used for user-space applications; the kernel is a large, standalone program with detailed and explicit requirements on how its pieces are put together. The build process also differs from how things were done with previous versions of the kernel; the new build system is simpler to use and produces more correct results, but it looks very different from what came before. The kernel build system is a complex beast, and we just look at a tiny piece of it. The files found in the *Documentation/kbuild* directory in the kernel source are required reading for anybody wanting to understand all that is really going on beneath the surface.

There are some prerequisites that you must get out of the way before you can build kernel modules. The first is to ensure that you have sufficiently current versions of the compiler, module utilities, and other necessary tools. The file *Documentation/Changes* in the kernel documentation directory always lists the required tool versions; you should consult it before going any further. Trying to build a kernel (and its modules) with the wrong tool versions can lead to no end of subtle, difficult problems. Note that, occasionally, a version of the compiler that is too new can be just as problematic as one that is too old; the kernel source makes a great many assumptions about the compiler, and new releases can sometimes break things for a while.

If you still do not have a kernel tree handy, or have not yet configured and built that kernel, now is the time to go do it. You cannot build loadable modules for a 2.6 kernel without this tree on your filesystem. It is also helpful (though not required) to be actually running the kernel that you are building for.

Once you have everything set up, creating a makefile for your module is straightforward. In fact, for the "hello world" example shown earlier in this chapter, a single line will suffice:

```
obj-m := hello.o
```

Readers who are familiar with *make*, but not with the 2.6 kernel build system, are likely to be wondering how this makefile works. The above line is not how a traditional makefile looks, after all. The answer, of course, is that the kernel build system handles the rest. The assignment above (which takes advantage of the extended syntax provided by GNU *make*) states that there is one module to be built from the object file *hello.o*. The resulting module is named *hello.ko* after being built from the object file.

If, instead, you have a module called *module.ko* that is generated from two source files (called, say, *file1.c* and *file2.c*), the correct incantation would be:

```
obj-m := module.o
module-objs := file1.o file2.o
```

For a makefile like those shown above to work, it must be invoked within the context of the larger kernel build system. If your kernel source tree is located in, say, your *~/kernel-2.6* directory, the *make* command required to build your module (typed in the directory containing the module source and makefile) would be:

```
make -C ~/kernel-2.6 M=`pwd` modules
```

This command starts by changing its directory to the one provided with the -C option (that is, your kernel source directory). There it finds the kernel's top-level makefile. The M= option causes that makefile to move back into your module source directory before trying to build the modules target. This target, in turn, refers to the list of modules found in the obj-m variable, which we've set to *module.o* in our examples.

Typing the previous *make* command can get tiresome after a while, so the kernel developers have developed a sort of makefile idiom, which makes life easier for those building modules outside of the kernel tree. The trick is to write your makefile as follows:

```
# If KERNELRELEASE is defined, we've been invoked from the
# kernel build system and can use its language.
ifneq ($(KERNELRELEASE),)
    obj-m := hello.o

# Otherwise we were called directly from the command
# line; invoke the kernel build system.
else

    KERNELDIR ?= /lib/modules/$(shell uname -r)/build
    PWD  := $(shell pwd)

default:
    $(MAKE) -C $(KERNELDIR) M=$(PWD) modules

endif
```

Once again, we are seeing the extended GNU *make* syntax in action. This makefile is read twice on a typical build. When the makefile is invoked from the command line, it notices that the KERNELRELEASE variable has not been set. It locates the kernel source directory by taking advantage of the fact that the symbolic link *build* in the installed modules directory points back at the kernel build tree. If you are not actually running the kernel that you are building for, you can supply a KERNELDIR= option on the command line, set the KERNELDIR environment variable, or rewrite the line that sets KERNELDIR in the makefile. Once the kernel source tree has been found, the makefile invokes the default: target, which runs a second *make* command (parameterized in the makefile as $(MAKE)) to invoke the kernel build system as described previously. On the second reading, the makefile sets obj-m, and the kernel makefiles take care of actually building the module.

This mechanism for building modules may strike you as a bit unwieldy and obscure. Once you get used to it, however, you will likely appreciate the capabilities that have been programmed into the kernel build system. Do note that the above is not a complete makefile; a real makefile includes the usual sort of targets for cleaning up unneeded files, installing modules, etc. See the makefiles in the example source directory for a complete example.

Loading and Unloading Modules

After the module is built, the next step is loading it into the kernel. As we've already pointed out, *insmod* does the job for you. The program loads the module code and data into the kernel, which, in turn, performs a function similar to that of *ld*, in that it links any unresolved symbol in the module to the symbol table of the kernel. Unlike the linker, however, the kernel doesn't modify the module's disk file, but rather an in-memory copy. *insmod* accepts a number of command-line options (for details, see the manpage), and it can assign values to parameters in your module before linking it to the current kernel. Thus, if a module is correctly designed, it can be configured at load time; load-time configuration gives the user more flexibility than compile-time configuration, which is still used sometimes. Load-time configuration is explained in the section "Module Parameters," later in this chapter.

Interested readers may want to look at how the kernel supports *insmod*: it relies on a system call defined in *kernel/module.c*. The function *sys_init_module* allocates kernel memory to hold a module (this memory is allocated with *vmalloc*; see the section "vmalloc and Friends" in Chapter 8); it then copies the module text into that memory region, resolves kernel references in the module via the kernel symbol table, and calls the module's initialization function to get everything going.

If you actually look in the kernel source, you'll find that the names of the system calls are prefixed with sys_. This is true for all system calls and no other functions; it's useful to keep this in mind when grepping for the system calls in the sources.

The *modprobe* utility is worth a quick mention. *modprobe*, like *insmod*, loads a module into the kernel. It differs in that it will look at the module to be loaded to see whether it references any symbols that are not currently defined in the kernel. If any such references are found, *modprobe* looks for other modules in the current module search path that define the relevant symbols. When *modprobe* finds those modules (which are needed by the module being loaded), it loads them into the kernel as well. If you use *insmod* in this situation instead, the command fails with an "unresolved symbols" message left in the system logfile.

As mentioned before, modules may be removed from the kernel with the *rmmod* utility. Note that module removal fails if the kernel believes that the module is still in use (e.g., a program still has an open file for a device exported by the modules), or if the kernel has been configured to disallow module removal. It is possible to configure the kernel to allow "forced" removal of modules, even when they appear to be busy. If you reach a point where you are considering using this option, however, things are likely to have gone wrong badly enough that a reboot may well be the better course of action.

The *lsmod* program produces a list of the modules currently loaded in the kernel. Some other information, such as any other modules making use of a specific module, is also provided. *lsmod* works by reading the */proc/modules* virtual file. Information on currently loaded modules can also be found in the sysfs virtual filesystem under */sys/module*.

Version Dependency

Bear in mind that your module's code has to be recompiled for each version of the kernel that it is linked to—at least, in the absence of modversions, not covered here as they are more for distribution makers than developers. Modules are strongly tied to the data structures and function prototypes defined in a particular kernel version; the interface seen by a module can change significantly from one kernel version to the next. This is especially true of development kernels, of course.

The kernel does not just assume that a given module has been built against the proper kernel version. One of the steps in the build process is to link your module against a file (called *vermagic.o*) from the current kernel tree; this object contains a fair amount of information about the kernel the module was built for, including the target kernel version, compiler version, and the settings of a number of important configuration variables. When an attempt is made to load a module, this information can be tested for compatibility with the running kernel. If things don't match, the module is not loaded; instead, you see something like:

```
# insmod hello.ko
Error inserting './hello.ko': -1 Invalid module format
```

A look in the system log file (*/var/log/messages* or whatever your system is configured to use) will reveal the specific problem that caused the module to fail to load.

If you need to compile a module for a specific kernel version, you will need to use the build system and source tree for that particular version. A simple change to the KERNELDIR variable in the example makefile shown previously does the trick.

Kernel interfaces often change between releases. If you are writing a module that is intended to work with multiple versions of the kernel (especially if it must work across major releases), you likely have to make use of macros and #ifdef constructs to make your code build properly. This edition of this book only concerns itself with one major version of the kernel, so you do not often see version tests in our example code. But the need for them does occasionally arise. In such cases, you want to make use of the definitions found in *linux/version.h*. This header file, automatically included by *linux/module.h*, defines the following macros:

UTS_RELEASE

> This macro expands to a string describing the version of this kernel tree. For
> example, "2.6.10".

LINUX_VERSION_CODE

> This macro expands to the binary representation of the kernel version, one byte
> for each part of the version release number. For example, the code for 2.6.10 is
> 132618 (i.e., 0x02060a).[*] With this information, you can (almost) easily deter-
> mine what version of the kernel you are dealing with.

KERNEL_VERSION(major,minor,release)

> This is the macro used to build an integer version code from the individual num-
> bers that build up a version number. For example, KERNEL_VERSION(2,6,10)
> expands to 132618. This macro is very useful when you need to compare the
> current version and a known checkpoint.

Most dependencies based on the kernel version can be worked around with preprocessor conditionals by exploiting KERNEL_VERSION and LINUX_VERSION_CODE. Version
dependency should, however, not clutter driver code with hairy #ifdef conditionals;
the best way to deal with incompatibilities is by confining them to a specific header
file. As a general rule, code which is explicitly version (or platform) dependent
should be hidden behind a low-level macro or function. High-level code can then
just call those functions without concern for the low-level details. Code written in
this way tends to be easier to read and more robust.

Platform Dependency

Each computer platform has its peculiarities, and kernel designers are free to exploit
all the peculiarities to achieve better performance in the target object file.

Unlike application developers, who must link their code with precompiled libraries
and stick to conventions on parameter passing, kernel developers can dedicate some
processor registers to specific roles, and they have done so. Moreover, kernel code
can be optimized for a specific processor in a CPU family to get the best from the target platform: unlike applications that are often distributed in binary format, a custom compilation of the kernel can be optimized for a specific computer set.

For example, the IA32 (x86) architecture has been subdivided into several different
processor types. The old 80386 processor is still supported (for now), even though
its instruction set is, by modern standards, quite limited. The more modern processors in this architecture have introduced a number of new capabilities, including
faster instructions for entering the kernel, interprocessor locking, copying data, etc.
Newer processors can also, when operated in the correct mode, employ 36-bit (or

---

[*] This allows up to 256 development versions between stable versions.

larger) physical addresses, allowing them to address more than 4 GB of physical memory. Other processor families have seen similar improvements. The kernel, depending on various configuration options, can be built to make use of these additional features.

Clearly, if a module is to work with a given kernel, it must be built with the same understanding of the target processor as that kernel was. Once again, the *vermagic.o* object comes in to play. When a module is loaded, the kernel checks the processor-specific configuration options for the module and makes sure they match the running kernel. If the module was compiled with different options, it is not loaded.

If you are planning to write a driver for general distribution, you may well be wondering just how you can possibly support all these different variations. The best answer, of course, is to release your driver under a GPL-compatible license and contribute it to the mainline kernel. Failing that, distributing your driver in source form and a set of scripts to compile it on the user's system may be the best answer. Some vendors have released tools to make this task easier. If you must distribute your driver in binary form, you need to look at the different kernels provided by your target distributions, and provide a version of the module for each. Be sure to take into account any errata kernels that may have been released since the distribution was produced. Then, there are licensing issues to be considered, as we discussed in the section "License Terms" in Chapter 1. As a general rule, distributing things in source form is an easier way to make your way in the world.

The Kernel Symbol Table

We've seen how *insmod* resolves undefined symbols against the table of public kernel symbols. The table contains the addresses of global kernel items—functions and variables—that are needed to implement modularized drivers. When a module is loaded, any symbol exported by the module becomes part of the kernel symbol table. In the usual case, a module implements its own functionality without the need to export any symbols at all. You need to export symbols, however, whenever other modules may benefit from using them.

New modules can use symbols exported by your module, and you can stack new modules on top of other modules. Module stacking is implemented in the mainstream kernel sources as well: the *msdos* filesystem relies on symbols exported by the *fat* module, and each input USB device module stacks on the *usbcore* and *input* modules.

Module stacking is useful in complex projects. If a new abstraction is implemented in the form of a device driver, it might offer a plug for hardware-specific implementations. For example, the video-for-linux set of drivers is split into a generic module that exports symbols used by lower-level device drivers for specific hardware. According to your setup, you load the generic video module and the specific module for your installed hardware. Support for parallel ports and the wide variety of attachable devices is handled in the same way, as is the USB kernel subsystem. Stacking in the parallel port subsystem is shown in Figure 2-2; the arrows show the communications between the modules and with the kernel programming interface.

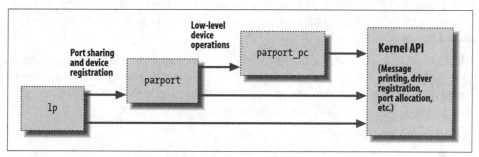

Figure 2-2. Stacking of parallel port driver modules

When using stacked modules, it is helpful to be aware of the *modprobe* utility. As we described earlier, *modprobe* functions in much the same way as *insmod*, but it also loads any other modules that are required by the module you want to load. Thus, one *modprobe* command can sometimes replace several invocations of *insmod* (although you'll still need *insmod* when loading your own modules from the current directory, because *modprobe* looks only in the standard installed module directories).

Using stacking to split modules into multiple layers can help reduce development time by simplifying each layer. This is similar to the separation between mechanism and policy that we discussed in Chapter 1.

The Linux kernel header files provide a convenient way to manage the visibility of your symbols, thus reducing namespace pollution (filling the namespace with names that may conflict with those defined elsewhere in the kernel) and promoting proper information hiding. If your module needs to export symbols for other modules to use, the following macros should be used.

```
EXPORT_SYMBOL(name);
EXPORT_SYMBOL_GPL(name);
```

Either of the above macros makes the given symbol available outside the module. The _GPL version makes the symbol available to GPL-licensed modules only. Symbols must be exported in the global part of the module's file, outside of any function, because the macros expand to the declaration of a special-purpose variable that is expected to be accessible globally. This variable is stored in a special part of the module executable (an "ELF section") that is used by the kernel at load time to find the variables exported by the module. (Interested readers can look at *<linux/module.h>* for the details, even though the details are not needed to make things work.)

Preliminaries

We are getting closer to looking at some actual module code. But first, we need to look at some other things that need to appear in your module source files. The kernel is a unique environment, and it imposes its own requirements on code that would interface with it.

Most kernel code ends up including a fairly large number of header files to get definitions of functions, data types, and variables. We'll examine these files as we come to them, but there are a few that are specific to modules, and must appear in every loadable module. Thus, just about all module code has the following:

```
#include <linux/module.h>
#include <linux/init.h>
```

module.h contains a great many definitions of symbols and functions needed by loadable modules. You need *init.h* to specify your initialization and cleanup functions, as we saw in the "hello world" example above, and which we revisit in the next section. Most modules also include *moduleparam.h* to enable the passing of parameters to the module at load time; we will get to that shortly.

It is not strictly necessary, but your module really should specify which license applies to its code. Doing so is just a matter of including a MODULE_LICENSE line:

```
MODULE_LICENSE("GPL");
```

The specific licenses recognized by the kernel are "GPL" (for any version of the GNU General Public License), "GPL v2" (for GPL version two only), "GPL and additional rights," "Dual BSD/GPL," "Dual MPL/GPL," and "Proprietary." Unless your module is explicitly marked as being under a free license recognized by the kernel, it is assumed to be proprietary, and the kernel is "tainted" when the module is loaded. As we mentioned in the section "License Terms" in Chapter 1, kernel developers tend to be unenthusiastic about helping users who experience problems after loading proprietary modules.

Other descriptive definitions that can be contained within a module include MODULE_AUTHOR (stating who wrote the module), MODULE_DESCRIPTION (a human-readable statement of what the module does), MODULE_VERSION (for a code revision number; see the comments in *<linux/module.h>* for the conventions to use in creating version strings), MODULE_ALIAS (another name by which this module can be known), and MODULE_DEVICE_TABLE (to tell user space about which devices the module supports). We'll discuss MODULE_ALIAS in Chapter 11 and MODULE_DEVICE_TABLE in Chapter 12.

The various MODULE_ declarations can appear anywhere within your source file outside of a function. A relatively recent convention in kernel code, however, is to put these declarations at the end of the file.

Initialization and Shutdown

As already mentioned, the module initialization function registers any facility offered by the module. By *facility*, we mean a new functionality, be it a whole driver or a new software abstraction, that can be accessed by an application. The actual definition of the initialization function always looks like:

```
static int __init initialization_function(void)
{
    /* Initialization code here */
}
module_init(initialization_function);
```

Initialization functions should be declared static, since they are not meant to be visible outside the specific file; there is no hard rule about this, though, as no function is exported to the rest of the kernel unless explicitly requested. The __init token in the definition may look a little strange; it is a hint to the kernel that the given function is used only at initialization time. The module loader drops the initialization function after the module is loaded, making its memory available for other uses. There is a similar tag (__initdata) for data used only during initialization. Use of __init and __initdata is optional, but it is worth the trouble. Just be sure not to use them for any function (or data structure) you will be using after initialization completes. You may also encounter __devinit and __devinitdata in the kernel source; these translate to __init and __initdata only if the kernel has not been configured for hotpluggable devices. We will look at hotplug support in Chapter 14.

The use of *module_init* is mandatory. This macro adds a special section to the module's object code stating where the module's initialization function is to be found. Without this definition, your initialization function is never called.

Modules can register many different types of facilities, including different kinds of devices, filesystems, cryptographic transforms, and more. For each facility, there is a specific kernel function that accomplishes this registration. The arguments passed to the kernel registration functions are usually pointers to data structures describing the new facility and the name of the facility being registered. The data structure usually contains pointers to module functions, which is how functions in the module body get called.

The items that can be registered go beyond the list of device types mentioned in Chapter 1. They include, among others, serial ports, miscellaneous devices, sysfs entries, */proc* files, executable domains, and line disciplines. Many of those registrable items support functions that aren't directly related to hardware but remain in the "software abstractions" field. Those items can be registered, because they are integrated into the driver's functionality anyway (like */proc* files and line disciplines for example).

There are other facilities that can be registered as add-ons for certain drivers, but their use is so specific that it's not worth talking about them; they use the stacking technique, as described in the section "The Kernel Symbol Table." If you want to probe further, you can grep for EXPORT_SYMBOL in the kernel sources, and find the entry points offered by different drivers. Most registration functions are prefixed with register_, so another possible way to find them is to grep for register_ in the kernel source.

The Cleanup Function

Every nontrivial module also requires a cleanup function, which unregisters interfaces and returns all resources to the system before the module is removed. This function is defined as:

```
static void __exit cleanup_function(void)
{
    /* Cleanup code here */
}

module_exit(cleanup_function);
```

The cleanup function has no value to return, so it is declared void. The __exit modifier marks the code as being for module unload only (by causing the compiler to place it in a special ELF section). If your module is built directly into the kernel, or if your kernel is configured to disallow the unloading of modules, functions marked __exit are simply discarded. For this reason, a function marked __exit can be called *only* at module unload or system shutdown time; any other use is an error. Once again, the *module_exit* declaration is necessary to enable to kernel to find your cleanup function.

If your module does not define a cleanup function, the kernel does not allow it to be unloaded.

Error Handling During Initialization

One thing you must always bear in mind when registering facilities with the kernel is that the registration could fail. Even the simplest action often requires memory allocation, and the required memory may not be available. So module code must always check return values, and be sure that the requested operations have actually succeeded.

If any errors occur when you register utilities, the first order of business is to decide whether the module can continue initializing itself anyway. Often, the module can continue to operate after a registration failure, with degraded functionality if necessary. Whenever possible, your module should press forward and provide what capabilities it can after things fail.

If it turns out that your module simply cannot load after a particular type of failure, you must undo any registration activities performed before the failure. Linux doesn't keep a per-module registry of facilities that have been registered, so the module must back out of everything itself if initialization fails at some point. If you ever fail to unregister what you obtained, the kernel is left in an unstable state; it contains internal pointers to code that no longer exists. In such situations, the only recourse, usually, is to reboot the system. You really do want to take care to do the right thing when an initialization error occurs.

Error recovery is sometimes best handled with the goto statement. We normally hate to use goto, but in our opinion, this is one situation where it is useful. Careful use of goto in error situations can eliminate a great deal of complicated, highly-indented, "structured" logic. Thus, in the kernel, goto is often used as shown here to deal with errors.

The following sample code (using fictitious registration and unregistration functions) behaves correctly if initialization fails at any point:

```
int __init my_init_function(void)
{
    int err;

    /* registration takes a pointer and a name */
    err = register_this(ptr1, "skull");
    if (err) goto fail_this;
    err = register_that(ptr2, "skull");
    if (err) goto fail_that;
    err = register_those(ptr3, "skull");
    if (err) goto fail_those;

    return 0; /* success */

  fail_those: unregister_that(ptr2, "skull");
  fail_that: unregister_this(ptr1, "skull");
  fail_this: return err; /* propagate the error */
}
```

This code attempts to register three (fictitious) facilities. The goto statement is used in case of failure to cause the unregistration of only the facilities that had been successfully registered before things went bad.

Another option, requiring no hairy goto statements, is keeping track of what has been successfully registered and calling your module's cleanup function in case of any error. The cleanup function unrolls only the steps that have been successfully accomplished. This alternative, however, requires more code and more CPU time, so in fast paths you still resort to goto as the best error-recovery tool.

The return value of *my_init_function*, err, is an error code. In the Linux kernel, error codes are negative numbers belonging to the set defined in *<linux/errno.h>*. If you want to generate your own error codes instead of returning what you get from other functions, you should include *<linux/errno.h>* in order to use symbolic values such as -ENODEV, -ENOMEM, and so on. It is always good practice to return appropriate error codes, because user programs can turn them to meaningful strings using *perror* or similar means.

Obviously, the module cleanup function must undo any registration performed by the initialization function, and it is customary (but not usually mandatory) to unregister facilities in the reverse order used to register them:

```
void __exit my_cleanup_function(void)
{
    unregister_those(ptr3, "skull");
    unregister_that(ptr2, "skull");
    unregister_this(ptr1, "skull");
    return;
}
```

If your initialization and cleanup are more complex than dealing with a few items, the goto approach may become difficult to manage, because all the cleanup code must be repeated within the initialization function, with several labels intermixed. Sometimes, therefore, a different layout of the code proves more successful.

What you'd do to minimize code duplication and keep everything streamlined is to call the cleanup function from within the initialization whenever an error occurs. The cleanup function then must check the status of each item before undoing its registration. In its simplest form, the code looks like the following:

```
struct something *item1;
struct somethingelse *item2;
int stuff_ok;

void my_cleanup(void)
{
    if (item1)
        release_thing(item1);
    if (item2)
        release_thing2(item2);
    if (stuff_ok)
        unregister_stuff();
    return;
}

int __init my_init(void)
{
    int err = -ENOMEM;

    item1 = allocate_thing(arguments);
    item2 = allocate_thing2(arguments2);
    if (!item2 || !item2)
        goto fail;
    err = register_stuff(item1, item2);
    if (!err)
```

```
        stuff_ok = 1;
    else
        goto fail;
    return 0; /* success */

fail:
    my_cleanup();
    return err;
}
```

As shown in this code, you may or may not need external flags to mark success of the initialization step, depending on the semantics of the registration/allocation function you call. Whether or not flags are needed, this kind of initialization scales well to a large number of items and is often better than the technique shown earlier. Note, however, that the cleanup function cannot be marked __exit when it is called by nonexit code, as in the previous example.

Module-Loading Races

Thus far, our discussion has skated over an important aspect of module loading: race conditions. If you are not careful in how you write your initialization function, you can create situations that can compromise the stability of the system as a whole. We will discuss race conditions later in this book; for now, a couple of quick points will have to suffice.

The first is that you should always remember that some other part of the kernel can make use of any facility you register immediately after that registration has completed. It is entirely possible, in other words, that the kernel will make calls into your module while your initialization function is still running. So your code must be prepared to be called as soon as it completes its first registration. Do not register any facility until all of your internal initialization needed to support that facility has been completed.

You must also consider what happens if your initialization function decides to fail, but some part of the kernel is already making use of a facility your module has registered. If this situation is possible for your module, you should seriously consider not failing the initialization at all. After all, the module has clearly succeeded in exporting something useful. If initialization must fail, it must carefully step around any possible operations going on elsewhere in the kernel until those operations have completed.

Module Parameters

Several parameters that a driver needs to know can change from system to system. These can vary from the device number to use (as we'll see in the next chapter) to numerous aspects of how the driver should operate. For example, drivers for SCSI adapters often have options controlling the use of tagged command queuing, and the Integrated Device Electronics (IDE) drivers allow user control of DMA operations. If your driver controls older hardware, it may also need to be told explicitly where to find that hardware's I/O ports or I/O memory addresses. The kernel supports these needs by making it possible for a driver to designate parameters that may be changed when the driver's module is loaded.

These parameter values can be assigned at load time by *insmod* or *modprobe*; the latter can also read parameter assignment from its configuration file (*/etc/modprobe.conf*). The commands accept the specification of several types of values on the command line. As a way of demonstrating this capability, imagine a much-needed enhancement to the "hello world" module (called *hellop*) shown at the beginning of this chapter. We add two parameters: an integer value called howmany and a character string called whom. Our vastly more functional module then, at load time, greets whom not just once, but howmany times. Such a module could then be loaded with a command line such as:

```
insmod hellop howmany=10 whom="Mom"
```

Upon being loaded that way, *hellop* would say "Hello, Mom" 10 times.

However, before *insmod* can change module parameters, the module must make them available. Parameters are declared with the module_param macro, which is defined in *moduleparam.h*. module_param takes three parameters: the name of the variable, its type, and a permissions mask to be used for an accompanying sysfs entry. The macro should be placed outside of any function and is typically found near the head of the source file. So *hellop* would declare its parameters and make them available to *insmod* as follows:

```
static char *whom = "world";
static int howmany = 1;
module_param(howmany, int, S_IRUGO);
module_param(whom, charp, S_IRUGO);
```

Numerous types are supported for module parameters:

bool
invbool

> A boolean (true or false) value (the associated variable should be of type int). The invbool type inverts the value, so that true values become false and vice versa.

charp

> A char pointer value. Memory is allocated for user-provided strings, and the pointer is set accordingly.

```
int
long
short
uint
ulong
ushort
```
> Basic integer values of various lengths. The versions starting with u are for unsigned values.

Array parameters, where the values are supplied as a comma-separated list, are also supported by the module loader. To declare an array parameter, use:

```
module_param_array(name,type,num,perm);
```

Where name is the name of your array (and of the parameter), type is the type of the array elements, num is an integer variable, and perm is the usual permissions value. If the array parameter is set at load time, num is set to the number of values supplied. The module loader refuses to accept more values than will fit in the array.

If you really need a type that does not appear in the list above, there are hooks in the module code that allow you to define them; see *moduleparam.h* for details on how to do that. All module parameters should be given a default value; *insmod* changes the value only if explicitly told to by the user. The module can check for explicit parameters by testing parameters against their default values.

The final *module_param* field is a permission value; you should use the definitions found in *<linux/stat.h>*. This value controls who can access the representation of the module parameter in sysfs. If perm is set to 0, there is no sysfs entry at all; otherwise, it appears under */sys/module** with the given set of permissions. Use S_IRUGO for a parameter that can be read by the world but cannot be changed; S_IRUGO|S_IWUSR allows root to change the parameter. Note that if a parameter is changed by sysfs, the value of that parameter as seen by your module changes, but your module is not notified in any other way. You should probably not make module parameters writable, unless you are prepared to detect the change and react accordingly.

Doing It in User Space

A Unix programmer who's addressing kernel issues for the first time might be nervous about writing a module. Writing a user program that reads and writes directly to the device ports may be easier.

Indeed, there are some arguments in favor of user-space programming, and sometimes writing a so-called user-space device driver is a wise alternative to kernel hacking. In this section, we discuss some of the reasons why you might write a driver in

---

* As of this writing, there is talk of moving parameters elsewhere within sysfs, however.

user space. This book is about kernel-space drivers, however, so we do not go beyond this introductory discussion.

The advantages of user-space drivers are:

- The full C library can be linked in. The driver can perform many exotic tasks without resorting to external programs (the utility programs implementing usage policies that are usually distributed along with the driver itself).

- The programmer can run a conventional debugger on the driver code without having to go through contortions to debug a running kernel.

- If a user-space driver hangs, you can simply kill it. Problems with the driver are unlikely to hang the entire system, unless the hardware being controlled is *really* misbehaving.

- User memory is swappable, unlike kernel memory. An infrequently used device with a huge driver won't occupy RAM that other programs could be using, except when it is actually in use.

- A well-designed driver program can still, like kernel-space drivers, allow concurrent access to a device.

- If you must write a closed-source driver, the user-space option makes it easier for you to avoid ambiguous licensing situations and problems with changing kernel interfaces.

For example, USB drivers can be written for user space; see the (still young) libusb project at libusb.sourceforge.net and "gadgetfs" in the kernel source. Another example is the X server: it knows exactly what the hardware can do and what it can't, and it offers the graphic resources to all X clients. Note, however, that there is a slow but steady drift toward frame-buffer-based graphics environments, where the X server acts only as a server based on a real kernel-space device driver for actual graphic manipulation.

Usually, the writer of a user-space driver implements a server process, taking over from the kernel the task of being the single agent in charge of hardware control. Client applications can then connect to the server to perform actual communication with the device; therefore, a smart driver process can allow concurrent access to the device. This is exactly how the X server works.

But the user-space approach to device driving has a number of drawbacks. The most important are:

- Interrupts are not available in user space. There are workarounds for this limitation on some platforms, such as the *vm86* system call on the IA32 architecture.

- Direct access to memory is possible only by *mmap*ping */dev/mem*, and only a privileged user can do that.

- Access to I/O ports is available only after calling *ioperm* or *iopl*. Moreover, not all platforms support these system calls, and access to */dev/port* can be too slow to be effective. Both the system calls and the device file are reserved to a privileged user.

- Response time is slower, because a context switch is required to transfer information or actions between the client and the hardware.

- Worse yet, if the driver has been swapped to disk, response time is unacceptably long. Using the *mlock* system call might help, but usually you'll need to lock many memory pages, because a user-space program depends on a lot of library code. *mlock*, too, is limited to privileged users.

- The most important devices can't be handled in user space, including, but not limited to, network interfaces and block devices.

As you see, user-space drivers can't do that much after all. Interesting applications nonetheless exist: for example, support for SCSI scanner devices (implemented by the *SANE* package) and CD writers (implemented by *cdrecord* and other tools). In both cases, user-level device drivers rely on the "SCSI generic" kernel driver, which exports low-level SCSI functionality to user-space programs so they can drive their own hardware.

One case in which working in user space might make sense is when you are beginning to deal with new and unusual hardware. This way you can learn to manage your hardware without the risk of hanging the whole system. Once you've done that, encapsulating the software in a kernel module should be a painless operation.

Quick Reference

This section summarizes the kernel functions, variables, macros, and */proc* files that we've touched on in this chapter. It is meant to act as a reference. Each item is listed after the relevant header file, if any. A similar section appears at the end of almost every chapter from here on, summarizing the new symbols introduced in the chapter. Entries in this section generally appear in the same order in which they were introduced in the chapter:

insmod
modprobe
rmmod
    User-space utilities that load modules into the running kernels and remove them.

```
#include <linux/init.h>
module_init(init_function);
module_exit(cleanup_function);
```
    Macros that designate a module's initialization and cleanup functions.

`__init`
`__initdata`
`__exit`
`__exitdata`

Markers for functions (`__init` and `__exit`) and data (`__initdata` and `__exitdata`) that are only used at module initialization or cleanup time. Items marked for initialization may be discarded once initialization completes; the exit items may be discarded if module unloading has not been configured into the kernel. These markers work by causing the relevant objects to be placed in a special ELF section in the executable file.

`#include <linux/sched.h>`

One of the most important header files. This file contains definitions of much of the kernel API used by the driver, including functions for sleeping and numerous variable declarations.

`struct task_struct *current;`

The current process.

`current->pid`
`current->comm`

The process ID and command name for the current process.

`obj-m`

A makefile symbol used by the kernel build system to determine which modules should be built in the current directory.

/sys/module
/proc/modules

/sys/module is a sysfs directory hierarchy containing information on currently-loaded modules. */proc/modules* is the older, single-file version of that information. Entries contain the module name, the amount of memory each module occupies, and the usage count. Extra strings are appended to each line to specify flags that are currently active for the module.

vermagic.o

An object file from the kernel source directory that describes the environment a module was built for.

`#include <linux/module.h>`

Required header. It must be included by a module source.

`#include <linux/version.h>`

A header file containing information on the version of the kernel being built.

`LINUX_VERSION_CODE`

Integer macro, useful to `#ifdef` version dependencies.

```
EXPORT_SYMBOL (symbol);
EXPORT_SYMBOL_GPL (symbol);
```
Macro used to export a symbol to the kernel. The second form exports without using versioning information, and the third limits the export to GPL-licensed modules.

```
MODULE_AUTHOR(author);
MODULE_DESCRIPTION(description);
MODULE_VERSION(version_string);
MODULE_DEVICE_TABLE(table_info);
MODULE_ALIAS(alternate_name);
```
Place documentation on the module in the object file.

```
module_init(init_function);
module_exit(exit_function);
```
Macros that declare a module's initialization and cleanup functions.

```
#include <linux/moduleparam.h>
module_param(variable, type, perm);
```
Macro that creates a module parameter that can be adjusted by the user when the module is loaded (or at boot time for built-in code). The type can be one of bool, charp, int, invbool, long, short, ushort, uint, ulong, or intarray.

```
#include <linux/kernel.h>
int printk(const char * fmt, ...);
```
The analogue of *printf* for kernel code.

CHAPTER 3
Char Drivers

The goal of this chapter is to write a complete char device driver. We develop a character driver because this class is suitable for most simple hardware devices. Char drivers are also easier to understand than block drivers or network drivers (which we get to in later chapters). Our ultimate aim is to write a *modularized* char driver, but we won't talk about modularization issues in this chapter.

Throughout the chapter, we present code fragments extracted from a real device driver: *scull* (Simple Character Utility for Loading Localities). *scull* is a char driver that acts on a memory area as though it were a device. In this chapter, because of that peculiarity of *scull*, we use the word *device* interchangeably with "the memory area used by *scull*."

The advantage of *scull* is that it isn't hardware dependent. *scull* just acts on some memory, allocated from the kernel. Anyone can compile and run *scull*, and *scull* is portable across the computer architectures on which Linux runs. On the other hand, the device doesn't do anything "useful" other than demonstrate the interface between the kernel and char drivers and allow the user to run some tests.

The Design of scull

The first step of driver writing is defining the capabilities (the mechanism) the driver will offer to user programs. Since our "device" is part of the computer's memory, we're free to do what we want with it. It can be a sequential or random-access device, one device or many, and so on.

To make *scull* useful as a template for writing real drivers for real devices, we'll show you how to implement several device abstractions on top of the computer memory, each with a different personality.

The *scull* source implements the following devices. Each kind of device implemented by the module is referred to as a *type*.

scull0 to scull3

> Four devices, each consisting of a memory area that is both global and persistent. Global means that if the device is opened multiple times, the data contained within the device is shared by all the file descriptors that opened it. Persistent means that if the device is closed and reopened, data isn't lost. This device can be fun to work with, because it can be accessed and tested using conventional commands, such as *cp*, *cat*, and shell I/O redirection.

scullpipe0 to scullpipe3

> Four FIFO (first-in-first-out) devices, which act like pipes. One process reads what another process writes. If multiple processes read the same device, they contend for data. The internals of *scullpipe* will show how blocking and nonblocking *read* and *write* can be implemented without having to resort to interrupts. Although real drivers synchronize with their devices using hardware interrupts, the topic of blocking and nonblocking operations is an important one and is separate from interrupt handling (covered in Chapter 10).

scullsingle
scullpriv
sculluid
scullwuid

> These devices are similar to *scull0* but with some limitations on when an *open* is permitted. The first (*scullsingle*) allows only one process at a time to use the driver, whereas *scullpriv* is private to each virtual console (or X terminal session), because processes on each console/terminal get different memory areas. *sculluid* and *scullwuid* can be opened multiple times, but only by one user at a time; the former returns an error of "Device Busy" if another user is locking the device, whereas the latter implements blocking *open*. These variations of *scull* would appear to be confusing policy and mechanism, but they are worth looking at, because some real-life devices require this sort of management.

Each of the *scull* devices demonstrates different features of a driver and presents different difficulties. This chapter covers the internals of *scull0* to *scull3*; the more advanced devices are covered in Chapter 6. *scullpipe* is described in the section "A Blocking I/O Example," and the others are described in "Access Control on a Device File."

Major and Minor Numbers

Char devices are accessed through names in the filesystem. Those names are called special files or device files or simply nodes of the filesystem tree; they are conventionally located in the */dev* directory. Special files for char drivers are identified by a "c" in the first column of the output of *ls –l*. Block devices appear in */dev* as well, but they are identified by a "b." The focus of this chapter is on char devices, but much of the following information applies to block devices as well.

If you issue the *ls* –*l* command, you'll see two numbers (separated by a comma) in the device file entries before the date of the last modification, where the file length normally appears. These numbers are the major and minor device number for the particular device. The following listing shows a few devices as they appear on a typical system. Their major numbers are 1, 4, 7, and 10, while the minors are 1, 3, 5, 64, 65, and 129.

```
crw-rw-rw-   1 root     root       1,   3 Apr 11  2002 null
crw-------   1 root     root      10,   1 Apr 11  2002 psaux
crw-------   1 root     root       4,   1 Oct 28 03:04 tty1
crw-rw-rw-   1 root     tty        4,  64 Apr 11  2002 ttys0
crw-rw----   1 root     uucp       4,  65 Apr 11  2002 ttyS1
crw--w----   1 vcsa     tty        7,   1 Apr 11  2002 vcs1
crw--w----   1 vcsa     tty        7, 129 Apr 11  2002 vcsa1
crw-rw-rw-   1 root     root       1,   5 Apr 11  2002 zero
```

Traditionally, the major number identifies the driver associated with the device. For example, */dev/null* and */dev/zero* are both managed by driver 1, whereas virtual consoles and serial terminals are managed by driver 4; similarly, both *vcs1* and *vcsa1* devices are managed by driver 7. Modern Linux kernels allow multiple drivers to share major numbers, but most devices that you will see are still organized on the one-major-one-driver principle.

The minor number is used by the kernel to determine exactly which device is being referred to. Depending on how your driver is written (as we will see below), you can either get a direct pointer to your device from the kernel, or you can use the minor number yourself as an index into a local array of devices. Either way, the kernel itself knows almost nothing about minor numbers beyond the fact that they refer to devices implemented by your driver.

The Internal Representation of Device Numbers

Within the kernel, the dev_t type (defined in *<linux/types.h>*) is used to hold device numbers—both the major and minor parts. As of Version 2.6.0 of the kernel, dev_t is a 32-bit quantity with 12 bits set aside for the major number and 20 for the minor number. Your code should, of course, never make any assumptions about the internal organization of device numbers; it should, instead, make use of a set of macros found in *<linux/kdev_t.h>*. To obtain the major or minor parts of a dev_t, use:

```
MAJOR(dev_t dev);
MINOR(dev_t dev);
```

If, instead, you have the major and minor numbers and need to turn them into a dev_t, use:

```
MKDEV(int major, int minor);
```

Note that the 2.6 kernel can accommodate a vast number of devices, while previous kernel versions were limited to 255 major and 255 minor numbers. One assumes that the wider range will be sufficient for quite some time, but the computing field is littered with erroneous assumptions of that nature. So you should expect that the format of dev_t could change again in the future; if you write your drivers carefully, however, these changes will not be a problem.

Allocating and Freeing Device Numbers

One of the first things your driver will need to do when setting up a char device is to obtain one or more device numbers to work with. The necessary function for this task is *register_chrdev_region*, which is declared in *<linux/fs.h>*:

```
int register_chrdev_region(dev_t first, unsigned int count,
                           char *name);
```

Here, first is the beginning device number of the range you would like to allocate. The minor number portion of first is often 0, but there is no requirement to that effect. count is the total number of contiguous device numbers you are requesting. Note that, if count is large, the range you request could spill over to the next major number; but everything will still work properly as long as the number range you request is available. Finally, name is the name of the device that should be associated with this number range; it will appear in */proc/devices* and sysfs.

As with most kernel functions, the return value from *register_chrdev_region* will be 0 if the allocation was successfully performed. In case of error, a negative error code will be returned, and you will not have access to the requested region.

register_chrdev_region works well if you know ahead of time exactly which device numbers you want. Often, however, you will not know which major numbers your device will use; there is a constant effort within the Linux kernel development community to move over to the use of dynamicly-allocated device numbers. The kernel will happily allocate a major number for you on the fly, but you must request this allocation by using a different function:

```
int alloc_chrdev_region(dev_t *dev, unsigned int firstminor,
                        unsigned int count, char *name);
```

With this function, dev is an output-only parameter that will, on successful completion, hold the first number in your allocated range. firstminor should be the requested first minor number to use; it is usually 0. The count and name parameters work like those given to *request_chrdev_region*.

Regardless of how you allocate your device numbers, you should free them when they are no longer in use. Device numbers are freed with:

```
void unregister_chrdev_region(dev_t first, unsigned int count);
```

The usual place to call *unregister_chrdev_region* would be in your module's cleanup function.

The above functions allocate device numbers for your driver's use, but they do not tell the kernel anything about what you will actually do with those numbers. Before a user-space program can access one of those device numbers, your driver needs to connect them to its internal functions that implement the device's operations. We will describe how this connection is accomplished shortly, but there are a couple of necessary digressions to take care of first.

Dynamic Allocation of Major Numbers

Some major device numbers are statically assigned to the most common devices. A list of those devices can be found in *Documentation/devices.txt* within the kernel source tree. The chances of a static number having already been assigned for the use of your new driver are small, however, and new numbers are not being assigned. So, as a driver writer, you have a choice: you can simply pick a number that appears to be unused, or you can allocate major numbers in a dynamic manner. Picking a number may work as long as the only user of your driver is you; once your driver is more widely deployed, a randomly picked major number will lead to conflicts and trouble.

Thus, for new drivers, we strongly suggest that you use dynamic allocation to obtain your major device number, rather than choosing a number randomly from the ones that are currently free. In other words, your drivers should almost certainly be using *alloc_chrdev_region* rather than *register_chrdev_region*.

The disadvantage of dynamic assignment is that you can't create the device nodes in advance, because the major number assigned to your module will vary. For normal use of the driver, this is hardly a problem, because once the number has been assigned, you can read it from */proc/devices*.*

To load a driver using a dynamic major number, therefore, the invocation of *insmod* can be replaced by a simple script that, after calling *insmod*, reads */proc/devices* in order to create the special file(s).

A typical */proc/devices* file looks like the following:

```
Character devices:
 1 mem
 2 pty
 3 ttyp
 4 ttyS
 6 lp
 7 vcs
10 misc
13 input
14 sound
```

---

* Even better device information can usually be obtained from sysfs, generally mounted on */sys* on 2.6-based systems. Getting *scull* to export information via sysfs is beyond the scope of this chapter, however; we'll return to this topic in Chapter 14.

```
  21 sg
180 usb

Block devices:
  2 fd
  8 sd
 11 sr
 65 sd
 66 sd
```

The script to load a module that has been assigned a dynamic number can, therefore, be written using a tool such as *awk* to retrieve information from */proc/devices* in order to create the files in */dev*.

The following script, *scull_load*, is part of the *scull* distribution. The user of a driver that is distributed in the form of a module can invoke such a script from the system's *rc.local* file or call it manually whenever the module is needed.

```
#!/bin/sh
module="scull"
device="scull"
mode="664"

# invoke insmod with all arguments we got
# and use a pathname, as newer modutils don't look in . by default
/sbin/insmod ./$module.ko $* || exit 1

# remove stale nodes
rm -f /dev/${device}[0-3]

major=$(awk "\\$2==\"$module\" {print \\$1}" /proc/devices)

mknod /dev/${device}0 c $major 0
mknod /dev/${device}1 c $major 1
mknod /dev/${device}2 c $major 2
mknod /dev/${device}3 c $major 3

# give appropriate group/permissions, and change the group.
# Not all distributions have staff, some have "wheel" instead.
group="staff"
grep -q '^staff:' /etc/group || group="wheel"

chgrp $group /dev/${device}[0-3]
chmod $mode  /dev/${device}[0-3]
```

The script can be adapted for another driver by redefining the variables and adjusting the *mknod* lines. The script just shown creates four devices because four is the default in the *scull* sources.

The last few lines of the script may seem obscure: why change the group and mode of a device? The reason is that the script must be run by the superuser, so newly created special files are owned by root. The permission bits default so that only root has write access, while anyone can get read access. Normally, a device node requires a different access policy, so in some way or another access rights must be changed. The default in our script is to give access to a group of users, but your needs may vary. In the section "Access Control on a Device File" in Chapter 6, the code for *scull-luid* demonstrates how the driver can enforce its own kind of authorization for device access.

A *scull_unload* script is also available to clean up the */dev* directory and remove the module.

As an alternative to using a pair of scripts for loading and unloading, you could write an init script, ready to be placed in the directory your distribution uses for these scripts.* As part of the *scull* source, we offer a fairly complete and configurable example of an init script, called *scull.init*; it accepts the conventional arguments—start, stop, and restart—and performs the role of both *scull_load* and *scull_unload*.

If repeatedly creating and destroying */dev* nodes sounds like overkill, there is a useful workaround. If you are loading and unloading only a single driver, you can just use *rmmod* and *insmod* after the first time you create the special files with your script: dynamic numbers are not randomized,† and you can count on the same number being chosen each time if you don't load any other (dynamic) modules. Avoiding lengthy scripts is useful during development. But this trick, clearly, doesn't scale to more than one driver at a time.

The best way to assign major numbers, in our opinion, is by defaulting to dynamic allocation while leaving yourself the option of specifying the major number at load time, or even at compile time. The *scull* implementation works in this way; it uses a global variable, scull_major, to hold the chosen number (there is also a scull_minor for the minor number). The variable is initialized to SCULL_MAJOR, defined in *scull.h*. The default value of SCULL_MAJOR in the distributed source is 0, which means "use dynamic assignment." The user can accept the default or choose a particular major number, either by modifying the macro before compiling or by specifying a value for scull_major on the *insmod* command line. Finally, by using the *scull_load* script, the user can pass arguments to *insmod* on *scull_load*'s command line.‡

Here's the code we use in *scull*'s source to get a major number:

```
if (scull_major) {
    dev = MKDEV(scull_major, scull_minor);
    result = register_chrdev_region(dev, scull_nr_devs, "scull");
} else {
    result = alloc_chrdev_region(&dev, scull_minor, scull_nr_devs,
```

---

* The Linux Standard Base specifies that init scripts should be placed in */etc/init.d*, but some distributions still place them elsewhere. In addition, if your script is to be run at boot time, you need to make a link to it from the appropriate run-level directory (i.e., *...*/rc3.d*).

† Though certain kernel developers have threatened to do exactly that in the future.

‡ The init script *scull.init* doesn't accept driver options on the command line, but it supports a configuration file, because it's designed for automatic use at boot and shutdown time.

```
                "scull");
        scull_major = MAJOR(dev);
    }
    if (result < 0) {
        printk(KERN_WARNING "scull: can't get major %d\n", scull_major);
        return result;
    }
```

Almost all of the sample drivers used in this book use similar code for their major number assignment.

Some Important Data Structures

As you can imagine, device number registration is just the first of many tasks that driver code must carry out. We will soon look at other important driver components, but one other digression is needed first. Most of the fundamental driver operations involve three important kernel data structures, called file_operations, file, and inode. A basic familiarity with these structures is required to be able to do much of anything interesting, so we will now take a quick look at each of them before getting into the details of how to implement the fundamental driver operations.

File Operations

So far, we have reserved some device numbers for our use, but we have not yet connected any of our driver's operations to those numbers. The file_operations structure is how a char driver sets up this connection. The structure, defined in *<linux/fs.h>*, is a collection of function pointers. Each open file (represented internally by a file structure, which we will examine shortly) is associated with its own set of functions (by including a field called f_op that points to a file_operations structure). The operations are mostly in charge of implementing the system calls and are therefore, named *open*, *read*, and so on. We can consider the file to be an "object" and the functions operating on it to be its "methods," using object-oriented programming terminology to denote actions declared by an object to act on itself. This is the first sign of object-oriented programming we see in the Linux kernel, and we'll see more in later chapters.

Conventionally, a file_operations structure or a pointer to one is called fops (or some variation thereof). Each field in the structure must point to the function in the driver that implements a specific operation, or be left NULL for unsupported operations. The exact behavior of the kernel when a NULL pointer is specified is different for each function, as the list later in this section shows.

The following list introduces all the operations that an application can invoke on a device. We've tried to keep the list brief so it can be used as a reference, merely summarizing each operation and the default kernel behavior when a NULL pointer is used.

As you read through the list of file_operations methods, you will note that a number of parameters include the string __user. This annotation is a form of documentation, noting that a pointer is a user-space address that cannot be directly dereferenced. For normal compilation, __user has no effect, but it can be used by external checking software to find misuse of user-space addresses.

The rest of the chapter, after describing some other important data structures, explains the role of the most important operations and offers hints, caveats, and real code examples. We defer discussion of the more complex operations to later chapters, because we aren't ready to dig into topics such as memory management, blocking operations, and asynchronous notification quite yet.

struct module *owner
> The first file_operations field is not an operation at all; it is a pointer to the module that "owns" the structure. This field is used to prevent the module from being unloaded while its operations are in use. Almost all the time, it is simply initialized to THIS_MODULE, a macro defined in *<linux/module.h>*.

loff_t (*llseek) (struct file *, loff_t, int);
> The *llseek* method is used to change the current read/write position in a file, and the new position is returned as a (positive) return value. The loff_t parameter is a "long offset" and is at least 64 bits wide even on 32-bit platforms. Errors are signaled by a negative return value. If this function pointer is NULL, seek calls will modify the position counter in the file structure (described in the section "The file Structure") in potentially unpredictable ways.

ssize_t (*read) (struct file *, char __user *, size_t, loff_t *);
> Used to retrieve data from the device. A null pointer in this position causes the *read* system call to fail with -EINVAL ("Invalid argument"). A nonnegative return value represents the number of bytes successfully read (the return value is a "signed size" type, usually the native integer type for the target platform).

ssize_t (*aio_read)(struct kiocb *, char __user *, size_t, loff_t);
> Initiates an asynchronous read—a read operation that might not complete before the function returns. If this method is NULL, all operations will be processed (synchronously) by *read* instead.

ssize_t (*write) (struct file *, const char __user *, size_t, loff_t *);
> Sends data to the device. If NULL, -EINVAL is returned to the program calling the *write* system call. The return value, if nonnegative, represents the number of bytes successfully written.

ssize_t (*aio_write)(struct kiocb *, const char __user *, size_t, loff_t *);
> Initiates an asynchronous write operation on the device.

int (*readdir) (struct file *, void *, filldir_t);
> This field should be NULL for device files; it is used for reading directories and is useful only for filesystems.

```
unsigned int (*poll) (struct file *, struct poll_table_struct *);
```
The *poll* method is the back end of three system calls: *poll*, *epoll*, and *select*, all of which are used to query whether a read or write to one or more file descriptors would block. The *poll* method should return a bit mask indicating whether non-blocking reads or writes are possible, and, possibly, provide the kernel with information that can be used to put the calling process to sleep until I/O becomes possible. If a driver leaves its *poll* method NULL, the device is assumed to be both readable and writable without blocking.

```
int (*ioctl) (struct inode *, struct file *, unsigned int, unsigned long);
```
The *ioctl* system call offers a way to issue device-specific commands (such as formatting a track of a floppy disk, which is neither reading nor writing). Additionally, a few *ioctl* commands are recognized by the kernel without referring to the fops table. If the device doesn't provide an *ioctl* method, the system call returns an error for any request that isn't predefined (-ENOTTY, "No such ioctl for device").

```
int (*mmap) (struct file *, struct vm_area_struct *);
```
mmap is used to request a mapping of device memory to a process's address space. If this method is NULL, the *mmap* system call returns -ENODEV.

```
int (*open) (struct inode *, struct file *);
```
Though this is always the first operation performed on the device file, the driver is not required to declare a corresponding method. If this entry is NULL, opening the device always succeeds, but your driver isn't notified.

```
int (*flush) (struct file *);
```
The *flush* operation is invoked when a process closes its copy of a file descriptor for a device; it should execute (and wait for) any outstanding operations on the device. This must not be confused with the *fsync* operation requested by user programs. Currently, *flush* is used in very few drivers; the SCSI tape driver uses it, for example, to ensure that all data written makes it to the tape before the device is closed. If *flush* is NULL, the kernel simply ignores the user application request.

```
int (*release) (struct inode *, struct file *);
```
This operation is invoked when the file structure is being released. Like *open*, *release* can be NULL.[*]

```
int (*fsync) (struct file *, struct dentry *, int);
```
This method is the back end of the *fsync* system call, which a user calls to flush any pending data. If this pointer is NULL, the system call returns -EINVAL.

---

[*] Note that *release* isn't invoked every time a process calls *close*. Whenever a file structure is shared (for example, after a *fork* or a *dup*), *release* won't be invoked until all copies are closed. If you need to flush pending data when any copy is closed, you should implement the *flush* method.

```
int (*aio_fsync)(struct kiocb *, int);
```
This is the asynchronous version of the *fsync* method.

```
int (*fasync) (int, struct file *, int);
```
This operation is used to notify the device of a change in its FASYNC flag. Asynchronous notification is an advanced topic and is described in Chapter 6. The field can be NULL if the driver doesn't support asynchronous notification.

```
int (*lock) (struct file *, int, struct file_lock *);
```
The *lock* method is used to implement file locking; locking is an indispensable feature for regular files but is almost never implemented by device drivers.

```
ssize_t (*readv) (struct file *, const struct iovec *, unsigned long, loff_t *);
ssize_t (*writev) (struct file *, const struct iovec *, unsigned long, loff_t *);
```
These methods implement scatter/gather read and write operations. Applications occasionally need to do a single read or write operation involving multiple memory areas; these system calls allow them to do so without forcing extra copy operations on the data. If these function pointers are left NULL, the *read* and *write* methods are called (perhaps more than once) instead.

```
ssize_t (*sendfile)(struct file *, loff_t *, size_t, read_actor_t, void *);
```
This method implements the read side of the *sendfile* system call, which moves the data from one file descriptor to another with a minimum of copying. It is used, for example, by a web server that needs to send the contents of a file out a network connection. Device drivers usually leave *sendfile* NULL.

```
ssize_t (*sendpage) (struct file *, struct page *, int, size_t, loff_t *,
   int);
```
sendpage is the other half of *sendfile*; it is called by the kernel to send data, one page at a time, to the corresponding file. Device drivers do not usually implement *sendpage*.

```
unsigned long (*get_unmapped_area)(struct file *, unsigned long, unsigned
   long, unsigned long, unsigned long);
```
The purpose of this method is to find a suitable location in the process's address space to map in a memory segment on the underlying device. This task is normally performed by the memory management code; this method exists to allow drivers to enforce any alignment requirements a particular device may have. Most drivers can leave this method NULL.

```
int (*check_flags)(int)
```
This method allows a module to check the flags passed to an *fcntl(F_SETFL...)* call.

```
int (*dir_notify)(struct file *, unsigned long);
```
This method is invoked when an application uses *fcntl* to request directory change notifications. It is useful only to filesystems; drivers need not implement *dir_notify*.

The *scull* device driver implements only the most important device methods. Its
file_operations structure is initialized as follows:

```
struct file_operations scull_fops = {
    .owner =    THIS_MODULE,
    .llseek =   scull_llseek,
    .read =     scull_read,
    .write =    scull_write,
    .ioctl =    scull_ioctl,
    .open =     scull_open,
    .release =  scull_release,
};
```

This declaration uses the standard C tagged structure initialization syntax. This syntax is preferred because it makes drivers more portable across changes in the definitions of the structures and, arguably, makes the code more compact and readable.
Tagged initialization allows the reordering of structure members; in some cases, substantial performance improvements have been realized by placing pointers to frequently accessed members in the same hardware cache line.

The file Structure

struct file, defined in *<linux/fs.h>*, is the second most important data structure
used in device drivers. Note that a file has nothing to do with the FILE pointers of
user-space programs. A FILE is defined in the C library and never appears in kernel
code. A struct file, on the other hand, is a kernel structure that never appears in
user programs.

The file structure represents an *open file*. (It is not specific to device drivers; every
open file in the system has an associated struct file in kernel space.) It is created by
the kernel on *open* and is passed to any function that operates on the file, until
the last *close*. After all instances of the file are closed, the kernel releases the data
structure.

In the kernel sources, a pointer to struct file is usually called either file or filp
("file pointer"). We'll consistently call the pointer filp to prevent ambiguities with
the structure itself. Thus, file refers to the structure and filp to a pointer to the
structure.

The most important fields of struct file are shown here. As in the previous section,
the list can be skipped on a first reading. However, later in this chapter, when we
face some real C code, we'll discuss the fields in more detail.

mode_t f_mode;
> The file mode identifies the file as either readable or writable (or both), by means
> of the bits FMODE_READ and FMODE_WRITE. You might want to check this field for
> read/write permission in your *open* or *ioctl* function, but you don't need to check
> permissions for *read* and *write*, because the kernel checks before invoking your

method. An attempt to read or write when the file has not been opened for that type of access is rejected without the driver even knowing about it.

loff_t f_pos;
> The current reading or writing position. loff_t is a 64-bit value on all platforms (long long in *gcc* terminology). The driver can read this value if it needs to know the current position in the file but should not normally change it; *read* and *write* should update a position using the pointer they receive as the last argument instead of acting on filp->f_pos directly. The one exception to this rule is in the *llseek* method, the purpose of which is to change the file position.

unsigned int f_flags;
> These are the file flags, such as O_RDONLY, O_NONBLOCK, and O_SYNC. A driver should check the O_NONBLOCK flag to see if nonblocking operation has been requested (we discuss nonblocking I/O in the section "Blocking and Nonblocking Operations" in Chapter 1); the other flags are seldom used. In particular, read/write permission should be checked using f_mode rather than f_flags. All the flags are defined in the header *<linux/fcntl.h>*.

struct file_operations *f_op;
> The operations associated with the file. The kernel assigns the pointer as part of its implementation of *open* and then reads it when it needs to dispatch any operations. The value in filp->f_op is never saved by the kernel for later reference; this means that you can change the file operations associated with your file, and the new methods will be effective after you return to the caller. For example, the code for *open* associated with major number 1 (*/dev/null*, */dev/zero*, and so on) substitutes the operations in filp->f_op depending on the minor number being opened. This practice allows the implementation of several behaviors under the same major number without introducing overhead at each system call. The ability to replace the file operations is the kernel equivalent of "method overriding" in object-oriented programming.

void *private_data;
> The *open* system call sets this pointer to NULL before calling the *open* method for the driver. You are free to make its own use of the field or to ignore it; you can use the field to point to allocated data, but then you must remember to free that memory in the *release* method before the file structure is destroyed by the kernel. private_data is a useful resource for preserving state information across system calls and is used by most of our sample modules.

struct dentry *f_dentry;
> The directory entry (*dentry*) structure associated with the file. Device driver writers normally need not concern themselves with dentry structures, other than to access the inode structure as filp->f_dentry->d_inode.

The real structure has a few more fields, but they aren't useful to device drivers. We can safely ignore those fields, because drivers never create file structures; they only access structures created elsewhere.

The inode Structure

The *inode* structure is used by the kernel internally to represent files. Therefore, it is different from the file structure that represents an open file descriptor. There can be numerous file structures representing multiple open descriptors on a single file, but they all point to a single inode structure.

The inode structure contains a great deal of information about the file. As a general rule, only two fields of this structure are of interest for writing driver code:

dev_t i_rdev;
> For inodes that represent device files, this field contains the actual device number.

struct cdev *i_cdev;
> struct cdev is the kernel's internal structure that represents char devices; this field contains a pointer to that structure when the inode refers to a char device file.

The type of i_rdev changed over the course of the 2.5 development series, breaking a lot of drivers. As a way of encouraging more portable programming, the kernel developers have added two macros that can be used to obtain the major and minor number from an inode:

```
unsigned int iminor(struct inode *inode);
unsigned int imajor(struct inode *inode);
```

In the interest of not being caught by the next change, these macros should be used instead of manipulating i_rdev directly.

Char Device Registration

As we mentioned, the kernel uses structures of type struct cdev to represent char devices internally. Before the kernel invokes your device's operations, you must allocate and register one or more of these structures.* To do so, your code should include <*linux/cdev.h*>, where the structure and its associated helper functions are defined.

There are two ways of allocating and initializing one of these structures. If you wish to obtain a standalone cdev structure at runtime, you may do so with code such as:

```
struct cdev *my_cdev = cdev_alloc();
my_cdev->ops = &my_fops;
```

---

* There is an older mechanism that avoids the use of cdev structures (which we discuss in the section "The Older Way"). New code should use the newer technique, however.

Chances are, however, that you will want to embed the cdev structure within a device-specific structure of your own; that is what *scull* does. In that case, you should initialize the structure that you have already allocated with:

```
void cdev_init(struct cdev *cdev, struct file_operations *fops);
```

Either way, there is one other struct cdev field that you need to initialize. Like the file_operations structure, struct cdev has an owner field that should be set to THIS_MODULE.

Once the cdev structure is set up, the final step is to tell the kernel about it with a call to:

```
int cdev_add(struct cdev *dev, dev_t num, unsigned int count);
```

Here, dev is the cdev structure, num is the first device number to which this device responds, and count is the number of device numbers that should be associated with the device. Often count is one, but there are situations where it makes sense to have more than one device number correspond to a specific device. Consider, for example, the SCSI tape driver, which allows user space to select operating modes (such as density) by assigning multiple minor numbers to each physical device.

There are a couple of important things to keep in mind when using *cdev_add*. The first is that this call can fail. If it returns a negative error code, your device has not been added to the system. It almost always succeeds, however, and that brings up the other point: as soon as *cdev_add* returns, your device is "live" and its operations can be called by the kernel. You should not call *cdev_add* until your driver is completely ready to handle operations on the device.

To remove a char device from the system, call:

```
void cdev_del(struct cdev *dev);
```

Clearly, you should not access the cdev structure after passing it to *cdev_del*.

Device Registration in scull

Internally, *scull* represents each device with a structure of type struct scull_dev. This structure is defined as:

```
struct scull_dev {
    struct scull_qset *data;  /* Pointer to first quantum set */
    int quantum;              /* the current quantum size */
    int qset;                 /* the current array size */
    unsigned long size;       /* amount of data stored here */
    unsigned int access_key;  /* used by sculluid and scullpriv */
    struct semaphore sem;     /* mutual exclusion semaphore    */
    struct cdev cdev;     /* Char device structure       */
};
```

We discuss the various fields in this structure as we come to them, but for now, we call attention to cdev, the struct cdev that interfaces our device to the kernel. This structure must be initialized and added to the system as described above; the *scull* code that handles this task is:

```
static void scull_setup_cdev(struct scull_dev *dev, int index)
{
    int err, devno = MKDEV(scull_major, scull_minor + index);

    cdev_init(&dev->cdev, &scull_fops);
    dev->cdev.owner = THIS_MODULE;
    dev->cdev.ops = &scull_fops;
    err = cdev_add (&dev->cdev, devno, 1);
    /* Fail gracefully if need be */
    if (err)
    printk(KERN_NOTICE "Error %d adding scull%d", err, index);
}
```

Since the cdev structure is embedded within struct scull_dev, *cdev_init* must be called to perform the initialization of that structure.

The Older Way

If you dig through much driver code in the 2.6 kernel, you may notice that quite a few char drivers do not use the cdev interface that we have just described. What you are seeing is older code that has not yet been upgraded to the 2.6 interface. Since that code works as it is, this upgrade may not happen for a long time. For completeness, we describe the older char device registration interface, but new code should not use it; this mechanism will likely go away in a future kernel.

The classic way to register a char device driver is with:

```
int register_chrdev(unsigned int major, const char *name,
                    struct file_operations *fops);
```

Here, major is the major number of interest, name is the name of the driver (it appears in */proc/devices*), and fops is the default file_operations structure. A call to *register_chrdev* registers minor numbers 0–255 for the given major, and sets up a default cdev structure for each. Drivers using this interface must be prepared to handle *open* calls on all 256 minor numbers (whether they correspond to real devices or not), and they cannot use major or minor numbers greater than 255.

If you use *register_chrdev*, the proper function to remove your device(s) from the system is:

```
int unregister_chrdev(unsigned int major, const char *name);
```

major and name must be the same as those passed to *register_chrdev*, or the call will fail.

open and release

Now that we've taken a quick look at the fields, we start using them in real *scull* functions.

The open Method

The *open* method is provided for a driver to do any initialization in preparation for later operations. In most drivers, *open* should perform the following tasks:

- Check for device-specific errors (such as device-not-ready or similar hardware problems)
- Initialize the device if it is being opened for the first time
- Update the f_op pointer, if necessary
- Allocate and fill any data structure to be put in filp->private_data

The first order of business, however, is usually to identify which device is being opened. Remember that the prototype for the *open* method is:

```
int (*open)(struct inode *inode, struct file *filp);
```

The *inode* argument has the information we need in the form of its i_cdev field, which contains the cdev structure we set up before. The only problem is that we do not normally want the cdev structure itself, we want the scull_dev structure that contains that cdev structure. The C language lets programmers play all sorts of tricks to make that kind of conversion; programming such tricks is error prone, however, and leads to code that is difficult for others to read and understand. Fortunately, in this case, the kernel hackers have done the tricky stuff for us, in the form of the *container_of* macro, defined in *<linux/kernel.h>*:

```
container_of(pointer, container_type, container_field);
```

This macro takes a pointer to a field of type container_field, within a structure of type container_type, and returns a pointer to the containing structure. In *scull_open*, this macro is used to find the appropriate device structure:

```
struct scull_dev *dev; /* device information */

dev = container_of(inode->i_cdev, struct scull_dev, cdev);
filp->private_data = dev; /* for other methods */
```

Once it has found the scull_dev structure, *scull* stores a pointer to it in the private_data field of the file structure for easier access in the future.

The other way to identify the device being opened is to look at the minor number stored in the inode structure. If you register your device with *register_chrdev*, you must use this technique. Be sure to use *iminor* to obtain the minor number from the inode structure, and make sure that it corresponds to a device that your driver is actually prepared to handle.

The (slightly simplified) code for *scull_open* is:

```
int scull_open(struct inode *inode, struct file *filp)
{
    struct scull_dev *dev; /* device information */

    dev = container_of(inode->i_cdev, struct scull_dev, cdev);
    filp->private_data = dev; /* for other methods */

    /* now trim to 0 the length of the device if open was write-only */
    if ( (filp->f_flags & O_ACCMODE) == O_WRONLY) {
        scull_trim(dev); /* ignore errors */
    }
    return 0;          /* success */
}
```

The code looks pretty sparse, because it doesn't do any particular device handling when *open* is called. It doesn't need to, because the *scull* device is global and persistent by design. Specifically, there's no action such as "initializing the device on first open," because we don't keep an open count for *scull*s.

The only real operation performed on the device is truncating it to a length of 0 when the device is opened for writing. This is performed because, by design, overwriting a *scull* device with a shorter file results in a shorter device data area. This is similar to the way opening a regular file for writing truncates it to zero length. The operation does nothing if the device is opened for reading.

We'll see later how a real initialization works when we look at the code for the other *scull* personalities.

The release Method

The role of the *release* method is the reverse of *open*. Sometimes you'll find that the method implementation is called *device_close* instead of *device_release*. Either way, the device method should perform the following tasks:

- Deallocate anything that *open* allocated in `filp->private_data`
- Shut down the device on last close

The basic form of *scull* has no hardware to shut down, so the code required is minimal:*

```
int scull_release(struct inode *inode, struct file *filp)
{
    return 0;
}
```

---

* The other flavors of the device are closed by different functions because *scull_open* substituted a different `filp->f_op` for each device. We'll discuss these as we introduce each flavor.

You may be wondering what happens when a device file is closed more times than it is opened. After all, the *dup* and *fork* system calls create copies of open files without calling *open*; each of those copies is then closed at program termination. For example, most programs don't open their *stdin* file (or device), but all of them end up closing it. How does a driver know when an open device file has *really* been closed?

The answer is simple: not every *close* system call causes the *release* method to be invoked. Only the calls that actually release the device data structure invoke the method—hence its name. The kernel keeps a counter of how many times a file structure is being used. Neither *fork* nor *dup* creates a new file structure (only *open* does that); they just increment the counter in the existing structure. The *close* system call executes the *release* method only when the counter for the file structure drops to 0, which happens when the structure is destroyed. This relationship between the *release* method and the *close* system call guarantees that your driver sees only one *release* call for each *open*.

Note that the *flush* method *is* called every time an application calls *close*. However, very few drivers implement *flush*, because usually there's nothing to perform at close time unless *release* is involved.

As you may imagine, the previous discussion applies even when the application terminates without explicitly closing its open files: the kernel automatically closes any file at process exit time by internally using the *close* system call.

scull's Memory Usage

Before introducing the *read* and *write* operations, we'd better look at how and why *scull* performs memory allocation. "How" is needed to thoroughly understand the code, and "why" demonstrates the kind of choices a driver writer needs to make, although *scull* is definitely not typical as a device.

This section deals only with the memory allocation policy in *scull* and doesn't show the hardware management skills you need to write real drivers. These skills are introduced in Chapters 9 and 10. Therefore, you can skip this section if you're not interested in understanding the inner workings of the memory-oriented *scull* driver.

The region of memory used by *scull*, also called a *device*, is variable in length. The more you write, the more it grows; trimming is performed by overwriting the device with a shorter file.

The *scull* driver introduces two core functions used to manage memory in the Linux kernel. These functions, defined in *<linux/slab.h>*, are:

```
void *kmalloc(size_t size, int flags);
void kfree(void *ptr);
```

A call to *kmalloc* attempts to allocate size bytes of memory; the return value is a pointer to that memory or NULL if the allocation fails. The flags argument is used to describe how the memory should be allocated; we examine those flags in detail in Chapter 8. For now, we always use GFP_KERNEL. Allocated memory should be freed with *kfree*. You should never pass anything to *kfree* that was not obtained from *kmalloc*. It is, however, legal to pass a NULL pointer to *kfree*.

kmalloc is not the most efficient way to allocate large areas of memory (see Chapter 8), so the implementation chosen for *scull* is not a particularly smart one. The source code for a smart implementation would be more difficult to read, and the aim of this section is to show *read* and *write*, not memory management. That's why the code just uses *kmalloc* and *kfree* without resorting to allocation of whole pages, although that approach would be more efficient.

On the flip side, we didn't want to limit the size of the "device" area, for both a philosophical reason and a practical one. Philosophically, it's always a bad idea to put arbitrary limits on data items being managed. Practically, *scull* can be used to temporarily eat up your system's memory in order to run tests under low-memory conditions. Running such tests might help you understand the system's internals. You can use the command *cp /dev/zero /dev/scull0* to eat all the real RAM with *scull*, and you can use the *dd* utility to choose how much data is copied to the *scull* device.

In *scull*, each device is a linked list of pointers, each of which points to a scull_dev structure. Each such structure can refer, by default, to at most four million bytes, through an array of intermediate pointers. The released source uses an array of 1000 pointers to areas of 4000 bytes. We call each memory area a *quantum* and the array (or its length) a *quantum set*. A *scull* device and its memory areas are shown in Figure 3-1.

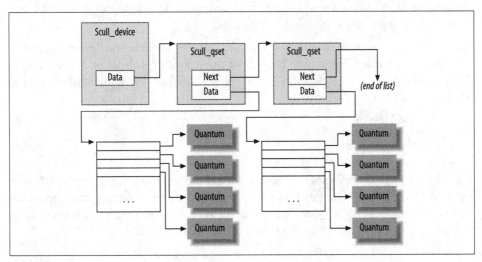

Figure 3-1. The layout of a scull device

The chosen numbers are such that writing a single byte in *scull* consumes 8000 or 12,000 thousand bytes of memory: 4000 for the quantum and 4000 or 8000 for the quantum set (according to whether a pointer is represented in 32 bits or 64 bits on the target platform). If, instead, you write a huge amount of data, the overhead of the linked list is not too bad. There is only one list element for every four megabytes of data, and the maximum size of the device is limited by the computer's memory size.

Choosing the appropriate values for the quantum and the quantum set is a question of policy, rather than mechanism, and the optimal sizes depend on how the device is used. Thus, the *scull* driver should not force the use of any particular values for the quantum and quantum set sizes. In *scull*, the user can change the values in charge in several ways: by changing the macros SCULL_QUANTUM and SCULL_QSET in *scull.h* at compile time, by setting the integer values scull_quantum and scull_qset at module load time, or by changing both the current and default values using *ioctl* at runtime.

Using a macro and an integer value to allow both compile-time and load-time configuration is reminiscent of how the major number is selected. We use this technique for whatever value in the driver is arbitrary or related to policy.

The only question left is how the default numbers have been chosen. In this particular case, the problem is finding the best balance between the waste of memory resulting from half-filled quanta and quantum sets and the overhead of allocation, deallocation, and pointer chaining that occurs if quanta and sets are small. Additionally, the internal design of *kmalloc* should be taken into account. (We won't pursue the point now, though; the innards of *kmalloc* are explored in Chapter 8.) The choice of default numbers comes from the assumption that massive amounts of data are likely to be written to *scull* while testing it, although normal use of the device will most likely transfer just a few kilobytes of data.

We have already seen the scull_dev structure that represents our device internally. That structure's quantum and qset fields hold the device's quantum and quantum set sizes, respectively. The actual data, however, is tracked by a different structure, which we call struct scull_qset:

```
struct scull_qset {
    void **data;
    struct scull_qset *next;
};
```

The next code fragment shows in practice how struct scull_dev and struct scull_qset are used to hold data. The function *scull_trim* is in charge of freeing the whole data area and is invoked by *scull_open* when the file is opened for writing. It simply walks through the list and frees any quantum and quantum set it finds.

```
int scull_trim(struct scull_dev *dev)
{
    struct scull_qset *next, *dptr;
    int qset = dev->qset;    /* "dev" is not-null */
    int i;
```

```
        for (dptr = dev->data; dptr; dptr = next) { /* all the list items */
            if (dptr->data) {
                for (i = 0; i < qset; i++)
                    kfree(dptr->data[i]);
                kfree(dptr->data);
                dptr->data = NULL;
            }
            next = dptr->next;
            kfree(dptr);
        }
        dev->size = 0;
        dev->quantum = scull_quantum;
        dev->qset = scull_qset;
        dev->data = NULL;
        return 0;
}
```

scull_trim is also used in the module cleanup function to return memory used by *scull* to the system.

read and write

The *read* and *write* methods both perform a similar task, that is, copying data from and to application code. Therefore, their prototypes are pretty similar, and it's worth introducing them at the same time:

```
ssize_t read(struct file *filp, char __user *buff,
    size_t count, loff_t *offp);
ssize_t write(struct file *filp, const char __user *buff,
    size_t count, loff_t *offp);
```

For both methods, filp is the file pointer and count is the size of the requested data transfer. The buff argument points to the user buffer holding the data to be written or the empty buffer where the newly read data should be placed. Finally, offp is a pointer to a "long offset type" object that indicates the file position the user is accessing. The return value is a "signed size type"; its use is discussed later.

Let us repeat that the buff argument to the *read* and *write* methods is a user-space pointer. Therefore, it cannot be directly dereferenced by kernel code. There are a few reasons for this restriction:

- Depending on which architecture your driver is running on, and how the kernel was configured, the user-space pointer may not be valid while running in kernel mode at all. There may be no mapping for that address, or it could point to some other, random data.

- Even if the pointer does mean the same thing in kernel space, user-space memory is paged, and the memory in question might not be resident in RAM when the system call is made. Attempting to reference the user-space memory directly could generate a page fault, which is something that kernel code is not allowed to do. The result would be an "oops," which would result in the death of the process that made the system call.

- The pointer in question has been supplied by a user program, which could be buggy or malicious. If your driver ever blindly dereferences a user-supplied pointer, it provides an open doorway allowing a user-space program to access or overwrite memory anywhere in the system. If you do not wish to be responsible for compromising the security of your users' systems, you cannot ever dereference a user-space pointer directly.

Obviously, your driver must be able to access the user-space buffer in order to get its job done. This access must always be performed by special, kernel-supplied functions, however, in order to be safe. We introduce some of those functions (which are defined in *<asm/uaccess.h>*) here, and the rest in the section "Using the ioctl Argument" in Chapter 1; they use some special, architecture-dependent magic to ensure that data transfers between kernel and user space happen in a safe and correct way.

The code for *read* and *write* in *scull* needs to copy a whole segment of data to or from the user address space. This capability is offered by the following kernel functions, which copy an arbitrary array of bytes and sit at the heart of most *read* and *write* implementations:

```
unsigned long copy_to_user(void __user *to,
                           const void *from,
                           unsigned long count);
unsigned long copy_from_user(void *to,
                             const void __user *from,
                             unsigned long count);
```

Although these functions behave like normal *memcpy* functions, a little extra care must be used when accessing user space from kernel code. The user pages being addressed might not be currently present in memory, and the virtual memory subsystem can put the process to sleep while the page is being transferred into place. This happens, for example, when the page must be retrieved from swap space. The net result for the driver writer is that any function that accesses user space must be reentrant, must be able to execute concurrently with other driver functions, and, in particular, must be in a position where it can legally sleep. We return to this subject in Chapter 5.

The role of the two functions is not limited to copying data to and from user-space: they also check whether the user space pointer is valid. If the pointer is invalid, no copy is performed; if an invalid address is encountered during the copy, on the other hand, only part of the data is copied. In both cases, the return value is the amount of memory still to be copied. The *scull* code looks for this error return, and returns -EFAULT to the user if it's not 0.

The topic of user-space access and invalid user space pointers is somewhat advanced and is discussed in Chapter 6. However, it's worth noting that if you don't need to check the user-space pointer you can invoke *__copy_to_user* and *__copy_from_user* instead. This is useful, for example, if you know you already checked the argument. Be careful, however; if, in fact, you do *not* check a user-space pointer that you pass to these functions, then you can create kernel crashes and/or security holes.

As far as the actual device methods are concerned, the task of the *read* method is to copy data from the device to user space (using *copy_to_user*), while the *write* method must copy data from user space to the device (using *copy_from_user*). Each *read* or *write* system call requests transfer of a specific number of bytes, but the driver is free to transfer less data—the exact rules are slightly different for reading and writing and are described later in this chapter.

Whatever the amount of data the methods transfer, they should generally update the file position at *offp to represent the current file position after successful completion of the system call. The kernel then propagates the file position change back into the file structure when appropriate. The *pread* and *pwrite* system calls have different semantics, however; they operate from a given file offset and do not change the file position as seen by any other system calls. These calls pass in a pointer to the user-supplied position, and discard the changes that your driver makes.

Figure 3-2 represents how a typical *read* implementation uses its arguments.

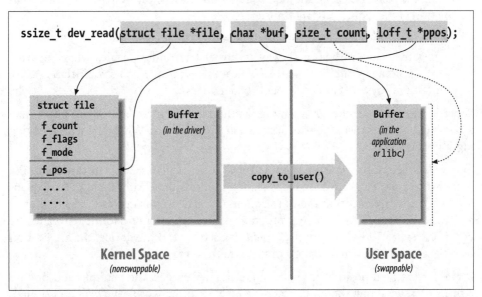

Figure 3-2. The arguments to read

Both the *read* and *write* methods return a negative value if an error occurs. A return value greater than or equal to 0, instead, tells the calling program how many bytes have been successfully transferred. If some data is transferred correctly and then an error happens, the return value must be the count of bytes successfully transferred, and the error does not get reported until the next time the function is called. Implementing this convention requires, of course, that your driver remember that the error has occurred so that it can return the error status in the future.

Although kernel functions return a negative number to signal an error, and the value of the number indicates the kind of error that occurred (as introduced in Chapter 2), programs that run in user space always see –1 as the error return value. They need to access the errno variable to find out what happened. The user-space behavior is dictated by the POSIX standard, but that standard does not make requirements on how the kernel operates internally.

The read Method

The return value for *read* is interpreted by the calling application program:

- If the value equals the count argument passed to the *read* system call, the requested number of bytes has been transferred. This is the optimal case.
- If the value is positive, but smaller than count, only part of the data has been transferred. This may happen for a number of reasons, depending on the device. Most often, the application program retries the read. For instance, if you read using the *fread* function, the library function reissues the system call until completion of the requested data transfer.
- If the value is 0, end-of-file was reached (and no data was read).
- A negative value means there was an error. The value specifies what the error was, according to <*linux/errno.h*>. Typical values returned on error include -EINTR (interrupted system call) or -EFAULT (bad address).

What is missing from the preceding list is the case of "there is no data, but it may arrive later." In this case, the *read* system call should block. We'll deal with blocking input in Chapter 6.

The *scull* code takes advantage of these rules. In particular, it takes advantage of the partial-read rule. Each invocation of *scull_read* deals only with a single data quantum, without implementing a loop to gather all the data; this makes the code shorter and easier to read. If the reading program really wants more data, it reiterates the call. If the standard I/O library (i.e., *fread*) is used to read the device, the application won't even notice the quantization of the data transfer.

If the current read position is greater than the device size, the *read* method of *scull* returns 0 to signal that there's no data available (in other words, we're at end-of-file). This situation can happen if process A is reading the device while process B opens it for writing, thus truncating the device to a length of 0. Process A suddenly finds itself past end-of-file, and the next *read* call returns 0.

Here is the code for *read* (ignore the calls to *down_interruptible* and *up* for now; we will get to them in the next chapter):

```c
ssize_t scull_read(struct file *filp, char __user *buf, size_t count,
                loff_t *f_pos)
{
    struct scull_dev *dev = filp->private_data;
    struct scull_qset *dptr;    /* the first listitem */
    int quantum = dev->quantum, qset = dev->qset;
    int itemsize = quantum * qset; /* how many bytes in the listitem */
    int item, s_pos, q_pos, rest;
    ssize_t retval = 0;

    if (down_interruptible(&dev->sem))
        return -ERESTARTSYS;
    if (*f_pos >= dev->size)
        goto out;
    if (*f_pos + count > dev->size)
        count = dev->size - *f_pos;

    /* find listitem, qset index, and offset in the quantum */
    item = (long)*f_pos / itemsize;
    rest = (long)*f_pos % itemsize;
    s_pos = rest / quantum; q_pos = rest % quantum;

    /* follow the list up to the right position (defined elsewhere) */
    dptr = scull_follow(dev, item);

    if (dptr == NULL || !dptr->data || ! dptr->data[s_pos])
        goto out; /* don't fill holes */

    /* read only up to the end of this quantum */
    if (count > quantum - q_pos)
        count = quantum - q_pos;

    if (copy_to_user(buf, dptr->data[s_pos] + q_pos, count)) {
        retval = -EFAULT;
        goto out;
    }
    *f_pos += count;
    retval = count;

  out:
    up(&dev->sem);
    return retval;
}
```

The write Method

write, like *read*, can transfer less data than was requested, according to the following rules for the return value:

- If the value equals count, the requested number of bytes has been transferred.
- If the value is positive, but smaller than count, only part of the data has been transferred. The program will most likely retry writing the rest of the data.
- If the value is 0, nothing was written. This result is not an error, and there is no reason to return an error code. Once again, the standard library retries the call to *write*. We'll examine the exact meaning of this case in Chapter 6, where blocking *write* is introduced.
- A negative value means an error occurred; as for *read*, valid error values are those defined in *<linux/errno.h>*.

Unfortunately, there may still be misbehaving programs that issue an error message and abort when a partial transfer is performed. This happens because some programmers are accustomed to seeing *write* calls that either fail or succeed completely, which is actually what happens most of the time and should be supported by devices as well. This limitation in the *scull* implementation could be fixed, but we didn't want to complicate the code more than necessary.

The *scull* code for *write* deals with a single quantum at a time, as the *read* method does:

```
ssize_t scull_write(struct file *filp, const char __user *buf, size_t count,
                loff_t *f_pos)
{
    struct scull_dev *dev = filp->private_data;
    struct scull_qset *dptr;
    int quantum = dev->quantum, qset = dev->qset;
    int itemsize = quantum * qset;
    int item, s_pos, q_pos, rest;
    ssize_t retval = -ENOMEM; /* value used in "goto out" statements */

    if (down_interruptible(&dev->sem))
        return -ERESTARTSYS;

    /* find listitem, qset index and offset in the quantum */
    item = (long)*f_pos / itemsize;
    rest = (long)*f_pos % itemsize;
    s_pos = rest / quantum; q_pos = rest % quantum;

    /* follow the list up to the right position */
    dptr = scull_follow(dev, item);
    if (dptr == NULL)
        goto out;
    if (!dptr->data) {
        dptr->data = kmalloc(qset * sizeof(char *), GFP_KERNEL);
        if (!dptr->data)
```

```
            goto out;
        memset(dptr->data, 0, qset * sizeof(char *));
    }
    if (!dptr->data[s_pos]) {
        dptr->data[s_pos] = kmalloc(quantum, GFP_KERNEL);
        if (!dptr->data[s_pos])
            goto out;
    }
    /* write only up to the end of this quantum */
    if (count > quantum - q_pos)
        count = quantum - q_pos;

    if (copy_from_user(dptr->data[s_pos]+q_pos, buf, count)) {
        retval = -EFAULT;
        goto out;
    }
    *f_pos += count;
    retval = count;

        /* update the size */
    if (dev->size < *f_pos)
        dev->size = *f_pos;

  out:
    up(&dev->sem);
    return retval;
}
```

readv and writev

Unix systems have long supported two system calls named *readv* and *writev*. These "vector" versions of *read* and *write* take an array of structures, each of which contains a pointer to a buffer and a length value. A *readv* call would then be expected to read the indicated amount into each buffer in turn. *writev*, instead, would gather together the contents of each buffer and put them out as a single write operation.

If your driver does not supply methods to handle the vector operations, *readv* and *writev* are implemented with multiple calls to your *read* and *write* methods. In many situations, however, greater efficiency is acheived by implementing *readv* and *writev* directly.

The prototypes for the vector operations are:

```
ssize_t (*readv) (struct file *filp, const struct iovec *iov,
                unsigned long count, loff_t *ppos);
ssize_t (*writev) (struct file *filp, const struct iovec *iov,
                unsigned long count, loff_t *ppos);
```

Here, the filp and ppos arguments are the same as for *read* and *write*. The iovec structure, defined in *<linux/uio.h>*, looks like:

```
struct iovec
{
```

```
        void __user *iov_base;
        __kernel_size_t iov_len;
    };
```

Each iovec describes one chunk of data to be transferred; it starts at iov_base (in user space) and is iov_len bytes long. The count parameter tells the method how many iovec structures there are. These structures are created by the application, but the kernel copies them into kernel space before calling the driver.

The simplest implementation of the vectored operations would be a straightforward loop that just passes the address and length out of each iovec to the driver's *read* or *write* function. Often, however, efficient and correct behavior requires that the driver do something smarter. For example, a *writev* on a tape drive should write the contents of all the iovec structures as a single record on the tape.

Many drivers, however, gain no benefit from implementing these methods themselves. Therefore, *scull* omits them. The kernel emulates them with *read* and *write*, and the end result is the same.

Playing with the New Devices

Once you are equipped with the four methods just described, the driver can be compiled and tested; it retains any data you write to it until you overwrite it with new data. The device acts like a data buffer whose length is limited only by the amount of real RAM available. You can try using *cp*, *dd*, and input/output redirection to test out the driver.

The *free* command can be used to see how the amount of free memory shrinks and expands according to how much data is written into *scull*.

To get more confident with reading and writing one quantum at a time, you can add a *printk* at an appropriate point in the driver and watch what happens while an application reads or writes large chunks of data. Alternatively, use the *strace* utility to monitor the system calls issued by a program, together with their return values. Tracing a *cp* or an *ls -l > /dev/scull0* shows quantized reads and writes. Monitoring (and debugging) techniques are presented in detail in Chapter 4

Quick Reference

This chapter introduced the following symbols and header files. The list of the fields in struct file_operations and struct file is not repeated here.

```
#include <linux/types.h>
dev_t
```
dev_t is the type used to represent device numbers within the kernel.

```
int MAJOR(dev_t dev);
int MINOR(dev_t dev);
```
Macros that extract the major and minor numbers from a device number.

```
dev_t MKDEV(unsigned int major, unsigned int minor);
```
Macro that builds a dev_t data item from the major and minor numbers.

```
#include <linux/fs.h>
```
The "filesystem" header is the header required for writing device drivers. Many important functions and data structures are declared in here.

```
int register_chrdev_region(dev_t first, unsigned int count, char *name)
int alloc_chrdev_region(dev_t *dev, unsigned int firstminor, unsigned int
  count, char *name)
void unregister_chrdev_region(dev_t first, unsigned int count);
```
Functions that allow a driver to allocate and free ranges of device numbers. *register_chrdev_region* should be used when the desired major number is known in advance; for dynamic allocation, use *alloc_chrdev_region* instead.

```
int register_chrdev(unsigned int major, const char *name, struct file_operations
  *fops);
```
The old (pre-2.6) char device registration routine. It is emulated in the 2.6 kernel but should not be used for new code. If the major number is not 0, it is used unchanged; otherwise a dynamic number is assigned for this device.

```
int unregister_chrdev(unsigned int major, const char *name);
```
Function that undoes a registration made with *register_chrdev*. Both major and the name string must contain the same values that were used to register the driver.

```
struct file_operations;
struct file;
struct inode;
```
Three important data structures used by most device drivers. The file_operations structure holds a char driver's methods; struct file represents an open file, and struct inode represents a file on disk.

```
#include <linux/cdev.h>
struct cdev *cdev_alloc(void);
void cdev_init(struct cdev *dev, struct file_operations *fops);
int cdev_add(struct cdev *dev, dev_t num, unsigned int count);
void cdev_del(struct cdev *dev);
```
Functions for the management of cdev structures, which represent char devices within the kernel.

```
#include <linux/kernel.h>
container_of(pointer, type, field);
```
A convenience macro that may be used to obtain a pointer to a structure from a pointer to some other structure contained within it.

```
#include <asm/uaccess.h>
```
This include file declares functions used by kernel code to move data to and from user space.

```
unsigned long copy_from_user (void *to, const void *from, unsigned long
    count);
unsigned long copy_to_user (void *to, const void *from, unsigned long count);
```
Copy data between user space and kernel space.

## CHAPTER 4

Debugging Techniques

Kernel programming brings its own, unique debugging challenges. Kernel code cannot be easily executed under a debugger, nor can it be easily traced, because it is a set of functionalities not related to a specific process. Kernel code errors can also be exceedingly hard to reproduce and can bring down the entire system with them, thus destroying much of the evidence that could be used to track them down.

This chapter introduces techniques you can use to monitor kernel code and trace errors under such trying circumstances.

Debugging Support in the Kernel

In Chapter 2, we recommended that you build and install your own kernel, rather than running the stock kernel that comes with your distribution. One of the strongest reasons for running your own kernel is that the kernel developers have built several debugging features into the kernel itself. These features can create extra output and slow performance, so they tend not to be enabled in production kernels from distributors. As a kernel developer, however, you have different priorities and will gladly accept the (minimal) overhead of the extra kernel debugging support.

Here, we list the configuration options that should be enabled for kernels used for development. Except where specified otherwise, all of these options are found under the "kernel hacking" menu in whatever kernel configuration tool you prefer. Note that some of these options are not supported by all architectures.

CONFIG_DEBUG_KERNEL
> This option just makes other debugging options available; it should be turned on but does not, by itself, enable any features.

CONFIG_DEBUG_SLAB
> This crucial option turns on several types of checks in the kernel memory allocation functions; with these checks enabled, it is possible to detect a number of memory overrun and missing initialization errors. Each byte of allocated memory

is set to 0xa5 before being handed to the caller and then set to 0x6b when it is freed. If you ever see either of those "poison" patterns repeating in output from your driver (or often in an oops listing), you'll know exactly what sort of error to look for. When debugging is enabled, the kernel also places special guard values before and after every allocated memory object; if those values ever get changed, the kernel knows that somebody has overrun a memory allocation, and it complains loudly. Various checks for more obscure errors are enabled as well.

CONFIG_DEBUG_PAGEALLOC

Full pages are removed from the kernel address space when freed. This option can slow things down significantly, but it can also quickly point out certain kinds of memory corruption errors.

CONFIG_DEBUG_SPINLOCK

With this option enabled, the kernel catches operations on uninitialized spinlocks and various other errors (such as unlocking a lock twice).

CONFIG_DEBUG_SPINLOCK_SLEEP

This option enables a check for attempts to sleep while holding a spinlock. In fact, it complains if you call a function that could potentially sleep, even if the call in question would not sleep.

CONFIG_INIT_DEBUG

Items marked with __init (or __initdata) are discarded after system initialization or module load time. This option enables checks for code that attempts to access initialization-time memory after initialization is complete.

CONFIG_DEBUG_INFO

This option causes the kernel to be built with full debugging information included. You'll need that information if you want to debug the kernel with *gdb*. You may also want to enable CONFIG_FRAME_POINTER if you plan to use *gdb*.

CONFIG_MAGIC_SYSRQ

Enables the "magic SysRq" key. We look at this key in the section "System Hangs," later in this chapter.

CONFIG_DEBUG_STACKOVERFLOW
CONFIG_DEBUG_STACK_USAGE

These options can help track down kernel stack overflows. A sure sign of a stack overflow is an oops listing without any sort of reasonable back trace. The first option adds explicit overflow checks to the kernel; the second causes the kernel to monitor stack usage and make some statistics available via the magic SysRq key.

CONFIG_KALLSYMS

This option (under "General setup/Standard features") causes kernel symbol information to be built into the kernel; it is enabled by default. The symbol information is used in debugging contexts; without it, an oops listing can give you a kernel traceback only in hexadecimal, which is not very useful.

CONFIG_IKCONFIG
CONFIG_IKCONFIG_PROC

> These options (found in the "General setup" menu) cause the full kernel config-uration state to be built into the kernel and to be made available via */proc*. Most kernel developers know which configuration they used and do not need these options (which make the kernel bigger). They can be useful, though, if you are trying to debug a problem in a kernel built by somebody else.

CONFIG_ACPI_DEBUG

> Under "Power management/ACPI." This option turns on verbose ACPI (Advanced Configuration and Power Interface) debugging information, which can be useful if you suspect a problem related to ACPI.

CONFIG_DEBUG_DRIVER

> Under "Device drivers." Turns on debugging information in the driver core, which can be useful for tracking down problems in the low-level support code. We'll look at the driver core in Chapter 14.

CONFIG_SCSI_CONSTANTS

> This option, found under "Device drivers/SCSI device support," builds in infor-mation for verbose SCSI error messages. If you are working on a SCSI driver, you probably want this option.

CONFIG_INPUT_EVBUG

> This option (under "Device drivers/Input device support") turns on verbose log-ging of input events. If you are working on a driver for an input device, this option may be helpful. Be aware of the security implications of this option, how-ever: it logs everything you type, including your passwords.

CONFIG_PROFILING

> This option is found under "Profiling support." Profiling is normally used for system performance tuning, but it can also be useful for tracking down some kernel hangs and related problems.

We will revisit some of the above options as we look at various ways of tracking down kernel problems. But first, we will look at the classic debugging technique: print statements.

Debugging by Printing

The most common debugging technique is monitoring, which in applications pro-gramming is done by calling *printf* at suitable points. When you are debugging ker-nel code, you can accomplish the same goal with *printk*.

printk

We used the *printk* function in earlier chapters with the simplifying assumption that it works like *printf*. Now it's time to introduce some of the differences.

One of the differences is that *printk* lets you classify messages according to their severity by associating different *loglevels*, or priorities, with the messages. You usually indicate the loglevel with a macro. For example, KERN_INFO, which we saw prepended to some of the earlier print statements, is one of the possible loglevels of the message. The loglevel macro expands to a string, which is concatenated to the message text at compile time; that's why there is no comma between the priority and the format string in the following examples. Here are two examples of *printk* commands, a debug message and a critical message:

```
printk(KERN_DEBUG "Here I am: %s:%i\n", __FILE__, __LINE__);
printk(KERN_CRIT "I'm trashed; giving up on %p\n", ptr);
```

There are eight possible loglevel strings, defined in the header *<linux/kernel.h>*; we list them in order of decreasing severity:

KERN_EMERG
: Used for emergency messages, usually those that precede a crash.

KERN_ALERT
: A situation requiring immediate action.

KERN_CRIT
: Critical conditions, often related to serious hardware or software failures.

KERN_ERR
: Used to report error conditions; device drivers often use KERN_ERR to report hardware difficulties.

KERN_WARNING
: Warnings about problematic situations that do not, in themselves, create serious problems with the system.

KERN_NOTICE
: Situations that are normal, but still worthy of note. A number of security-related conditions are reported at this level.

KERN_INFO
: Informational messages. Many drivers print information about the hardware they find at startup time at this level.

KERN_DEBUG
: Used for debugging messages.

Each string (in the macro expansion) represents an integer in angle brackets. Integers range from 0 to 7, with smaller values representing higher priorities.

A *printk* statement with no specified priority defaults to DEFAULT_MESSAGE_LOGLEVEL, specified in *kernel/printk.c* as an integer. In the 2.6.10 kernel, DEFAULT_MESSAGE_LOGLEVEL is KERN_WARNING, but that has been known to change in the past.

Based on the loglevel, the kernel may print the message to the current console, be it a text-mode terminal, a serial port, or a parallel printer. If the priority is less than the integer variable console_loglevel, the message is delivered to the console one line at a time (nothing is sent unless a trailing newline is provided). If both *klogd* and *syslogd* are running on the system, kernel messages are appended to */var/log/messages* (or otherwise treated depending on your *syslogd* configuration), independent of console_loglevel. If *klogd* is not running, the message won't reach user space unless you read */proc/kmsg* (which is often most easily done with the *dmesg* command). When using *klogd*, you should remember that it doesn't save consecutive identical lines; it only saves the first such line and, at a later time, the number of repetitions it received.

The variable console_loglevel is initialized to DEFAULT_CONSOLE_LOGLEVEL and can be modified through the *sys_syslog* system call. One way to change it is by specifying the *-c* switch when invoking *klogd*, as specified in the *klogd* manpage. Note that to change the current value, you must first kill *klogd* and then restart it with the *-c* option. Alternatively, you can write a program to change the console loglevel. You'll find a version of such a program in *misc-progs/setlevel.c* in the source files provided on O'Reilly's FTP site. The new level is specified as an integer value between 1 and 8, inclusive. If it is set to 1, only messages of level 0 (KERN_EMERG) reach the console; if it is set to 8, all messages, including debugging ones, are displayed.

It is also possible to read and modify the console loglevel using the text file */proc/sys/kernel/printk*. The file hosts four integer values: the current loglevel, the default level for messages that lack an explicit loglevel, the minimum allowed loglevel, and the boot-time default loglevel. Writing a single value to this file changes the current loglevel to that value; thus, for example, you can cause all kernel messages to appear at the console by simply entering:

```
# echo 8 > /proc/sys/kernel/printk
```

It should now be apparent why the *hello.c* sample had the KERN_ALERT; markers; they are there to make sure that the messages appear on the console.

Redirecting Console Messages

Linux allows for some flexibility in console logging policies by letting you send messages to a specific virtual console (if your console lives on the text screen). By default, the "console" is the current virtual terminal. To select a different virtual terminal to receive messages, you can issue ioctl(TIOCLINUX) on any console device. The following program, *setconsole*, can be used to choose which console receives kernel messages; it must be run by the superuser and is available in the *misc-progs* directory.

The following is the program in its entirety. You should invoke it with a single argument specifying the number of the console that is to receive messages.

```c
int main(int argc, char **argv)
{
    char bytes[2] = {11,0}; /* 11 is the TIOCLINUX cmd number */

    if (argc==2) bytes[1] = atoi(argv[1]); /* the chosen console */
    else {
        fprintf(stderr, "%s: need a single arg\n",argv[0]); exit(1);
    }
    if (ioctl(STDIN_FILENO, TIOCLINUX, bytes)<0) {     /* use stdin */
        fprintf(stderr,"%s: ioctl(stdin, TIOCLINUX): %s\n",
                    argv[0], strerror(errno));
        exit(1);
    }
    exit(0);
}
```

setconsole uses the special *ioctl* command TIOCLINUX, which implements Linux-specific functions. To use TIOCLINUX, you pass it an argument that is a pointer to a byte array. The first byte of the array is a number that specifies the requested subcommand, and the following bytes are subcommand specific. In *setconsole*, subcommand 11 is used, and the next byte (stored in bytes[1]) identifies the virtual console. The complete description of TIOCLINUX can be found in *drivers/char/tty_io.c*, in the kernel sources.

How Messages Get Logged

The *printk* function writes messages into a circular buffer that is __LOG_BUF_LEN bytes long: a value from 4 KB to 1 MB chosen while configuring the kernel. The function then wakes any process that is waiting for messages, that is, any process that is sleeping in the *syslog* system call or that is reading */proc/kmsg*. These two interfaces to the logging engine are almost equivalent, but note that reading from */proc/kmsg* consumes the data from the log buffer, whereas the *syslog* system call can optionally return log data while leaving it for other processes as well. In general, reading the */proc* file is easier and is the default behavior for *klogd*. The *dmesg* command can be used to look at the content of the buffer without flushing it; actually, the command returns to *stdout* the whole content of the buffer, whether or not it has already been read.

If you happen to read the kernel messages by hand, after stopping *klogd*, you'll find that the */proc* file looks like a FIFO, in that the reader blocks, waiting for more data. Obviously, you can't read messages this way if *klogd* or another process is already reading the same data, because you'll contend for it.

If the circular buffer fills up, *printk* wraps around and starts adding new data to the beginning of the buffer, overwriting the oldest data. Therefore, the logging process loses the oldest data. This problem is negligible compared with the advantages of using such a circular buffer. For example, a circular buffer allows the system to run even without a logging process, while minimizing memory waste by overwriting old data should nobody read it. Another feature of the Linux approach to messaging is that *printk* can be invoked from anywhere, even from an interrupt handler, with no limit on how much data can be printed. The only disadvantage is the possibility of losing some data.

If the *klogd* process is running, it retrieves kernel messages and dispatches them to *syslogd*, which in turn checks */etc/syslog.conf* to find out how to deal with them. *syslogd* differentiates between messages according to a facility and a priority; allowable values for both the facility and the priority are defined in *<sys/syslog.h>*. Kernel messages are logged by the LOG_KERN facility at a priority corresponding to the one used in *printk* (for example, LOG_ERR is used for KERN_ERR messages). If *klogd* isn't running, data remains in the circular buffer until someone reads it or the buffer overflows.

If you want to avoid clobbering your system log with the monitoring messages from your driver, you can either specify the *–f* (file) option to *klogd* to instruct it to save messages to a specific file, or customize */etc/syslog.conf* to suit your needs. Yet another possibility is to take the brute-force approach: kill *klogd* and verbosely print messages on an unused virtual terminal,* or issue the command *cat /proc/kmsg* from an unused *xterm*.

Turning the Messages On and Off

During the early stages of driver development, *printk* can help considerably in debugging and testing new code. When you officially release the driver, on the other hand, you should remove, or at least disable, such print statements. Unfortunately, you're likely to find that as soon as you think you no longer need the messages and remove them, you implement a new feature in the driver (or somebody finds a bug), and you want to turn at least one of the messages back on. There are several ways to solve both issues, to globally enable or disable your debug messages and to turn individual messages on or off.

Here we show one way to code *printk* calls so you can turn them on and off individually or globally; the technique depends on defining a macro that resolves to a *printk* (or *printf*) call when you want it to:

- Each print statement can be enabled or disabled by removing or adding a single letter to the macro's name.
- All the messages can be disabled at once by changing the value of the CFLAGS variable before compiling.

---

* For example, use *setlevel 8; setconsole 10* to set up terminal 10 to display messages.

- The same print statement can be used in kernel code and user-level code, so that the driver and test programs can be managed in the same way with regard to extra messages.

The following code fragment implements these features and comes directly from the header *scull.h*:

```
#undef PDEBUG              /* undef it, just in case */
#ifdef SCULL_DEBUG
# ifdef __KERNEL__
    /* This one if debugging is on, and kernel space */
#   define PDEBUG(fmt, args...) printk( KERN_DEBUG "scull: " fmt, ## args)
# else
    /* This one for user space */
#   define PDEBUG(fmt, args...) fprintf(stderr, fmt, ## args)
# endif
#else
#  define PDEBUG(fmt, args...) /* not debugging: nothing */
#endif

#undef PDEBUGG
#define PDEBUGG(fmt, args...) /* nothing: it's a placeholder */
```

The symbol PDEBUG is defined or undefined, depending on whether SCULL_DEBUG is defined, and displays information in whatever manner is appropriate to the environment where the code is running: it uses the kernel call *printk* when it's in the kernel and the *libc* call *fprintf* to the standard error when run in user space. The PDEBUGG symbol, on the other hand, does nothing; it can be used to easily "comment" print statements without removing them entirely.

To simplify the process further, add the following lines to your makefile:

```
# Comment/uncomment the following line to disable/enable debugging
DEBUG = y

# Add your debugging flag (or not) to CFLAGS
ifeq ($(DEBUG),y)
  DEBFLAGS = -O -g -DSCULL_DEBUG # "-O" is needed to expand inlines
else
  DEBFLAGS = -O2
endif

CFLAGS += $(DEBFLAGS)
```

The macros shown in this section depend on a *gcc* extension to the ANSI C preprocessor that supports macros with a variable number of arguments. This *gcc* dependency shouldn't be a problem, because the kernel proper depends heavily on *gcc* features anyway. In addition, the makefile depends on GNU's version of *make*; once again, the kernel already depends on GNU *make*, so this dependency is not a problem.

If you're familiar with the C preprocessor, you can expand on the given definitions to implement the concept of a "debug level," defining different levels and assigning an integer (or bit mask) value to each level to determine how verbose it should be.

But every driver has its own features and monitoring needs. The art of good programming is in choosing the best trade-off between flexibility and efficiency, and we can't tell what is the best for you. Remember that preprocessor conditionals (as well as constant expressions in the code) are executed at compile time, so you must recompile to turn messages on or off. A possible alternative is to use C conditionals, which are executed at runtime and, therefore, permit you to turn messaging on and off during program execution. This is a nice feature, but it requires additional processing every time the code is executed, which can affect performance even when the messages are disabled. Sometimes this performance hit is unacceptable.

The macros shown in this section have proven themselves useful in a number of situations, with the only disadvantage being the requirement to recompile a module after any changes to its messages.

Rate Limiting

If you are not careful, you can find yourself generating thousands of messages with *printk*, overwhelming the console and, possibly, overflowing the system log file. When using a slow console device (e.g., a serial port), an excessive message rate can also slow down the system or just make it unresponsive. It can be very hard to get a handle on what is wrong with a system when the console is spewing out data nonstop. Therefore, you should be very careful about what you print, especially in production versions of drivers and especially once initialization is complete. In general, production code should never print anything during normal operation; printed output should be an indication of an exceptional situation requiring attention.

On the other hand, you may want to emit a log message if a device you are driving stops working. But you should be careful not to overdo things. An unintelligent process that continues forever in the face of failures can generate thousands of retries per second; if your driver prints a "my device is broken" message every time, it could create vast amounts of output and possibly hog the CPU if the console device is slow—no interrupts can be used to driver the console, even if it is a serial port or a line printer.

In many cases, the best behavior is to set a flag saying, "I have already complained about this," and not print any further messages once the flag gets set. In others, though, there are reasons to emit an occasional "the device is still broken" notice. The kernel has provided a function that can be helpful in such cases:

```
int printk_ratelimit(void);
```

This function should be called before you consider printing a message that could be repeated often. If the function returns a nonzero value, go ahead and print your message, otherwise skip it. Thus, typical calls look like this:

```
if (printk_ratelimit( ))
    printk(KERN_NOTICE "The printer is still on fire\n");
```

printk_ratelimit works by tracking how many messages are sent to the console. When the level of output exceeds a threshold, *printk_ratelimit* starts returning 0 and causing messages to be dropped.

The behavior of *printk_ratelimit* can be customized by modifying */proc/sys/kernel/ printk_ratelimit* (the number of seconds to wait before re-enabling messages) and are */proc/sys/kernel/printk_ratelimit_burst* (the number of messages accepted before rate-limiting).

Printing Device Numbers

Occasionally, when printing a message from a driver, you will want to print the device number associated withp the hardware of interest. It is not particularly hard to print the major and minor numbers, but, in the interest of consistency, the kernel provides a couple of utility macros (defined in *<linux/kdev_t.h>*) for this purpose:

```
int print_dev_t(char *buffer, dev_t dev);
char *format_dev_t(char *buffer, dev_t dev);
```

Both macros encode the device number into the given buffer; the only difference is that *print_dev_t* returns the number of characters printed, while *format_dev_t* returns buffer; therefore, it can be used as a parameter to a *printk* call directly, although one must remember that *printk* doesn't flush until a trailing newline is provided. The buffer should be large enough to hold a device number; given that 64-bit device numbers are a distinct possibility in future kernel releases, the buffer should probably be at least 20 bytes long.

Debugging by Querying

The previous section described how *printk* works and how it can be used. What it didn't talk about are its disadvantages.

A massive use of *printk* can slow down the system noticeably, even if you lower *console_loglevel* to avoid loading the console device, because *syslogd* keeps syncing its output files; thus, every line that is printed causes a disk operation. This is the right implementation from *syslogd*'s perspective. It tries to write everything to disk in case the system crashes right after printing the message; however, you don't want to slow down your system just for the sake of debugging messages. This problem can be solved by prefixing the name of your log file as it appears in */etc/syslogd.conf* with a hyphen.* The problem with changing the configuration file is that the modification will likely remain there after you are done debugging, even though during normal system operation you do want messages to be flushed to disk as soon as possible. An alternative to such a permanent change is running a program other than *klogd* (such as *cat /proc/kmsg*, as suggested earlier), but this may not provide a suitable environment for normal system operation.

More often than not, the best way to get relevant information is to query the system when you need the information, instead of continually producing data. In fact, every Unix system provides many tools for obtaining system information: *ps*, *netstat*, *vmstat*, and so on.

A few techniques are available to driver developers for querying the system: creating a file in the */proc* filesystem, using the *ioctl* driver method, and exporting attributes via *sysfs*. The use of *sysfs* requires quite some background on the driver model. It is discussed in Chapter 14.

Using the /proc Filesystem

The */proc* filesystem is a special, software-created filesystem that is used by the kernel to export information to the world. Each file under */proc* is tied to a kernel function that generates the file's "contents" on the fly when the file is read. We have already seen some of these files in action; */proc/modules*, for example, always returns a list of the currently loaded modules.

/proc is heavily used in the Linux system. Many utilities on a modern Linux distribution, such as *ps*, *top*, and *uptime*, get their information from */proc*. Some device drivers also export information via */proc*, and yours can do so as well. The */proc* filesystem is dynamic, so your module can add or remove entries at any time.

Fully featured */proc* entries can be complicated beasts; among other things, they can be written to as well as read from. Most of the time, however, */proc* entries are read-only files. This section concerns itself with the simple read-only case. Those who are interested in implementing something more complicated can look here for the basics; the kernel source may then be consulted for the full picture.

Before we continue, however, we should mention that adding files under */proc* is discouraged. The */proc* filesystem is seen by the kernel developers as a bit of an uncontrolled mess that has gone far beyond its original purpose (which was to provide information about the processes running in the system). The recommended way of making information available in new code is via sysfs. As suggested, working with sysfs requires an understanding of the Linux device model, however, and we do not

---

* The hyphen, or minus sign, is a "magic" marker to prevent *syslogd* from flushing the file to disk at every new message, documented in *syslog.conf(5)*, a manpage worth reading.

get to that until Chapter 14. Meanwhile, files under *proc* are slightly easier to create, and they are entirely suitable for debugging purposes, so we cover them here.

Implementing files in /proc

All modules that work with *proc* should include *<linux/proc_fs.h>* to define the proper functions.

To create a read-only *proc* file, your driver must implement a function to produce the data when the file is read. When some process reads the file (using the *read* system call), the request reaches your module by means of this function. We'll look at this function first and get to the registration interface later in this section.

When a process reads from your *proc* file, the kernel allocates a page of memory (i.e., PAGE_SIZE bytes) where the driver can write data to be returned to user space. That buffer is passed to your function, which is a method called *read_proc*:

```
int (*read_proc)(char *page, char **start, off_t offset, int count,
                 int *eof, void *data);
```

The page pointer is the buffer where you'll write your data; start is used by the function to say where the interesting data has been written in page (more on this later); offset and count have the same meaning as for the *read* method. The eof argument points to an integer that must be set by the driver to signal that it has no more data to return, while data is a driver-specific data pointer you can use for internal bookkeeping.

This function should return the number of bytes of data actually placed in the page buffer, just like the *read* method does for other files. Other output values are *eof and *start. eof is a simple flag, but the use of the start value is somewhat more complicated; its purpose is to help with the implementation of large (greater than one page) *proc* files.

The start parameter has a somewhat unconventional use. Its purpose is to indicate where (within page) the data to be returned to the user is found. When your *proc_read* method is called, *start will be NULL. If you leave it NULL, the kernel assumes that the data has been put into page as if offset were 0; in other words, it assumes a simpleminded version of *proc_read*, which places the entire contents of the virtual file in page without paying attention to the offset parameter. If, instead, you set *start to a non-NULL value, the kernel assumes that the data pointed to by *start takes offset into account and is ready to be returned directly to the user. In general, simple *proc_read* methods that return tiny amounts of data just ignore start. More complex methods set *start to page and only place data beginning at the requested offset there.

There has long been another major issue with *proc* files, which start is meant to solve as well. Sometimes the ASCII representation of kernel data structures changes between successive calls to *read*, so the reader process could find inconsistent data from one call to the next. If *start is set to a small integer value, the caller uses it to increment filp->f_pos independently of the amount of data you return, thus making f_pos an internal record number of your *read_proc* procedure. If, for example, your *read_proc* function is returning information from a big array of structures, and five of those structures were returned in the first call, *start could be set to 5. The next call provides that same value as the offset; the driver then knows to start returning data from the sixth structure in the array. This is acknowledged as a "hack" by its authors and can be seen in *fs/proc/generic.c*.

Note that there is a better way to implement large */proc* files; it's called seq_file, and we'll discuss it shortly. First, though, it is time for an example. Here is a simple (if somewhat ugly) *read_proc* implementation for the *scull* device:

```
int scull_read_procmem(char *buf, char **start, off_t offset,
                int count, int *eof, void *data)
{
    int i, j, len = 0;
    int limit = count - 80; /* Don't print more than this */

    for (i = 0; i < scull_nr_devs && len <= limit; i++) {
        struct scull_dev *d = &scull_devices[i];
        struct scull_qset *qs = d->data;
        if (down_interruptible(&d->sem))
            return -ERESTARTSYS;
        len += sprintf(buf+len,"\nDevice %i: qset %i, q %i, sz %li\n",
                i, d->qset, d->quantum, d->size);
        for (; qs && len <= limit; qs = qs->next) { /* scan the list */
            len += sprintf(buf + len, "  item at %p, qset at %p\n",
                    qs, qs->data);
            if (qs->data && !qs->next) /* dump only the last item */
                for (j = 0; j < d->qset; j++) {
                    if (qs->data[j])
                        len += sprintf(buf + len,
                            "    % 4i: %8p\n",
                            j, qs->data[j]);
                }
        }
        up(&scull_devices[i].sem);
    }
    *eof = 1;
    return len;
}
```

This is a fairly typical *read_proc* implementation. It assumes that there will never be a need to generate more than one page of data and so ignores the start and offset values. It is, however, careful not to overrun its buffer, just in case.

An older interface

If you read through the kernel source, you may encounter code implementing */proc* files with an older interface:

```
int (*get_info)(char *page, char **start, off_t offset, int count);
```

All of the arguments have the same meaning as they do for *read_proc*, but the eof and data arguments are missing. This interface is still supported, but it could go away in the future; new code should use the *read_proc* interface instead.

Creating your /proc file

Once you have a *read_proc* function defined, you need to connect it to an entry in the */proc* hierarchy. This is done with a call to *create_proc_read_entry*:

```
struct proc_dir_entry *create_proc_read_entry(const char *name,
                          mode_t mode, struct proc_dir_entry *base,
                          read_proc_t *read_proc, void *data);
```

Here, name is the name of the file to create, mode is the protection mask for the file (it can be passed as 0 for a system-wide default), base indicates the directory in which the file should be created (if base is NULL, the file is created in the */proc* root), read_proc is the *read_proc* function that implements the file, and data is ignored by the kernel (but passed to *read_proc*). Here is the call used by *scull* to make its */proc* function available as */proc/scullmem*:

```
create_proc_read_entry("scullmem", 0 /* default mode */,
        NULL /* parent dir */, scull_read_procmem,
        NULL /* client data */);
```

Here, we create a file called *scullmem* directly under */proc*, with the default, world-readable protections.

The directory entry pointer can be used to create entire directory hierarchies under */proc*. Note, however, that an entry may be more easily placed in a subdirectory of */proc* simply by giving the directory name as part of the name of the entry—as long as the directory itself already exists. For example, an (often ignored) convention says that */proc* entries associated with device drivers should go in the subdirectory *driver/*; *scull* could place its entry there simply by giving its name as *driver/scullmem*.

Entries in */proc*, of course, should be removed when the module is unloaded. *remove_proc_entry* is the function that undoes what *create_proc_read_entry* already did:

```
remove_proc_entry("scullmem", NULL /* parent dir */);
```

Failure to remove entries can result in calls at unwanted times, or, if your module has been unloaded, kernel crashes.

When using */proc* files as shown, you must remember a few nuisances of the implementation—no surprise its use is discouraged nowadays.

The most important problem is with removal of */proc* entries. Such removal may well happen while the file is in use, as there is no owner associated to */proc* entries, so using them doesn't act on the module's reference count. This problem is simply triggered by running *sleep 100 < /proc/myfile* just before removing the module, for example.

Another issue is about registering two entries with the same name. The kernel trusts the driver and doesn't check if the name is already registered, so if you are not careful you might end up with two or more entries with the same name. This is a problem known to happen in classrooms, and such entries are indistinguishable, both when you access them and when you call *remove_proc_entry*.

The seq_file interface

As we noted above, the implementation of large files under */proc* is a little awkward. Over time, */proc* methods have become notorious for buggy implementations when the amount of output grows large. As a way of cleaning up the */proc* code and making life easier for kernel programmers, the seq_file interface was added. This interface provides a simple set of functions for the implementation of large kernel virtual files.

The seq_file interface assumes that you are creating a virtual file that steps through a sequence of items that must be returned to user space. To use seq_file, you must create a simple "iterator" object that can establish a position within the sequence, step forward, and output one item in the sequence. It may sound complicated, but, in fact, the process is quite simple. We'll step through the creation of a */proc* file in the *scull* driver to show how it is done.

The first step, inevitably, is the inclusion of *<linux/seq_file.h>*. Then you must create four iterator methods, called *start*, *next*, *stop*, and *show*.

The *start* method is always called first. The prototype for this function is:

```
void *start(struct seq_file *sfile, loff_t *pos);
```

The sfile argument can almost always be ignored. pos is an integer position indicating where the reading should start. The interpretation of the position is entirely up to the implementation; it need not be a byte position in the resulting file. Since seq_file implementations typically step through a sequence of interesting items, the position is often interpreted as a cursor pointing to the next item in the sequence. The *scull* driver interprets each device as one item in the sequence, so the incoming pos is simply an index into the scull_devices array. Thus, the *start* method used in *scull* is:

```
static void *scull_seq_start(struct seq_file *s, loff_t *pos)
{
    if (*pos >= scull_nr_devs)
        return NULL;   /* No more to read */
    return scull_devices + *pos;
}
```

The return value, if non-NULL, is a private value that can be used by the iterator implementation.

The *next* function should move the iterator to the next position, returning NULL if there is nothing left in the sequence. This method's prototype is:

```
void *next(struct seq_file *sfile, void *v, loff_t *pos);
```

Here, v is the iterator as returned from the previous call to *start* or *next*, and pos is the current position in the file. *next* should increment the value pointed to by pos; depending on how your iterator works, you might (though probably won't) want to increment pos by more than one. Here's what *scull* does:

```
static void *scull_seq_next(struct seq_file *s, void *v, loff_t *pos)
{
    (*pos)++;
    if (*pos >= scull_nr_devs)
        return NULL;
    return scull_devices + *pos;
}
```

When the kernel is done with the iterator, it calls *stop* to clean up:

```
void stop(struct seq_file *sfile, void *v);
```

The *scull* implementation has no cleanup work to do, so its *stop* method is empty.

It is worth noting that the seq_file code, by design, does not sleep or perform other nonatomic tasks between the calls to *start* and *stop*. You are also guaranteed to see one *stop* call sometime shortly after a call to *start*. Therefore, it is safe for your *start* method to acquire semaphores or spinlocks. As long as your other seq_file methods are atomic, the whole sequence of calls is atomic. (If this paragraph does not make sense to you, come back to it after you've read the next chapter.)

In between these calls, the kernel calls the *show* method to actually output something interesting to the user space. This method's prototype is:

```
int show(struct seq_file *sfile, void *v);
```

This method should create output for the item in the sequence indicated by the iterator v. It should not use *printk*, however; instead, there is a special set of functions for seq_file output:

int seq_printf(struct seq_file *sfile, const char *fmt, ...);
> This is the *printf* equivalent for seq_file implementations; it takes the usual format string and additional value arguments. You must also pass it the seq_file structure given to the *show* function, however. If *seq_printf* returns a nonzero value, it means that the buffer has filled, and output is being discarded. Most implementations ignore the return value, however.

int seq_putc(struct seq_file *sfile, char c);
int seq_puts(struct seq_file *sfile, const char *s);
> These are the equivalents of the user-space *putc* and *puts* functions.

int seq_escape(struct seq_file *m, const char *s, const char *esc);
> This function is equivalent to *seq_puts* with the exception that any character in s that is also found in esc is printed in octal format. A common value for esc is " \t\n\\", which keeps embedded white space from messing up the output and possibly confusing shell scripts.

```
int seq_path(struct seq_file *sfile, struct vfsmount *m, struct dentry
  *dentry, char *esc);
```
This function can be used for outputting the file name associated with a given
directory entry. It is unlikely to be useful in device drivers; we have included it
here for completeness.

Getting back to our example; the *show* method used in *scull* is:

```
static int scull_seq_show(struct seq_file *s, void *v)
{
    struct scull_dev *dev = (struct scull_dev *) v;
    struct scull_qset *d;
    int i;

    if (down_interruptible(&dev->sem))
        return -ERESTARTSYS;
    seq_printf(s, "\nDevice %i: qset %i, q %i, sz %li\n",
            (int) (dev - scull_devices), dev->qset,
            dev->quantum, dev->size);
    for (d = dev->data; d; d = d->next) { /* scan the list */
        seq_printf(s, "  item at %p, qset at %p\n", d, d->data);
        if (d->data && !d->next) /* dump only the last item */
            for (i = 0; i < dev->qset; i++) {
                if (d->data[i])
                    seq_printf(s, "    % 4i: %8p\n",
                            i, d->data[i]);
            }
    }
    up(&dev->sem);
    return 0;
}
```

Here, we finally interpret our "iterator" value, which is simply a pointer to a scull_dev
structure.

Now that it has a full set of iterator operations, *scull* must package them up and
connect them to a file in */proc*. The first step is done by filling in a seq_operations
structure:

```
static struct seq_operations scull_seq_ops = {
    .start = scull_seq_start,
    .next  = scull_seq_next,
    .stop  = scull_seq_stop,
    .show  = scull_seq_show
};
```

With that structure in place, we must create a file implementation that the kernel
understands. We do not use the *read_proc* method described previously; when using
seq_file, it is best to connect in to */proc* at a slightly lower level. That means creating a file_operations structure (yes, the same structure used for char drivers) implementing all of the operations needed by the kernel to handle reads and seeks on the

file. Fortunately, this task is straightforward. The first step is to create an *open* method that connects the file to the `seq_file` operations:

```
static int scull_proc_open(struct inode *inode, struct file *file)
{
    return seq_open(file, &scull_seq_ops);
}
```

The call to *seq_open* connects the `file` structure with our sequence operations defined above. As it turns out, *open* is the only file operation we must implement ourselves, so we can now set up our `file_operations` structure:

```
static struct file_operations scull_proc_ops = {
    .owner   = THIS_MODULE,
    .open    = scull_proc_open,
    .read    = seq_read,
    .llseek  = seq_lseek,
    .release = seq_release
};
```

Here we specify our own *open* method, but use the canned methods *seq_read*, *seq_lseek*, and *seq_release* for everything else.

The final step is to create the actual file in */proc*:

```
entry = create_proc_entry("scullseq", 0, NULL);
if (entry)
    entry->proc_fops = &scull_proc_ops;
```

Rather than using *create_proc_read_entry*, we call the lower-level *create_proc_entry*, which has this prototype:

```
struct proc_dir_entry *create_proc_entry(const char *name,
                      mode_t mode,
                      struct proc_dir_entry *parent);
```

The arguments are the same as their equivalents in *create_proc_read_entry*: the name of the file, its protections, and the parent directory.

With the above code, *scull* has a new */proc* entry that looks much like the previous one. It is superior, however, because it works regardless of how large its output becomes, it handles seeks properly, and it is generally easier to read and maintain. We recommend the use of `seq_file` for the implementation of files that contain more than a very small number of lines of output.

The ioctl Method

ioctl, which we show you how to use in Chapter 1, is a system call that acts on a file descriptor; it receives a number that identifies a command to be performed and (optionally) another argument, usually a pointer. As an alternative to using the */proc* filesystem, you can implement a few *ioctl* commands tailored for debugging. These commands can copy relevant data structures from the driver to user space where you can examine them.

Using *ioctl* this way to get information is somewhat more difficult than using */proc*, because you need another program to issue the *ioctl* and display the results. This program must be written, compiled, and kept in sync with the module you're testing. On the other hand, the driver-side code can be easier than what is needed to implement a */proc* file.

There are times when *ioctl* is the best way to get information, because it runs faster than reading */proc*. If some work must be performed on the data before it's written to the screen, retrieving the data in binary form is more efficient than reading a text file. In addition, *ioctl* doesn't require splitting data into fragments smaller than a page.

Another interesting advantage of the *ioctl* approach is that information-retrieval commands can be left in the driver even when debugging would otherwise be disabled. Unlike a */proc* file, which is visible to anyone who looks in the directory (and too many people are likely to wonder "what that strange file is"), undocumented *ioctl* commands are likely to remain unnoticed. In addition, they will still be there should something weird happen to the driver. The only drawback is that the module will be slightly bigger.

Debugging by Watching

Sometimes minor problems can be tracked down by watching the behavior of an application in user space. Watching programs can also help in building confidence that a driver is working correctly. For example, we were able to feel confident about *scull* after looking at how its *read* implementation reacted to read requests for different amounts of data.

There are various ways to watch a user-space program working. You can run a debugger on it to step through its functions, add print statements, or run the program under *strace*. Here we'll discuss just the last technique, which is most interesting when the real goal is examining kernel code.

The *strace* command is a powerful tool that shows all the system calls issued by a user-space program. Not only does it show the calls, but it can also show the arguments to the calls and their return values in symbolic form. When a system call fails, both the symbolic value of the error (e.g., ENOMEM) and the corresponding string (Out of memory) are displayed. *strace* has many command-line options; the most useful of which are -*t* to display the time *when* each call is executed, -*T* to display the time spent in the call, -*e* to limit the types of calls traced, and -*o* to redirect the output to a file. By default, *strace* prints tracing information on stderr.

strace receives information from the kernel itself. This means that a program can be traced regardless of whether or not it was compiled with debugging support (the -*g* option to *gcc*) and whether or not it is stripped. You can also attach tracing to a running process, similar to the way a debugger can connect to a running process and control it.

The trace information is often used to support bug reports sent to application developers, but it's also invaluable to kernel programmers. We've seen how driver code executes by reacting to system calls; *strace* allows us to check the consistency of input and output data of each call.

For example, the following screen dump shows (most of) the last lines of running the command *strace ls /dev > /dev/scull0*:

```
open("/dev", O_RDONLY|O_NONBLOCK|O_LARGEFILE|O_DIRECTORY) = 3
fstat64(3, {st_mode=S_IFDIR|0755, st_size=24576, ...}) = 0
fcntl64(3, F_SETFD, FD_CLOEXEC)           = 0
getdents64(3, /* 141 entries */, 4096)    = 4088
[...]
getdents64(3, /* 0 entries */, 4096)      = 0
close(3)                                  = 0
[...]
fstat64(1, {st_mode=S_IFCHR|0664, st_rdev=makedev(254, 0), ...}) = 0
write(1, "MAKEDEV\nadmmidi0\nadmmidi1\nadmmid"..., 4096) = 4000
write(1, "b\nptywc\nptywd\nptywe\nptywf\nptyx0\n"..., 96) = 96
write(1, "b\nptyxc\nptyxd\nptyxe\nptyxf\nptyy0\n"..., 4096) = 3904
write(1, "s17\nvcs18\nvcs19\nvcs2\nvcs20\nvcs21"..., 192) = 192
write(1, "\nvcs47\nvcs48\nvcs49\nvcs5\nvcs50\nvc"..., 673) = 673
close(1)                                  = 0
exit_group(0)                             = ?
```

It's apparent from the first *write* call that after *ls* finished looking in the target directory, it tried to write 4 KB. Strangely (for *ls*), only 4000 bytes were written, and the operation was retried. However, we know that the *write* implementation in *scull* writes a single quantum at a time, so we could have expected the partial write. After a few steps, everything sweeps through, and the program exits successfully.

As another example, let's *read* the *scull* device (using the *wc* command):

```
[...]
open("/dev/scull0", O_RDONLY|O_LARGEFILE) = 3
fstat64(3, {st_mode=S_IFCHR|0664, st_rdev=makedev(254, 0), ...}) = 0
read(3, "MAKEDEV\nadmmidi0\nadmmidi1\nadmmid"..., 16384) = 4000
read(3, "b\nptywc\nptywd\nptywe\nptywf\nptyx0\n"..., 16384) = 4000
read(3, "s17\nvcs18\nvcs19\nvcs2\nvcs20\nvcs21"..., 16384) = 865
read(3, "", 16384)                        = 0
fstat64(1, {st_mode=S_IFCHR|0620, st_rdev=makedev(136, 1), ...}) = 0
write(1, "8865 /dev/scull0\n", 17)        = 17
close(3)                                  = 0
exit_group(0)                             = ?
```

As expected, *read* is able to retrieve only 4000 bytes at a time, but the total amount of data is the same that was written in the previous example. It's interesting to note how retries are organized in this example, as opposed to the previous trace. *wc* is optimized for fast reading and, therefore, bypasses the standard library, trying to read more data with a single system call. You can see from the read lines in the trace how *wc* tried to read 16 KB at a time.

Linux experts can find much useful information in the output of *strace*. If you're put off by all the symbols, you can limit yourself to watching how the file methods (*open*, *read*, and so on) work with the efile flag.

Personally, we find *strace* most useful for pinpointing runtime errors from system calls. Often the *perror* call in the application or demo program isn't verbose enough to be useful for debugging, and being able to tell exactly which arguments to which system call triggered the error can be a great help.

Debugging System Faults

Even if you've used all the monitoring and debugging techniques, sometimes bugs remain in the driver, and the system faults when the driver is executed. When this happens, it's important to be able to collect as much information as possible to solve the problem.

Note that "fault" doesn't mean "panic." The Linux code is robust enough to respond gracefully to most errors: a fault usually results in the destruction of the current process while the system goes on working. The system *can* panic, and it may if a fault happens outside of a process's context or if some vital part of the system is compromised. But when the problem is due to a driver error, it usually results only in the sudden death of the process unlucky enough to be using the driver. The only unrecoverable damage when a process is destroyed is that some memory allocated to the process's context is lost; for instance, dynamic lists allocated by the driver through *kmalloc* might be lost. However, since the kernel calls the *close* operation for any open device when a process dies, your driver can release what was allocated by the *open* method.

Even though an oops usually does not bring down the entire system, you may well find yourself needing to reboot after one happens. A buggy driver can leave hardware in an unusable state, leave kernel resources in an inconsistent state, or, in the worst case, corrupt kernel memory in random places. Often you can simply unload your buggy driver and try again after an oops. If, however, you see anything that suggests that the system as a whole is not well, your best bet is usually to reboot immediately.

We've already said that when kernel code misbehaves, an informative message is printed on the console. The next section explains how to decode and use such messages. Even though they appear rather obscure to the novice, processor dumps are full of interesting information, often sufficient to pinpoint a program bug without the need for additional testing.

Oops Messages

Most bugs show themselves in NULL pointer dereferences or by the use of other incorrect pointer values. The usual outcome of such bugs is an oops message.

Almost any address used by the processor is a virtual address and is mapped to physical addresses through a complex structure of page tables (the exceptions are physical addresses used with the memory management subsystem itself). When an invalid pointer is dereferenced, the paging mechanism fails to map the pointer to a physical address, and the processor signals a *page fault* to the operating system. If the address is not valid, the kernel is not able to "page in" the missing address; it (usually) generates an oops if this happens while the processor is in supervisor mode.

An oops displays the processor status at the time of the fault, including the contents of the CPU registers and other seemingly incomprehensible information. The message is generated by *printk* statements in the fault handler (*arch/*/kernel/traps.c*) and is dispatched as described earlier in the section "printk."

Let's look at one such message. Here's what results from dereferencing a NULL pointer on a PC running Version 2.6 of the kernel. The most relevant information here is the instruction pointer (EIP), the address of the faulty instruction.

```
Unable to handle kernel NULL pointer dereference at virtual address 00000000
 printing eip:
d083a064
Oops: 0002 [#1]
SMP
CPU:    0
EIP:     0060:[<d083a064>]    Not tainted
EFLAGS: 00010246    (2.6.6)
EIP is at faulty_write+0x4/0x10 [faulty]
eax: 00000000   ebx: 00000000   ecx: 00000000   edx: 00000000
esi: cf8b2460   edi: cf8b2480   ebp: 00000005   esp: c31c5f74
ds: 007b   es: 007b   ss: 0068
Process bash (pid: 2086, threadinfo=c31c4000 task=cfa0a6c0)
Stack: c0150558 cf8b2460 080e9408 00000005 cf8b2480 00000000 cf8b2460 cf8b2460
       ffffffff7 080e9408 c31c4000 c0150682 cf8b2460 080e9408 00000005 cf8b2480
       00000000 00000001 00000005 c0103f8f 00000001 080e9408 00000005 00000005
Call Trace:
 [<c0150558>] vfs_write+0xb8/0x130
 [<c0150682>] sys_write+0x42/0x70
 [<c0103f8f>] syscall_call+0x7/0xb

Code: 89 15 00 00 00 00 c3 90 8d 74 26 00 83 ec 0c b8 00 a6 83 d0
```

This message was generated by writing to a device owned by the *faulty* module, a module built deliberately to demonstrate failures. The implementation of the *write* method of *faulty.c* is trivial:

```
ssize_t faulty_write (struct file *filp, const char __user *buf, size_t count,
       loff_t *pos)
{
```

```
    /* make a simple fault by dereferencing a NULL pointer */
    *(int *)0 = 0;
    return 0;
}
```

As you can see, what we do here is dereference a NULL pointer. Since 0 is never a valid pointer value, a fault occurs, which the kernel turns into the oops message shown earlier. The calling process is then killed.

The *faulty* module has a different fault condition in its *read* implementation:

```
ssize_t faulty_read(struct file *filp, char __user *buf,
            size_t count, loff_t *pos)
{
    int ret;
    char stack_buf[4];

    /* Let's try a buffer overflow  */
    memset(stack_buf, 0xff, 20);
    if (count > 4)
        count = 4; /* copy 4 bytes to the user */
    ret = copy_to_user(buf, stack_buf, count);
    if (!ret)
        return count;
    return ret;
}
```

This method copies a string into a local variable; unfortunately, the string is longer than the destination array. The resulting buffer overflow causes an oops when the function returns. Since the return instruction brings the instruction pointer to nowhere land, this kind of fault is much harder to trace, and you can get something such as the following:

```
EIP:    0010:[<00000000>]
Unable to handle kernel paging request at virtual address ffffffff
 printing eip:
ffffffff
Oops: 0000 [#5]
SMP
CPU:    0
EIP:    0060:[<ffffffff>]     Not tainted
EFLAGS: 00010296    (2.6.6)
EIP is at 0xffffffff
eax: 0000000c   ebx: ffffffff   ecx: 00000000   edx: bfffda7c
esi: cf434f00   edi: ffffffff   ebp: 00002000   esp: c27fff78
ds: 007b   es: 007b   ss: 0068
Process head (pid: 2331, threadinfo=c27fe000 task=c3226150)
Stack: ffffffff bfffda70 00002000 cf434f20 00000001 00000286 cf434f00 fffffff7
       bfffda70 c27fe000 c0150612 cf434f00 bfffda70 00002000 cf434f20 00000000
       00000003 00002000 c0103f8f 00000003 bfffda70 00002000 00002000 bfffda70
Call Trace:
 [<c0150612>] sys_read+0x42/0x70
 [<c0103f8f>] syscall_call+0x7/0xb

Code:  Bad EIP value.
```

In this case, we see only part of the call stack (*vfs_read* and *faulty_read* are missing), and the kernel complains about a "bad EIP value." That complaint, and the offending address (ffffffff) listed at the beginning are both hints that the kernel stack has been corrupted.

In general, when you are confronted with an oops, the first thing to do is to look at the location where the problem happened, which is usually listed separately from the call stack. In the first oops shown above, the relevant line is:

```
EIP is at faulty_write+0x4/0x10 [faulty]
```

Here we see that we were in the function *faulty_write*, which is located in the *faulty* module (which is listed in square brackets). The hex numbers indicate that the instruction pointer was 4 bytes into the function, which appears to be 10 (hex) bytes long. Often that is enough to figure out what the problem is.

If you need more information, the call stack shows you how you got to where things fell apart. The stack itself is printed in hex form; with a bit of work, you can often determine the values of local variables and function parameters from the stack listing. Experienced kernel developers can benefit from a certain amount of pattern recognition here; for example, if we look at the stack listing from the *faulty_read* oops:

```
Stack: ffffffff bfffda70 00002000 cf434f20 00000001 00000286 cf434f00 ffffff7
       bfffda70 c27fe000 c0150612 cf434f00 bfffda70 00002000 cf434f20 00000000
       00000003 00002000 c0103f8f 00000003 bfffda70 00002000 00002000 bfffda70
```

The ffffffff at the top of the stack is part of our string that broke things. On the x86 architecture, by default, the user-space stack starts just below 0xc0000000; thus, the recurring value 0xbfffda70 is probably a user-space stack address; it is, in fact, the address of the buffer passed to the *read* system call, replicated each time it is passed down the kernel call chain. On the x86 (again, by default), kernel space starts at 0xc0000000, so values above that are almost certainly kernel-space addresses, and so on.

Finally, when looking at oops listings, always be on the lookout for the "slab poisoning" values discussed at the beginning of this chapter. Thus, for example, if you get a kernel oops where the offending address is 0xa5a5a5a5, you are almost certainly forgetting to initialize dynamic memory somewhere.

Please note that you see a symbolic call stack (as shown above) only if your kernel is built with the CONFIG_KALLSYMS option turned on. Otherwise, you see a bare, hexadecimal listing, which is far less useful until you have decoded it in other ways.

System Hangs

Although most bugs in kernel code end up as oops messages, sometimes they can completely hang the system. If the system hangs, no message is printed. For example, if the code enters an endless loop, the kernel stops scheduling,* and the system doesn't respond to any action, including the magic Ctrl-Alt-Del combination. You have two choices for dealing with system hangs—either prevent them beforehand or be able to debug them after the fact.

You can prevent an endless loop by inserting *schedule* invocations at strategic points. The *schedule* call (as you might guess) invokes the scheduler and, therefore, allows other processes to steal CPU time from the current process. If a process is looping in kernel space due to a bug in your driver, the *schedule* calls enable you to kill the process after tracing what is happening.

You should be aware, of course, that any call to *schedule* may create an additional source of reentrant calls to your driver, since it allows other processes to run. This reentrancy should not normally be a problem, assuming that you have used suitable locking in your driver. Be sure, however, not to call *schedule* any time that your driver is holding a spinlock.

If your driver really hangs the system, and you don't know where to insert *schedule* calls, the best way to go may be to add some print messages and write them to the console (by changing the console_loglevel value if need be).

Sometimes the system may appear to be hung, but it isn't. This can happen, for example, if the keyboard remains locked in some strange way. These false hangs can be detected by looking at the output of a program you keep running for just this purpose. A clock or system load meter on your display is a good status monitor; as long as it continues to update, the scheduler is working.

An indispensable tool for many lockups is the "magic SysRq key," which is available on most architectures. Magic SysRq is invoked with the combination of the Alt and SysRq keys on the PC keyboard, or with other special keys on other platforms (see *Documentation/sysrq.txt* for details), and is available on the serial console as well. A third key, pressed along with these two, performs one of a number of useful actions:

r   Turns off keyboard raw mode; useful in situations where a crashed application (such as the X server) may have left your keyboard in a strange state.

k   Invokes the "secure attention key" (SAK) function. SAK kills all processes running on the current console, leaving you with a clean terminal.

s   Performs an emergency synchronization of all disks.

u   Umount. Attempts to remount all disks in a read-only mode. This operation, usually invoked immediately after *s*, can save a lot of filesystem checking time in cases where the system is in serious trouble.

---

* Actually, multiprocessor systems still schedule on the other processors, and even a uniprocessor machine might reschedule if kernel preemption is enabled. For the most common case (uniprocessor with preemption disabled), however, the system stops scheduling altogether.

b   Boot. Immediately reboots the system. Be sure to synchronize and remount the disks first.

p   Prints processor registers information.

t   Prints the current task list.

m   Prints memory information.

Other magic SysRq functions exist; see *sysrq.txt* in the *Documentation* directory of the kernel source for the full list. Note that magic SysRq must be explicitly enabled in the kernel configuration and that most distributions do not enable it, for obvious security reasons. For a system used to develop drivers, however, enabling magic SysRq is worth the trouble of building a new kernel in itself. Magic SysRq may be disabled at runtime with a command such as the following:

```
echo 0 > /proc/sys/kernel/sysrq
```

You should consider disabling it if unprivileged users can reach your system keyboard, to prevent accidental or willing damages. Some previous kernel versions had *sysrq* disabled by default, so you needed to enable it at runtime by writing 1 to that same */proc/sys* file.

The *sysrq* operations are exceedingly useful, so they have been made available to system administrators who can't reach the console. The file */proc/sysrq-trigger* is a write-only entry point, where you can trigger a specific *sysrq* action by writing the associated command character; you can then collect any output data from the kernel logs. This entry point to *sysrq* is always working, even if *sysrq* is disabled on the console.

If you are experiencing a "live hang," in which your driver is stuck in a loop but the system as a whole is still functioning, there are a couple of techniques worth knowing. Often, the SysRq *p* function points the finger directly at the guilty routine. Failing that, you can also use the kernel profiling function. Build a kernel with profiling enabled, and boot it with `profile=2` on the command line. Reset the profile counters with the *readprofile* utility, then send your driver into its loop. After a little while, use *readprofile* again to see where the kernel is spending its time. Another more advanced alternative is *oprofile*, that you may consider as well. The file *Documentation/basic_profiling.txt* tells you everything you need to know to get started with the profilers.

One precaution worth using when chasing system hangs is to mount all your disks as read-only (or unmount them). If the disks are read-only or unmounted, there's no risk of damaging the filesystem or leaving it in an inconsistent state. Another possibility is using a computer that mounts all of its filesystems via NFS, the network file system. The "NFS-Root" capability must be enabled in the kernel, and special parameters must be passed at boot time. In this case, you'll avoid filesystem corruption without even resorting to SysRq, because filesystem coherence is managed by the NFS server, which is not brought down by your device driver.

Debuggers and Related Tools

The last resort in debugging modules is using a debugger to step through the code, watching the value of variables and machine registers. This approach is time-consuming and should be avoided whenever possible. Nonetheless, the fine-grained perspective on the code that is achieved through a debugger is sometimes invaluable.

Using an interactive debugger on the kernel is a challenge. The kernel runs in its own address space on behalf of all the processes on the system. As a result, a number of common capabilities provided by user-space debuggers, such as breakpoints and single-stepping, are harder to come by in the kernel. In this section we look at several ways of debugging the kernel; each of them has advantages and disadvantages.

Using gdb

gdb can be quite useful for looking at the system internals. Proficient use of the debugger at this level requires some confidence with *gdb* commands, some understanding of assembly code for the target platform, and the ability to match source code and optimized assembly.

The debugger must be invoked as though the kernel were an application. In addition to specifying the filename for the ELF kernel image, you need to provide the name of a core file on the command line. For a running kernel, that core file is the kernel core image, */proc/kcore*. A typical invocation of *gdb* looks like the following:

```
gdb /usr/src/linux/vmlinux /proc/kcore
```

The first argument is the name of the uncompressed ELF kernel executable, not the *zImage* or *bzImage* or anything built specifically for the boot environment.

The second argument on the *gdb* command line is the name of the core file. Like any file in */proc*, */proc/kcore* is generated when it is read. When the *read* system call executes in the */proc* filesystem, it maps to a data-generation function rather than a data-retrieval one; we've already exploited this feature in the section "Using the /proc Filesystem" earlier in this chapter. *kcore* is used to represent the kernel "executable" in the format of a core file; it is a huge file, because it represents the whole kernel address space, which corresponds to all physical memory. From within *gdb*, you can look at kernel variables by issuing the standard *gdb* commands. For example, p jiffies prints the number of clock ticks from system boot to the current time.

When you print data from *gdb*, the kernel is still running, and the various data items have different values at different times; *gdb*, however, optimizes access to the core file by caching data that has already been read. If you try to look at the jiffies variable once again, you'll get the same answer as before. Caching values to avoid extra disk access is a correct behavior for conventional core files but is inconvenient when a "dynamic" core image is used. The solution is to issue the command *core-file /proc/kcore* whenever you want to flush the *gdb* cache; the debugger gets ready to use a new core file and discards any old information. You won't, however, always need to issue *core-file* when reading a new datum; *gdb* reads the core in chunks of a few kilobytes and caches only chunks it has already referenced.

Numerous capabilities normally provided by *gdb* are not available when you are working with the kernel. For example, *gdb* is not able to modify kernel data; it expects to be running a program to be debugged under its own control before playing with its memory image. It is also not possible to set breakpoints or watchpoints, or to single-step through kernel functions.

Note that, in order to have symbol information available for *gdb*, you must compile your kernel with the `CONFIG_DEBUG_INFO` option set. The result is a far larger kernel image on disk, but, without that information, digging through kernel variables is almost impossible.

With the debugging information available, you can learn a lot about what is going on inside the kernel. *gdb* happily prints out structures, follows pointers, etc. One thing that is harder, however, is examining modules. Since modules are not part of the *vmlinux* image passed to *gdb*, the debugger knows nothing about them. Fortunately, as of kernel 2.6.7, it is possible to teach *gdb* what it needs to know to examine loadable modules.

Linux loadable modules are ELF-format executable images; as such, they have been divided up into numerous sections. A typical module can contain a dozen or more sections, but there are typically three that are relevant in a debugging session:

`.text`
> This section contains the executable code for the module. The debugger must know where this section is to be able to give tracebacks or set breakpoints. (Neither of these operations is relevant when running the debugger on */proc/kcore*, but they can useful when working with *kgdb*, described below).

`.bss`
`.data`
> These two sections hold the module's variables. Any variable that is not initialized at compile time ends up in `.bss`, while those that are initialized go into `.data`.

Making *gdb* work with loadable modules requires informing the debugger about where a given module's sections have been loaded. That information is available in sysfs, under */sys/module*. For example, after loading the *scull* module, the directory */sys/module/scull/sections* contains files with names such as *.text*; the content of each file is the base address for that section.

We are now in a position to issue a *gdb* command telling it about our module. The command we need is `add-symbol-file`; this command takes as parameters the name of the module object file, the *.text* base address, and a series of optional parameters describing where any other sections of interest have been put. After digging through the module section data in sysfs, we can construct a command such as:

```
(gdb) add-symbol-file .../scull.ko 0xd0832000 \
        -s .bss 0xd0837100 \
        -s .data 0xd0836be0
```

We have included a small script in the sample source (*gdbline*) that can create this command for a given module.

We can now use *gdb* to examine variables in our loadable module. Here is a quick example taken from a *scull* debugging session:

```
(gdb) add-symbol-file scull.ko 0xd0832000 \
        -s .bss 0xd0837100 \
        -s .data 0xd0836be0
add symbol table from file "scull.ko" at
        .text_addr = 0xd0832000
        .bss_addr = 0xd0837100
        .data_addr = 0xd0836be0
(y or n) y
Reading symbols from scull.ko...done.
(gdb) p scull_devices[0]
$1 = {data = 0xcfd66c50,
        quantum = 4000,
        qset = 1000,
        size = 20881,
        access_key = 0,
        ...}
```

Here we see that the first *scull* device currently holds 20,881 bytes. If we wanted, we could follow the data chain, or look at anything else of interest in the module.

One other useful trick worth knowing about is this:

```
(gdb) print *(address)
```

Here, fill in a hex address for address; the output is a file and line number for the code corresponding to that address. This technique may be useful, for example, to find out where a function pointer really points.

We still cannot perform typical debugging tasks like setting breakpoints or modifying data; to perform those operations, we need to use a tool like *kdb* (described next) or *kgdb* (which we get to shortly).

The kdb Kernel Debugger

Many readers may be wondering why the kernel does not have any more advanced debugging features built into it. The answer, quite simply, is that Linus does not believe in interactive debuggers. He fears that they lead to poor fixes, those which patch up symptoms rather than addressing the real cause of problems. Thus, no built-in debuggers.

Other kernel developers, however, see an occasional use for interactive debugging tools. One such tool is the *kdb* built-in kernel debugger, available as a nonofficial patch from *oss.sgi.com*. To use *kdb*, you must obtain the patch (be sure to get a version that matches your kernel version), apply it, and rebuild and reinstall the kernel. Note that, as of this writing, *kdb* works only on IA-32 (x86) systems (though a version for the IA-64 existed for a while in the mainline kernel source before being removed).

Once you are running a *kdb*-enabled kernel, there are a couple of ways to enter the debugger. Pressing the Pause (or Break) key on the console starts up the debugger. *kdb* also starts up when a kernel oops happens or when a breakpoint is hit. In any case, you see a message that looks something like this:

```
Entering kdb (0xc0347b80) on processor 0 due to Keyboard Entry
[0]kdb>
```

Note that just about everything the kernel does stops when *kdb* is running. Nothing else should be running on a system where you invoke *kdb*; in particular, you should not have networking turned on—unless, of course, you are debugging a network driver. It is generally a good idea to boot the system in single-user mode if you will be using *kdb*.

As an example, consider a quick *scull* debugging session. Assuming that the driver is already loaded, we can tell *kdb* to set a breakpoint in *scull_read* as follows:

```
[0]kdb> bp scull_read
Instruction(i) BP #0 at 0xcd087c5dc (scull_read)
    is enabled globally adjust 1
[0]kdb> go
```

The *bp* command tells *kdb* to stop the next time the kernel enters *scull_read*. You then type **go** to continue execution. After putting something into one of the *scull* devices, we can attempt to read it by running *cat* under a shell on another terminal, yielding the following:

```
Instruction(i) breakpoint #0 at 0xd087c5dc (adjusted)
0xd087c5dc scull_read:         int3

Entering kdb (current=0xcf09f890, pid 1575) on processor 0 due to
Breakpoint @ 0xd087c5dc
[0]kdb>
```

We are now positioned at the beginning of *scull_read*. To see how we got there, we can get a stack trace:

```
[0]kdb> bt
    ESP      EIP        Function (args)
0xcdbddf74 0xd087c5dc [scull]scull_read
0xcdbddf78 0xc0150718 vfs_read+0xb8
0xcdbddfa4 0xc01509c2 sys_read+0x42
0xcdbddfc4 0xc0103fcf syscall_call+0x7
[0]kdb>
```

kdb attempts to print out the arguments to every function in the call trace. It gets confused, however, by optimization tricks used by the compiler. Therefore, it fails to print the arguments to *scull_read*.

Time to look at some data. The *mds* command manipulates data; we can query the value of the scull_devices pointer with a command such as:

```
[0]kdb> mds scull_devices 1
0xd0880de8 cf36ac00   ....
```

Here we asked for one (4-byte) word of data starting at the location of scull_devices; the answer tells us that our device array is at the address 0xd0880de8; the first device structure itself is at 0xcf36ac00. To look at that device structure, we need to use that address:

```
[0]kdb> mds cf36ac00
0xcf36ac00 ce137dbc ....
0xcf36ac04 00000fa0 ....
0xcf36ac08 000003e8 ....
0xcf36ac0c 0000009b ....
0xcf36ac10 00000000 ....
0xcf36ac14 00000001 ....
0xcf36ac18 00000000 ....
0xcf36ac1c 00000001 ....
```

The eight lines here correspond to the beginning part of the scull_dev structure. Therefore, we see that the memory for the first device is allocated at 0xce137dbc, the quantum is 4000 (hex fa0), the quantum set size is 1000 (hex 3e8), and there are currently 155 (hex 9b) bytes stored in the device.

kdb can change data as well. Suppose we wanted to trim some of the data from the device:

```
[0]kdb> mm cf26ac0c 0x50
0xcf26ac0c = 0x50
```

A subsequent *cat* on the device will now return less data than before.

kdb has a number of other capabilities, including single-stepping (by instructions, not lines of C source code), setting breakpoints on data access, disassembling code, stepping through linked lists, accessing register data, and more. After you have applied the *kdb* patch, a full set of manual pages can be found in the *Documentation/kdb* directory in your kernel source tree.

The kgdb Patches

The two interactive debugging approaches we have looked at so far (using *gdb* on */proc/kcore* and *kdb*) both fall short of the sort of environment that user-space application developers have become used to. Wouldn't it be nice if there were a true debugger for the kernel that supported features like changing variables, breakpoints, etc.?

As it turns out, such a solution does exist. There are, as of this writing, two separate patches in circulation that allow *gdb*, with full capabilities, to be run against the kernel. Confusingly, both of these patches are called *kgdb*. They work by separating the system running the test kernel from the system running the debugger; the two are typically connected via a serial cable. Therefore, the developer can run *gdb* on his or her stable desktop system, while operating on a kernel running on a sacrificial test box. Setting up *gdb* in this mode takes a little time at the outset, but that investment can pay off quickly when a difficult bug shows up.

These patches are in a strong state of flux, and may even be merged at some point, so we avoid saying much about them beyond where they are and their basic features. Interested readers are encouraged to look and see the current state of affairs.

The first *kgdb* patch is currently found in the -mm kernel tree—the staging area for patches on their way into the 2.6 mainline. This version of the patch supports the x86, SuperH, ia64, x86_64, SPARC, and 32-bit PPC architectures. In addition to the usual mode of operation over a serial port, this version of *kgdb* can also communicate over a local-area network. It is simply a matter of enabling the Ethernet mode and booting with the kgdboe parameter set to indicate the IP address from which debugging commands can originate. The documentation under *Documentation/i386/ kgdb* describes how to set things up.*

As an alternative, you can use the *kgdb* patch found on *http://kgdb.sf.net/*. This version of the debugger does not support the network communication mode (though that is said to be under development), but it does have some built-in support for working with loadable modules. It supports the x86, x86_64, PowerPC, and S/390 architectures.

The User-Mode Linux Port

User-Mode Linux (UML) is an interesting concept. It is structured as a separate port of the Linux kernel with its own *arch/um* subdirectory. It does not run on a new type of hardware, however; instead, it runs on a virtual machine implemented on the Linux system call interface. Thus, UML allows the Linux kernel to run as a separate, user-mode process on a Linux system.

Having a copy of the kernel running as a user-mode process brings a number of advantages. Because it is running on a constrained, virtual processor, a buggy kernel cannot damage the "real" system. Different hardware and software configurations can be tried easily on the same box. And, perhaps most significantly for kernel developers, the user-mode kernel can be easily manipulated with *gdb* or another debugger.

---

* It does neglect to point out that you should have your network adapter driver built into the kernel, however, or the debugger fails to find it at boot time and will shut itself down.

After all, it is just another process. UML clearly has the potential to accelerate kernel development.

However, UML has a big shortcoming from the point of view of driver writers: the user-mode kernel has no access to the host system's hardware. Thus, while it can be useful for debugging most of the sample drivers in this book, UML is not yet useful for debugging drivers that have to deal with real hardware.

See *http://user-mode-linux.sf.net/* for more information on UML.

The Linux Trace Toolkit

The Linux Trace Toolkit (LTT) is a kernel patch and a set of related utilities that allow the tracing of events in the kernel. The trace includes timing information and can create a reasonably complete picture of what happened over a given period of time. Thus, it can be used not only for debugging but also for tracking down performance problems.

LTT, along with extensive documentation, can be found at *http://www.opersys.com/LTT*.

Dynamic Probes

Dynamic Probes (or DProbes) is a debugging tool released (under the GPL) by IBM for Linux on the IA-32 architecture. It allows the placement of a "probe" at almost any place in the system, in both user and kernel space. The probe consists of some code (written in a specialized, stack-oriented language) that is executed when control hits the given point. This code can report information back to user space, change registers, or do a number of other things. The useful feature of DProbes is that once the capability has been built into the kernel, probes can be inserted anywhere within a running system without kernel builds or reboots. DProbes can also work with the LTT to insert new tracing events at arbitrary locations.

The DProbes tool can be downloaded from IBM's open source site: *http://oss.software.ibm.com*.

CHAPTER 5

Concurrency and Race Conditions

Thus far, we have paid little attention to the problem of concurrency—i.e., what happens when the system tries to do more than one thing at once. The management of concurrency is, however, one of the core problems in operating systems programming. Concurrency-related bugs are some of the easiest to create and some of the hardest to find. Even expert Linux kernel programmers end up creating concurrency-related bugs on occasion.

In early Linux kernels, there were relatively few sources of concurrency. Symmetric multiprocessing (SMP) systems were not supported by the kernel, and the only cause of concurrent execution was the servicing of hardware interrupts. That approach offers simplicity, but it no longer works in a world that prizes performance on systems with more and more processors, and that insists that the system respond to events quickly. In response to the demands of modern hardware and applications, the Linux kernel has evolved to a point where many more things are going on simultaneously. This evolution has resulted in far greater performance and scalability. It has also, however, significantly complicated the task of kernel programming. Device driver programmers must now factor concurrency into their designs from the beginning, and they must have a strong understanding of the facilities provided by the kernel for concurrency management.

The purpose of this chapter is to begin the process of creating that understanding. To that end, we introduce facilities that are immediately applied to the *scull* driver from Chapter 3. Other facilities presented here are not put to use for some time yet. But first, we take a look at what could go wrong with our simple *scull* driver and how to avoid these potential problems.

Pitfalls in scull

Let us take a quick look at a fragment of the *scull* memory management code. Deep down inside the *write* logic, *scull* must decide whether the memory it requires has been allocated yet or not. One piece of the code that handles this task is:

```
if (!dptr->data[s_pos]) {
    dptr->data[s_pos] = kmalloc(quantum, GFP_KERNEL);
    if (!dptr->data[s_pos])
        goto out;
}
```

Suppose for a moment that two processes (we'll call them "A" and "B") are independently attempting to write to the same offset within the same *scull* device. Each process reaches the if test in the first line of the fragment above at the same time. If the pointer in question is NULL, each process will decide to allocate memory, and each will assign the resulting pointer to dptr->data[s_pos]. Since both processes are assigning to the same location, clearly only one of the assignments will prevail.

What will happen, of course, is that the process that completes the assignment second will "win." If process A assigns first, its assignment will be overwritten by process B. At that point, *scull* will forget entirely about the memory that A allocated; it only has a pointer to B's memory. The memory allocated by A, thus, will be dropped and never returned to the system.

This sequence of events is a demonstration of a *race condition*. Race conditions are a result of uncontrolled access to shared data. When the wrong access pattern happens, something unexpected results. For the race condition discussed here, the result is a memory leak. That is bad enough, but race conditions can often lead to system crashes, corrupted data, or security problems as well. Programmers can be tempted to disregard race conditions as extremely low probability events. But, in the computing world, one-in-a-million events can happen every few seconds, and the consequences can be grave.

We will eliminate race conditions from *scull* shortly, but first we need to take a more general view of concurrency.

Concurrency and Its Management

In a modern Linux system, there are numerous sources of concurrency and, therefore, possible race conditions. Multiple user-space processes are running, and they can access your code in surprising combinations of ways. SMP systems can be executing your code simultaneously on different processors. Kernel code is preemptible; your driver's code can lose the processor at any time, and the process that replaces it could also be running in your driver. Device interrupts are asynchronous events that can cause concurrent execution of your code. The kernel also provides various mechanisms for delayed code execution, such as workqueues, tasklets, and timers, which can cause your code to run at any time in ways unrelated to what the current process is doing. In the modern, hot-pluggable world, your device could simply disappear while you are in the middle of working with it.

Avoidance of race conditions can be an intimidating task. In a world where anything can happen at any time, how does a driver programmer avoid the creation of absolute chaos? As it turns out, most race conditions can be avoided through some thought, the kernel's concurrency control primitives, and the application of a few basic principles. We'll start with the principles first, then get into the specifics of how to apply them.

Race conditions come about as a result of shared access to resources. When two threads of execution* have a reason to work with the same data structures (or hardware resources), the potential for mixups always exists. So the first rule of thumb to keep in mind as you design your driver is to avoid shared resources whenever possible. If there is no concurrent access, there can be no race conditions. So carefully-written kernel code should have a minimum of sharing. The most obvious application of this idea is to avoid the use of global variables. If you put a resource in a place where more than one thread of execution can find it, there should be a strong reason for doing so.

The fact of the matter is, however, that such sharing is often required. Hardware resources are, by their nature, shared, and software resources also must often be available to more than one thread. Bear in mind as well that global variables are far from the only way to share data; any time your code passes a pointer to some other part of the kernel, it is potentially creating a new sharing situation. Sharing is a fact of life.

Here is the hard rule of resource sharing: any time that a hardware or software resource is shared beyond a single thread of execution, and the possibility exists that one thread could encounter an inconsistent view of that resource, you must explicitly manage access to that resource. In the *scull* example above, process B's view of the situation is inconsistent; unaware that process A has already allocated memory for the (shared) device, it performs its own allocation and overwrites A's work. In this case, we must control access to the *scull* data structure. We need to arrange things so that the code either sees memory that has been allocated or knows that no memory has been *or will be* allocated by anybody else. The usual technique for access management is called *locking* or *mutual exclusion*—making sure that only one thread of execution can manipulate a shared resource at any time. Much of the rest of this chapter will be devoted to locking.

---

* For the purposes of this chapter, a "thread" of execution is any context that is running code. Each process is clearly a thread of execution, but so is an interrupt handler or other code running in response to an asynchronous kernel event.

First, however, we must briefly consider one other important rule. When kernel code creates an object that will be shared with any other part of the kernel, that object must continue to exist (and function properly) until it is known that no outside references to it exist. The instant that *scull* makes its devices available, it must be prepared to handle requests on those devices. And *scull* must continue to be able to handle requests on its devices until it knows that no reference (such as open userspace files) to those devices exists. Two requirements come out of this rule: no object can be made available to the kernel until it is in a state where it can function properly, and references to such objects must be tracked. In most cases, you'll find that the kernel handles reference counting for you, but there are always exceptions.

Following the above rules requires planning and careful attention to detail. It is easy to be surprised by concurrent access to resources you hadn't realized were shared. With some effort, however, most race conditions can be headed off before they bite you—or your users.

Semaphores and Mutexes

So let us look at how we can add locking to *scull*. Our goal is to make our operations on the *scull* data structure *atomic*, meaning that the entire operation happens at once as far as other threads of execution are concerned. For our memory leak example, we need to ensure that if one thread finds that a particular chunk of memory must be allocated, it has the opportunity to perform that allocation before any other thread can make that test. To this end, we must set up *critical sections*: code that can be executed by only one thread at any given time.

Not all critical sections are the same, so the kernel provides different primitives for different needs. In this case, every access to the *scull* data structure happens in process context as a result of a direct user request; no accesses will be made from interrupt handlers or other asynchronous contexts. There are no particular latency (response time) requirements; application programmers understand that I/O requests are not usually satisfied immediately. Furthermore, the *scull* is not holding any other critical system resource while it is accessing its own data structures. What all this means is that if the *scull* driver goes to sleep while waiting for its turn to access the data structure, nobody is going to mind.

"Go to sleep" is a well-defined term in this context. When a Linux process reaches a point where it cannot make any further processes, it goes to sleep (or "blocks"), yielding the processor to somebody else until some future time when it can get work done again. Processes often sleep when waiting for I/O to complete. As we get deeper into the kernel, we will encounter a number of situations where we cannot sleep. The *write* method in *scull* is not one of those situations, however. So we can use a locking mechanism that might cause the process to sleep while waiting for access to the critical section.

Just as importantly, we will be performing an operation (memory allocation with *kmalloc*) that could sleep—so sleeps are a possibility in any case. If our critical sections are to work properly, we must use a locking primitive that works when a thread that owns the lock sleeps. Not all locking mechanisms can be used where sleeping is a possibility (we'll see some that don't later in this chapter). For our present needs, however, the mechanism that fits best is a *semaphore*.

Semaphores are a well-understood concept in computer science. At its core, a semaphore is a single integer value combined with a pair of functions that are typically called *P* and *V*. A process wishing to enter a critical section will call *P* on the relevant semaphore; if the semaphore's value is greater than zero, that value is decremented by one and the process continues. If, instead, the semaphore's value is 0 (or less), the process must wait until somebody else releases the semaphore. Unlocking a semaphore is accomplished by calling *V*; this function increments the value of the semaphore and, if necessary, wakes up processes that are waiting.

When semaphores are used for *mutual exclusion*—keeping multiple processes from running within a critical section simultaneously—their value will be initially set to 1. Such a semaphore can be held only by a single process or thread at any given time. A semaphore used in this mode is sometimes called a *mutex*, which is, of course, an abbreviation for "mutual exclusion." Almost all semaphores found in the Linux kernel are used for mutual exclusion.

The Linux Semaphore Implementation

The Linux kernel provides an implementation of semaphores that conforms to the above semantics, although the terminology is a little different. To use semaphores, kernel code must include *<asm/semaphore.h>*. The relevant type is struct semaphore; actual semaphores can be declared and initialized in a few ways. One is to create a semaphore directly, then set it up with *sema_init*:

```
void sema_init(struct semaphore *sem, int val);
```

where val is the initial value to assign to a semaphore.

Usually, however, semaphores are used in a mutex mode. To make this common case a little easier, the kernel has provided a set of helper functions and macros. Thus, a mutex can be declared and initialized with one of the following:

```
DECLARE_MUTEX(name);
DECLARE_MUTEX_LOCKED(name);
```

Here, the result is a semaphore variable (called name) that is initialized to 1 (with DECLARE_MUTEX) or 0 (with DECLARE_MUTEX_LOCKED). In the latter case, the mutex starts out in a locked state; it will have to be explicitly unlocked before any thread will be allowed access.

If the mutex must be initialized at runtime (which is the case if it is allocated dynamically, for example), use one of the following:

```
void init_MUTEX(struct semaphore *sem);
void init_MUTEX_LOCKED(struct semaphore *sem);
```

In the Linux world, the *P* function is called *down*—or some variation of that name. Here, "down" refers to the fact that the function decrements the value of the semaphore and, perhaps after putting the caller to sleep for a while to wait for the semaphore to become available, grants access to the protected resources. There are three versions of *down*:

```
void down(struct semaphore *sem);
int down_interruptible(struct semaphore *sem);
int down_trylock(struct semaphore *sem);
```

down decrements the value of the semaphore and waits as long as need be. *down_interruptible* does the same, but the operation is interruptible. The interruptible version is almost always the one you will want; it allows a user-space process that is waiting on a semaphore to be interrupted by the user. You do not, as a general rule, want to use noninterruptible operations unless there truly is no alternative. Noninterruptible operations are a good way to create unkillable processes (the dreaded "D state" seen in *ps*), and annoy your users. Using *down_interruptible* requires some extra care, however, if the operation is interrupted, the function returns a nonzero value, and the caller does *not* hold the semaphore. Proper use of *down_interruptible* requires always checking the return value and responding accordingly.

The final version (*down_trylock*) never sleeps; if the semaphore is not available at the time of the call, *down_trylock* returns immediately with a nonzero return value.

Once a thread has successfully called one of the versions of *down*, it is said to be "holding" the semaphore (or to have "taken out" or "acquired" the semaphore). That thread is now entitled to access the critical section protected by the semaphore. When the operations requiring mutual exclusion are complete, the semaphore must be returned. The Linux equivalent to *V* is *up*:

```
void up(struct semaphore *sem);
```

Once *up* has been called, the caller no longer holds the semaphore.

As you would expect, any thread that takes out a semaphore is required to release it with one (and only one) call to *up*. Special care is often required in error paths; if an error is encountered while a semaphore is held, that semaphore must be released before returning the error status to the caller. Failure to free a semaphore is an easy error to make; the result (processes hanging in seemingly unrelated places) can be hard to reproduce and track down.

Using Semaphores in scull

The semaphore mechanism gives *scull* a tool that can be used to avoid race conditions while accessing the scull_dev data structure. But it is up to us to use that tool correctly. The keys to proper use of locking primitives are to specify exactly which resources are to be protected and to make sure that every access to those resources uses the proper locking. In our example driver, everything of interest is contained within the scull_dev structure, so that is the logical scope for our locking regime.

Let's look again at that structure:

```
struct scull_dev {
    struct scull_qset *data;  /* Pointer to first quantum set */
    int quantum;              /* the current quantum size */
    int qset;                 /* the current array size */
    unsigned long size;       /* amount of data stored here */
    unsigned int access_key;  /* used by sculluid and scullpriv */
    struct semaphore sem;     /* mutual exclusion semaphore    */
    struct cdev cdev;     /* Char device structure       */
};
```

Toward the bottom of the structure is a member called sem which is, of course, our semaphore. We have chosen to use a separate semaphore for each virtual *scull* device. It would have been equally correct to use a single, global semaphore. The various *scull* devices share no resources in common, however, and there is no reason to make one process wait while another process is working with a different *scull* device. Using a separate semaphore for each device allows operations on different devices to proceed in parallel and, therefore, improves performance.

Semaphores must be initialized before use. *scull* performs this initialization at load time in this loop:

```
for (i = 0; i < scull_nr_devs; i++) {
    scull_devices[i].quantum = scull_quantum;
    scull_devices[i].qset = scull_qset;
    init_MUTEX(&scull_devices[i].sem);
    scull_setup_cdev(&scull_devices[i], i);
}
```

Note that the semaphore must be initialized *before* the *scull* device is made available to the rest of the system. Therefore, *init_MUTEX* is called before *scull_setup_cdev*. Performing these operations in the opposite order would create a race condition where the semaphore could be accessed before it is ready.

Next, we must go through the code and make sure that no accesses to the scull_dev data structure are made without holding the semaphore. Thus, for example, *scull_write* begins with this code:

```
if (down_interruptible(&dev->sem))
    return -ERESTARTSYS;
```

Note the check on the return value of *down_interruptible*; if it returns nonzero, the operation was interrupted. The usual thing to do in this situation is to return -ERESTARTSYS. Upon seeing this return code, the higher layers of the kernel will either restart the call from the beginning or return the error to the user. If you return -ERESTARTSYS, you must first undo any user-visible changes that might have been made, so that the right thing happens when the system call is retried. If you cannot undo things in this manner, you should return -EINTR instead.

scull_write must release the semaphore whether or not it was able to carry out its other tasks successfully. If all goes well, execution falls into the final few lines of the function:

```
out:
  up(&dev->sem);
  return retval;
```

This code frees the semaphore and returns whatever status is called for. There are several places in *scull_write* where things can go wrong; these include memory allocation failures or a fault while trying to copy data from user space. In those cases, the code performs a goto out, ensuring that the proper cleanup is done.

Reader/Writer Semaphores

Semaphores perform mutual exclusion for all callers, regardless of what each thread may want to do. Many tasks break down into two distinct types of work, however: tasks that only need to read the protected data structures and those that must make changes. It is often possible to allow multiple concurrent readers, as long as nobody is trying to make any changes. Doing so can optimize performance significantly; read-only tasks can get their work done in parallel without having to wait for other readers to exit the critical section.

The Linux kernel provides a special type of semaphore called a *rwsem* (or "reader/writer semaphore") for this situation. The use of rwsems in drivers is relatively rare, but they are occasionally useful.

Code using rwsems must include *<linux/rwsem.h>*. The relevant data type for reader/writer semaphores is struct rw_semaphore; an rwsem must be explicitly initialized at runtime with:

```
void init_rwsem(struct rw_semaphore *sem);
```

A newly initialized rwsem is available for the next task (reader or writer) that comes along. The interface for code needing read-only access is:

```
void down_read(struct rw_semaphore *sem);
int down_read_trylock(struct rw_semaphore *sem);
void up_read(struct rw_semaphore *sem);
```

A call to *down_read* provides read-only access to the protected resources, possibly concurrently with other readers. Note that *down_read* may put the calling process into an uninterruptible sleep. *down_read_trylock* will not wait if read access is unavailable; it returns nonzero if access was granted, 0 otherwise. Note that the convention for *down_read_trylock* differs from that of most kernel functions, where success is indicated by a return value of 0. A rwsem obtained with *down_read* must eventually be freed with *up_read*.

The interface for writers is similar:

```
void down_write(struct rw_semaphore *sem);
int down_write_trylock(struct rw_semaphore *sem);
void up_write(struct rw_semaphore *sem);
void downgrade_write(struct rw_semaphore *sem);
```

down_write, *down_write_trylock*, and *up_write* all behave just like their reader counterparts, except, of course, that they provide write access. If you have a situation where a writer lock is needed for a quick change, followed by a longer period of read-only access, you can use *downgrade_write* to allow other readers in once you have finished making changes.

An rwsem allows either one writer or an unlimited number of readers to hold the semaphore. Writers get priority; as soon as a writer tries to enter the critical section, no readers will be allowed in until all writers have completed their work. This implementation can lead to reader *starvation*—where readers are denied access for a long time—if you have a large number of writers contending for the semaphore. For this reason, rwsems are best used when write access is required only rarely, and writer access is held for short periods of time.

Completions

A common pattern in kernel programming involves initiating some activity outside of the current thread, then waiting for that activity to complete. This activity can be the creation of a new kernel thread or user-space process, a request to an existing process, or some sort of hardware-based action. It such cases, it can be tempting to use a semaphore for synchronization of the two tasks, with code such as:

```
struct semaphore sem;

init_MUTEX_LOCKED(&sem);
start_external_task(&sem);
down(&sem);
```

The external task can then call up(&sem) when its work is done.

As is turns out, semaphores are not the best tool to use in this situation. In normal use, code attempting to lock a semaphore finds that semaphore available almost all the time; if there is significant contention for the semaphore, performance suffers and the locking scheme needs to be reviewed. So semaphores have been heavily optimized for the "available" case. When used to communicate task completion in the way shown above, however, the thread calling *down* will almost always have to wait; performance will suffer accordingly. Semaphores can also be subject to a (difficult) race condition when used in this way if they are declared as automatic variables. In some cases, the semaphore could vanish before the process calling *up* is finished with it.

These concerns inspired the addition of the "completion" interface in the 2.4.7 kernel. Completions are a lightweight mechanism with one task: allowing one thread to tell another that the job is done. To use completions, your code must include *<linux/completion.h>*. A completion can be created with:

```
DECLARE_COMPLETION(my_completion);
```

Or, if the completion must be created and initialized dynamically:

```
struct completion my_completion;
/* ... */
init_completion(&my_completion);
```

Waiting for the completion is a simple matter of calling:

```
void wait_for_completion(struct completion *c);
```

Note that this function performs an uninterruptible wait. If your code calls *wait_for_completion* and nobody ever completes the task, the result will be an unkillable process.[*]

On the other side, the actual completion event may be signalled by calling one of the following:

```
void complete(struct completion *c);
void complete_all(struct completion *c);
```

The two functions behave differently if more than one thread is waiting for the same completion event. *complete* wakes up only one of the waiting threads while *complete_all* allows all of them to proceed. In most cases, there is only one waiter, and the two functions will produce an identical result.

A completion is normally a one-shot device; it is used once then discarded. It is possible, however, to reuse completion structures if proper care is taken. If *complete_all* is not used, a completion structure can be reused without any problems as long as there is no ambiguity about what event is being signalled. If you use *complete_all*, however, you must reinitialize the completion structure before reusing it. The macro:

```
INIT_COMPLETION(struct completion c);
```

can be used to quickly perform this reinitialization.

As an example of how completions may be used, consider the *complete* module, which is included in the example source. This module defines a device with simple semantics: any process trying to read from the device will wait (using *wait_for_completion*)

---

[*] As of this writing, patches adding interruptible versions were in circulation but had not been merged into the mainline.

until some other process writes to the device. The code which implements this behavior is:

```
DECLARE_COMPLETION(comp);

ssize_t complete_read (struct file *filp, char __user *buf, size_t count, loff_t
*pos)
{
    printk(KERN_DEBUG "process %i (%s) going to sleep\n",
            current->pid, current->comm);
    wait_for_completion(&comp);
    printk(KERN_DEBUG "awoken %i (%s)\n", current->pid, current->comm);
    return 0; /* EOF */
}

ssize_t complete_write (struct file *filp, const char __user *buf, size_t count,
        loff_t *pos)
{
    printk(KERN_DEBUG "process %i (%s) awakening the readers...\n",
            current->pid, current->comm);
    complete(&comp);
    return count; /* succeed, to avoid retrial */
}
```

It is possible to have multiple processes "reading" from this device at the same time. Each write to the device will cause exactly one read operation to complete, but there is no way to know which one it will be.

A typical use of the completion mechanism is with kernel thread termination at module exit time. In the prototypical case, some of the driver internal workings is performed by a kernel thread in a while (1) loop. When the module is ready to be cleaned up, the exit function tells the thread to exit and then waits for completion. To this aim, the kernel includes a specific function to be used by the thread:

```
void complete_and_exit(struct completion *c, long retval);
```

Spinlocks

Semaphores are a useful tool for mutual exclusion, but they are not the only such tool provided by the kernel. Instead, most locking is implemented with a mechanism called a *spinlock*. Unlike semaphores, spinlocks may be used in code that cannot sleep, such as interrupt handlers. When properly used, spinlocks offer higher performance than semaphores in general. They do, however, bring a different set of constraints on their use.

Spinlocks are simple in concept. A spinlock is a mutual exclusion device that can have only two values: "locked" and "unlocked." It is usually implemented as a single bit in an integer value. Code wishing to take out a particular lock tests the relevant bit. If the lock is available, the "locked" bit is set and the code continues into the critical section. If, instead, the lock has been taken by somebody else, the code goes into a tight loop where it repeatedly checks the lock until it becomes available. This loop is the "spin" part of a spinlock.

Of course, the real implementation of a spinlock is a bit more complex than the description above. The "test and set" operation must be done in an atomic manner so that only one thread can obtain the lock, even if several are spinning at any given time. Care must also be taken to avoid deadlocks on *hyperthreaded* processors— chips that implement multiple, virtual CPUs sharing a single processor core and cache. So the actual spinlock implementation is different for every architecture that Linux supports. The core concept is the same on all systems, however, when there is contention for a spinlock, the processors that are waiting execute a tight loop and accomplish no useful work.

Spinlocks are, by their nature, intended for use on multiprocessor systems, although a uniprocessor workstation running a preemptive kernel behaves like SMP, as far as concurrency is concerned. If a nonpreemptive uniprocessor system ever went into a spin on a lock, it would spin forever; no other thread would ever be able to obtain the CPU to release the lock. For this reason, spinlock operations on uniprocessor systems without preemption enabled are optimized to do nothing, with the exception of the ones that change the IRQ masking status. Because of preemption, even if you never expect your code to run on an SMP system, you still need to implement proper locking.

Introduction to the Spinlock API

The required include file for the spinlock primitives is *<linux/spinlock.h>*. An actual lock has the type spinlock_t. Like any other data structure, a spinlock must be initialized. This initialization may be done at compile time as follows:

```
spinlock_t my_lock = SPIN_LOCK_UNLOCKED;
```

or at runtime with:

```
void spin_lock_init(spinlock_t *lock);
```

Before entering a critical section, your code must obtain the requisite lock with:

```
void spin_lock(spinlock_t *lock);
```

Note that all spinlock waits are, by their nature, uninterruptible. Once you call *spin_lock*, you will spin until the lock becomes available.

To release a lock that you have obtained, pass it to:

```
void spin_unlock(spinlock_t *lock);
```

There are many other spinlock functions, and we will look at them all shortly. But none of them depart from the core idea shown by the functions listed above. There is very little that one can do with a lock, other than lock and release it. However, there are a few rules about how you must work with spinlocks. We will take a moment to look at those before getting into the full spinlock interface.

Spinlocks and Atomic Context

Imagine for a moment that your driver acquires a spinlock and goes about its business within its critical section. Somewhere in the middle, your driver loses the processor. Perhaps it has called a function (*copy_from_user*, say) that puts the process to sleep. Or, perhaps, kernel preemption kicks in, and a higher-priority process pushes your code aside. Your code is now holding a lock that it will not release any time in the foreseeable future. If some other thread tries to obtain the same lock, it will, in the best case, wait (spinning in the processor) for a very long time. In the worst case, the system could deadlock entirely.

Most readers would agree that this scenario is best avoided. Therefore, the core rule that applies to spinlocks is that any code must, while holding a spinlock, be atomic. It cannot sleep; in fact, it cannot relinquish the processor for any reason except to service interrupts (and sometimes not even then).

The kernel preemption case is handled by the spinlock code itself. Any time kernel code holds a spinlock, preemption is disabled on the relevant processor. Even uniprocessor systems must disable preemption in this way to avoid race conditions. That is why proper locking is required even if you never expect your code to run on a multiprocessor machine.

Avoiding sleep while holding a lock can be more difficult; many kernel functions can sleep, and this behavior is not always well documented. Copying data to or from user space is an obvious example: the required user-space page may need to be swapped in from the disk before the copy can proceed, and that operation clearly requires a sleep. Just about any operation that must allocate memory can sleep; *kmalloc* can decide to give up the processor, and wait for more memory to become available unless it is explicitly told not to. Sleeps can happen in surprising places; writing code that will execute under a spinlock requires paying attention to every function that you call.

Here's another scenario: your driver is executing and has just taken out a lock that controls access to its device. While the lock is held, the device issues an interrupt, which causes your interrupt handler to run. The interrupt handler, before accessing the device, must also obtain the lock. Taking out a spinlock in an interrupt handler is a legitimate thing to do; that is one of the reasons that spinlock operations do not sleep. But what happens if the interrupt routine executes in the same processor as the code that took out the lock originally? While the interrupt handler is spinning, the noninterrupt code will not be able to run to release the lock. That processor will spin forever.

Avoiding this trap requires disabling interrupts (on the local CPU only) while the spinlock is held. There are variants of the spinlock functions that will disable interrupts for you (we'll see them in the next section). However, a complete discussion of interrupts must wait until Chapter 10.

The last important rule for spinlock usage is that spinlocks must always be held for the minimum time possible. The longer you hold a lock, the longer another processor may have to spin waiting for you to release it, and the chance of it having to spin at all is greater. Long lock hold times also keep the current processor from scheduling, meaning that a higher priority process—which really should be able to get the CPU—may have to wait. The kernel developers put a great deal of effort into reducing kernel latency (the time a process may have to wait to be scheduled) in the 2.5 development series. A poorly written driver can wipe out all that progress just by holding a lock for too long. To avoid creating this sort of problem, make a point of keeping your lock-hold times short.

The Spinlock Functions

We have already seen two functions, *spin_lock* and *spin_unlock*, that manipulate spinlocks. There are several other functions, however, with similar names and purposes. We will now present the full set. This discussion will take us into ground we will not be able to cover properly for a few chapters yet; a complete understanding of the spinlock API requires an understanding of interrupt handling and related concepts.

There are actually four functions that can lock a spinlock:

```
void spin_lock(spinlock_t *lock);
void spin_lock_irqsave(spinlock_t *lock, unsigned long flags);
void spin_lock_irq(spinlock_t *lock);
void spin_lock_bh(spinlock_t *lock)
```

We have already seen how *spin_lock* works. *spin_lock_irqsave* disables interrupts (on the local processor only) before taking the spinlock; the previous interrupt state is stored in flags. If you are absolutely sure nothing else might have already disabled interrupts on your processor (or, in other words, you are sure that you should enable interrupts when you release your spinlock), you can use *spin_lock_irq* instead and not have to keep track of the flags. Finally, *spin_lock_bh* disables software interrupts before taking the lock, but leaves hardware interrupts enabled.

If you have a spinlock that can be taken by code that runs in (hardware or software) interrupt context, you must use one of the forms of *spin_lock* that disables interrupts. Doing otherwise can deadlock the system, sooner or later. If you do not access your lock in a hardware interrupt handler, but you do via software interrupts (in code that runs out of a tasklet, for example, a topic covered in Chapter 7), you can use *spin_lock_bh* to safely avoid deadlocks while still allowing hardware interrupts to be serviced.

There are also four ways to release a spinlock; the one you use must correspond to the function you used to take the lock:

```
void spin_unlock(spinlock_t *lock);
void spin_unlock_irqrestore(spinlock_t *lock, unsigned long flags);
void spin_unlock_irq(spinlock_t *lock);
void spin_unlock_bh(spinlock_t *lock);
```

Each *spin_unlock* variant undoes the work performed by the corresponding *spin_lock* function. The `flags` argument passed to *spin_unlock_irqrestore* must be the same variable passed to *spin_lock_irqsave*. You must also call *spin_lock_irqsave* and *spin_unlock_irqrestore* in the same function; otherwise, your code may break on some architectures.

There is also a set of nonblocking spinlock operations:

```
int spin_trylock(spinlock_t *lock);
int spin_trylock_bh(spinlock_t *lock);
```

These functions return nonzero on success (the lock was obtained), 0 otherwise. There is no "try" version that disables interrupts.

Reader/Writer Spinlocks

The kernel provides a reader/writer form of spinlocks that is directly analogous to the reader/writer semaphores we saw earlier in this chapter. These locks allow any number of readers into a critical section simultaneously, but writers must have exclusive access. Reader/writer locks have a type of `rwlock_t`, defined in *<linux/spinlock.h>*. They can be declared and initialized in two ways:

```
rwlock_t my_rwlock = RW_LOCK_UNLOCKED; /* Static way */

rwlock_t my_rwlock;
rwlock_init(&my_rwlock);   /* Dynamic way */
```

The list of functions available should look reasonably familiar by now. For readers, the following functions are available:

```
void read_lock(rwlock_t *lock);
void read_lock_irqsave(rwlock_t *lock, unsigned long flags);
void read_lock_irq(rwlock_t *lock);
void read_lock_bh(rwlock_t *lock);

void read_unlock(rwlock_t *lock);
void read_unlock_irqrestore(rwlock_t *lock, unsigned long flags);
void read_unlock_irq(rwlock_t *lock);
void read_unlock_bh(rwlock_t *lock);
```

Interestingly, there is no *read_trylock*.

The functions for write access are similar:

```
void write_lock(rwlock_t *lock);
void write_lock_irqsave(rwlock_t *lock, unsigned long flags);
```

```
void write_lock_irq(rwlock_t *lock);
void write_lock_bh(rwlock_t *lock);
int write_trylock(rwlock_t *lock);

void write_unlock(rwlock_t *lock);
void write_unlock_irqrestore(rwlock_t *lock, unsigned long flags);
void write_unlock_irq(rwlock_t *lock);
void write_unlock_bh(rwlock_t *lock);
```

Reader/writer locks can starve readers just as rwsems can. This behavior is rarely a problem; however, if there is enough lock contention to bring about starvation, performance is poor anyway.

Locking Traps

Many years of experience with locks—experience that predates Linux—have shown that locking can be very hard to get right. Managing concurrency is an inherently tricky undertaking, and there are many ways of making mistakes. In this section, we take a quick look at things that can go wrong.

Ambiguous Rules

As has already been said above, a proper locking scheme requires clear and explicit rules. When you create a resource that can be accessed concurrently, you should define which lock will control that access. Locking should really be laid out at the beginning; it can be a hard thing to retrofit in afterward. Time taken at the outset usually is paid back generously at debugging time.

As you write your code, you will doubtless encounter several functions that all require access to structures protected by a specific lock. At this point, you must be careful: if one function acquires a lock and then calls another function that also attempts to acquire the lock, your code deadlocks. Neither semaphores nor spinlocks allow a lock holder to acquire the lock a second time; should you attempt to do so, things simply hang.

To make your locking work properly, you have to write some functions with the assumption that their caller has already acquired the relevant lock(s). Usually, only your internal, static functions can be written in this way; functions called from outside must handle locking explicitly. When you write internal functions that make assumptions about locking, do yourself (and anybody else who works with your code) a favor and document those assumptions explicitly. It can be very hard to come back months later and figure out whether you need to hold a lock to call a particular function or not.

In the case of *scull*, the design decision taken was to require all functions invoked directly from system calls to acquire the semaphore applying to the device structure that is accessed. All internal functions, which are only called from other *scull* functions, can then assume that the semaphore has been properly acquired.

Lock Ordering Rules

In systems with a large number of locks (and the kernel is becoming such a system), it is not unusual for code to need to hold more than one lock at once. If some sort of computation must be performed using two different resources, each of which has its own lock, there is often no alternative to acquiring both locks.

Taking multiple locks can be dangerous, however. If you have two locks, called *Lock1* and *Lock2*, and code needs to acquire both at the same time, you have a potential deadlock. Just imagine one thread locking *Lock1* while another simultaneously takes *Lock2*. Then each thread tries to get the one it doesn't have. Both threads will deadlock.

The solution to this problem is usually simple: when multiple locks must be acquired, they should always be acquired in the same order. As long as this convention is followed, simple deadlocks like the one described above can be avoided. However, following lock ordering rules can be easier said than done. It is very rare that such rules are actually written down anywhere. Often the best you can do is to see what other code does.

A couple of rules of thumb can help. If you must obtain a lock that is local to your code (a device lock, say) along with a lock belonging to a more central part of the kernel, take your lock first. If you have a combination of semaphores and spinlocks, you must, of course, obtain the semaphore(s) first; calling *down* (which can sleep) while holding a spinlock is a serious error. But most of all, try to avoid situations where you need more than one lock.

Fine- Versus Coarse-Grained Locking

The first Linux kernel that supported multiprocessor systems was 2.0; it contained exactly one spinlock. The *big kernel lock* turned the entire kernel into one large critical section; only one CPU could be executing kernel code at any given time. This lock solved the concurrency problem well enough to allow the kernel developers to address all of the other issues involved in supporting SMP. But it did not scale very well. Even a two-processor system could spend a significant amount of time simply waiting for the big kernel lock. The performance of a four-processor system was not even close to that of four independent machines.

So, subsequent kernel releases have included finer-grained locking. In 2.2, one spinlock controlled access to the block I/O subsystem; another worked for networking, and so on. A modern kernel can contain thousands of locks, each protecting one small resource. This sort of fine-grained locking can be good for scalability; it allows each processor to work on its specific task without contending for locks used by other processors. Very few people miss the big kernel lock.*

Fine-grained locking comes at a cost, however. In a kernel with thousands of locks, it can be very hard to know which locks you need—and in which order you should acquire them—to perform a specific operation. Remember that locking bugs can be very difficult to find; more locks provide more opportunities for truly nasty locking bugs to creep into the kernel. Fine-grained locking can bring a level of complexity that, over the long term, can have a large, adverse effect on the maintainability of the kernel.

Locking in a device driver is usually relatively straightforward; you can have a single lock that covers everything you do, or you can create one lock for every device you manage. As a general rule, you should start with relatively coarse locking unless you have a real reason to believe that contention could be a problem. Resist the urge to optimize prematurely; the real performance constraints often show up in unexpected places.

If you do suspect that lock contention is hurting performance, you may find the *lockmeter* tool useful. This patch (available at *http://oss.sgi.com/projects/lockmeter/*) instruments the kernel to measure time spent waiting in locks. By looking at the report, you are able to determine quickly whether lock contention is truly the problem or not.

Alternatives to Locking

The Linux kernel provides a number of powerful locking primitives that can be used to keep the kernel from tripping over its own feet. But, as we have seen, the design and implementation of a locking scheme is not without its pitfalls. Often there is no alternative to semaphores and spinlocks; they may be the only way to get the job done properly. There are situations, however, where atomic access can be set up without the need for full locking. This section looks at other ways of doing things.

Lock-Free Algorithms

Sometimes, you can recast your algorithms to avoid the need for locking altogether. A number of reader/writer situations—if there is only one writer—can often work in this manner. If the writer takes care that the view of the data structure, as seen by the reader, is always consistent, it may be possible to create a lock-free data structure.

A data structure that can often be useful for lockless producer/consumer tasks is the *circular buffer*. This algorithm involves a producer placing data into one end of an

---

* This lock still exists in 2.6, though it covers very little of the kernel now. If you stumble across a *lock_kernel* call, you have found the big kernel lock. Do not even think about using it in any new code, however.

array, while the consumer removes data from the other. When the end of the array is reached, the producer wraps back around to the beginning. So a circular buffer requires an array and two index values to track where the next new value goes and which value should be removed from the buffer next.

When carefully implemented, a circular buffer requires no locking in the absence of multiple producers or consumers. The producer is the only thread that is allowed to modify the write index and the array location it points to. As long as the writer stores a new value into the buffer before updating the write index, the reader will always see a consistent view. The reader, in turn, is the only thread that can access the read index and the value it points to. With a bit of care to ensure that the two pointers do not overrun each other, the producer and the consumer can access the buffer concurrently with no race conditions.

Figure 5-1 shows circular buffer in several states of fill. This buffer has been defined such that an empty condition is indicated by the read and write pointers being equal, while a full condition happens whenever the write pointer is immediately behind the read pointer (being careful to account for a wrap!). When carefully programmed, this buffer can be used without locks.

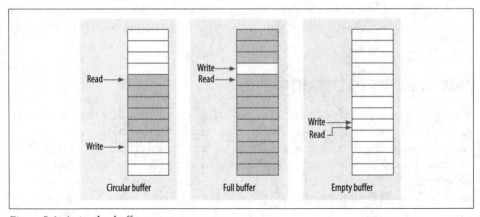

Figure 5-1. A circular buffer

Circular buffers show up reasonably often in device drivers. Networking adaptors, in particular, often use circular buffers to exchange data (packets) with the processor. Note that, as of 2.6.10, there is a generic circular buffer implementation available in the kernel; see *<linux/kfifo.h>* for information on how to use it.

Atomic Variables

Sometimes, a shared resource is a simple integer value. Suppose your driver maintains a shared variable n_op that tells how many device operations are currently outstanding. Normally, even a simple operation such as:

```
n_op++;
```

would require locking. Some processors might perform that sort of increment in an atomic manner, but you can't count on it. But a full locking regime seems like overhead for a simple integer value. For cases like this, the kernel provides an atomic integer type called atomic_t, defined in *<asm/atomic.h>*.

An atomic_t holds an int value on all supported architectures. Because of the way this type works on some processors, however, the full integer range may not be available; thus, you should not count on an atomic_t holding more than 24 bits. The following operations are defined for the type and are guaranteed to be atomic with respect to all processors of an SMP computer. The operations are very fast, because they compile to a single machine instruction whenever possible.

```
void atomic_set(atomic_t *v, int i);
atomic_t v = ATOMIC_INIT(0);
```
> Set the atomic variable v to the integer value i. You can also initialize atomic values at compile time with the ATOMIC_INIT macro.

```
int atomic_read(atomic_t *v);
```
> Return the current value of v.

```
void atomic_add(int i, atomic_t *v);
```
> Add i to the atomic variable pointed to by v. The return value is void, because there is an extra cost to returning the new value, and most of the time there's no need to know it.

```
void atomic_sub(int i, atomic_t *v);
```
> Subtract i from *v.

```
void atomic_inc(atomic_t *v);
void atomic_dec(atomic_t *v);
```
> Increment or decrement an atomic variable.

```
int atomic_inc_and_test(atomic_t *v);
int atomic_dec_and_test(atomic_t *v);
int atomic_sub_and_test(int i, atomic_t *v);
```
> Perform the specified operation and test the result; if, after the operation, the atomic value is 0, then the return value is true; otherwise, it is false. Note that there is no *atomic_add_and_test*.

```
int atomic_add_negative(int i, atomic_t *v);
```
> Add the integer variable i to v. The return value is true if the result is negative, false otherwise.

```
int atomic_add_return(int i, atomic_t *v);
int atomic_sub_return(int i, atomic_t *v);
int atomic_inc_return(atomic_t *v);
int atomic_dec_return(atomic_t *v);
```
> Behave just like *atomic_add* and friends, with the exception that they return the new value of the atomic variable to the caller.

As stated earlier, `atomic_t` data items must be accessed only through these functions. If you pass an atomic item to a function that expects an integer argument, you'll get a compiler error.

You should also bear in mind that `atomic_t` values work only when the quantity in question is truly atomic. Operations requiring multiple `atomic_t` variables still require some other sort of locking. Consider the following code:

```
atomic_sub(amount, &first_atomic);
atomic_add(amount, &second_atomic);
```

There is a period of time where the `amount` has been subtracted from the first atomic value but not yet added to the second. If that state of affairs could create trouble for code that might run between the two operations, some form of locking must be employed.

Bit Operations

The `atomic_t` type is good for performing integer arithmetic. It doesn't work as well, however, when you need to manipulate individual bits in an atomic manner. For that purpose, instead, the kernel offers a set of functions that modify or test single bits atomically. Because the whole operation happens in a single step, no interrupt (or other processor) can interfere.

Atomic bit operations are very fast, since they perform the operation using a single machine instruction without disabling interrupts whenever the underlying platform can do that. The functions are architecture dependent and are declared in *<asm/bitops.h>*. They are guaranteed to be atomic even on SMP computers and are useful to keep coherence across processors.

Unfortunately, data typing in these functions is architecture dependent as well. The nr argument (describing which bit to manipulate) is usually defined as `int` but is `unsigned long` for a few architectures. The address to be modified is usually a pointer to `unsigned long`, but a few architectures use `void *` instead.

The available bit operations are:

`void set_bit(nr, void *addr);`
> Sets bit number nr in the data item pointed to by `addr`.

`void clear_bit(nr, void *addr);`
> Clears the specified bit in the `unsigned long` datum that lives at `addr`. Its semantics are otherwise the same as *set_bit*.

`void change_bit(nr, void *addr);`
> Toggles the bit.

```
test_bit(nr, void *addr);
```
This function is the only bit operation that doesn't need to be atomic; it simply returns the current value of the bit.

```
int test_and_set_bit(nr, void *addr);
int test_and_clear_bit(nr, void *addr);
int test_and_change_bit(nr, void *addr);
```
Behave atomically like those listed previously, except that they also return the previous value of the bit.

When these functions are used to access and modify a shared flag, you don't have to do anything except call them; they perform their operations in an atomic manner. Using bit operations to manage a lock variable that controls access to a shared variable, on the other hand, is a little more complicated and deserves an example. Most modern code does not use bit operations in this way, but code like the following still exists in the kernel.

A code segment that needs to access a shared data item tries to atomically acquire a lock using either *test_and_set_bit* or *test_and_clear_bit*. The usual implementation is shown here; it assumes that the lock lives at bit nr of address addr. It also assumes that the bit is 0 when the lock is free or nonzero when the lock is busy.

```
/* try to set lock */
while (test_and_set_bit(nr, addr) != 0)
    wait_for_a_while();

/* do your work */

/* release lock, and check... */
if (test_and_clear_bit(nr, addr) == 0)
    something_went_wrong(); /* already released: error */
```

If you read through the kernel source, you find code that works like this example. It is, however, far better to use spinlocks in new code; spinlocks are well debugged, they handle issues like interrupts and kernel preemption, and others reading your code do not have to work to understand what you are doing.

seqlocks

The 2.6 kernel contains a couple of new mechanisms that are intended to provide fast, lockless access to a shared resource. Seqlocks work in situations where the resource to be protected is small, simple, and frequently accessed, and where write access is rare but must be fast. Essentially, they work by allowing readers free access to the resource but requiring those readers to check for collisions with writers and, when such a collision happens, retry their access. Seqlocks generally cannot be used to protect data structures involving pointers, because the reader may be following a pointer that is invalid while the writer is changing the data structure.

Seqlocks are defined in *<linux/seqlock.h>*. There are the two usual methods for initializing a seqlock (which has type `seqlock_t`):

```
seqlock_t lock1 = SEQLOCK_UNLOCKED;

seqlock_t lock2;
seqlock_init(&lock2);
```

Read access works by obtaining an (unsigned) integer sequence value on entry into the critical section. On exit, that sequence value is compared with the current value; if there is a mismatch, the read access must be retried. As a result, reader code has a form like the following:

```
unsigned int seq;

do {
    seq = read_seqbegin(&the_lock);
    /* Do what you need to do */
} while read_seqretry(&the_lock, seq);
```

This sort of lock is usually used to protect some sort of simple computation that requires multiple, consistent values. If the test at the end of the computation shows that a concurrent write occurred, the results can be simply discarded and recomputed.

If your seqlock might be accessed from an interrupt handler, you should use the IRQ-safe versions instead:

```
unsigned int read_seqbegin_irqsave(seqlock_t *lock,
                                    unsigned long flags);
int read_seqretry_irqrestore(seqlock_t *lock, unsigned int seq,
                             unsigned long flags);
```

Writers must obtain an exclusive lock to enter the critical section protected by a seqlock. To do so, call:

```
void write_seqlock(seqlock_t *lock);
```

The write lock is implemented with a spinlock, so all the usual constraints apply. Make a call to:

```
void write_sequnlock(seqlock_t *lock);
```

to release the lock. Since spinlocks are used to control write access, all of the usual variants are available:

```
void write_seqlock_irqsave(seqlock_t *lock, unsigned long flags);
void write_seqlock_irq(seqlock_t *lock);
void write_seqlock_bh(seqlock_t *lock);

void write_sequnlock_irqrestore(seqlock_t *lock, unsigned long flags);
void write_sequnlock_irq(seqlock_t *lock);
void write_sequnlock_bh(seqlock_t *lock);
```

There is also a *write_tryseqlock* that returns nonzero if it was able to obtain the lock.

Read-Copy-Update

Read-copy-update (RCU) is an advanced mutual exclusion scheme that can yield high performance in the right conditions. Its use in drivers is rare but not unknown, so it is worth a quick overview here. Those who are interested in the full details of the RCU algorithm can find them in the white paper published by its creator (*http://www.rdrop.com/users/paulmck/rclock/intro/rclock_intro.html*).

RCU places a number of constraints on the sort of data structure that it can protect. It is optimized for situations where reads are common and writes are rare. The resources being protected should be accessed via pointers, and all references to those resources must be held only by atomic code. When the data structure needs to be changed, the writing thread makes a copy, changes the copy, then aims the relevant pointer at the new version—thus, the name of the algorithm. When the kernel is sure that no references to the old version remain, it can be freed.

As an example of real-world use of RCU, consider the network routing tables. Every outgoing packet requires a check of the routing tables to determine which interface should be used. The check is fast, and, once the kernel has found the target interface, it no longer needs the routing table entry. RCU allows route lookups to be performed without locking, with significant performance benefits. The Starmode radio IP driver in the kernel also uses RCU to keep track of its list of devices.

Code using RCU should include *<linux/rcupdate.h>*.

On the read side, code using an RCU-protected data structure should bracket its references with calls to *rcu_read_lock* and *rcu_read_unlock*. As a result, RCU code tends to look like:

```
struct my_stuff *stuff;

rcu_read_lock();
stuff = find_the_stuff(args...);
do_something_with(stuff);
rcu_read_unlock();
```

The *rcu_read_lock* call is fast; it disables kernel preemption but does not wait for anything. The code that executes while the read "lock" is held must be atomic. No reference to the protected resource may be used after the call to *rcu_read_unlock*.

Code that needs to change the protected structure has to carry out a few steps. The first part is easy; it allocates a new structure, copies data from the old one if need be, then replaces the pointer that is seen by the read code. At this point, for the purposes of the read side, the change is complete; any code entering the critical section sees the new version of the data.

All that remains is to free the old version. The problem, of course, is that code running on other processors may still have a reference to the older data, so it cannot be freed immediately. Instead, the write code must wait until it knows that no such reference can exist. Since all code holding references to this data structure must (by the rules) be atomic, we know that once every processor on the system has been scheduled at least once, all references must be gone. So that is what RCU does; it sets aside a callback that waits until all processors have scheduled; that callback is then run to perform the cleanup work.

Code that changes an RCU-protected data structure must get its cleanup callback by allocating a struct rcu_head, although it doesn't need to initialize that structure in any way. Often, that structure is simply embedded within the larger resource that is protected by RCU. After the change to that resource is complete, a call should be made to:

```
void call_rcu(struct rcu_head *head, void (*func)(void *arg), void *arg);
```

The given func is called when it is safe to free the resource; it is passed to the same arg that was passed to *call_rcu*. Usually, the only thing func needs to do is to call *kfree*.

The full RCU interface is more complex than we have seen here; it includes, for example, utility functions for working with protected linked lists. See the relevant header files for the full story.

Quick Reference

This chapter has introduced a substantial set of symbols for the management of concurrency. The most important of these are summarized here:

#include <asm/semaphore.h>
> The include file that defines semaphores and the operations on them.

DECLARE_MUTEX(name);
DECLARE_MUTEX_LOCKED(name);
> Two macros for declaring and initializing a semaphore used in mutual exclusion mode.

void init_MUTEX(struct semaphore *sem);
void init_MUTEX_LOCKED(struct semaphore *sem);
> These two functions can be used to initialize a semaphore at runtime.

void down(struct semaphore *sem);
int down_interruptible(struct semaphore *sem);
int down_trylock(struct semaphore *sem);
void up(struct semaphore *sem);
> Lock and unlock a semaphore. *down* puts the calling process into an uninterruptible sleep if need be; *down_interruptible*, instead, can be interrupted by a signal. *down_trylock* does not sleep; instead, it returns immediately if the semaphore is unavailable. Code that locks a semaphore must eventually unlock it with *up*.

```
struct rw_semaphore;
init_rwsem(struct rw_semaphore *sem);
```
The reader/writer version of semaphores and the function that initializes it.

```
void down_read(struct rw_semaphore *sem);
int down_read_trylock(struct rw_semaphore *sem);
void up_read(struct rw_semaphore *sem);
```
Functions for obtaining and releasing read access to a reader/writer semaphore.

```
void down_write(struct rw_semaphore *sem)
int down_write_trylock(struct rw_semaphore *sem)
void up_write(struct rw_semaphore *sem)
void downgrade_write(struct rw_semaphore *sem)
```
Functions for managing write access to a reader/writer semaphore.

```
#include <linux/completion.h>
DECLARE_COMPLETION(name);
init_completion(struct completion *c);
INIT_COMPLETION(struct completion c);
```
The include file describing the Linux completion mechanism, and the normal methods for initializing completions. INIT_COMPLETION should be used only to reinitialize a completion that has been previously used.

```
void wait_for_completion(struct completion *c);
```
Wait for a completion event to be signalled.

```
void complete(struct completion *c);
void complete_all(struct completion *c);
```
Signal a completion event. *complete* wakes, at most, one waiting thread, while *complete_all* wakes all waiters.

```
void complete_and_exit(struct completion *c, long retval);
```
Signals a completion event by calling *complete* and calls *exit* for the current thread.

```
#include <linux/spinlock.h>
spinlock_t lock = SPIN_LOCK_UNLOCKED;
spin_lock_init(spinlock_t *lock);
```
The include file defining the spinlock interface and the two ways of initializing locks.

```
void spin_lock(spinlock_t *lock);
void spin_lock_irqsave(spinlock_t *lock, unsigned long flags);
void spin_lock_irq(spinlock_t *lock);
void spin_lock_bh(spinlock_t *lock);
```
The various ways of locking a spinlock and, possibly, disabling interrupts.

```
int spin_trylock(spinlock_t *lock);
int spin_trylock_bh(spinlock_t *lock);
```
Nonspinning versions of the above functions; these return 0 in case of failure to obtain the lock, nonzero otherwise.

```
void spin_unlock(spinlock_t *lock);
void spin_unlock_irqrestore(spinlock_t *lock, unsigned long flags);
void spin_unlock_irq(spinlock_t *lock);
void spin_unlock_bh(spinlock_t *lock);
```
The corresponding ways of releasing a spinlock.

```
rwlock_t lock = RW_LOCK_UNLOCKED
rwlock_init(rwlock_t *lock);
```
The two ways of initializing reader/writer locks.

```
void read_lock(rwlock_t *lock);
void read_lock_irqsave(rwlock_t *lock, unsigned long flags);
void read_lock_irq(rwlock_t *lock);
void read_lock_bh(rwlock_t *lock);
```
Functions for obtaining read access to a reader/writer lock.

```
void read_unlock(rwlock_t *lock);
void read_unlock_irqrestore(rwlock_t *lock, unsigned long flags);
void read_unlock_irq(rwlock_t *lock);
void read_unlock_bh(rwlock_t *lock);
```
Functions for releasing read access to a reader/writer spinlock.

```
void write_lock(rwlock_t *lock);
void write_lock_irqsave(rwlock_t *lock, unsigned long flags);
void write_lock_irq(rwlock_t *lock);
void write_lock_bh(rwlock_t *lock);
```
Functions for obtaining write access to a reader/writer lock.

```
void write_unlock(rwlock_t *lock);
void write_unlock_irqrestore(rwlock_t *lock, unsigned long flags);
void write_unlock_irq(rwlock_t *lock);
void write_unlock_bh(rwlock_t *lock);
```
Functions for releasing write access to a reader/writer spinlock.

```
#include <asm/atomic.h>
atomic_t v = ATOMIC_INIT(value);
void atomic_set(atomic_t *v, int i);
int atomic_read(atomic_t *v);
void atomic_add(int i, atomic_t *v);
void atomic_sub(int i, atomic_t *v);
void atomic_inc(atomic_t *v);
void atomic_dec(atomic_t *v);
int atomic_inc_and_test(atomic_t *v);
int atomic_dec_and_test(atomic_t *v);
int atomic_sub_and_test(int i, atomic_t *v);
int atomic_add_negative(int i, atomic_t *v);
int atomic_add_return(int i, atomic_t *v);
int atomic_sub_return(int i, atomic_t *v);
int atomic_inc_return(atomic_t *v);
int atomic_dec_return(atomic_t *v);
```
Atomically access integer variables. The atomic_t variables must be accessed only through these functions.

```
#include <asm/bitops.h>
void set_bit(nr, void *addr);
void clear_bit(nr, void *addr);
void change_bit(nr, void *addr);
test_bit(nr, void *addr);
int test_and_set_bit(nr, void *addr);
int test_and_clear_bit(nr, void *addr);
int test_and_change_bit(nr, void *addr);
```
Atomically access bit values; they can be used for flags or lock variables. Using these functions prevents any race condition related to concurrent access to the bit.

```
#include <linux/seqlock.h>
seqlock_t lock = SEQLOCK_UNLOCKED;
seqlock_init(seqlock_t *lock);
```
The include file defining seqlocks and the two ways of initializing them.

```
unsigned int read_seqbegin(seqlock_t *lock);
unsigned int read_seqbegin_irqsave(seqlock_t *lock, unsigned long flags);
int read_seqretry(seqlock_t *lock, unsigned int seq);
int read_seqretry_irqrestore(seqlock_t *lock, unsigned int seq, unsigned long
  flags);
```
Functions for obtaining read access to a seqlock-protected resources.

```
void write_seqlock(seqlock_t *lock);
void write_seqlock_irqsave(seqlock_t *lock, unsigned long flags);
void write_seqlock_irq(seqlock_t *lock);
void write_seqlock_bh(seqlock_t *lock);
int write_tryseqlock(seqlock_t *lock);
```
Functions for obtaining write access to a seqlock-protected resource.

```
void write_sequnlock(seqlock_t *lock);
void write_sequnlock_irqrestore(seqlock_t *lock, unsigned long flags);
void write_sequnlock_irq(seqlock_t *lock);
void write_sequnlock_bh(seqlock_t *lock);
```
Functions for releasing write access to a seqlock-protected resource.

```
#include <linux/rcupdate.h>
```
The include file required to use the read-copy-update (RCU) mechanism.

```
void rcu_read_lock;
void rcu_read_unlock;
```
Macros for obtaining atomic read access to a resource protected by RCU.

```
void call_rcu(struct rcu_head *head, void (*func)(void *arg), void *arg);
```
Arranges for a callback to run after all processors have been scheduled and an RCU-protected resource can be safely freed.

Advanced Char Driver Operations

In Chapter 3, we built a complete device driver that the user can write to and read from. But a real device usually offers more functionality than synchronous *read* and *write*. Now that we're equipped with debugging tools should something go awry—and a firm understanding of concurrency issues to help keep things from going awry—we can safely go ahead and create a more advanced driver.

This chapter examines a few concepts that you need to understand to write fully featured char device drivers. We start with implementing the *ioctl* system call, which is a common interface used for device control. Then we proceed to various ways of synchronizing with user space; by the end of this chapter you have a good idea of how to put processes to sleep (and wake them up), implement nonblocking I/O, and inform user space when your devices are available for reading or writing. We finish with a look at how to implement a few different device access policies within drivers.

The ideas discussed here are demonstrated by way of a couple of modified versions of the *scull* driver. Once again, everything is implemented using in-memory virtual devices, so you can try out the code yourself without needing to have any particular hardware. By now, you may be wanting to get your hands dirty with real hardware, but that will have to wait until Chapter 9.

ioctl

Most drivers need—in addition to the ability to read and write the device—the ability to perform various types of hardware control via the device driver. Most devices can perform operations beyond simple data transfers; user space must often be able to request, for example, that the device lock its door, eject its media, report error information, change a baud rate, or self destruct. These operations are usually supported via the *ioctl* method, which implements the system call by the same name.

In user space, the *ioctl* system call has the following prototype:

```
int ioctl(int fd, unsigned long cmd, ...);
```

The prototype stands out in the list of Unix system calls because of the dots, which usually mark the function as having a variable number of arguments. In a real system, however, a system call can't actually have a variable number of arguments. System calls must have a well-defined prototype, because user programs can access them only through hardware "gates." Therefore, the dots in the prototype represent not a variable number of arguments but a single optional argument, traditionally identified as char *argp. The dots are simply there to prevent type checking during compilation. The actual nature of the third argument depends on the specific control command being issued (the second argument). Some commands take no arguments, some take an integer value, and some take a pointer to other data. Using a pointer is the way to pass arbitrary data to the *ioctl* call; the device is then able to exchange any amount of data with user space.

The unstructured nature of the *ioctl* call has caused it to fall out of favor among kernel developers. Each *ioctl* command is, essentially, a separate, usually undocumented system call, and there is no way to audit these calls in any sort of comprehensive manner. It is also difficult to make the unstructured *ioctl* arguments work identically on all systems; for example, consider 64-bit systems with a user-space process running in 32-bit mode. As a result, there is strong pressure to implement miscellaneous control operations by just about any other means. Possible alternatives include embedding commands into the data stream (we will discuss this approach later in this chapter) or using virtual filesystems, either sysfs or driver-specific filesystems. (We will look at sysfs in Chapter 14.) However, the fact remains that *ioctl* is often the easiest and most straightforward choice for true device operations.

The *ioctl* driver method has a prototype that differs somewhat from the user-space version:

```
int (*ioctl) (struct inode *inode, struct file *filp,
              unsigned int cmd, unsigned long arg);
```

The inode and filp pointers are the values corresponding to the file descriptor fd passed on by the application and are the same parameters passed to the *open* method. The cmd argument is passed from the user unchanged, and the optional arg argument is passed in the form of an unsigned long, regardless of whether it was given by the user as an integer or a pointer. If the invoking program doesn't pass a third argument, the arg value received by the driver operation is undefined. Because type checking is disabled on the extra argument, the compiler can't warn you if an invalid argument is passed to *ioctl*, and any associated bug would be difficult to spot.

As you might imagine, most *ioctl* implementations consist of a big switch statement that selects the correct behavior according to the cmd argument. Different commands have different numeric values, which are usually given symbolic names to simplify coding. The symbolic name is assigned by a preprocessor definition. Custom drivers usually declare such symbols in their header files; *scull.h* declares them for *scull*. User programs must, of course, include that header file as well to have access to those symbols.

Choosing the ioctl Commands

Before writing the code for *ioctl*, you need to choose the numbers that correspond to commands. The first instinct of many programmers is to choose a set of small numbers starting with 0 or 1 and going up from there. There are, however, good reasons for not doing things that way. The *ioctl* command numbers should be unique across the system in order to prevent errors caused by issuing the right command to the wrong device. Such a mismatch is not unlikely to happen, and a program might find itself trying to change the baud rate of a non-serial-port input stream, such as a FIFO or an audio device. If each *ioctl* number is unique, the application gets an EINVAL error rather than succeeding in doing something unintended.

To help programmers create unique *ioctl* command codes, these codes have been split up into several bitfields. The first versions of Linux used 16-bit numbers: the top eight were the "magic" numbers associated with the device, and the bottom eight were a sequential number, unique within the device. This happened because Linus was "clueless" (his own word); a better division of bitfields was conceived only later. Unfortunately, quite a few drivers still use the old convention. They have to: changing the command codes would break no end of binary programs, and that is not something the kernel developers are willing to do.

To choose *ioctl* numbers for your driver according to the Linux kernel convention, you should first check *include/asm/ioctl.h* and *Documentation/ioctl-number.txt*. The header defines the bitfields you will be using: type (magic number), ordinal number, direction of transfer, and size of argument. The *ioctl-number.txt* file lists the magic numbers used throughout the kernel,* so you'll be able to choose your own magic number and avoid overlaps. The text file also lists the reasons why the convention should be used.

The approved way to define *ioctl* command numbers uses four bitfields, which have the following meanings. New symbols introduced in this list are defined in *<linux/ioctl.h>*.

type
: The magic number. Just choose one number (after consulting *ioctl-number.txt*) and use it throughout the driver. This field is eight bits wide (_IOC_TYPEBITS).

number
: The ordinal (sequential) number. It's eight bits (_IOC_NRBITS) wide.

---

* Maintenance of this file has been somewhat scarce as of late, however.

direction

    The direction of data transfer, if the particular command involves a data transfer. The possible values are _IOC_NONE (no data transfer), _IOC_READ, _IOC_WRITE, and _IOC_READ|_IOC_WRITE (data is transferred both ways). Data transfer is seen from the application's point of view; _IOC_READ means reading *from* the device, so the driver must write to user space. Note that the field is a bit mask, so _IOC_READ and _IOC_WRITE can be extracted using a logical AND operation.

size

    The size of user data involved. The width of this field is architecture dependent, but is usually 13 or 14 bits. You can find its value for your specific architecture in the macro _IOC_SIZEBITS. It's not mandatory that you use the size field—the kernel does not check it—but it is a good idea. Proper use of this field can help detect user-space programming errors and enable you to implement backward compatibility if you ever need to change the size of the relevant data item. If you need larger data structures, however, you can just ignore the size field. We'll see how this field is used soon.

The header file *<asm/ioctl.h>*, which is included by *<linux/ioctl.h>*, defines macros that help set up the command numbers as follows: _IO(type,nr) (for a command that has no argument), _IOR(type,nr,datatype) (for reading data from the driver), _IOW(type,nr,datatype) (for writing data), and _IOWR(type,nr,datatype) (for bidirectional transfers). The type and number fields are passed as arguments, and the size field is derived by applying *sizeof* to the datatype argument.

The header also defines macros that may be used in your driver to decode the numbers: _IOC_DIR(nr), _IOC_TYPE(nr), _IOC_NR(nr), and _IOC_SIZE(nr). We won't go into any more detail about these macros because the header file is clear, and sample code is shown later in this section.

Here is how some *ioctl* commands are defined in *scull*. In particular, these commands set and get the driver's configurable parameters.

```
/* Use 'k' as magic number */
#define SCULL_IOC_MAGIC  'k'
/* Please use a different 8-bit number in your code */

#define SCULL_IOCRESET    _IO(SCULL_IOC_MAGIC, 0)

/*
 * S means "Set" through a ptr,
 * T means "Tell" directly with the argument value
 * G means "Get": reply by setting through a pointer
 * Q means "Query": response is on the return value
 * X means "eXchange": switch G and S atomically
 * H means "sHift": switch T and Q atomically
 */
#define SCULL_IOCSQUANTUM _IOW(SCULL_IOC_MAGIC,  1, int)
#define SCULL_IOCSQSET    _IOW(SCULL_IOC_MAGIC,  2, int)
```

```
#define SCULL_IOCTQUANTUM _IO(SCULL_IOC_MAGIC,   3)
#define SCULL_IOCTQSET    _IO(SCULL_IOC_MAGIC,   4)
#define SCULL_IOCGQUANTUM _IOR(SCULL_IOC_MAGIC,  5, int)
#define SCULL_IOCGQSET    _IOR(SCULL_IOC_MAGIC,  6, int)
#define SCULL_IOCQQUANTUM _IO(SCULL_IOC_MAGIC,   7)
#define SCULL_IOCQQSET    _IO(SCULL_IOC_MAGIC,   8)
#define SCULL_IOCXQUANTUM _IOWR(SCULL_IOC_MAGIC, 9, int)
#define SCULL_IOCXQSET    _IOWR(SCULL_IOC_MAGIC,10, int)
#define SCULL_IOCHQUANTUM _IO(SCULL_IOC_MAGIC,  11)
#define SCULL_IOCHQSET    _IO(SCULL_IOC_MAGIC,  12)

#define SCULL_IOC_MAXNR 14
```

The actual source file defines a few extra commands that have not been shown here.

We chose to implement both ways of passing integer arguments: by pointer and by explicit value (although, by an established convention, *ioctl* should exchange values by pointer). Similarly, both ways are used to return an integer number: by pointer or by setting the return value. This works as long as the return value is a positive integer; as you know by now, on return from any system call, a positive value is preserved (as we saw for *read* and *write*), while a negative value is considered an error and is used to set errno in user space.[*]

The "exchange" and "shift" operations are not particularly useful for *scull*. We implemented "exchange" to show how the driver can combine separate operations into a single atomic one, and "shift" to pair "tell" and "query." There are times when atomic test-and-set operations like these are needed, in particular, when applications need to set or release locks.

The explicit ordinal number of the command has no specific meaning. It is used only to tell the commands apart. Actually, you could even use the same ordinal number for a read command and a write command, since the actual *ioctl* number is different in the "direction" bits, but there is no reason why you would want to do so. We chose not to use the ordinal number of the command anywhere but in the declaration, so we didn't assign a symbolic value to it. That's why explicit numbers appear in the definition given previously. The example shows one way to use the command numbers, but you are free to do it differently.

With the exception of a small number of predefined commands (to be discussed shortly), the value of the *ioctl* cmd argument is not currently used by the kernel, and it's quite unlikely it will be in the future. Therefore, you could, if you were feeling lazy, avoid the complex declarations shown earlier and explicitly declare a set of scalar numbers. On the other hand, if you did, you wouldn't benefit from using the bit-fields, and you would encounter difficulties if you ever submitted your code for

---

[*] Actually, all *libc* implementations currently in use (including uClibc) consider as error codes only values in the range −4095 to −1. Unfortunately, being able to return large negative numbers but not small ones is not very useful.

inclusion in the mainline kernel. The header *<linux/kd.h>* is an example of this old-fashioned approach, using 16-bit scalar values to define the *ioctl* commands. That source file relied on scalar numbers because it used the conventions obeyed at that time, not out of laziness. Changing it now would cause gratuitous incompatibility.

The Return Value

The implementation of *ioctl* is usually a `switch` statement based on the command number. But what should the `default` selection be when the command number doesn't match a valid operation? The question is controversial. Several kernel functions return `-EINVAL` ("Invalid argument"), which makes sense because the command argument is indeed not a valid one. The POSIX standard, however, states that if an inappropriate *ioctl* command has been issued, then `-ENOTTY` should be returned. This error code is interpreted by the C library as "inappropriate ioctl for device," which is usually exactly what the programmer needs to hear. It's still pretty common, though, to return `-EINVAL` in response to an invalid *ioctl* command.

The Predefined Commands

Although the *ioctl* system call is most often used to act on devices, a few commands are recognized by the kernel. Note that these commands, when applied to your device, are decoded *before* your own file operations are called. Thus, if you choose the same number for one of your *ioctl* commands, you won't ever see any request for that command, and the application gets something unexpected because of the conflict between the *ioctl* numbers.

The predefined commands are divided into three groups:

- Those that can be issued on any file (regular, device, FIFO, or socket)
- Those that are issued only on regular files
- Those specific to the filesystem type

Commands in the last group are executed by the implementation of the hosting filesystem (this is how the *chattr* command works). Device driver writers are interested only in the first group of commands, whose magic number is "T." Looking at the workings of the other groups is left to the reader as an exercise; *ext2_ioctl* is a most interesting function (and easier to understand than one might expect), because it implements the append-only flag and the immutable flag.

The following *ioctl* commands are predefined for any file, including device-special files:

FIOCLEX
> Set the close-on-exec flag (File IOctl CLose on EXec). Setting this flag causes the file descriptor to be closed when the calling process executes a new program.

FIONCLEX
> Clear the close-on-exec flag (File IOctl Not CLos on EXec). The command restores the common file behavior, undoing what FIOCLEX above does.

FIOASYNC
> Set or reset asynchronous notification for the file (as discussed in the section "Asynchronous Notification," later in this chapter). Note that kernel versions up to Linux 2.2.4 incorrectly used this command to modify the O_SYNC flag. Since both actions can be accomplished through *fcntl*, nobody actually uses the FIOASYNC command, which is reported here only for completeness.

FIOQSIZE
> This command returns the size of a file or directory; when applied to a device file, however, it yields an ENOTTY error return.

FIONBIO
> "File IOctl Non-Blocking I/O" (described in the section "Blocking and Non-blocking Operations"). This call modifies the O_NONBLOCK flag in filp->f_flags. The third argument to the system call is used to indicate whether the flag is to be set or cleared. (We'll look at the role of the flag later in this chapter.) Note that the usual way to change this flag is with the *fcntl* system call, using the *F_SETFL* command.

The last item in the list introduced a new system call, *fcntl*, which looks like *ioctl*. In fact, the *fcntl* call is very similar to *ioctl* in that it gets a command argument and an extra (optional) argument. It is kept separate from *ioctl* mainly for historical reasons: when Unix developers faced the problem of controlling I/O operations, they decided that files and devices were different. At the time, the only devices with *ioctl* implementations were ttys, which explains why -ENOTTY is the standard reply for an incorrect *ioctl* command. Things have changed, but *fcntl* remains a separate system call.

Using the ioctl Argument

Another point we need to cover before looking at the *ioctl* code for the *scull* driver is how to use the extra argument. If it is an integer, it's easy: it can be used directly. If it is a pointer, however, some care must be taken.

When a pointer is used to refer to user space, we must ensure that the user address is valid. An attempt to access an unverified user-supplied pointer can lead to incorrect behavior, a kernel oops, system corruption, or security problems. It is the driver's responsibility to make proper checks on every user-space address it uses and to return an error if it is invalid.

In Chapter 3, we looked at the *copy_from_user* and *copy_to_user* functions, which can be used to safely move data to and from user space. Those functions can be used in *ioctl* methods as well, but *ioctl* calls often involve small data items that can be more efficiently manipulated through other means. To start, address verification (without transferring data) is implemented by the function *access_ok*, which is declared in *<asm/uaccess.h>*:

```
int access_ok(int type, const void *addr, unsigned long size);
```

The first argument should be either VERIFY_READ or VERIFY_WRITE, depending on whether the action to be performed is reading the user-space memory area or writing it. The addr argument holds a user-space address, and size is a byte count. If *ioctl*, for instance, needs to read an integer value from user space, size is sizeof(int). If you need to both read and write at the given address, use VERIFY_WRITE, since it is a superset of VERIFY_READ.

Unlike most kernel functions, *access_ok* returns a boolean value: 1 for success (access is OK) and 0 for failure (access is not OK). If it returns false, the driver should usually return -EFAULT to the caller.

There are a couple of interesting things to note about *access_ok*. First, it does not do the complete job of verifying memory access; it only checks to see that the memory reference is in a region of memory that the process might reasonably have access to. In particular, *access_ok* ensures that the address does not point to kernel-space memory. Second, most driver code need not actually call *access_ok*. The memory-access routines described later take care of that for you. Nonetheless, we demonstrate its use so that you can see how it is done.

The *scull* source exploits the bitfields in the *ioctl* number to check the arguments before the switch:

```
int err = 0, tmp;
int retval = 0;

/*
 * extract the type and number bitfields, and don't decode
 * wrong cmds: return ENOTTY (inappropriate ioctl) before access_ok()
 */
if (_IOC_TYPE(cmd) != SCULL_IOC_MAGIC) return -ENOTTY;
if (_IOC_NR(cmd) > SCULL_IOC_MAXNR) return -ENOTTY;

/*
 * the direction is a bitmask, and VERIFY_WRITE catches R/W
 * transfers. `Type' is user-oriented, while
```

```
 * access_ok is kernel-oriented, so the concept of "read" and
 * "write" is reversed
 */
if (_IOC_DIR(cmd) & _IOC_READ)
    err = !access_ok(VERIFY_WRITE, (void __user *)arg, _IOC_SIZE(cmd));
else if (_IOC_DIR(cmd) & _IOC_WRITE)
    err = !access_ok(VERIFY_READ, (void __user *)arg, _IOC_SIZE(cmd));
if (err) return -EFAULT;
```

After calling *access_ok*, the driver can safely perform the actual transfer. In addition to the *copy_from_user* and *copy_to_user* functions, the programmer can exploit a set of functions that are optimized for the most used data sizes (one, two, four, and eight bytes). These functions are described in the following list and are defined in *<asm/ uaccess.h>*:

put_user(datum, ptr)

__put_user(datum, ptr)

> These macros write the datum to user space; they are relatively fast and should be called instead of *copy_to_user* whenever single values are being transferred. The macros have been written to allow the passing of any type of pointer to *put_user*, as long as it is a user-space address. The size of the data transfer depends on the type of the ptr argument and is determined at compile time using the sizeof and typeof compiler builtins. As a result, if ptr is a char pointer, one byte is transferred, and so on for two, four, and possibly eight bytes.

> *put_user* checks to ensure that the process is able to write to the given memory address. It returns 0 on success, and -EFAULT on error. *__put_user* performs less checking (it does not call *access_ok*), but can still fail if the memory pointed to is not writable by the user. Thus, *__put_user* should only be used if the memory region has already been verified with *access_ok*.

> As a general rule, you call *__put_user* to save a few cycles when you are implementing a *read* method, or when you copy several items and, thus, call *access_ok* just once before the first data transfer, as shown above for *ioctl*.

get_user(local, ptr)

__get_user(local, ptr)

> These macros are used to retrieve a single datum from user space. They behave like *put_user* and *__put_user*, but transfer data in the opposite direction. The value retrieved is stored in the local variable local; the return value indicates whether the operation succeeded. Again, *__get_user* should only be used if the address has already been verified with *access_ok*.

If an attempt is made to use one of the listed functions to transfer a value that does not fit one of the specific sizes, the result is usually a strange message from the compiler, such as "conversion to non-scalar type requested." In such cases, *copy_to_user* or *copy_from_user* must be used.

Capabilities and Restricted Operations

Access to a device is controlled by the permissions on the device file(s), and the driver is not normally involved in permissions checking. There are situations, however, where any user is granted read/write permission on the device, but some control operations should still be denied. For example, not all users of a tape drive should be able to set its default block size, and a user who has been granted read/write access to a disk device should probably still be denied the ability to format it. In cases like these, the driver must perform additional checks to be sure that the user is capable of performing the requested operation.

Unix systems have traditionally restricted privileged operations to the superuser account. This meant that privilege was an all-or-nothing thing—the superuser can do absolutely anything, but all other users are highly restricted. The Linux kernel provides a more flexible system called *capabilities*. A capability-based system leaves the all-or-nothing mode behind and breaks down privileged operations into separate subgroups. In this way, a particular user (or program) can be empowered to perform a specific privileged operation without giving away the ability to perform other, unrelated operations. The kernel uses capabilities exclusively for permissions management and exports two system calls *capget* and *capset*, to allow them to be managed from user space.

The full set of capabilities can be found in *<linux/capability.h>*. These are the only capabilities known to the system; it is not possible for driver authors or system administrators to define new ones without modifying the kernel source. A subset of those capabilities that might be of interest to device driver writers includes the following:

CAP_DAC_OVERRIDE
> The ability to override access restrictions (data access control, or DAC) on files and directories.

CAP_NET_ADMIN
> The ability to perform network administration tasks, including those that affect network interfaces.

CAP_SYS_MODULE
> The ability to load or remove kernel modules.

CAP_SYS_RAWIO
> The ability to perform "raw" I/O operations. Examples include accessing device ports or communicating directly with USB devices.

CAP_SYS_ADMIN
> A catch-all capability that provides access to many system administration operations.

CAP_SYS_TTY_CONFIG
> The ability to perform tty configuration tasks.

Before performing a privileged operation, a device driver should check that the calling process has the appropriate capability; failure to do so could result user processes performing unauthorized operations with bad results on system stability or security. Capability checks are performed with the *capable* function (defined in *<linux/sched.h>*):

```
int capable(int capability);
```

In the *scull* sample driver, any user is allowed to query the quantum and quantum set sizes. Only privileged users, however, may change those values, since inappropriate values could badly affect system performance. When needed, the *scull* implementation of *ioctl* checks a user's privilege level as follows:

```
if (! capable (CAP_SYS_ADMIN))
    return -EPERM;
```

In the absence of a more specific capability for this task, CAP_SYS_ADMIN was chosen for this test.

The Implementation of the ioctl Commands

The *scull* implementation of *ioctl* only transfers the configurable parameters of the device and turns out to be as easy as the following:

```
switch(cmd) {

  case SCULL_IOCRESET:
    scull_quantum = SCULL_QUANTUM;
    scull_qset = SCULL_QSET;
    break;

  case SCULL_IOCSQUANTUM: /* Set: arg points to the value */
    if (! capable (CAP_SYS_ADMIN))
        return -EPERM;
    retval = __get_user(scull_quantum, (int __user *)arg);
    break;

  case SCULL_IOCTQUANTUM: /* Tell: arg is the value */
    if (! capable (CAP_SYS_ADMIN))
        return -EPERM;
    scull_quantum = arg;
    break;

  case SCULL_IOCGQUANTUM: /* Get: arg is pointer to result */
    retval = __put_user(scull_quantum, (int __user *)arg);
    break;

  case SCULL_IOCQQUANTUM: /* Query: return it (it's positive) */
    return scull_quantum;

  case SCULL_IOCXQUANTUM: /* eXchange: use arg as pointer */
    if (! capable (CAP_SYS_ADMIN))
```

```
            return -EPERM;
        tmp = scull_quantum;
        retval = __get_user(scull_quantum, (int __user *)arg);
        if (retval == 0)
            retval = __put_user(tmp, (int __user *)arg);
        break;

      case SCULL_IOCHQUANTUM: /* sHift: like Tell + Query */
        if (! capable (CAP_SYS_ADMIN))
            return -EPERM;
        tmp = scull_quantum;
        scull_quantum = arg;
        return tmp;

      default:  /* redundant, as cmd was checked against MAXNR */
        return -ENOTTY;
    }
    return retval;
```

scull also includes six entries that act on scull_qset. These entries are identical to the
ones for scull_quantum and are not worth showing in print.

The six ways to pass and receive arguments look like the following from the caller's
point of view (i.e., from user space):

```
int quantum;

ioctl(fd,SCULL_IOCSQUANTUM, &quantum);          /* Set by pointer */
ioctl(fd,SCULL_IOCTQUANTUM, quantum);           /* Set by value */

ioctl(fd,SCULL_IOCGQUANTUM, &quantum);          /* Get by pointer */
quantum = ioctl(fd,SCULL_IOCQQUANTUM);          /* Get by return value */

ioctl(fd,SCULL_IOCXQUANTUM, &quantum);          /* Exchange by pointer */
quantum = ioctl(fd,SCULL_IOCHQUANTUM, quantum); /* Exchange by value */
```

Of course, a normal driver would not implement such a mix of calling modes. We
have done so here only to demonstrate the different ways in which things could be
done. Normally, however, data exchanges would be consistently performed, either
through pointers or by value, and mixing of the two techniques would be avoided.

Device Control Without ioctl

Sometimes controlling the device is better accomplished by writing control
sequences to the device itself. For example, this technique is used in the console
driver, where so-called escape sequences are used to move the cursor, change the
default color, or perform other configuration tasks. The benefit of implementing
device control this way is that the user can control the device just by writing data,
without needing to use (or sometimes write) programs built just for configuring the
device. When devices can be controlled in this manner, the program issuing commands
often need not even be running on the same system as the device it is controlling.

For example, the *setterm* program acts on the console (or another terminal) configuration by printing escape sequences. The controlling program can live on a different computer from the controlled device, because a simple redirection of the data stream does the configuration job. This is what happens every time you run a remote tty session: escape sequences are printed remotely but affect the local tty; the technique is not restricted to ttys, though.

The drawback of controlling by printing is that it adds policy constraints to the device; for example, it is viable only if you are sure that the control sequence can't appear in the data being written to the device during normal operation. This is only partly true for ttys. Although a text display is meant to display only ASCII characters, sometimes control characters can slip through in the data being written and can, therefore, affect the console setup. This can happen, for example, when you *cat* a binary file to the screen; the resulting mess can contain anything, and you often end up with the wrong font on your console.

Controlling by write *is* definitely the way to go for those devices that don't transfer data but just respond to commands, such as robotic devices.

For instance, a driver written for fun by one of your authors moves a camera on two axes. In this driver, the "device" is simply a pair of old stepper motors, which can't really be read from or written to. The concept of "sending a data stream" to a stepper motor makes little or no sense. In this case, the driver interprets what is being written as ASCII commands and converts the requests to sequences of impulses that manipulate the stepper motors. The idea is similar, somewhat, to the AT commands you send to the modem in order to set up communication, the main difference being that the serial port used to communicate with the modem must transfer real data as well. The advantage of direct device control is that you can use *cat* to move the camera without writing and compiling special code to issue the *ioctl* calls.

When writing command-oriented drivers, there's no reason to implement the *ioctl* method. An additional command in the interpreter is easier to implement and use.

Sometimes, though, you might choose to act the other way around: instead of turning the *write* method into an interpreter and avoiding *ioctl*, you might choose to avoid *write* altogether and use *ioctl* commands exclusively, while accompanying the driver with a specific command-line tool to send those commands to the driver. This approach moves the complexity from kernel space to user space, where it may be easier to deal with, and helps keep the driver small while denying use of simple *cat* or *echo* commands.

Blocking I/O

Back in Chapter 3, we looked at how to implement the *read* and *write* driver methods. At that point, however, we skipped over one important issue: how does a driver respond if it cannot immediately satisfy the request? A call to *read* may come when no data is available, but more is expected in the future. Or a process could attempt to *write*, but your device is not ready to accept the data, because your output buffer is full. The calling process usually does not care about such issues; the programmer simply expects to call *read* or *write* and have the call return after the necessary work has been done. So, in such cases, your driver should (by default) *block* the process, putting it to sleep until the request can proceed.

This section shows how to put a process to sleep and wake it up again later on. As usual, however, we have to explain a few concepts first.

Introduction to Sleeping

What does it mean for a process to "sleep"? When a process is put to sleep, it is marked as being in a special state and removed from the scheduler's run queue. Until something comes along to change that state, the process will not be scheduled on any CPU and, therefore, will not run. A sleeping process has been shunted off to the side of the system, waiting for some future event to happen.

Causing a process to sleep is an easy thing for a Linux device driver to do. There are, however, a couple of rules that you must keep in mind to be able to code sleeps in a safe manner.

The first of these rules is: never sleep when you are running in an atomic context. We got an introduction to atomic operation in Chapter 5; an atomic context is simply a state where multiple steps must be performed without any sort of concurrent access. What that means, with regard to sleeping, is that your driver cannot sleep while holding a spinlock, seqlock, or RCU lock. You also cannot sleep if you have disabled interrupts. It *is* legal to sleep while holding a semaphore, but you should look very carefully at any code that does so. If code sleeps while holding a semaphore, any other thread waiting for that semaphore also sleeps. So any sleeps that happen while holding semaphores should be short, and you should convince yourself that, by holding the semaphore, you are not blocking the process that will eventually wake you up.

Another thing to remember with sleeping is that, when you wake up, you never know how long your process may have been out of the CPU or what may have changed in the mean time. You also do not usually know if another process may have been sleeping for the same event; that process may wake before you and grab whatever resource you were waiting for. The end result is that you can make no assumptions about the state of the system after you wake up, and you must check to ensure that the condition you were waiting for is, indeed, true.

One other relevant point, of course, is that your process cannot sleep unless it is assured that somebody else, somewhere, will wake it up. The code doing the awakening must also be able to find your process to be able to do its job. Making sure that a wakeup happens is a matter of thinking through your code and knowing, for each sleep, exactly what series of events will bring that sleep to an end. Making it possible for your sleeping process to be found is, instead, accomplished through a data structure called a *wait queue*. A wait queue is just what it sounds like: a list of processes, all waiting for a specific event.

In Linux, a wait queue is managed by means of a "wait queue head," a structure of type `wait_queue_head_t`, which is defined in *<linux/wait.h>*. A wait queue head can be defined and initialized statically with:

```
DECLARE_WAIT_QUEUE_HEAD(name);
```

or dynamicly as follows:

```
wait_queue_head_t my_queue;
init_waitqueue_head(&my_queue);
```

We will return to the structure of wait queues shortly, but we know enough now to take a first look at sleeping and waking up.

Simple Sleeping

When a process sleeps, it does so in expectation that some condition will become true in the future. As we noted before, any process that sleeps must check to be sure that the condition it was waiting for is really true when it wakes up again. The simplest way of sleeping in the Linux kernel is a macro called *wait_event* (with a few variants); it combines handling the details of sleeping with a check on the condition a process is waiting for. The forms of *wait_event* are:

```
wait_event(queue, condition)
wait_event_interruptible(queue, condition)
wait_event_timeout(queue, condition, timeout)
wait_event_interruptible_timeout(queue, condition, timeout)
```

In all of the above forms, queue is the wait queue head to use. Notice that it is passed "by value." The condition is an arbitrary boolean expression that is evaluated by the macro before and after sleeping; until condition evaluates to a true value, the process continues to sleep. Note that condition may be evaluated an arbitrary number of times, so it should not have any side effects.

If you use *wait_event*, your process is put into an uninterruptible sleep which, as we have mentioned before, is usually not what you want. The preferred alternative is *wait_event_interruptible*, which can be interrupted by signals. This version returns an integer value that you should check; a nonzero value means your sleep was interrupted by some sort of signal, and your driver should probably return -ERESTARTSYS. The final versions (*wait_event_timeout* and *wait_event_interruptible_timeout*) wait for a limited time; after that time period (expressed in jiffies, which we will discuss in Chapter 7) expires, the macros return with a value of 0 regardless of how condition evaluates.

The other half of the picture, of course, is waking up. Some other thread of execution (a different process, or an interrupt handler, perhaps) has to perform the wakeup for you, since your process is, of course, asleep. The basic function that wakes up sleeping processes is called *wake_up*. It comes in several forms (but we look at only two of them now):

```
void wake_up(wait_queue_head_t *queue);
void wake_up_interruptible(wait_queue_head_t *queue);
```

wake_up wakes up all processes waiting on the given queue (though the situation is a little more complicated than that, as we will see later). The other form (*wake_up_interruptible*) restricts itself to processes performing an interruptible sleep. In general, the two are indistinguishable (if you are using interruptible sleeps); in practice, the convention is to use *wake_up* if you are using *wait_event* and *wake_up_interruptible* if you use *wait_event_interruptible*.

We now know enough to look at a simple example of sleeping and waking up. In the sample source, you can find a module called *sleepy*. It implements a device with simple behavior: any process that attempts to read from the device is put to sleep. Whenever a process writes to the device, all sleeping processes are awakened. This behavior is implemented with the following *read* and *write* methods:

```
static DECLARE_WAIT_QUEUE_HEAD(wq);
static int flag = 0;

ssize_t sleepy_read (struct file *filp, char __user *buf, size_t count, loff_t *pos)
{
    printk(KERN_DEBUG "process %i (%s) going to sleep\n",
            current->pid, current->comm);
    wait_event_interruptible(wq, flag != 0);
    flag = 0;
    printk(KERN_DEBUG "awoken %i (%s)\n", current->pid, current->comm);
    return 0; /* EOF */
}

ssize_t sleepy_write (struct file *filp, const char __user *buf, size_t count,
        loff_t *pos)
{
    printk(KERN_DEBUG "process %i (%s) awakening the readers...\n",
            current->pid, current->comm);
    flag = 1;
    wake_up_interruptible(&wq);
    return count; /* succeed, to avoid retrial */
}
```

Note the use of the flag variable in this example. Since *wait_event_interruptible* checks for a condition that must become true, we use flag to create that condition.

It is interesting to consider what happens if *two* processes are waiting when *sleepy_write* is called. Since *sleepy_read* resets flag to 0 once it wakes up, you might think that the second process to wake up would immediately go back to sleep. On a single-processor system, that is almost always what happens. But it is important to understand why you cannot count on that behavior. The *wake_up_interruptible* call *will* cause both sleeping processes to wake up. It is entirely possible that they will both note that flag is nonzero before either has the opportunity to reset it. For this trivial module, this race condition is unimportant. In a real driver, this kind of race can create rare crashes that are difficult to diagnose. If correct operation required that exactly one process see the nonzero value, it would have to be tested in an atomic manner. We will see how a real driver handles such situations shortly. But first we have to cover one other topic.

Blocking and Nonblocking Operations

One last point we need to touch on before we look at the implementation of full-featured *read* and *write* methods is deciding when to put a process to sleep. There are times when implementing proper Unix semantics requires that an operation not block, even if it cannot be completely carried out.

There are also times when the calling process informs you that it does not *want* to block, whether or not its I/O can make any progress at all. Explicitly nonblocking I/O is indicated by the O_NONBLOCK flag in filp->f_flags. The flag is defined in *<linux/fcntl.h>*, which is automatically included by *<linux/fs.h>*. The flag gets its name from "open-nonblock," because it can be specified at open time (and originally could be specified only there). If you browse the source code, you find some references to an O_NDELAY flag; this is an alternate name for O_NONBLOCK, accepted for compatibility with System V code. The flag is cleared by default, because the normal behavior of a process waiting for data is just to sleep. In the case of a blocking operation, which is the default, the following behavior should be implemented in order to adhere to the standard semantics:

- If a process calls *read* but no data is (yet) available, the process must block. The process is awakened as soon as some data arrives, and that data is returned to the caller, even if there is less than the amount requested in the count argument to the method.

- If a process calls *write* and there is no space in the buffer, the process must block, and it must be on a different wait queue from the one used for reading. When some data has been written to the hardware device, and space becomes free in the output buffer, the process is awakened and the *write* call succeeds, although the data may be only partially written if there isn't room in the buffer for the count bytes that were requested.

Both these statements assume that there are both input and output buffers; in practice, almost every device driver has them. The input buffer is required to avoid losing data that arrives when nobody is reading. In contrast, data can't be lost on *write*, because if the system call doesn't accept data bytes, they remain in the user-space buffer. Even so, the output buffer is almost always useful for squeezing more performance out of the hardware.

The performance gain of implementing an output buffer in the driver results from the reduced number of context switches and user-level/kernel-level transitions. Without an output buffer (assuming a slow device), only one or a few characters are accepted by each system call, and while one process sleeps in *write*, another process runs (that's one context switch). When the first process is awakened, it resumes (another context switch), *write* returns (kernel/user transition), and the process reiterates the system call to write more data (user/kernel transition); the call blocks and the loop continues. The addition of an output buffer allows the driver to accept larger chunks of data with each *write* call, with a corresponding increase in performance. If that buffer is big enough, the *write* call succeeds on the first attempt—the buffered data will be pushed out to the device later—without control needing to go back to user space for a second or third *write* call. The choice of a suitable size for the output buffer is clearly device-specific.

We don't use an input buffer in *scull*, because data is already available when *read* is issued. Similarly, no output buffer is used, because data is simply copied to the memory area associated with the device. Essentially, the device *is* a buffer, so the implementation of additional buffers would be superfluous. We'll see the use of buffers in Chapter 10.

The behavior of *read* and *write* is different if O_NONBLOCK is specified. In this case, the calls simply return -EAGAIN ("try it again") if a process calls *read* when no data is available or if it calls *write* when there's no space in the buffer.

As you might expect, nonblocking operations return immediately, allowing the application to poll for data. Applications must be careful when using the *stdio* functions while dealing with nonblocking files, because they can easily mistake a nonblocking return for EOF. They always have to check errno.

Naturally, O_NONBLOCK is meaningful in the *open* method also. This happens when the call can actually block for a long time; for example, when opening (for read access) a FIFO that has no writers (yet), or accessing a disk file with a pending lock. Usually, opening a device either succeeds or fails, without the need to wait for external events. Sometimes, however, opening the device requires a long initialization, and you may choose to support O_NONBLOCK in your *open* method by returning immediately with -EAGAIN if the flag is set, after starting the device initialization process. The driver may also implement a blocking *open* to support access policies in a way similar to file locks. We'll see one such implementation in the section "Blocking open as an Alternative to EBUSY" later in this chapter.

Some drivers may also implement special semantics for O_NONBLOCK; for example, an open of a tape device usually blocks until a tape has been inserted. If the tape drive is opened with O_NONBLOCK, the open succeeds immediately regardless of whether the media is present or not.

Only the *read*, *write*, and *open* file operations are affected by the nonblocking flag.

A Blocking I/O Example

Finally, we get to an example of a real driver method that implements blocking I/O. This example is taken from the *scullpipe* driver; it is a special form of *scull* that implements a pipe-like device.

Within a driver, a process blocked in a *read* call is awakened when data arrives; usually the hardware issues an interrupt to signal such an event, and the driver awakens waiting processes as part of handling the interrupt. The *scullpipe* driver works differently, so that it can be run without requiring any particular hardware or an interrupt handler. We chose to use another process to generate the data and wake the reading process; similarly, reading processes are used to wake writer processes that are waiting for buffer space to become available.

The device driver uses a device structure that contains two wait queues and a buffer. The size of the buffer is configurable in the usual ways (at compile time, load time, or runtime).

```
struct scull_pipe {
        wait_queue_head_t inq, outq;       /* read and write queues */
        char *buffer, *end;                /* begin of buf, end of buf */
        int buffersize;                    /* used in pointer arithmetic */
        char *rp, *wp;                     /* where to read, where to write */
        int nreaders, nwriters;            /* number of openings for r/w */
        struct fasync_struct *async_queue; /* asynchronous readers */
        struct semaphore sem;              /* mutual exclusion semaphore */
        struct cdev cdev;                  /* Char device structure */
};
```

The *read* implementation manages both blocking and nonblocking input and looks like this:

```
static ssize_t scull_p_read (struct file *filp, char __user *buf, size_t count,
                loff_t *f_pos)
{
    struct scull_pipe *dev = filp->private_data;

    if (down_interruptible(&dev->sem))
        return -ERESTARTSYS;

    while (dev->rp == dev->wp) { /* nothing to read */
        up(&dev->sem); /* release the lock */
        if (filp->f_flags & O_NONBLOCK)
            return -EAGAIN;
        PDEBUG("\"%s\" reading: going to sleep\n", current->comm);
        if (wait_event_interruptible(dev->inq, (dev->rp != dev->wp)))
            return -ERESTARTSYS; /* signal: tell the fs layer to handle it */
        /* otherwise loop, but first reacquire the lock */
        if (down_interruptible(&dev->sem))
            return -ERESTARTSYS;
    }
    /* ok, data is there, return something */
```

```
        if (dev->wp > dev->rp)
            count = min(count, (size_t)(dev->wp - dev->rp));
        else /* the write pointer has wrapped, return data up to dev->end */
            count = min(count, (size_t)(dev->end - dev->rp));
        if (copy_to_user(buf, dev->rp, count)) {
            up (&dev->sem);
            return -EFAULT;
        }
        dev->rp += count;
        if (dev->rp == dev->end)
            dev->rp = dev->buffer; /* wrapped */
        up (&dev->sem);

        /* finally, awake any writers and return */
        wake_up_interruptible(&dev->outq);
        PDEBUG("\"%s\" did read %li bytes\n",current->comm, (long)count);
        return count;
    }
```

As you can see, we left some PDEBUG statements in the code. When you compile the driver, you can enable messaging to make it easier to follow the interaction of different processes.

Let us look carefully at how *scull_p_read* handles waiting for data. The while loop tests the buffer with the device semaphore held. If there is data there, we know we can return it to the user immediately without sleeping, so the entire body of the loop is skipped. If, instead, the buffer is empty, we must sleep. Before we can do that, however, we must drop the device semaphore; if we were to sleep holding it, no writer would ever have the opportunity to wake us up. Once the semaphore has been dropped, we make a quick check to see if the user has requested non-blocking I/O, and return if so. Otherwise, it is time to call *wait_event_interruptible*.

Once we get past that call, something has woken us up, but we do not know what. One possibility is that the process received a signal. The if statement that contains the *wait_event_interruptible* call checks for this case. This statement ensures the proper and expected reaction to signals, which could have been responsible for waking up the process (since we were in an interruptible sleep). If a signal has arrived and it has not been blocked by the process, the proper behavior is to let upper layers of the kernel handle the event. To this end, the driver returns -ERESTARTSYS to the caller; this value is used internally by the virtual filesystem (VFS) layer, which either restarts the system call or returns -EINTR to user space. We use the same type of check to deal with signal handling for every *read* and *write* implementation.

However, even in the absence of a signal, we do not yet know for sure that there is data there for the taking. Somebody else could have been waiting for data as well, and they might win the race and get the data first. So we must acquire the device semaphore again; only then can we test the read buffer again (in the while loop) and truly know that we can return the data in the buffer to the user. The end result of all this code is that, when we exit from the while loop, we know that the semaphore is held and the buffer contains data that we can use.

Just for completeness, let us note that *scull_p_read* can sleep in another spot after we take the device semaphore: the call to *copy_to_user*. If *scull* sleeps while copying data between kernel and user space, it sleeps with the device semaphore held. Holding the semaphore in this case is justified since it does not deadlock the system (we know that the kernel will perform the copy to user space and wakes us up without trying to lock the same semaphore in the process), and since it is important that the device memory array not change while the driver sleeps.

Advanced Sleeping

Many drivers are able to meet their sleeping requirements with the functions we have covered so far. There are situations, however, that call for a deeper understanding of how the Linux wait queue mechanism works. Complex locking or performance requirements can force a driver to use lower-level functions to effect a sleep. In this section, we look at the lower level to get an understanding of what is really going on when a process sleeps.

How a process sleeps

If you look inside *<linux/wait.h>*, you see that the data structure behind the wait_queue_head_t type is quite simple; it consists of a spinlock and a linked list. What goes on to that list is a wait queue entry, which is declared with the type wait_queue_t. This structure contains information about the sleeping process and exactly how it would like to be woken up.

The first step in putting a process to sleep is usually the allocation and initialization of a wait_queue_t structure, followed by its addition to the proper wait queue. When everything is in place, whoever is charged with doing the wakeup will be able to find the right processes.

The next step is to set the state of the process to mark it as being asleep. There are several task states defined in *<linux/sched.h>*. TASK_RUNNING means that the process is able to run, although it is not necessarily executing in the processor at any specific moment. There are two states that indicate that a process is asleep: TASK_INTERRUPTIBLE and TASK_UNINTERRUPTIBLE; they correspond, of course, to the two types of sleep. The other states are not normally of concern to driver writers.

In the 2.6 kernel, it is not normally necessary for driver code to manipulate the process state directly. However, should you need to do so, the call to use is:

```
void set_current_state(int new_state);
```

In older code, you often see something like this instead:

```
current->state = TASK_INTERRUPTIBLE;
```

But changing current directly in that manner is discouraged; such code breaks easily when data structures change. The above code does show, however, that changing the current state of a process does not, by itself, put it to sleep. By changing the current state, you have changed the way the scheduler treats a process, but you have not yet yielded the processor.

Giving up the processor is the final step, but there is one thing to do first: you must check the condition you are sleeping for first. Failure to do this check invites a race condition; what happens if the condition came true while you were engaged in the above process, and some other thread has just tried to wake you up? You could miss the wakeup altogether and sleep longer than you had intended. Consequently, down inside code that sleeps, you typically see something such as:

```
if (!condition)
    schedule( );
```

By checking our condition *after* setting the process state, we are covered against all possible sequences of events. If the condition we are waiting for had come about before setting the process state, we notice in this check and not actually sleep. If the wakeup happens thereafter, the process is made runnable whether or not we have actually gone to sleep yet.

The call to *schedule* is, of course, the way to invoke the scheduler and yield the CPU. Whenever you call this function, you are telling the kernel to consider which process should be running and to switch control to that process if necessary. So you never know how long it will be before *schedule* returns to your code.

After the `if` test and possible call to (and return from) *schedule*, there is some cleanup to be done. Since the code no longer intends to sleep, it must ensure that the task state is reset to TASK_RUNNING. If the code just returned from *schedule*, this step is unnecessary; that function does not return until the process is in a runnable state. But if the call to *schedule* was skipped because it was no longer necessary to sleep, the process state will be incorrect. It is also necessary to remove the process from the wait queue, or it may be awakened more than once.

Manual sleeps

In previous versions of the Linux kernel, nontrivial sleeps required the programmer to handle all of the above steps manually. It was a tedious process involving a fair amount of error-prone boilerplate code. Programmers can still code a manual sleep in that manner if they want to; *<linux/sched.h>* contains all the requisite definitions, and the kernel source abounds with examples. There is an easier way, however.

The first step is the creation and initialization of a wait queue entry. That is usually done with this macro:

```
DEFINE_WAIT(my_wait);
```

in which name is the name of the wait queue entry variable. You can also do things in two steps:

```
wait_queue_t my_wait;
init_wait(&my_wait);
```

But it is usually easier to put a DEFINE_WAIT line at the top of the loop that implements your sleep.

The next step is to add your wait queue entry to the queue, and set the process state. Both of those tasks are handled by this function:

```
void prepare_to_wait(wait_queue_head_t *queue,
                     wait_queue_t *wait,
                     int state);
```

Here, queue and wait are the wait queue head and the process entry, respectively. state is the new state for the process; it should be either TASK_INTERRUPTIBLE (for interruptible sleeps, which is usually what you want) or TASK_UNINTERRUPTIBLE (for uninterruptible sleeps).

After calling *prepare_to_wait*, the process can call *schedule*—after it has checked to be sure it still needs to wait. Once *schedule* returns, it is cleanup time. That task, too, is handled by a special function:

```
void finish_wait(wait_queue_head_t *queue, wait_queue_t *wait);
```

Thereafter, your code can test its state and see if it needs to wait again.

We are far past due for an example. Previously we looked at the *read* method for *scullpipe*, which uses *wait_event*. The *write* method in the same driver does its waiting with *prepare_to_wait* and *finish_wait*, instead. Normally you would not mix methods within a single driver in this way, but we did so in order to be able to show both ways of handling sleeps.

First, for completeness, let's look at the *write* method itself:

```
/* How much space is free? */
static int spacefree(struct scull_pipe *dev)
{
    if (dev->rp == dev->wp)
        return dev->buffersize - 1;
    return ((dev->rp + dev->buffersize - dev->wp) % dev->buffersize) - 1;
}

static ssize_t scull_p_write(struct file *filp, const char __user *buf, size_t count,
                loff_t *f_pos)
{
    struct scull_pipe *dev = filp->private_data;
    int result;

    if (down_interruptible(&dev->sem))
        return -ERESTARTSYS;
```

```
    /* Make sure there's space to write */
    result = scull_getwritespace(dev, filp);
    if (result)
        return result; /* scull_getwritespace called up(&dev->sem) */

    /* ok, space is there, accept something */
    count = min(count, (size_t)spacefree(dev));
    if (dev->wp >= dev->rp)
        count = min(count, (size_t)(dev->end - dev->wp)); /* to end-of-buf */
    else /* the write pointer has wrapped, fill up to rp-1 */
        count = min(count, (size_t)(dev->rp - dev->wp - 1));
    PDEBUG("Going to accept %li bytes to %p from %p\n", (long)count, dev->wp, buf);
    if (copy_from_user(dev->wp, buf, count)) {
        up (&dev->sem);
        return -EFAULT;
    }
    dev->wp += count;
    if (dev->wp == dev->end)
        dev->wp = dev->buffer; /* wrapped */
    up(&dev->sem);

    /* finally, awake any reader */
    wake_up_interruptible(&dev->inq);  /* blocked in read() and select() */

    /* and signal asynchronous readers, explained late in chapter 5 */
    if (dev->async_queue)
        kill_fasync(&dev->async_queue, SIGIO, POLL_IN);
    PDEBUG("\"%s\" did write %li bytes\n",current->comm, (long)count);
    return count;
}
```

This code looks similar to the *read* method, except that we have pushed the code that sleeps into a separate function called *scull_getwritespace*. Its job is to ensure that there is space in the buffer for new data, sleeping if need be until that space comes available. Once the space is there, *scull_p_write* can simply copy the user's data there, adjust the pointers, and wake up any processes that may have been waiting to read data.

The code that handles the actual sleep is:

```
/* Wait for space for writing; caller must hold device semaphore.  On
 * error the semaphore will be released before returning. */
static int scull_getwritespace(struct scull_pipe *dev, struct file *filp)
{
    while (spacefree(dev) == 0) { /* full */
        DEFINE_WAIT(wait);

        up(&dev->sem);
        if (filp->f_flags & O_NONBLOCK)
            return -EAGAIN;
```

```
        PDEBUG("\"%s\" writing: going to sleep\n",current->comm);
        prepare_to_wait(&dev->outq, &wait, TASK_INTERRUPTIBLE);
        if (spacefree(dev) == 0)
            schedule();
        finish_wait(&dev->outq, &wait);
        if (signal_pending(current))
            return -ERESTARTSYS; /* signal: tell the fs layer to handle it */
        if (down_interruptible(&dev->sem))
            return -ERESTARTSYS;
    }
    return 0;
}
```

Note once again the containing while loop. If space is available without sleeping, this function simply returns. Otherwise, it must drop the device semaphore and wait. The code uses *DEFINE_WAIT* to set up a wait queue entry and *prepare_to_wait* to get ready for the actual sleep. Then comes the obligatory check on the buffer; we must handle the case in which space becomes available in the buffer after we have entered the while loop (and dropped the semaphore) but before we put ourselves onto the wait queue. Without that check, if the reader processes were able to completely empty the buffer in that time, we could miss the only wakeup we would ever get and sleep forever. Having satisfied ourselves that we must sleep, we can call *schedule*.

It is worth looking again at this case: what happens if the wakeup happens between the test in the if statement and the call to *schedule*? In that case, all is well. The wakeup resets the process state to TASK_RUNNING and *schedule* returns—although not necessarily right away. As long as the test happens after the process has put itself on the wait queue and changed its state, things will work.

To finish up, we call *finish_wait*. The call to *signal_pending* tells us whether we were awakened by a signal; if so, we need to return to the user and let them try again later. Otherwise, we reacquire the semaphore, and test again for free space as usual.

Exclusive waits

We have seen that when a process calls *wake_up* on a wait queue, all processes waiting on that queue are made runnable. In many cases, that is the correct behavior. In others, however, it is possible to know ahead of time that only one of the processes being awakened will succeed in obtaining the desired resource, and the rest will simply have to sleep again. Each one of those processes, however, has to obtain the processor, contend for the resource (and any governing locks), and explicitly go back to sleep. If the number of processes in the wait queue is large, this "thundering herd" behavior can seriously degrade the performance of the system.

In response to real-world thundering herd problems, the kernel developers added an "exclusive wait" option to the kernel. An exclusive wait acts very much like a normal sleep, with two important differences:

- When a wait queue entry has the WQ_FLAG_EXCLUSIVE flag set, it is added to the end of the wait queue. Entries without that flag are, instead, added to the beginning.
- When *wake_up* is called on a wait queue, it stops after waking the first process that has the WQ_FLAG_EXCLUSIVE flag set.

The end result is that processes performing exclusive waits are awakened one at a time, in an orderly manner, and do not create thundering herds. The kernel still wakes up all nonexclusive waiters every time, however.

Employing exclusive waits within a driver is worth considering if two conditions are met: you expect significant contention for a resource, and waking a single process is sufficient to completely consume the resource when it becomes available. Exclusive waits work well for the Apache web server, for example; when a new connection comes in, exactly one of the (often many) Apache processes on the system should wake up to deal with it. We did not use exclusive waits in the *scullpipe* driver, however; it is rare to see readers contending for data (or writers for buffer space), and we cannot know that one reader, once awakened, will consume all of the available data.

Putting a process into an interruptible wait is a simple matter of calling *prepare_to_ wait_exclusive*:

```
void prepare_to_wait_exclusive(wait_queue_head_t *queue,
                               wait_queue_t *wait,
                               int state);
```

This call, when used in place of *prepare_to_wait*, sets the "exclusive" flag in the wait queue entry and adds the process to the end of the wait queue. Note that there is no way to perform exclusive waits with *wait_event* and its variants.

The details of waking up

The view we have presented of the wakeup process is simpler than what really happens inside the kernel. The actual behavior that results when a process is awakened is controlled by a function in the wait queue entry. The default wakeup function[*] sets the process into a runnable state and, possibly, performs a context switch to that process if it has a higher priority. Device drivers should never need to supply a different wake function; should yours prove to be the exception, see *<linux/wait.h>* for information on how to do it.

---

[*] It has the imaginative name *default_wake_function*.

We have not yet seen all the variations of *wake_up*. Most driver writers never need the others, but, for completeness, here is the full set:

```
wake_up(wait_queue_head_t *queue);
wake_up_interruptible(wait_queue_head_t *queue);
```

> *wake_up* awakens every process on the queue that is not in an exclusive wait, and exactly one exclusive waiter, if it exists. *wake_up_interruptible* does the same, with the exception that it skips over processes in an uninterruptible sleep. These functions can, before returning, cause one or more of the processes awakened to be scheduled (although this does not happen if they are called from an atomic context).

```
wake_up_nr(wait_queue_head_t *queue, int nr);
wake_up_interruptible_nr(wait_queue_head_t *queue, int nr);
```

> These functions perform similarly to *wake_up*, except they can awaken up to nr exclusive waiters, instead of just one. Note that passing 0 is interpreted as asking for *all* of the exclusive waiters to be awakened, rather than none of them.

```
wake_up_all(wait_queue_head_t *queue);
wake_up_interruptible_all(wait_queue_head_t *queue);
```

> This form of *wake_up* awakens all processes whether they are performing an exclusive wait or not (though the interruptible form still skips processes doing uninterruptible waits).

```
wake_up_interruptible_sync(wait_queue_head_t *queue);
```

> Normally, a process that is awakened may preempt the current process and be scheduled into the processor before *wake_up* returns. In other words, a call to *wake_up* may not be atomic. If the process calling *wake_up* is running in an atomic context (it holds a spinlock, for example, or is an interrupt handler), this rescheduling does not happen. Normally, that protection is adequate. If, however, you need to explicitly ask to not be scheduled out of the processor at this time, you can use the "sync" variant of *wake_up_interruptible*. This function is most often used when the caller is about to reschedule anyway, and it is more efficient to simply finish what little work remains first.

If all of the above is not entirely clear on a first reading, don't worry. Very few drivers ever need to call anything except *wake_up_interruptible*.

Ancient history: sleep_on

If you spend any time digging through the kernel source, you will likely encounter two functions that we have neglected to discuss so far:

```
void sleep_on(wait_queue_head_t *queue);
void interruptible_sleep_on(wait_queue_head_t *queue);
```

As you might expect, these functions unconditionally put the current process to sleep on the given queue. These functions are strongly deprecated, however, and you should never use them. The problem is obvious if you think about it: *sleep_on* offers no way to protect against race conditions. There is always a window between when your code decides it must sleep and when *sleep_on* actually effects that sleep. A wakeup that arrives during that window is missed. For this reason, code that calls *sleep_on* is never entirely safe.

Current plans call for *sleep_on* and its variants (there are a couple of time-out forms we haven't shown) to be removed from the kernel in the not-too-distant future.

Testing the Scullpipe Driver

We have seen how the *scullpipe* driver implements blocking I/O. If you wish to try it out, the source to this driver can be found with the rest of the book examples. Blocking I/O in action can be seen by opening two windows. The first can run a command such as cat /dev/scullpipe. If you then, in another window, copy a file to */dev/scullpipe*, you should see that file's contents appear in the first window.

Testing nonblocking activity is trickier, because the conventional programs available to a shell don't perform nonblocking operations. The *misc-progs* source directory contains the following simple program, called *nbtest*, for testing nonblocking operations. All it does is copy its input to its output, using nonblocking I/O and delaying between retries. The delay time is passed on the command line and is one second by default.

```
int main(int argc, char **argv)
{
    int delay = 1, n, m = 0;

    if (argc > 1)
        delay=atoi(argv[1]);
    fcntl(0, F_SETFL, fcntl(0,F_GETFL) | O_NONBLOCK); /* stdin */
    fcntl(1, F_SETFL, fcntl(1,F_GETFL) | O_NONBLOCK); /* stdout */

    while (1) {
        n = read(0, buffer, 4096);
        if (n >= 0)
            m = write(1, buffer, n);
        if ((n < 0 || m < 0) && (errno != EAGAIN))
            break;
        sleep(delay);
    }
    perror(n < 0 ? "stdin" : "stdout");
    exit(1);
}
```

If you run this program under a process tracing utility such as *strace*, you can see the success or failure of each operation, depending on whether data is available when the operation is tried.

poll and select

Applications that use nonblocking I/O often use the *poll*, *select*, and *epoll* system calls as well. *poll*, *select*, and *epoll* have essentially the same functionality: each allow a process to determine whether it can read from or write to one or more open files without blocking. These calls can also block a process until any of a given set of file descriptors becomes available for reading or writing. Therefore, they are often used in applications that must use multiple input or output streams without getting stuck on any one of them. The same functionality is offered by multiple functions, because two were implemented in Unix almost at the same time by two different groups: *select* was introduced in BSD Unix, whereas *poll* was the System V solution. The *epoll* call* was added in 2.5.45 as a way of making the polling function scale to thousands of file descriptors.

Support for any of these calls requires support from the device driver. This support (for all three calls) is provided through the driver's *poll* method. This method has the following prototype:

```
unsigned int (*poll) (struct file *filp, poll_table *wait);
```

The driver method is called whenever the user-space program performs a *poll*, *select*, or *epoll* system call involving a file descriptor associated with the driver. The device method is in charge of these two steps:

1. Call *poll_wait* on one or more wait queues that could indicate a change in the poll status. If no file descriptors are currently available for I/O, the kernel causes the process to wait on the wait queues for all file descriptors passed to the system call.

2. Return a bit mask describing the operations (if any) that could be immediately performed without blocking.

Both of these operations are usually straightforward and tend to look very similar from one driver to the next. They rely, however, on information that only the driver can provide and, therefore, must be implemented individually by each driver.

The poll_table structure, the second argument to the *poll* method, is used within the kernel to implement the *poll*, *select*, and *epoll* calls; it is declared in *<linux/poll.h>*, which must be included by the driver source. Driver writers do not need to know anything about its internals and must use it as an opaque object; it is passed to the driver method so that the driver can load it with every wait queue that could wake up the process and change the status of the *poll* operation. The driver adds a wait queue to the poll_table structure by calling the function *poll_wait*:

```
void poll_wait (struct file *, wait_queue_head_t *, poll_table *);
```

---

* Actually, *epoll* is a set of three calls that together can be used to achieve the polling functionality. For our purposes, though, we can think of it as a single call.

The second task performed by the *poll* method is returning the bit mask describing which operations could be completed immediately; this is also straightforward. For example, if the device has data available, a *read* would complete without sleeping; the *poll* method should indicate this state of affairs. Several flags (defined via *<linux/poll.h>*) are used to indicate the possible operations:

POLLIN
> This bit must be set if the device can be read without blocking.

POLLRDNORM
> This bit must be set if "normal" data is available for reading. A readable device returns (POLLIN | POLLRDNORM).

POLLRDBAND
> This bit indicates that out-of-band data is available for reading from the device. It is currently used only in one place in the Linux kernel (the DECnet code) and is not generally applicable to device drivers.

POLLPRI
> High-priority data (out-of-band) can be read without blocking. This bit causes *select* to report that an exception condition occurred on the file, because *select* reports out-of-band data as an exception condition.

POLLHUP
> When a process reading this device sees end-of-file, the driver must set POLLHUP (hang-up). A process calling *select* is told that the device is readable, as dictated by the *select* functionality.

POLLERR
> An error condition has occurred on the device. When *poll* is invoked, the device is reported as both readable and writable, since both *read* and *write* return an error code without blocking.

POLLOUT
> This bit is set in the return value if the device can be written to without blocking.

POLLWRNORM
> This bit has the same meaning as POLLOUT, and sometimes it actually is the same number. A writable device returns (POLLOUT | POLLWRNORM).

POLLWRBAND
> Like POLLRDBAND, this bit means that data with nonzero priority can be written to the device. Only the datagram implementation of *poll* uses this bit, since a datagram can transmit out-of-band data.

It's worth repeating that POLLRDBAND and POLLWRBAND are meaningful only with file descriptors associated with sockets: device drivers won't normally use these flags.

The description of *poll* takes up a lot of space for something that is relatively simple to use in practice. Consider the *scullpipe* implementation of the *poll* method:

```
static unsigned int scull_p_poll(struct file *filp, poll_table *wait)
{
    struct scull_pipe *dev = filp->private_data;
    unsigned int mask = 0;

    /*
     * The buffer is circular; it is considered full
     * if "wp" is right behind "rp" and empty if the
     * two are equal.
     */
    down(&dev->sem);
    poll_wait(filp, &dev->inq,  wait);
    poll_wait(filp, &dev->outq, wait);
    if (dev->rp != dev->wp)
        mask |= POLLIN | POLLRDNORM;    /* readable */
    if (spacefree(dev))
        mask |= POLLOUT | POLLWRNORM;    /* writable */
    up(&dev->sem);
    return mask;
}
```

This code simply adds the two *scullpipe* wait queues to the poll_table, then sets the appropriate mask bits depending on whether data can be read or written.

The *poll* code as shown is missing end-of-file support, because *scullpipe* does not support an end-of-file condition. For most real devices, the *poll* method should return POLLHUP if no more data is (or will become) available. If the caller used the *select* system call, the file is reported as readable. Regardless of whether *poll* or *select* is used, the application knows that it can call *read* without waiting forever, and the *read* method returns, 0 to signal end-of-file.

With real FIFOs, for example, the reader sees an end-of-file when all the writers close the file, whereas in *scullpipe* the reader never sees end-of-file. The behavior is different because a FIFO is intended to be a communication channel between two processes, while *scullpipe* is a trash can where everyone can put data as long as there's at least one reader. Moreover, it makes no sense to reimplement what is already available in the kernel, so we chose to implement a different behavior in our example.

Implementing end-of-file in the same way as FIFOs do would mean checking dev->nwriters, both in *read* and in *poll*, and reporting end-of-file (as just described) if no process has the device opened for writing. Unfortunately, though, with this implementation, if a reader opened the *scullpipe* device before the writer, it would see end-of-file without having a chance to wait for data. The best way to fix this problem would be to implement blocking within *open* like real FIFOs do; this task is left as an exercise for the reader.

Interaction with read and write

The purpose of the *poll* and *select* calls is to determine in advance if an I/O operation will block. In that respect, they complement *read* and *write*. More important, *poll* and *select* are useful, because they let the application wait simultaneously for several data streams, although we are not exploiting this feature in the *scull* examples.

A correct implementation of the three calls is essential to make applications work correctly: although the following rules have more or less already been stated, we summarize them here.

Reading data from the device

- If there is data in the input buffer, the *read* call should return immediately, with no noticeable delay, even if less data is available than the application requested, and the driver is sure the remaining data will arrive soon. You can always return less data than you're asked for if this is convenient for any reason (we did it in *scull*), provided you return at least one byte. In this case, *poll* should return POLLIN|POLLRDNORM.

- If there is no data in the input buffer, by default *read* must block until at least one byte is there. If O_NONBLOCK is set, on the other hand, *read* returns immediately with a return value of -EAGAIN (although some old versions of System V return 0 in this case). In these cases, *poll* must report that the device is unreadable until at least one byte arrives. As soon as there is some data in the buffer, we fall back to the previous case.

- If we are at end-of-file, *read* should return immediately with a return value of 0, independent of O_NONBLOCK. *poll* should report POLLHUP in this case.

Writing to the device

- If there is space in the output buffer, *write* should return without delay. It can accept less data than the call requested, but it must accept at least one byte. In this case, *poll* reports that the device is writable by returning POLLOUT|POLLWRNORM.

- If the output buffer is full, by default *write* blocks until some space is freed. If O_NONBLOCK is set, *write* returns immediately with a return value of -EAGAIN (older System V Unices returned 0). In these cases, *poll* should report that the file is not writable. If, on the other hand, the device is not able to accept any more data, *write* returns -ENOSPC ("No space left on device"), independently of the setting of O_NONBLOCK.

- Never make a *write* call wait for data transmission before returning, even if O_NONBLOCK is clear. This is because many applications use *select* to find out whether a *write* will block. If the device is reported as writable, the call must not block. If the program using the device wants to ensure that the data it enqueues in the output buffer is actually transmitted, the driver must provide an *fsync* method. For instance, a removable device should have an *fsync* entry point.

Although this is a good set of general rules, one should also recognize that each device is unique and that sometimes the rules must be bent slightly. For example, record-oriented devices (such as tape drives) cannot execute partial writes.

Flushing pending output

We've seen how the *write* method by itself doesn't account for all data output needs. The *fsync* function, invoked by the system call of the same name, fills the gap. This method's prototype is

```
int (*fsync) (struct file *file, struct dentry *dentry, int datasync);
```

If some application ever needs to be assured that data has been sent to the device, the *fsync* method must be implemented regardless of whether O_NONBLOCK is set. A call to *fsync* should return only when the device has been completely flushed (i.e., the output buffer is empty), even if that takes some time. The datasync argument is used to distinguish between the *fsync* and *fdatasync* system calls; as such, it is only of interest to filesystem code and can be ignored by drivers.

The *fsync* method has no unusual features. The call isn't time critical, so every device driver can implement it to the author's taste. Most of the time, char drivers just have a NULL pointer in their fops. Block devices, on the other hand, always implement the method with the general-purpose *block_fsync*, which, in turn, flushes all the blocks of the device, waiting for I/O to complete.

The Underlying Data Structure

The actual implementation of the *poll* and *select* system calls is reasonably simple, for those who are interested in how it works; *epoll* is a bit more complex but is built on the same mechanism. Whenever a user application calls *poll*, *select*, or *epoll_ctl*,[*] the kernel invokes the *poll* method of all files referenced by the system call, passing the same poll_table to each of them. The poll_table structure is just a wrapper around a function that builds the actual data structure. That structure, for *poll* and *select*, is a linked list of memory pages containing poll_table_entry structures. Each poll_table_entry holds the struct file and wait_queue_head_t pointers passed to *poll_wait*, along with an associated wait queue entry. The call to *poll_wait* sometimes also adds the process to the given wait queue. The whole structure must be maintained by the kernel so that the process can be removed from all of those queues before *poll* or *select* returns.

If none of the drivers being polled indicates that I/O can occur without blocking, the *poll* call simply sleeps until one of the (perhaps many) wait queues it is on wakes it up.

---

[*] This is the function that sets up the internal data structure for future calls to *epoll_wait*.

What's interesting in the implementation of *poll* is that the driver's *poll* method may be called with a NULL pointer as a poll_table argument. This situation can come about for a couple of reasons. If the application calling *poll* has provided a timeout value of 0 (indicating that no wait should be done), there is no reason to accumulate wait queues, and the system simply does not do it. The poll_table pointer is also set to NULL immediately after any driver being *poll*ed indicates that I/O is possible. Since the kernel knows at that point that no wait will occur, it does not build up a list of wait queues.

When the *poll* call completes, the poll_table structure is deallocated, and all wait queue entries previously added to the poll table (if any) are removed from the table and their wait queues.

We tried to show the data structures involved in polling in Figure 6-1; the figure is a simplified representation of the real data structures, because it ignores the multipage nature of a poll table and disregards the file pointer that is part of each poll_table_entry. The reader interested in the actual implementation is urged to look in *<linux/poll.h>* and *fs/select.c*.

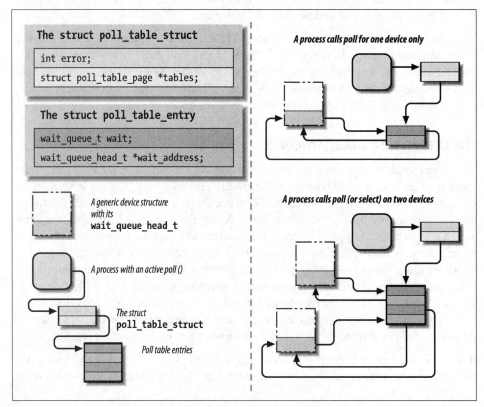

Figure 6-1. The data structures behind poll

At this point, it is possible to understand the motivation behind the new *epoll* system call. In a typical case, a call to *poll* or *select* involves only a handful of file descriptors, so the cost of setting up the data structure is small. There are applications out there, however, that work with thousands of file descriptors. At that point, setting up and tearing down this data structure between every I/O operation becomes prohibitively expensive. The *epoll* system call family allows this sort of application to set up the internal kernel data structure exactly once and to use it many times.

Asynchronous Notification

Although the combination of blocking and nonblocking operations and the *select* method are sufficient for querying the device most of the time, some situations aren't efficiently managed by the techniques we've seen so far.

Let's imagine a process that executes a long computational loop at low priority but needs to process incoming data as soon as possible. If this process is responding to new observations available from some sort of data acquisition peripheral, it would like to know immediately when new data is available. This application could be written to call *poll* regularly to check for data, but, for many situations, there is a better way. By enabling asynchronous notification, this application can receive a signal whenever data becomes available and need not concern itself with polling.

User programs have to execute two steps to enable asynchronous notification from an input file. First, they specify a process as the "owner" of the file. When a process invokes the F_SETOWN command using the *fcntl* system call, the process ID of the owner process is saved in filp->f_owner for later use. This step is necessary for the kernel to know just whom to notify. In order to actually enable asynchronous notification, the user programs must set the FASYNC flag in the device by means of the F_SETFL *fcntl* command.

After these two calls have been executed, the input file can request delivery of a SIGIO signal whenever new data arrives. The signal is sent to the process (or process group, if the value is negative) stored in filp->f_owner.

For example, the following lines of code in a user program enable asynchronous notification to the current process for the stdin input file:

```
signal(SIGIO, &input_handler); /* dummy sample; sigaction( ) is better */
fcntl(STDIN_FILENO, F_SETOWN, getpid( ));
oflags = fcntl(STDIN_FILENO, F_GETFL);
fcntl(STDIN_FILENO, F_SETFL, oflags | FASYNC);
```

The program named *asynctest* in the sources is a simple program that reads stdin as shown. It can be used to test the asynchronous capabilities of *scullpipe*. The program is similar to *cat* but doesn't terminate on end-of-file; it responds only to input, not to the absence of input.

Note, however, that not all the devices support asynchronous notification, and you can choose not to offer it. Applications usually assume that the asynchronous capability is available only for sockets and ttys.

There is one remaining problem with input notification. When a process receives a SIGIO, it doesn't know which input file has new input to offer. If more than one file is enabled to asynchronously notify the process of pending input, the application must still resort to *poll* or *select* to find out what happened.

The Driver's Point of View

A more relevant topic for us is how the device driver can implement asynchronous signaling. The following list details the sequence of operations from the kernel's point of view:

1. When F_SETOWN is invoked, nothing happens, except that a value is assigned to filp->f_owner.

2. When F_SETFL is executed to turn on FASYNC, the driver's *fasync* method is called. This method is called whenever the value of FASYNC is changed in filp->f_flags to notify the driver of the change, so it can respond properly. The flag is cleared by default when the file is opened. We'll look at the standard implementation of the driver method later in this section.

3. When data arrives, all the processes registered for asynchronous notification must be sent a SIGIO signal.

While implementing the first step is trivial—there's nothing to do on the driver's part—the other steps involve maintaining a dynamic data structure to keep track of the different asynchronous readers; there might be several. This dynamic data structure, however, doesn't depend on the particular device involved, and the kernel offers a suitable general-purpose implementation so that you don't have to rewrite the same code in every driver.

The general implementation offered by Linux is based on one data structure and two functions (which are called in the second and third steps described earlier). The header that declares related material is *<linux/fs.h>* (nothing new here), and the data structure is called struct fasync_struct. As with wait queues, we need to insert a pointer to the structure in the device-specific data structure.

The two functions that the driver calls correspond to the following prototypes:

```
int fasync_helper(int fd, struct file *filp,
        int mode, struct fasync_struct **fa);
void kill_fasync(struct fasync_struct **fa, int sig, int band);
```

fasync_helper is invoked to add or remove entries from the list of interested processes when the FASYNC flag changes for an open file. All of its arguments except the last are provided to the *fasync* method and can be passed through directly. kill_fasync is used to signal the interested processes when data arrives. Its arguments are the signal to send (usually SIGIO) and the band, which is almost always POLL_IN* (but that may be used to send "urgent" or out-of-band data in the networking code).

Here's how *scullpipe* implements the *fasync* method:

```
static int scull_p_fasync(int fd, struct file *filp, int mode)
{
    struct scull_pipe *dev = filp->private_data;

    return fasync_helper(fd, filp, mode, &dev->async_queue);
}
```

It's clear that all the work is performed by *fasync_helper*. It wouldn't be possible, however, to implement the functionality without a method in the driver, because the helper function needs to access the correct pointer to struct fasync_struct * (here &dev->async_queue), and only the driver can provide the information.

When data arrives, then, the following statement must be executed to signal asynchronous readers. Since new data for the *scullpipe* reader is generated by a process issuing a *write*, the statement appears in the *write* method of *scullpipe*.

```
if (dev->async_queue)
    kill_fasync(&dev->async_queue, SIGIO, POLL_IN);
```

Note that some devices also implement asynchronous notification to indicate when the device can be written; in this case, of course, *kill_fasync* must be called with a mode of POLL_OUT.

It might appear that we're done, but there's still one thing missing. We must invoke our *fasync* method when the file is closed to remove the file from the list of active asynchronous readers. Although this call is required only if filp->f_flags has FASYNC set, calling the function anyway doesn't hurt and is the usual implementation. The following lines, for example, are part of the *release* method for *scullpipe*:

```
/* remove this filp from the asynchronously notified filp's */
scull_p_fasync(-1, filp, 0);
```

The data structure underlying asynchronous notification is almost identical to the structure struct wait_queue, because both situations involve waiting on an event. The difference is that struct file is used in place of struct task_struct. The struct file in the queue is then used to retrieve f_owner, in order to signal the process.

Seeking a Device

One of the last things we need to cover in this chapter is the *llseek* method, which is useful (for some devices) and easy to implement.

---

* POLL_IN is a symbol used in the asynchronous notification code; it is equivalent to POLLIN|POLLRDNORM.

The llseek Implementation

The *llseek* method implements the *lseek* and *llseek* system calls. We have already stated that if the *llseek* method is missing from the device's operations, the default implementation in the kernel performs seeks by modifying filp->f_pos, the current reading/writing position within the file. Please note that for the *lseek* system call to work correctly, the *read* and *write* methods must cooperate by using and updating the offset item they receive as an argument.

You may need to provide your own *llseek* method if the seek operation corresponds to a physical operation on the device. A simple example can be seen in the *scull* driver:

```
loff_t scull_llseek(struct file *filp, loff_t off, int whence)
{
    struct scull_dev *dev = filp->private_data;
    loff_t newpos;

    switch(whence) {
      case 0: /* SEEK_SET */
        newpos = off;
        break;

      case 1: /* SEEK_CUR */
        newpos = filp->f_pos + off;
        break;

      case 2: /* SEEK_END */
        newpos = dev->size + off;
        break;

      default: /* can't happen */
        return -EINVAL;
    }
    if (newpos < 0) return -EINVAL;
    filp->f_pos = newpos;
    return newpos;
}
```

The only device-specific operation here is retrieving the file length from the device. In *scull* the *read* and *write* methods cooperate as needed, as shown in Chapter 3.

Although the implementation just shown makes sense for *scull*, which handles a well-defined data area, most devices offer a data flow rather than a data area (just think about the serial ports or the keyboard), and seeking those devices does not make sense. If this is the case for your device, you can't just refrain from declaring the *llseek* operation, because the default method allows seeking. Instead, you should inform the kernel that your device does not support *llseek* by calling *nonseekable_open* in your *open* method:

```
int nonseekable_open(struct inode *inode; struct file *filp);
```

This call marks the given `filp` as being nonseekable; the kernel never allows an *lseek* call on such a file to succeed. By marking the file in this way, you can also be assured that no attempts will be made to seek the file by way of the *pread* and *pwrite* system calls.

For completeness, you should also set the *llseek* method in your `file_operations` structure to the special helper function *no_llseek*, which is defined in *<linux/fs.h>*.

Access Control on a Device File

Offering access control is sometimes vital for the reliability of a device node. Not only should unauthorized users not be permitted to use the device (a restriction is enforced by the filesystem permission bits), but sometimes only one authorized user should be allowed to open the device at a time.

The problem is similar to that of using ttys. In that case, the *login* process changes the ownership of the device node whenever a user logs into the system, in order to prevent other users from interfering with or sniffing the tty data flow. However, it's impractical to use a privileged program to change the ownership of a device every time it is opened just to grant unique access to it.

None of the code shown up to now implements any access control beyond the filesystem permission bits. If the *open* system call forwards the request to the driver, *open* succeeds. We now introduce a few techniques for implementing some additional checks.

Every device shown in this section has the same behavior as the bare *scull* device (that is, it implements a persistent memory area) but differs from *scull* in access control, which is implemented in the *open* and *release* operations.

Single-Open Devices

The brute-force way to provide access control is to permit a device to be opened by only one process at a time (single openness). This technique is best avoided because it inhibits user ingenuity. A user might want to run different processes on the same device, one reading status information while the other is writing data. In some cases, users can get a lot done by running a few simple programs through a shell script, as long as they can access the device concurrently. In other words, implementing a single-open behavior amounts to creating policy, which may get in the way of what your users want to do.

Allowing only a single process to open a device has undesirable properties, but it is also the easiest access control to implement for a device driver, so it's shown here. The source code is extracted from a device called *scullsingle*.

The *scullsingle* device maintains an `atomic_t` variable called `scull_s_available`; that variable is initialized to a value of one, indicating that the device is indeed available. The *open* call decrements and tests `scull_s_available` and refuses access if somebody else already has the device open:

```
static atomic_t scull_s_available = ATOMIC_INIT(1);

static int scull_s_open(struct inode *inode, struct file *filp)
{
    struct scull_dev *dev = &scull_s_device; /* device information */

    if (! atomic_dec_and_test (&scull_s_available)) {
        atomic_inc(&scull_s_available);
        return -EBUSY; /* already open */
    }

    /* then, everything else is copied from the bare scull device */
    if ( (filp->f_flags & O_ACCMODE) == O_WRONLY)
        scull_trim(dev);
    filp->private_data = dev;
    return 0;          /* success */
}
```

The *release* call, on the other hand, marks the device as no longer busy:

```
static int scull_s_release(struct inode *inode, struct file *filp)
{
    atomic_inc(&scull_s_available); /* release the device */
    return 0;
}
```

Normally, we recommend that you put the open flag `scull_s_available` within the device structure (Scull_Dev here) because, conceptually, it belongs to the device. The *scull* driver, however, uses standalone variables to hold the flag so it can use the same device structure and methods as the bare *scull* device and minimize code duplication.

Restricting Access to a Single User at a Time

The next step beyond a single-open device is to let a single user open a device in multiple processes but allow only one user to have the device open at a time. This solution makes it easy to test the device, since the user can read and write from several processes at once, but assumes that the user takes some responsibility for maintaining the integrity of the data during multiple accesses. This is accomplished by adding checks in the *open* method; such checks are performed *after* the normal permission checking and can only make access more restrictive than that specified by the owner and group permission bits. This is the same access policy as that used for ttys, but it doesn't resort to an external privileged program.

Those access policies are a little trickier to implement than single-open policies. In this case, two items are needed: an open count and the uid of the "owner" of the device. Once again, the best place for such items is within the device structure; our example uses global variables instead, for the reason explained earlier for *scullsingle*. The name of the device is *sculluid*.

The *open* call grants access on first open but remembers the owner of the device. This means that a user can open the device multiple times, thus allowing cooperating processes to work concurrently on the device. At the same time, no other user can open it, thus avoiding external interference. Since this version of the function is almost identical to the preceding one, only the relevant part is reproduced here:

```
spin_lock(&scull_u_lock);
if (scull_u_count &&
        (scull_u_owner != current->uid) &&  /* allow user */
        (scull_u_owner != current->euid) && /* allow whoever did su */
        !capable(CAP_DAC_OVERRIDE)) { /* still allow root */
    spin_unlock(&scull_u_lock);
    return -EBUSY;   /* -EPERM would confuse the user */
}

if (scull_u_count == 0)
    scull_u_owner = current->uid; /* grab it */

scull_u_count++;
spin_unlock(&scull_u_lock);
```

Note that the *sculluid* code has two variables (scull_u_owner and scull_u_count) that control access to the device and that could be accessed concurrently by multiple processes. To make these variables safe, we control access to them with a spinlock (scull_u_lock). Without that locking, two (or more) processes could test scull_u_count at the same time, and both could conclude that they were entitled to take ownership of the device. A spinlock is indicated here, because the lock is held for a very short time, and the driver does nothing that could sleep while holding the lock.

We chose to return -EBUSY and not -EPERM, even though the code is performing a permission check, in order to point a user who is denied access in the right direction. The reaction to "Permission denied" is usually to check the mode and owner of the /dev file, while "Device busy" correctly suggests that the user should look for a process already using the device.

This code also checks to see if the process attempting the open has the ability to override file access permissions; if so, the open is allowed even if the opening process is not the owner of the device. The CAP_DAC_OVERRIDE capability fits the task well in this case.

The *release* method looks like the following:

```
static int scull_u_release(struct inode *inode, struct file *filp)
{
    spin_lock(&scull_u_lock);
    scull_u_count--; /* nothing else */
```

```
    spin_unlock(&scull_u_lock);
    return 0;
}
```

Once again, we must obtain the lock prior to modifying the count to ensure that we do not race with another process.

Blocking open as an Alternative to EBUSY

When the device isn't accessible, returning an error is usually the most sensible approach, but there are situations in which the user would prefer to wait for the device.

For example, if a data communication channel is used both to transmit reports on a regular, scheduled basis (using *crontab*) and for casual usage according to people's needs, it's much better for the scheduled operation to be slightly delayed rather than fail just because the channel is currently busy.

This is one of the choices that the programmer must make when designing a device driver, and the right answer depends on the particular problem being solved.

The alternative to EBUSY, as you may have guessed, is to implement blocking *open*. The *scullwuid* device is a version of *sculluid* that waits for the device on *open* instead of returning -EBUSY. It differs from *sculluid* only in the following part of the *open* operation:

```
spin_lock(&scull_w_lock);
while (! scull_w_available( )) {
    spin_unlock(&scull_w_lock);
    if (filp->f_flags & O_NONBLOCK) return -EAGAIN;
    if (wait_event_interruptible (scull_w_wait, scull_w_available( )))
        return -ERESTARTSYS; /* tell the fs layer to handle it */
    spin_lock(&scull_w_lock);
}
if (scull_w_count == 0)
    scull_w_owner = current->uid; /* grab it */
scull_w_count++;
spin_unlock(&scull_w_lock);
```

The implementation is based once again on a wait queue. If the device is not currently available, the process attempting to open it is placed on the wait queue until the owning process closes the device.

The *release* method, then, is in charge of awakening any pending process:

```
static int scull_w_release(struct inode *inode, struct file *filp)
{
    int temp;

    spin_lock(&scull_w_lock);
    scull_w_count--;
    temp = scull_w_count;
    spin_unlock(&scull_w_lock);
```

```
        if (temp == 0)
            wake_up_interruptible_sync(&scull_w_wait); /* awake other uid's */
        return 0;
}
```

Here is an example of where calling *wake_up_interruptible_sync* makes sense. When we do the wakeup, we are just about to return to user space, which is a natural scheduling point for the system. Rather than potentially reschedule when we do the wakeup, it is better to just call the "sync" version and finish our job.

The problem with a blocking-open implementation is that it is really unpleasant for the interactive user, who has to keep guessing what is going wrong. The interactive user usually invokes standard commands, such as *cp* and *tar*, and can't just add O_NONBLOCK to the *open* call. Someone who's making a backup using the tape drive in the next room would prefer to get a plain "device or resource busy" message instead of being left to guess why the hard drive is so silent today, while *tar* should be scanning it.

This kind of problem (a need for different, incompatible policies for the same device) is often best solved by implementing one device node for each access policy. An example of this practice can be found in the Linux tape driver, which provides multiple device files for the same device. Different device files will, for example, cause the drive to record with or without compression, or to automatically rewind the tape when the device is closed.

Cloning the Device on open

Another technique to manage access control is to create different private copies of the device, depending on the process opening it.

Clearly, this is possible only if the device is not bound to a hardware object; *scull* is an example of such a "software" device. The internals of */dev/tty* use a similar technique in order to give its process a different "view" of what the */dev* entry point represents. When copies of the device are created by the software driver, we call them *virtual devices*—just as virtual consoles use a single physical tty device.

Although this kind of access control is rarely needed, the implementation can be enlightening in showing how easily kernel code can change the application's perspective of the surrounding world (i.e., the computer).

The */dev/scullpriv* device node implements virtual devices within the *scull* package. The *scullpriv* implementation uses the device number of the process's controlling tty as a key to access the virtual device. Nonetheless, you can easily modify the sources to use any integer value for the key; each choice leads to a different policy. For example, using the uid leads to a different virtual device for each user, while using a pid key creates a new device for each process accessing it.

The decision to use the controlling terminal is meant to enable easy testing of the device using I/O redirection: the device is shared by all commands run on the same virtual terminal and is kept separate from the one seen by commands run on another terminal.

The *open* method looks like the following code. It must look for the right virtual device and possibly create one. The final part of the function is not shown because it is copied from the bare *scull*, which we've already seen.

```
/* The clone-specific data structure includes a key field */

struct scull_listitem {
    struct scull_dev device;
    dev_t key;
    struct list_head list;

};

/* The list of devices, and a lock to protect it */
static LIST_HEAD(scull_c_list);
static spinlock_t scull_c_lock = SPIN_LOCK_UNLOCKED;

/* Look for a device or create one if missing */
static struct scull_dev *scull_c_lookfor_device(dev_t key)
{
    struct scull_listitem *lptr;

    list_for_each_entry(lptr, &scull_c_list, list) {
        if (lptr->key == key)
            return &(lptr->device);
    }

    /* not found */
    lptr = kmalloc(sizeof(struct scull_listitem), GFP_KERNEL);
    if (!lptr)
        return NULL;

    /* initialize the device */
    memset(lptr, 0, sizeof(struct scull_listitem));
    lptr->key = key;
    scull_trim(&(lptr->device)); /* initialize it */
    init_MUTEX(&(lptr->device.sem));

    /* place it in the list */
    list_add(&lptr->list, &scull_c_list);

    return &(lptr->device);
}

static int scull_c_open(struct inode *inode, struct file *filp)
{
    struct scull_dev *dev;
```

```
    dev_t key;

    if (!current->signal->tty) {
        PDEBUG("Process \"%s\" has no ctl tty\n", current->comm);
        return -EINVAL;
    }
    key = tty_devnum(current->signal->tty);

    /* look for a scullc device in the list */
    spin_lock(&scull_c_lock);
    dev = scull_c_lookfor_device(key);
    spin_unlock(&scull_c_lock);

    if (!dev)
        return -ENOMEM;

    /* then, everything else is copied from the bare scull device */
```

The *release* method does nothing special. It would normally release the device on last close, but we chose not to maintain an open count in order to simplify the testing of the driver. If the device were released on last close, you wouldn't be able to read the same data after writing to the device, unless a background process were to keep it open. The sample driver takes the easier approach of keeping the data, so that at the next *open*, you'll find it there. The devices are released when *scull_cleanup* is called.

This code uses the generic Linux linked list mechanism in preference to reimplementing the same capability from scratch. Linux lists are discussed in Chapter 11.

Here's the *release* implementation for */dev/scullpriv*, which closes the discussion of device methods.

```
static int scull_c_release(struct inode *inode, struct file *filp)
{
    /*
     * Nothing to do, because the device is persistent.
     * A `real' cloned device should be freed on last close
     */
    return 0;
}
```

Quick Reference

This chapter introduced the following symbols and header files:

#include <linux/ioctl.h>

Declares all the macros used to define *ioctl* commands. It is currently included by *<linux/fs.h>*.

```
_IOC_NRBITS
_IOC_TYPEBITS
_IOC_SIZEBITS
_IOC_DIRBITS
```
The number of bits available for the different bitfields of *ioctl* commands. There are also four macros that specify the MASKs and four that specify the SHIFTs, but they're mainly for internal use. _IOC_SIZEBITS is an important value to check, because it changes across architectures.

```
_IOC_NONE
_IOC_READ
_IOC_WRITE
```
The possible values for the "direction" bitfield. "Read" and "write" are different bits and can be ORed to specify read/write. The values are 0-based.

```
_IOC(dir,type,nr,size)
_IO(type,nr)
_IOR(type,nr,size)
_IOW(type,nr,size)
_IOWR(type,nr,size)
```
Macros used to create an *ioctl* command.

```
_IOC_DIR(nr)
_IOC_TYPE(nr)
_IOC_NR(nr)
_IOC_SIZE(nr)
```
Macros used to decode a command. In particular, _IOC_TYPE(nr) is an OR combination of _IOC_READ and _IOC_WRITE.

```
#include <asm/uaccess.h>
int access_ok(int type, const void *addr, unsigned long size);
```
Checks that a pointer to user space is actually usable. *access_ok* returns a nonzero value if the access should be allowed.

```
VERIFY_READ
VERIFY_WRITE
```
The possible values for the type argument in *access_ok*. VERIFY_WRITE is a superset of VERIFY_READ.

```
#include <asm/uaccess.h>
int put_user(datum,ptr);
int get_user(local,ptr);
int __put_user(datum,ptr);
int __get_user(local,ptr);
```
Macros used to store or retrieve a datum to or from user space. The number of bytes being transferred depends on sizeof(*ptr). The regular versions call

access_ok first, while the qualified versions (*__put_user* and *__get_user*) assume
that *access_ok* has already been called.

```
#include <linux/capability.h>
```
Defines the various `CAP_` symbols describing the capabilities a user-space process
may have.

```
int capable(int capability);
```
Returns nonzero if the process has the given capability.

```
#include <linux/wait.h>
typedef struct { /* ... */ } wait_queue_head_t;
void init_waitqueue_head(wait_queue_head_t *queue);
DECLARE_WAIT_QUEUE_HEAD(queue);
```
The defined type for Linux wait queues. A `wait_queue_head_t` must be explicitly
initialized with either *init_waitqueue_head* at runtime or *DECLARE_WAIT_
QUEUE_HEAD* at compile time.

```
void wait_event(wait_queue_head_t q, int condition);
int wait_event_interruptible(wait_queue_head_t q, int condition);
int wait_event_timeout(wait_queue_head_t q, int condition, int time);
int wait_event_interruptible_timeout(wait_queue_head_t q, int condition,
  int time);
```
Cause the process to sleep on the given queue until the given condition evalu-
ates to a true value.

```
void wake_up(struct wait_queue **q);
void wake_up_interruptible(struct wait_queue **q);
void wake_up_nr(struct wait_queue **q, int nr);
void wake_up_interruptible_nr(struct wait_queue **q, int nr);
void wake_up_all(struct wait_queue **q);
void wake_up_interruptible_all(struct wait_queue **q);
void wake_up_interruptible_sync(struct wait_queue **q);
```
Wake processes that are sleeping on the queue q. The *_interruptible* form wakes
only interruptible processes. Normally, only one exclusive waiter is awakened,
but that behavior can be changed with the *_nr* or *_all* forms. The *_sync* version
does not reschedule the CPU before returning.

```
#include <linux/sched.h>
set_current_state(int state);
```
Sets the execution state of the current process. `TASK_RUNNING` means it is ready to
run, while the sleep states are `TASK_INTERRUPTIBLE` and `TASK_UNINTERRUPTIBLE`.

```
void schedule(void);
```
Selects a runnable process from the run queue. The chosen process can be
current or a different one.

```
typedef struct { /* ... */ } wait_queue_t;
init_waitqueue_entry(wait_queue_t *entry, struct task_struct *task);
```
The `wait_queue_t` type is used to place a process onto a wait queue.

```
void prepare_to_wait(wait_queue_head_t *queue, wait_queue_t *wait, int state);
void prepare_to_wait_exclusive(wait_queue_head_t *queue, wait_queue_t *wait,
  int state);
void finish_wait(wait_queue_head_t *queue, wait_queue_t *wait);
```
Helper functions that can be used to code a manual sleep.

```
void sleep_on(wiat_queue_head_t *queue);
void interruptible_sleep_on(wiat_queue_head_t *queue);
```
Obsolete and deprecated functions that unconditionally put the current process to sleep.

```
#include <linux/poll.h>
void poll_wait(struct file *filp, wait_queue_head_t *q, poll_table *p)
```
Places the current process into a wait queue without scheduling immediately. It is designed to be used by the *poll* method of device drivers.

```
int fasync_helper(struct inode *inode, struct file *filp, int mode, struct
  fasync_struct **fa);
```
A "helper" for implementing the *fasync* device method. The `mode` argument is the same value that is passed to the method, while `fa` points to a device-specific `fasync_struct *`.

```
void kill_fasync(struct fasync_struct *fa, int sig, int band);
```
If the driver supports asynchronous notification, this function can be used to send a signal to processes registered in `fa`.

```
int nonseekable_open(struct inode *inode, struct file *filp);
loff_t no_llseek(struct file *file, loff_t offset, int whence);
```
nonseekable_open should be called in the *open* method of any device that does not support seeking. Such devices should also use *no_llseek* as their *llseek* method.

## CHAPTER 7

Time, Delays, and Deferred Work

At this point, we know the basics of how to write a full-featured char module. Real-world drivers, however, need to do more than implement the operations that control a device; they have to deal with issues such as timing, memory management, hardware access, and more. Fortunately, the kernel exports a number of facilities to ease the task of the driver writer. In the next few chapters, we'll describe some of the kernel resources you can use. This chapter leads the way by describing how timing issues are addressed. Dealing with time involves the following tasks, in order of increasing complexity:

- Measuring time lapses and comparing times
- Knowing the current time
- Delaying operation for a specified amount of time
- Scheduling asynchronous functions to happen at a later time

Measuring Time Lapses

The kernel keeps track of the flow of time by means of timer interrupts. Interrupts are covered in detail in Chapter 10.

Timer interrupts are generated by the system's timing hardware at regular intervals; this interval is programmed at boot time by the kernel according to the value of HZ, which is an architecture-dependent value defined in *<linux/param.h>* or a subplatform file included by it. Default values in the distributed kernel source range from 50 to 1200 ticks per second on real hardware, down to 24 for software simulators. Most platforms run at 100 or 1000 interrupts per second; the popular x86 PC defaults to 1000, although it used to be 100 in previous versions (up to and including 2.4). As a general rule, even if you know the value of HZ, you should never count on that specific value when programming.

It is possible to change the value of HZ for those who want systems with a different clock interrupt frequency. If you change HZ in the header file, you need to recompile the kernel and all modules with the new value. You might want to raise HZ to get a more fine-grained resolution in your asynchronous tasks, if you are willing to pay the overhead of the extra timer interrupts to achieve your goals. Actually, raising HZ to 1000 was pretty common with x86 industrial systems using Version 2.4 or 2.2 of the kernel. With current versions, however, the best approach to the timer interrupt is to keep the default value for HZ, by virtue of our complete trust in the kernel developers, who have certainly chosen the best value. Besides, some internal calculations are currently implemented only for HZ in the range from 12 to 1535 (see *<linux/timex.h>* and RFC-1589).

Every time a timer interrupt occurs, the value of an internal kernel counter is incremented. The counter is initialized to 0 at system boot, so it represents the number of clock ticks since last boot. The counter is a 64-bit variable (even on 32-bit architectures) and is called jiffies_64. However, driver writers normally access the jiffies variable, an unsigned long that is the same as either jiffies_64 or its least significant bits. Using jiffies is usually preferred because it is faster, and accesses to the 64-bit jiffies_64 value are not necessarily atomic on all architectures.

In addition to the low-resolution kernel-managed jiffy mechanism, some CPU platforms feature a high-resolution counter that software can read. Although its actual use varies somewhat across platforms, it's sometimes a very powerful tool.

Using the jiffies Counter

The counter and the utility functions to read it live in *<linux/jiffies.h>*, although you'll usually just include *<linux/sched.h>*, that automatically pulls *jiffies.h* in. Needless to say, both jiffies and jiffies_64 must be considered read-only.

Whenever your code needs to remember the current value of jiffies, it can simply access the unsigned long variable, which is declared as volatile to tell the compiler not to optimize memory reads. You need to read the current counter whenever your code needs to calculate a future time stamp, as shown in the following example:

```
#include <linux/jiffies.h>
unsigned long j, stamp_1, stamp_half, stamp_n;

j = jiffies;                            /* read the current value */
stamp_1    = j + HZ;                    /* 1 second in the future */
stamp_half = j + HZ/2;                  /* half a second */
stamp_n    = j + n * HZ / 1000;         /* n milliseconds */
```

This code has no problem with jiffies wrapping around, as long as different values are compared in the right way. Even though on 32-bit platforms the counter wraps around only once every 50 days when HZ is 1000, your code should be prepared to face that event. To compare your cached value (like stamp_1 above) and the current value, you should use one of the following macros:

```
#include <linux/jiffies.h>
int time_after(unsigned long a, unsigned long b);
```

```
int time_before(unsigned long a, unsigned long b);
int time_after_eq(unsigned long a, unsigned long b);
int time_before_eq(unsigned long a, unsigned long b);
```

The first evaluates true when *a*, as a snapshot of `jiffies`, represents a time after *b*, the second evaluates true when time *a* is before time *b*, and the last two compare for "after or equal" and "before or equal." The code works by converting the values to signed long, subtracting them, and comparing the result. If you need to know the difference between two instances of `jiffies` in a safe way, you can use the same trick: `diff = (long)t2 - (long)t1;`.

You can convert a jiffies difference to milliseconds trivially through:

```
msec = diff * 1000 / HZ;
```

Sometimes, however, you need to exchange time representations with user space programs that tend to represent time values with `struct timeval` and `struct timespec`. The two structures represent a precise time quantity with two numbers: seconds and microseconds are used in the older and popular `struct timeval`, and seconds and nanoseconds are used in the newer `struct timespec`. The kernel exports four helper functions to convert time values expressed as jiffies to and from those structures:

```
#include <linux/time.h>

unsigned long timespec_to_jiffies(struct timespec *value);
void jiffies_to_timespec(unsigned long jiffies, struct timespec *value);
unsigned long timeval_to_jiffies(struct timeval *value);
void jiffies_to_timeval(unsigned long jiffies, struct timeval *value);
```

Accessing the 64-bit jiffy count is not as straightforward as accessing `jiffies`. While on 64-bit computer architectures the two variables are actually one, access to the value is not atomic for 32-bit processors. This means you might read the wrong value if both halves of the variable get updated while you are reading them. It's extremely unlikely you'll ever need to read the 64-bit counter, but in case you do, you'll be glad to know that the kernel exports a specific helper function that does the proper locking for you:

```
#include <linux/jiffies.h>
u64 get_jiffies_64(void);
```

In the above prototype, the `u64` type is used. This is one of the types defined by *<linux/types.h>*, discussed in Chapter 11, and represents an unsigned 64-bit type.

If you're wondering how 32-bit platforms update both the 32-bit and 64-bit counters at the same time, read the linker script for your platform (look for a file whose name matches *vmlinux*.lds*). There, the `jiffies` symbol is defined to access the least significant word of the 64-bit value, according to whether the platform is little-endian or big-endian. Actually, the same trick is used for 64-bit platforms, so that the `unsigned long` and `u64` variables are accessed at the same address.

Finally, note that the actual clock frequency is almost completely hidden from user space. The macro HZ always expands to 100 when user-space programs include *param.h*, and every counter reported to user space is converted accordingly. This applies to *clock(3)*, *times(2)*, and any related function. The only evidence available to users of the HZ value is how fast timer interrupts happen, as shown in */proc/interrupts*. For example, you can obtain HZ by dividing this count by the system uptime reported in */proc/uptime*.

Processor-Specific Registers

If you need to measure very short time intervals or you need extremely high precision in your figures, you can resort to platform-dependent resources, a choice of precision over portability.

In modern processors, the pressing demand for empirical performance figures is thwarted by the intrinsic unpredictability of instruction timing in most CPU designs due to cache memories, instruction scheduling, and branch prediction. As a response, CPU manufacturers introduced a way to count clock cycles as an easy and reliable way to measure time lapses. Therefore, most modern processors include a counter register that is steadily incremented once at each clock cycle. Nowadays, this clock counter is the only reliable way to carry out high-resolution timekeeping tasks.

The details differ from platform to platform: the register may or may not be readable from user space, it may or may not be writable, and it may be 64 or 32 bits wide. In the last case, you must be prepared to handle overflows just like we did with the jiffy counter. The register may even not exist for your platform, or it can be implemented in an external device by the hardware designer, if the CPU lacks the feature and you are dealing with a special-purpose computer.

Whether or not the register can be zeroed, we strongly discourage resetting it, even when hardware permits. You might not, after all, be the only user of the counter at any given time; on some platforms supporting SMP, for example, the kernel depends on such a counter to be synchronized across processors. Since you can always measure differences between values, as long as that difference doesn't exceed the overflow time, you can get the work done without claiming exclusive ownership of the register by modifying its current value.

The most renowned counter register is the TSC (timestamp counter), introduced in x86 processors with the Pentium and present in all CPU designs ever since—including the x86_64 platform. It is a 64-bit register that counts CPU clock cycles; it can be read from both kernel space and user space.

After including *<asm/msr.h>* (an x86-specific header whose name stands for "machine-specific registers"), you can use one of these macros:

```
rdtsc(low32,high32);
rdtscl(low32);
rdtscll(var64);
```

The first macro atomically reads the 64-bit value into two 32-bit variables; the next one ("read low half") reads the low half of the register into a 32-bit variable, discarding the high half; the last reads the 64-bit value into a long long variable, hence, the name. All of these macros store values into their arguments.

Reading the low half of the counter is enough for most common uses of the TSC. A 1-GHz CPU overflows it only once every 4.2 seconds, so you won't need to deal with multiregister variables if the time lapse you are benchmarking reliably takes less time. However, as CPU frequencies rise over time and as timing requirements increase, you'll most likely need to read the 64-bit counter more often in the future.

As an example using only the low half of the register, the following lines measure the execution of the instruction itself:

```
unsigned long ini, end;
rdtscl(ini); rdtscl(end);
printk("time lapse: %li\n", end - ini);
```

Some of the other platforms offer similar functionality, and kernel headers offer an architecture-independent function that you can use instead of *rdtsc*. It is called *get_cycles*, defined in *<asm/timex.h>* (included by *<linux/timex.h>*). Its prototype is:

```
#include <linux/timex.h>
cycles_t get_cycles(void);
```

This function is defined for every platform, and it always returns 0 on the platforms that have no cycle-counter register. The cycles_t type is an appropriate unsigned type to hold the value read.

Despite the availability of an architecture-independent function, we'd like to take the opportunity to show an example of inline assembly code. To this aim, we implement a *rdtscl* function for MIPS processors that works in the same way as the x86 one.

We base the example on MIPS because most MIPS processors feature a 32-bit counter as register 9 of their internal "coprocessor 0." To access the register, readable only from kernel space, you can define the following macro that executes a "move from coprocessor 0" assembly instruction:*

```
#define rdtscl(dest) \
    __asm__ __volatile__("mfc0 %0,$9; nop" : "=r" (dest))
```

With this macro in place, the MIPS processor can execute the same code shown earlier for the x86.

---

* The trailing *nop* instruction is required to prevent the compiler from accessing the target register in the instruction immediately following *mfc0*. This kind of interlock is typical of RISC processors, and the compiler can still schedule useful instructions in the delay slots. In this case, we use *nop* because inline assembly is a black box for the compiler and no optimization can be performed.

With *gcc* inline assembly, the allocation of general-purpose registers is left to the compiler. The macro just shown uses %0 as a placeholder for "argument 0," which is later specified as "any register (r) used as output (=)." The macro also states that the output register must correspond to the C expression dest. The syntax for inline assembly is very powerful but somewhat complex, especially for architectures that have constraints on what each register can do (namely, the x86 family). The syntax is described in the *gcc* documentation, usually available in the *info* documentation tree.

The short C-code fragment shown in this section has been run on a K7-class x86 processor and a MIPS VR4181 (using the macro just described). The former reported a time lapse of 11 clock ticks and the latter just 2 clock ticks. The small figure was expected, since RISC processors usually execute one instruction per clock cycle.

There is one other thing worth knowing about timestamp counters: they are not necessarily synchronized across processors in an SMP system. To be sure of getting a coherent value, you should disable preemption for code that is querying the counter.

Knowing the Current Time

Kernel code can always retrieve a representation of the current time by looking at the value of jiffies. Usually, the fact that the value represents only the time since the last boot is not relevant to the driver, because its life is limited to the system uptime. As shown, drivers can use the current value of jiffies to calculate time intervals across events (for example, to tell double-clicks from single-clicks in input device drivers or calculate timeouts). In short, looking at jiffies is almost always sufficient when you need to measure time intervals. If you need very precise measurements for short time lapses, processor-specific registers come to the rescue (although they bring in serious portability issues).

It's quite unlikely that a driver will ever need to know the wall-clock time, expressed in months, days, and hours; the information is usually needed only by user programs such as *cron* and *syslogd*. Dealing with real-world time is usually best left to user space, where the C library offers better support; besides, such code is often too policy-related to belong in the kernel. There *is* a kernel function that turns a wall-clock time into a jiffies value, however:

```
#include <linux/time.h>
unsigned long mktime (unsigned int year, unsigned int mon,
                      unsigned int day, unsigned int hour,
                      unsigned int min, unsigned int sec);
```

To repeat: dealing directly with wall-clock time in a driver is often a sign that policy is being implemented and should therefore be questioned.

While you won't have to deal with human-readable representations of the time, sometimes you need to deal with absolute timestamp even in kernel space. To this aim, *<linux/time.h>* exports the *do_gettimeofday* function. When called, it fills a struct timeval pointer—the same one used in the *gettimeofday* system call—with the familiar seconds and microseconds values. The prototype for *do_gettimeofday* is:

```
#include <linux/time.h>
void do_gettimeofday(struct timeval *tv);
```

The source states that *do_gettimeofday* has "near microsecond resolution," because it asks the timing hardware what fraction of the current jiffy has already elapsed. The precision varies from one architecture to another, however, since it depends on the actual hardware mechanisms in use. For example, some *m68knommu* processors, Sun3 systems, and other *m68k* systems cannot offer more than jiffy resolution. Pentium systems, on the other hand, offer very fast and precise subtick measures by reading the timestamp counter described earlier in this chapter.

The current time is also available (though with jiffy granularity) from the xtime variable, a struct timespec value. Direct use of this variable is discouraged because it is difficult to atomically access both the fields. Therefore, the kernel offers the utility function *current_kernel_time*:

```
#include <linux/time.h>
struct timespec current_kernel_time(void);
```

Code for retrieving the current time in the various ways it is available within the *jit* ("just in time") module in the source files provided on O'Reilly's FTP site. *jit* creates a file called */proc/currentime*, which returns the following items in ASCII when read:

- The current jiffies and jiffies_64 values as hex numbers
- The current time as returned by *do_gettimeofday*
- The timespec returned by *current_kernel_time*

We chose to use a dynamic */proc* file to keep the boilerplate code to a minimum—it's not worth creating a whole device just to return a little textual information.

The file returns text lines continuously as long as the module is loaded; each *read* system call collects and returns one set of data, organized in two lines for better readability. Whenever you read multiple data sets in less than a timer tick, you'll see the difference between *do_gettimeofday*, which queries the hardware, and the other values that are updated only when the timer ticks.

```
phon% head -8 /proc/currentime
0x00bdbc1f 0x0000000100bdbc1f 1062370899.630126
                              1062370899.629161488
0x00bdbc1f 0x0000000100bdbc1f 1062370899.630150
                              1062370899.629161488
0x00bdbc20 0x0000000100bdbc20 1062370899.630208
                              1062370899.630161336
0x00bdbc20 0x0000000100bdbc20 1062370899.630233
                              1062370899.630161336
```

In the screenshot above, there are two interesting things to note. First, the *current_kernel_time* value, though expressed in nanoseconds, has only clock-tick granularity;

do_gettimeofday consistently reports a later time but not later than the next timer tick. Second, the 64-bit jiffies counter has the least-significant bit of the upper 32-bit word set. This happens because the default value for INITIAL_JIFFIES, used at boot time to initialize the counter, forces a low-word overflow a few minutes after boot time to help detect problems related to that very overflow. This initial bias in the counter has no effect, because jiffies is unrelated to wall-clock time. In */proc/ uptime*, where the kernel extracts the uptime from the counter, the initial bias is removed before conversion.

Delaying Execution

Device drivers often need to delay the execution of a particular piece of code for a period of time, usually to allow the hardware to accomplish some task. In this section we cover a number of different techniques for achieving delays. The circumstances of each situation determine which technique is best to use; we go over them all, and point out the advantages and disadvantages of each.

One important thing to consider is how the delay you need compares with the clock tick, considering the range of HZ across the various platforms. Delays that are reliably longer than the clock tick, and don't suffer from its coarse granularity, can make use of the system clock. Very short delays typically must be implemented with software loops. In between these two cases lies a gray area. In this chapter, we use the phrase "long" delay to refer to a multiple-jiffy delay, which can be as low as a few milliseconds on some platforms, but is still long as seen by the CPU and the kernel.

The following sections talk about the different delays by taking a somewhat long path from various intuitive but inappropriate solutions to the right solution. We chose this path because it allows a more in-depth discussion of kernel issues related to timing. If you are eager to find the right code, just skim through the section.

Long Delays

Occasionally a driver needs to delay execution for relatively long periods—more than one clock tick. There are a few ways of accomplishing this sort of delay; we start with the simplest technique, then proceed to the more advanced techniques.

Busy waiting

If you want to delay execution by a multiple of the clock tick, allowing some slack in the value, the easiest (though not recommended) implementation is a loop that monitors the jiffy counter. The *busy-waiting* implementation usually looks like the following code, where j1 is the value of jiffies at the expiration of the delay:

```
while (time_before(jiffies, j1))
    cpu_relax( );
```

The call to *cpu_relax* invokes an architecture-specific way of saying that you're not doing much with the processor at the moment. On many systems it does nothing at all; on symmetric multithreaded ("hyperthreaded") systems, it may yield the core to the other thread. In any case, this approach should definitely be avoided whenever possible. We show it here because on occasion you might want to run this code to better understand the internals of other code.

So let's look at how this code works. The loop is guaranteed to work because jiffies is declared as volatile by the kernel headers and, therefore, is fetched from memory any time some C code accesses it. Although technically correct (in that it works as designed), this busy loop severely degrades system performance. If you didn't configure your kernel for preemptive operation, the loop completely locks the processor for the duration of the delay; the scheduler never preempts a process that is running in kernel space, and the computer looks completely dead until time j1 is reached. The problem is less serious if you are running a preemptive kernel, because, unless the code is holding a lock, some of the processor's time can be recovered for other uses. Busy waits are still expensive on preemptive systems, however.

Still worse, if interrupts happen to be disabled when you enter the loop, jiffies won't be updated, and the while condition remains true forever. Running a preemptive kernel won't help either, and you'll be forced to hit the big red button.

This implementation of delaying code is available, like the following ones, in the *jit* module. The */proc/jit** files created by the module delay a whole second each time you read a line of text, and lines are guaranteed to be 20 bytes each. If you want to test the busy-wait code, you can read */proc/jitbusy*, which busy-loops for one second for each line it returns.

 Be sure to read, at most, one line (or a few lines) at a time from */proc/jitbusy*. The simplified kernel mechanism to register */proc* files invokes the *read* method over and over to fill the data buffer the user requested. Therefore, a command such as *cat /proc/jitbusy*, if it reads 4 KB at a time, freezes the computer for 205 seconds.

The suggested command to read */proc/jitbusy* is *dd bs=20 < /proc/jitbusy*, optionally specifying the number of blocks as well. Each 20-byte line returned by the file represents the value the jiffy counter had before and after the delay. This is a sample run on an otherwise unloaded computer:

```
phon% dd bs=20 count=5 < /proc/jitbusy
    1686518    1687518
    1687519    1688519
    1688520    1689520
    1689520    1690520
    1690521    1691521
```

All looks good: delays are exactly one second (1000 jiffies), and the next *read* system call starts immediately after the previous one is over. But let's see what happens on a system with a large number of CPU-intensive processes running (and nonpreemptive kernel):

```
phon% dd bs=20 count=5 < /proc/jitbusy
  1911226    1912226
  1913323    1914323
  1919529    1920529
  1925632    1926632
  1931835    1932835
```

Here, each *read* system call delays exactly one second, but the kernel can take more than 5 seconds before scheduling the *dd* process so it can issue the next system call. That's expected in a multitasking system; CPU time is shared between all running processes, and a CPU-intensive process has its dynamic priority reduced. (A discussion of scheduling policies is outside the scope of this book.)

The test under load shown above has been performed while running the *load50* sample program. This program forks a number of processes that do nothing, but do it in a CPU-intensive way. The program is part of the sample files accompanying this book, and forks 50 processes by default, although the number can be specified on the command line. In this chapter, and elsewhere in the book, the tests with a loaded system have been performed with *load50* running in an otherwise idle computer.

If you repeat the command while running a preemptible kernel, you'll find no noticeable difference on an otherwise idle CPU and the following behavior under load:

```
phon% dd bs=20 count=5 < /proc/jitbusy
  14940680   14942777
  14942778   14945430
  14945431   14948491
  14948492   14951960
  14951961   14955840
```

Here, there is no significant delay between the end of a system call and the beginning of the next one, but the individual delays are far longer than one second: up to 3.8 seconds in the example shown and increasing over time. These values demonstrate that the process has been interrupted during its delay, scheduling other processes. The gap between system calls is not the only scheduling option for this process, so no special delay can be seen there.

Yielding the processor

As we have seen, busy waiting imposes a heavy load on the system as a whole; we would like to find a better technique. The first change that comes to mind is to explicitly release the CPU when we're not interested in it. This is accomplished by calling the *schedule* function, declared in *<linux/sched.h>*:

```
while (time_before(jiffies, j1)) {
    schedule( );
}
```

This loop can be tested by reading */proc/jitsched* as we read */proc/jitbusy* above. However, is still isn't optimal. The current process does nothing but release the CPU, but it remains in the run queue. If it is the only runnable process, it actually runs (it calls the scheduler, which selects the same process, which calls the scheduler, which...). In other words, the load of the machine (the average number of running processes) is at least one, and the idle task (process number 0, also called *swapper* for historical reasons) never runs. Though this issue may seem irrelevant, running the idle task when the computer is idle relieves the processor's workload, decreasing its temperature and increasing its lifetime, as well as the duration of the batteries if the computer happens to be your laptop. Moreover, since the process is actually executing during the delay, it is accountable for all the time it consumes.

The behavior of */proc/jitsched* is actually similar to running */proc/jitbusy* under a preemptive kernel. This is a sample run, on an unloaded system:

```
phon% dd bs=20 count=5 < /proc/jitsched
  1760205    1761207
  1761209    1762211
  1762212    1763212
  1763213    1764213
  1764214    1765217
```

It's interesting to note that each *read* sometimes ends up waiting a few clock ticks more than requested. This problem gets worse and worse as the system gets busy, and the driver could end up waiting longer than expected. Once a process releases the processor with *schedule*, there are no guarantees that the process will get the processor back anytime soon. Therefore, calling *schedule* in this manner is not a safe solution to the driver's needs, in addition to being bad for the computing system as a whole. If you test *jitsched* while running *load50*, you can see that the delay associated to each line is extended by a few seconds, because other processes are using the CPU when the timeout expires.

Timeouts

The suboptimal delay loops shown up to now work by watching the jiffy counter without telling anyone. But the best way to implement a delay, as you may imagine, is usually to ask the kernel to do it for you. There are two ways of setting up jiffy-based timeouts, depending on whether your driver is waiting for other events or not.

If your driver uses a wait queue to wait for some other event, but you also want to be sure that it runs within a certain period of time, it can use *wait_event_timeout* or *wait_event_interruptible_timeout*:

```
#include <linux/wait.h>
long wait_event_timeout(wait_queue_head_t q, condition, long timeout);
long wait_event_interruptible_timeout(wait_queue_head_t q,
                    condition, long timeout);
```

These functions sleep on the given wait queue, but they return after the timeout (expressed in jiffies) expires. Thus, they implement a bounded sleep that does not go on forever. Note that the timeout value represents the number of jiffies to wait, not an absolute time value. The value is represented by a signed number, because it sometimes is the result of a subtraction, although the functions complain through a *printk* statement if the provided timeout is negative. If the timeout expires, the functions return 0; if the process is awakened by another event, it returns the remaining delay expressed in jiffies. The return value is never negative, even if the delay is greater than expected because of system load.

The */proc/jitqueue* file shows a delay based on *wait_event_interruptible_timeout*, although the module has no event to wait for, and uses 0 as a condition:

```
wait_queue_head_t wait;
init_waitqueue_head (&wait);
wait_event_interruptible_timeout(wait, 0, delay);
```

The observed behaviour, when reading */proc/jitqueue*, is nearly optimal, even under load:

```
phon% dd bs=20 count=5 < /proc/jitqueue
  2027024  2028024
  2028025  2029025
  2029026  2030026
  2030027  2031027
  2031028  2032028
```

Since the reading process (*dd* above) is not in the run queue while waiting for the timeout, you see no difference in behavior whether the code is run in a preemptive kernel or not.

wait_event_timeout and *wait_event_interruptible_timeout* were designed with a hardware driver in mind, where execution could be resumed in either of two ways: either somebody calls *wake_up* on the wait queue, or the timeout expires. This doesn't apply to *jitqueue*, as nobody ever calls *wake_up* on the wait queue (after all, no other code even knows about it), so the process always wakes up when the timeout expires. To accommodate for this very situation, where you want to delay execution waiting for no specific event, the kernel offers the *schedule_timeout* function so you can avoid declaring and using a superfluous wait queue head:

```
#include <linux/sched.h>
signed long schedule_timeout(signed long timeout);
```

Here, timeout is the number of jiffies to delay. The return value is 0 unless the function returns before the given timeout has elapsed (in response to a signal). *schedule_timeout* requires that the caller first set the current process state, so a typical call looks like:

```
set_current_state(TASK_INTERRUPTIBLE);
schedule_timeout (delay);
```

The previous lines (from */proc/jitschedto*) cause the process to sleep until the given time has passed. Since *wait_event_interruptible_timeout* relies on *schedule_timeout* internally, we won't bother showing the numbers *jitschedto* returns, because they are the same as those of *jitqueue*. Once again, it is worth noting that an extra time interval could pass between the expiration of the timeout and when your process is actually scheduled to execute.

In the example just shown, the first line calls *set_current_state* to set things up so that the scheduler won't run the current process again until the timeout places it back in TASK_RUNNING state. To achieve an uninterruptible delay, use TASK_UNINTERRUPTIBLE instead. If you forget to change the state of the current process, a call to *schedule_timeout* behaves like a call to *schedule* (i.e., the *jitsched* behavior), setting up a timer that is not used.

If you want to play with the four *jit* files under different system situations or different kernels, or try other ways to delay execution, you may want to configure the amount of the delay when loading the module by setting the *delay* module parameter.

Short Delays

When a device driver needs to deal with latencies in its hardware, the delays involved are usually a few dozen microseconds at most. In this case, relying on the clock tick is definitely not the way to go.

The kernel functions *ndelay*, *udelay*, and *mdelay* serve well for short delays, delaying execution for the specified number of nanoseconds, microseconds, or milliseconds respectively.* Their prototypes are:

```
#include <linux/delay.h>
void ndelay(unsigned long nsecs);
void udelay(unsigned long usecs);
void mdelay(unsigned long msecs);
```

The actual implementations of the functions are in *<asm/delay.h>*, being architecture-specific, and sometimes build on an external function. Every architecture implements *udelay*, but the other functions may or may not be defined; if they are not, *<linux/delay.h>* offers a default version based on *udelay*. In all cases, the delay achieved is at least the requested value but could be more; actually, no platform currently achieves nanosecond precision, although several ones offer submicrosecond

---

* The u in *udelay* represents the Greek letter mu and stands for *micro*.

precision. Delaying more than the requested value is usually not a problem, as short delays in a driver are usually needed to wait for the hardware, and the requirements are to wait for *at least* a given time lapse.

The implementation of *udelay* (and possibly *ndelay* too) uses a software loop based on the processor speed calculated at boot time, using the integer variable `loops_per_jiffy`. If you want to look at the actual code, however, be aware that the *x86* implementation is quite a complex one because of the different timing sources it uses, based on what CPU type is running the code.

To avoid integer overflows in loop calculations, *udelay* and *ndelay* impose an upper bound in the value passed to them. If your module fails to load and displays an unresolved symbol, *__bad_udelay*, it means you called *udelay* with too large an argument. Note, however, that the compile-time check can be performed only on constant values and that not all platforms implement it. As a general rule, if you are trying to delay for thousands of nanoseconds, you should be using *udelay* rather than *ndelay*; similarly, millisecond-scale delays should be done with *mdelay* and not one of the finer-grained functions.

It's important to remember that the three delay functions are busy-waiting; other tasks can't be run during the time lapse. Thus, they replicate, though on a different scale, the behavior of *jitbusy*. Thus, these functions should only be used when there is no practical alternative.

There is another way of achieving millisecond (and longer) delays that does not involve busy waiting. The file *<linux/delay.h>* declares these functions:

```
void msleep(unsigned int millisecs);
unsigned long msleep_interruptible(unsigned int millisecs);
void ssleep(unsigned int seconds)
```

The first two functions puts the calling process to sleep for the given number of millisecs. A call to *msleep* is uninterruptible; you can be sure that the process sleeps for at least the given number of milliseconds. If your driver is sitting on a wait queue and you want a wakeup to break the sleep, use *msleep_interruptible*. The return value from *msleep_interruptible* is normally 0; if, however, the process is awakened early, the return value is the number of milliseconds remaining in the originally requested sleep period. A call to *ssleep* puts the process into an uninterruptible sleep for the given number of seconds.

In general, if you can tolerate longer delays than requested, you should use *schedule_timeout*, *msleep*, or *ssleep*.

Kernel Timers

Whenever you need to schedule an action to happen later, without blocking the current process until that time arrives, kernel timers are the tool for you. These timers are used to schedule execution of a function at a particular time in the future, based on the clock tick, and can be used for a variety of tasks; for example, polling a device by checking its state at regular intervals when the hardware can't fire interrupts. Other typical uses of kernel timers are turning off the floppy motor or finishing another lengthy shut down operation. In such cases, delaying the return from *close* would impose an unnecessary (and surprising) cost on the application program. Finally, the kernel itself uses the timers in several situations, including the implementation of *schedule_timeout*.

A kernel timer is a data structure that instructs the kernel to execute a user-defined function with a user-defined argument at a user-defined time. The implementation resides in *<linux/timer.h>* and *kernel/timer.c* and is described in detail in the section "The Implementation of Kernel Timers."

The functions scheduled to run almost certainly do *not* run while the process that registered them is executing. They are, instead, run asynchronously. Until now, everything we have done in our sample drivers has run in the context of a process executing system calls. When a timer runs, however, the process that scheduled it could be asleep, executing on a different processor, or quite possibly has exited altogether.

This asynchronous execution resembles what happens when a hardware interrupt happens (which is discussed in detail in Chapter 10). In fact, kernel timers are run as the result of a "software interrupt." When running in this sort of atomic context, your code is subject to a number of constraints. Timer functions must be atomic in all the ways we discussed in the section "Spinlocks and Atomic Context" in Chapter 1, but there are some additional issues brought about by the lack of a process context. We will introduce these constraints now; they will be seen again in several places in later chapters. Repetition is called for because the rules for atomic contexts must be followed assiduously, or the system will find itself in deep trouble.

A number of actions require the context of a process in order to be executed. When you are outside of process context (i.e., in interrupt context), you must observe the following rules:

- No access to user space is allowed. Because there is no process context, there is no path to the user space associated with any particular process.

- The current pointer is not meaningful in atomic mode and cannot be used since the relevant code has no connection with the process that has been interrupted.

- No sleeping or scheduling may be performed. Atomic code may not call *schedule* or a form of *wait_event*, nor may it call any other function that could sleep. For example, calling *kmalloc(..., GFP_KERNEL)* is against the rules. Semaphores also must not be used since they can sleep.

Kernel code can tell if it is running in interrupt context by calling the function *in_interrupt()*, which takes no parameters and returns nonzero if the processor is currently running in interrupt context, either hardware interrupt or software interrupt.

A function related to *in_interrupt()* is *in_atomic()*. Its return value is nonzero whenever scheduling is not allowed; this includes hardware and software interrupt contexts as well as any time when a spinlock is held. In the latter case, current may be valid, but access to user space is forbidden, since it can cause scheduling to happen. Whenever you are using *in_interrupt()*, you should really consider whether *in_atomic()* is what you actually mean. Both functions are declared in *<asm/hardirq.h>*

One other important feature of kernel timers is that a task can reregister itself to run again at a later time. This is possible because each `timer_list` structure is unlinked from the list of active timers before being run and can, therefore, be immediately re-linked elsewhere. Although rescheduling the same task over and over might appear to be a pointless operation, it is sometimes useful. For example, it can be used to implement the polling of devices.

It's also worth knowing that in an SMP system, the timer function is executed by the same CPU that registered it, to achieve better cache locality whenever possible. Therefore, a timer that reregisters itself always runs on the same CPU.

An important feature of timers that should not be forgotten, though, is that they are a potential source of race conditions, even on uniprocessor systems. This is a direct result of their being asynchronous with other code. Therefore, any data structures accessed by the timer function should be protected from concurrent access, either by being atomic types (discussed in the section "Atomic Variables" in Chapter 1) or by using spinlocks (discussed in Chapter 5).

The Timer API

The kernel provides drivers with a number of functions to declare, register, and remove kernel timers. The following excerpt shows the basic building blocks:

```
#include <linux/timer.h>
struct timer_list {
        /* ... */
        unsigned long expires;
        void (*function)(unsigned long);
        unsigned long data;
};

void init_timer(struct timer_list *timer);
struct timer_list TIMER_INITIALIZER(_function, _expires, _data);

void add_timer(struct timer_list * timer);
int del_timer(struct timer_list * timer);
```

The data structure includes more fields than the ones shown, but those three are the ones that are meant to be accessed from outside the timer code iteslf. The expires field represents the jiffies value when the timer is expected to run; at that time, the function *function* is called with data as an argument. If you need to pass multiple items in the argument, you can bundle them as a single data structure and pass a pointer cast to unsigned long, a safe practice on all supported architectures and pretty common in memory management (as discussed in Chapter 15). The expires value is not a jiffies_64 item because timers are not expected to expire very far in the future, and 64-bit operations are slow on 32-bit platforms.

The structure must be initialized before use. This step ensures that all the fields are properly set up, including the ones that are opaque to the caller. Initialization can be performed by calling *init_timer* or assigning TIMER_INITIALIZER to a static structure, according to your needs. After initialization, you can change the three public fields before calling *add_timer*. To disable a registered timer before it expires, call *del_timer*.

The *jit* module includes a sample file, */proc/jitimer* (for "just in timer"), that returns one header line and six data lines. The data lines represent the current environment where the code is running; the first one is generated by the *read* file operation and the others by a timer. The following output was recorded while compiling a kernel:

```
phon% cat /proc/jitimer
   time  delta inirq    pid  cpu command
33565837     0     0   1269    0 cat
33565847    10     1   1271    0 sh
33565857    10     1   1273    0 cpp0
33565867    10     1   1273    0 cpp0
33565877    10     1   1274    0 cc1
33565887    10     1   1274    0 cc1
```

In this output, the time field is the value of jiffies when the code runs, delta is the change in jiffies since the previous line, inirq is the Boolean value returned by *in_interrupt*, pid and command refer to the current process, and cpu is the number of the CPU being used (always 0 on uniprocessor systems).

If you read */proc/jitimer* while the system is unloaded, you'll find that the context of the timer is process 0, the idle task, which is called "swapper" mainly for historical reasons.

The timer used to generate */proc/jitimer* data is run every 10 jiffies by default, but you can change the value by setting the tdelay (timer delay) parameter when loading the module.

The following code excerpt shows the part of *jit* related to the *jitimer* timer. When a process attempts to read our file, we set up the timer as follows:

```
unsigned long j = jiffies;

/* fill the data for our timer function */
data->prevjiffies = j;
```

```
        data->buf = buf2;
        data->loops = JIT_ASYNC_LOOPS;

        /* register the timer */
        data->timer.data = (unsigned long)data;
        data->timer.function = jit_timer_fn;
        data->timer.expires = j + tdelay; /* parameter */
        add_timer(&data->timer);

        /* wait for the buffer to fill */
        wait_event_interruptible(data->wait, !data->loops);
```

The actual timer function looks like this:

```
        void jit_timer_fn(unsigned long arg)
        {
            struct jit_data *data = (struct jit_data *)arg;
            unsigned long j = jiffies;
            data->buf += sprintf(data->buf, "%9li  %3li     %i    %6i   %i   %s\n",
                        j, j - data->prevjiffies, in_interrupt() ? 1 : 0,
                        current->pid, smp_processor_id(), current->comm);

            if (--data->loops) {
                data->timer.expires += tdelay;
                data->prevjiffies = j;
                add_timer(&data->timer);
            } else {
                wake_up_interruptible(&data->wait);
            }
        }
```

The timer API includes a few more functions than the ones introduced above. The
following set completes the list of kernel offerings:

int mod_timer(struct timer_list *timer, unsigned long expires);
> Updates the expiration time of a timer, a common task for which a timeout
> timer is used (again, the motor-off floppy timer is a typical example). *mod_timer*
> can be called on inactive timers as well, where you normally use *add_timer*.

int del_timer_sync(struct timer_list *timer);
> Works like *del_timer*, but also guarantees that when it returns, the timer func-
> tion is not running on any CPU. *del_timer_sync* is used to avoid race conditions
> on SMP systems and is the same as *del_timer* in UP kernels. This function should
> be preferred over *del_timer* in most situations. This function can sleep if it is
> called from a nonatomic context but busy waits in other situations. Be very care-
> ful about calling *del_timer_sync* while holding locks; if the timer function
> attempts to obtain the same lock, the system can deadlock. If the timer function
> reregisters itself, the caller must first ensure that this reregistration will not hap-
> pen; this is usually accomplished by setting a "shutting down" flag, which is
> checked by the timer function.

```
int timer_pending(const struct timer_list * timer);
```
Returns true or false to indicate whether the timer is currently scheduled to run by reading one of the opaque fields of the structure.

The Implementation of Kernel Timers

Although you won't need to know how kernel timers are implemented in order to use them, the implementation is interesting, and a look at its internals is worthwhile.

The implementation of the timers has been designed to meet the following requirements and assumptions:

- Timer management must be as lightweight as possible.
- The design should scale well as the number of active timers increases.
- Most timers expire within a few seconds or minutes at most, while timers with long delays are pretty rare.
- A timer should run on the same CPU that registered it.

The solution devised by kernel developers is based on a per-CPU data structure. The timer_list structure includes a pointer to that data structure in its base field. If base is NULL, the timer is not scheduled to run; otherwise, the pointer tells which data structure (and, therefore, which CPU) runs it. Per-CPU data items are described in the section "Per-CPU Variables" in Chapter 8.

Whenever kernel code registers a timer (via add_timer or mod_timer), the operation is eventually performed by internal_add_timer (in kernel/timer.c) which, in turn, adds the new timer to a double-linked list of timers within a "cascading table" associated to the current CPU.

The cascading table works like this: if the timer expires in the next 0 to 255 jiffies, it is added to one of the 256 lists devoted to short-range timers using the least significant bits of the expires field. If it expires farther in the future (but before 16,384 jiffies), it is added to one of 64 lists based on bits 9–14 of the expires field. For timers expiring even farther, the same trick is used for bits 15–20, 21–26, and 27–31. Timers with an expire field pointing still farther in the future (something that can happen only on 64-bit platforms) are hashed with a delay value of 0xffffffff, and timers with expires in the past are scheduled to run at the next timer tick. (A timer that is already expired may sometimes be registered in high-load situations, especially if you run a preemptible kernel.)

When __run_timers is fired, it executes all pending timers for the current timer tick. If jiffies is currently a multiple of 256, the function also rehashes one of the next-level lists of timers into the 256 short-term lists, possibly cascading one or more of the other levels as well, according to the bit representation of jiffies.

This approach, while exceedingly complex at first sight, performs very well both with few timers and with a large number of them. The time required to manage each active timer is independent of the number of timers already registered and is limited to a few logic operations on the binary representation of its expires field. The only cost associated with this implementation is the memory for the 512 list heads (256 short-term lists and 4 groups of 64 more lists)—i.e., 4 KB of storage.

The function *__run_timers*, as shown by */proc/jitimer*, is run in atomic context. In addition to the limitations we already described, this brings in an interesting feature: the timer expires at just the right time, even if you are not running a preemptible kernel, and the CPU is busy in kernel space. You can see what happens when you read */proc/jitbusy* in the background and */proc/jitimer* in the foreground. Although the system appears to be locked solid by the busy-waiting system call, the kernel timers still work fine.

Keep in mind, however, that a kernel timer is far from perfect, as it suffers from jitter and other artifacts induced by hardware interrupts, as well as other timers and other asynchronous tasks. While a timer associated with simple digital I/O can be enough for simple tasks like running a stepper motor or other amateur electronics, it is usually not suitable for production systems in industrial environments. For such tasks, you'll most likely need to resort to a real-time kernel extension.

Tasklets

Another kernel facility related to timing issues is the *tasklet* mechanism. It is mostly used in interrupt management (we'll see it again in Chapter 10.)

Tasklets resemble kernel timers in some ways. They are always run at interrupt time, they always run on the same CPU that schedules them, and they receive an unsigned long argument. Unlike kernel timers, however, you can't ask to execute the function at a specific time. By scheduling a tasklet, you simply ask for it to be executed at a later time chosen by the kernel. This behavior is especially useful with interrupt handlers, where the hardware interrupt must be managed as quickly as possible, but most of the data management can be safely delayed to a later time. Actually, a tasklet, just like a kernel timer, is executed (in atomic mode) in the context of a "soft interrupt," a kernel mechanism that executes asynchronous tasks with hardware interrupts enabled.

A tasklet exists as a data structure that must be initialized before use. Initialization can be performed by calling a specific function or by declaring the structure using certain macros:

```
#include <linux/interrupt.h>

struct tasklet_struct {
    /* ... */
```

```
        void (*func)(unsigned long);
        unsigned long data;
};

void tasklet_init(struct tasklet_struct *t,
        void (*func)(unsigned long), unsigned long data);
DECLARE_TASKLET(name, func, data);
DECLARE_TASKLET_DISABLED(name, func, data);
```

Tasklets offer a number of interesting features:

- A tasklet can be disabled and re-enabled later; it won't be executed until it is enabled as many times as it has been disabled.

- Just like timers, a tasklet can reregister itself.

- A tasklet can be scheduled to execute at normal priority or high priority. The latter group is always executed first.

- Tasklets may be run immediately if the system is not under heavy load but never later than the next timer tick.

- A tasklets can be concurrent with other tasklets but is strictly serialized with respect to itself—the same tasklet never runs simultaneously on more than one processor. Also, as already noted, a tasklet always runs on the same CPU that schedules it.

The *jit* module includes two files, */proc/jitasklet* and */proc/jitasklethi*, that return the same data as */proc/jitimer*, introduced in the section "Kernel Timers." When you read one of the files, you get back a header and six data lines. The first data line describes the context of the calling process, and the other lines describe the context of successive runs of a tasklet procedure. This is a sample run while compiling a kernel:

```
phon% cat /proc/jitasklet
   time   delta  inirq    pid   cpu command
 6076139     0      0     4370   0  cat
 6076140     1      1     4368   0  cc1
 6076141     1      1     4368   0  cc1
 6076141     0      1        2   0  ksoftirqd/0
 6076141     0      1        2   0  ksoftirqd/0
 6076141     0      1        2   0  ksoftirqd/0
```

As confirmed by the above data, the tasklet is run at the next timer tick as long as the CPU is busy running a process, but it is run immediately when the CPU is otherwise idle. The kernel provides a set of *ksoftirqd* kernel threads, one per CPU, just to run "soft interrupt" handlers, such as the *tasklet_action* function. Thus, the final three runs of the tasklet take place in the context of the *ksoftirqd* kernel thread associated to CPU 0. The *jitasklethi* implementation uses a high-priority tasklet, explained in an upcoming list of functions.

The actual code in *jit* that implements */proc/jitasklet* and */proc/jitasklethi* is almost identical to the code that implements */proc/jitimer*, but it uses the tasklet calls instead

of the timer ones. The following list lays out in detail the kernel interface to tasklets
after the tasklet structure has been initialized:

`void tasklet_disable(struct tasklet_struct *t);`

This function disables the given tasklet. The tasklet may still be scheduled with
tasklet_schedule, but its execution is deferred until the tasklet has been enabled
again. If the tasklet is currently running, this function busy-waits until the tasklet
exits; thus, after calling *tasklet_disable*, you can be sure that the tasklet is not
running anywhere in the system.

`void tasklet_disable_nosync(struct tasklet_struct *t);`

Disable the tasklet, but without waiting for any currently-running function to
exit. When it returns, the tasklet is disabled and won't be scheduled in the future
until re-enabled, but it may be still running on another CPU when the function
returns.

`void tasklet_enable(struct tasklet_struct *t);`

Enables a tasklet that had been previously disabled. If the tasklet has already
been scheduled, it will run soon. A call to *tasklet_enable* must match each call to
tasklet_disable, as the kernel keeps track of the "disable count" for each tasklet.

`void tasklet_schedule(struct tasklet_struct *t);`

Schedule the tasklet for execution. If a tasklet is scheduled again before it has a
chance to run, it runs only once. However, if it is scheduled *while* it runs, it runs
again after it completes; this ensures that events occurring while other events are
being processed receive due attention. This behavior also allows a tasklet to
reschedule itself.

`void tasklet_hi_schedule(struct tasklet_struct *t);`

Schedule the tasklet for execution with higher priority. When the soft interrupt
handler runs, it deals with high-priority tasklets before other soft interrupt tasks,
including "normal" tasklets. Ideally, only tasks with low-latency requirements
(such as filling the audio buffer) should use this function, to avoid the additional latencies introduced by other soft interrupt handlers. Actually, */proc/
jitasklethi* shows no human-visible difference from */proc/jitasklet*.

`void tasklet_kill(struct tasklet_struct *t);`

This function ensures that the tasklet is not scheduled to run again; it is usually
called when a device is being closed or the module removed. If the tasklet is
scheduled to run, the function waits until it has executed. If the tasklet resched-
ules itself, you must prevent it from rescheduling itself before calling *tasklet_kill*,
as with *del_timer_sync*.

Tasklets are implemented in *kernel/softirq.c*. The two tasklet lists (normal and high-
priority) are declared as per-CPU data structures, using the same CPU-affinity mechanism used by kernel timers. The data structure used in tasklet management is a simple linked list, because tasklets have none of the sorting requirements of kernel
timers.

Workqueues

Workqueues are, superficially, similar to tasklets; they allow kernel code to request that a function be called at some future time. There are, however, some significant differences between the two, including:

- Tasklets run in software interrupt context with the result that all tasklet code must be atomic. Instead, workqueue functions run in the context of a special kernel process; as a result, they have more flexibility. In particular, workqueue functions can sleep.

- Tasklets always run on the processor from which they were originally submitted. Workqueues work in the same way, by default.

- Kernel code can request that the execution of workqueue functions be delayed for an explicit interval.

The key difference between the two is that tasklets execute quickly, for a short period of time, and in atomic mode, while workqueue functions may have higher latency but need not be atomic. Each mechanism has situations where it is appropriate.

Workqueues have a type of struct workqueue_struct, which is defined in *<linux/workqueue.h>*. A workqueue must be explicitly created before use, using one of the following two functions:

```
struct workqueue_struct *create_workqueue(const char *name);
struct workqueue_struct *create_singlethread_workqueue(const char *name);
```

Each workqueue has one or more dedicated processes ("kernel threads"), which run functions submitted to the queue. If you use *create_workqueue*, you get a workqueue that has a dedicated thread for each processor on the system. In many cases, all those threads are simply overkill; if a single worker thread will suffice, create the workqueue with *create_singlethread_workqueue* instead.

To submit a task to a workqueue, you need to fill in a work_struct structure. This can be done at compile time as follows:

```
DECLARE_WORK(name, void (*function)(void *), void *data);
```

Where name is the name of the structure to be declared, function is the function that is to be called from the workqueue, and data is a value to pass to that function. If you need to set up the work_struct structure at runtime, use the following two macros:

```
INIT_WORK(struct work_struct *work, void (*function)(void *), void *data);
PREPARE_WORK(struct work_struct *work, void (*function)(void *), void *data);
```

INIT_WORK does a more thorough job of initializing the structure; you should use it the first time that structure is set up. *PREPARE_WORK* does almost the same job, but it does not initialize the pointers used to link the work_struct structure into the workqueue. If there is any possibility that the structure may currently be submitted to a workqueue, and you need to change that structure, use *PREPARE_WORK* rather than *INIT_WORK*.

There are two functions for submitting work to a workqueue:

```
int queue_work(struct workqueue_struct *queue, struct work_struct *work);
int queue_delayed_work(struct workqueue_struct *queue,
                       struct work_struct *work, unsigned long delay);
```

Either one adds work to the given queue. If *queue_delayed_work* is used, however, the actual work is not performed until at least delay jiffies have passed. The return value from these functions is 0 if the work was successfully added to the queue; a nonzero result means that this work_struct structure was already waiting in the queue, and was not added a second time.

At some time in the future, the work function will be called with the given data value. The function will be running in the context of the worker thread, so it can sleep if need be—although you should be aware of how that sleep might affect any other tasks submitted to the same workqueue. What the function cannot do, however, is access user space. Since it is running inside a kernel thread, there simply is no user space to access.

Should you need to cancel a pending workqueue entry, you may call:

```
int cancel_delayed_work(struct work_struct *work);
```

The return value is nonzero if the entry was canceled before it began execution. The kernel guarantees that execution of the given entry will not be initiated after a call to *cancel_delayed_work*. If *cancel_delayed_work* returns 0, however, the entry may have already been running on a different processor, and might still be running after a call to *cancel_delayed_work*. To be absolutely sure that the work function is not running anywhere in the system after *cancel_delayed_work* returns 0, you must follow that call with a call to:

```
void flush_workqueue(struct workqueue_struct *queue);
```

After *flush_workqueue* returns, no work function submitted prior to the call is running anywhere in the system.

When you are done with a workqueue, you can get rid of it with:

```
void destroy_workqueue(struct workqueue_struct *queue);
```

The Shared Queue

A device driver, in many cases, does not need its own workqueue. If you only submit tasks to the queue occasionally, it may be more efficient to simply use the shared, default workqueue that is provided by the kernel. If you use this queue, however, you must be aware that you will be sharing it with others. Among other things, that means that you should not monopolize the queue for long periods of time (no long sleeps), and it may take longer for your tasks to get their turn in the processor.

The *jiq* ("just in queue") module exports two files that demonstrate the use of the shared workqueue. They use a single work_struct structure, which is set up this way:

```
static struct work_struct jiq_work;

    /* this line is in jiq_init() */
    INIT_WORK(&jiq_work, jiq_print_wq, &jiq_data);
```

When a process reads */proc/jiqwq*, the module initiates a series of trips through the shared workqueue with no delay. The function it uses is:

```
int schedule_work(struct work_struct *work);
```

Note that a different function is used when working with the shared queue; it requires only the work_struct structure for an argument. The actual code in *jiq* looks like this:

```
prepare_to_wait(&jiq_wait, &wait, TASK_INTERRUPTIBLE);
schedule_work(&jiq_work);
schedule();
finish_wait(&jiq_wait, &wait);
```

The actual work function prints out a line just like the *jit* module does, then, if need be, resubmits the work_struct structure into the workqueue. Here is *jiq_print_wq* in its entirety:

```
static void jiq_print_wq(void *ptr)
{
    struct clientdata *data = (struct clientdata *) ptr;

    if (! jiq_print (ptr))
        return;

    if (data->delay)
        schedule_delayed_work(&jiq_work, data->delay);
    else
        schedule_work(&jiq_work);
}
```

If the user is reading the delayed device (*/proc/jiqwqdelay*), the work function resubmits itself in the delayed mode with *schedule_delayed_work*:

```
int schedule_delayed_work(struct work_struct *work, unsigned long delay);
```

If you look at the output from these two devices, it looks something like:

```
% cat /proc/jiqwq
    time delta preempt   pid cpu command
 1113043    0      0      7   1 events/1
 1113043    0      0      7   1 events/1
 1113043    0      0      7   1 events/1
 1113043    0      0      7   1 events/1
 1113043    0      0      7   1 events/1
% cat /proc/jiqwqdelay
    time delta preempt   pid cpu command
 1122066    1      0      6   0 events/0
```

```
1122067    1    0    6    0 events/0
1122068    1    0    6    0 events/0
1122069    1    0    6    0 events/0
1122070    1    0    6    0 events/0
```

When /proc/jiqwq is read, there is no obvious delay between the printing of each line. When, instead, /proc/jiqwqdelay is read, there is a delay of exactly one jiffy between each line. In either case, we see the same process name printed; it is the name of the kernel thread that implements the shared workqueue. The CPU number is printed after the slash; we never know which CPU will be running when the /proc file is read, but the work function will always run on the same processor thereafter.

If you need to cancel a work entry submitted to the shared queue, you may use *cancel_delayed_work*, as described above. Flushing the shared workqueue requires a separate function, however:

```
void flush_scheduled_work(void);
```

Since you do not know who else might be using this queue, you never really know how long it might take for *flush_scheduled_work* to return.

Quick Reference

This chapter introduced the following symbols.

Timekeeping

```
#include <linux/param.h>
HZ
```
The HZ symbol specifies the number of clock ticks generated per second.

```
#include <linux/jiffies.h>
volatile unsigned long jiffies
u64 jiffies_64
```
The jiffies_64 variable is incremented once for each clock tick; thus, it's incremented HZ times per second. Kernel code most often refers to jiffies, which is the same as jiffies_64 on 64-bit platforms and the least significant half of it on 32-bit platforms.

```
int time_after(unsigned long a, unsigned long b);
int time_before(unsigned long a, unsigned long b);
int time_after_eq(unsigned long a, unsigned long b);
int time_before_eq(unsigned long a, unsigned long b);
```
These Boolean expressions compare jiffies in a safe way, without problems in case of counter overflow and without the need to access jiffies_64.

```
u64 get_jiffies_64(void);
```
Retrieves jiffies_64 without race conditions.

```
#include <linux/time.h>
unsigned long timespec_to_jiffies(struct timespec *value);
void jiffies_to_timespec(unsigned long jiffies, struct timespec *value);
unsigned long timeval_to_jiffies(struct timeval *value);
void jiffies_to_timeval(unsigned long jiffies, struct timeval *value);
```
Converts time representations between jiffies and other representations.

```
#include <asm/msr.h>
rdtsc(low32,high32);
rdtscl(low32);
rdtscll(var32);
```
x86-specific macros to read the timestamp counter. They read it as two 32-bit halves, read only the lower half, or read all of it into a long long variable.

```
#include <linux/timex.h>
cycles_t get_cycles(void);
```
Returns the timestamp counter in a platform-independent way. If the CPU offers no timestamp feature, 0 is returned.

```
#include <linux/time.h>
unsigned long mktime(year, mon, day, h, m, s);
```
Returns the number of seconds since the Epoch, based on the six unsigned int arguments.

```
void do_gettimeofday(struct timeval *tv);
```
Returns the current time, as seconds and microseconds since the Epoch, with the best resolution the hardware can offer. On most platforms the resolution is one microsecond or better, although some platforms offer only jiffies resolution.

```
struct timespec current_kernel_time(void);
```
Returns the current time with the resolution of one jiffy.

Delays

```
#include <linux/wait.h>
long wait_event_interruptible_timeout(wait_queue_head_t *q, condition, signed
  long timeout);
```
Puts the current process to sleep on the wait queue, installing a timeout value expressed in jiffies. Use *schedule_timeout* (below) for noninterruptible sleeps.

```
#include <linux/sched.h>
signed long schedule_timeout(signed long timeout);
```
Calls the scheduler after ensuring that the current process is awakened at timeout expiration. The caller must invoke *set_current_state* first to put itself in an interruptible or noninterruptible sleep state.

```
#include <linux/delay.h>
void ndelay(unsigned long nsecs);
void udelay(unsigned long usecs);
void mdelay(unsigned long msecs);
```
Introduces delays of an integer number of nanoseconds, microseconds, and milliseconds. The delay achieved is at least the requested value, but it can be more. The argument to each function must not exceed a platform-specific limit (usually a few thousands).

```
void msleep(unsigned int millisecs);
unsigned long msleep_interruptible(unsigned int millisecs);
void ssleep(unsigned int seconds);
```
Puts the process to sleep for the given number of milliseconds (or seconds, in the case of *ssleep*).

Kernel Timers

```
#include <asm/hardirq.h>
int in_interrupt(void);
int in_atomic(void);
```
Returns a Boolean value telling whether the calling code is executing in interrupt context or atomic context. Interrupt context is outside of a process context, either during hardware or software interrupt processing. Atomic context is when you can't schedule either an interrupt context or a process's context with a spinlock held.

```
#include <linux/timer.h>
void init_timer(struct timer_list * timer);
struct timer_list TIMER_INITIALIZER(_function, _expires, _data);
```
This function and the static declaration of the timer structure are the two ways to initialize a timer_list data structure.

```
void add_timer(struct timer_list * timer);
```
Registers the timer structure to run on the current CPU.

```
int mod_timer(struct timer_list *timer, unsigned long expires);
```
Changes the expiration time of an already scheduled timer structure. It can also act as an alternative to *add_timer*.

```
int timer_pending(struct timer_list * timer);
```
Macro that returns a Boolean value stating whether the timer structure is already registered to run.

```
void del_timer(struct timer_list * timer);
void del_timer_sync(struct timer_list * timer);
```
Removes a timer from the list of active timers. The latter function ensures that the timer is not currently running on another CPU.

Tasklets

```
#include <linux/interrupt.h>
DECLARE_TASKLET(name, func, data);
DECLARE_TASKLET_DISABLED(name, func, data);
void tasklet_init(struct tasklet_struct *t, void (*func)(unsigned long),
  unsigned long data);
```
> The first two macros declare a tasklet structure, while the *tasklet_init* function initializes a tasklet structure that has been obtained by allocation or other means. The second DECLARE macro marks the tasklet as disabled.

```
void tasklet_disable(struct tasklet_struct *t);
void tasklet_disable_nosync(struct tasklet_struct *t);
void tasklet_enable(struct tasklet_struct *t);
```
> Disables and reenables a tasklet. Each *disable* must be matched with an *enable* (you can disable the tasklet even if it's already disabled). The function *tasklet_disable* waits for the tasklet to terminate if it is running on another CPU. The *nosync* version doesn't take this extra step.

```
void tasklet_schedule(struct tasklet_struct *t);
void tasklet_hi_schedule(struct tasklet_struct *t);
```
> Schedules a tasklet to run, either as a "normal" tasklet or a high-priority one. When soft interrupts are executed, high-priority tasklets are dealt with first, while normal tasklets run last.

```
void tasklet_kill(struct tasklet_struct *t);
```
> Removes the tasklet from the list of active ones, if it's scheduled to run. Like *tasklet_disable*, the function may block on SMP systems waiting for the tasklet to terminate if it's currently running on another CPU.

Workqueues

```
#include <linux/workqueue.h>
struct workqueue_struct;
struct work_struct;
```
> The structures representing a workqueue and a work entry, respectively.

```
struct workqueue_struct *create_workqueue(const char *name);
struct workqueue_struct *create_singlethread_workqueue(const char *name);
void destroy_workqueue(struct workqueue_struct *queue);
```
> Functions for creating and destroying workqueues. A call to *create_workqueue* creates a queue with a worker thread on each processor in the system; instead, *create_singlethread_workqueue* creates a workqueue with a single worker process.

```
DECLARE_WORK(name, void (*function)(void *), void *data);
INIT_WORK(struct work_struct *work, void (*function)(void *), void *data);
PREPARE_WORK(struct work_struct *work, void (*function)(void *), void *data);
```
Macros that declare and initialize workqueue entries.

```
int queue_work(struct workqueue_struct *queue, struct work_struct *work);
int queue_delayed_work(struct workqueue_struct *queue, struct work_struct
  *work, unsigned long delay);
```
Functions that queue work for execution from a workqueue.

```
int cancel_delayed_work(struct work_struct *work);
void flush_workqueue(struct workqueue_struct *queue);
```
Use *cancel_delayed_work* to remove an entry from a workqueue; *flush_workqueue* ensures that no workqueue entries are running anywhere in the system.

```
int schedule_work(struct work_struct *work);
int schedule_delayed_work(struct work_struct *work, unsigned long delay);
void flush_scheduled_work(void);
```
Functions for working with the shared workqueue.

## CHAPTER 8

Allocating Memory

Thus far, we have used *kmalloc* and *kfree* for the allocation and freeing of memory. The Linux kernel offers a richer set of memory allocation primitives, however. In this chapter, we look at other ways of using memory in device drivers and how to optimize your system's memory resources. We do not get into how the different architectures actually administer memory. Modules are not involved in issues of segmentation, paging, and so on, since the kernel offers a unified memory management interface to the drivers. In addition, we won't describe the internal details of memory management in this chapter, but defer it to Chapter 15.

The Real Story of kmalloc

The *kmalloc* allocation engine is a powerful tool and easily learned because of its similarity to *malloc*. The function is fast (unless it blocks) and doesn't clear the memory it obtains; the allocated region still holds its previous content.* The allocated region is also contiguous in physical memory. In the next few sections, we talk in detail about *kmalloc*, so you can compare it with the memory allocation techniques that we discuss later.

The Flags Argument

Remember that the prototype for *kmalloc* is:

```
#include <linux/slab.h>

void *kmalloc(size_t size, int flags);
```

---

* Among other things, this implies that you should explicitly clear any memory that might be exposed to user space or written to a device; otherwise, you risk disclosing information that should be kept private.

The first argument to *kmalloc* is the size of the block to be allocated. The second argument, the allocation flags, is much more interesting, because it controls the behavior of *kmalloc* in a number of ways.

The most commonly used flag, GFP_KERNEL, means that the allocation (internally performed by calling, eventually, *__get_free_pages*, which is the source of the GFP_ prefix) is performed on behalf of a process running in kernel space. In other words, this means that the calling function is executing a system call on behalf of a process. Using GFP_KERNEL means that *kmalloc* can put the current process to sleep waiting for a page when called in low-memory situations. A function that allocates memory using GFP_KERNEL must, therefore, be reentrant and cannot be running in atomic context. While the current process sleeps, the kernel takes proper action to locate some free memory, either by flushing buffers to disk or by swapping out memory from a user process.

GFP_KERNEL isn't always the right allocation flag to use; sometimes *kmalloc* is called from outside a process's context. This type of call can happen, for instance, in interrupt handlers, tasklets, and kernel timers. In this case, the current process should not be put to sleep, and the driver should use a flag of GFP_ATOMIC instead. The kernel normally tries to keep some free pages around in order to fulfill atomic allocation. When GFP_ATOMIC is used, *kmalloc* can use even the last free page. If that last page does not exist, however, the allocation fails.

Other flags can be used in place of or in addition to GFP_KERNEL and GFP_ATOMIC, although those two cover most of the needs of device drivers. All the flags are defined in *<linux/gfp.h>*, and individual flags are prefixed with a double underscore, such as __GFP_DMA. In addition, there are symbols that represent frequently used combinations of flags; these lack the prefix and are sometimes called *allocation priorities*. The latter include:

GFP_ATOMIC
> Used to allocate memory from interrupt handlers and other code outside of a process context. Never sleeps.

GFP_KERNEL
> Normal allocation of kernel memory. May sleep.

GFP_USER
> Used to allocate memory for user-space pages; it may sleep.

GFP_HIGHUSER
> Like GFP_USER, but allocates from high memory, if any. High memory is described in the next subsection.

GFP_NOIO
GFP_NOFS
> These flags function like GFP_KERNEL, but they add restrictions on what the kernel can do to satisfy the request. A GFP_NOFS allocation is not allowed to perform

any filesystem calls, while GFP_NOIO disallows the initiation of any I/O at all. They are used primarily in the filesystem and virtual memory code where an allocation may be allowed to sleep, but recursive filesystem calls would be a bad idea.

The allocation flags listed above can be augmented by an ORing in any of the following flags, which change how the allocation is carried out:

__GFP_DMA

This flag requests allocation to happen in the DMA-capable memory zone. The exact meaning is platform-dependent and is explained in the following section.

__GFP_HIGHMEM

This flag indicates that the allocated memory may be located in high memory.

__GFP_COLD

Normally, the memory allocator tries to return "cache warm" pages—pages that are likely to be found in the processor cache. Instead, this flag requests a "cold" page, which has not been used in some time. It is useful for allocating pages for DMA reads, where presence in the processor cache is not useful. See the section "Direct Memory Access" in Chapter 1 for a full discussion of how to allocate DMA buffers.

__GFP_NOWARN

This rarely used flag prevents the kernel from issuing warnings (with *printk*) when an allocation cannot be satisfied.

__GFP_HIGH

This flag marks a high-priority request, which is allowed to consume even the last pages of memory set aside by the kernel for emergencies.

__GFP_REPEAT
__GFP_NOFAIL
__GFP_NORETRY

These flags modify how the allocator behaves when it has difficulty satisfying an allocation. __GFP_REPEAT means "try a little harder" by repeating the attempt— but the allocation can still fail. The __GFP_NOFAIL flag tells the allocator never to fail; it works as hard as needed to satisfy the request. Use of __GFP_NOFAIL is very strongly discouraged; there will probably never be a valid reason to use it in a device driver. Finally, __GFP_NORETRY tells the allocator to give up immediately if the requested memory is not available.

Memory zones

Both __GFP_DMA and __GFP_HIGHMEM have a platform-dependent role, although their use is valid for all platforms.

The Linux kernel knows about a minimum of three *memory zones*: DMA-capable memory, normal memory, and high memory. While allocation normally happens in the *normal* zone, setting either of the bits just mentioned requires memory to be allocated from a different zone. The idea is that every computer platform that must know about special memory ranges (instead of considering all RAM equivalents) will fall into this abstraction.

DMA-capable memory is memory that lives in a preferential address range, where peripherals can perform DMA access. On most sane platforms, all memory lives in this zone. On the x86, the DMA zone is used for the first 16 MB of RAM, where legacy ISA devices can perform DMA; PCI devices have no such limit.

High memory is a mechanism used to allow access to (relatively) large amounts of memory on 32-bit platforms. This memory cannot be directly accessed from the kernel without first setting up a special mapping and is generally harder to work with. If your driver uses large amounts of memory, however, it will work better on large systems if it can use high memory. See the section "High and Low Memory" in Chapter 1 for a detailed description of how high memory works and how to use it.

Whenever a new page is allocated to fulfill a memory allocation request, the kernel builds a list of zones that can be used in the search. If __GFP_DMA is specified, only the DMA zone is searched: if no memory is available at low addresses, allocation fails. If no special flag is present, both normal and DMA memory are searched; if __GFP_HIGHMEM is set, all three zones are used to search a free page. (Note, however, that *kmalloc* cannot allocate high memory.)

The situation is more complicated on nonuniform memory access (NUMA) systems. As a general rule, the allocator attempts to locate memory local to the processor performing the allocation, although there are ways of changing that behavior.

The mechanism behind memory zones is implemented in *mm/page_alloc.c*, while initialization of the zone resides in platform-specific files, usually in *mm/init.c* within the *arch* tree. We'll revisit these topics in Chapter 15.

The Size Argument

The kernel manages the system's *physical* memory, which is available only in page-sized chunks. As a result, *kmalloc* looks rather different from a typical user-space *malloc* implementation. A simple, heap-oriented allocation technique would quickly run into trouble; it would have a hard time working around the page boundaries. Thus, the kernel uses a special page-oriented allocation technique to get the best use from the system's RAM.

Linux handles memory allocation by creating a set of pools of memory objects of fixed sizes. Allocation requests are handled by going to a pool that holds sufficiently large objects and handing an entire memory chunk back to the requester. The memory management scheme is quite complex, and the details of it are not normally all that interesting to device driver writers.

The one thing driver developers should keep in mind, though, is that the kernel can allocate only certain predefined, fixed-size byte arrays. If you ask for an arbitrary amount of memory, you're likely to get slightly more than you asked for, up to twice as much. Also, programmers should remember that the smallest allocation that *kmalloc* can handle is as big as 32 or 64 bytes, depending on the page size used by the system's architecture.

There is an upper limit to the size of memory chunks that can be allocated by *kmalloc*. That limit varies depending on architecture and kernel configuration options. If your code is to be completely portable, it cannot count on being able to allocate anything larger than 128 KB. If you need more than a few kilobytes, however, there are better ways than *kmalloc* to obtain memory, which we describe later in this chapter.

Lookaside Caches

A device driver often ends up allocating many objects of the same size, over and over. Given that the kernel already maintains a set of memory pools of objects that are all the same size, why not add some special pools for these high-volume objects? In fact, the kernel does implement a facility to create this sort of pool, which is often called a *lookaside cache*. Device drivers normally do not exhibit the sort of memory behavior that justifies using a lookaside cache, but there can be exceptions; the USB and SCSI drivers in Linux 2.6 use caches.

The cache manager in the Linux kernel is sometimes called the "slab allocator." For that reason, its functions and types are declared in *<linux/slab.h>*. The slab allocator implements caches that have a type of kmem_cache_t; they are created with a call to *kmem_cache_create*:

```
kmem_cache_t *kmem_cache_create(const char *name, size_t size,
                                size_t offset,
                                unsigned long flags,
                                void (*constructor)(void *, kmem_cache_t *,
                                                unsigned long flags),
                                void (*destructor)(void *, kmem_cache_t *,
                                                unsigned long flags));
```

The function creates a new cache object that can host any number of memory areas all of the same size, specified by the size argument. The name argument is associated with this cache and functions as housekeeping information usable in tracking problems; usually, it is set to the name of the type of structure that is cached. The cache keeps a pointer to the name, rather than copying it, so the driver should pass in a pointer to a name in static storage (usually the name is just a literal string). The name cannot contain blanks.

The offset is the offset of the first object in the page; it can be used to ensure a particular alignment for the allocated objects, but you most likely will use 0 to request the default value. flags controls how allocation is done and is a bit mask of the following flags:

SLAB_NO_REAP

Setting this flag protects the cache from being reduced when the system is looking for memory. Setting this flag is normally a bad idea; it is important to avoid restricting the memory allocator's freedom of action unnecessarily.

SLAB_HWCACHE_ALIGN

This flag requires each data object to be aligned to a cache line; actual alignment depends on the cache layout of the host platform. This option can be a good choice if your cache contains items that are frequently accessed on SMP machines. The padding required to achieve cache line alignment can end up wasting significant amounts of memory, however.

SLAB_CACHE_DMA

This flag requires each data object to be allocated in the DMA memory zone.

There is also a set of flags that can be used during the debugging of cache allocations; see *mm/slab.c* for the details. Usually, however, these flags are set globally via a kernel configuration option on systems used for development.

The constructor and destructor arguments to the function are optional functions (but there can be no destructor without a constructor); the former can be used to initialize newly allocated objects, and the latter can be used to "clean up" objects prior to their memory being released back to the system as a whole.

Constructors and destructors can be useful, but there are a few constraints that you should keep in mind. A constructor is called when the memory for a set of objects is allocated; because that memory may hold several objects, the constructor may be called multiple times. You cannot assume that the constructor will be called as an immediate effect of allocating an object. Similarly, destructors can be called at some unknown future time, not immediately after an object has been freed. Constructors and destructors may or may not be allowed to sleep, according to whether they are passed the SLAB_CTOR_ATOMIC flag (where CTOR is short for *constructor*).

For convenience, a programmer can use the same function for both the constructor and destructor; the slab allocator always passes the SLAB_CTOR_CONSTRUCTOR flag when the callee is a constructor.

Once a cache of objects is created, you can allocate objects from it by calling *kmem_cache_alloc*:

```
void *kmem_cache_alloc(kmem_cache_t *cache, int flags);
```

Here, the cache argument is the cache you have created previously; the flags are the same as you would pass to *kmalloc* and are consulted if *kmem_cache_alloc* needs to go out and allocate more memory itself.

To free an object, use *kmem_cache_free*:

```
void kmem_cache_free(kmem_cache_t *cache, const void *obj);
```

When driver code is finished with the cache, typically when the module is unloaded, it should free its cache as follows:

```
int kmem_cache_destroy(kmem_cache_t *cache);
```

The destroy operation succeeds only if all objects allocated from the cache have been returned to it. Therefore, a module should check the return status from *kmem_cache_destroy*; a failure indicates some sort of memory leak within the module (since some of the objects have been dropped).

One side benefit to using lookaside caches is that the kernel maintains statistics on cache usage. These statistics may be obtained from */proc/slabinfo*.

A scull Based on the Slab Caches: scullc

Time for an example. *scullc* is a cut-down version of the *scull* module that implements only the bare device—the persistent memory region. Unlike *scull*, which uses *kmalloc*, *scullc* uses memory caches. The size of the quantum can be modified at compile time and at load time, but not at runtime—that would require creating a new memory cache, and we didn't want to deal with these unneeded details.

scullc is a complete example that can be used to try out the slab allocator. It differs from *scull* only in a few lines of code. First, we must declare our own slab cache:

```
/* declare one cache pointer: use it for all devices */
kmem_cache_t *scullc_cache;
```

The creation of the slab cache is handled (at module load time) in this way:

```
/* scullc_init: create a cache for our quanta */
scullc_cache = kmem_cache_create("scullc", scullc_quantum,
        0, SLAB_HWCACHE_ALIGN, NULL, NULL); /* no ctor/dtor */
if (!scullc_cache) {
    scullc_cleanup( );
    return -ENOMEM;
}
```

This is how it allocates memory quanta:

```
/* Allocate a quantum using the memory cache */
if (!dptr->data[s_pos]) {
    dptr->data[s_pos] = kmem_cache_alloc(scullc_cache, GFP_KERNEL);
    if (!dptr->data[s_pos])
        goto nomem;
    memset(dptr->data[s_pos], 0, scullc_quantum);
}
```

And these lines release memory:

```
for (i = 0; i < qset; i++)
if (dptr->data[i])
        kmem_cache_free(scullc_cache, dptr->data[i]);
```

Finally, at module unload time, we have to return the cache to the system:

```
/* scullc_cleanup: release the cache of our quanta */
if (scullc_cache)
    kmem_cache_destroy(scullc_cache);
```

The main differences in passing from *scull* to *scullc* are a slight speed improvement and better memory use. Since quanta are allocated from a pool of memory fragments of exactly the right size, their placement in memory is as dense as possible, as opposed to *scull* quanta, which bring in an unpredictable memory fragmentation.

Memory Pools

There are places in the kernel where memory allocations cannot be allowed to fail. As a way of guaranteeing allocations in those situations, the kernel developers created an abstraction known as a *memory pool* (or "mempool"). A memory pool is really just a form of a lookaside cache that tries to always keep a list of free memory around for use in emergencies.

A memory pool has a type of mempool_t (defined in <*linux/mempool.h*>); you can create one with *mempool_create*:

```
mempool_t *mempool_create(int min_nr,
                          mempool_alloc_t *alloc_fn,
                          mempool_free_t *free_fn,
                          void *pool_data);
```

The min_nr argument is the minimum number of allocated objects that the pool should always keep around. The actual allocation and freeing of objects is handled by alloc_fn and free_fn, which have these prototypes:

```
typedef void *(mempool_alloc_t)(int gfp_mask, void *pool_data);
typedef void (mempool_free_t)(void *element, void *pool_data);
```

The final parameter to *mempool_create* (pool_data) is passed to alloc_fn and free_fn.

If need be, you can write special-purpose functions to handle memory allocations for mempools. Usually, however, you just want to let the kernel slab allocator handle that task for you. There are two functions (*mempool_alloc_slab* and *mempool_free_slab*) that perform the impedance matching between the memory pool allocation prototypes and *kmem_cache_alloc* and *kmem_cache_free*. Thus, code that sets up memory pools often looks like the following:

```
cache = kmem_cache_create(. . .);
pool = mempool_create(MY_POOL_MINIMUM,
                      mempool_alloc_slab, mempool_free_slab,
                      cache);
```

Once the pool has been created, objects can be allocated and freed with:

```
void *mempool_alloc(mempool_t *pool, int gfp_mask);
void mempool_free(void *element, mempool_t *pool);
```

When the mempool is created, the allocation function will be called enough times to create a pool of preallocated objects. Thereafter, calls to *mempool_alloc* attempt to acquire additional objects from the allocation function; should that allocation fail, one of the preallocated objects (if any remain) is returned. When an object is freed with *mempool_free*, it is kept in the pool if the number of preallocated objects is currently below the minimum; otherwise, it is to be returned to the system.

A mempool can be resized with:

```
int mempool_resize(mempool_t *pool, int new_min_nr, int gfp_mask);
```

This call, if successful, resizes the pool to have at least new_min_nr objects.

If you no longer need a memory pool, return it to the system with:

```
void mempool_destroy(mempool_t *pool);
```

You must return all allocated objects before destroying the mempool, or a kernel oops results.

If you are considering using a mempool in your driver, please keep one thing in mind: mempools allocate a chunk of memory that sits in a list, idle and unavailable for any real use. It is easy to consume a great deal of memory with mempools. In almost every case, the preferred alternative is to do without the mempool and simply deal with the possibility of allocation failures instead. If there is any way for your driver to respond to an allocation failure in a way that does not endanger the integrity of the system, do things that way. Use of mempools in driver code should be rare.

get_free_page and Friends

If a module needs to allocate big chunks of memory, it is usually better to use a page-oriented technique. Requesting whole pages also has other advantages, which are introduced in Chapter 15.

To allocate pages, the following functions are available:

get_zeroed_page(unsigned int flags);
> Returns a pointer to a new page and fills the page with zeros.

__get_free_page(unsigned int flags);
> Similar to *get_zeroed_page*, but doesn't clear the page.

__get_free_pages(unsigned int flags, unsigned int order);
> Allocates and returns a pointer to the first byte of a memory area that is potentially several (physically contiguous) pages long but doesn't zero the area.

The flags argument works in the same way as with *kmalloc*; usually either GFP_KERNEL or GFP_ATOMIC is used, perhaps with the addition of the __GFP_DMA flag (for memory that can be used for ISA direct-memory-access operations) or __GFP_HIGHMEM when high memory can be used.* order is the base-two logarithm of the number of pages you are requesting or freeing (i.e., log2N). For example, order is 0 if you want one page and 3 if you request eight pages. If order is too big (no contiguous area of that size is available), the page allocation fails. The *get_order* function, which takes an integer argument, can be used to extract the order from a size (that must be a power of two) for the hosting platform. The maximum allowed value for order is 10 or 11 (corresponding to 1024 or 2048 pages), depending on the architecture. The chances of an order-10 allocation succeeding on anything other than a freshly booted system with a lot of memory are small, however.

If you are curious, */proc/buddyinfo* tells you how many blocks of each order are available for each memory zone on the system.

When a program is done with the pages, it can free them with one of the following functions. The first function is a macro that falls back on the second:

```
void free_page(unsigned long addr);
void free_pages(unsigned long addr, unsigned long order);
```

If you try to free a different number of pages from what you allocated, the memory map becomes corrupted, and the system gets in trouble at a later time.

It's worth stressing that *__get_free_pages* and the other functions can be called at any time, subject to the same rules we saw for *kmalloc*. The functions can fail to allocate memory in certain circumstances, particularly when GFP_ATOMIC is used. Therefore, the program calling these allocation functions must be prepared to handle an allocation failure.

Although kmalloc(GFP_KERNEL) sometimes fails when there is no available memory, the kernel does its best to fulfill allocation requests. Therefore, it's easy to degrade system responsiveness by allocating too much memory. For example, you can bring the computer down by pushing too much data into a *scull* device; the system starts crawling while it tries to swap out as much as possible in order to fulfill the *kmalloc* request. Since every resource is being sucked up by the growing device, the computer is soon rendered unusable; at that point, you can no longer even start a new process to try to deal with the problem. We don't address this issue in *scull*, since it is just a sample module and not a real tool to put into a multiuser system. As a programmer, you must be careful nonetheless, because a module is privileged code and can open new security holes in the system (the most likely is a denial-of-service hole like the one just outlined).

---

* Although *alloc_pages* (described shortly) should really be used for allocating high-memory pages, for reasons we can't really get into until Chapter 15.

A scull Using Whole Pages: scullp

In order to test page allocation for real, we have released the *scullp* module together with other sample code. It is a reduced *scull*, just like *scullc* introduced earlier.

Memory quanta allocated by *scullp* are whole pages or page sets: the `scullp_order` variable defaults to 0 but can be changed at either compile or load time.

The following lines show how it allocates memory:

```
/* Here's the allocation of a single quantum */
if (!dptr->data[s_pos]) {
    dptr->data[s_pos] =
        (void *)__get_free_pages(GFP_KERNEL, dptr->order);
    if (!dptr->data[s_pos])
        goto nomem;
    memset(dptr->data[s_pos], 0, PAGE_SIZE << dptr->order);
}
```

The code to deallocate memory in *scullp* looks like this:

```
/* This code frees a whole quantum-set */
for (i = 0; i < qset; i++)
    if (dptr->data[i])
        free_pages((unsigned long)(dptr->data[i]),
                dptr->order);
```

At the user level, the perceived difference is primarily a speed improvement and better memory use, because there is no internal fragmentation of memory. We ran some tests copying 4 MB from *scull0* to *scull1* and then from *scullp0* to *scullp1*; the results showed a slight improvement in kernel-space processor usage.

The performance improvement is not dramatic, because *kmalloc* is designed to be fast. The main advantage of page-level allocation isn't actually speed, but rather more efficient memory usage. Allocating by pages wastes no memory, whereas using *kmalloc* wastes an unpredictable amount of memory because of allocation granularity.

But the biggest advantage of the *__get_free_page* functions is that the pages obtained are completely yours, and you could, in theory, assemble the pages into a linear area by appropriate tweaking of the page tables. For example, you can allow a user process to *mmap* memory areas obtained as single unrelated pages. We discuss this kind of operation in Chapter 15, where we show how *scullp* offers memory mapping, something that *scull* cannot offer.

The alloc_pages Interface

For completeness, we introduce another interface for memory allocation, even though we will not be prepared to use it until after Chapter 15. For now, suffice it to say that `struct page` is an internal kernel structure that describes a page of memory. As we will see, there are many places in the kernel where it is necessary to work with page structures; they are especially useful in any situation where you might be dealing with high memory, which does not have a constant address in kernel space.

The *real* core of the Linux page allocator is a function called *alloc_pages_node*:

```
struct page *alloc_pages_node(int nid, unsigned int flags,
                              unsigned int order);
```

This function also has two variants (which are simply macros); these are the versions that you will most likely use:

```
struct page *alloc_pages(unsigned int flags, unsigned int order);
struct page *alloc_page(unsigned int flags);
```

The core function, *alloc_pages_node*, takes three arguments. nid is the NUMA node ID[*] whose memory should be allocated, flags is the usual GFP_ allocation flags, and order is the size of the allocation. The return value is a pointer to the first of (possibly many) page structures describing the allocated memory, or, as usual, NULL on failure.

alloc_pages simplifies the situation by allocating the memory on the current NUMA node (it calls *alloc_pages_node* with the return value from *numa_node_id* as the nid parameter). And, of course, *alloc_page* omits the order parameter and allocates a single page.

To release pages allocated in this manner, you should use one of the following:

```
void __free_page(struct page *page);
void __free_pages(struct page *page, unsigned int order);
void free_hot_page(struct page *page);
void free_cold_page(struct page *page);
```

If you have specific knowledge of whether a single page's contents are likely to be resident in the processor cache, you should communicate that to the kernel with *free_hot_page* (for cache-resident pages) or *free_cold_page*. This information helps the memory allocator optimize its use of memory across the system.

vmalloc and Friends

The next memory allocation function that we show you is *vmalloc*, which allocates a contiguous memory region in the *virtual* address space. Although the pages are not consecutive in physical memory (each page is retrieved with a separate call to *alloc_page*), the kernel sees them as a contiguous range of addresses. *vmalloc* returns 0 (the NULL address) if an error occurs, otherwise, it returns a pointer to a linear memory area of size at least size.

---

[*] NUMA (nonuniform memory access) computers are multiprocessor systems where memory is "local" to specific groups of processors ("nodes"). Access to local memory is faster than access to nonlocal memory. On such systems, allocating memory on the correct node is important. Driver authors do not normally have to worry about NUMA issues, however.

We describe *vmalloc* here because it is one of the fundamental Linux memory allocation mechanisms. We should note, however, that use of *vmalloc* is discouraged in most situations. Memory obtained from *vmalloc* is slightly less efficient to work with, and, on some architectures, the amount of address space set aside for *vmalloc* is relatively small. Code that uses *vmalloc* is likely to get a chilly reception if submitted for inclusion in the kernel. If possible, you should work directly with individual pages rather than trying to smooth things over with *vmalloc*.

That said, let's see how *vmalloc* works. The prototypes of the function and its relatives (*ioremap*, which is not strictly an allocation function, is discussed later in this section) are as follows:

```
#include <linux/vmalloc.h>

void *vmalloc(unsigned long size);
void vfree(void * addr);
void *ioremap(unsigned long offset, unsigned long size);
void iounmap(void * addr);
```

It's worth stressing that memory addresses returned by *kmalloc* and *_get_free_pages* are also virtual addresses. Their actual value is still massaged by the MMU (the memory management unit, usually part of the CPU) before it is used to address physical memory.* *vmalloc* is not different in how it uses the hardware, but rather in how the kernel performs the allocation task.

The (virtual) address range used by *kmalloc* and *__get_free_pages* features a one-to-one mapping to physical memory, possibly shifted by a constant PAGE_OFFSET value; the functions don't need to modify the page tables for that address range. The address range used by *vmalloc* and *ioremap*, on the other hand, is completely synthetic, and each allocation builds the (virtual) memory area by suitably setting up the page tables.

This difference can be perceived by comparing the pointers returned by the allocation functions. On some platforms (for example, the x86), addresses returned by *vmalloc* are just beyond the addresses that *kmalloc* uses. On other platforms (for example, MIPS, IA-64, and x86_64), they belong to a completely different address range. Addresses available for *vmalloc* are in the range from VMALLOC_START to VMALLOC_END. Both symbols are defined in *<asm/pgtable.h>*.

Addresses allocated by *vmalloc* can't be used outside of the microprocessor, because they make sense only on top of the processor's MMU. When a driver needs a real physical address (such as a DMA address, used by peripheral hardware to drive the system's bus), you can't easily use *vmalloc*. The right time to call *vmalloc* is when

---

* Actually, some architectures define ranges of "virtual" addresses as reserved to address physical memory. When this happens, the Linux kernel takes advantage of the feature, and both the kernel and *__get_free_pages* addresses lie in one of those memory ranges. The difference is transparent to device drivers and other code that is not directly involved with the memory-management kernel subsystem.

you are allocating memory for a large sequential buffer that exists only in software. It's important to note that *vmalloc* has more overhead than *__get_free_pages*, because it must both retrieve the memory and build the page tables. Therefore, it doesn't make sense to call *vmalloc* to allocate just one page.

An example of a function in the kernel that uses *vmalloc* is the *create_module* system call, which uses *vmalloc* to get space for the module being created. Code and data of the module are later copied to the allocated space using *copy_from_user*. In this way, the module appears to be loaded into contiguous memory. You can verify, by looking in */proc/kallsyms*, that kernel symbols exported by modules lie in a different memory range from symbols exported by the kernel proper.

Memory allocated with *vmalloc* is released by *vfree*, in the same way that *kfree* releases memory allocated by *kmalloc*.

Like *vmalloc*, *ioremap* builds new page tables; unlike *vmalloc*, however, it doesn't actually allocate any memory. The return value of *ioremap* is a special virtual address that can be used to access the specified physical address range; the virtual address obtained is eventually released by calling *iounmap*.

ioremap is most useful for mapping the (physical) address of a PCI buffer to (virtual) kernel space. For example, it can be used to access the frame buffer of a PCI video device; such buffers are usually mapped at high physical addresses, outside of the address range for which the kernel builds page tables at boot time. PCI issues are explained in more detail in Chapter 12.

It's worth noting that for the sake of portability, you should not directly access addresses returned by *ioremap* as if they were pointers to memory. Rather, you should always use *readb* and the other I/O functions introduced in Chapter 9. This requirement applies because some platforms, such as the Alpha, are unable to directly map PCI memory regions to the processor address space because of differences between PCI specs and Alpha processors in how data is transferred.

Both *ioremap* and *vmalloc* are page oriented (they work by modifying the page tables); consequently, the relocated or allocated size is rounded up to the nearest page boundary. *ioremap* simulates an unaligned mapping by "rounding down" the address to be remapped and by returning an offset into the first remapped page.

One minor drawback of *vmalloc* is that it can't be used in atomic context because, internally, it uses *kmalloc(GFP_KERNEL)* to acquire storage for the page tables, and therefore could sleep. This shouldn't be a problem—if the use of *__get_free_page* isn't good enough for an interrupt handler, the software design needs some cleaning up.

A scull Using Virtual Addresses: scullv

Sample code using *vmalloc* is provided in the *scullv* module. Like *scullp*, this module is a stripped-down version of *scull* that uses a different allocation function to obtain space for the device to store data.

The module allocates memory 16 pages at a time. The allocation is done in large chunks to achieve better performance than *scullp* and to show something that takes too long with other allocation techniques to be feasible. Allocating more than one page with __*get_free_pages* is failure prone, and even when it succeeds, it can be slow. As we saw earlier, *vmalloc* is faster than other functions in allocating several pages, but somewhat slower when retrieving a single page, because of the overhead of page-table building. *scullv* is designed like *scullp*. order specifies the "order" of each allocation and defaults to 4. The only difference between *scullv* and *scullp* is in allocation management. These lines use *vmalloc* to obtain new memory:

```
/* Allocate a quantum using virtual addresses */
if (!dptr->data[s_pos]) {
    dptr->data[s_pos] =
        (void *)vmalloc(PAGE_SIZE << dptr->order);
    if (!dptr->data[s_pos])
        goto nomem;
    memset(dptr->data[s_pos], 0, PAGE_SIZE << dptr->order);
}
```

and these lines release memory:

```
/* Release the quantum-set */
for (i = 0; i < qset; i++)
    if (dptr->data[i])
        vfree(dptr->data[i]);
```

If you compile both modules with debugging enabled, you can look at their data allocation by reading the files they create in */proc*. This snapshot was taken on an x86_64 system:

```
salma% cat /tmp/bigfile > /dev/scullp0; head -5 /proc/scullpmem
Device 0: qset 500, order 0, sz 1535135
  item at 000001001847da58, qset at 000001001db4c000
      0:1001db56000
      1:1003d1c7000

salma% cat /tmp/bigfile > /dev/scullv0; head -5 /proc/scullvmem

Device 0: qset 500, order 4, sz 1535135
  item at 000001001847da58, qset at 0000010013dea000
      0:ffffff0001177000
      1:ffffff0001188000
```

The following output, instead, came from an x86 system:

```
rudo% cat /tmp/bigfile > /dev/scullp0; head -5 /proc/scullpmem

Device 0: qset 500, order 0, sz 1535135
   item at ccf80e00, qset at cf7b9800
        0:ccc58000
        1:cccdd000

rudo% cat /tmp/bigfile > /dev/scullv0; head -5 /proc/scullvmem

Device 0: qset 500, order 4, sz 1535135
   item at cfab4800, qset at cf8e4000
        0:d087a000
        1:d08d2000
```

The values show two different behaviors. On x86_64, physical addresses and virtual addresses are mapped to completely different address ranges (0x100 and 0xffffff00), while on x86 computers, *vmalloc* returns virtual addresses just above the mapping used for physical memory.

Per-CPU Variables

Per-CPU variables are an interesting 2.6 kernel feature. When you create a per-CPU variable, each processor on the system gets its own copy of that variable. This may seem like a strange thing to want to do, but it has its advantages. Access to per-CPU variables requires (almost) no locking, because each processor works with its own copy. Per-CPU variables can also remain in their respective processors' caches, which leads to significantly better performance for frequently updated quantities.

A good example of per-CPU variable use can be found in the networking subsystem. The kernel maintains no end of counters tracking how many of each type of packet was received; these counters can be updated thousands of times per second. Rather than deal with the caching and locking issues, the networking developers put the statistics counters into per-CPU variables. Updates are now lockless and fast. On the rare occasion that user space requests to see the values of the counters, it is a simple matter to add up each processor's version and return the total.

The declarations for per-CPU variables can be found in *<linux/percpu.h>*. To create a per-CPU variable at compile time, use this macro:

```
DEFINE_PER_CPU(type, name);
```

If the variable (to be called name) is an array, include the dimension information with the type. Thus, a per-CPU array of three integers would be created with:

```
DEFINE_PER_CPU(int[3], my_percpu_array);
```

Per-CPU variables can be manipulated without explicit locking—almost. Remember that the 2.6 kernel is preemptible; it would not do for a processor to be preempted in the middle of a critical section that modifies a per-CPU variable. It also would not be good if your process were to be moved to another processor in the middle of a per-CPU variable access. For this reason, you must explicitly use the *get_cpu_var* macro to access the current processor's copy of a given variable, and call *put_cpu_var* when you are done. The call to *get_cpu_var* returns an lvalue for the current processor's version of the variable and disables preemption. Since an lvalue is returned, it can be assigned to or operated on directly. For example, one counter in the networking code is incremented with these two statements:

```
get_cpu_var(sockets_in_use)++;
put_cpu_var(sockets_in_use);
```

You can access another processor's copy of the variable with:

```
per_cpu(variable, int cpu_id);
```

If you write code that involves processors reaching into each other's per-CPU variables, you, of course, have to implement a locking scheme that makes that access safe.

Dynamically allocated per-CPU variables are also possible. These variables can be allocated with:

```
void *alloc_percpu(type);
void *__alloc_percpu(size_t size, size_t align);
```

In most cases, *alloc_percpu* does the job; you can call *__alloc_percpu* in cases where a particular alignment is required. In either case, a per-CPU variable can be returned to the system with *free_percpu*. Access to a dynamically allocated per-CPU variable is done via *per_cpu_ptr*:

```
per_cpu_ptr(void *per_cpu_var, int cpu_id);
```

This macro returns a pointer to the version of per_cpu_var corresponding to the given cpu_id. If you are simply reading another CPU's version of the variable, you can dereference that pointer and be done with it. If, however, you are manipulating the current processor's version, you probably need to ensure that you cannot be moved out of that processor first. If the entirety of your access to the per-CPU variable happens with a spinlock held, all is well. Usually, however, you need to use *get_cpu* to block preemption while working with the variable. Thus, code using dynamic per-CPU variables tends to look like this:

```
int cpu;

cpu = get_cpu( )
ptr = per_cpu_ptr(per_cpu_var, cpu);
/* work with ptr */
put_cpu( );
```

When using compile-time per-CPU variables, the *get_cpu_var* and *put_cpu_var* macros take care of these details. Dynamic per-CPU variables require more explicit protection.

Per-CPU variables can be exported to modules, but you must use a special version of the macros:

```
EXPORT_PER_CPU_SYMBOL(per_cpu_var);
EXPORT_PER_CPU_SYMBOL_GPL(per_cpu_var);
```

To access such a variable within a module, declare it with:

```
DECLARE_PER_CPU(type, name);
```

The use of *DECLARE_PER_CPU* (instead of *DEFINE_PER_CPU*) tells the compiler that an external reference is being made.

If you want to use per-CPU variables to create a simple integer counter, take a look at the canned implementation in *<linux/percpu_counter.h>*. Finally, note that some architectures have a limited amount of address space available for per-CPU variables. If you create per-CPU variables in your code, you should try to keep them small.

Obtaining Large Buffers

As we have noted in previous sections, allocations of large, contiguous memory buffers are prone to failure. System memory fragments over time, and chances are that a truly large region of memory will simply not be available. Since there are usually ways of getting the job done without huge buffers, the kernel developers have not put a high priority on making large allocations work. Before you try to obtain a large memory area, you should really consider the alternatives. By far the best way of performing large I/O operations is through scatter/gather operations, which we discuss in the section "Scatter-gather mappings" in Chapter 1.

Acquiring a Dedicated Buffer at Boot Time

If you really need a huge buffer of physically contiguous memory, the best approach is often to allocate it by requesting memory at boot time. Allocation at boot time is the only way to retrieve consecutive memory pages while bypassing the limits imposed by *__get_free_pages* on the buffer size, both in terms of maximum allowed size and limited choice of sizes. Allocating memory at boot time is a "dirty" technique, because it bypasses all memory management policies by reserving a private memory pool. This technique is inelegant and inflexible, but it is also the least prone to failure. Needless to say, a module can't allocate memory at boot time; only drivers directly linked to the kernel can do that.

One noticeable problem with boot-time allocation is that it is not a feasible option for the average user, since this mechanism is available only for code linked in the kernel image. A device driver using this kind of allocation can be installed or replaced only by rebuilding the kernel and rebooting the computer.

When the kernel is booted, it gains access to all the physical memory available in the system. It then initializes each of its subsystems by calling that subsystem's initialization function, allowing initialization code to allocate a memory buffer for private use by reducing the amount of RAM left for normal system operation.

Boot-time memory allocation is performed by calling one of these functions:

```
#include <linux/bootmem.h>
void *alloc_bootmem(unsigned long size);
void *alloc_bootmem_low(unsigned long size);
void *alloc_bootmem_pages(unsigned long size);
void *alloc_bootmem_low_pages(unsigned long size);
```

The functions allocate either whole pages (if they end with _pages) or non-page-aligned memory areas. The allocated memory may be high memory unless one of the _low versions is used. If you are allocating this buffer for a device driver, you probably want to use it for DMA operations, and that is not always possible with high memory; thus, you probably want to use one of the _low variants.

It is rare to free memory allocated at boot time; you will almost certainly be unable to get it back later if you want it. There is an interface to free this memory, however:

```
void free_bootmem(unsigned long addr, unsigned long size);
```

Note that partial pages freed in this manner are not returned to the system—but, if you are using this technique, you have probably allocated a fair number of whole pages to begin with.

If you must use boot-time allocation, you need to link your driver directly into the kernel. See the files in the kernel source under *Documentation/kbuild* for more information on how this should be done.

Quick Reference

The functions and symbols related to memory allocation are:

```
#include <linux/slab.h>
void *kmalloc(size_t size, int flags);
void kfree(void *obj);
```
   The most frequently used interface to memory allocation.

```
#include <linux/mm.h>
GFP_USER
GFP_KERNEL
GFP_NOFS
GFP_NOIO
GFP_ATOMIC
```
   Flags that control how memory allocations are performed, from the least restrictive to the most. The GFP_USER and GFP_KERNEL priorities allow the current process

to be put to sleep to satisfy the request. `GFP_NOFS` and `GFP_NOIO` disable filesystem operations and all I/O operations, respectively, while `GFP_ATOMIC` allocations cannot sleep at all.

`__GFP_DMA`
`__GFP_HIGHMEM`
`__GFP_COLD`
`__GFP_NOWARN`
`__GFP_HIGH`
`__GFP_REPEAT`
`__GFP_NOFAIL`
`__GFP_NORETRY`

These flags modify the kernel's behavior when allocating memory.

```
#include <linux/malloc.h>
kmem_cache_t *kmem_cache_create(char *name, size_t size, size_t offset,
  unsigned long flags, constructor(), destructor());
int kmem_cache_destroy(kmem_cache_t *cache);
```

Create and destroy a slab cache. The cache can be used to allocate several objects of the same size.

`SLAB_NO_REAP`
`SLAB_HWCACHE_ALIGN`
`SLAB_CACHE_DMA`

Flags that can be specified while creating a cache.

`SLAB_CTOR_ATOMIC`
`SLAB_CTOR_CONSTRUCTOR`

Flags that the allocator can pass to the constructor and the destructor functions.

```
void *kmem_cache_alloc(kmem_cache_t *cache, int flags);
void kmem_cache_free(kmem_cache_t *cache, const void *obj);
```

Allocate and release a single object from the cache.

/proc/slabinfo

A virtual file containing statistics on slab cache usage.

```
#include <linux/mempool.h>
mempool_t *mempool_create(int min_nr, mempool_alloc_t *alloc_fn, mempool_free_t
  *free_fn, void *data);
void mempool_destroy(mempool_t *pool);
```

Functions for the creation of memory pools, which try to avoid memory allocation failures by keeping an "emergency list" of allocated items.

```
void *mempool_alloc(mempool_t *pool, int gfp_mask);
void mempool_free(void *element, mempool_t *pool);
```

Functions for allocating items from (and returning them to) memory pools.

```
unsigned long get_zeroed_page(int flags);
unsigned long __get_free_page(int flags);
unsigned long __get_free_pages(int flags, unsigned long order);
```
The page-oriented allocation functions. *get_zeroed_page* returns a single, zero-filled page. All the other versions of the call do not initialize the contents of the returned page(s).

```
int get_order(unsigned long size);
```
Returns the allocation order associated to *size* in the current platform, according to PAGE_SIZE. The argument must be a power of two, and the return value is at least 0.

```
void free_page(unsigned long addr);
void free_pages(unsigned long addr, unsigned long order);
```
Functions that release page-oriented allocations.

```
struct page *alloc_pages_node(int nid, unsigned int flags, unsigned int order);
struct page *alloc_pages(unsigned int flags, unsigned int order);
struct page *alloc_page(unsigned int flags);
```
All variants of the lowest-level page allocator in the Linux kernel.

```
void __free_page(struct page *page);
void __free_pages(struct page *page, unsigned int order);
void free_hot_page(struct page *page);
void free_cold_page(struct page *page);
```
Various ways of freeing pages allocated with one of the forms of *alloc_page*.

```
#include <linux/vmalloc.h>
void * vmalloc(unsigned long size);
void vfree(void * addr);
#include <asm/io.h>
void * ioremap(unsigned long offset, unsigned long size);
void iounmap(void *addr);
```
Functions that allocate or free a contiguous *virtual* address space. *ioremap* accesses physical memory through virtual addresses, while *vmalloc* allocates free pages. Regions mapped with *ioremap* are freed with *iounmap*, while pages obtained from *vmalloc* are released with *vfree*.

```
#include <linux/percpu.h>
DEFINE_PER_CPU(type, name);
DECLARE_PER_CPU(type, name);
```
Macros that define and declare per-CPU variables.

```
per_cpu(variable, int cpu_id)
get_cpu_var(variable)
put_cpu_var(variable)
```
Macros that provide access to statically declared per-CPU variables.

```
void *alloc_percpu(type);
void *__alloc_percpu(size_t size, size_t align);
void free_percpu(void *variable);
```
Functions that perform runtime allocation and freeing of per-CPU variables.

```
int get_cpu();
void put_cpu();
per_cpu_ptr(void *variable, int cpu_id)
```
get_cpu obtains a reference to the current processor (therefore, preventing pre-emption and movement to another processor) and returns the ID number of the processor; *put_cpu* returns that reference. To access a dynamically allocated per-CPU variable, use *per_cpu_ptr* with the ID of the CPU whose version should be accessed. Manipulations of the current CPU's version of a dynamic, per-CPU variable should probably be surrounded by calls to *get_cpu* and *put_cpu*.

```
#include <linux/bootmem.h>
void *alloc_bootmem(unsigned long size);
void *alloc_bootmem_low(unsigned long size);
void *alloc_bootmem_pages(unsigned long size);
void *alloc_bootmem_low_pages(unsigned long size);
void free_bootmem(unsigned long addr, unsigned long size);
```
Functions (which can be used only by drivers directly linked into the kernel) that perform allocation and freeing of memory at system bootstrap time.

Communicating with Hardware

Although playing with *scull* and similar toys is a good introduction to the software interface of a Linux device driver, implementing a *real* device requires hardware. The driver is the abstraction layer between software concepts and hardware circuitry; as such, it needs to talk with both of them. Up until now, we have examined the internals of software concepts; this chapter completes the picture by showing you how a driver can access I/O ports and I/O memory while being portable across Linux platforms.

This chapter continues in the tradition of staying as independent of specific hardware as possible. However, where specific examples are needed, we use simple digital I/O ports (such as the standard PC parallel port) to show how the I/O instructions work and normal frame-buffer video memory to show memory-mapped I/O.

We chose simple digital I/O because it is the easiest form of an input/output port. Also, the parallel port implements raw I/O and is available in most computers: data bits written to the device appear on the output pins, and voltage levels on the input pins are directly accessible by the processor. In practice, you have to connect LEDs or a printer to the port to actually *see* the results of a digital I/O operation, but the underlying hardware is extremely easy to use.

I/O Ports and I/O Memory

Every peripheral device is controlled by writing and reading its registers. Most of the time a device has several registers, and they are accessed at consecutive addresses, either in the memory address space or in the I/O address space.

At the hardware level, there is no conceptual difference between memory regions and I/O regions: both of them are accessed by asserting electrical signals on the address bus and control bus (i.e., the *read* and *write* signals)* and by reading from or writing to the data bus.

While some CPU manufacturers implement a single address space in their chips, others decided that peripheral devices are different from memory and, therefore, deserve a separate address space. Some processors (most notably the x86 family) have separate *read* and *write* electrical lines for I/O ports and special CPU instructions to access ports.

Because peripheral devices are built to fit a peripheral bus, and the most popular I/O buses are modeled on the personal computer, even processors that do not have a separate address space for I/O ports must fake reading and writing I/O ports when accessing some peripheral devices, usually by means of external chipsets or extra circuitry in the CPU core. The latter solution is common within tiny processors meant for embedded use.

For the same reason, Linux implements the concept of I/O ports on all computer platforms it runs on, even on platforms where the CPU implements a single address space. The implementation of port access sometimes depends on the specific make and model of the host computer (because different models use different chipsets to map bus transactions into memory address space).

Even if the peripheral bus has a separate address space for I/O ports, not all devices map their registers to I/O ports. While use of I/O ports is common for ISA peripheral boards, most PCI devices map registers into a memory address region. This I/O memory approach is generally preferred, because it doesn't require the use of special-purpose processor instructions; CPU cores access memory much more efficiently, and the compiler has much more freedom in register allocation and addressing-mode selection when accessing memory.

I/O Registers and Conventional Memory

Despite the strong similarity between hardware registers and memory, a programmer accessing I/O registers must be careful to avoid being tricked by CPU (or compiler) optimizations that can modify the expected I/O behavior.

The main difference between I/O registers and RAM is that I/O operations have side effects, while memory operations have none: the only effect of a memory write is storing a value to a location, and a memory read returns the last value written there. Because memory access speed is so critical to CPU performance, the no-side-effects case has been optimized in several ways: values are cached and read/write instructions are reordered.

---

* Not all computer platforms use a *read* and a *write* signal; some have different means to address external circuits. The difference is irrelevant at software level, however, and we'll assume all have *read* and *write* to simplify the discussion.

The compiler can cache data values into CPU registers without writing them to memory, and even if it stores them, both write and read operations can operate on cache memory without ever reaching physical RAM. Reordering can also happen both at the compiler level and at the hardware level: often a sequence of instructions can be executed more quickly if it is run in an order different from that which appears in the program text, for example, to prevent interlocks in the RISC pipeline. On CISC processors, operations that take a significant amount of time can be executed concurrently with other, quicker ones.

These optimizations are transparent and benign when applied to conventional memory (at least on uniprocessor systems), but they can be fatal to correct I/O operations, because they interfere with those "side effects" that are the main reason why a driver accesses I/O registers. The processor cannot anticipate a situation in which some other process (running on a separate processor, or something happening inside an I/O controller) depends on the order of memory access. The compiler or the CPU may just try to outsmart you and reorder the operations you request; the result can be strange errors that are very difficult to debug. Therefore, a driver must ensure that no caching is performed and no read or write reordering takes place when accessing registers.

The problem with hardware caching is the easiest to face: the underlying hardware is already configured (either automatically or by Linux initialization code) to disable any hardware cache when accessing I/O regions (whether they are memory or port regions).

The solution to compiler optimization and hardware reordering is to place a *memory barrier* between operations that must be visible to the hardware (or to another processor) in a particular order. Linux provides four macros to cover all possible ordering needs:

```
#include <linux/kernel.h>
void barrier(void)
```
> This function tells the compiler to insert a memory barrier but has no effect on the hardware. Compiled code stores to memory all values that are currently modified and resident in CPU registers, and rereads them later when they are needed. A call to *barrier* prevents compiler optimizations across the barrier but leaves the hardware free to do its own reordering.

```
#include <asm/system.h>
void rmb(void);
void read_barrier_depends(void);
void wmb(void);
void mb(void);
```
> These functions insert hardware memory barriers in the compiled instruction flow; their actual instantiation is platform dependent. An *rmb* (read memory barrier) guarantees that any reads appearing before the barrier are completed

prior to the execution of any subsequent read. *wmb* guarantees ordering in write operations, and the *mb* instruction guarantees both. Each of these functions is a superset of *barrier*.

read_barrier_depends is a special, weaker form of read barrier. Whereas *rmb* prevents the reordering of all reads across the barrier, *read_barrier_depends* blocks only the reordering of reads that depend on data from other reads. The distinction is subtle, and it does not exist on all architectures. Unless you understand exactly what is going on, and you have a reason to believe that a full read barrier is exacting an excessive performance cost, you should probably stick to using *rmb*.

```
void smp_rmb(void);
void smp_read_barrier_depends(void);
void smp_wmb(void);
void smp_mb(void);
```

These versions of the barrier macros insert hardware barriers only when the kernel is compiled for SMP systems; otherwise, they all expand to a simple *barrier* call.

A typical usage of memory barriers in a device driver may have this sort of form:

```
writel(dev->registers.addr, io_destination_address);
writel(dev->registers.size, io_size);
writel(dev->registers.operation, DEV_READ);
wmb( );
writel(dev->registers.control, DEV_GO);
```

In this case, it is important to be sure that all of the device registers controlling a particular operation have been properly set prior to telling it to begin. The memory barrier enforces the completion of the writes in the necessary order.

Because memory barriers affect performance, they should be used only where they are really needed. The different types of barriers can also have different performance characteristics, so it is worthwhile to use the most specific type possible. For example, on the x86 architecture, *wmb()* currently does nothing, since writes outside the processor are not reordered. Reads are reordered, however, so *mb()* is slower than *wmb()*.

It is worth noting that most of the other kernel primitives dealing with synchronization, such as spinlock and atomic_t operations, also function as memory barriers. Also worthy of note is that some peripheral buses (such as the PCI bus) have caching issues of their own; we discuss those when we get to them in later chapters.

Some architectures allow the efficient combination of an assignment and a memory barrier. The kernel provides a few macros that perform this combination; in the default case, they are defined as follows:

```
#define set_mb(var, value)  do {var = value; mb( );}  while 0
#define set_wmb(var, value) do {var = value; wmb( );} while 0
#define set_rmb(var, value) do {var = value; rmb( );} while 0
```

Where appropriate, *<asm/system.h>* defines these macros to use architecture-specific instructions that accomplish the task more quickly. Note that *set_rmb* is defined only by a small number of architectures. (The use of a do...while construct is a standard C idiom that causes the expanded macro to work as a normal C statement in all contexts.)

Using I/O Ports

I/O ports are the means by which drivers communicate with many devices, at least part of the time. This section covers the various functions available for making use of I/O ports; we also touch on some portability issues.

I/O Port Allocation

As you might expect, you should not go off and start pounding on I/O ports without first ensuring that you have exclusive access to those ports. The kernel provides a registration interface that allows your driver to claim the ports it needs. The core function in that interface is *request_region*:

```
#include <linux/ioport.h>
struct resource *request_region(unsigned long first, unsigned long n,
                                const char *name);
```

This function tells the kernel that you would like to make use of n ports, starting with first. The name parameter should be the name of your device. The return value is non-NULL if the allocation succeeds. If you get NULL back from *request_region*, you will not be able to use the desired ports.

All port allocations show up in */proc/ioports*. If you are unable to allocate a needed set of ports, that is the place to look to see who got there first.

When you are done with a set of I/O ports (at module unload time, perhaps), they should be returned to the system with:

```
void release_region(unsigned long start, unsigned long n);
```

There is also a function that allows your driver to check to see whether a given set of I/O ports is available:

```
int check_region(unsigned long first, unsigned long n);
```

Here, the return value is a negative error code if the given ports are not available. This function is deprecated because its return value provides no guarantee of whether an allocation would succeed; checking and later allocating are not an atomic operation. We list it here because several drivers are still using it, but you should always use *request_region*, which performs the required locking to ensure that the allocation is done in a safe, atomic manner.

Manipulating I/O ports

After a driver has requested the range of I/O ports it needs to use in its activities, it must read and/or write to those ports. To this end, most hardware differentiates between 8-bit, 16-bit, and 32-bit ports. Usually you can't mix them like you normally do with system memory access.*

A C program, therefore, must call different functions to access different size ports. As suggested in the previous section, computer architectures that support only memory-mapped I/O registers fake port I/O by remapping port addresses to memory addresses, and the kernel hides the details from the driver in order to ease portability. The Linux kernel headers (specifically, the architecture-dependent header *<asm/io.h>*) define the following inline functions to access I/O ports:

```
unsigned inb(unsigned port);
void outb(unsigned char byte, unsigned port);
```
> Read or write byte ports (eight bits wide). The port argument is defined as unsigned long for some platforms and unsigned short for others. The return type of *inb* is also different across architectures.

```
unsigned inw(unsigned port);
void outw(unsigned short word, unsigned port);
```
> These functions access 16-bit ports (one word wide); they are not available when compiling for the S390 platform, which supports only byte I/O.

```
unsigned inl(unsigned port);
void outl(unsigned longword, unsigned port);
```
> These functions access 32-bit ports. longword is declared as either unsigned long or unsigned int, according to the platform. Like word I/O, "long" I/O is not available on S390.

> From now on, when we use unsigned without further type specifications, we are referring to an architecture-dependent definition whose exact nature is not relevant. The functions are almost always portable, because the compiler automatically casts the values during assignment—their being unsigned helps prevent compile-time warnings. No information is lost with such casts as long as the programmer assigns sensible values to avoid overflow. We stick to this convention of "incomplete typing" throughout this chapter.

Note that no 64-bit port I/O operations are defined. Even on 64-bit architectures, the port address space uses a 32-bit (maximum) data path.

---

* Sometimes I/O ports are arranged like memory, and you can (for example) bind two 8-bit writes into a single 16-bit operation. This applies, for instance, to PC video boards. But generally, you can't count on this feature.

I/O Port Access from User Space

The functions just described are primarily meant to be used by device drivers, but they can also be used from user space, at least on PC-class computers. The GNU C library defines them in *<sys/io.h>*. The following conditions should apply in order for *inb* and friends to be used in user-space code:

- The program must be compiled with the *-O* option to force expansion of inline functions.

- The *ioperm* or *iopl* system calls must be used to get permission to perform I/O operations on ports. *ioperm* gets permission for individual ports, while *iopl* gets permission for the entire I/O space. Both of these functions are x86-specific.

- The program must run as root to invoke *ioperm* or *iopl*.* Alternatively, one of its ancestors must have gained port access running as root.

If the host platform has no *ioperm* and no *iopl* system calls, user space can still access I/O ports by using the */dev/port* device file. Note, however, that the meaning of the file is very platform-specific and not likely useful for anything but the PC.

The sample sources *misc-progs/inp.c* and *misc-progs/outp.c* are a minimal tool for reading and writing ports from the command line, in user space. They expect to be installed under multiple names (e.g., *inb*, *inw*, and *inl* and manipulates byte, word, or long ports depending on which name was invoked by the user). They use *ioperm* or *iopl* under x86, */dev/port* on other platforms.

The programs can be made setuid root, if you want to live dangerously and play with your hardware without acquiring explicit privileges. Please do not install them setuid on a production system, however; they are a security hole by design.

String Operations

In addition to the single-shot in and out operations, some processors implement special instructions to transfer a sequence of bytes, words, or longs to and from a single I/O port or the same size. These are the so-called *string instructions*, and they perform the task more quickly than a C-language loop can do. The following macros implement the concept of string I/O either by using a single machine instruction or by executing a tight loop if the target processor has no instruction that performs string I/O. The macros are not defined at all when compiling for the S390 platform. This should not be a portability problem, since this platform doesn't usually share device drivers with other platforms, because its peripheral buses are different.

---

* Technically, it must have the CAP_SYS_RAWIO capability, but that is the same as running as root on most current systems.

The prototypes for string functions are:

```
void insb(unsigned port, void *addr, unsigned long count);
void outsb(unsigned port, void *addr, unsigned long count);
```
Read or write count bytes starting at the memory address addr. Data is read from or written to the single port port.

```
void insw(unsigned port, void *addr, unsigned long count);
void outsw(unsigned port, void *addr, unsigned long count);
```
Read or write 16-bit values to a single 16-bit port.

```
void insl(unsigned port, void *addr, unsigned long count);
void outsl(unsigned port, void *addr, unsigned long count);
```
Read or write 32-bit values to a single 32-bit port.

There is one thing to keep in mind when using the string functions: they move a straight byte stream to or from the port. When the port and the host system have different byte ordering rules, the results can be surprising. Reading a port with *inw* swaps the bytes, if need be, to make the value read match the host ordering. The string functions, instead, do not perform this swapping.

Pausing I/O

Some platforms—most notably the i386—can have problems when the processor tries to transfer data too quickly to or from the bus. The problems can arise when the processor is overclocked with respect to the peripheral bus (think ISA here) and can show up when the device board is too slow. The solution is to insert a small delay after each I/O instruction if another such instruction follows. On the x86, the pause is achieved by performing an out b instruction to port 0x80 (normally but not always unused), or by busy waiting. See the *io.h* file under your platform's *asm* subdirectory for details.

If your device misses some data, or if you fear it might miss some, you can use pausing functions in place of the normal ones. The pausing functions are exactly like those listed previously, but their names end in *_p*; they are called *inb_p*, *outb_p*, and so on. The functions are defined for most supported architectures, although they often expand to the same code as nonpausing I/O, because there is no need for the extra pause if the architecture runs with a reasonably modern peripheral bus.

Platform Dependencies

I/O instructions are, by their nature, highly processor dependent. Because they work with the details of how the processor handles moving data in and out, it is very hard to hide the differences between systems. As a consequence, much of the source code related to port I/O is platform-dependent.

You can see one of the incompatibilities, data typing, by looking back at the list of functions, where the arguments are typed differently based on the architectural differences between platforms. For example, a port is unsigned short on the x86 (where the processor supports a 64-KB I/O space), but unsigned long on other platforms, whose ports are just special locations in the same address space as memory.

Other platform dependencies arise from basic structural differences in the processors and are, therefore, unavoidable. We won't go into detail about the differences, because we assume that you won't be writing a device driver for a particular system without understanding the underlying hardware. Instead, here is an overview of the capabilities of the architectures supported by the kernel:

IA-32 (x86)
x86_64
   The architecture supports all the functions described in this chapter. Port numbers are of type unsigned short.

IA-64 (Itanium)
   All functions are supported; ports are unsigned long (and memory-mapped). String functions are implemented in C.

Alpha
   All the functions are supported, and ports are memory-mapped. The implementation of port I/O is different in different Alpha platforms, according to the chipset they use. String functions are implemented in C and defined in *arch/alpha/lib/io.c*. Ports are unsigned long.

ARM
   Ports are memory-mapped, and all functions are supported; string functions are implemented in C. Ports are of type unsigned int.

Cris
   This architecture does not support the I/O port abstraction even in an emulated mode; the various port operations are defined to do nothing at all.

M68k
M68k-nommu
   Ports are memory-mapped. String functions are supported, and the port type is unsigned char *.

MIPS
MIPS64
   The MIPS port supports all the functions. String operations are implemented with tight assembly loops, because the processor lacks machine-level string I/O. Ports are memory-mapped; they are unsigned long.

PA-RISC
   All of the functions are supported; ports are int on PCI-based systems and unsigned short on EISA systems, except for string operations, which use unsigned long port numbers.

PowerPC
PowerPC64

All the functions are supported; ports have type unsigned `char *` on 32-bit systems and unsigned `long` on 64-bit systems.

S390

Similar to the M68k, the header for this platform supports only byte-wide port I/O with no string operations. Ports are `char` pointers and are memory-mapped.

Super-H

Ports are unsigned `int` (memory-mapped), and all the functions are supported.

SPARC
SPARC64

Once again, I/O space is memory-mapped. Versions of the port functions are defined to work with unsigned `long` ports.

The curious reader can extract more information from the *io.h* files, which sometimes define a few architecture-specific functions in addition to those we describe in this chapter. Be warned that some of these files are rather difficult reading, however.

It's interesting to note that no processor outside the x86 family features a different address space for ports, even though several of the supported families are shipped with ISA and/or PCI slots (and both buses implement separate I/O and memory address spaces).

Moreover, some processors (most notably the early Alphas) lack instructions that move one or two bytes at a time.* Therefore, their peripheral chipsets simulate 8-bit and 16-bit I/O accesses by mapping them to special address ranges in the memory address space. Thus, an *inb* and an *inw* instruction that act on the same port are implemented by two 32-bit memory reads that operate on different addresses. Fortunately, all of this is hidden from the device driver writer by the internals of the macros described in this section, but we feel it's an interesting feature to note. If you want to probe further, look for examples in *include/asm-alpha/core_lca.h*.

How I/O operations are performed on each platform is well described in the programmer's manual for each platform; those manuals are usually available for download as PDFs on the Web.

---

* Single-byte I/O is not as important as one may imagine, because it is a rare operation. To read/write a single byte to any address space, you need to implement a data path connecting the low bits of the register-set data bus to any byte position in the external data bus. These data paths require additional logic gates that get in the way of every data transfer. Dropping byte-wide loads and stores can benefit overall system performance.

An I/O Port Example

The sample code we use to show port I/O from within a device driver acts on general-purpose digital I/O ports; such ports are found in most computer systems.

A digital I/O port, in its most common incarnation, is a byte-wide I/O location, either memory-mapped or port-mapped. When you write a value to an output location, the electrical signal seen on output pins is changed according to the individual bits being written. When you read a value from the input location, the current logic level seen on input pins is returned as individual bit values.

The actual implementation and software interface of such I/O ports varies from system to system. Most of the time, I/O pins are controlled by two I/O locations: one that allows selecting what pins are used as input and what pins are used as output and one in which you can actually read or write logic levels. Sometimes, however, things are even simpler, and the bits are hardwired as either input or output (but, in this case, they're no longer called "general-purpose I/O"); the parallel port found on all personal computers is one such not-so-general-purpose I/O port. Either way, the I/O pins are usable by the sample code we introduce shortly.

An Overview of the Parallel Port

Because we expect most readers to be using an x86 platform in the form called "personal computer," we feel it is worth explaining how the PC parallel port is designed. The parallel port is the peripheral interface of choice for running digital I/O sample code on a personal computer. Although most readers probably have parallel port specifications available, we summarize them here for your convenience.

The parallel interface, in its minimal configuration (we overlook the ECP and EPP modes) is made up of three 8-bit ports. The PC standard starts the I/O ports for the first parallel interface at 0x378 and for the second at 0x278. The first port is a bidirectional data register; it connects directly to pins 2–9 on the physical connector. The second port is a read-only status register; when the parallel port is being used for a printer, this register reports several aspects of printer status, such as being online, out of paper, or busy. The third port is an output-only control register, which, among other things, controls whether interrupts are enabled.

The signal levels used in parallel communications are standard transistor-transistor logic (TTL) levels: 0 and 5 volts, with the logic threshold at about 1.2 volts. You can count on the ports at least meeting the standard TTL LS current ratings, although most modern parallel ports do better in both current and voltage ratings.

The parallel connector is not isolated from the computer's internal circuitry, which is useful if you want to connect logic gates directly to the port. But you have to be careful to do the wiring correctly; the parallel port circuitry is easily damaged when you play with your own custom circuitry, unless you add optoisolators to your circuit. You can choose to use plug-in parallel ports if you fear you'll damage your motherboard.

The bit specifications are outlined in Figure 9-1. You can access 12 output bits and 5 input bits, some of which are logically inverted over the course of their signal path. The only bit with no associated signal pin is bit 4 (0x10) of port 2, which enables interrupts from the parallel port. We use this bit as part of our implementation of an interrupt handler in Chapter 10.

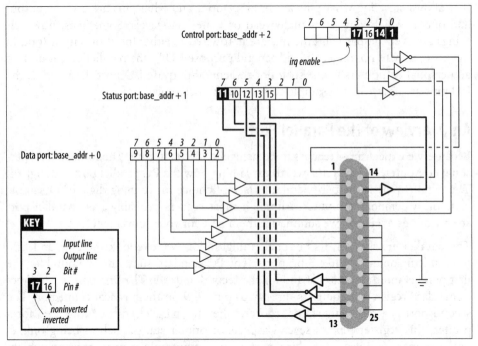

Figure 9-1. The pinout of the parallel port

A Sample Driver

The driver we introduce is called *short* (Simple Hardware Operations and Raw Tests). All it does is read and write a few 8-bit ports, starting from the one you select at load time. By default, it uses the port range assigned to the parallel interface of the PC. Each device node (with a unique minor number) accesses a different port. The *short* driver doesn't do anything useful; it just isolates for external use as a single instruction acting on a port. If you are not used to port I/O, you can use *short* to get familiar with it; you can measure the time it takes to transfer data through a port or play other games.

For *short* to work on your system, it must have free access to the underlying hardware device (by default, the parallel interface); thus, no other driver may have allocated it. Most modern distributions set up the parallel port drivers as modules that are loaded only when needed, so contention for the I/O addresses is not usually a problem. If, however, you get a "can't get I/O address" error from *short* (on the console or in the system log file), some other driver has probably already taken the port. A quick look at */proc/ioports* usually tells you which driver is getting in the way. The same caveat applies to other I/O devices if you are not using the parallel interface.

From now on, we just refer to "the parallel interface" to simplify the discussion. However, you can set the base module parameter at load time to redirect *short* to other I/O devices. This feature allows the sample code to run on any Linux platform where you have access to a digital I/O interface that is accessible via *outb* and *inb* (even though the actual hardware is memory-mapped on all platforms but the x86). Later, in the section "Using I/O Memory," we show how *short* can be used with generic memory-mapped digital I/O as well.

To watch what happens on the parallel connector and if you have a bit of an inclination to work with hardware, you can solder a few LEDs to the output pins. Each LED should be connected in series to a 1-KΩ resistor leading to a ground pin (unless, of course, your LEDs have the resistor built in). If you connect an output pin to an input pin, you'll generate your own input to be read from the input ports.

Note that you cannot just connect a printer to the parallel port and see data sent to *short*. This driver implements simple access to the I/O ports and does not perform the handshake that printers need to operate on the data. In the next chapter, we show a sample driver (called *shortprint*), that is capable of driving parallel printers; that driver uses interrupts, however, so we can't get to it quite yet.

If you are going to view parallel data by soldering LEDs to a D-type connector, we suggest that you not use pins 9 and 10, because we connect them together later to run the sample code shown in Chapter 10.

As far as *short* is concerned, */dev/short0* writes to and reads from the 8-bit port located at the I/O address base (0x378 unless changed at load time). */dev/short1* writes to the 8-bit port located at base + 1, and so on up to base + 7.

The actual output operation performed by */dev/short0* is based on a tight loop using *outb*. A memory barrier instruction is used to ensure that the output operation actually takes place and is not optimized away:

```
while (count--) {
    outb(*(ptr++), port);
    wmb( );
}
```

You can run the following command to light your LEDs:

```
echo  -n "any string"  > /dev/short0
```

Each LED monitors a single bit of the output port. Remember that only the last character written remains steady on the output pins long enough to be perceived by your eyes. For that reason, we suggest that you prevent automatic insertion of a trailing newline by passing the *-n* option to *echo*.

Reading is performed by a similar function, built around *inb* instead of *outb*. In order to read "meaningful" values from the parallel port, you need to have some hardware connected to the input pins of the connector to generate signals. If there is no signal, you read an endless stream of identical bytes. If you choose to read from an output port, you most likely get back the last value written to the port (this applies to the parallel interface and to most other digital I/O circuits in common use). Thus, those uninclined to get out their soldering irons can read the current output value on port 0x378 by running a command such as:

```
dd if=/dev/short0 bs=1 count=1 | od -t x1
```

To demonstrate the use of all the I/O instructions, there are three variations of each *short* device: */dev/short0* performs the loop just shown, */dev/short0p* uses *outb_p* and *inb_p* in place of the "fast" functions, and */dev/short0s* uses the string instructions. There are eight such devices, from *short0* to *short7*. Although the PC parallel interface has only three ports, you may need more of them if using a different I/O device to run your tests.

The *short* driver performs an absolute minimum of hardware control but is adequate to show how the I/O port instructions are used. Interested readers may want to look at the source for the *parport* and *parport_pc* modules to see how complicated this device can get in real life in order to support a range of devices (printers, tape backup, network interfaces) on the parallel port.

Using I/O Memory

Despite the popularity of I/O ports in the x86 world, the main mechanism used to communicate with devices is through memory-mapped registers and device memory. Both are called *I/O memory* because the difference between registers and memory is transparent to software.

I/O memory is simply a region of RAM-like locations that the device makes available to the processor over the bus. This memory can be used for a number of purposes, such as holding video data or Ethernet packets, as well as implementing device registers that behave just like I/O ports (i.e., they have side effects associated with reading and writing them).

The way to access I/O memory depends on the computer architecture, bus, and device being used, although the principles are the same everywhere. The discussion in this chapter touches mainly on ISA and PCI memory, while trying to convey general information as well. Although access to PCI memory is introduced here, a thorough discussion of PCI is deferred to Chapter 12.

Depending on the computer platform and bus being used, I/O memory may or may not be accessed through page tables. When access passes though page tables, the kernel must first arrange for the physical address to be visible from your driver, and this usually means that you must call *ioremap* before doing any I/O. If no page tables are needed, I/O memory locations look pretty much like I/O ports, and you can just read and write to them using proper wrapper functions.

Whether or not *ioremap* is required to access I/O memory, direct use of pointers to I/O memory is discouraged. Even though (as introduced in the section "I/O Ports and I/O Memory") I/O memory is addressed like normal RAM at hardware level, the extra care outlined in the section "I/O Registers and Conventional Memory" suggests avoiding normal pointers. The wrapper functions used to access I/O memory are safe on all platforms and are optimized away whenever straight pointer dereferencing can perform the operation.

Therefore, even though dereferencing a pointer works (for now) on the x86, failure to use the proper macros hinders the portability and readability of the driver.

I/O Memory Allocation and Mapping

I/O memory regions must be allocated prior to use. The interface for allocation of memory regions (defined in *<linux/ioport.h>*) is:

```
struct resource *request_mem_region(unsigned long start, unsigned long len,
                                     char *name);
```

This function allocates a memory region of len bytes, starting at start. If all goes well, a non-NULL pointer is returned; otherwise the return value is NULL. All I/O memory allocations are listed in */proc/iomem*.

Memory regions should be freed when no longer needed:

```
void release_mem_region(unsigned long start, unsigned long len);
```

There is also an old function for checking I/O memory region availability:

```
int check_mem_region(unsigned long start, unsigned long len);
```

But, as with *check_region*, this function is unsafe and should be avoided.

Allocation of I/O memory is not the only required step before that memory may be accessed. You must also ensure that this I/O memory has been made accessible to the kernel. Getting at I/O memory is not just a matter of dereferencing a pointer; on many systems, I/O memory is not directly accessible in this way at all. So a mapping must be set up first. This is the role of the *ioremap* function, introduced in the section "vmalloc and Friends" in Chapter 1. The function is designed specifically to assign virtual addresses to I/O memory regions.

Once equipped with *ioremap* (and *iounmap*), a device driver can access any I/O memory address, whether or not it is directly mapped to virtual address space. Remember, though, that the addresses returned from *ioremap* should not be dereferenced directly; instead, accessor functions provided by the kernel should be used. Before we get into those functions, we'd better review the *ioremap* prototypes and introduce a few details that we passed over in the previous chapter.

The functions are called according to the following definition:

```
#include <asm/io.h>
void *ioremap(unsigned long phys_addr, unsigned long size);
void *ioremap_nocache(unsigned long phys_addr, unsigned long size);
void iounmap(void * addr);
```

First of all, you notice the new function *ioremap_nocache*. We didn't cover it in Chapter 8, because its meaning is definitely hardware related. Quoting from one of the kernel headers: "It's useful if some control registers are in such an area, and write combining or read caching is not desirable." Actually, the function's implementation is identical to *ioremap* on most computer platforms: in situations where all of I/O memory is already visible through noncacheable addresses, there's no reason to implement a separate, noncaching version of *ioremap*.

Accessing I/O Memory

On some platforms, you may get away with using the return value from *ioremap* as a pointer. Such use is not portable, and, increasingly, the kernel developers have been working to eliminate any such use. The proper way of getting at I/O memory is via a set of functions (defined via *<asm/io.h>*) provided for that purpose.

To read from I/O memory, use one of the following:

```
unsigned int ioread8(void *addr);
unsigned int ioread16(void *addr);
unsigned int ioread32(void *addr);
```

Here, addr should be an address obtained from *ioremap* (perhaps with an integer offset); the return value is what was read from the given I/O memory.

There is a similar set of functions for writing to I/O memory:

```
void iowrite8(u8 value, void *addr);
void iowrite16(u16 value, void *addr);
void iowrite32(u32 value, void *addr);
```

If you must read or write a series of values to a given I/O memory address, you can use the repeating versions of the functions:

```
void ioread8_rep(void *addr, void *buf, unsigned long count);
void ioread16_rep(void *addr, void *buf, unsigned long count);
```

```
void ioread32_rep(void *addr, void *buf, unsigned long count);
void iowrite8_rep(void *addr, const void *buf, unsigned long count);
void iowrite16_rep(void *addr, const void *buf, unsigned long count);
void iowrite32_rep(void *addr, const void *buf, unsigned long count);
```

These functions read or write count values from the given buf to the given addr. Note that count is expressed in the size of the data being written; *ioread32_rep* reads count 32-bit values starting at buf.

The functions described above perform all I/O to the given addr. If, instead, you need to operate on a block of I/O memory, you can use one of the following:

```
void memset_io(void *addr, u8 value, unsigned int count);
void memcpy_fromio(void *dest, void *source, unsigned int count);
void memcpy_toio(void *dest, void *source, unsigned int count);
```

These functions behave like their C library analogs.

If you read through the kernel source, you see many calls to an older set of functions when I/O memory is being used. These functions still work, but their use in new code is discouraged. Among other things, they are less safe because they do not perform the same sort of type checking. Nonetheless, we describe them here:

unsigned readb(address);

unsigned readw(address);

unsigned readl(address);

> These macros are used to retrieve 8-bit, 16-bit, and 32-bit data values from I/O memory.

void writeb(unsigned value, address);

void writew(unsigned value, address);

void writel(unsigned value, address);

> Like the previous functions, these functions (macros) are used to write 8-bit, 16-bit, and 32-bit data items.

Some 64-bit platforms also offer *readq* and *writeq*, for quad-word (8-byte) memory operations on the PCI bus. The *quad-word* nomenclature is a historical leftover from the times when all real processors had 16-bit words. Actually, the *L* naming used for 32-bit values has become incorrect too, but renaming everything would confuse things even more.

Ports as I/O Memory

Some hardware has an interesting feature: some versions use I/O ports, while others use I/O memory. The registers exported to the processor are the same in either case, but the access method is different. As a way of making life easier for drivers dealing with this kind of hardware, and as a way of minimizing the apparent differences between I/O port and memory accesses, the 2.6 kernel provides a function called *ioport_map*:

```
void *ioport_map(unsigned long port, unsigned int count);
```

This function remaps count I/O ports and makes them appear to be I/O memory. From that point thereafter, the driver may use *ioread8* and friends on the returned addresses and forget that it is using I/O ports at all.

This mapping should be undone when it is no longer needed:

```
void ioport_unmap(void *addr);
```

These functions make I/O ports look like memory. Do note, however, that the I/O ports must still be allocated with *request_region* before they can be remapped in this way.

Reusing short for I/O Memory

The *short* sample module, introduced earlier to access I/O ports, can be used to access I/O memory as well. To this aim, you must tell it to use I/O memory at load time; also, you need to change the base address to make it point to your I/O region.

For example, this is how we used *short* to light the debug LEDs on a MIPS development board:

```
mips.root# ./short_load use_mem=1 base=0xb7ffffc0
mips.root# echo -n 7 > /dev/short0
```

Use of *short* for I/O memory is the same as it is for I/O ports.

The following fragment shows the loop used by *short* in writing to a memory location:

```
while (count--) {
    iowrite8(*ptr++, address);
    wmb( );
}
```

Note the use of a write memory barrier here. Because *iowrite8* likely turns into a direct assignment on many architectures, the memory barrier is needed to ensure that the writes happen in the expected order.

short uses *inb* and *outb* to show how that is done. It would be a straightforward exercise for the reader, however, to change *short* to remap I/O ports with *ioport_map*, and simplify the rest of the code considerably.

ISA Memory Below 1 MB

One of the most well-known I/O memory regions is the ISA range found on personal computers. This is the memory range between 640 KB (0xA0000) and 1 MB (0x100000). Therefore, it appears right in the middle of regular system RAM. This positioning may seem a little strange; it is an artifact of a decision made in the early 1980s, when 640 KB of memory seemed like more than anybody would ever be able to use.

This memory range belongs to the non-directly-mapped class of memory.* You can read/write a few bytes in that memory range using the *short* module as explained previously, that is, by setting use_mem at load time.

Although ISA I/O memory exists only in x86-class computers, we think it's worth spending a few words and a sample driver on it.

We are not going to discuss PCI memory in this chapter, since it is the cleanest kind of I/O memory: once you know the physical address, you can simply remap and access it. The "problem" with PCI I/O memory is that it doesn't lend itself to a working example for this chapter, because we can't know in advance the physical addresses your PCI memory is mapped to, or whether it's safe to access either of those ranges. We chose to describe the ISA memory range, because it's both less clean and more suitable to running sample code.

To demonstrate access to ISA memory, we use yet another silly little module (part of the sample sources). In fact, this one is called *silly*, as an acronym for Simple Tool for Unloading and Printing ISA Data, or something like that.

The module supplements the functionality of *short* by giving access to the whole 384-KB memory space and by showing all the different I/O functions. It features four device nodes that perform the same task using different data transfer functions. The *silly* devices act as a window over I/O memory, in a way similar to */dev/mem*. You can read and write data, and *lseek* to an arbitrary I/O memory address.

Because *silly* provides access to ISA memory, it must start by mapping the physical ISA addresses into kernel virtual addresses. In the early days of the Linux kernel, one could simply assign a pointer to an ISA address of interest, then dereference it directly. In the modern world, though, we must work with the virtual memory system and remap the memory range first. This mapping is done with *ioremap*, as explained earlier for *short*:

```
#define ISA_BASE    0xA0000
#define ISA_MAX     0x100000  /* for general memory access */

    /* this line appears in silly_init */
    io_base = ioremap(ISA_BASE, ISA_MAX - ISA_BASE);
```

ioremap returns a pointer value that can be used with *ioread8* and the other functions explained in the section "Accessing I/O Memory."

Let's look back at our sample module to see how these functions might be used. */dev/sillyb*, featuring minor number 0, accesses I/O memory with *ioread8* and *iowrite8*. The following code shows the implementation for *read*, which makes the address

---

* Actually, this is not completely true. The memory range is so small and so frequently used that the kernel builds page tables at boot time to access those addresses. However, the virtual address used to access them is not the same as the physical address, and thus *ioremap* is needed anyway.

range 0xA0000-0xFFFFF available as a virtual file in the range 0-0x5FFFF. The *read* function is structured as a switch statement over the different access modes; here is the *sillyb* case:

```
case M_8:
  while (count) {
      *ptr = ioread8(add);
      add++;
      count--;
      ptr++;
  }
  break;
```

The next two devices are */dev/sillyw* (minor number 1) and */dev/sillyl* (minor number 2). They act like */dev/sillyb*, except that they use 16-bit and 32-bit functions. Here's the *write* implementation of *sillyl*, again part of a switch:

```
case M_32:
  while (count >= 4) {
      iowrite8(*(u32 *)ptr, add);
      add += 4;
      count -= 4;
      ptr += 4;
  }
  break;
```

The last device is */dev/sillycp* (minor number 3), which uses the *memcpy_*io* functions to perform the same task. Here's the core of its *read* implementation:

```
case M_memcpy:
  memcpy_fromio(ptr, add, count);
  break;
```

Because *ioremap* was used to provide access to the ISA memory area, *silly* must invoke *iounmap* when the module is unloaded:

```
iounmap(io_base);
```

isa_readb and Friends

A look at the kernel source will turn up another set of routines with names such as *isa_readb*. In fact, each of the functions just described has an *isa_* equivalent. These functions provide access to ISA memory without the need for a separate *ioremap* step. The word from the kernel developers, however, is that these functions are intended to be temporary driver-porting aids and that they may go away in the future. Therefore, you should avoid using them.

Quick Reference

This chapter introduced the following symbols related to hardware management:

#include <linux/kernel.h>
void barrier(void)
> This "software" memory barrier requests the compiler to consider all memory volatile across this instruction.

#include <asm/system.h>
void rmb(void);
void read_barrier_depends(void);
void wmb(void);
void mb(void);
> Hardware memory barriers. They request the CPU (and the compiler) to check-point all memory reads, writes, or both across this instruction.

#include <asm/io.h>
unsigned inb(unsigned port);
void outb(unsigned char byte, unsigned port);
unsigned inw(unsigned port);
void outw(unsigned short word, unsigned port);
unsigned inl(unsigned port);
void outl(unsigned doubleword, unsigned port);
> Functions that are used to read and write I/O ports. They can also be called by user-space programs, provided they have the right privileges to access ports.

unsigned inb_p(unsigned port);
...
> If a small delay is needed after an I/O operation, you can use the six pausing counterparts of the functions introduced in the previous entry; these pausing functions have names ending in _p.

void insb(unsigned port, void *addr, unsigned long count);
void outsb(unsigned port, void *addr, unsigned long count);
void insw(unsigned port, void *addr, unsigned long count);
void outsw(unsigned port, void *addr, unsigned long count);
void insl(unsigned port, void *addr, unsigned long count);
void outsl(unsigned port, void *addr, unsigned long count);
> The "string functions" are optimized to transfer data from an input port to a region of memory, or the other way around. Such transfers are performed by reading or writing the same port count times.

```
#include <linux/ioport.h>
struct resource *request_region(unsigned long start, unsigned long len, char
    *name);
void release_region(unsigned long start, unsigned long len);
int check_region(unsigned long start, unsigned long len);
```
Resource allocators for I/O ports. The (deprecated) *check* function returns 0 for success and less than 0 in case of error.

```
struct resource *request_mem_region(unsigned long start, unsigned long len,
    char *name);
void release_mem_region(unsigned long start, unsigned long len);
int check_mem_region(unsigned long start, unsigned long len);
```
Functions that handle resource allocation for memory regions.

```
#include <asm/io.h>
void *ioremap(unsigned long phys_addr, unsigned long size);
void *ioremap_nocache(unsigned long phys_addr, unsigned long size);
void iounmap(void *virt_addr);
```
ioremap remaps a physical address range into the processor's virtual address space, making it available to the kernel. *iounmap* frees the mapping when it is no longer needed.

```
#include <asm/io.h>
unsigned int ioread8(void *addr);
unsigned int ioread16(void *addr);
unsigned int ioread32(void *addr);
void iowrite8(u8 value, void *addr);
void iowrite16(u16 value, void *addr);
void iowrite32(u32 value, void *addr);
```
Accessor functions that are used to work with I/O memory.

```
void ioread8_rep(void *addr, void *buf, unsigned long count);
void ioread16_rep(void *addr, void *buf, unsigned long count);
void ioread32_rep(void *addr, void *buf, unsigned long count);
void iowrite8_rep(void *addr, const void *buf, unsigned long count);
void iowrite16_rep(void *addr, const void *buf, unsigned long count);
void iowrite32_rep(void *addr, const void *buf, unsigned long count);
```
"Repeating" versions of the I/O memory primitives.

```
unsigned readb(address);
unsigned readw(address);
unsigned readl(address);
void writeb(unsigned value, address);
void writew(unsigned value, address);
void writel(unsigned value, address);
memset_io(address, value, count);
memcpy_fromio(dest, source, nbytes);
memcpy_toio(dest, source, nbytes);
```
Older, type-unsafe functions for accessing I/O memory.

```
void *ioport_map(unsigned long port, unsigned int count);
void ioport_unmap(void *addr);
```
A driver author that wants to treat I/O ports as if they were I/O memory may pass those ports to *ioport_map*. The mapping should be done (with *ioport_unmap*) when no longer needed.

CHAPTER 10
Interrupt Handling

Although some devices can be controlled using nothing but their I/O regions, most real devices are a bit more complicated than that. Devices have to deal with the external world, which often includes things such as spinning disks, moving tape, wires to distant places, and so on. Much has to be done in a time frame that is different from, and far slower than, that of the processor. Since it is almost always undesirable to have the processor wait on external events, there must be a way for a device to let the processor know when something has happened.

That way, of course, is interrupts. An *interrupt* is simply a signal that the hardware can send when it wants the processor's attention. Linux handles interrupts in much the same way that it handles signals in user space. For the most part, a driver need only register a handler for its device's interrupts, and handle them properly when they arrive. Of course, underneath that simple picture there is some complexity; in particular, interrupt handlers are somewhat limited in the actions they can perform as a result of how they are run.

It is difficult to demonstrate the use of interrupts without a real hardware device to generate them. Thus, the sample code used in this chapter works with the parallel port. Such ports are starting to become scarce on modern hardware, but, with luck, most people are still able to get their hands on a system with an available port. We'll be working with the *short* module from the previous chapter; with some small additions it can generate and handle interrupts from the parallel port. The module's name, *short*, actually means *short int* (it is C, isn't it?), to remind us that it handles *int*errupts.

Before we get into the topic, however, it is time for one cautionary note. Interrupt handlers, by their nature, run concurrently with other code. Thus, they inevitably raise issues of concurrency and contention for data structures and hardware. If you succumbed to the temptation to pass over the discussion in Chapter 5, we understand. But we also recommend that you turn back and have another look now. A solid understanding of concurrency control techniques is vital when working with interrupts.

Preparing the Parallel Port

Although the parallel interface is simple, it can trigger interrupts. This capability is used by the printer to notify the *lp* driver that it is ready to accept the next character in the buffer.

Like most devices, the parallel port doesn't actually generate interrupts before it's instructed to do so; the parallel standard states that setting bit 4 of port 2 (0x37a, 0x27a, or whatever) enables interrupt reporting. A simple *outb* call to set the bit is performed by *short* at module initialization.

Once interrupts are enabled, the parallel interface generates an interrupt whenever the electrical signal at pin 10 (the so-called ACK bit) changes from low to high. The simplest way to force the interface to generate interrupts (short of hooking up a printer to the port) is to connect pins 9 and 10 of the parallel connector. A short length of wire inserted into the appropriate holes in the parallel port connector on the back of your system creates this connection. The pinout of the parallel port is shown in Figure 9-1.

Pin 9 is the most significant bit of the parallel data byte. If you write binary data to */dev/short0*, you generate several interrupts. Writing ASCII text to the port won't generate any interrupts, though, because the ASCII character set has no entries with the top bit set.

If you'd rather avoid wiring pins together, but you do have a printer at hand, you can run the sample interrupt handler using a real printer, as shown later. However, note that the probing functions we introduce depend on the jumper between pin 9 and 10 being in place, and you need it to experiment with probing using our code.

Installing an Interrupt Handler

If you want to actually "see" interrupts being generated, writing to the hardware device isn't enough; a software handler must be configured in the system. If the Linux kernel hasn't been told to expect your interrupt, it simply acknowledges and ignores it.

Interrupt lines are a precious and often limited resource, particularly when there are only 15 or 16 of them. The kernel keeps a registry of interrupt lines, similar to the registry of I/O ports. A module is expected to request an interrupt channel (or IRQ, for interrupt request) before using it and to release it when finished. In many situations, modules are also expected to be able to share interrupt lines with other drivers, as we will see. The following functions, declared in *<linux/interrupt.h>*, implement the interrupt registration interface:

```
int request_irq(unsigned int irq,
                irqreturn_t (*handler)(int, void *, struct pt_regs *),
                unsigned long flags,
```

```
                const char *dev_name,
                void *dev_id);

    void free_irq(unsigned int irq, void *dev_id);
```

The value returned from *request_irq* to the requesting function is either 0 to indicate success or a negative error code, as usual. It's not uncommon for the function to return -EBUSY to signal that another driver is already using the requested interrupt line. The arguments to the functions are as follows:

unsigned int irq
> The interrupt number being requested.

irqreturn_t (*handler)(int, void *, struct pt_regs *)
> The pointer to the handling function being installed. We discuss the arguments to this function and its return value later in this chapter.

unsigned long flags
> As you might expect, a bit mask of options (described later) related to interrupt management.

const char *dev_name
> The string passed to *request_irq* is used in */proc/interrupts* to show the owner of the interrupt (see the next section).

void *dev_id
> Pointer used for shared interrupt lines. It is a unique identifier that is used when the interrupt line is freed and that may also be used by the driver to point to its own private data area (to identify which device is interrupting). If the interrupt is not shared, dev_id can be set to NULL, but it a good idea anyway to use this item to point to the device structure. We'll see a practical use for dev_id in the section "Implementing a Handler."

The bits that can be set in flags are as follows:

SA_INTERRUPT
> When set, this indicates a "fast" interrupt handler. Fast handlers are executed with interrupts disabled on the current processor (the topic is covered in the section "Fast and Slow Handlers").

SA_SHIRQ
> This bit signals that the interrupt can be shared between devices. The concept of sharing is outlined in the section "Interrupt Sharing."

SA_SAMPLE_RANDOM
> This bit indicates that the generated interrupts can contribute to the entropy pool used by */dev/random* and */dev/urandom*. These devices return truly random numbers when read and are designed to help application software choose secure keys for encryption. Such random numbers are extracted from an entropy pool that is contributed by various random events. If your device generates interrupts at truly random times, you should set this flag. If, on the other hand, your interrupts are

predictable (for example, vertical blanking of a frame grabber), the flag is not worth setting—it wouldn't contribute to system entropy anyway. Devices that could be influenced by attackers should not set this flag; for example, network drivers can be subjected to predictable packet timing from outside and should not contribute to the entropy pool. See the comments in *drivers/char/random.c* for more information.

The interrupt handler can be installed either at driver initialization or when the device is first opened. Although installing the interrupt handler from within the module's initialization function might sound like a good idea, it often isn't, especially if your device does not share interrupts. Because the number of interrupt lines is limited, you don't want to waste them. You can easily end up with more devices in your computer than there are interrupts. If a module requests an IRQ at initialization, it prevents any other driver from using the interrupt, even if the device holding it is never used. Requesting the interrupt at device open, on the other hand, allows some sharing of resources.

It is possible, for example, to run a frame grabber on the same interrupt as a modem, as long as you don't use the two devices at the same time. It is quite common for users to load the module for a special device at system boot, even if the device is rarely used. A data acquisition gadget might use the same interrupt as the second serial port. While it's not too hard to avoid connecting to your Internet service provider (ISP) during data acquisition, being forced to unload a module in order to use the modem is really unpleasant.

The correct place to call *request_irq* is when the device is first opened, *before* the hardware is instructed to generate interrupts. The place to call *free_irq* is the last time the device is closed, *after* the hardware is told not to interrupt the processor any more. The disadvantage of this technique is that you need to keep a per-device open count so that you know when interrupts can be disabled.

This discussion notwithstanding, *short* requests its interrupt line at load time. This was done so that you can run the test programs without having to run an extra process to keep the device open. *short*, therefore, requests the interrupt from within its initialization function (*short_init*) instead of doing it in *short_open*, as a real device driver would.

The interrupt requested by the following code is short_irq. The actual assignment of the variable (i.e., determining which IRQ to use) is shown later, since it is not relevant to the current discussion. short_base is the base I/O address of the parallel interface being used; register 2 of the interface is written to enable interrupt reporting.

```
if (short_irq >= 0) {
    result = request_irq(short_irq, short_interrupt,
            SA_INTERRUPT, "short", NULL);
    if (result) {
        printk(KERN_INFO "short: can't get assigned irq %i\n",
                short_irq);
```

```
        short_irq = -1;
    }
    else { /* actually enable it -- assume this *is* a parallel port */
        outb(0x10,short_base+2);
    }
}
```

The code shows that the handler being installed is a fast handler (SA_INTERRUPT), doesn't support interrupt sharing (SA_SHIRQ is missing), and doesn't contribute to system entropy (SA_SAMPLE_RANDOM is missing, too). The *outb* call then enables interrupt reporting for the parallel port.

For what it's worth, the i386 and x86_64 architectures define a function for querying the availability of an interrupt line:

```
int can_request_irq(unsigned int irq, unsigned long flags);
```

This function returns a nonzero value if an attempt to allocate the given interrupt succeeds. Note, however, that things can always change between calls to *can_request_irq* and *request_irq*.

The /proc Interface

Whenever a hardware interrupt reaches the processor, an internal counter is incremented, providing a way to check whether the device is working as expected. Reported interrupts are shown in */proc/interrupts*. The following snapshot was taken on a two-processor Pentium system:

```
root@montalcino:/bike/corbet/write/ldd3/src/short# m /proc/interrupts
           CPU0       CPU1
   0:    4848108         34    IO-APIC-edge   timer
   2:          0          0        XT-PIC     cascade
   8:          3          1    IO-APIC-edge   rtc
  10:       4335          1    IO-APIC-level  aic7xxx
  11:       8903          0    IO-APIC-level  uhci_hcd
  12:         49          1    IO-APIC-edge   i8042
 NMI:          0          0
 LOC:    4848187    4848186
 ERR:          0
 MIS:          0
```

The first column is the IRQ number. You can see from the IRQs that are missing that the file shows only interrupts corresponding to installed handlers. For example, the first serial port (which uses interrupt number 4) is not shown, indicating that the modem isn't being used. In fact, even if the modem had been used earlier but wasn't in use at the time of the snapshot, it would not show up in the file; the serial ports are well behaved and release their interrupt handlers when the device is closed.

The */proc/interrupts* display shows how many interrupts have been delivered to each CPU on the system. As you can see from the output, the Linux kernel generally handles interrupts on the first CPU as a way of maximizing cache locality.* The last two columns give information on the programmable interrupt controller that handles the interrupt (and that a driver writer does not need to worry about), and the name(s) of the device(s) that have registered handlers for the interrupt (as specified in the dev_name argument to *request_irq*).

The */proc* tree contains another interrupt-related file, */proc/stat*; sometimes you'll find one file more useful and sometimes you'll prefer the other. */proc/stat* records several low-level statistics about system activity, including (but not limited to) the number of interrupts received since system boot. Each line of *stat* begins with a text string that is the key to the line; the intr mark is what we are looking for. The following (truncated) snapshot was taken shortly after the previous one:

```
intr 5167833 5154006 2 0 2 4907 0 2 68 4 0 4406 9291 50 0 0
```

The first number is the total of all interrupts, while each of the others represents a single IRQ line, starting with interrupt 0. All of the counts are summed across all processors in the system. This snapshot shows that interrupt number 4 has been used 4907 times, even though no handler is *currently* installed. If the driver you're testing acquires and releases the interrupt at each open and close cycle, you may find */proc/stat* more useful than */proc/interrupts*.

Another difference between the two files is that *interrupts* is not architecture dependent (except, perhaps, for a couple of lines at the end), whereas *stat* is; the number of fields depends on the hardware underlying the kernel. The number of available interrupts varies from as few as 15 on the SPARC to as many as 256 on the IA-64 and a few other systems. It's interesting to note that the number of interrupts defined on the x86 is currently 224, not 16 as you may expect; this, as explained in *include/asm-i386/irq.h*, depends on Linux using the architectural limit instead of an implementation-specific limit (such as the 16 interrupt sources of the old-fashioned PC interrupt controller).

The following is a snapshot of */proc/interrupts* taken on an IA-64 system. As you can see, besides different hardware routing of common interrupt sources, the output is very similar to that from the 32-bit system shown earlier.

```
         CPU0      CPU1
 27:      1705     34141  IO-SAPIC-level  qla1280
 40:         0         0          SAPIC  perfmon
 43:       913      6960  IO-SAPIC-level  eth0
 47:     26722       146  IO-SAPIC-level  usb-uhci
 64:         3         6  IO-SAPIC-edge   ide0
 80:         4         2  IO-SAPIC-edge   keyboard
 89:         0         0  IO-SAPIC-edge   PS/2 Mouse
239:   5606341   5606052          SAPIC  timer
```

---

* Although, some larger systems explicitly use interrupt balancing schemes to spread the interrupt load across the system.

```
254:        67575       52815         SAPIC  IPI
NMI:            0           0
ERR:            0
```

Autodetecting the IRQ Number

One of the most challenging problems for a driver at initialization time can be how to determine which IRQ line is going to be used by the device. The driver needs the information in order to correctly install the handler. Even though a programmer could require the user to specify the interrupt number at load time, this is a bad practice, because most of the time the user doesn't know the number, either because he didn't configure the jumpers or because the device is jumperless. Most users want their hardware to "just work" and are not interested in issues like interrupt numbers. So autodetection of the interrupt number is a basic requirement for driver usability.

Sometimes autodetection depends on the knowledge that some devices feature a default behavior that rarely, if ever, changes. In this case, the driver might assume that the default values apply. This is exactly how *short* behaves by default with the parallel port. The implementation is straightforward, as shown by *short* itself:

```
if (short_irq < 0) /* not yet specified: force the default on */
    switch(short_base) {
        case 0x378: short_irq = 7; break;
        case 0x278: short_irq = 2; break;
        case 0x3bc: short_irq = 5; break;
    }
```

The code assigns the interrupt number according to the chosen base I/O address, while allowing the user to override the default at load time with something like:

```
insmod ./short.ko irq=x
```

short_base defaults to 0x378, so short_irq defaults to 7.

Some devices are more advanced in design and simply "announce" which interrupt they're going to use. In this case, the driver retrieves the interrupt number by reading a status byte from one of the device's I/O ports or PCI configuration space. When the target device is one that has the ability to tell the driver which interrupt it is going to use, autodetecting the IRQ number just means probing the device, with no additional work required to probe the interrupt. Most modern hardware works this way, fortunately; for example, the PCI standard solves the problem by requiring peripheral devices to declare what interrupt line(s) they are going to use. The PCI standard is discussed in Chapter 12.

Unfortunately, not every device is programmer friendly, and autodetection might require some probing. The technique is quite simple: the driver tells the device to generate interrupts and watches what happens. If everything goes well, only one interrupt line is activated.

Although probing is simple in theory, the actual implementation might be unclear. We look at two ways to perform the task: calling kernel-defined helper functions and implementing our own version.

Kernel-assisted probing

The Linux kernel offers a low-level facility for probing the interrupt number. It works for only nonshared interrupts, but most hardware that is capable of working in a shared interrupt mode provides better ways of finding the configured interrupt number anyway. The facility consists of two functions, declared in *<linux/interrupt.h>* (which also describes the probing machinery):

unsigned long probe_irq_on(void);
> This function returns a bit mask of unassigned interrupts. The driver must preserve the returned bit mask, and pass it to *probe_irq_off* later. After this call, the driver should arrange for its device to generate at least one interrupt.

int probe_irq_off(unsigned long);
> After the device has requested an interrupt, the driver calls this function, passing as its argument the bit mask previously returned by *probe_irq_on*. *probe_irq_off* returns the number of the interrupt that was issued after "probe_on." If no interrupts occurred, 0 is returned (therefore, IRQ 0 can't be probed for, but no custom device can use it on any of the supported architectures anyway). If more than one interrupt occurred (ambiguous detection), *probe_irq_off* returns a negative value.

The programmer should be careful to enable interrupts on the device *after* the call to *probe_irq_on* and to disable them *before* calling *probe_irq_off*. Additionally, you must remember to service the pending interrupt in your device after *probe_irq_off*.

The *short* module demonstrates how to use such probing. If you load the module with probe=1, the following code is executed to detect your interrupt line, provided pins 9 and 10 of the parallel connector are bound together:

```
int count = 0;
do {
    unsigned long mask;

    mask = probe_irq_on();
    outb_p(0x10,short_base+2); /* enable reporting */
    outb_p(0x00,short_base);   /* clear the bit */
    outb_p(0xFF,short_base);    /* set the bit: interrupt! */
    outb_p(0x00,short_base+2); /* disable reporting */
    udelay(5);  /* give it some time */
    short_irq = probe_irq_off(mask);

    if (short_irq == 0) { /* none of them? */
        printk(KERN_INFO "short: no irq reported by probe\n");
        short_irq = -1;
    }
```

```
    /*
     * if more than one line has been activated, the result is
     * negative. We should service the interrupt (no need for lpt port)
     * and loop over again. Loop at most five times, then give up
     */
} while (short_irq < 0 && count++ < 5);
if (short_irq < 0)
    printk("short: probe failed %i times, giving up\n", count);
```

Note the use of *udelay* before calling *probe_irq_off*. Depending on the speed of your processor, you may have to wait for a brief period to give the interrupt time to actually be delivered.

Probing might be a lengthy task. While this is not true for *short*, probing a frame grabber, for example, requires a delay of at least 20 ms (which is ages for the processor), and other devices might take even longer. Therefore, it's best to probe for the interrupt line only once, at module initialization, independently of whether you install the handler at device open (as you should) or within the initialization function (which is not recommended).

It's interesting to note that on some platforms (PowerPC, M68k, most MIPS implementations, and both SPARC versions) probing is unnecessary, and, therefore, the previous functions are just empty placeholders, sometimes called "useless ISA nonsense." On other platforms, probing is implemented only for ISA devices. Anyway, most architectures define the functions (even if they are empty) to ease porting existing device drivers.

Do-it-yourself probing

Probing can also be implemented in the driver itself without too much trouble. It is a rare driver that must implement its own probing, but seeing how it works gives some insight into the process. To that end, the *short* module performs do-it-yourself detection of the IRQ line if it is loaded with probe=2.

The mechanism is the same as the one described earlier: enable all unused interrupts, then wait and see what happens. We can, however, exploit our knowledge of the device. Often a device can be configured to use one IRQ number from a set of three or four; probing just those IRQs enables us to detect the right one, without having to test for all possible IRQs.

The *short* implementation assumes that 3, 5, 7, and 9 are the only possible IRQ values. These numbers are actually the values that some parallel devices allow you to select.

The following code probes by testing all "possible" interrupts and looking at what happens. The trials array lists the IRQs to try and has 0 as the end marker; the tried array is used to keep track of which handlers have actually been registered by this driver.

```
int trials[ ] = {3, 5, 7, 9, 0};
int tried[ ]  = {0, 0, 0, 0, 0};
int i, count = 0;

/*
 * install the probing handler for all possible lines. Remember
 * the result (0 for success, or -EBUSY) in order to only free
 * what has been acquired
 */
for (i = 0; trials[i]; i++)
    tried[i] = request_irq(trials[i], short_probing,
            SA_INTERRUPT, "short probe", NULL);

do {
    short_irq = 0; /* none got, yet */
    outb_p(0x10,short_base+2); /* enable */
    outb_p(0x00,short_base);
    outb_p(0xFF,short_base); /* toggle the bit */
    outb_p(0x00,short_base+2); /* disable */
    udelay(5);  /* give it some time */

    /* the value has been set by the handler */
    if (short_irq == 0) { /* none of them? */
        printk(KERN_INFO "short: no irq reported by probe\n");
    }
    /*
     * If more than one line has been activated, the result is
     * negative. We should service the interrupt (but the lpt port
     * doesn't need it) and loop over again. Do it at most 5 times
     */
} while (short_irq <=0 && count++ < 5);

/* end of loop, uninstall the handler */
for (i = 0; trials[i]; i++)
    if (tried[i] == 0)
        free_irq(trials[i], NULL);

if (short_irq < 0)
    printk("short: probe failed %i times, giving up\n", count);
```

You might not know in advance what the "possible" IRQ values are. In that case, you need to probe all the free interrupts, instead of limiting yourself to a few trials[ ]. To probe for all interrupts, you have to probe from IRQ 0 to IRQ NR_IRQS-1, where NR_IRQS is defined in *<asm/irq.h>* and is platform dependent.

Now we are missing only the probing handler itself. The handler's role is to update short_irq according to which interrupts are actually received. A 0 value in short_irq means "nothing yet," while a negative value means "ambiguous." These values were chosen to be consistent with *probe_irq_off* and to allow the same code to call either kind of probing within *short.c*.

```
irqreturn_t short_probing(int irq, void *dev_id, struct pt_regs *regs)
{
```

```
        if (short_irq == 0) short_irq = irq;    /* found */
        if (short_irq != irq) short_irq = -irq; /* ambiguous */
        return IRQ_HANDLED;
    }
```

The arguments to the handler are described later. Knowing that irq is the interrupt being handled should be sufficient to understand the function just shown.

Fast and Slow Handlers

Older versions of the Linux kernel took great pains to distinguish between "fast" and "slow" interrupts. Fast interrupts were those that could be handled very quickly, whereas handling slow interrupts took significantly longer. Slow interrupts could be sufficiently demanding of the processor, and it was worthwhile to reenable interrupts while they were being handled. Otherwise, tasks requiring quick attention could be delayed for too long.

In modern kernels, most of the differences between fast and slow interrupts have disappeared. There remains only one: fast interrupts (those that were requested with the SA_INTERRUPT flag) are executed with all other interrupts disabled on the current processor. Note that other processors can still handle interrupts, although you will never see two processors handling the same IRQ at the same time.

So, which type of interrupt should your driver use? On modern systems, SA_INTERRUPT is intended only for use in a few, specific situations such as timer interrupts. Unless you have a strong reason to run your interrupt handler with other interrupts disabled, you should not use SA_INTERRUPT.

This description should satisfy most readers, although someone with a taste for hardware and some experience with her computer might be interested in going deeper. If you don't care about the internal details, you can skip to the next section.

The internals of interrupt handling on the x86

This description has been extrapolated from *arch/i386/kernel/irq.c*, *arch/i386/kernel/apic.c*, *arch/i386/kernel/entry.S*, *arch/i386/kernel/i8259.c*, and *include/asm-i386/hw_irq.h* as they appear in the 2.6 kernels; although the general concepts remain the same, the hardware details differ on other platforms.

The lowest level of interrupt handling can be found in *entry.S*, an assembly-language file that handles much of the machine-level work. By way of a bit of assembler trickery and some macros, a bit of code is assigned to every possible interrupt. In each case, the code pushes the interrupt number on the stack and jumps to a common segment, which calls *do_IRQ*, defined in *irq.c*.

The first thing *do_IRQ* does is to acknowledge the interrupt so that the interrupt controller can go on to other things. It then obtains a spinlock for the given IRQ number, thus preventing any other CPU from handling this IRQ. It clears a couple of status bits (including one called IRQ_WAITING that we'll look at shortly) and then looks up the handler(s) for this particular IRQ. If there is no handler, there's nothing to do; the spinlock is released, any pending software interrupts are handled, and *do_IRQ* returns.

Usually, however, if a device is interrupting, there is at least one handler registered for its IRQ as well. The function *handle_IRQ_event* is called to actually invoke the handlers. If the handler is of the slow variety (SA_INTERRUPT is not set), interrupts are reenabled in the hardware, and the handler is invoked. Then it's just a matter of cleaning up, running software interrupts, and getting back to regular work. The "regular work" may well have changed as a result of an interrupt (the handler could *wake_up* a process, for example), so the last thing that happens on return from an interrupt is a possible rescheduling of the processor.

Probing for IRQs is done by setting the IRQ_WAITING status bit for each IRQ that currently lacks a handler. When the interrupt happens, *do_IRQ* clears that bit and then returns, because no handler is registered. *probe_irq_off*, when called by a driver, needs to search for only the IRQ that no longer has IRQ_WAITING set.

Implementing a Handler

So far, we've learned to register an interrupt handler but not to write one. Actually, there's nothing unusual about a handler—it's ordinary C code.

The only peculiarity is that a handler runs at interrupt time and, therefore, suffers some restrictions on what it can do. These restrictions are the same as those we saw with kernel timers. A handler can't transfer data to or from user space, because it doesn't execute in the context of a process. Handlers also cannot do anything that would sleep, such as calling *wait_event*, allocating memory with anything other than GFP_ATOMIC, or locking a semaphore. Finally, handlers cannot call *schedule*.

The role of an interrupt handler is to give feedback to its device about interrupt reception and to read or write data according to the meaning of the interrupt being serviced. The first step usually consists of clearing a bit on the interface board; most hardware devices won't generate other interrupts until their "interrupt-pending" bit has been cleared. Depending on how your hardware works, this step may need to be performed last instead of first; there is no catch-all rule here. Some devices don't require this step, because they don't have an "interrupt-pending" bit; such devices are a minority, although the parallel port is one of them. For that reason, *short* does not have to clear such a bit.

A typical task for an interrupt handler is awakening processes sleeping on the device if the interrupt signals the event they're waiting for, such as the arrival of new data.

To stick with the frame grabber example, a process could acquire a sequence of images by continuously reading the device; the *read* call blocks before reading each frame, while the interrupt handler awakens the process as soon as each new frame arrives. This assumes that the grabber interrupts the processor to signal successful arrival of each new frame.

The programmer should be careful to write a routine that executes in a minimum amount of time, independent of its being a fast or slow handler. If a long computation needs to be performed, the best approach is to use a tasklet or workqueue to schedule computation at a safer time (we'll look at how work can be deferred in this manner in the section "Top and Bottom Halves.")

Our sample code in *short* responds to the interrupt by calling *do_gettimeofday* and printing the current time into a page-sized circular buffer. It then awakens any reading process, because there is now data available to be read.

```
irqreturn_t short_interrupt(int irq, void *dev_id, struct pt_regs *regs)
{
    struct timeval tv;
    int written;

    do_gettimeofday(&tv);

        /* Write a 16 byte record. Assume PAGE_SIZE is a multiple of 16 */
    written = sprintf((char *)short_head,"%08u.%06u\n",
            (int)(tv.tv_sec % 100000000), (int)(tv.tv_usec));
    BUG_ON(written != 16);
    short_incr_bp(&short_head, written);
    wake_up_interruptible(&short_queue); /* awake any reading process */
    return IRQ_HANDLED;
}
```

This code, though simple, represents the typical job of an interrupt handler. It, in turn, calls *short_incr_bp*, which is defined as follows:

```
static inline void short_incr_bp(volatile unsigned long *index, int delta)
{
    unsigned long new = *index + delta;
    barrier();  /* Don't optimize these two together */
    *index = (new >= (short_buffer + PAGE_SIZE)) ? short_buffer : new;
}
```

This function has been carefully written to wrap a pointer into the circular buffer without ever exposing an incorrect value. The *barrier* call is there to block compiler optimizations across the other two lines of the function. Without the barrier, the compiler might decide to optimize out the new variable and assign directly to *index. That optimization could expose an incorrect value of the index for a brief period in the case where it wraps. By taking care to prevent in inconsistent value from ever being visible to other threads, we can manipulate the circular buffer pointers safely without locks.

The device file used to read the buffer being filled at interrupt time is */dev/shortint*. This device special file, together with */dev/shortprint*, wasn't introduced in

Chapter 9, because its use is specific to interrupt handling. The internals of */dev/shortint* are specifically tailored for interrupt generation and reporting. Writing to the device generates one interrupt every other byte; reading the device gives the time when each interrupt was reported.

If you connect together pins 9 and 10 of the parallel connector, you can generate interrupts by raising the high bit of the parallel data byte. This can be accomplished by writing binary data to */dev/short0* or by writing anything to */dev/shortint*.[*]

The following code implements *read* and *write* for */dev/shortint*:

```
ssize_t short_i_read (struct file *filp, char __user *buf, size_t count,
    loff_t *f_pos)
{
    int count0;
    DEFINE_WAIT(wait);

    while (short_head == short_tail) {
        prepare_to_wait(&short_queue, &wait, TASK_INTERRUPTIBLE);
        if (short_head == short_tail)
            schedule( );
        finish_wait(&short_queue, &wait);
        if (signal_pending (current))  /* a signal arrived */
            return -ERESTARTSYS; /* tell the fs layer to handle it */
    }
    /* count0 is the number of readable data bytes */
    count0 = short_head - short_tail;
    if (count0 < 0) /* wrapped */
        count0 = short_buffer + PAGE_SIZE - short_tail;
    if (count0 < count) count = count0;

    if (copy_to_user(buf, (char *)short_tail, count))
        return -EFAULT;
    short_incr_bp (&short_tail, count);
    return count;
}

ssize_t short_i_write (struct file *filp, const char __user *buf, size_t count,
        loff_t *f_pos)
{
    int written = 0, odd = *f_pos & 1;
    unsigned long port = short_base; /* output to the parallel data latch */
    void *address = (void *) short_base;

    if (use_mem) {
        while (written < count)
            iowrite8(0xff * ((++written + odd) & 1), address);
    } else {
```

---

[*] The *shortint* device accomplishes its task by alternately writing 0x00 and 0xff to the parallel port.

```
        while (written < count)
            outb(0xff * ((++written + odd) & 1), port);
    }

    *f_pos += count;
    return written;
}
```

The other device special file, */dev/shortprint*, uses the parallel port to drive a printer; you can use it if you want to avoid connecting pins 9 and 10 of a D-25 connector. The *write* implementation of *shortprint* uses a circular buffer to store data to be printed, while the *read* implementation is the one just shown (so you can read the time your printer takes to eat each character).

In order to support printer operation, the interrupt handler has been slightly modified from the one just shown, adding the ability to send the next data byte to the printer if there is more data to transfer.

Handler Arguments and Return Value

Though *short* ignores them, three arguments are passed to an interrupt handler: irq, dev_id, and regs. Let's look at the role of each.

The interrupt number (int irq) is useful as information you may print in your log messages, if any. The second argument, void *dev_id, is a sort of client data; a void * argument is passed to *request_irq*, and this same pointer is then passed back as an argument to the handler when the interrupt happens. You usually pass a pointer to your device data structure in dev_id, so a driver that manages several instances of the same device doesn't need any extra code in the interrupt handler to find out which device is in charge of the current interrupt event.

Typical use of the argument in an interrupt handler is as follows:

```
static irqreturn_t sample_interrupt(int irq, void *dev_id, struct pt_regs
                        *regs)
{
    struct sample_dev *dev = dev_id;

    /* now `dev' points to the right hardware item */
    /* .... */
}
```

The typical *open* code associated with this handler looks like this:

```
static void sample_open(struct inode *inode, struct file *filp)
{
    struct sample_dev *dev = hwinfo + MINOR(inode->i_rdev);
    request_irq(dev->irq, sample_interrupt,
                0 /* flags */, "sample", dev /* dev_id */);
    /*....*/
    return 0;
}
```

The last argument, struct pt_regs *regs, is rarely used. It holds a snapshot of the processor's context before the processor entered interrupt code. The registers can be used for monitoring and debugging; they are not normally needed for regular device driver tasks.

Interrupt handlers should return a value indicating whether there was actually an interrupt to handle. If the handler found that its device did, indeed, need attention, it should return IRQ_HANDLED; otherwise the return value should be IRQ_NONE. You can also generate the return value with this macro:

```
IRQ_RETVAL(handled)
```

where handled is nonzero if you were able to handle the interrupt. The return value is used by the kernel to detect and suppress spurious interrupts. If your device gives you no way to tell whether it really interrupted, you should return IRQ_HANDLED.

Enabling and Disabling Interrupts

There are times when a device driver must block the delivery of interrupts for a (hopefully short) period of time (we saw one such situation in the section "Spin-locks" in Chapter 5). Often, interrupts must be blocked while holding a spinlock to avoid deadlocking the system. There are ways of disabling interrupts that do not involve spinlocks. But before we discuss them, note that disabling interrupts should be a relatively rare activity, even in device drivers, and this technique should never be used as a mutual exclusion mechanism within a driver.

Disabling a single interrupt

Sometimes (but rarely!) a driver needs to disable interrupt delivery for a specific interrupt line. The kernel offers three functions for this purpose, all declared in *<asm/irq.h>*. These functions are part of the kernel API, so we describe them, but their use is discouraged in most drivers. Among other things, you cannot disable shared interrupt lines, and, on modern systems, shared interrupts are the norm. That said, here they are:

```
void disable_irq(int irq);
void disable_irq_nosync(int irq);
void enable_irq(int irq);
```

Calling any of these functions may update the mask for the specified irq in the programmable interrupt controller (PIC), thus disabling or enabling the specified IRQ across all processors. Calls to these functions can be nested—if *disable_irq* is called twice in succession, two *enable_irq* calls are required before the IRQ is truly reenabled. It is possible to call these functions from an interrupt handler, but enabling your own IRQ while handling it is not usually good practice.

disable_irq not only disables the given interrupt but also waits for a currently executing interrupt handler, if any, to complete. Be aware that if the thread calling *disable_irq* holds any resources (such as spinlocks) that the interrupt handler needs, the system can deadlock. *disable_irq_nosync* differs from *disable_irq* in that it returns immediately. Thus, using *disable_irq_nosync* is a little faster but may leave your driver open to race conditions.

But why disable an interrupt? Sticking to the parallel port, let's look at the *plip* network interface. A *plip* device uses the bare-bones parallel port to transfer data. Since only five bits can be read from the parallel connector, they are interpreted as four data bits and a clock/handshake signal. When the first four bits of a packet are transmitted by the initiator (the interface sending the packet), the clock line is raised, causing the receiving interface to interrupt the processor. The *plip* handler is then invoked to deal with newly arrived data.

After the device has been alerted, the data transfer proceeds, using the handshake line to clock new data to the receiving interface (this might not be the best implementation, but it is necessary for compatibility with other packet drivers using the parallel port). Performance would be unbearable if the receiving interface had to handle two interrupts for every byte received. Therefore, the driver disables the interrupt during the reception of the packet; instead, a poll-and-delay loop is used to bring in the data.

Similarly, because the handshake line from the receiver to the transmitter is used to acknowledge data reception, the transmitting interface disables its IRQ line during packet transmission.

Disabling all interrupts

What if you need to disable *all* interrupts? In the 2.6 kernel, it is possible to turn off all interrupt handling on the current processor with either of the following two functions (which are defined in *<asm/system.h>*):

```
void local_irq_save(unsigned long flags);
void local_irq_disable(void);
```

A call to *local_irq_save* disables interrupt delivery on the current processor after saving the current interrupt state into flags. Note that flags is passed directly, not by pointer. *local_irq_disable* shuts off local interrupt delivery without saving the state; you should use this version only if you know that interrupts have not already been disabled elsewhere.

Turning interrupts back on is accomplished with:

```
void local_irq_restore(unsigned long flags);
void local_irq_enable(void);
```

The first version restores that state which was stored into flags by *local_irq_save*, while *local_irq_enable* enables interrupts unconditionally. Unlike *disable_irq*, *local_irq_disable* does not keep track of multiple calls. If more than one function in the call chain might need to disable interrupts, *local_irq_save* should be used.

In the 2.6 kernel, there is no way to disable all interrupts globally across the entire system. The kernel developers have decided that the cost of shutting off all interrupts is too high and that there is no need for that capability in any case. If you are working with an older driver that makes calls to functions such as *cli* and *sti*, you need to update it to use proper locking before it will work under 2.6.

Top and Bottom Halves

One of the main problems with interrupt handling is how to perform lengthy tasks within a handler. Often a substantial amount of work must be done in response to a device interrupt, but interrupt handlers need to finish up quickly and not keep interrupts blocked for long. These two needs (work and speed) conflict with each other, leaving the driver writer in a bit of a bind.

Linux (along with many other systems) resolves this problem by splitting the interrupt handler into two halves. The so-called *top half* is the routine that actually responds to the interrupt—the one you register with *request_irq*. The *bottom half* is a routine that is scheduled by the top half to be executed later, at a safer time. The big difference between the top-half handler and the bottom half is that all interrupts are enabled during execution of the bottom half—that's why it runs at a safer time. In the typical scenario, the top half saves device data to a device-specific buffer, schedules its bottom half, and exits: this operation is very fast. The bottom half then performs whatever other work is required, such as awakening processes, starting up another I/O operation, and so on. This setup permits the top half to service a new interrupt while the bottom half is still working.

Almost every serious interrupt handler is split this way. For instance, when a network interface reports the arrival of a new packet, the handler just retrieves the data and pushes it up to the protocol layer; actual processing of the packet is performed in a bottom half.

The Linux kernel has two different mechanisms that may be used to implement bottom-half processing, both of which were introduced in Chapter 7. Tasklets are often the preferred mechanism for bottom-half processing; they are very fast, but all tasklet code must be atomic. The alternative to tasklets is workqueues, which may have a higher latency but that are allowed to sleep.

The following discussion works, once again, with the *short* driver. When loaded with a module option, *short* can be told to do interrupt processing in a top/bottom-half mode with either a tasklet or workqueue handler. In this case, the top half executes quickly; it simply remembers the current time and schedules the bottom half processing. The bottom half is then charged with encoding this time and awakening any user processes that may be waiting for data.

Tasklets

Remember that tasklets are a special function that may be scheduled to run, in software interrupt context, at a system-determined safe time. They may be scheduled to run multiple times, but tasklet scheduling is not cumulative; the tasklet runs only once, even if it is requested repeatedly before it is launched. No tasklet ever runs in parallel with itself, since they run only once, but tasklets can run in parallel with other tasklets on SMP systems. Thus, if your driver has multiple tasklets, they must employ some sort of locking to avoid conflicting with each other.

Tasklets are also guaranteed to run on the same CPU as the function that first schedules them. Therefore, an interrupt handler can be secure that a tasklet does not begin executing before the handler has completed. However, another interrupt can certainly be delivered while the tasklet is running, so locking between the tasklet and the interrupt handler may still be required.

Tasklets must be declared with the DECLARE_TASKLET macro:

```
DECLARE_TASKLET(name, function, data);
```

name is the name to be given to the tasklet, *function* is the function that is called to execute the tasklet (it takes one unsigned long argument and returns void), and data is an unsigned long value to be passed to the *tasklet* function.

The *short* driver declares its tasklet as follows:

```
void short_do_tasklet(unsigned long);
DECLARE_TASKLET(short_tasklet, short_do_tasklet, 0);
```

The function *tasklet_schedule* is used to schedule a tasklet for running. If *short* is loaded with tasklet=1, it installs a different interrupt handler that saves data and schedules the tasklet as follows:

```
irqreturn_t short_tl_interrupt(int irq, void *dev_id, struct pt_regs *regs)
{
    do_gettimeofday((struct timeval *) tv_head); /* cast to stop 'volatile' warning
*/
    short_incr_tv(&tv_head);
    tasklet_schedule(&short_tasklet);
    short_wq_count++; /* record that an interrupt arrived */
    return IRQ_HANDLED;
}
```

The actual tasklet routine, *short_do_tasklet*, will be executed shortly (so to speak) at the system's convenience. As mentioned earlier, this routine performs the bulk of the work of handling the interrupt; it looks like this:

```
void short_do_tasklet (unsigned long unused)
{
    int savecount = short_wq_count, written;
    short_wq_count = 0; /* we have already been removed from the queue */
    /*
     * The bottom half reads the tv array, filled by the top half,
```

```
 * and prints it to the circular text buffer, which is then consumed
 * by reading processes
 */

/* First write the number of interrupts that occurred before this bh */
written = sprintf((char *)short_head,"bh after %6i\n",savecount);
short_incr_bp(&short_head, written);

/*
 * Then, write the time values. Write exactly 16 bytes at a time,
 * so it aligns with PAGE_SIZE
 */

do {
    written = sprintf((char *)short_head,"%08u.%06u\n",
            (int)(tv_tail->tv_sec % 100000000),
            (int)(tv_tail->tv_usec));
    short_incr_bp(&short_head, written);
    short_incr_tv(&tv_tail);
} while (tv_tail != tv_head);

wake_up_interruptible(&short_queue); /* awake any reading process */
}
```

Among other things, this tasklet makes a note of how many interrupts have arrived since it was last called. A device such as *short* can generate a great many interrupts in a brief period, so it is not uncommon for several to arrive before the bottom half is executed. Drivers must always be prepared for this possibility and must be able to determine how much work there is to perform from the information left by the top half.

Workqueues

Recall that workqueues invoke a function at some future time in the context of a special worker process. Since the *workqueue* function runs in process context, it can sleep if need be. You cannot, however, copy data into user space from a workqueue, unless you use the advanced techniques we demonstrate in Chapter 15; the worker process does not have access to any other process's address space.

The *short* driver, if loaded with the wq option set to a nonzero value, uses a workqueue for its bottom-half processing. It uses the system default workqueue, so there is no special setup code required; if your driver has special latency requirements (or might sleep for a long time in the *workqueue* function), you may want to create your own, dedicated workqueue. We do need a work_struct structure, which is declared and initialized with the following:

```
static struct work_struct short_wq;

    /* this line is in short_init( ) */
    INIT_WORK(&short_wq, (void (*)(void *)) short_do_tasklet, NULL);
```

Our worker function is *short_do_tasklet*, which we have already seen in the previous section.

When working with a workqueue, *short* establishes yet another interrupt handler that looks like this:

```
irqreturn_t short_wq_interrupt(int irq, void *dev_id, struct pt_regs *regs)
{
    /* Grab the current time information. */
    do_gettimeofday((struct timeval *) tv_head);
    short_incr_tv(&tv_head);

    /* Queue the bh. Don't worry about multiple enqueueing */
    schedule_work(&short_wq);

    short_wq_count++; /* record that an interrupt arrived */
    return IRQ_HANDLED;
}
```

As you can see, the interrupt handler looks very much like the tasklet version, with the exception that it calls *schedule_work* to arrange the bottom-half processing.

Interrupt Sharing

The notion of an IRQ conflict is almost synonymous with the PC architecture. In the past, IRQ lines on the PC have not been able to serve more than one device, and there have never been enough of them. As a result, frustrated users have often spent much time with their computer case open, trying to find a way to make all of their peripherals play well together.

Modern hardware, of course, has been designed to allow the sharing of interrupts; the PCI bus requires it. Therefore, the Linux kernel supports interrupt sharing on all buses, even those (such as the ISA bus) where sharing has traditionally not been supported. Device drivers for the 2.6 kernel should be written to work with shared interrupts if the target hardware can support that mode of operation. Fortunately, working with shared interrupts is easy, most of the time.

Installing a Shared Handler

Shared interrupts are installed through *request_irq* just like nonshared ones, but there are two differences:

- The SA_SHIRQ bit must be specified in the flags argument when requesting the interrupt.

- The dev_id argument *must* be unique. Any pointer into the module's address space will do, but dev_id definitely cannot be set to NULL.

The kernel keeps a list of shared handlers associated with the interrupt, and dev_id can be thought of as the signature that differentiates between them. If two drivers were to register NULL as their signature on the same interrupt, things might get mixed up at unload time, causing the kernel to oops when an interrupt arrived. For this reason, modern kernels complain loudly if passed a NULL dev_id when registering shared interrupts. When a shared interrupt is requested, *request_irq* succeeds if one of the following is true:

- The interrupt line is free.
- All handlers already registered for that line have also specified that the IRQ is to be shared.

Whenever two or more drivers are sharing an interrupt line and the hardware interrupts the processor on that line, the kernel invokes every handler registered for that interrupt, passing each its own dev_id. Therefore, a shared handler must be able to recognize its own interrupts and should quickly exit when its own device has not interrupted. Be sure to return IRQ_NONE whenever your handler is called and finds that the device is not interrupting.

If you need to probe for your device before requesting the IRQ line, the kernel can't help you. No probing function is available for shared handlers. The standard probing mechanism works if the line being used is free, but if the line is already held by another driver with sharing capabilities, the probe fails, even if your driver would have worked perfectly. Fortunately, most hardware designed for interrupt sharing is also able to tell the processor which interrupt it is using, thus eliminating the need for explicit probing.

Releasing the handler is performed in the normal way, using *free_irq*. Here the dev_id argument is used to select the correct handler to release from the list of shared handlers for the interrupt. That's why the dev_id pointer must be unique.

A driver using a shared handler needs to be careful about one more thing: it can't play with *enable_irq* or *disable_irq*. If it does, things might go haywire for other devices sharing the line; disabling another device's interrupts for even a short time may create latencies that are problematic for that device and it's user. Generally, the programmer must remember that his driver doesn't own the IRQ, and its behavior should be more "social" than is necessary if one owns the interrupt line.

Running the Handler

As suggested earlier, when the kernel receives an interrupt, all the registered handlers are invoked. A shared handler must be able to distinguish between interrupts that it needs to handle and interrupts generated by other devices.

Loading *short* with the option *shared=1* installs the following handler instead of the default:

```
irqreturn_t short_sh_interrupt(int irq, void *dev_id, struct pt_regs *regs)
{
    int value, written;
    struct timeval tv;

    /* If it wasn't short, return immediately */
    value = inb(short_base);
    if (!(value & 0x80))
        return IRQ_NONE;

    /* clear the interrupting bit */
    outb(value & 0x7F, short_base);

    /* the rest is unchanged */

    do_gettimeofday(&tv);
    written = sprintf((char *)short_head,"%08u.%06u\n",
            (int)(tv.tv_sec % 100000000), (int)(tv.tv_usec));
    short_incr_bp(&short_head, written);
    wake_up_interruptible(&short_queue); /* awake any reading process */
    return IRQ_HANDLED;
}
```

An explanation is due here. Since the parallel port has no "interrupt-pending" bit to check, the handler uses the ACK bit for this purpose. If the bit is high, the interrupt being reported is for *short*, and the handler clears the bit.

The handler resets the bit by zeroing the high bit of the parallel interface's data port—*short* assumes that pins 9 and 10 are connected together. If one of the other devices sharing the IRQ with *short* generates an interrupt, *short* sees that its own line is still inactive and does nothing.

A full-featured driver probably splits the work into top and bottom halves, of course, but that's easy to add and does not have any impact on the code that implements sharing. A real driver would also likely use the dev_id argument to determine which, of possibly many, devices might be interrupting.

Note that if you are using a printer (instead of the jumper wire) to test interrupt management with *short*, this shared handler won't work as advertised, because the printer protocol doesn't allow for sharing, and the driver can't know whether the interrupt was from the printer.

The /proc Interface and Shared Interrupts

Installing shared handlers in the system doesn't affect */proc/stat*, which doesn't even know about handlers. However, */proc/interrupts* changes slightly.

All the handlers installed for the same interrupt number appear on the same line of
/proc/interrupts. The following output (from an x86_64 system) shows how shared
interrupt handlers are displayed:

```
               CPU0
   0:     892335412        XT-PIC  timer
   1:        453971        XT-PIC  i8042
   2:             0        XT-PIC  cascade
   5:             0        XT-PIC  libata, ehci_hcd
   8:             0        XT-PIC  rtc
   9:             0        XT-PIC  acpi
  10:      11365067        XT-PIC  ide2, uhci_hcd, uhci_hcd, SysKonnect SK-98xx, EMU10K1
  11:       4391962        XT-PIC  uhci_hcd, uhci_hcd
  12:           224        XT-PIC  i8042
  14:       2787721        XT-PIC  ide0
  15:        203048        XT-PIC  ide1
 NMI:         41234
 LOC:     892193503
 ERR:           102
 MIS:             0
```

This system has several shared interrupt lines. IRQ 5 is used for the serial ATA and
IEEE 1394 controllers; IRQ 10 has several devices, including an IDE controller, two
USB controllers, an Ethernet interface, and a sound card; and IRQ 11 also is used by
two USB controllers.

Interrupt-Driven I/O

Whenever a data transfer to or from the managed hardware might be delayed for any
reason, the driver writer should implement buffering. Data buffers help to detach
data transmission and reception from the *write* and *read* system calls, and overall system performance benefits.

A good buffering mechanism leads to *interrupt-driven I/O*, in which an input buffer is
filled at interrupt time and is emptied by processes that read the device; an output
buffer is filled by processes that write to the device and is emptied at interrupt time.
An example of interrupt-driven output is the implementation of */dev/shortprint*.

For interrupt-driven data transfer to happen successfully, the hardware should be
able to generate interrupts with the following semantics:

- For input, the device interrupts the processor when new data has arrived and is
  ready to be retrieved by the system processor. The actual actions to perform
  depend on whether the device uses I/O ports, memory mapping, or DMA.

- For output, the device delivers an interrupt either when it is ready to accept new
  data or to acknowledge a successful data transfer. Memory-mapped and DMA-
  capable devices usually generate interrupts to tell the system they are done with
  the buffer.

The timing relationships between a *read* or *write* and the actual arrival of data were introduced in the section "Blocking and Nonblocking Operations" in Chapter 6.

A Write-Buffering Example

We have mentioned the *shortprint* driver a couple of times; now it is time to actually take a look. This module implements a very simple, output-oriented driver for the parallel port; it is sufficient, however, to enable the printing of files. If you chose to test this driver out, however, remember that you must pass the printer a file in a format it understands; not all printers respond well when given a stream of arbitrary data.

The *shortprint* driver maintains a one-page circular output buffer. When a user-space process writes data to the device, that data is fed into the buffer, but the *write* method does not actually perform any I/O. Instead, the core of *shortp_write* looks like this:

```
while (written < count) {
    /* Hang out until some buffer space is available. */
    space = shortp_out_space( );
    if (space <= 0) {
        if (wait_event_interruptible(shortp_out_queue,
                (space = shortp_out_space( )) > 0))
            goto out;
    }

    /* Move data into the buffer. */
    if ((space + written) > count)
        space = count - written;
    if (copy_from_user((char *) shortp_out_head, buf, space)) {
        up(&shortp_out_sem);
        return -EFAULT;
    }
    shortp_incr_out_bp(&shortp_out_head, space);
    buf += space;
    written += space;

    /* If no output is active, make it active. */
    spin_lock_irqsave(&shortp_out_lock, flags);
    if (! shortp_output_active)
        shortp_start_output( );
    spin_unlock_irqrestore(&shortp_out_lock, flags);
}

out:
    *f_pos += written;
```

A semaphore (shortp_out_sem) controls access to the circular buffer; *shortp_write* obtains that semaphore just prior to the code fragment above. While holding the semaphore, it attempts to feed data into the circular buffer. The function *shortp_out_space* returns the amount of contiguous space available (so there is no need to worry about buffer wraps); if that amount is 0, the driver waits until some space is freed. It then copies as much data as it can into the buffer.

Once there is data to output, *shortp_write* must ensure that the data is written to the device. The actual writing is done by way of a *workqueue* function; *shortp_write* must kick that function off if it is not already running. After obtaining a separate spinlock that controls access to variables used on the consumer side of the output buffer (including shortp_output_active), it calls *shortp_start_output* if need be. Then it's just a matter of noting how much data was "written" to the buffer and returning.

The function that starts the output process looks like the following:

```
static void shortp_start_output(void)
{
    if (shortp_output_active) /* Should never happen */
        return;

    /* Set up our 'missed interrupt' timer */
    shortp_output_active = 1;
    shortp_timer.expires = jiffies + TIMEOUT;
    add_timer(&shortp_timer);

    /*  And get the process going. */
    queue_work(shortp_workqueue, &shortp_work);
}
```

The reality of dealing with hardware is that you can, occasionally, lose an interrupt from the device. When this happens, you really do not want your driver to stop forevermore until the system is rebooted; that is not a user-friendly way of doing things. It is far better to realize that an interrupt has been missed, pick up the pieces, and go on. To that end, *shortprint* sets a kernel timer whenever it outputs data to the device. If the timer expires, we may have missed an interrupt. We look at the timer function shortly, but, for the moment, let's stick with the main output functionality. That is implemented in our *workqueue* function, which, as you can see above, is scheduled here. The core of that function looks like the following:

```
spin_lock_irqsave(&shortp_out_lock, flags);

/* Have we written everything? */
if (shortp_out_head == shortp_out_tail) { /* empty */
    shortp_output_active = 0;
    wake_up_interruptible(&shortp_empty_queue);
    del_timer(&shortp_timer);
}
/* Nope, write another byte */
else
    shortp_do_write( );

/* If somebody's waiting, maybe wake them up. */
if (((PAGE_SIZE + shortp_out_tail - shortp_out_head) % PAGE_SIZE) > SP_MIN_SPACE)
{
```

```
        wake_up_interruptible(&shortp_out_queue);
    }
    spin_unlock_irqrestore(&shortp_out_lock, flags);
```

Since we are dealing with the output side's shared variables, we must obtain the spinlock. Then we look to see whether there is any more data to send out; if not, we note that output is no longer active, delete the timer, and wake up anybody who might have been waiting for the queue to become completely empty (this sort of wait is done when the device is closed). If, instead, there remains data to write, we call *shortp_do_write* to actually send a byte to the hardware.

Then, since we may have freed space in the output buffer, we consider waking up any processes waiting to add more data to that buffer. We do not perform that wakeup unconditionally, however; instead, we wait until a minimum amount of space is available. There is no point in awakening a writer every time we take one byte out of the buffer; the cost of awakening the process, scheduling it to run, and putting it back to sleep is too high for that. Instead, we should wait until that process is able to move a substantial amount of data into the buffer at once. This technique is common in buffering, interrupt-driven drivers.

For completeness, here is the code that actually writes the data to the port:

```
static void shortp_do_write(void)
{
    unsigned char cr = inb(shortp_base + SP_CONTROL);

    /* Something happened; reset the timer */
    mod_timer(&shortp_timer, jiffies + TIMEOUT);

    /* Strobe a byte out to the device */
    outb_p(*shortp_out_tail, shortp_base+SP_DATA);
    shortp_incr_out_bp(&shortp_out_tail, 1);
    if (shortp_delay)
        udelay(shortp_delay);
    outb_p(cr | SP_CR_STROBE, shortp_base+SP_CONTROL);
    if (shortp_delay)
        udelay(shortp_delay);
    outb_p(cr & ~SP_CR_STROBE, shortp_base+SP_CONTROL);
}
```

Here, we reset the timer to reflect the fact that we have made some progress, strobe the byte out to the device, and update the circular buffer pointer.

The *workqueue* function does not resubmit itself directly, so only a single byte will be written to the device. At some point, the printer will, in its slow way, consume the byte and become ready for the next one; it will then interrupt the processor. The interrupt handler used in *shortprint* is short and simple:

```
static irqreturn_t shortp_interrupt(int irq, void *dev_id, struct pt_regs *regs)
{
    if (! shortp_output_active)
        return IRQ_NONE;
```

```
    /* Remember the time, and farm off the rest to the workqueue function */
    do_gettimeofday(&shortp_tv);
    queue_work(shortp_workqueue, &shortp_work);
    return IRQ_HANDLED;
}
```

Since the parallel port does not require an explicit interrupt acknowledgment, all the interrupt handler really needs to do is to tell the kernel to run the *workqueue* function again.

What if the interrupt never comes? The driver code that we have seen thus far would simply come to a halt. To keep that from happening, we set a timer back a few pages ago. The function that is executed when that timer expires is:

```
static void shortp_timeout(unsigned long unused)
{
    unsigned long flags;
    unsigned char status;

    if (! shortp_output_active)
        return;
    spin_lock_irqsave(&shortp_out_lock, flags);
    status = inb(shortp_base + SP_STATUS);

    /* If the printer is still busy we just reset the timer */
    if ((status & SP_SR_BUSY) == 0 || (status & SP_SR_ACK)) {
        shortp_timer.expires = jiffies + TIMEOUT;
        add_timer(&shortp_timer);
        spin_unlock_irqrestore(&shortp_out_lock, flags);
        return;
    }

    /* Otherwise we must have dropped an interrupt. */
    spin_unlock_irqrestore(&shortp_out_lock, flags);
    shortp_interrupt(shortp_irq, NULL, NULL);
}
```

If no output is supposed to be active, the timer function simply returns; this keeps the timer from resubmitting itself when things are being shut down. Then, after taking the lock, we query the status of the port; if it claims to be busy, it simply hasn't gotten around to interrupting us yet, so we reset the timer and return. Printers can, at times, take a very long time to make themselves ready; consider the printer that runs out of paper while everybody is gone over a long weekend. In such situations, there is nothing to do other than to wait patiently until something changes.

If, however, the printer claims to be ready, we must have missed its interrupt. In that case, we simply invoke our interrupt handler manually to get the output process moving again.

The *shortprint* driver does not support reading from the port; instead, it behaves like *shortint* and returns interrupt timing information. The implementation of an interrupt-driven *read* method would be very similar to what we have seen, however. Data from the device would be read into a driver buffer; it would be copied out to user space only when a significant amount of data has accumulated in the buffer, the full *read* request has been satisfied, or some sort of timeout occurs.

Quick Reference

These symbols related to interrupt management were introduced in this chapter:

```
#include <linux/interrupt.h>
int request_irq(unsigned int irq, irqreturn_t (*handler)( ), unsigned long
    flags, const char *dev_name, void *dev_id);
void free_irq(unsigned int irq, void *dev_id);
```
> Calls that register and unregister an interrupt handler.

```
#include <linux/irq.h.h>
int can_request_irq(unsigned int irq, unsigned long flags);
```
> This function, available on the i386 and x86_64 architectures, returns a nonzero value if an attempt to allocate the given interrupt line succeeds.

```
#include <asm/signal.h>
SA_INTERRUPT
SA_SHIRQ
SA_SAMPLE_RANDOM
```
> Flags for *request_irq*. SA_INTERRUPT requests installation of a fast handler (as opposed to a slow one). SA_SHIRQ installs a shared handler, and the third flag asserts that interrupt timestamps can be used to generate system entropy.

```
/proc/interrupts
/proc/stat
```
> Filesystem nodes that report information about hardware interrupts and installed handlers.

```
unsigned long probe_irq_on(void);
int probe_irq_off(unsigned long);
```
> Functions used by the driver when it has to probe to determine which interrupt line is being used by a device. The result of *probe_irq_on* must be passed back to *probe_irq_off* after the interrupt has been generated. The return value of *probe_irq_off* is the detected interrupt number.

```
IRQ_NONE
IRQ_HANDLED
IRQ_RETVAL(int x)
```
> The possible return values from an interrupt handler, indicating whether an actual interrupt from the device was present.

```
void disable_irq(int irq);
void disable_irq_nosync(int irq);
void enable_irq(int irq);
```
A driver can enable and disable interrupt reporting. If the hardware tries to generate an interrupt while interrupts are disabled, the interrupt is lost forever. A driver using a shared handler must not use these functions.

```
void local_irq_save(unsigned long flags);
void local_irq_restore(unsigned long flags);
```
Use *local_irq_save* to disable interrupts on the local processor and remember their previous state. The flags can be passed to *local_irq_restore* to restore the previous interrupt state.

```
void local_irq_disable(void);
void local_irq_enable(void);
```
Functions that unconditionally disable and enable interrupts on the current processor.

CHAPTER 11

Data Types in the Kernel

Before we go on to more advanced topics, we need to stop for a quick note on portability issues. Modern versions of the Linux kernel are highly portable, running on numerous different architectures. Given the multiplatform nature of Linux, drivers intended for serious use should be portable as well.

But a core issue with kernel code is being able both to access data items of known length (for example, filesystem data structures or registers on device boards) and to exploit the capabilities of different processors (32-bit and 64-bit architectures, and possibly 16 bit as well).

Several of the problems encountered by kernel developers while porting x86 code to new architectures have been related to incorrect data typing. Adherence to strict data typing and compiling with the *-Wall -Wstrict-prototypes* flags can prevent most bugs.

Data types used by kernel data are divided into three main classes: standard C types such as int, explicitly sized types such as u32, and types used for specific kernel objects, such as pid_t. We are going to see when and how each of the three typing classes should be used. The final sections of the chapter talk about some other typical problems you might run into when porting driver code from the x86 to other platforms, and introduce the generalized support for linked lists exported by recent kernel headers.

If you follow the guidelines we provide, your driver should compile and run even on platforms on which you are unable to test it.

Use of Standard C Types

Although most programmers are accustomed to freely using standard types like int and long, writing device drivers requires some care to avoid typing conflicts and obscure bugs.

The problem is that you can't use the standard types when you need "a 2-byte filler" or "something representing a 4-byte string," because the normal C data types are not the same size on all architectures. To show the data size of the various C types, the *datasize* program has been included in the sample files provided on O'Reilly's FTP site in the directory *misc-progs*. This is a sample run of the program on an i386 system (the last four types shown are introduced in the next section):

```
morgana% misc-progs/datasize
arch   Size:  char  short  int  long  ptr long-long  u8 u16 u32 u64
i686           1      2     4     4    4      8        1   2   4   8
```

The program can be used to show that long integers and pointers feature a different size on 64-bit platforms, as demonstrated by running the program on different Linux computers:

```
arch   Size:  char  short  int  long  ptr long-long  u8 u16 u32 u64
i386           1      2     4     4    4      8        1   2   4   8
alpha          1      2     4     8    8      8        1   2   4   8
armv4l         1      2     4     4    4      8        1   2   4   8
ia64           1      2     4     8    8      8        1   2   4   8
m68k           1      2     4     4    4      8        1   2   4   8
mips           1      2     4     4    4      8        1   2   4   8
ppc            1      2     4     4    4      8        1   2   4   8
sparc          1      2     4     4    4      8        1   2   4   8
sparc64        1      2     4     4    4      8        1   2   4   8
x86_64         1      2     4     8    8      8        1   2   4   8
```

It's interesting to note that the SPARC 64 architecture runs with a 32-bit user space, so pointers are 32 bits wide there, even though they are 64 bits wide in kernel space. This can be verified by loading the *kdatasize* module (available in the directory *misc-modules* within the sample files). The module reports size information at load time using *printk* and returns an error (so there's no need to unload it):

```
kernel: arch   Size:  char short int long  ptr long-long u8 u16 u32 u64
kernel: sparc64         1    2    4   8    8      8       1   2   4   8
```

Although you must be careful when mixing different data types, sometimes there are good reasons to do so. One such situation is for memory addresses, which are special as far as the kernel is concerned. Although, conceptually, addresses are pointers, memory administration is often better accomplished by using an unsigned integer type; the kernel treats physical memory like a huge array, and a memory address is just an index into the array. Furthermore, a pointer is easily dereferenced; when dealing directly with memory addresses, you almost never want to dereference them in this manner. Using an integer type prevents this dereferencing, thus avoiding bugs. Therefore, generic memory addresses in the kernel are usually unsigned long, exploiting the fact that pointers and long integers are always the same size, at least on all the platforms currently supported by Linux.

For what it's worth, the C99 standard defines the intptr_t and uintptr_t types for an integer variable that can hold a pointer value. These types are almost unused in the 2.6 kernel, however.

Assigning an Explicit Size to Data Items

Sometimes kernel code requires data items of a specific size, perhaps to match predefined binary structures,* to communicate with user space, or to align data within structures by inserting "padding" fields (but refer to the section "Data Alignment" for information about alignment issues).

The kernel offers the following data types to use whenever you need to know the size of your data. All the types are declared in *<asm/types.h>*, which, in turn, is included by *<linux/types.h>*:

```
u8;    /* unsigned byte (8 bits) */
u16;   /* unsigned word (16 bits) */
u32;   /* unsigned 32-bit value */
u64;   /* unsigned 64-bit value */
```

The corresponding signed types exist, but are rarely needed; just replace u with s in the name if you need them.

If a user-space program needs to use these types, it can prefix the names with a double underscore: __u8 and the other types are defined independent of __KERNEL__. If, for example, a driver needs to exchange binary structures with a program running in user space by means of *ioctl*, the header files should declare 32-bit fields in the structures as __u32.

It's important to remember that these types are Linux specific, and using them hinders porting software to other Unix flavors. Systems with recent compilers support the C99-standard types, such as uint8_t and uint32_t; if portability is a concern, those types can be used in favor of the Linux-specific variety.

You might also note that sometimes the kernel uses conventional types, such as unsigned int, for items whose dimension is architecture independent. This is usually done for backward compatibility. When u32 and friends were introduced in Version 1.1.67, the developers couldn't change existing data structures to the new types because the compiler issues a warning when there is a type mismatch between the structure field and the value being assigned to it.† Linus didn't expect the operating system (OS) he wrote for his own use to become multiplatform; as a result, old structures are sometimes loosely typed.

---

* This happens when reading partition tables, when executing a binary file, or when decoding a network packet.

† As a matter of fact, the compiler signals type inconsistencies even if the two types are just different names for the same object, such as unsigned long and u32 on the PC.

Interface-Specific Types

Some of the commonly used data types in the kernel have their own typedef statements, thus preventing any portability problems. For example, a process identifier (pid) is usually pid_t instead of int. Using pid_t masks any possible difference in the actual data typing. We use the expression *interface-specific* to refer to a type defined by a library in order to provide an interface to a specific data structure.

Note that, in recent times, relatively few new interface-specific types have been defined. Use of the typedef statement has gone out of favor among many kernel developers, who would rather see the real type information used directly in the code, rather than hidden behind a user-defined type. Many older interface-specific types remain in the kernel, however, and they will not be going away anytime soon.

Even when no interface-specific type is defined, it's always important to use the proper data type in a way consistent with the rest of the kernel. A jiffy count, for instance, is always unsigned long, independent of its actual size, so the unsigned long type should always be used when working with jiffies. In this section we concentrate on use of _t types.

Many _t types are defined in *<linux/types.h>*, but the list is rarely useful. When you need a specific type, you'll find it in the prototype of the functions you need to call or in the data structures you use.

Whenever your driver uses functions that require such "custom" types and you don't follow the convention, the compiler issues a warning; if you use the -*Wall* compiler flag and are careful to remove all the warnings, you can feel confident that your code is portable.

The main problem with _t data items is that when you need to print them, it's not always easy to choose the right *printk* or *printf* format, and warnings you resolve on one architecture reappear on another. For example, how would you print a size_t, that is unsigned long on some platforms and unsigned int on some others?

Whenever you need to print some interface-specific data, the best way to do it is by casting the value to the biggest possible type (usually long or unsigned long) and then printing it through the corresponding format. This kind of tweaking won't generate errors or warnings because the format matches the type, and you won't lose data bits because the cast is either a null operation or an extension of the item to a bigger data type.

In practice, the data items we're talking about aren't usually meant to be printed, so the issue applies only to debugging messages. Most often, the code needs only to store and compare the interface-specific types, in addition to passing them as arguments to library or kernel functions.

Although _t types are the correct solution for most situations, sometimes the right type doesn't exist. This happens for some old interfaces that haven't yet been cleaned up.

The one ambiguous point we've found in the kernel headers is data typing for I/O functions, which is loosely defined (see the section "Platform Dependencies" in Chapter 9). The loose typing is mainly there for historical reasons, but it can create problems when writing code. For example, one can get into trouble by swapping the arguments to functions like *outb*; if there were a port_t type, the compiler would find this type of error.

Other Portability Issues

In addition to data typing, there are a few other software issues to keep in mind when writing a driver if you want it to be portable across Linux platforms.

A general rule is to be suspicious of explicit constant values. Usually the code has been parameterized using preprocessor macros. This section lists the most important portability problems. Whenever you encounter other values that have been parameterized, you can find hints in the header files and in the device drivers distributed with the official kernel.

Time Intervals

When dealing with time intervals, don't assume that there are 1000 jiffies per second. Although this is currently true for the i386 architecture, not every Linux platform runs at this speed. The assumption can be false even for the x86 if you play with the HZ value (as some people do), and nobody knows what will happen in future kernels. Whenever you calculate time intervals using jiffies, scale your times using HZ (the number of timer interrupts per second). For example, to check against a time-out of half a second, compare the elapsed time against HZ/2. More generally, the number of jiffies corresponding to msec milliseconds is always msec*HZ/1000.

Page Size

When playing games with memory, remember that a memory page is PAGE_SIZE bytes, not 4 KB. Assuming that the page size is 4 KB and hardcoding the value is a common error among PC programmers, instead, supported platforms show page sizes from 4 KB to 64 KB, and sometimes they differ between different implementations of the same platform. The relevant macros are PAGE_SIZE and PAGE_SHIFT. The latter contains the number of bits to shift an address to get its page number. The number currently is 12 or greater for pages that are 4 KB and larger. The macros are defined in *<asm/page.h>*; user-space programs can use the *getpagesize* library function if they ever need the information.

Let's look at a nontrivial situation. If a driver needs 16 KB for temporary data, it shouldn't specify an order of 2 to *get_free_pages*. You need a portable solution. Such a solution, fortunately, has been written by the kernel developers and is called *get_order*:

```
#include <asm/page.h>
int order = get_order(16*1024);
buf = get_free_pages(GFP_KERNEL, order);
```

Remember that the argument to *get_order* must be a power of two.

Byte Order

Be careful not to make assumptions about byte ordering. Whereas the PC stores multibyte values low-byte first (little end first, thus little-endian), some high-level platforms work the other way (big-endian). Whenever possible, your code should be written such that it does not care about byte ordering in the data it manipulates. However, sometimes a driver needs to build an integer number out of single bytes or do the opposite, or it must communicate with a device that expects a specific order.

The include file *<asm/byteorder.h>* defines either __BIG_ENDIAN or __LITTLE_ENDIAN, depending on the processor's byte ordering. When dealing with byte ordering issues, you could code a bunch of #ifdef __LITTLE_ENDIAN conditionals, but there is a better way. The Linux kernel defines a set of macros that handle conversions between the processor's byte ordering and that of the data you need to store or load in a specific byte order. For example:

```
u32 cpu_to_le32 (u32);
u32 le32_to_cpu (u32);
```

These two macros convert a value from whatever the CPU uses to an unsigned, little-endian, 32-bit quantity and back. They work whether your CPU is big-endian or little-endian and, for that matter, whether it is a 32-bit processor or not. They return their argument unchanged in cases where there is no work to be done. Use of these macros makes it easy to write portable code without having to use a lot of conditional compilation constructs.

There are dozens of similar routines; you can see the full list in *<linux/byteorder/big_endian.h>* and *<linux/byteorder/little_endian.h>*. After a while, the pattern is not hard to follow. *be64_to_cpu* converts an unsigned, big-endian, 64-bit value to the internal CPU representation. *le16_to_cpus*, instead, handles signed, little-endian, 16-bit quantities. When dealing with pointers, you can also use functions like *cpu_to_le32p*, which take a pointer to the value to be converted rather than the value itself. See the include file for the rest.

Data Alignment

The last problem worth considering when writing portable code is how to access unaligned data—for example, how to read a 4-byte value stored at an address that isn't a multiple of 4 bytes. i386 users often access unaligned data items, but not all architectures permit it. Many modern architectures generate an exception every time the program tries unaligned data transfers; data transfer is handled by the exception handler, with a great performance penalty. If you need to access unaligned data, you should use the following macros:

```
#include <asm/unaligned.h>
get_unaligned(ptr);
put_unaligned(val, ptr);
```

These macros are typeless and work for every data item, whether it's one, two, four, or eight bytes long. They are defined with any kernel version.

Another issue related to alignment is portability of data structures across platforms. The same data structure (as defined in the C-language source file) can be compiled differently on different platforms. The compiler arranges structure fields to be aligned according to conventions that differ from platform to platform.

In order to write data structures for data items that can be moved across architectures, you should always enforce natural alignment of the data items in addition to standardizing on a specific endianness. *Natural alignment* means storing data items at an address that is a multiple of their size (for instance, 8-byte items go in an address multiple of 8). To enforce natural alignment while preventing the compiler to arrange the fields in unpredictable ways, you should use filler fields that avoid leaving holes in the data structure.

To show how alignment is enforced by the compiler, the *dataalign* program is distributed in the *misc-progs* directory of the sample code, and an equivalent *kdataalign* module is part of *misc-modules*. This is the output of the program on several platforms and the output of the module on the SPARC64:

```
arch  Align:  char  short  int  long   ptr  long-long   u8  u16  u32  u64
i386              1      2    4     4     4         4     1    2    4    4
i686              1      2    4     4     4         4     1    2    4    4
alpha             1      2    4     8     8         8     1    2    4    8
armv4l            1      2    4     4     4         4     1    2    4    4
ia64              1      2    4     8     8         8     1    2    4    8
mips              1      2    4     4     4         8     1    2    4    8
ppc               1      2    4     4     4         8     1    2    4    8
sparc             1      2    4     4     4         8     1    2    4    8
sparc64           1      2    4     4     4         8     1    2    4    8
x86_64            1      2    4     8     8         8     1    2    4    8

kernel: arch  Align: char short int long  ptr long-long u8 u16 u32 u64
kernel: sparc64         1     2    4    8    8         8    1   2   4   8
```

It's interesting to note that not all platforms align 64-bit values on 64-bit boundaries, so you need filler fields to enforce alignment and ensure portability.

Finally, be aware that the compiler may quietly insert padding into structures itself to ensure that every field is aligned for good performance on the target processor. If you are defining a structure that is intended to match a structure expected by a device, this automatic padding may thwart your attempt. The way around this problem is to tell the compiler that the structure must be "packed," with no fillers added. For example, the kernel header file *<linux/edd.h>* defines several data structures used in interfacing with the x86 BIOS, and it includes the following definition:

```
struct {
        u16 id;
        u64 lun;
        u16 reserved1;
        u32 reserved2;
} __attribute__ ((packed)) scsi;
```

Without the __attribute__ ((packed)), the lun field would be preceded by two filler bytes or six if we compile the structure on a 64-bit platform.

Pointers and Error Values

Many internal kernel functions return a pointer value to the caller. Many of those functions can also fail. In most cases, failure is indicated by returning a NULL pointer value. This technique works, but it is unable to communicate the exact nature of the problem. Some interfaces really need to return an actual error code so that the caller can make the right decision based on what actually went wrong.

A number of kernel interfaces return this information by encoding the error code in a pointer value. Such functions must be used with care, since their return value cannot simply be compared against NULL. To help in the creation and use of this sort of interface, a small set of functions has been made available (in *<linux/err.h>*).

A function returning a pointer type can return an error value with:

```
void *ERR_PTR(long error);
```

where error is the usual negative error code. The caller can use *IS_ERR* to test whether a returned pointer is an error code or not:

```
long IS_ERR(const void *ptr);
```

If you need the actual error code, it can be extracted with:

```
long PTR_ERR(const void *ptr);
```

You should use *PTR_ERR* only on a value for which *IS_ERR* returns a true value; any other value is a valid pointer.

Linked Lists

Operating system kernels, like many other programs, often need to maintain lists of data structures. The Linux kernel has, at times, been host to several linked list implementations at the same time. To reduce the amount of duplicated code, the kernel developers have created a standard implementation of circular, doubly linked lists; others needing to manipulate lists are encouraged to use this facility.

When working with the linked list interface, you should always bear in mind that the list functions perform no locking. If there is a possibility that your driver could attempt to perform concurrent operations on the same list, it is your responsibility to implement a locking scheme. The alternatives (corrupted list structures, data loss, kernel panics) tend to be difficult to diagnose.

To use the list mechanism, your driver must include the file *<linux/list.h>*. This file defines a simple structure of type list_head:

```
struct list_head {
    struct list_head *next, *prev;
};
```

Linked lists used in real code are almost invariably made up of some type of structure, each one describing one entry in the list. To use the Linux list facility in your code, you need only embed a list_head inside the structures that make up the list. If your driver maintains a list of things to do, say, its declaration would look something like this:

```
struct todo_struct {
    struct list_head list;
    int priority; /* driver specific */
    /* ... add other driver-specific fields */
};
```

The head of the list is usually a standalone list_head structure. Figure 11-1 shows how the simple struct list_head is used to maintain a list of data structures.

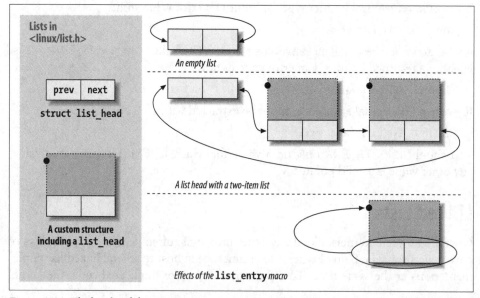

Figure 11-1. The list_head data structure

List heads must be initialized prior to use with the INIT_LIST_HEAD macro. A "things to do" list head could be declared and initialized with:

```
struct list_head todo_list;

INIT_LIST_HEAD(&todo_list);
```

Alternatively, lists can be initialized at compile time:

```
LIST_HEAD(todo_list);
```

Several functions are defined in *<linux/list.h>* that work with lists:

list_add(struct list_head *new, struct list_head *head);
: Adds the new entry immediately after the list head—normally at the beginning of the list. Therefore, it can be used to build stacks. Note, however, that the head need not be the nominal head of the list; if you pass a list_head structure that happens to be in the middle of the list somewhere, the new entry goes immediately after it. Since Linux lists are circular, the head of the list is not generally different from any other entry.

list_add_tail(struct list_head *new, struct list_head *head);
: Adds a new entry just before the given list head—at the end of the list, in other words. *list_add_tail* can, thus, be used to build first-in first-out queues.

list_del(struct list_head *entry);
list_del_init(struct list_head *entry);
: The given entry is removed from the list. If the entry might ever be reinserted into another list, you should use *list_del_init*, which reinitializes the linked list pointers.

list_move(struct list_head *entry, struct list_head *head);
list_move_tail(struct list_head *entry, struct list_head *head);
: The given entry is removed from its current list and added to the beginning of head. To put the entry at the end of the new list, use *list_move_tail* instead.

list_empty(struct list_head *head);
: Returns a nonzero value if the given list is empty.

list_splice(struct list_head *list, struct list_head *head);
: Joins two lists by inserting list immediately after head.

The list_head structures are good for implementing a list of like structures, but the invoking program is usually more interested in the larger structures that make up the list as a whole. A macro, *list_entry*, is provided that maps a list_head structure pointer back into a pointer to the structure that contains it. It is invoked as follows:

```
list_entry(struct list_head *ptr, type_of_struct, field_name);
```

where ptr is a pointer to the struct list_head being used, type_of_struct is the type of the structure containing the ptr, and field_name is the name of the list field within the structure. In our `todo_struct` structure from before, the list field is called simply `list`. Thus, we would turn a list entry into its containing structure with a line such as:

```
struct todo_struct *todo_ptr =
    list_entry(listptr, struct todo_struct, list);
```

The *list_entry* macro takes a little getting used to but is not that hard to use.

The traversal of linked lists is easy: one need only follow the `prev` and `next` pointers. As an example, suppose we want to keep the list of `todo_struct` items sorted in descending priority order. A function to add a new entry would look something like this:

```
void todo_add_entry(struct todo_struct *new)
{
    struct list_head *ptr;
    struct todo_struct *entry;

    for (ptr = todo_list.next; ptr != &todo_list; ptr = ptr->next) {
        entry = list_entry(ptr, struct todo_struct, list);
        if (entry->priority < new->priority) {
            list_add_tail(&new->list, ptr);
            return;
        }
    }
    list_add_tail(&new->list, &todo_struct)
}
```

However, as a general rule, it is better to use one of a set of predefined macros for creating loops that iterate through lists. The previous loop, for example, could be coded as:

```
void todo_add_entry(struct todo_struct *new)
{
    struct list_head *ptr;
    struct todo_struct *entry;

    list_for_each(ptr, &todo_list) {
        entry = list_entry(ptr, struct todo_struct, list);
        if (entry->priority < new->priority) {
            list_add_tail(&new->list, ptr);
            return;
        }
    }
    list_add_tail(&new->list, &todo_struct)
}
```

Using the provided macros helps avoid simple programming errors; the developers of these macros have also put some effort into ensuring that they perform well. A few variants exist:

list_for_each(struct list_head *cursor, struct list_head *list)
> This macro creates a for loop that executes once with cursor pointing at each successive entry in the list. Be careful about changing the list while iterating through it.

list_for_each_prev(struct list_head *cursor, struct list_head *list)
> This version iterates backward through the list.

list_for_each_safe(struct list_head *cursor, struct list_head *next, struct list_head *list)
> If your loop may delete entries in the list, use this version. It simply stores the next entry in the list in next at the beginning of the loop, so it does not get confused if the entry pointed to by cursor is deleted.

list_for_each_entry(type *cursor, struct list_head *list, member)
list_for_each_entry_safe(type *cursor, type *next, struct list_head *list, member)
> These macros ease the process of dealing with a list containing a given type of structure. Here, cursor is a pointer to the containing structure type, and member is the name of the list_head structure within the containing structure. With these macros, there is no need to put list_entry calls inside the loop.

If you look inside *<linux/list.h>*, you see some additional declarations. The hlist type is a doubly linked list with a separate, single-pointer list head type; it is often used for creation of hash tables and similar structures. There are also macros for iterating through both types of lists that are intended to work with the read-copy-update mechanism (described in the section "Read-Copy-Update" in Chapter 5). These primitives are unlikely to be useful in device drivers; see the header file if you would like more information on how they work.

Quick Reference

The following symbols were introduced in this chapter:

#include <linux/types.h>
typedef u8;
typedef u16;
typedef u32;
typedef u64;
> Types guaranteed to be 8-, 16-, 32-, and 64-bit unsigned integer values. The equivalent signed types exist as well. In user space, you can refer to the types as __u8, __u16, and so forth.

```
#include <asm/page.h>
PAGE_SIZE
PAGE_SHIFT
```
Symbols that define the number of bytes per page for the current architecture and the number of bits in the page offset (12 for 4-KB pages and 13 for 8-KB pages).

```
#include <asm/byteorder.h>
__LITTLE_ENDIAN
__BIG_ENDIAN
```
Only one of the two symbols is defined, depending on the architecture.

```
#include <asm/byteorder.h>
u32 __cpu_to_le32 (u32);
u32 __le32_to_cpu (u32);
```
Functions that convert between known byte orders and that of the processor. There are more than 60 such functions; see the various files in *include/linux/ byteorder/* for a full list and the ways in which they are defined.

```
#include <asm/unaligned.h>
get_unaligned(ptr);
put_unaligned(val, ptr);
```
Some architectures need to protect unaligned data access using these macros. The macros expand to normal pointer dereferencing for architectures that permit you to access unaligned data.

```
#include <linux/err.h>
void *ERR_PTR(long error);
long PTR_ERR(const void *ptr);
long IS_ERR(const void *ptr);
```
Functions allow error codes to be returned by functions that return a pointer value.

```
#include <linux/list.h>
list_add(struct list_head *new, struct list_head *head);
list_add_tail(struct list_head *new, struct list_head *head);
list_del(struct list_head *entry);
list_del_init(struct list_head *entry);
list_empty(struct list_head *head);
list_entry(entry, type, member);
list_move(struct list_head *entry, struct list_head *head);
list_move_tail(struct list_head *entry, struct list_head *head);
list_splice(struct list_head *list, struct list_head *head);
```
Functions that manipulate circular, doubly linked lists.

```
list_for_each(struct list_head *cursor, struct list_head *list)
list_for_each_prev(struct list_head *cursor, struct list_head *list)
list_for_each_safe(struct list_head *cursor, struct list_head *next, struct
  list_head *list)
list_for_each_entry(type *cursor, struct list_head *list, member)
list_for_each_entry_safe(type *cursor, type *next struct list_head *list,
  member)
```

Convenience macros for iterating through linked lists.

CHAPTER 12
PCI Drivers

While Chapter 9 introduced the lowest levels of hardware control, this chapter provides an overview of the higher-level bus architectures. A bus is made up of both an electrical interface and a programming interface. In this chapter, we deal with the programming interface.

This chapter covers a number of bus architectures. However, the primary focus is on the kernel functions that access Peripheral Component Interconnect (PCI) peripherals, because these days the PCI bus is the most commonly used peripheral bus on desktops and bigger computers. The bus is the one that is best supported by the kernel. ISA is still common for electronic hobbyists and is described later, although it is pretty much a bare-metal kind of bus, and there isn't much to say in addition to what is covered in Chapters 9 and 10.

The PCI Interface

Although many computer users think of PCI as a way of laying out electrical wires, it is actually a complete set of specifications defining how different parts of a computer should interact.

The PCI specification covers most issues related to computer interfaces. We are not going to cover it all here; in this section, we are mainly concerned with how a PCI driver can find its hardware and gain access to it. The probing techniques discussed in the sections "Module Parameters" in Chapter 2 and "Autodetecting the IRQ Number" in Chapter 10 can be used with PCI devices, but the specification offers an alternative that is preferable to probing.

The PCI architecture was designed as a replacement for the ISA standard, with three main goals: to get better performance when transferring data between the computer and its peripherals, to be as platform independent as possible, and to simplify adding and removing peripherals to the system.

The PCI bus achieves better performance by using a higher clock rate than ISA; its clock runs at 25 or 33 MHz (its actual rate being a factor of the system clock), and 66-MHz and even 133-MHz implementations have recently been deployed as well. Moreover, it is equipped with a 32-bit data bus, and a 64-bit extension has been included in the specification. Platform independence is often a goal in the design of a computer bus, and it's an especially important feature of PCI, because the PC world has always been dominated by processor-specific interface standards. PCI is currently used extensively on IA-32, Alpha, PowerPC, SPARC64, and IA-64 systems, and some other platforms as well.

What is most relevant to the driver writer, however, is PCI's support for autodetection of interface boards. PCI devices are jumperless (unlike most older peripherals) and are automatically configured at boot time. Then, the device driver must be able to access configuration information in the device in order to complete initialization. This happens without the need to perform any probing.

PCI Addressing

Each PCI peripheral is identified by a *bus* number, a *device* number, and a *function* number. The PCI specification permits a single system to host up to 256 buses, but because 256 buses are not sufficient for many large systems, Linux now supports PCI *domains*. Each PCI domain can host up to 256 buses. Each bus hosts up to 32 devices, and each device can be a multifunction board (such as an audio device with an accompanying CD-ROM drive) with a maximum of eight functions. Therefore, each function can be identified at hardware level by a 16-bit address, or key. Device drivers written for Linux, though, don't need to deal with those binary addresses, because they use a specific data structure, called pci_dev, to act on the devices.

Most recent workstations feature at least two PCI buses. Plugging more than one bus in a single system is accomplished by means of *bridges*, special-purpose PCI peripherals whose task is joining two buses. The overall layout of a PCI system is a tree where each bus is connected to an upper-layer bus, up to bus 0 at the root of the tree. The CardBus PC-card system is also connected to the PCI system via bridges. A typical PCI system is represented in Figure 12-1, where the various bridges are highlighted.

The 16-bit hardware addresses associated with PCI peripherals, although mostly hidden in the struct pci_dev object, are still visible occasionally, especially when lists of devices are being used. One such situation is the output of *lspci* (part of the *pciutils* package, available with most distributions) and the layout of information in */proc/pci* and */proc/bus/pci*. The sysfs representation of PCI devices also shows this addressing scheme, with the addition of the PCI domain information.* When the hardware address is displayed, it can be shown as two values (an 8-bit bus number and an 8-bit

---

* Some architectures also display the PCI domain information in the */proc/pci* and */proc/bus/pci* files.

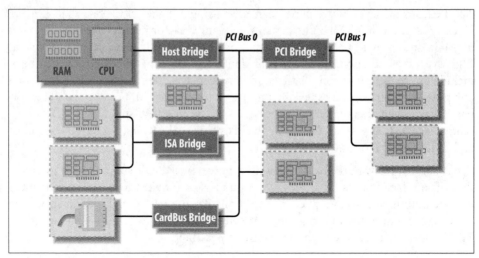

Figure 12-1. Layout of a typical PCI system

device and function number), as three values (bus, device, and function), or as four values (domain, bus, device, and function); all the values are usually displayed in hexadecimal.

For example, */proc/bus/pci/devices* uses a single 16-bit field (to ease parsing and sorting), while */proc/bus/busnumber* splits the address into three fields. The following shows how those addresses appear, showing only the beginning of the output lines:

```
$ lspci | cut -d: -f1-3
0000:00:00.0 Host bridge
0000:00:00.1 RAM memory
0000:00:00.2 RAM memory
0000:00:02.0 USB Controller
0000:00:04.0 Multimedia audio controller
0000:00:06.0 Bridge
0000:00:07.0 ISA bridge
0000:00:09.0 USB Controller
0000:00:09.1 USB Controller
0000:00:09.2 USB Controller
0000:00:0c.0 CardBus bridge
0000:00:0f.0 IDE interface
0000:00:10.0 Ethernet controller
0000:00:12.0 Network controller
0000:00:13.0 FireWire (IEEE 1394)
0000:00:14.0 VGA compatible controller
$ cat /proc/bus/pci/devices | cut -f1
0000
0001
0002
0010
0020
0030
```

```
0038
0048
0049
004a
0060
0078
0080
0090
0098
00a0
$ tree /sys/bus/pci/devices/
/sys/bus/pci/devices/
|-- 0000:00:00.0 -> ../../../devices/pci0000:00/0000:00:00.0
|-- 0000:00:00.1 -> ../../../devices/pci0000:00/0000:00:00.1
|-- 0000:00:00.2 -> ../../../devices/pci0000:00/0000:00:00.2
|-- 0000:00:02.0 -> ../../../devices/pci0000:00/0000:00:02.0
|-- 0000:00:04.0 -> ../../../devices/pci0000:00/0000:00:04.0
|-- 0000:00:06.0 -> ../../../devices/pci0000:00/0000:00:06.0
|-- 0000:00:07.0 -> ../../../devices/pci0000:00/0000:00:07.0
|-- 0000:00:09.0 -> ../../../devices/pci0000:00/0000:00:09.0
|-- 0000:00:09.1 -> ../../../devices/pci0000:00/0000:00:09.1
|-- 0000:00:09.2 -> ../../../devices/pci0000:00/0000:00:09.2
|-- 0000:00:0c.0 -> ../../../devices/pci0000:00/0000:00:0c.0
|-- 0000:00:0f.0 -> ../../../devices/pci0000:00/0000:00:0f.0
|-- 0000:00:10.0 -> ../../../devices/pci0000:00/0000:00:10.0
|-- 0000:00:12.0 -> ../../../devices/pci0000:00/0000:00:12.0
|-- 0000:00:13.0 -> ../../../devices/pci0000:00/0000:00:13.0
`-- 0000:00:14.0 -> ../../../devices/pci0000:00/0000:00:14.0
```

All three lists of devices are sorted in the same order, since *lspci* uses the */proc* files as its source of information. Taking the VGA video controller as an example, 0x00a0 means 0000:00:14.0 when split into domain (16 bits), bus (8 bits), device (5 bits) and function (3 bits).

The hardware circuitry of each peripheral board answers queries pertaining to three address spaces: memory locations, I/O ports, and configuration registers. The first two address spaces are shared by all the devices on the same PCI bus (i.e., when you access a memory location, all the devices on that PCI bus see the bus cycle at the same time). The configuration space, on the other hand, exploits *geographical addressing*. Configuration queries address only one slot at a time, so they never collide.

As far as the driver is concerned, memory and I/O regions are accessed in the usual ways via *inb*, *readb*, and so forth. Configuration transactions, on the other hand, are performed by calling specific kernel functions to access configuration registers. With regard to interrupts, every PCI slot has four interrupt pins, and each device function can use one of them without being concerned about how those pins are routed to the CPU. Such routing is the responsibility of the computer platform and is implemented outside of the PCI bus. Since the PCI specification requires interrupt lines to be shareable, even a processor with a limited number of IRQ lines, such as the x86, can host many PCI interface boards (each with four interrupt pins).

The I/O space in a PCI bus uses a 32-bit address bus (leading to 4 GB of I/O ports), while the memory space can be accessed with either 32-bit or 64-bit addresses. 64-bit addresses are available on more recent platforms. Addresses are supposed to be unique to one device, but software may erroneously configure two devices to the same address, making it impossible to access either one. But this problem never occurs unless a driver is willingly playing with registers it shouldn't touch. The good news is that every memory and I/O address region offered by the interface board can be remapped by means of configuration transactions. That is, the firmware initializes PCI hardware at system boot, mapping each region to a different address to avoid collisions.* The addresses to which these regions are currently mapped can be read from the configuration space, so the Linux driver can access its devices without probing. After reading the configuration registers, the driver can safely access its hardware.

The PCI configuration space consists of 256 bytes for each device function (except for PCI Express devices, which have 4 KB of configuration space for each function), and the layout of the configuration registers is standardized. Four bytes of the configuration space hold a unique function ID, so the driver can identify its device by looking for the specific ID for that peripheral.† In summary, each device board is geographically addressed to retrieve its configuration registers; the information in those registers can then be used to perform normal I/O access, without the need for further geographic addressing.

It should be clear from this description that the main innovation of the PCI interface standard over ISA is the configuration address space. Therefore, in addition to the usual driver code, a PCI driver needs the ability to access the configuration space, in order to save itself from risky probing tasks.

For the remainder of this chapter, we use the word *device* to refer to a device function, because each function in a multifunction board acts as an independent entity. When we refer to a device, we mean the tuple "domain number, bus number, device number, and function number."

Boot Time

To see how PCI works, we start from system boot, since that's when the devices are configured.

---

* Actually, that configuration is not restricted to the time the system boots; hotpluggable devices, for example, cannot be available at boot time and appear later instead. The main point here is that the device driver must not change the address of I/O or memory regions.

† You'll find the ID of any device in its own hardware manual. A list is included in the file *pci.ids*, part of the *pciutils* package and the kernel sources; it doesn't pretend to be complete but just lists the most renowned vendors and devices. The kernel version of this file will not be included in future kernel series.

When power is applied to a PCI device, the hardware remains inactive. In other words, the device responds only to configuration transactions. At power on, the device has no memory and no I/O ports mapped in the computer's address space; every other device-specific feature, such as interrupt reporting, is disabled as well.

Fortunately, every PCI motherboard is equipped with PCI-aware firmware, called the BIOS, NVRAM, or PROM, depending on the platform. The firmware offers access to the device configuration address space by reading and writing registers in the PCI controller.

At system boot, the firmware (or the Linux kernel, if so configured) performs configuration transactions with every PCI peripheral in order to allocate a safe place for each address region it offers. By the time a device driver accesses the device, its memory and I/O regions have already been mapped into the processor's address space. The driver can change this default assignment, but it never needs to do that.

As suggested, the user can look at the PCI device list and the devices' configuration registers by reading */proc/bus/pci/devices* and */proc/bus/pci/*/**. The former is a text file with (hexadecimal) device information, and the latter are binary files that report a snapshot of the configuration registers of each device, one file per device. The individual PCI device directories in the sysfs tree can be found in */sys/bus/pci/devices*. A PCI device directory contains a number of different files:

```
$ tree /sys/bus/pci/devices/0000:00:10.0
/sys/bus/pci/devices/0000:00:10.0
|-- class
|-- config
|-- detach_state
|-- device
|-- irq
|-- power
|   `-- state
|-- resource
|-- subsystem_device
|-- subsystem_vendor
`-- vendor
```

The file *config* is a binary file that allows the raw PCI config information to be read from the device (just like the */proc/bus/pci/*/** provides.) The files *vendor*, *device*, *subsystem_device*, *subsystem_vendor*, and *class* all refer to the specific values of this PCI device (all PCI devices provide this information.) The file *irq* shows the current IRQ assigned to this PCI device, and the file *resource* shows the current memory resources allocated by this device.

Configuration Registers and Initialization

In this section, we look at the configuration registers that PCI devices contain. All PCI devices feature at least a 256-byte address space. The first 64 bytes are standardized, while the rest are device dependent. Figure 12-2 shows the layout of the device-independent configuration space.

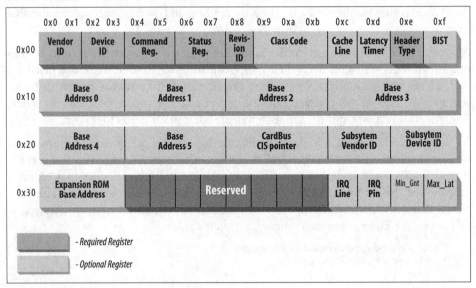

Figure 12-2. The standardized PCI configuration registers

As the figure shows, some of the PCI configuration registers are required and some are optional. Every PCI device must contain meaningful values in the required registers, whereas the contents of the optional registers depend on the actual capabilities of the peripheral. The optional fields are not used unless the contents of the required fields indicate that they are valid. Thus, the required fields assert the board's capabilities, including whether the other fields are usable.

It's interesting to note that the PCI registers are always little-endian. Although the standard is designed to be architecture independent, the PCI designers sometimes show a slight bias toward the PC environment. The driver writer should be careful about byte ordering when accessing multibyte configuration registers; code that works on the PC might not work on other platforms. The Linux developers have taken care of the byte-ordering problem (see the next section, "Accessing the Configuration Space"), but the issue must be kept in mind. If you ever need to convert data from host order to PCI order or vice versa, you can resort to the functions defined in *<asm/byteorder.h>*, introduced in Chapter 11, knowing that PCI byte order is little-endian.

Describing all the configuration items is beyond the scope of this book. Usually, the technical documentation released with each device describes the supported registers. What we're interested in is how a driver can look for its device and how it can access the device's configuration space.

Three or five PCI registers identify a device: vendorID, deviceID, and class are the three that are always used. Every PCI manufacturer assigns proper values to these read-only registers, and the driver can use them to look for the device. Additionally, the fields subsystem vendorID and subsystem deviceID are sometimes set by the vendor to further differentiate similar devices.

Let's look at these registers in more detail:

vendorID
> This 16-bit register identifies a hardware manufacturer. For instance, every Intel device is marked with the same vendor number, 0x8086. There is a global registry of such numbers, maintained by the PCI Special Interest Group, and manufacturers must apply to have a unique number assigned to them.

deviceID
> This is another 16-bit register, selected by the manufacturer; no official registration is required for the device ID. This ID is usually paired with the vendor ID to make a unique 32-bit identifier for a hardware device. We use the word *signature* to refer to the vendor and device ID pair. A device driver usually relies on the signature to identify its device; you can find what value to look for in the hardware manual for the target device.

class
> Every peripheral device belongs to a *class*. The class register is a 16-bit value whose top 8 bits identify the "base class" (or *group*). For example, "ethernet" and "token ring" are two classes belonging to the "network" group, while the "serial" and "parallel" classes belong to the "communication" group. Some drivers can support several similar devices, each of them featuring a different signature but all belonging to the same class; these drivers can rely on the class register to identify their peripherals, as shown later.

subsystem vendorID
subsystem deviceID
> These fields can be used for further identification of a device. If the chip is a generic interface chip to a local (onboard) bus, it is often used in several completely different roles, and the driver must identify the actual device it is talking with. The subsystem identifiers are used to this end.

Using these different identifiers, a PCI driver can tell the kernel what kind of devices it supports. The struct pci_device_id structure is used to define a list of the different types of PCI devices that a driver supports. This structure contains the following fields:

`__u32 vendor;`
`__u32 device;`
> These specify the PCI vendor and device IDs of a device. If a driver can handle any vendor or device ID, the value `PCI_ANY_ID` should be used for these fields.

`__u32 subvendor;`
`__u32 subdevice;`
> These specify the PCI subsystem vendor and subsystem device IDs of a device. If a driver can handle any type of subsystem ID, the value `PCI_ANY_ID` should be used for these fields.

`__u32 class;`
`__u32 class_mask;`
> These two values allow the driver to specify that it supports a type of PCI class device. The different classes of PCI devices (a VGA controller is one example) are described in the PCI specification. If a driver can handle any type of subsystem ID, the value `PCI_ANY_ID` should be used for these fields.

`kernel_ulong_t driver_data;`
> This value is not used to match a device but is used to hold information that the PCI driver can use to differentiate between different devices if it wants to.

There are two helper macros that should be used to initialize a struct `pci_device_id` structure:

`PCI_DEVICE(vendor, device)`
> This creates a struct `pci_device_id` that matches only the specific vendor and device ID. The macro sets the `subvendor` and `subdevice` fields of the structure to `PCI_ANY_ID`.

`PCI_DEVICE_CLASS(device_class, device_class_mask)`
> This creates a struct `pci_device_id` that matches a specific PCI class.

An example of using these macros to define the type of devices a driver supports can be found in the following kernel files:

```
drivers/usb/host/ehci-hcd.c:

static const struct pci_device_id pci_ids[] = { {
        /* handle any USB 2.0 EHCI controller */
        PCI_DEVICE_CLASS(((PCI_CLASS_SERIAL_USB << 8) | 0x20), ~0),
        .driver_data =  (unsigned long) &ehci_driver,
        },
        { /* end: all zeroes */ }
};

drivers/i2c/busses/i2c-i810.c:
```

```
static struct pci_device_id i810_ids[] = {
    { PCI_DEVICE(PCI_VENDOR_ID_INTEL, PCI_DEVICE_ID_INTEL_82810_IG1) },
    { PCI_DEVICE(PCI_VENDOR_ID_INTEL, PCI_DEVICE_ID_INTEL_82810_IG3) },
    { PCI_DEVICE(PCI_VENDOR_ID_INTEL, PCI_DEVICE_ID_INTEL_82810E_IG) },
    { PCI_DEVICE(PCI_VENDOR_ID_INTEL, PCI_DEVICE_ID_INTEL_82815_CGC) },
    { PCI_DEVICE(PCI_VENDOR_ID_INTEL, PCI_DEVICE_ID_INTEL_82845G_IG) },
    { 0, },
};
```

These examples create a list of struct pci_device_id structures, with an empty structure set to all zeros as the last value in the list. This array of IDs is used in the struct pci_driver (described below), and it is also used to tell user space which devices this specific driver supports.

MODULE_DEVICE_TABLE

This pci_device_id structure needs to be exported to user space to allow the hotplug and module loading systems know what module works with what hardware devices. The macro MODULE_DEVICE_TABLE accomplishes this. An example is:

```
MODULE_DEVICE_TABLE(pci, i810_ids);
```

This statement creates a local variable called __mod_pci_device_table that points to the list of struct pci_device_id. Later in the kernel build process, the depmod program searches all modules for the symbol __mod_pci_device_table. If that symbol is found, it pulls the data out of the module and adds it to the file */lib/modules/KERNEL_VERSION/modules.pcimap*. After depmod completes, all PCI devices that are supported by modules in the kernel are listed, along with their module names, in that file. When the kernel tells the hotplug system that a new PCI device has been found, the hotplug system uses the *modules.pcimap* file to find the proper driver to load.

Registering a PCI Driver

The main structure that all PCI drivers must create in order to be registered with the kernel properly is the struct pci_driver structure. This structure consists of a number of function callbacks and variables that describe the PCI driver to the PCI core. Here are the fields in this structure that a PCI driver needs to be aware of:

const char *name;
> The name of the driver. It must be unique among all PCI drivers in the kernel and is normally set to the same name as the module name of the driver. It shows up in sysfs under */sys/bus/pci/drivers/* when the driver is in the kernel.

const struct pci_device_id *id_table;
> Pointer to the struct pci_device_id table described earlier in this chapter.

```
int (*probe) (struct pci_dev *dev, const struct pci_device_id *id);
```
Pointer to the probe function in the PCI driver. This function is called by the PCI core when it has a struct pci_dev that it thinks this driver wants to control. A pointer to the struct pci_device_id that the PCI core used to make this decision is also passed to this function. If the PCI driver claims the struct pci_dev that is passed to it, it should initialize the device properly and return 0. If the driver does not want to claim the device, or an error occurs, it should return a negative error value. More details about this function follow later in this chapter.

```
void (*remove) (struct pci_dev *dev);
```
Pointer to the function that the PCI core calls when the struct pci_dev is being removed from the system, or when the PCI driver is being unloaded from the kernel. More details about this function follow later in this chapter.

```
int (*suspend) (struct pci_dev *dev, u32 state);
```
Pointer to the function that the PCI core calls when the struct pci_dev is being suspended. The suspend state is passed in the state variable. This function is optional; a driver does not have to provide it.

```
int (*resume) (struct pci_dev *dev);
```
Pointer to the function that the PCI core calls when the struct pci_dev is being resumed. It is always called after suspend has been called. This function is optional; a driver does not have to provide it.

In summary, to create a proper struct pci_driver structure, only four fields need to be initialized:

```
static struct pci_driver pci_driver = {
    .name = "pci_skel",
    .id_table = ids,
    .probe = probe,
    .remove = remove,
};
```

To register the struct pci_driver with the PCI core, a call to *pci_register_driver* is made with a pointer to the struct pci_driver. This is traditionally done in the module initialization code for the PCI driver:

```
static int __init pci_skel_init(void)
{
    return pci_register_driver(&pci_driver);
}
```

Note that the *pci_register_driver* function either returns a negative error number or 0 if everything was registered successfully. It does not return the number of devices that were bound to the driver or an error number if no devices were bound to the driver. This is a change from kernels prior to the 2.6 release and was done because of the following situations:

- On systems that support PCI hotplug, or CardBus systems, a PCI device can appear or disappear at any point in time. It is helpful if drivers can be loaded before the device appears, to reduce the time it takes to initialize a device.

- The 2.6 kernel allows new PCI IDs to be dynamically allocated to a driver after it has been loaded. This is done through the file new_id that is created in all PCI driver directories in sysfs. This is very useful if a new device is being used that the kernel doesn't know about just yet. A user can write the PCI ID values to the *new_id* file, and then the driver binds to the new device. If a driver was not allowed to load until a device was present in the system, this interface would not be able to work.

When the PCI driver is to be unloaded, the struct pci_driver needs to be unregistered from the kernel. This is done with a call to *pci_unregister_driver*. When this call happens, any PCI devices that were currently bound to this driver are removed, and the *remove* function for this PCI driver is called before the *pci_unregister_driver* function returns.

```
static void __exit pci_skel_exit(void)
{
    pci_unregister_driver(&pci_driver);
}
```

Old-Style PCI Probing

In older kernel versions, the function, *pci_register_driver*, was not always used by PCI drivers. Instead, they would either walk the list of PCI devices in the system by hand, or they would call a function that could search for a specific PCI device. The ability to walk the list of PCI devices in the system within a driver has been removed from the 2.6 kernel in order to prevent drivers from crashing the kernel if they happened to modify the PCI device lists while a device was being removed at the same time.

If the ability to find a specific PCI device is really needed, the following functions are available:

```
struct pci_dev *pci_get_device(unsigned int vendor, unsigned int device,
                     struct pci_dev *from);
```
This function scans the list of PCI devices currently present in the system, and if the input arguments match the specified vendor and device IDs, it increments the reference count on the struct pci_dev variable found, and returns it to the caller. This prevents the structure from disappearing without any notice and ensures that the kernel does not oops. After the driver is done with the struct pci_dev returned by the function, it must call the function *pci_dev_put* to decre-

ment the usage count properly back to allow the kernel to clean up the device if it is removed.

The from argument is used to get hold of multiple devices with the same signature; the argument should point to the last device that has been found, so that the search can continue instead of restarting from the head of the list. To find the first device, from is specified as NULL. If no (further) device is found, NULL is returned.

An example of how to use this function properly is:

```
struct pci_dev *dev;
dev = pci_get_device(PCI_VENDOR_FOO, PCI_DEVICE_FOO, NULL);
if (dev) {
    /* Use the PCI device */
    ...
    pci_dev_put(dev);
}
```

This function can not be called from interrupt context. If it is, a warning is printed out to the system log.

struct pci_dev *pci_get_subsys(unsigned int vendor, unsigned int device, unsigned int ss_vendor, unsigned int ss_device, struct pci_dev *from);
This function works just like *pci_get_device*, but it allows the subsystem vendor and subsystem device IDs to be specified when looking for the device.

This function can not be called from interrupt context. If it is, a warning is printed out to the system log.

struct pci_dev *pci_get_slot(struct pci_bus *bus, unsigned int devfn);
This function searches the list of PCI devices in the system on the specified struct pci_bus for the specified device and function number of the PCI device. If a device is found that matches, its reference count is incremented and a pointer to it is returned. When the caller is finished accessing the struct pci_dev, it must call *pci_dev_put*.

All of these functions can not be called from interrupt context. If they are, a warning is printed out to the system log.

Enabling the PCI Device

In the *probe* function for the PCI driver, before the driver can access any device resource (I/O region or interrupt) of the PCI device, the driver must call the *pci_enable_device* function:

int pci_enable_device(struct pci_dev *dev);
This function actually enables the device. It wakes up the device and in some cases also assigns its interrupt line and I/O regions. This happens, for example, with CardBus devices (which have been made completely equivalent to PCI at the driver level).

Accessing the Configuration Space

After the driver has detected the device, it usually needs to read from or write to the three address spaces: memory, port, and configuration. In particular, accessing the configuration space is vital to the driver, because it is the only way it can find out where the device is mapped in memory and in the I/O space.

Because the microprocessor has no way to access the configuration space directly, the computer vendor has to provide a way to do it. To access configuration space, the CPU must write and read registers in the PCI controller, but the exact implementation is vendor dependent and not relevant to this discussion, because Linux offers a standard interface to access the configuration space.

As far as the driver is concerned, the configuration space can be accessed through 8-bit, 16-bit, or 32-bit data transfers. The relevant functions are prototyped in *<linux/pci.h>*:

```
int pci_read_config_byte(struct pci_dev *dev, int where, u8 *val);
int pci_read_config_word(struct pci_dev *dev, int where, u16 *val);
int pci_read_config_dword(struct pci_dev *dev, int where, u32 *val);
```
> Read one, two, or four bytes from the configuration space of the device identified by dev. The where argument is the byte offset from the beginning of the configuration space. The value fetched from the configuration space is returned through the val pointer, and the return value of the functions is an error code. The *word* and *dword* functions convert the value just read from little-endian to the native byte order of the processor, so you need not deal with byte ordering.

```
int pci_write_config_byte(struct pci_dev *dev, int where, u8 val);
int pci_write_config_word(struct pci_dev *dev, int where, u16 val);
int pci_write_config_dword(struct pci_dev *dev, int where, u32 val);
```
> Write one, two, or four bytes to the configuration space. The device is identified by dev as usual, and the value being written is passed as val. The *word* and *dword* functions convert the value to little-endian before writing to the peripheral device.

All of the previous functions are implemented as inline functions that really call the following functions. Feel free to use these functions instead of the above in case the driver does not have access to a struct pci_dev at any paticular moment in time:

```
int pci_bus_read_config_byte (struct pci_bus *bus, unsigned int devfn, int
  where, u8 *val);
int pci_bus_read_config_word (struct pci_bus *bus, unsigned int devfn, int
  where, u16 *val);
int pci_bus_read_config_dword (struct pci_bus *bus, unsigned int devfn, int
  where, u32 *val);
```
> Just like the *pci_read_* functions, but struct pci_bus * and devfn variables are needed instead of a struct pci_dev *.

```
int pci_bus_write_config_byte (struct pci_bus *bus, unsigned int devfn, int
    where, u8 val);
int pci_bus_write_config_word (struct pci_bus *bus, unsigned int devfn, int
    where, u16 val);
int pci_bus_write_config_dword (struct pci_bus *bus, unsigned int devfn, int
    where, u32 val);
```

> Just like the *pci_write_* functions, but struct pci_bus * and devfn variables are
> needed instead of a struct pci_dev *.

The best way to address the configuration variables using the *pci_read_* functions is by means of the symbolic names defined in *<linux/pci.h>*. For example, the following small function retrieves the revision ID of a device by passing the symbolic name for where to *pci_read_config_byte*:

```
static unsigned char skel_get_revision(struct pci_dev *dev)
{
    u8 revision;

    pci_read_config_byte(dev, PCI_REVISION_ID, &revision);
    return revision;
}
```

Accessing the I/O and Memory Spaces

A PCI device implements up to six I/O address regions. Each region consists of either memory or I/O locations. Most devices implement their I/O registers in memory regions, because it's generally a saner approach (as explained in the section "I/O Ports and I/O Memory," in Chapter 9). However, unlike normal memory, I/O registers should not be cached by the CPU because each access can have side effects. The PCI device that implements I/O registers as a memory region marks the difference by setting a "memory-is-prefetchable" bit in its configuration register.[*] If the memory region is marked as prefetchable, the CPU can cache its contents and do all sorts of optimization with it; nonprefetchable memory access, on the other hand, can't be optimized because each access can have side effects, just as with I/O ports. Peripherals that map their control registers to a memory address range declare that range as nonprefetchable, whereas something like video memory on PCI boards is prefetchable. In this section, we use the word *region* to refer to a generic I/O address space that is memory-mapped or port-mapped.

An interface board reports the size and current location of its regions using configuration registers—the six 32-bit registers shown in Figure 12-2, whose symbolic names are PCI_BASE_ADDRESS_0 through PCI_BASE_ADDRESS_5. Since the I/O space defined by PCI is a 32-bit address space, it makes sense to use the same configuration interface

---

[*] The information lives in one of the low-order bits of the base address PCI registers. The bits are defined in *<linux/pci.h>*.

for memory and I/O. If the device uses a 64-bit address bus, it can declare regions in the 64-bit memory space by using two consecutive `PCI_BASE_ADDRESS` registers for each region, low bits first. It is possible for one device to offer both 32-bit regions and 64-bit regions.

In the kernel, the I/O regions of PCI devices have been integrated into the generic resource management. For this reason, you don't need to access the configuration variables in order to know where your device is mapped in memory or I/O space. The preferred interface for getting region information consists of the following functions:

`unsigned long pci_resource_start(struct pci_dev *dev, int bar);`
> The function returns the first address (memory address or I/O port number) associated with one of the six PCI I/O regions. The region is selected by the integer bar (the base address register), ranging from 0–5 (inclusive).

`unsigned long pci_resource_end(struct pci_dev *dev, int bar);`
> The function returns the last address that is part of the I/O region number bar. Note that this is the last usable address, not the first address after the region.

`unsigned long pci_resource_flags(struct pci_dev *dev, int bar);`
> This function returns the flags associated with this resource.

Resource flags are used to define some features of the individual resource. For PCI resources associated with PCI I/O regions, the information is extracted from the base address registers, but can come from elsewhere for resources not associated with PCI devices.

All resource flags are defined in *<linux/ioport.h>*; the most important are:

`IORESOURCE_IO`
`IORESOURCE_MEM`
> If the associated I/O region exists, one and only one of these flags is set.

`IORESOURCE_PREFETCH`
`IORESOURCE_READONLY`
> These flags tell whether a memory region is prefetchable and/or write protected. The latter flag is never set for PCI resources.

By making use of the *pci_resource_* functions, a device driver can completely ignore the underlying PCI registers, since the system already used them to structure resource information.

PCI Interrupts

As far as interrupts are concerned, PCI is easy to handle. By the time Linux boots, the computer's firmware has already assigned a unique interrupt number to the device, and the driver just needs to use it. The interrupt number is stored in configuration register 60 (`PCI_INTERRUPT_LINE`), which is one byte wide. This allows for as many as 256 interrupt lines, but the actual limit depends on the CPU being used. The driver doesn't need to bother checking the interrupt number, because the value found in PCI_INTERRUPT_LINE is guaranteed to be the right one.

If the device doesn't support interrupts, register 61 (PCI_INTERRUPT_PIN) is 0; otherwise, it's nonzero. However, since the driver knows if its device is interrupt driven or not, it doesn't usually need to read PCI_INTERRUPT_PIN.

Thus, PCI-specific code for dealing with interrupts just needs to read the configuration byte to obtain the interrupt number that is saved in a local variable, as shown in the following code. Beyond that, the information in Chapter 10 applies.

```
result = pci_read_config_byte(dev, PCI_INTERRUPT_LINE, &myirq);
if (result) {
    /* deal with error */
}
```

The rest of this section provides additional information for the curious reader but isn't needed for writing drivers.

A PCI connector has four interrupt pins, and peripheral boards can use any or all of them. Each pin is individually routed to the motherboard's interrupt controller, so interrupts can be shared without any electrical problems. The interrupt controller is then responsible for mapping the interrupt wires (pins) to the processor's hardware; this platform-dependent operation is left to the controller in order to achieve platform independence in the bus itself.

The read-only configuration register located at PCI_INTERRUPT_PIN is used to tell the computer which single pin is actually used. It's worth remembering that each device board can host up to eight devices; each device uses a single interrupt pin and reports it in its own configuration register. Different devices on the same device board can use different interrupt pins or share the same one.

The PCI_INTERRUPT_LINE register, on the other hand, is read/write. When the computer is booted, the firmware scans its PCI devices and sets the register for each device according to how the interrupt pin is routed for its PCI slot. The value is assigned by the firmware, because only the firmware knows how the motherboard routes the different interrupt pins to the processor. For the device driver, however, the PCI_INTERRUPT_LINE register is read-only. Interestingly, recent versions of the Linux kernel under some circumstances can assign interrupt lines without resorting to the BIOS.

Hardware Abstractions

We complete the discussion of PCI by taking a quick look at how the system handles the plethora of PCI controllers available on the marketplace. This is just an informational section, meant to show the curious reader how the object-oriented layout of the kernel extends down to the lowest levels.

The mechanism used to implement hardware abstraction is the usual structure containing methods. It's a powerful technique that adds just the minimal overhead of dereferencing a pointer to the normal overhead of a function call. In the case of PCI management, the only hardware-dependent operations are the ones that read and write configuration registers, because everything else in the PCI world is accomplished by directly reading and writing the I/O and memory address spaces, and those are under direct control of the CPU.

Thus, the relevant structure for configuration register access includes only two fields:

```
struct pci_ops {
    int (*read)(struct pci_bus *bus, unsigned int devfn, int where, int size,
            u32 *val);
    int (*write)(struct pci_bus *bus, unsigned int devfn, int where, int size,
            u32 val);
};
```

The structure is defined in *<linux/pci.h>* and used by *drivers/pci/pci.c*, where the actual public functions are defined.

The two functions that act on the PCI configuration space have more overhead than dereferencing a pointer; they use cascading pointers due to the high object-orientedness of the code, but the overhead is not an issue in operations that are performed quite rarely and never in speed-critical paths. The actual implementation of *pci_read_config_byte(dev, where, val)*, for instance, expands to:

```
dev->bus->ops->read(bus, devfn, where, 8, val);
```

The various PCI buses in the system are detected at system boot, and that's when the struct pci_bus items are created and associated with their features, including the ops field.

Implementing hardware abstraction via "hardware operations" data structures is typical in the Linux kernel. One important example is the struct alpha_machine_vector data structure. It is defined in *<asm-alpha/machvec.h>* and takes care of everything that may change across different Alpha-based computers.

A Look Back: ISA

The ISA bus is quite old in design and is a notoriously poor performer, but it still holds a good part of the market for extension devices. If speed is not important and you want to support old motherboards, an ISA implementation is preferable to PCI. An additional advantage of this old standard is that if you are an electronic hobbyist, you can easily build your own ISA devices, something definitely not possible with PCI.

On the other hand, a great disadvantage of ISA is that it's tightly bound to the PC architecture; the interface bus has all the limitations of the 80286 processor and causes endless pain to system programmers. The other great problem with the ISA design (inherited from the original IBM PC) is the lack of geographical addressing, which has led to many problems and lengthy unplug-rejumper-plug-test cycles to add new devices. It's interesting to note that even the oldest Apple II computers were already exploiting geographical addressing, and they featured jumperless expansion boards.

Despite its great disadvantages, ISA is still used in several unexpected places. For example, the VR41xx series of MIPS processors used in several palmtops features an ISA-compatible expansion bus, strange as it seems. The reason behind these unexpected uses of ISA is the extreme low cost of some legacy hardware, such as 8390-based Ethernet cards, so a CPU with ISA electrical signaling can easily exploit the awful, but cheap, PC devices.

Hardware Resources

An ISA device can be equipped with I/O ports, memory areas, and interrupt lines.

Even though the x86 processors support 64 KB of I/O port memory (i.e., the processor asserts 16 address lines), some old PC hardware decodes only the lowest 10 address lines. This limits the usable address space to 1024 ports, because any address in the range 1 KB to 64 KB is mistaken for a low address by any device that decodes only the low address lines. Some peripherals circumvent this limitation by mapping only one port into the low kilobyte and using the high address lines to select between different device registers. For example, a device mapped at 0x340 can safely use port 0x740, 0xB40, and so on.

If the availability of I/O ports is limited, memory access is still worse. An ISA device can use only the memory range between 640 KB and 1 MB and between 15 MB and 16 MB for I/O register and device control. The 640-KB to 1-MB range is used by the PC BIOS, by VGA-compatible video boards, and by various other devices, leaving little space available for new devices. Memory at 15 MB, on the other hand, is not directly supported by Linux, and hacking the kernel to support it is a waste of programming time nowadays.

The third resource available to ISA device boards is interrupt lines. A limited number of interrupt lines is routed to the ISA bus, and they are shared by all the interface boards. As a result, if devices aren't properly configured, they can find themselves using the same interrupt lines.

Although the original ISA specification doesn't allow interrupt sharing across devices, most device boards allow it.* Interrupt sharing at the software level is described in the section "Interrupt Sharing," in Chapter 10.

ISA Programming

As far as programming is concerned, there's no specific aid in the kernel or the BIOS to ease access to ISA devices (like there is, for example, for PCI). The only facilities you can use are the registries of I/O ports and IRQ lines, described in the section "Installing an Interrupt Handler" in Chapter 10.

The programming techniques shown throughout the first part of this book apply to ISA devices; the driver can probe for I/O ports, and the interrupt line must be auto-detected with one of the techniques shown in the section "Autodetecting the IRQ Number" in Chapter 10.

The helper functions *isa_readb* and friends have been briefly introduced in the section "Using I/O Memory" in Chapter 9, and there's nothing more to say about them.

The Plug-and-Play Specification

Some new ISA device boards follow peculiar design rules and require a special initialization sequence intended to simplify installation and configuration of add-on interface boards. The specification for the design of these boards is called *plug and play* (PnP) and consists of a cumbersome rule set for building and configuring jumperless ISA devices. PnP devices implement relocatable I/O regions; the PC's BIOS is responsible for the relocation—reminiscent of PCI.

In short, the goal of PnP is to obtain the same flexibility found in PCI devices without changing the underlying electrical interface (the ISA bus). To this end, the specs define a set of device-independent configuration registers and a way to geographically address the interface boards, even though the physical bus doesn't carry per-board (geographical) wiring—every ISA signal line connects to every available slot.

Geographical addressing works by assigning a small integer, called the *card select number* (CSN), to each PnP peripheral in the computer. Each PnP device features a unique serial identifier, 64 bits wide, that is hardwired into the peripheral board. CSN assignment uses the unique serial number to identify the PnP devices. But the CSNs can be assigned safely only at boot time, which requires the BIOS to be PnP

---

* The problem with interrupt sharing is a matter of electrical engineering: if a device drives the signal line inactive—by applying a low-impedance voltage level—the interrupt can't be shared. If, on the other hand, the device uses a pull-up resistor to the inactive logic level, sharing is possible. This is the norm nowadays. However, there's still a potential risk of losing interrupt events since ISA interrupts are edge triggered instead of level triggered. Edge-triggered interrupts are easier to implement in hardware but don't lend themselves to safe sharing.

aware. For this reason, old computers require the user to obtain and insert a specific configuration diskette, even if the device is PnP capable.

Interface boards following the PnP specs are complicated at the hardware level. They are much more elaborate than PCI boards and require complex software. It's not unusual to have difficulty installing these devices, and even if the installation goes well, you still face the performance constraints and the limited I/O space of the ISA bus. It's much better to install PCI devices whenever possible and enjoy the new technology instead.

If you are interested in the PnP configuration software, you can browse *drivers/net/ 3c509.c*, whose probing function deals with PnP devices. The 2.6 kernel saw a lot of work in the PnP device support area, so a lot of the inflexible interfaces have been cleaned up compared to previous kernel releases.

PC/104 and PC/104+

Currently in the industrial world, two bus architectures are quite fashionable: PC/104 and PC/104+. Both are standard in PC-class single-board computers.

Both standards refer to specific form factors for printed circuit boards, as well as electrical/mechanical specifications for board interconnections. The practical advantage of these buses is that they allow circuit boards to be stacked vertically using a plug-and-socket kind of connector on one side of the device.

The electrical and logical layout of the two buses is identical to ISA (PC/104) and PCI (PC/104+), so software won't notice any difference between the usual desktop buses and these two.

Other PC Buses

PCI and ISA are the most commonly used peripheral interfaces in the PC world, but they aren't the only ones. Here's a summary of the features of other buses found in the PC market.

MCA

Micro Channel Architecture (MCA) is an IBM standard used in PS/2 computers and some laptops. At the hardware level, Micro Channel has more features than ISA. It supports multimaster DMA, 32-bit address and data lines, shared interrupt lines, and geographical addressing to access per-board configuration registers. Such registers are called *Programmable Option Select* (POS), but they don't have all the features of the PCI registers. Linux support for Micro Channel includes functions that are exported to modules.

A device driver can read the integer value MCA_bus to see if it is running on a Micro Channel computer. If the symbol is a preprocessor macro, the macro MCA_bus__is_a_macro is defined as well. If MCA_bus__is_a_macro is undefined, then MCA_bus is an integer variable exported to modularized code. Both MCA_BUS and MCA_bus__is_a_macro are defined in *<asm/processor.h>*.

EISA

The Extended ISA (EISA) bus is a 32-bit extension to ISA, with a compatible interface connector; ISA device boards can be plugged into an EISA connector. The additional wires are routed under the ISA contacts.

Like PCI and MCA, the EISA bus is designed to host jumperless devices, and it has the same features as MCA: 32-bit address and data lines, multimaster DMA, and shared interrupt lines. EISA devices are configured by software, but they don't need any particular operating system support. EISA drivers already exist in the Linux kernel for Ethernet devices and SCSI controllers.

An EISA driver checks the value EISA_bus to determine if the host computer carries an EISA bus. Like MCA_bus, EISA_bus is either a macro or a variable, depending on whether EISA_bus__is_a_macro is defined. Both symbols are defined in *<asm/processor.h>*.

The kernel has full EISA support for devices with sysfs and resource management functionality. This is located in the *drivers/eisa* directory.

VLB

Another extension to ISA is the VESA Local Bus (VLB) interface bus, which extends the ISA connectors by adding a third lengthwise slot. A device can just plug into this extra connector (without plugging in the two associated ISA connectors), because the VLB slot duplicates all important signals from the ISA connectors. Such "standalone" VLB peripherals not using the ISA slot are rare, because most devices need to reach the back panel so that their external connectors are available.

The VESA bus is much more limited in its capabilities than the EISA, MCA, and PCI buses and is disappearing from the market. No special kernel support exists for VLB. However, both the Lance Ethernet driver and the IDE disk driver in Linux 2.0 can deal with VLB versions of their devices.

SBus

While most computers nowadays are equipped with a PCI or ISA interface bus, most older SPARC-based workstations use SBus to connect their peripherals.

SBus is quite an advanced design, although it has been around for a long time. It is meant to be processor independent (even though only SPARC computers use it) and is optimized for I/O peripheral boards. In other words, you can't plug additional RAM into SBus slots (RAM expansion boards have long been forgotten even in the ISA world, and PCI does not support them either). This optimization is meant to simplify the design of both hardware devices and system software, at the expense of some additional complexity in the motherboard.

This I/O bias of the bus results in peripherals using *virtual* addresses to transfer data, thus bypassing the need to allocate a contiguous DMA buffer. The motherboard is responsible for decoding the virtual addresses and mapping them to physical addresses. This requires attaching an MMU (memory management unit) to the bus; the chipset in charge of the task is called IOMMU. Although somehow more complex than using physical addresses on the interface bus, this design is greatly simplified by the fact that SPARC processors have always been designed by keeping the MMU core separate from the CPU core (either physically or at least conceptually). Actually, this design choice is shared by other smart processor designs and is beneficial overall. Another feature of this bus is that device boards exploit massive geographical addressing, so there's no need to implement an address decoder in every peripheral or to deal with address conflicts.

SBus peripherals use the Forth language in their PROMs to initialize themselves. Forth was chosen because the interpreter is lightweight and, therefore, can be easily implemented in the firmware of any computer system. In addition, the SBus specification outlines the boot process, so that compliant I/O devices fit easily into the system and are recognized at system boot. This was a great step to support multiplatform devices; it's a completely different world from the PC-centric ISA stuff we were used to. However, it didn't succeed for a variety of commercial reasons.

Although current kernel versions offer quite full-featured support for SBus devices, the bus is used so little nowadays that it's not worth covering in detail here. Interested readers can look at source files in *arch/sparc/kernel* and *arch/sparc/mm*.

NuBus

Another interesting, but nearly forgotten, interface bus is NuBus. It is found on older Mac computers (those with the M68k family of CPUs).

All of the bus is memory-mapped (like everything with the M68k), and the devices are only geographically addressed. This is good and typical of Apple, as the much older Apple II already had a similar bus layout. What is bad is that it's almost impossible to find documentation on NuBus, due to the close-everything policy Apple has always followed with its Mac computers (and unlike the previous Apple II, whose source code and schematics were available at little cost).

The file *drivers/nubus/nubus.c* includes almost everything we know about this bus, and it's interesting reading; it shows how much hard reverse engineering developers had to do.

External Buses

One of the most recent entries in the field of interface buses is the whole class of external buses. This includes USB, FireWire, and IEEE1284 (parallel-port-based external bus). These interfaces are somewhat similar to older and not-so-external technology, such as PCMCIA/CardBus and even SCSI.

Conceptually, these buses are neither full-featured interface buses (like PCI is) nor dumb communication channels (like the serial ports are). It's hard to classify the software that is needed to exploit their features, as it's usually split into two levels: the driver for the hardware controller (like drivers for PCI SCSI adaptors or PCI controllers introduced in the section "The PCI Interface") and the driver for the specific "client" device (like *sd.c* handles generic SCSI disks and so-called PCI drivers deal with cards plugged in the bus).

Quick Reference

This section summarizes the symbols introduced in the chapter:

#include <linux/pci.h>
> Header that includes symbolic names for the PCI registers and several vendor and device ID values.

struct pci_dev;
> Structure that represents a PCI device within the kernel.

struct pci_driver;
> Structure that represents a PCI driver. All PCI drivers must define this.

struct pci_device_id;
> Structure that describes the types of PCI devices this driver supports.

int pci_register_driver(struct pci_driver *drv);
int pci_module_init(struct pci_driver *drv);
void pci_unregister_driver(struct pci_driver *drv);
> Functions that register or unregister a PCI driver from the kernel.

```
struct pci_dev *pci_find_device(unsigned int vendor, unsigned int device,
                            struct pci_dev *from);
struct pci_dev *pci_find_device_reverse(unsigned int vendor, unsigned int
                                device, const struct pci_dev *from);
struct pci_dev *pci_find_subsys (unsigned int vendor, unsigned int device,
    unsigned int ss_vendor, unsigned int ss_device, const struct pci_dev *from);
struct pci_dev *pci_find_class(unsigned int class, struct pci_dev *from);
```
> Functions that search the device list for devices with a specific signature or those belonging to a specific class. The return value is NULL if none is found. from is used to continue a search; it must be NULL the first time you call either function, and it must point to the device just found if you are searching for more devices. These functions are not recommended to be used, use the pci_get_ variants instead.

```
struct pci_dev *pci_get_device(unsigned int vendor, unsigned int device,
                            struct pci_dev *from);
struct pci_dev *pci_get_subsys(unsigned int vendor, unsigned int device,
    unsigned int ss_vendor, unsigned int ss_device, struct pci_dev *from);
struct pci_dev *pci_get_slot(struct pci_bus *bus, unsigned int devfn);
```
> Functions that search the device list for devices with a specific signature or belonging to a specific class. The return value is NULL if none is found. from is used to continue a search; it must be NULL the first time you call either function, and it must point to the device just found if you are searching for more devices. The structure returned has its reference count incremented, and after the caller is finished with it, the function *pci_dev_put* must be called.

```
int pci_read_config_byte(struct pci_dev *dev, int where, u8 *val);
int pci_read_config_word(struct pci_dev *dev, int where, u16 *val);
int pci_read_config_dword(struct pci_dev *dev, int where, u32 *val);
int pci_write_config_byte (struct pci_dev *dev, int where, u8 *val);
int pci_write_config_word (struct pci_dev *dev, int where, u16 *val);
int pci_write_config_dword (struct pci_dev *dev, int where, u32 *val);
```
> Functions that read or write a PCI configuration register. Although the Linux kernel takes care of byte ordering, the programmer must be careful about byte ordering when assembling multibyte values from individual bytes. The PCI bus is little-endian.

```
int pci_enable_device(struct pci_dev *dev);
```
> Enables a PCI device.

```
unsigned long pci_resource_start(struct pci_dev *dev, int bar);
unsigned long pci_resource_end(struct pci_dev *dev, int bar);
unsigned long pci_resource_flags(struct pci_dev *dev, int bar);
```
> Functions that handle PCI device resources.

## CHAPTER 13

USB Drivers

The universal serial bus (USB) is a connection between a host computer and a number of peripheral devices. It was originally created to replace a wide range of slow and different buses—the parallel, serial, and keyboard connections—with a single bus type that all devices could connect to.* USB has grown beyond these slow connections and now supports almost every type of device that can be connected to a PC. The latest revision of the USB specification added high-speed connections with a theoretical speed limit of 480 MBps.

Topologically, a USB subsystem is not laid out as a bus; it is rather a tree built out of several point-to-point links. The links are four-wire cables (ground, power, and two signal wires) that connect a device and a hub, just like twisted-pair Ethernet. The USB host controller is in charge of asking every USB device if it has any data to send. Because of this topology, a USB device can never start sending data without first being asked to by the host controller. This configuration allows for a very easy plug-and-play type of system, whereby devices can be automatically configured by the host computer.

The bus is very simple at the technological level, as it's a single-master implementation in which the host computer polls the various peripheral devices. Despite this intrinsic limitation, the bus has some interesting features, such as the ability for a device to request a fixed bandwidth for its data transfers in order to reliably support video and audio I/O. Another important feature of USB is that it acts merely as a communication channel between the device and the host, without requiring specific meaning or structure to the data it delivers.†

---

* Portions of this chapter are based on the in-kernel documentation for the Linux kernel USB code, which were written by the kernel USB developers and released under the GPL.

† Actually, some structure is there, but it mostly reduces to a requirement for the communication to fit into one of a few predefined classes: a keyboard won't allocate bandwidth, for example, while some video cameras will.

The USB protocol specifications define a set of standards that any device of a specific type can follow. If a device follows that standard, then a special driver for that device is not necessary. These different types are called classes and consist of things like storage devices, keyboards, mice, joysticks, network devices, and modems. Other types of devices that do not fit into these classes require a special vendor-specific driver to be written for that specific device. Video devices and USB-to-serial devices are a good example where there is no defined standard, and a driver is needed for every different device from different manufacturers.

These features, together with the inherent hotplug capability of the design, make USB a handy, low-cost mechanism to connect (and disconnect) several devices to the computer without the need to shut the system down, open the cover, and swear over screws and wires.

The Linux kernel supports two main types of USB drivers: drivers on a host system and drivers on a device. The USB drivers for a host system control the USB devices that are plugged into it, from the host's point of view (a common USB host is a desktop computer.) The USB drivers in a device, control how that single device looks to the host computer as a USB device. As the term "USB device drivers" is very confusing, the USB developers have created the term "USB gadget drivers" to describe the drivers that control a USB device that connects to a computer (remember that Linux also runs in those tiny embedded devices, too.) This chapter details how the USB system that runs on a desktop computer works. USB gadget drivers are outside the realm of this book at this point in time.

As Figure 13-1 shows, USB drivers live between the different kernel subsytems (block, net, char, etc.) and the USB hardware controllers. The USB core provides an interface for USB drivers to use to access and control the USB hardware, without having to worry about the different types of USB hardware controllers that are present on the system.

USB Device Basics

A USB device is a very complex thing, as described in the official USB documentation (available at *http://www.usb.org*). Fortunately, the Linux kernel provides a subsystem called the *USB core* to handle most of the complexity. This chapter describes the interaction between a driver and the USB core. Figure 13-2 shows how USB devices consist of configurations, interfaces, and endpoints and how USB drivers bind to USB interfaces, not the entire USB device.

Endpoints

The most basic form of USB communication is through something called an *endpoint*. A USB endpoint can carry data in only one direction, either from the host

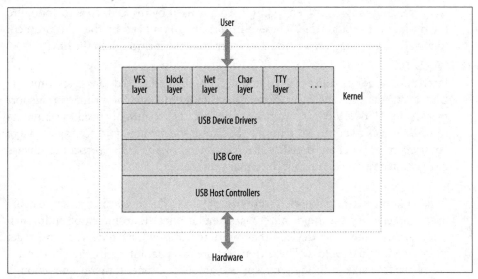

Figure 13-1. USB driver overview

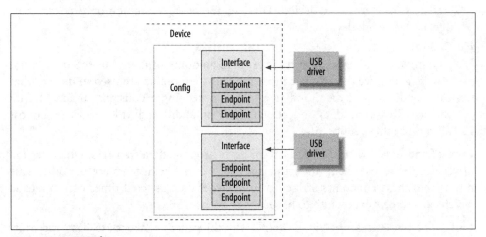

Figure 13-2. USB device overview

computer to the device (called an *OUT* endpoint) or from the device to the host computer (called an *IN* endpoint). Endpoints can be thought of as unidirectional pipes.

A USB endpoint can be one of four different types that describe how the data is transmitted:

CONTROL

Control endpoints are used to allow access to different parts of the USB device. They are commonly used for configuring the device, retrieving information about the device, sending commands to the device, or retrieving status reports about the device. These endpoints are usually small in size. Every USB device has a control endpoint called "endpoint 0" that is used by the USB core to configure the device at insertion time. These transfers are guaranteed by the USB protocol to always have enough reserved bandwidth to make it through to the device.

INTERRUPT

Interrupt endpoints transfer small amounts of data at a fixed rate every time the USB host asks the device for data. These endpoints are the primary transport method for USB keyboards and mice. They are also commonly used to send data to USB devices to control the device, but are not generally used to transfer large amounts of data. These transfers are guaranteed by the USB protocol to always have enough reserved bandwidth to make it through.

BULK

Bulk endpoints transfer large amounts of data. These endpoints are usually much larger (they can hold more characters at once) than interrupt endpoints. They are common for devices that need to transfer any data that must get through with no data loss. These transfers are not guaranteed by the USB protocol to always make it through in a specific amount of time. If there is not enough room on the bus to send the whole BULK packet, it is split up across multiple transfers to or from the device. These endpoints are common on printers, storage, and network devices.

ISOCHRONOUS

Isochronous endpoints also transfer large amounts of data, but the data is not always guaranteed to make it through. These endpoints are used in devices that can handle loss of data, and rely more on keeping a constant stream of data flowing. Real-time data collections, such as audio and video devices, almost always use these endpoints.

Control and bulk endpoints are used for asynchronous data transfers, whenever the driver decides to use them. Interrupt and isochronous endpoints are periodic. This means that these endpoints are set up to transfer data at fixed times continuously, which causes their bandwidth to be reserved by the USB core.

USB endpoints are described in the kernel with the structure struct usb_host_endpoint. This structure contains the real endpoint information in another structure called struct usb_endpoint_descriptor. The latter structure contains all of the USB-specific data in the exact format that the device itself specified. The fields of this structure that drivers care about are:

bEndpointAddress

This is the USB address of this specific endpoint. Also included in this 8-bit value is the direction of the endpoint. The bitmasks USB_DIR_OUT and USB_DIR_IN can be placed against this field to determine if the data for this endpoint is directed to the device or to the host.

bmAttributes

This is the type of endpoint. The bitmask USB_ENDPOINT_XFERTYPE_MASK should be placed against this value in order to determine if the endpoint is of type

USB_ENDPOINT_XFER_ISOC, USB_ENDPOINT_XFER_BULK, or of type USB_ENDPOINT_
XFER_INT. These macros define a isochronous, bulk, and interrupt endpoint,
respectively.

wMaxPacketSize

This is the maximum size in bytes that this endpoint can handle at once. Note
that it is possible for a driver to send amounts of data to an endpoint that is bigger than this value, but the data will be divided up into wMaxPacketSize chunks
when actually transmitted to the device. For high-speed devices, this field can be
used to support a high-bandwidth mode for the endpoint by using a few extra
bits in the upper part of the value. See the USB specification for more details
about how this is done.

bInterval

If this endpoint is of type interrupt, this value is the interval setting for the endpoint—that is, the time between interrupt requests for the endpoint. The value is
represented in milliseconds.

The fields of this structure do not have a "traditional" Linux kernel naming scheme.
This is because these fields directly correspond to the field names in the USB specification. The USB kernel programmers felt that it was more important to use the specified names, so as to reduce confusion when reading the specification, than it was to
have variable names that look familiar to Linux programmers.

Interfaces

USB endpoints are bundled up into *interfaces*. USB interfaces handle only one type of
a USB logical connection, such as a mouse, a keyboard, or a audio stream. Some USB
devices have multiple interfaces, such as a USB speaker that might consist of two
interfaces: a USB keyboard for the buttons and a USB audio stream. Because a USB
interface represents basic functionality, each USB driver controls an interface; so, for
the speaker example, Linux needs two different drivers for one hardware device.

USB interfaces may have alternate settings, which are different choices for parameters of the interface. The initial state of a interface is in the first setting, numbered 0.
Alternate settings can be used to control individual endpoints in different ways, such
as to reserve different amounts of USB bandwidth for the device. Each device with an
isochronous endpoint uses alternate settings for the same interface.

USB interfaces are described in the kernel with the struct usb_interface structure.
This structure is what the USB core passes to USB drivers and is what the USB driver
then is in charge of controlling. The important fields in this structure are:

struct usb_host_interface *altsetting

An array of interface structures containing all of the alternate settings that may
be selected for this interface. Each struct usb_host_interface consists of a set of

endpoint configurations as defined by the struct usb_host_endpoint structure described above. Note that these interface structures are in no particular order.

unsigned num_altsetting

> The number of alternate settings pointed to by the altsetting pointer.

struct usb_host_interface *cur_altsetting

> A pointer into the array altsetting, denoting the currently active setting for this interface.

int minor

> If the USB driver bound to this interface uses the USB major number, this variable contains the minor number assigned by the USB core to the interface. This is valid only after a successful call to usb_register_dev (described later in this chapter).

There are other fields in the struct usb_interface structure, but USB drivers do not need to be aware of them.

Configurations

USB interfaces are themselves bundled up into *configurations*. A USB device can have multiple configurations and might switch between them in order to change the state of the device. For example, some devices that allow firmware to be downloaded to them contain multiple configurations to accomplish this. A single configuration can be enabled only at one point in time. Linux does not handle multiple configuration USB devices very well, but, thankfully, they are rare.

Linux describes USB configurations with the structure struct usb_host_config and entire USB devices with the structure struct usb_device. USB device drivers do not generally ever need to read or write to any values in these structures, so they are not defined in detail here. The curious reader can find descriptions of them in the file *include/linux/usb.h* in the kernel source tree.

A USB device driver commonly has to convert data from a given struct usb_interface structure into a struct usb_device structure that the USB core needs for a wide range of function calls. To do this, the function *interface_to_usbdev* is provided. Hopefully, in the future, all USB calls that currently need a struct usb_device will be converted to take a struct usb_interface parameter and will not require the drivers to do the conversion.

So to summarize, USB devices are quite complex and are made up of lots of different logical units. The relationships among these units can be simply described as follows:

- Devices usually have one or more configurations.
- Configurations often have one or more interfaces.
- Interfaces usually have one or more settings.
- Interfaces have zero or more endpoints.

USB and Sysfs

Due to the complexity of a single USB physical device, the representation of that device in sysfs is also quite complex. Both the physical USB device (as represented by a struct usb_device) and the individual USB interfaces (as represented by a struct usb_interface) are shown in sysfs as individual devices. (This is because both of those structures contain a struct device structure.) As an example, for a simple USB mouse that contains only one USB interface, the following would be the sysfs directory tree for that device:

```
/sys/devices/pci0000:00/0000:00:09.0/usb2/2-1
|-- 2-1:1.0
|   |-- bAlternateSetting
|   |-- bInterfaceClass
|   |-- bInterfaceNumber
|   |-- bInterfaceProtocol
|   |-- bInterfaceSubClass
|   |-- bNumEndpoints
|   |-- detach_state
|   |-- iInterface
|   `-- power
|       `-- state
|-- bConfigurationValue
|-- bDeviceClass
|-- bDeviceProtocol
|-- bDeviceSubClass
|-- bMaxPower
|-- bNumConfigurations
|-- bNumInterfaces
|-- bcdDevice
|-- bmAttributes
|-- detach_state
|-- devnum
|-- idProduct
|-- idVendor
|-- maxchild
|-- power
|   `-- state
|-- speed
`-- version
```

The struct usb_device is represented in the tree at:

```
/sys/devices/pci0000:00/0000:00:09.0/usb2/2-1
```

while the USB interface for the mouse—the interface that the USB mouse driver is bound to—is located at the directory:

```
/sys/devices/pci0000:00/0000:00:09.0/usb2/2-1/2-1:1.0
```

To help understand what this long device path means, we describe how the kernel labels the USB devices.

The first USB device is a root hub. This is the USB controller, usually contained in a PCI device. The controller is so named because it controls the whole USB bus connected to it. The controller is a bridge between the PCI bus and the USB bus, as well as being the first USB device on that bus.

All root hubs are assigned a unique number by the USB core. In our example, the root hub is called usb2, as it is the second root hub that was registered with the USB core. There is no limit on the number of root hubs that can be contained in a single system at any time.

Every device that is on a USB bus takes the number of the root hub as the first number in its name. That is followed by a - character and then the number of the port that the device is plugged into. As the device in our example is plugged into the first port, a 1 is added to the name. So the device name for the main USB mouse device is 2-1. Because this USB device contains one interface, that causes another device in the tree to be added to the sysfs path. The naming scheme for USB interfaces is the device name up to this point: in our example, it's 2-1 followed by a colon and the USB configuration number, then a period and the interface number. So for this example, the device name is 2-1:1.0 because it is the first configuration and has interface number zero.

So to summarize, the USB sysfs device naming scheme is:

    root_hub-hub_port:config.interface

As the devices go further down in the USB tree, and as more and more USB hubs are used, the hub port number is added to the string following the previous hub port number in the chain. For a two-deep tree, the device name looks like:

    root_hub-hub_port-hub_port:config.interface

As can be seen in the previous directory listing of the USB device and interface, all of the USB specific information is available directly through sysfs (for example, the idVendor, idProduct, and bMaxPower information). One of these files, *bConfigurationValue*, can be written to in order to change the active USB configuration that is being used. This is useful for devices that have multiple configurations, when the kernel is unable to determine what configuration to select in order to properly operate the device. A number of USB modems need to have the proper configuration value written to this file in order to have the correct USB driver bind to the device.

Sysfs does not expose all of the different parts of a USB device, as it stops at the interface level. Any alternate configurations that the device may contain are not shown, as well as the details of the endpoints associated with the interfaces. This information can be found in the *usbfs* filesystem, which is mounted in the */proc/bus/usb/* directory on the system. The file */proc/bus/usb/devices* does show all of the same information exposed in sysfs, as well as the alternate configuration and endpoint information for all USB devices that are present in the system. *usbfs* also allows user-space programs to directly talk to USB devices, which has enabled a lot of kernel drivers to be moved out to user space, where it is easier to maintain and debug. The USB scanner driver is a good example of this, as it is no longer present in the kernel because its functionality is now contained in the user-space SANE library programs.

USB Urbs

The USB code in the Linux kernel communicates with all USB devices using something called a *urb* (USB request block). This request block is described with the struct urb structure and can be found in the *include/linux/usb.h* file.

A urb is used to send or receive data to or from a specific USB endpoint on a specific USB device in an asynchronous manner. It is used much like a kiocb structure is used in the filesystem async I/O code or as a struct skbuff is used in the networking code. A USB device driver may allocate many urbs for a single endpoint or may reuse a single urb for many different endpoints, depending on the need of the driver. Every endpoint in a device can handle a queue of urbs, so that multiple urbs can be sent to the same endpoint before the queue is empty. The typical lifecycle of a urb is as follows:

- Created by a USB device driver.
- Assigned to a specific endpoint of a specific USB device.
- Submitted to the USB core, by the USB device driver.
- Submitted to the specific USB host controller driver for the specified device by the USB core.
- Processed by the USB host controller driver that makes a USB transfer to the device.
- When the urb is completed, the USB host controller driver notifies the USB device driver.

Urbs can also be canceled any time by the driver that submitted the urb, or by the USB core if the device is removed from the system. urbs are dynamically created and contain an internal reference count that enables them to be automatically freed when the last user of the urb releases it.

The procedure described in this chapter for handling urbs is useful, because it permits streaming and other complex, overlapping communications that allow drivers to achieve the highest possible data transfer speeds. But less cumbersome procedures are available if you just want to send individual bulk or control messages and do not care about data throughput rates. (See the section "USB Transfers Without Urbs.")

struct urb

The fields of the struct urb structure that matter to a USB device driver are:

struct usb_device *dev
> Pointer to the struct usb_device to which this urb is sent. This variable must be initialized by the USB driver before the urb can be sent to the USB core.

unsigned int pipe
> Endpoint information for the specific struct usb_device that this urb is to be sent to. This variable must be initialized by the USB driver before the urb can be sent to the USB core.

> To set fields of this structure, the driver uses the following functions as appropriate, depending on the direction of traffic. Note that every endpoint can be of only one type.

unsigned int usb_sndctrlpipe(struct usb_device *dev, unsigned int endpoint)
> Specifies a control OUT endpoint for the specified USB device with the specified endpoint number.

unsigned int usb_rcvctrlpipe(struct usb_device *dev, unsigned int endpoint)
> Specifies a control IN endpoint for the specified USB device with the specified endpoint number.

unsigned int usb_sndbulkpipe(struct usb_device *dev, unsigned int endpoint)
> Specifies a bulk OUT endpoint for the specified USB device with the specified endpoint number.

unsigned int usb_rcvbulkpipe(struct usb_device *dev, unsigned int endpoint)
> Specifies a bulk IN endpoint for the specified USB device with the specified endpoint number.

unsigned int usb_sndintpipe(struct usb_device *dev, unsigned int endpoint)
> Specifies an interrupt OUT endpoint for the specified USB device with the specified endpoint number.

unsigned int usb_rcvintpipe(struct usb_device *dev, unsigned int endpoint)
> Specifies an interrupt IN endpoint for the specified USB device with the specified endpoint number.

```
unsigned int usb_sndisocpipe(struct usb_device *dev, unsigned int
    endpoint)
```
Specifies an isochronous OUT endpoint for the specified USB device with the specified endpoint number.

```
unsigned int usb_rcvisocpipe(struct usb_device *dev, unsigned int
    endpoint)
```
Specifies an isochronous IN endpoint for the specified USB device with the specified endpoint number.

`unsigned int transfer_flags`

This variable can be set to a number of different bit values, depending on what the USB driver wants to happen to the urb. The available values are:

URB_SHORT_NOT_OK

When set, it specifies that any short read on an IN endpoint that might occur should be treated as an error by the USB core. This value is useful only for urbs that are to be read from the USB device, not for write urbs.

URB_ISO_ASAP

If the urb is isochronous, this bit can be set if the driver wants the urb to be scheduled, as soon as the bandwidth utilization allows it to be, and to set the start_frame variable in the urb at that point. If this bit is not set for an isochronous urb, the driver must specify the start_frame value and must be able to recover properly if the transfer cannot start at that moment. See the upcoming section about isochronous urbs for more information.

URB_NO_TRANSFER_DMA_MAP

Should be set when the urb contains a DMA buffer to be transferred. The USB core uses the buffer pointed to by the transfer_dma variable and not the buffer pointed to by the transfer_buffer variable.

URB_NO_SETUP_DMA_MAP

Like the URB_NO_TRANSFER_DMA_MAP bit, this bit is used for control urbs that have a DMA buffer already set up. If it is set, the USB core uses the buffer pointed to by the setup_dma variable instead of the setup_packet variable.

URB_ASYNC_UNLINK

If set, the call to *usb_unlink_urb* for this urb returns almost immediately, and the urb is unlinked in the background. Otherwise, the function waits until the urb is completely unlinked and finished before returning. Use this bit with care, because it can make synchronization issues very difficult to debug.

URB_NO_FSBR

Used by only the UHCI USB Host controller driver and tells it to not try to do Front Side Bus Reclamation logic. This bit should generally not be set, because machines with a UHCI host controller create a lot of CPU overhead, and the PCI bus is saturated waiting on a urb that sets this bit.

URB_ZERO_PACKET

If set, a bulk out urb finishes by sending a short packet containing no data when the data is aligned to an endpoint packet boundary. This is needed by some broken USB devices (such as a number of USB to IR devices) in order to work properly.

URB_NO_INTERRUPT

If set, the hardware may not generate an interrupt when the urb is finished. This bit should be used with care and only when queuing multiple urbs to the same endpoint. The USB core functions use this in order to do DMA buffer transfers.

void *transfer_buffer

Pointer to the buffer to be used when sending data to the device (for an OUT urb) or when receiving data from the device (for an IN urb). In order for the host controller to properly access this buffer, it must be created with a call to kmalloc, not on the stack or statically. For control endpoints, this buffer is for the data stage of the transfer.

dma_addr_t transfer_dma

Buffer to be used to transfer data to the USB device using DMA.

int transfer_buffer_length

The length of the buffer pointed to by the transfer_buffer or the transfer_dma variable (as only one can be used for a urb). If this is 0, neither transfer buffers are used by the USB core.

For an OUT endpoint, if the endpoint maximum size is smaller than the value specified in this variable, the transfer to the USB device is broken up into smaller chunks in order to properly transfer the data. This large transfer occurs in consecutive USB frames. It is much faster to submit a large block of data in one urb, and have the USB host controller split it up into smaller pieces, than it is to send smaller buffers in consecutive order.

unsigned char *setup_packet

Pointer to the setup packet for a control urb. It is transferred before the data in the transfer buffer. This variable is valid only for control urbs.

dma_addr_t setup_dma

DMA buffer for the setup packet for a control urb. It is transferred before the data in the normal transfer buffer. This variable is valid only for control urbs.

usb_complete_t complete

> Pointer to the completion handler function that is called by the USB core when the urb is completely transferred or when an error occurs to the urb. Within this function, the USB driver may inspect the urb, free it, or resubmit it for another transfer. (See the section "Completing Urbs: The Completion Callback Handler" for more details about the completion handler.)
>
> The usb_complete_t typedef is defined as:
>
> ```
> typedef void (*usb_complete_t)(struct urb *, struct pt_regs *);
> ```

void *context

> Pointer to a data blob that can be set by the USB driver. It can be used in the completion handler when the urb is returned to the driver. See the following section for more details about this variable.

int actual_length

> When the urb is finished, this variable is set to the actual length of the data either sent by the urb (for OUT urbs) or received by the urb (for IN urbs.) For IN urbs, this must be used instead of the transfer_buffer_length variable, because the data received could be smaller than the whole buffer size.

int status

> When the urb is finished, or being processed by the USB core, this variable is set to the current status of the urb. The only time a USB driver can safely access this variable is in the urb completion handler function (described in the section "Completing Urbs: The Completion Callback Handler"). This restriction is to prevent race conditions that occur while the urb is being processed by the USB core. For isochronous urbs, a successful value (0) in this variable merely indicates whether the urb has been unlinked. To obtain a detailed status on isochronous urbs, the iso_frame_desc variables should be checked.
>
> Valid values for this variable include:
>
> 0
>> The urb transfer was successful.
>
> -ENOENT
>> The urb was stopped by a call to *usb_kill_urb*.
>
> -ECONNRESET
>> The urb was unlinked by a call to *usb_unlink_urb*, and the transfer_flags variable of the urb was set to URB_ASYNC_UNLINK.
>
> -EINPROGRESS
>> The urb is still being processed by the USB host controllers. If your driver ever sees this value, it is a bug in your driver.
>
> -EPROTO
>> One of the following errors occurred with this urb:
>> - A bitstuff error happened during the transfer.
>> - No response packet was received in time by the hardware.

-EILSEQ

> There was a CRC mismatch in the urb transfer.

-EPIPE

> The endpoint is now stalled. If the endpoint involved is not a control endpoint, this error can be cleared through a call to the function *usb_clear_halt*.

-ECOMM

> Data was received faster during the transfer than it could be written to system memory. This error value happens only for an IN urb.

-ENOSR

> Data could not be retrieved from the system memory during the transfer fast enough to keep up with the requested USB data rate. This error value happens only for an OUT urb.

-EOVERFLOW

> A "babble" error happened to the urb. A "babble" error occurs when the endpoint receives more data than the endpoint's specified maximum packet size.

-EREMOTEIO

> Occurs only if the URB_SHORT_NOT_OK flag is set in the urb's transfer_flags variable and means that the full amount of data requested by the urb was not received.

-ENODEV

> The USB device is now gone from the system.

-EXDEV

> Occurs only for a isochronous urb and means that the transfer was only partially completed. In order to determine what was transferred, the driver must look at the individual frame status.

-EINVAL

> Something very bad happened with the urb. The USB kernel documentation describes what this value means:
>
> > ISO madness, if this happens: Log off and go home
>
> It also can happen if a parameter is incorrectly set in the urb stucture or if an incorrect function parameter in the *usb_submit_urb* call submitted the urb to the USB core.

-ESHUTDOWN

> There was a severe error with the USB host controller driver; it has now been disabled, or the device was disconnected from the system, and the urb was submitted after the device was removed. It can also occur if the configuration was changed for the device, while the urb was submitted to the device.

Generally, the error values -EPROTO, -EILSEQ, and -EOVERFLOW indicate hardware problems with the device, the device firmware, or the cable connecting the device to the computer.

int start_frame

Sets or returns the initial frame number for isochronous transfers to use.

int interval

The interval at which the urb is polled. This is valid only for interrupt or isochronous urbs. The value's units differ depending on the speed of the device. For low-speed and full-speed devices, the units are frames, which are equivalent to milliseconds. For devices, the units are in microframes, which is equivalent to units of 1/8 milliseconds. This value must be set by the USB driver for isochronous or interrupt urbs before the urb is sent to the USB core.

int number_of_packets

Valid only for isochronous urbs and specifies the number of isochronous transfer buffers to be handled by this urb. This value must be set by the USB driver for isochronous urbs before the urb is sent to the USB core.

int error_count

Set by the USB core only for isochronous urbs after their completion. It specifies the number of isochronous transfers that reported any type of error.

struct usb_iso_packet_descriptor iso_frame_desc[0]

Valid only for isochronous urbs. This variable is an array of the struct usb_iso_packet_descriptor structures that make up this urb. This structure allows a single urb to define a number of isochronous transfers at once. It is also used to collect the transfer status of each individual transfer.

The struct usb_iso_packet_descriptor is made up of the following fields:

unsigned int offset

The offset into the transfer buffer (starting at 0 for the first byte) where this packet's data is located.

unsigned int length

The length of the transfer buffer for this packet.

unsigned int actual_length

The length of the data received into the transfer buffer for this isochronous packet.

unsigned int status

The status of the individual isochronous transfer of this packet. It can take the same return values as the main struct urb structure's status variable.

Creating and Destroying Urbs

The struct urb structure must never be created statically in a driver or within another structure, because that would break the reference counting scheme used by the USB core for urbs. It must be created with a call to the *usb_alloc_urb* function. This function has the prototype:

```
struct urb *usb_alloc_urb(int iso_packets, int mem_flags);
```

The first parameter, iso_packets, is the number of isochronous packets this urb should contain. If you do not want to create an isochronous urb, this variable should be set to 0. The second parameter, mem_flags, is the same type of flag that is passed to the *kmalloc* function call to allocate memory from the kernel (see the section "The Flags Argument" in Chapter 8 for the details on these flags). If the function is successful in allocating enough space for the urb, a pointer to the urb is returned to the caller. If the return value is NULL, some error occurred within the USB core, and the driver needs to clean up properly.

After a urb has been created, it must be properly initialized before it can be used by the USB core. See the next sections for how to initialize different types of urbs.

In order to tell the USB core that the driver is finished with the urb, the driver must call the *usb_free_urb* function. This function only has one argument:

```
void usb_free_urb(struct urb *urb);
```

The argument is a pointer to the struct urb you want to release. After this function is called, the urb structure is gone, and the driver cannot access it any more.

Interrupt urbs

The function *usb_fill_int_urb* is a helper function to properly initialize a urb to be sent to a interrupt endpoint of a USB device:

```
void usb_fill_int_urb(struct urb *urb, struct usb_device *dev,
                      unsigned int pipe, void *transfer_buffer,
                      int buffer_length, usb_complete_t complete,
                      void *context, int interval);
```

This function contains a lot of parameters:

struct urb *urb
> A pointer to the urb to be initialized.

struct usb_device *dev
> The USB device to which this urb is to be sent.

unsigned int pipe
> The specific endpoint of the USB device to which this urb is to be sent. This value is created with the previously mentioned *usb_sndintpipe* or *usb_rcvintpipe* functions.

void *transfer_buffer
> A pointer to the buffer from which outgoing data is taken or into which incoming data is received. Note that this can not be a static buffer and must be created with a call to *kmalloc*.

int buffer_length
> The length of the buffer pointed to by the transfer_buffer pointer.

usb_complete_t complete
> Pointer to the completion handler that is called when this urb is completed.

void *context
> Pointer to the blob that is added to the urb structure for later retrieval by the completion handler function.

int interval
> The interval at which that this urb should be scheduled. See the previous description of the struct urb structure to find the proper units for this value.

Bulk urbs

Bulk urbs are initialized much like interrupt urbs. The function that does this is *usb_fill_bulk_urb*, and it looks like:

```
void usb_fill_bulk_urb(struct urb *urb, struct usb_device *dev,
                       unsigned int pipe, void *transfer_buffer,
                       int buffer_length, usb_complete_t complete,
                       void *context);
```

The function parameters are all the same as in the *usb_fill_int_urb* function. However, there is no interval parameter because bulk urbs have no interval value. Please note that the unsigned int pipe variable must be initialized with a call to the *usb_sndbulkpipe* or *usb_rcvbulkpipe* function.

The *usb_fill_int_urb* function does not set the transfer_flags variable in the urb, so any modification to this field has to be done by the driver itself.

Control urbs

Control urbs are initialized almost the same way as bulk urbs, with a call to the function *usb_fill_control_urb*:

```
void usb_fill_control_urb(struct urb *urb, struct usb_device *dev,
                          unsigned int pipe, unsigned char *setup_packet,
                          void *transfer_buffer, int buffer_length,
                          usb_complete_t complete, void *context);
```

The function parameters are all the same as in the *usb_fill_bulk_urb* function, except that there is a new parameter, unsigned char *setup_packet, which must point to the setup packet data that is to be sent to the endpoint. Also, the unsigned int pipe variable must be initialized with a call to the *usb_sndctrlpipe* or *usb_rcvictrlpipe* function.

The *usb_fill_control_urb* function does not set the transfer_flags variable in the urb, so any modification to this field has to be done by the driver itself. Most drivers do not use this function, as it is much simpler to use the synchronous API calls as described in the section "USB Transfers Without Urbs."

Isochronous urbs

Isochronous urbs unfortunately do not have an initializer function like the interrupt, control, and bulk urbs do. So they must be initialized "by hand" in the driver before they can be submitted to the USB core. The following is an example of how to properly initialize this type of urb. It was taken from the *konicawc.c* kernel driver located in the *drivers/usb/media* directory in the main kernel source tree.

```
urb->dev = dev;
urb->context = uvd;
urb->pipe = usb_rcvisocpipe(dev, uvd->video_endp-1);
urb->interval = 1;
urb->transfer_flags = URB_ISO_ASAP;
urb->transfer_buffer = cam->sts_buf[i];
urb->complete = konicawc_isoc_irq;
urb->number_of_packets = FRAMES_PER_DESC;
urb->transfer_buffer_length = FRAMES_PER_DESC;
for (j=0; j < FRAMES_PER_DESC; j++) {
        urb->iso_frame_desc[j].offset = j;
        urb->iso_frame_desc[j].length = 1;
}
```

Submitting Urbs

Once the urb has been properly created and initialized by the USB driver, it is ready to be submitted to the USB core to be sent out to the USB device. This is done with a call to the function *usb_submit_urb*:

```
int usb_submit_urb(struct urb *urb, int mem_flags);
```

The urb parameter is a pointer to the urb that is to be sent to the device. The mem_flags parameter is equivalent to the same parameter that is passed to the *kmalloc* call and is used to tell the USB core how to allocate any memory buffers at this moment in time.

After a urb has been submitted to the USB core successfully, it should never try to access any fields of the urb structure until the *complete* function is called.

Because the function *usb_submit_urb* can be called at any time (including from within an interrupt context), the specification of the mem_flags variable must be correct. There are really only three valid values that should be used, depending on when *usb_submit_urb* is being called:

GFP_ATOMIC
> This value should be used whenever the following are true:
> - The caller is within a urb completion handler, an interrupt, a bottom half, a tasklet, or a timer callback.
> - The caller is holding a spinlock or rwlock. Note that if a semaphore is being held, this value is not necessary.
> - The current->state is not TASK_RUNNING. The state is always TASK_RUNNING unless the driver has changed the current state itself.

`GFP_NOIO`
> This value should be used if the driver is in the block I/O patch. It should also be used in the error handling path of all storage-type devices.

`GFP_KERNEL`
> This should be used for all other situations that do not fall into one of the previously mentioned categories.

Completing Urbs: The Completion Callback Handler

If the call to *usb_submit_urb* was successful, transferring control of the urb to the USB core, the function returns 0; otherwise, a negative error number is returned. If the function succeeds, the completion handler of the urb (as specified by the *complete* function pointer) is called exactly once when the urb is completed. When this function is called, the USB core is finished with the URB, and control of it is now returned to the device driver.

There are only three ways a urb can be finished and have the *complete* function called:

- The urb is successfully sent to the device, and the device returns the proper acknowledgment. For an OUT urb, the data was successfully sent, and for an IN urb, the requested data was successfully received. If this has happened, the status variable in the urb is set to 0.

- Some kind of error happened when sending or receiving data from the device. This is noted by the error value in the status variable in the urb structure.

- The urb was "unlinked" from the USB core. This happens either when the driver tells the USB core to cancel a submitted urb with a call to *usb_unlink_urb* or *usb_kill_urb*, or when a device is removed from the system and a urb had been submitted to it.

An example of how to test for the different return values within a urb completion call is shown later in this chapter.

Canceling Urbs

To stop a urb that has been submitted to the USB core, the functions *usb_kill_urb* or *usb_unlink_urb* should be called:

```
int usb_kill_urb(struct urb *urb);
int usb_unlink_urb(struct urb *urb);
```

The urb parameter for both of these functions is a pointer to the urb that is to be canceled.

When the function is *usb_kill_urb*, the urb lifecycle is stopped. This function is usually used when the device is disconnected from the system, in the disconnect callback.

For some drivers, the *usb_unlink_urb* function should be used to tell the USB core to stop an urb. This function does not wait for the urb to be fully stopped before returning to the caller. This is useful for stopping the urb while in an interrupt handler or when a spinlock is held, as waiting for a urb to fully stop requires the ability for the USB core to put the calling process to sleep. This function requires that the URB_ASYNC_UNLINK flag value be set in the urb that is being asked to be stopped in order to work properly.

Writing a USB Driver

The approach to writing a USB device driver is similar to a pci_driver: the driver registers its driver object with the USB subsystem and later uses vendor and device identifiers to tell if its hardware has been installed.

What Devices Does the Driver Support?

The struct usb_device_id structure provides a list of different types of USB devices that this driver supports. This list is used by the USB core to decide which driver to give a device to, and by the hotplug scripts to decide which driver to automatically load when a specific device is plugged into the system.

The struct usb_device_id structure is defined with the following fields:

__u16 match_flags
> Determines which of the following fields in the structure the device should be matched against. This is a bit field defined by the different USB_DEVICE_ID_MATCH_* values specified in the *include/linux/mod_devicetable.h* file. This field is usually never set directly but is initialized by the USB_DEVICE type macros described later.

__u16 idVendor
> The USB vendor ID for the device. This number is assigned by the USB forum to its members and cannot be made up by anyone else.

__u16 idProduct
> The USB product ID for the device. All vendors that have a vendor ID assigned to them can manage their product IDs however they choose to.

__u16 bcdDevice_lo
__u16 bcdDevice_hi
> Define the low and high ends of the range of the vendor-assigned product version number. The bcdDevice_hi value is inclusive; its value is the number of the highest-numbered device. Both of these values are expressed in binary-coded

decimal (BCD) form. These variables, combined with the idVendor and idProduct, are used to define a specific version of a device.

`__u8 bDeviceClass`
`__u8 bDeviceSubClass`
`__u8 bDeviceProtocol`

Define the class, subclass, and protocol of the device, respectively. These numbers are assigned by the USB forum and are defined in the USB specification. These values specify the behavior for the whole device, including all interfaces on this device.

`__u8 bInterfaceClass`
`__u8 bInterfaceSubClass`
`__u8 bInterfaceProtocol`

Much like the device-specific values above, these define the class, subclass, and protocol of the individual interface, respectively. These numbers are assigned by the USB forum and are defined in the USB specification.

`kernel_ulong_t driver_info`

This value is not used to match against, but it holds information that the driver can use to differentiate the different devices from each other in the probe callback function to the USB driver.

As with PCI devices, there are a number of macros that are used to initialize this structure:

`USB_DEVICE(vendor, product)`

Creates a struct usb_device_id that can be used to match only the specified vendor and product ID values. This is very commonly used for USB devices that need a specific driver.

`USB_DEVICE_VER(vendor, product, lo, hi)`

Creates a struct usb_device_id that can be used to match only the specified vendor and product ID values within a version range.

`USB_DEVICE_INFO(class, subclass, protocol)`

Creates a struct usb_device_id that can be used to match a specific class of USB devices.

`USB_INTERFACE_INFO(class, subclass, protocol)`

Creates a struct usb_device_id that can be used to match a specific class of USB interfaces.

So, for a simple USB device driver that controls only a single USB device from a single vendor, the struct usb_device_id table would be defined as:

```
/* table of devices that work with this driver */
static struct usb_device_id skel_table [ ] = {
    { USB_DEVICE(USB_SKEL_VENDOR_ID, USB_SKEL_PRODUCT_ID) },
    { }                    /* Terminating entry */
};
MODULE_DEVICE_TABLE (usb, skel_table);
```

As with a PCI driver, the `MODULE_DEVICE_TABLE` macro is necessary to allow user-space tools to figure out what devices this driver can control. But for USB drivers, the string usb must be the first value in the macro.

Registering a USB Driver

The main structure that all USB drivers must create is a `struct usb_driver`. This structure must be filled out by the USB driver and consists of a number of function callbacks and variables that describe the USB driver to the USB core code:

`struct module *owner`

> Pointer to the module owner of this driver. The USB core uses it to properly reference count this USB driver so that it is not unloaded at inopportune moments. The variable should be set to the `THIS_MODULE` macro.

`const char *name`

> Pointer to the name of the driver. It must be unique among all USB drivers in the kernel and is normally set to the same name as the module name of the driver. It shows up in sysfs under */sys/bus/usb/drivers/* when the driver is in the kernel.

`const struct usb_device_id *id_table`

> Pointer to the `struct usb_device_id` table that contains a list of all of the different kinds of USB devices this driver can accept. If this variable is not set, the probe function callback in the USB driver is never called. If you want your driver always to be called for every USB device in the system, create a entry that sets only the `driver_info` field:
>
> ```
> static struct usb_device_id usb_ids[ ] = {
>     {.driver_info = 42},
>     { }
> };
> ```

`int (*probe) (struct usb_interface *intf, const struct usb_device_id *id)`

> Pointer to the probe function in the USB driver. This function (described in the section "probe and disconnect in Detail") is called by the USB core when it thinks it has a `struct usb_interface` that this driver can handle. A pointer to the `struct usb_device_id` that the USB core used to make this decision is also passed to this function. If the USB driver claims the `struct usb_interface` that is passed to it, it should initialize the device properly and return 0. If the driver does not want to claim the device, or an error occurs, it should return a negative error value.

`void (*disconnect) (struct usb_interface *intf)`

> Pointer to the disconnect function in the USB driver. This function (described in the section "probe and disconnect in Detail") is called by the USB core when the `struct usb_interface` has been removed from the system or when the driver is being unloaded from the USB core.

So, to create a value struct usb_driver structure, only five fields need to be initialized:

```
static struct usb_driver skel_driver = {
    .owner = THIS_MODULE,
    .name = "skeleton",
    .id_table = skel_table,
    .probe = skel_probe,
    .disconnect = skel_disconnect,
};
```

The struct usb_driver does contain a few more callbacks, which are generally not used very often, and are not required in order for a USB driver to work properly:

int (*ioctl) (struct usb_interface *intf, unsigned int code, void *buf)
Pointer to an *ioctl* function in the USB driver. If it is present, it is called when a user-space program makes a *ioctl* call on the *usbfs* filesystem device entry associated with a USB device attached to this USB driver. In pratice, only the USB hub driver uses this ioctl, as there is no other real need for any other USB driver to use it.

int (*suspend) (struct usb_interface *intf, u32 state)
Pointer to a suspend function in the USB driver. It is called when the device is to be suspended by the USB core.

int (*resume) (struct usb_interface *intf)
Pointer to a resume function in the USB driver. It is called when the device is being resumed by the USB core.

To register the struct usb_driver with the USB core, a call to *usb_register_driver* is made with a pointer to the struct usb_driver. This is traditionally done in the module initialization code for the USB driver:

```
static int __init usb_skel_init(void)
{
    int result;

    /* register this driver with the USB subsystem */
    result = usb_register(&skel_driver);
    if (result)
        err("usb_register failed. Error number %d", result);

    return result;
}
```

When the USB driver is to be unloaded, the struct usb_driver needs to be unregistered from the kernel. This is done with a call to *usb_deregister_driver*. When this call happens, any USB interfaces that were currently bound to this driver are disconnected, and the *disconnect* function is called for them.

```
static void __exit usb_skel_exit(void)
{
    /* deregister this driver with the USB subsystem */
    usb_deregister(&skel_driver);
}
```

probe and disconnect in Detail

In the struct usb_driver structure described in the previous section, the driver specified two functions that the USB core calls at appropriate times. The *probe* function is
called when a device is installed that the USB core thinks this driver should handle;
the *probe* function should perform checks on the information passed to it about the
device and decide whether the driver is really appropriate for that device. The *disconnect* function is called when the driver should no longer control the device for some
reason and can do clean-up.

Both the *probe* and *disconnect* function callbacks are called in the context of the USB
hub kernel thread, so it is legal to sleep within them. However, it is recommended
that the majority of work be done when the device is opened by a user if possible, in
order to keep the USB probing time to a minimum. This is because the USB core
handles the addition and removal of USB devices within a single thread, so any slow
device driver can cause the USB device detection time to slow down and become
noticeable by the user.

In the *probe* function callback, the USB driver should initialize any local structures
that it might use to manage the USB device. It should also save any information that
it needs about the device to the local structure, as it is usually easier to do so at this
time. As an example, USB drivers usually want to detect what the endpoint address
and buffer sizes are for the device, as they are needed in order to communicate with
the device. Here is some example code that detects both IN and OUT endpoints of
BULK type and saves some information about them in a local device structure:

```
/* set up the endpoint information */
/* use only the first bulk-in and bulk-out endpoints */
iface_desc = interface->cur_altsetting;
for (i = 0; i < iface_desc->desc.bNumEndpoints; ++i) {
    endpoint = &iface_desc->endpoint[i].desc;

    if (!dev->bulk_in_endpointAddr &&
        (endpoint->bEndpointAddress & USB_DIR_IN) &&
        ((endpoint->bmAttributes & USB_ENDPOINT_XFERTYPE_MASK)
                == USB_ENDPOINT_XFER_BULK)) {
        /* we found a bulk in endpoint */
        buffer_size = endpoint->wMaxPacketSize;
        dev->bulk_in_size = buffer_size;
        dev->bulk_in_endpointAddr = endpoint->bEndpointAddress;
        dev->bulk_in_buffer = kmalloc(buffer_size, GFP_KERNEL);
        if (!dev->bulk_in_buffer) {
            err("Could not allocate bulk_in_buffer");
            goto error;
        }
    }

    if (!dev->bulk_out_endpointAddr &&
        !(endpoint->bEndpointAddress & USB_DIR_IN) &&
        ((endpoint->bmAttributes & USB_ENDPOINT_XFERTYPE_MASK)
```

```
            == USB_ENDPOINT_XFER_BULK)) {
        /* we found a bulk out endpoint */
        dev->bulk_out_endpointAddr = endpoint->bEndpointAddress;
    }
}
if (!(dev->bulk_in_endpointAddr && dev->bulk_out_endpointAddr)) {
    err("Could not find both bulk-in and bulk-out endpoints");
    goto error;
}
```

This block of code first loops over every endpoint that is present in this interface and assigns a local pointer to the endpoint structure to make it easier to access later:

```
for (i = 0; i < iface_desc->desc.bNumEndpoints; ++i) {
    endpoint = &iface_desc->endpoint[i].desc;
```

Then, after we have an endpoint, and we have not found a bulk IN type endpoint already, we look to see if this endpoint's direction is IN. That can be tested by seeing whether the bitmask USB_DIR_IN is contained in the bEndpointAddress endpoint variable. If this is true, we determine whether the endpoint type is bulk or not, by first masking off the bmAttributes variable with the USB_ENDPOINT_XFERTYPE_MASK bitmask, and then checking if it matches the value USB_ENDPOINT_XFER_BULK:

```
if (!dev->bulk_in_endpointAddr &&
    (endpoint->bEndpointAddress & USB_DIR_IN) &&
    ((endpoint->bmAttributes & USB_ENDPOINT_XFERTYPE_MASK)
            == USB_ENDPOINT_XFER_BULK)) {
```

If all of these tests are true, the driver knows it found the proper type of endpoint and can save the information about the endpoint that it will later need to communicate over it in a local structure:

```
/* we found a bulk in endpoint */
buffer_size = endpoint->wMaxPacketSize;
dev->bulk_in_size = buffer_size;
dev->bulk_in_endpointAddr = endpoint->bEndpointAddress;
dev->bulk_in_buffer = kmalloc(buffer_size, GFP_KERNEL);
if (!dev->bulk_in_buffer) {
    err("Could not allocate bulk_in_buffer");
    goto error;
}
```

Because the USB driver needs to retrieve the local data structure that is associated with this struct usb_interface later in the lifecycle of the device, the function *usb_set_intfdata* can be called:

```
/* save our data pointer in this interface device */
usb_set_intfdata(interface, dev);
```

This function accepts a pointer to any data type and saves it in the struct usb_interface structure for later access. To retrieve the data, the function *usb_get_intfdata* should be called:

```
struct usb_skel *dev;
struct usb_interface *interface;
```

```
    int subminor;
    int retval = 0;

    subminor = iminor(inode);

    interface = usb_find_interface(&skel_driver, subminor);
    if (!interface) {
        err ("%s - error, can't find device for minor %d",
            __FUNCTION__, subminor);
        retval = -ENODEV;
        goto exit;
    }

    dev = usb_get_intfdata(interface);
    if (!dev) {
        retval = -ENODEV;
        goto exit;
    }
```

usb_get_intfdata is usually called in the *open* function of the USB driver and again in the *disconnect* function. Thanks to these two functions, USB drivers do not need to keep a static array of pointers that store the individual device structures for all current devices in the system. The indirect reference to device information allows an unlimited number of devices to be supported by any USB driver.

If the USB driver is not associated with another type of subsystem that handles the user interaction with the device (such as input, tty, video, etc.), the driver can use the USB major number in order to use the traditional char driver interface with user space. To do this, the USB driver must call the *usb_register_dev* function in the *probe* function when it wants to register a device with the USB core. Make sure that the device and driver are in a proper state to handle a user wanting to access the device as soon as this function is called.

```
    /* we can register the device now, as it is ready */
    retval = usb_register_dev(interface, &skel_class);
    if (retval) {
        /* something prevented us from registering this driver */
        err("Not able to get a minor for this device.");
        usb_set_intfdata(interface, NULL);
        goto error;
    }
```

The *usb_register_dev* function requires a pointer to a struct usb_interface and a pointer to a struct usb_class_driver. This struct usb_class_driver is used to define a number of different parameters that the USB driver wants the USB core to know when registering for a minor number. This structure consists of the following variables:

char *name

> The name that sysfs uses to describe the device. A leading pathname, if present, is used only in devfs and is not covered in this book. If the number of the device needs to be in the name, the characters %d should be in the name string. For

---

example, to create the devfs name usb/foo1 and the sysfs class name foo1, the name string should be set to usb/foo%d.

struct file_operations *fops;
> Pointer to the struct file_operations that this driver has defined to use to register as the character device. See Chapter 3 for more information about this structure.

mode_t mode;
> The mode for the devfs file to be created for this driver; unused otherwise. A typical setting for this variable would be the value S_IRUSR combined with the value S_IWUSR, which would provide only read and write access by the owner of the device file.

int minor_base;
> This is the start of the assigned minor range for this driver. All devices associated with this driver are created with unique, increasing minor numbers beginning with this value. Only 16 devices are allowed to be associated with this driver at any one time unless the CONFIG_USB_DYNAMIC_MINORS configuration option has been enabled for the kernel. If so, this variable is ignored, and all minor numbers for the device are allocated on a first-come, first-served manner. It is recommended that systems that have enabled this option use a program such as *udev* to manage the device nodes in the system, as a static */dev* tree will not work properly.

When the USB device is disconnected, all resources associated with the device should be cleaned up, if possible. At this time, if *usb_register_dev* has been called to allocate a minor number for this USB device during the *probe* function, the function *usb_deregister_dev* must be called to give the minor number back to the USB core.

In the *disconnect* function, it is also important to retrieve from the interface any data that was previously set with a call to *usb_set_intfdata*. Then set the data pointer in the struct usb_interface structure to NULL to prevent any further mistakes in accessing the data improperly:

```
static void skel_disconnect(struct usb_interface *interface)
{
    struct usb_skel *dev;
    int minor = interface->minor;

    /* prevent skel_open() from racing skel_disconnect() */
    lock_kernel();

    dev = usb_get_intfdata(interface);
    usb_set_intfdata(interface, NULL);

    /* give back our minor */
    usb_deregister_dev(interface, &skel_class);

    unlock_kernel();
```

```
        /* decrement our usage count */
        kref_put(&dev->kref, skel_delete);

        info("USB Skeleton #%d now disconnected", minor);
}
```

Note the call to *lock_kernel* in the previous code snippet. This takes the big kernel lock, so that the *disconnect* callback does not encounter a race condition with the open call when trying to get a pointer to the correct interface data structure. Because the open is called with the big kernel lock taken, if the *disconnect* also takes that same lock, only one portion of the driver can access and then set the interface data pointer.

Just before the *disconnect* function is called for a USB device, all urbs that are currently in transmission for the device are canceled by the USB core, so the driver does not have to explicitly call *usb_kill_urb* for these urbs. If a driver tries to submit a urb to a USB device after it has been disconnected with a call to *usb_submit_urb*, the submission will fail with an error value of -EPIPE.

Submitting and Controlling a Urb

When the driver has data to send to the USB device (as typically happens in a driver's write function), a urb must be allocated for transmitting the data to the device:

```
urb = usb_alloc_urb(0, GFP_KERNEL);
if (!urb) {
    retval = -ENOMEM;
    goto error;
}
```

After the urb is allocated successfully, a DMA buffer should also be created to send the data to the device in the most efficient manner, and the data that is passed to the driver should be copied into that buffer:

```
buf = usb_buffer_alloc(dev->udev, count, GFP_KERNEL, &urb->transfer_dma);
if (!buf) {
    retval = -ENOMEM;
    goto error;
}
if (copy_from_user(buf, user_buffer, count)) {
    retval = -EFAULT;
    goto error;
}
```

Once the data is properly copied from the user space into the local buffer, the urb must be initialized correctly before it can be submitted to the USB core:

```
/* initialize the urb properly */
usb_fill_bulk_urb(urb, dev->udev,
        usb_sndbulkpipe(dev->udev, dev->bulk_out_endpointAddr),
        buf, count, skel_write_bulk_callback, dev);
urb->transfer_flags |= URB_NO_TRANSFER_DMA_MAP;
```

Now that the urb is properly allocated, the data is properly copied, and the urb is properly initialized, it can be submitted to the USB core to be transmitted to the device:

```
/* send the data out the bulk port */
retval = usb_submit_urb(urb, GFP_KERNEL);
if (retval) {
    err("%s - failed submitting write urb, error %d", __FUNCTION__, retval);
    goto error;
}
```

After the urb is successfully transmitted to the USB device (or something happens in transmission), the urb callback is called by the USB core. In our example, we initialized the urb to point to the function *skel_write_bulk_callback*, and that is the function that is called:

```
static void skel_write_bulk_callback(struct urb *urb, struct pt_regs *regs)
{
    /* sync/async unlink faults aren't errors */
    if (urb->status &&
        !(urb->status == -ENOENT ||
          urb->status == -ECONNRESET ||
          urb->status == -ESHUTDOWN)) {
        dbg("%s - nonzero write bulk status received: %d",
            __FUNCTION__, urb->status);
    }

    /* free up our allocated buffer */
    usb_buffer_free(urb->dev, urb->transfer_buffer_length,
            urb->transfer_buffer, urb->transfer_dma);
}
```

The first thing the callback function does is check the status of the urb to determine if this urb completed successfully or not. The error values, -ENOENT, -ECONNRESET, and -ESHUTDOWN are not real transmission errors, just reports about conditions accompanying a successful transmission. (See the list of possible errors for urbs detailed in the section "struct urb.") Then the callback frees up the allocated buffer that was assigned to this urb to transmit.

It's common for another urb to be submitted to the device while the urb callback function is running. This is useful when streaming data to a device. Remember that the urb callback is running in interrupt context, so it should do any memory allocation, hold any semaphores, or do anything else that could cause the process to sleep. When submitting a urb from within a callback, use the GFP_ATOMIC flag to tell the USB core to not sleep if it needs to allocate new memory chunks during the submission process.

USB Transfers Without Urbs

Sometimes a USB driver does not want to go through all of the hassle of creating a struct urb, initializing it, and then waiting for the urb completion function to run, just to send or receive some simple USB data. Two functions are available to provide a simpler interface.

usb_bulk_msg

usb_bulk_msg creates a USB bulk urb and sends it to the specified device, then waits for it to complete before returning to the caller. It is defined as:

```
int usb_bulk_msg(struct usb_device *usb_dev, unsigned int pipe,
                 void *data, int len, int *actual_length,
                 int timeout);
```

The parameters of this function are:

struct usb_device *usb_dev
: A pointer to the USB device to send the bulk message to.

unsigned int pipe
: The specific endpoint of the USB device to which this bulk message is to be sent. This value is created with a call to either *usb_sndbulkpipe* or *usb_rcvbulkpipe*.

void *data
: A pointer to the data to send to the device if this is an OUT endpoint. If this is an IN endpoint, this is a pointer to where the data should be placed after being read from the device.

int len
: The length of the buffer that is pointed to by the data parameter.

int *actual_length
: A pointer to where the function places the actual number of bytes that have either been transferred to the device or received from the device, depending on the direction of the endpoint.

int timeout
: The amount of time, in jiffies, that should be waited before timing out. If this value is 0, the function waits forever for the message to complete.

If the function is successful, the return value is 0; otherwise, a negative error number is returned. This error number matches up with the error numbers previously described for urbs in the section "struct urb." If successful, the actual_length parameter contains the number of bytes that were transferred or received from this message.

The following is an example of using this function call:

```
/* do a blocking bulk read to get data from the device */
retval = usb_bulk_msg(dev->udev,
            usb_rcvbulkpipe(dev->udev, dev->bulk_in_endpointAddr),
```

```
            dev->bulk_in_buffer,
            min(dev->bulk_in_size, count),
            &count, HZ*10);

    /* if the read was successful, copy the data to user space */
    if (!retval) {
        if (copy_to_user(buffer, dev->bulk_in_buffer, count))
            retval = -EFAULT;
        else
            retval = count;
    }
```

This example shows a simple bulk read from an IN endpoint. If the read is success-ful, the data is then copied to user space. This is typically done in a read function for a USB driver.

The *usb_bulk_msg* function cannot be called from within interrupt context or with a spinlock held. Also, this function cannot be canceled by any other function, so be careful when using it; make sure that your driver's *disconnect* knows enough to wait for the call to complete before allowing itself to be unloaded from memory.

usb_control_msg

The *usb_control_msg* function works just like the *usb_bulk_msg* function, except it allows a driver to send and receive USB control messages:

```
int usb_control_msg(struct usb_device *dev, unsigned int pipe,
                    __u8 request, __u8 requesttype,
                    __u16 value, __u16 index,
                    void *data, __u16 size, int timeout);
```

The parameters of this function are almost the same as *usb_bulk_msg*, with a few important differences:

struct usb_device *dev
  A pointer to the USB device to send the control message to.

unsigned int pipe
  The specific endpoint of the USB device that this control message is to be sent to. This value is created with a call to either *usb_sndctrlpipe* or *usb_rcvctrlpipe*.

__u8 request
  The USB request value for the control message.

__u8 requesttype
  The USB request type value for the control message

__u16 value
  The USB message value for the control message.

__u16 index
  The USB message index value for the control message.

```
void *data
```
> A pointer to the data to send to the device if this is an OUT endpoint. If this is
> an IN endpoint, this is a pointer to where the data should be placed after being
> read from the device.

```
__u16 size
```
> The size of the buffer that is pointed to by the data parameter.

```
int timeout
```
> The amount of time, in jiffies, that should be waited before timing out. If this
> value is 0, the function will wait forever for the message to complete.

If the function is successful, it returns the number of bytes that were transferred to or
from the device. If it is not successful, it returns a negative error number.

The parameters request, requesttype, value, and index all directly map to the USB
specification for how a USB control message is defined. For more information on the
valid values for these parameters and how they are used, see Chapter 9 of the USB
specification.

Like the function *usb_bulk_msg*, the function *usb_control_msg* cannot be called from
within interrupt context or with a spinlock held. Also, this function cannot be canceled by any other function, so be careful when using it; make sure that your driver
disconnect function knows enough to wait for the call to complete before allowing
itself to be unloaded from memory.

Other USB Data Functions

A number of helper functions in the USB core can be used to retrieve standard information from all USB devices. These functions cannot be called from within interrupt
context or with a spinlock held.

The function *usb_get_descriptor* retrieves the specified USB descriptor from the specified device. The function is defined as:

```
int usb_get_descriptor(struct usb_device *dev, unsigned char type,
                       unsigned char index, void *buf, int size);
```

This function can be used by a USB driver to retrieve from the struct usb_device
structure any of the device descriptors that are not already present in the existing
struct usb_device and struct usb_interface structures, such as audio descriptors or
other class specific information. The parameters of the function are:

```
struct usb_device *usb_dev
```
> A pointer to the USB device that the descriptor should be retrieved from.

```
unsigned char type
```
> The descriptor type. This type is described in the USB specification and can be
> one of the following types:
> ```
> USB_DT_DEVICE
> USB_DT_CONFIG
> ```

```
USB_DT_STRING
USB_DT_INTERFACE
USB_DT_ENDPOINT
USB_DT_DEVICE_QUALIFIER
USB_DT_OTHER_SPEED_CONFIG
USB_DT_INTERFACE_POWER
USB_DT_OTG
USB_DT_DEBUG
USB_DT_INTERFACE_ASSOCIATION
USB_DT_CS_DEVICE
USB_DT_CS_CONFIG
USB_DT_CS_STRING
USB_DT_CS_INTERFACE
USB_DT_CS_ENDPOINT
```

unsigned char index
> The number of the descriptor that should be retrieved from the device.

void *buf
> A pointer to the buffer to which you copy the descriptor.

int size
> The size of the memory pointed to by the buf variable.

If this function is successful, it returns the number of bytes read from the device. Otherwise, it returns a negative error number returned by the underlying call to *usb_control_msg* that this function makes.

One of the more common uses for the *usb_get_descriptor* call is to retrieve a string from the USB device. Because this is quite common, there is a helper function for it called *usb_get_string*:

```
int usb_get_string(struct usb_device *dev, unsigned short langid,
                   unsigned char index, void *buf, int size);
```

If successful, this function returns the number of bytes received by the device for the string. Otherwise, it returns a negative error number returned by the underlying call to *usb_control_msg* that this function makes.

If this function is successful, it returns a string encoded in the UTF-16LE format (Unicode, 16 bits per character, in little-endian byte order) in the buffer pointed to by the buf parameter. As this format is usually not very useful, there is another function, called *usb_string*, that returns a string that is read from a USB device and is already converted into an ISO 8859-1 format string. This character set is a 8-bit subset of Unicode and is the most common format for strings in English and other Western European languages. As this is typically the format that the USB device's strings are in, it is recommended that the *usb_string* function be used instead of the *usb_get_string* function.

Quick Reference

This section summarizes the symbols introduced in the chapter:

#include <linux/usb.h>
> Header file where everything related to USB resides. It must be included by all USB device drivers.

struct usb_driver;
> Structure that describes a USB driver.

struct usb_device_id;
> Structure that describes the types of USB devices this driver supports.

int usb_register(struct usb_driver *d);
void usb_deregister(struct usb_driver *d);
> Functions used to register and unregister a USB driver from the USB core.

struct usb_device *interface_to_usbdev(struct usb_interface *intf);
> Retrieves the controlling struct usb_device * out of a struct usb_interface *.

struct usb_device;
> Structure that controls an entire USB device.

struct usb_interface;
> Main USB device structure that all USB drivers use to communicate with the USB core.

void usb_set_intfdata(struct usb_interface *intf, void *data);
void *usb_get_intfdata(struct usb_interface *intf);
> Functions to set and get access to the private data pointer section within the struct usb_interface.

struct usb_class_driver;
> A structure that describes a USB driver that wants to use the USB major number to communicate with user-space programs.

int usb_register_dev(struct usb_interface *intf, struct usb_class_driver *class_driver);
void usb_deregister_dev(struct usb_interface *intf, struct usb_class_driver *class_driver);
> Functions used to register and unregister a specific struct usb_interface * structure with a struct usb_class_driver * structure.

struct urb;
> Structure that describes a USB data transmission.

struct urb *usb_alloc_urb(int iso_packets, int mem_flags);
void usb_free_urb(struct urb *urb);
> Functions used to create and destroy a struct usb urb *.

```
int usb_submit_urb(struct urb *urb, int mem_flags);
int usb_kill_urb(struct urb *urb);
int usb_unlink_urb(struct urb *urb);
```
   Functions used to start and stop a USB data transmission.

```
void usb_fill_int_urb(struct urb *urb, struct usb_device *dev, unsigned int
  pipe, void *transfer_buffer, int buffer_length, usb_complete_t complete,
  void *context, int interval);
void usb_fill_bulk_urb(struct urb *urb, struct usb_device *dev, unsigned int
  pipe, void *transfer_buffer, int buffer_length, usb_complete_t complete,
  void *context);
void usb_fill_control_urb(struct urb *urb, struct usb_device *dev, unsigned
  int pipe, unsigned char *setup_packet, void *transfer_buffer, int
  buffer_ length, usb_complete_t complete, void *context);
```
   Functions used to initialize a struct urb before it is submitted to the USB core.

```
int usb_bulk_msg(struct usb_device *usb_dev, unsigned int pipe, void *data,
  int len, int *actual_length, int timeout);
int usb_control_msg(struct usb_device *dev, unsigned int pipe, __u8 request,
  __u8 requesttype, __u16 value, __u16 index, void *data, __u16 size,
  int timeout);
```
   Functions used to send or receive USB data without having to use a struct urb.

CHAPTER 14
The Linux Device Model

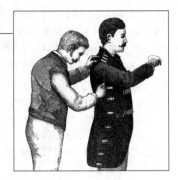

One of the stated goals for the 2.5 development cycle was the creation of a unified device model for the kernel. Previous kernels had no single data structure to which they could turn to obtain information about how the system is put together. Despite this lack of information, things worked well for some time. The demands of newer systems, with their more complicated topologies and need to support features such as power management, made it clear, however, that a general abstraction describing the structure of the system was needed.

The 2.6 device model provides that abstraction. It is now used within the kernel to support a wide variety of tasks, including:

Power management and system shutdown

These require an understanding of the system's structure. For example, a USB host adaptor cannot be shut down before dealing with all of the devices connected to that adaptor. The device model enables a traversal of the system's hardware in the right order.

Communications with user space

The implementation of the sysfs virtual filesystem is tightly tied into the device model and exposes the structure represented by it. The provision of information about the system to user space and knobs for changing operating parameters is increasingly done through sysfs and, therefore, through the device model.

Hotpluggable devices

Computer hardware is increasingly dynamic; peripherals can come and go at the whim of the user. The hotplug mechanism used within the kernel to handle and (especially) communicate with user space about the plugging and unplugging of devices is managed through the device model.

Device classes

Many parts of the system have little interest in how devices are connected, but they need to know what kinds of devices are available. The device model includes a mechanism for assigning devices to *classes*, which describe those devices at a higher, functional level and allow them to be discovered from user space.

Object lifecycles

Many of the functions described above, including hotplug support and sysfs, complicate the creation and manipulation of objects created within the kernel. The implementation of the device model required the creation of a set of mechanisms for dealing with object lifecycles, their relationships to each other, and their representation in user space.

The Linux device model is a complex data structure. For example, consider Figure 14-1, which shows (in simplified form) a tiny piece of the device model structure associated with a USB mouse. Down the center of the diagram, we see the part of the core "devices" tree that shows how the mouse is connected to the system. The "bus" tree tracks what is connected to each bus, while the subtree under "classes" concerns itself with the functions provided by the devices, regardless of how they are connected. The device model tree on even a simple system contains hundreds of nodes like those shown in the diagram; it is a difficult data structure to visualize as a whole.

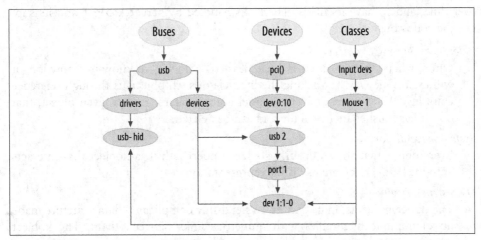

Figure 14-1. A small piece of the device model

For the most part, the Linux device model code takes care of all these considerations without imposing itself upon driver authors. It sits mostly in the background; direct interaction with the device model is generally handled by bus-level logic and various other kernel subsystems. As a result, many driver authors can ignore the device model entirely, and trust it to take care of itself.

There are times, however, when an understanding of the device model is a good thing to have. There are times when the device model "leaks out" from behind the other layers; for example, the generic DMA code (which we encounter in

Chapter 15) works with struct device. You may want to use some of the capabilities provided by the device model, such as the reference counting and related features provided by kobjects. Communication with user space via sysfs is also a device model function; this chapter explains how that communication works.

We start, however, with a bottom-up presentation of the device model. The complexity of the device model makes it hard to understand by starting with a high-level view. Our hope is that, by showing how the low-level device components work, we can prepare you for the challenge of grasping how those components are used to build the larger structure.

For many readers, this chapter can be treated as advanced material that need not be read the first time through. Those who are interested in how the Linux device model works are encouraged to press ahead, however, as we get into the low-level details.

Kobjects, Ksets, and Subsystems

The *kobject* is the fundamental structure that holds the device model together. It was initially conceived as a simple reference counter, but its responsibilities have grown over time, and so have its fields. The tasks handled by struct kobject and its supporting code now include:

Reference counting of objects
> Often, when a kernel object is created, there is no way to know just how long it will exist. One way of tracking the lifecycle of such objects is through reference counting. When no code in the kernel holds a reference to a given object, that object has finished its useful life and can be deleted.

Sysfs representation
> Every object that shows up in sysfs has, underneath it, a kobject that interacts with the kernel to create its visible representation.

Data structure glue
> The device model is, in its entirety, a fiendishly complicated data structure made up of multiple hierarchies with numerous links between them. The kobject implements this structure and holds it together.

Hotplug event handling
> The kobject subsystem handles the generation of events that notify user space about the comings and goings of hardware on the system.

One might conclude from the preceding list that the kobject is a complicated structure. One would be right. By looking at one piece at a time, however, it is possible to understand this structure and how it works.

Kobject Basics

A kobject has the type struct kobject; it is defined in *<linux/kobject.h>*. That file also includes declarations for a number of other structures related to kobjects and, of course, a long list of functions for manipulating them.

Embedding kobjects

Before we get into the details, it is worth taking a moment to understand how kobjects are used. If you look back at the list of functions handled by kobjects, you see that they are all services performed on behalf of other objects. A kobject, in other words, is of little interest on its own; it exists only to tie a higher-level object into the device model.

Thus, it is rare (even unknown) for kernel code to create a standalone kobject; instead, kobjects are used to control access to a larger, domain-specific object. To this end, kobjects are found embedded in other structures. If you are used to thinking of things in object-oriented terms, kobjects can be seen as a top-level, abstract class from which other classes are derived. A kobject implements a set of capabilities that are not particularly useful by themselves but that are nice to have in other objects. The C language does not allow for the direct expression of inheritance, so other techniques—such as embedding one structure in another—must be used.

As an example, let's look back at struct cdev, which we encountered in Chapter 3. That structure, as found in the 2.6.10 kernel, looks like this:

```
struct cdev {
    struct kobject kobj;
    struct module *owner;
    struct file_operations *ops;
    struct list_head list;
    dev_t dev;
    unsigned int count;
};
```

As we can see, the cdev structure has a kobject embedded within it. If you have one of these structures, finding its embedded kobject is just a matter of using the kobj field. Code that works with kobjects often has the opposite problem, however: given a struct kobject pointer, what is the pointer to the containing structure? You should avoid tricks (such as assuming that the kobject is at the beginning of the structure), and, instead, use the *container_of* macro (introduced in the section "The open Method" in Chapter 3). So the way to convert a pointer to a struct kobject called kp embedded within a struct cdev would be:

```
struct cdev *device = container_of(kp, struct cdev, kobj);
```

Programmers often define a simple macro for "back-casting" kobject pointers to the containing type.

Kobject initialization

This book has presented a number of types with simple mechanisms for initialization at compile or runtime. The initialization of a kobject is a bit more complicated, especially when all of its functions are used. Regardless of how a kobject is used, however, a few steps must be performed.

The first of those is to simply set the entire kobject to 0, usually with a call to *memset*. Often this initialization happens as part of the zeroing of the structure into which the kobject is embedded. Failure to zero out a kobject often leads to very strange crashes further down the line; it is not a step you want to skip.

The next step is to set up some of the internal fields with a call to *kobject_init( )*:

```
void kobject_init(struct kobject *kobj);
```

Among other things, *kobject_init* sets the kobject's reference count to one. Calling *kobject_init* is not sufficient, however. Kobject users must, at a minimum, set the name of the kobject; this is the name that is used in sysfs entries. If you dig through the kernel source, you can find the code that copies a string directly into the kobject's name field, but that approach should be avoided. Instead, use:

```
int kobject_set_name(struct kobject *kobj, const char *format, ...);
```

This function takes a *printk*-style variable argument list. Believe it or not, it is actually possible for this operation to fail (it may try to allocate memory); conscientious code should check the return value and react accordingly.

The other kobject fields that should be set, directly or indirectly, by the creator are ktype, kset, and parent. We will get to these later in this chapter.

Reference count manipulation

One of the key functions of a kobject is to serve as a reference counter for the object in which it is embedded. As long as references to the object exist, the object (and the code that supports it) must continue to exist. The low-level functions for manipulating a kobject's reference counts are:

```
struct kobject *kobject_get(struct kobject *kobj);
void kobject_put(struct kobject *kobj);
```

A successful call to *kobject_get* increments the kobject's reference counter and returns a pointer to the kobject. If, however, the kobject is already in the process of being destroyed, the operation fails, and *kobject_get* returns NULL. This return value must always be tested, or no end of unpleasant race conditions could result.

When a reference is released, the call to *kobject_put* decrements the reference count and, possibly, frees the object. Remember that *kobject_init* sets the reference count to one; so when you create a kobject, you should make sure that the corresponding *kobject_put* call is made when that initial reference is no longer needed.

Note that, in many cases, the reference count in the kobject itself may not be sufficient to prevent race conditions. The existence of a kobject (and its containing structure) may well, for example, require the continued existence of the module that created that kobject. It would not do to unload that module while the kobject is still being passed around. That is why the cdev structure we saw above contains a struct module pointer. Reference counting for struct cdev is implemented as follows:

```
struct kobject *cdev_get(struct cdev *p)
{
    struct module *owner = p->owner;
    struct kobject *kobj;

    if (owner && !try_module_get(owner))
        return NULL;
    kobj = kobject_get(&p->kobj);
    if (!kobj)
        module_put(owner);
    return kobj;
}
```

Creating a reference to a cdev structure requires creating a reference also to the module that owns it. So *cdev_get* uses *try_module_get* to attempt to increment that module's usage count. If that operation succeeds, *kobject_get* is used to increment the kobject's reference count as well. That operation could fail, of course, so the code checks the return value from *kobject_get* and releases its reference to the module if things don't work out.

Release functions and kobject types

One important thing still missing from the discussion is what happens to a kobject when its reference count reaches 0. The code that created the kobject generally does not know when that will happen; if it did, there would be little point in using a reference count in the first place. Even predictable object life cycles become more complicated when sysfs is brought in; user-space programs can keep a reference to a kobject (by keeping one of its associated sysfs files open) for an arbitrary period of time.

The end result is that a structure protected by a kobject cannot be freed at any single, predictable point in the driver's lifecycle, but in code that must be prepared to run at whatever moment the kobject's reference count goes to 0. The reference count is not under the direct control of the code that created the kobject. So that code must be notified asynchronously whenever the last reference to one of its kobjects goes away.

This notification is done through a kobject's *release* method. Usually, this method has a form such as:

```
void my_object_release(struct kobject *kobj)
{
    struct my_object *mine = container_of(kobj, struct my_object, kobj);
```

```
        /* Perform any additional cleanup on this object, then... */
        kfree(mine);
}
```

One important point cannot be overstated: every kobject must have a *release* method, and the kobject must persist (in a consistent state) until that method is called. If these constraints are not met, the code is flawed. It risks freeing the object when it is still in use, or it fails to release the object after the last reference is returned.

Interestingly, the *release* method is not stored in the kobject itself; instead, it is associated with the type of the structure that contains the kobject. This type is tracked with a structure of type struct kobj_type, often simply called a "ktype." This structure looks like the following:

```
struct kobj_type {
    void (*release)(struct kobject *);
    struct sysfs_ops *sysfs_ops;
    struct attribute **default_attrs;
};
```

The release field in struct kobj_type is, of course, a pointer to the *release* method for this type of kobject. We will come back to the other two fields (sysfs_ops and default_attrs) later in this chapter.

Every kobject needs to have an associated kobj_type structure. Confusingly, the pointer to this structure can be found in two different places. The kobject structure itself contains a field (called ktype) that can contain this pointer. If, however, this kobject is a member of a kset, the kobj_type pointer is provided by that kset instead. (We will look at ksets in the next section.) Meanwhile, the macro:

```
struct kobj_type *get_ktype(struct kobject *kobj);
```

finds the kobj_type pointer for a given kobject.

Kobject Hierarchies, Ksets, and Subsystems

The kobject structure is often used to link together objects into a hierarchical structure that matches the structure of the subsystem being modeled. There are two separate mechanisms for this linking: the parent pointer and ksets.

The parent field in struct kobject is a pointer to another kobject—the one representing the next level up in the hierarchy. If, for example, a kobject represents a USB device, its parent pointer may indicate the object representing the hub into which the device is plugged.

The main use for the parent pointer is to position the object in the sysfs hierarchy. We'll see how this works in the section "Low-Level Sysfs Operations."

Ksets

In many ways, a kset looks like an extension of the kobj_type structure; a kset is a collection of kobjects embedded within structures of the same type. However, while struct kobj_type concerns itself with the type of an object, struct kset is concerned with aggregation and collection. The two concepts have been separated so that objects of identical type can appear in distinct sets.

Therefore, the main function of a kset is containment; it can be thought of as the top-level container class for kobjects. In fact, each kset contains its own kobject internally, and it can, in many ways, be treated the same way as a kobject. It is worth noting that ksets are always represented in sysfs; once a kset has been set up and added to the system, there will be a sysfs directory for it. Kobjects do not necessarily show up in sysfs, but every kobject that is a member of a kset is represented there.

Adding a kobject to a kset is usually done when the object is created; it is a two-step process. The kobject's kset field must be pointed at the kset of interest; then the kobject should be passed to:

```
int kobject_add(struct kobject *kobj);
```

As always, programmers should be aware that this function can fail (in which case it returns a negative error code) and respond accordingly. There is a convenience function provided by the kernel:

```
extern int kobject_register(struct kobject *kobj);
```

This function is simply a combination of *kobject_init* and *kobject_add*.

When a kobject is passed to *kobject_add*, its reference count is incremented. Containment within the kset is, after all, a reference to the object. At some point, the kobject will probably have to be removed from the kset to clear that reference; that is done with:

```
void kobject_del(struct kobject *kobj);
```

There is also a *kobject_unregister* function, which is a combination of *kobject_del* and *kobject_put*.

A kset keeps its children in a standard kernel linked list. In almost all cases, the contained kobjects also have pointers to the kset (or, strictly, its embedded kobject) in their parent's fields. So, typically, a kset and its kobjects look something like what you see in Figure 14-2. Bear in mind that:

- All of the contained kobjects in the diagram are actually embedded within some other type, possibly even other ksets.
- It is not required that a kobject's parent be the containing kset (although any other organization would be strange and rare).

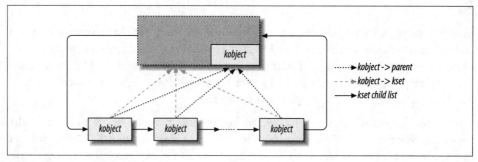

Figure 14-2. A simple kset hierarchy

Operations on ksets

For initialization and setup, ksets have an interface very similar to that of kobjects. The following functions exist:

```
void kset_init(struct kset *kset);
int kset_add(struct kset *kset);
int kset_register(struct kset *kset);
void kset_unregister(struct kset *kset);
```

For the most part, these functions just call the analogous *kobject_* function on the kset's embedded kobject.

To manage the reference counts of ksets, the situation is about the same:

```
struct kset *kset_get(struct kset *kset);
void kset_put(struct kset *kset);
```

A kset also has a name, which is stored in the embedded kobject. So, if you have a kset called my_set, you would set its name with:

```
kobject_set_name(&my_set->kobj, "The name");
```

Ksets also have a pointer (in the ktype field) to the kobj_type structure describing the kobjects it contains. This type is used in preference to the ktype field in a kobject itself. As a result, in typical usage, the ktype field in struct kobject is left NULL, because the same field within the kset is the one actually used.

Finally, a kset contains a subsystem pointer (called subsys). So it's time to talk about subsystems.

Subsystems

A subsystem is a representation for a high-level portion of the kernel as a whole. Subsystems usually (but not always) show up at the top of the sysfs hierarchy. Some example subsystems in the kernel include block_subsys (*/sys/block*, for block devices), devices_subsys (*/sys/devices*, the core device hierarchy), and a specific subsystem for every bus type known to the kernel. A driver author almost never needs to create a new subsystem; if you feel tempted to do so, think again. What you probably want, in the end, is to add a new class, as discussed in the section "Classes."

A subsystem is represented by a simple structure:

```
struct subsystem {
    struct kset kset;
    struct rw_semaphore rwsem;
};
```

A subsystem, thus, is really just a wrapper around a kset, with a semaphore thrown in.

Every kset must belong to a subsystem. The subsystem membership helps establish the kset's position in the hierarchy, but, more importantly, the subsystem's rwsem semaphore is used to serialize access to a kset's internal-linked list. This membership is represented by the subsys pointer in struct kset. Thus, one can find each kset's containing subsystem from the kset's structure, but one cannot find the multiple ksets contained in a subsystem directly from the subsystem structure.

Subsystems are often declared with a special macro:

```
decl_subsys(name, struct kobj_type *type,
            struct kset_hotplug_ops *hotplug_ops);
```

This macro creates a struct subsystem with a name formed by taking the name given to the macro and appending _subsys to it. The macro also initializes the internal kset with the given type and hotplug_ops. (We discuss hotplug operations later in this chapter.)

Subsystems have the usual list of setup and teardown functions:

```
void subsystem_init(struct subsystem *subsys);
int subsystem_register(struct subsystem *subsys);
void subsystem_unregister(struct subsystem *subsys);
struct subsystem *subsys_get(struct subsystem *subsys)
void subsys_put(struct subsystem *subsys);
```

Most of these operations just act upon the subsystem's kset.

Low-Level Sysfs Operations

Kobjects are the mechanism behind the sysfs virtual filesystem. For every directory found in sysfs, there is a kobject lurking somewhere within the kernel. Every kobject of interest also exports one or more *attributes*, which appear in that kobject's sysfs directory as files containing kernel-generated information. This section examines how kobjects and sysfs interact at a low level.

Code that works with sysfs should include *<linux/sysfs.h>*.

Getting a kobject to show up in sysfs is simply a matter of calling *kobject_add*. We have already seen that function as the way to add a kobject to a kset; creating entries in sysfs is also part of its job. There are a couple of things worth knowing about how the sysfs entry is created:

- Sysfs entries for kobjects are always directories, so a call to *kobject_add* results in the creation of a directory in sysfs. Usually that directory contains one or more attributes; we see how attributes are specified shortly.

- The name assigned to the kobject (with *kobject_set_name*) is the name used for the sysfs directory. Thus, kobjects that appear in the same part of the sysfs hierarchy must have unique names. Names assigned to kobjects should also be reasonable file names: they cannot contain the slash character, and the use of white space is strongly discouraged.

- The sysfs entry is located in the directory corresponding to the kobject's parent pointer. If parent is NULL when *kobject_add* is called, it is set to the kobject embedded in the new kobject's kset; thus, the sysfs hierarchy usually matches the internal hierarchy created with ksets. If both parent and kset are NULL, the sysfs directory is created at the top level, which is almost certainly not what you want.

Using the mechanisms we have described so far, we can use a kobject to create an empty directory in sysfs. Usually, you want to do something a little more interesting than that, so it is time to look at the implementation of attributes.

Default Attributes

When created, every kobject is given a set of default attributes. These attributes are specified by way of the kobj_type structure. That structure, remember, looks like this:

```
struct kobj_type {
    void (*release)(struct kobject *);
    struct sysfs_ops *sysfs_ops;
    struct attribute **default_attrs;
};
```

The default_attrs field lists the attributes to be created for every kobject of this type, and sysfs_ops provides the methods to implement those attributes. We start with default_attrs, which points to an array of pointers to attribute structures:

```
struct attribute {
    char *name;
    struct module *owner;
    mode_t mode;
};
```

In this structure, name is the name of the attribute (as it appears within the kobject's sysfs directory), owner is a pointer to the module (if any) that is responsible for the implementation of this attribute, and mode is the protection bits that are to be applied to this attribute. The mode is usually S_IRUGO for read-only attributes; if the attribute is writable, you can toss in S_IWUSR to give write access to root only (the macros for modes are defined in *<linux/stat.h>*). The last entry in the default_attrs list must be zero-filled.

The default_attrs array says what the attributes are but does not tell sysfs how to actually implement those attributes. That task falls to the kobj_type->sysfs_ops field, which points to a structure defined as:

```
struct sysfs_ops {
    ssize_t (*show)(struct kobject *kobj, struct attribute *attr,
                    char *buffer);
    ssize_t (*store)(struct kobject *kobj, struct attribute *attr,
                    const char *buffer, size_t size);
};
```

Whenever an attribute is read from user space, the *show* method is called with a pointer to the kobject and the appropriate attribute structure. That method should encode the value of the given attribute into buffer, being sure not to overrun it (it is PAGE_SIZE bytes), and return the actual length of the returned data. The conventions for sysfs state that each attribute should contain a single, human-readable value; if you have a lot of information to return, you may want to consider splitting it into multiple attributes.

The same *show* method is used for all attributes associated with a given kobject. The attr pointer passed into the function can be used to determine which attribute is being requested. Some *show* methods include a series of tests on the attribute name. Other implementations embed the attribute structure within another structure that contains the information needed to return the attribute's value; in this case, *container_of* may be used within the *show* method to obtain a pointer to the embedding structure.

The *store* method is similar; it should decode the data stored in buffer (size contains the length of that data, which does not exceed PAGE_SIZE), store and respond to the new value in whatever way makes sense, and return the number of bytes actually decoded. The *store* method can be called only if the attribute's permissions allow writes. When writing a *store* method, never forget that you are receiving arbitrary information from user space; you should validate it very carefully before taking any action in response. If the incoming data does not match expectations, return a negative error value rather than possibly doing something unwanted and unrecoverable. If your device exports a self_destruct attribute, you should require that a specific string be written there to invoke that functionality; an accidental, random write should yield only an error.

Nondefault Attributes

In many cases, the kobject type's default_attrs field describes all the attributes that kobject will ever have. But that's not a restriction in the design; attributes can be added and removed to kobjects at will. If you wish to add a new attribute to a kobject's sysfs directory, simply fill in an attribute structure and pass it to:

```
int sysfs_create_file(struct kobject *kobj, struct attribute *attr);
```

If all goes well, the file is created with the name given in the attribute structure, and the return value is 0; otherwise, the usual negative error code is returned.

Note that the same *show()* and *store()* functions are called to implement operations on the new attribute. Before you add a new, nondefault attribute to a kobject, you should take whatever steps are necessary to ensure that those functions know how to implement that attribute.

To remove an attribute, call:

```
int sysfs_remove_file(struct kobject *kobj, struct attribute *attr);
```

After the call, the attribute no longer appears in the kobject's sysfs entry. Do be aware, however, that a user-space process could have an open file descriptor for that attribute and that *show* and *store* calls are still possible after the attribute has been removed.

Binary Attributes

The sysfs conventions call for all attributes to contain a single value in a human-readable text format. That said, there is an occasional, rare need for the creation of attributes that can handle larger chunks of binary data. That need really only comes about when data must be passed, untouched, between user space and the device. For example, uploading firmware to devices requires this feature. When such a device is encountered in the system, a user-space program can be started (via the hotplug mechanism); that program then passes the firmware code to the kernel via a binary sysfs attribute, as is shown in the section "The Kernel Firmware Interface."

Binary attributes are described with a bin_attribute structure:

```
struct bin_attribute {
    struct attribute attr;
    size_t size;
    ssize_t (*read)(struct kobject *kobj, char *buffer,
                    loff_t pos, size_t size);
    ssize_t (*write)(struct kobject *kobj, char *buffer,
                    loff_t pos, size_t size);
};
```

Here, attr is an attribute structure giving the name, owner, and permissions for the binary attribute, and size is the maximum size of the binary attribute (or 0 if there is no maximum). The *read* and *write* methods work similarly to the normal char driver equivalents; they can be called multiple times for a single load with a maximum of one page worth of data in each call. There is no way for sysfs to signal the last of a set of write operations, so code implementing a binary attribute must be able to determine the end of the data some other way.

Binary attributes must be created explicitly; they cannot be set up as default attributes. To create a binary attribute, call:

```
int sysfs_create_bin_file(struct kobject *kobj,
                          struct bin_attribute *attr);
```

Binary attributes can be removed with:

```
int sysfs_remove_bin_file(struct kobject *kobj,
                          struct bin_attribute *attr);
```

Symbolic Links

The sysfs filesystem has the usual tree structure, reflecting the hierarchical organization of the kobjects it represents. The relationships between objects in the kernel are often more complicated than that, however. For example, one sysfs subtree (/sys/devices) represents all of the devices known to the system, while other subtrees (under /sys/bus) represent the device drivers. These trees do not, however, represent the relationships between the drivers and the devices they manage. Showing these additional relationships requires extra pointers which, in sysfs, are implemented through symbolic links.

Creating a symbolic link within sysfs is easy:

```
int sysfs_create_link(struct kobject *kobj, struct kobject *target,
                      char *name);
```

This function creates a link (called name) pointing to target's sysfs entry as an attribute of kobj. It is a relative link, so it works regardless of where sysfs is mounted on any particular system.

The link persists even if target is removed from the system. If you are creating symbolic links to other kobjects, you should probably have a way of knowing about changes to those kobjects, or some sort of assurance that the target kobjects will not disappear. The consequences (dead symbolic links within sysfs) are not particularly grave, but they are not representative of the best programming style and can cause confusion in user space.

Symbolic links can be removed with:

```
void sysfs_remove_link(struct kobject *kobj, char *name);
```

Hotplug Event Generation

A *hotplug event* is a notification to user space from the kernel that something has changed in the system's configuration. They are generated whenever a kobject is created or destroyed. Such events are generated, for example, when a digital camera is plugged in with a USB cable, when a user switches console modes, or when a disk is repartitioned. Hotplug events turn into an invocation of */sbin/hotplug*, which can respond to each event by loading drivers, creating device nodes, mounting partitions, or taking any other action that is appropriate.

The last major kobject function we look at is the generation of these events. The actual event generation takes place when a kobject is passed to *kobject_add* or *kobject_del*. Before the event is handed to user space, code associated with the kobject (or, more specifically, the kset to which it belongs) has the opportunity to add information for user space or to disable event generation entirely.

Hotplug Operations

Actual control of hotplug events is exercised by way of a set of methods stored in the kset_hotplug_ops structure:

```
struct kset_hotplug_ops {
    int (*filter)(struct kset *kset, struct kobject *kobj);
    char *(*name)(struct kset *kset, struct kobject *kobj);
    int (*hotplug)(struct kset *kset, struct kobject *kobj,
                   char **envp, int num_envp, char *buffer,
                   int buffer_size);
};
```

A pointer to this structure is found in the hotplug_ops field of the kset structure. If a given kobject is not contained within a kset, the kernel searchs up through the hierarchy (via the parent pointer) until it finds a kobject that *does* have a kset; that kset's hotplug operations are then used.

The *filter* hotplug operation is called whenever the kernel is considering generating an event for a given kobject. If *filter* returns 0, the event is not created. This method, therefore, gives the kset code an opportunity to decide which events should be passed on to user space and which should not.

As an example of how this method might be used, consider the block subsystem. There are at least three types of kobjects used there, representing disks, partitions, and request queues. User space may want to react to the addition of a disk or a partition, but it does not normally care about request queues. So the *filter* method allows event generation only for kobjects representing disks and partitions. It looks like this:

```
static int block_hotplug_filter(struct kset *kset, struct kobject *kobj)
{
    struct kobj_type *ktype = get_ktype(kobj);

    return ((ktype == &ktype_block) || (ktype == &ktype_part));
}
```

Here, a quick test on the type of kobject is sufficient to decide whether the event should be generated or not.

When the user-space hotplug program is invoked, it is passed to the name of the relevant subsystem as its one and only parameter. The *name* hotplug method is charged with providing that name. It should return a simple string suitable for passing to user space.

Everything else that the hotplug script might want to know is passed in the environment. The final hotplug method (*hotplug*) gives an opportunity to add useful environment variables prior to the invocation of that script. Again, this method's prototype is:

```
int (*hotplug)(struct kset *kset, struct kobject *kobj,
               char **envp, int num_envp, char *buffer,
               int buffer_size);
```

As usual, kset and kobject describe the object for which the event is being generated. The envp array is a place to store additional environment variable definitions (in the usual NAME=value format); it has num_envp entries available. The variables themselves should be encoded into buffer, which is buffer_size bytes long. If you add any variables to envp, be sure to add a NULL entry after your last addition so that the kernel knows where the end is. The return value should normally be 0; any nonzero return aborts the generation of the hotplug event.

The generation of hotplug events (like much of the work in the device model) is usually handled by logic at the bus driver level.

Buses, Devices, and Drivers

So far, we have seen a great deal of low-level infrastructures and a relative shortage of examples. We try to make up for that in the rest of this chapter as we get into the higher levels of the Linux device model. To that end, we introduce a new virtual bus, which we call *lddbus*,[*] and modify the *scullp* driver to "connect" to that bus.

Once again, much of the material covered here will never be needed by many driver authors. Details at this level are generally handled at the bus level, and few authors need to add a new bus type. This information is useful, however, for anybody wondering what is happening inside the PCI, USB, etc. layers or who needs to make changes at that level.

Buses

A bus is a channel between the processor and one or more devices. For the purposes of the device model, all devices are connected via a bus, even if it is an internal, virtual, "platform" bus. Buses can plug into each other—a USB controller is usually a

---

[*] The logical name for this bus, of course, would have been "sbus," but that name was already taken by a real, physical bus.

PCI device, for example. The device model represents the actual connections between buses and the devices they control.

In the Linux device model, a bus is represented by the bus_type structure, defined in *<linux/device.h>*. This structure looks like:

```
struct bus_type {
    char *name;
    struct subsystem subsys;
    struct kset drivers;
    struct kset devices;
    int (*match)(struct device *dev, struct device_driver *drv);
    struct device *(*add)(struct device * parent, char * bus_id);
    int (*hotplug) (struct device *dev, char **envp,
                    int num_envp, char *buffer, int buffer_size);
    /* Some fields omitted */
};
```

The name field is the name of the bus, something such as pci. You can see from the structure that each bus is its own subsystem; these subsystems do not live at the top level in sysfs, however. Instead, they are found underneath the bus subsystem. A bus contains two ksets, representing the known drivers for that bus and all devices plugged into the bus. Then, there is a set of methods that we will get to shortly.

Bus registration

As we mentioned, the example source includes a virtual bus implementation called *lddbus*. This bus sets up its bus_type structure as follows:

```
struct bus_type ldd_bus_type = {
    .name = "ldd",
    .match = ldd_match,
    .hotplug  = ldd_hotplug,
};
```

Note that very few of the bus_type fields require initialization; most of that is handled by the device model core. We do have to specify the name of the bus, however, and any methods that go along with it.

Inevitably, a new bus must be registered with the system via a call to *bus_register*. The *lddbus* code does so in this way:

```
ret = bus_register(&ldd_bus_type);
if (ret)
    return ret;
```

This call can fail, of course, so the return value must always be checked. If it succeeds, the new bus subsystem has been added to the system; it is visible in sysfs under */sys/bus*, and it is possible to start adding devices.

Should it be necessary to remove a bus from the system (when the associated module is removed, for example), *bus_unregister* should be called:

```
void bus_unregister(struct bus_type *bus);
```

Bus methods

There are several methods defined for the bus_type structure; they allow the bus code to serve as an intermediary between the device core and individual drivers. The methods defined in the 2.6.10 kernel are:

int (*match)(struct device *device, struct device_driver *driver);
> This method is called, perhaps multiple times, whenever a new device or driver is added for this bus. It should return a nonzero value if the given device can be handled by the given driver. (We get to the details of the device and device_driver structures shortly). This function must be handled at the bus level, because that is where the proper logic exists; the core kernel cannot know how to match devices and drivers for every possible bus type.

int (*hotplug) (struct device *device, char **envp, int num_envp, char *buffer, int buffer_size);
> This method allows the bus to add variables to the environment prior to the generation of a hotplug event in user space. The parameters are the same as for the kset *hotplug* method (described in the earlier section "Hotplug Event Generation").

The *lddbus* driver has a very simple *match* function, which simply compares the driver and device names:

```
static int ldd_match(struct device *dev, struct device_driver *driver)
{
    return !strncmp(dev->bus_id, driver->name, strlen(driver->name));
}
```

When real hardware is involved, the *match* function usually makes some sort of comparison between the hardware ID provided by the device itself and the IDs supported by the driver.

The *lddbus hotplug* method looks like this:

```
static int ldd_hotplug(struct device *dev, char **envp, int num_envp,
        char *buffer, int buffer_size)
{
    envp[0] = buffer;
    if (snprintf(buffer, buffer_size, "LDDBUS_VERSION=%s",
                Version) >= buffer_size)
        return -ENOMEM;
    envp[1] = NULL;
    return 0;
}
```

Here, we add in the current revision number of the *lddbus* source, just in case anybody is curious.

Iterating over devices and drivers

If you are writing bus-level code, you may find yourself having to perform some operation on all devices or drivers that have been registered with your bus. It may be tempting to dig directly into the structures in the bus_type structure, but it is better to use the helper functions that have been provided.

To operate on every device known to the bus, use:

```
int bus_for_each_dev(struct bus_type *bus, struct device *start,
                     void *data, int (*fn)(struct device *, void *));
```

This function iterates over every device on bus, passing the associated device structure to fn, along with the value passed in as data. If start is NULL, the iteration begins with the first device on the bus; otherwise iteration starts with the first device after start. If fn returns a nonzero value, iteration stops and that value is returned from *bus_for_each_dev*.

There is a similar function for iterating over drivers:

```
int bus_for_each_drv(struct bus_type *bus, struct device_driver *start,
                     void *data, int (*fn)(struct device_driver *, void *));
```

This function works just like *bus_for_each_dev*, except, of course, that it works with drivers instead.

It should be noted that both of these functions hold the bus subsystem's reader/writer semaphore for the duration of the work. So an attempt to use the two of them together will deadlock—each will be trying to obtain the same semaphore. Operations that modify the bus (such as unregistering devices) will also lock up. So, use the *bus_for_each* functions with some care.

Bus attributes

Almost every layer in the Linux device model provides an interface for the addition of attributes, and the bus layer is no exception. The bus_attribute type is defined in *<linux/device.h>* as follows:

```
struct bus_attribute {
    struct attribute attr;
    ssize_t (*show)(struct bus_type *bus, char *buf);
    ssize_t (*store)(struct bus_type *bus, const char *buf,
                     size_t count);
};
```

We have already seen struct attribute in the section "Default Attributes." The bus_attribute type also includes two methods for displaying and setting the value of the attribute. Most device model layers above the kobject level work this way.

A convenience macro has been provided for the compile-time creation and initialization of bus_attribute structures:

```
BUS_ATTR(name, mode, show, store);
```

This macro declares a structure, generating its name by prepending the string bus_attr_ to the given name.

Any attributes belonging to a bus should be created explicitly with *bus_create_file*:

```
int bus_create_file(struct bus_type *bus, struct bus_attribute *attr);
```

Attributes can also be removed with:

```
void bus_remove_file(struct bus_type *bus, struct bus_attribute *attr);
```

The *lddbus* driver creates a simple attribute file containing, once again, the source version number. The *show* method and bus_attribute structure are set up as follows:

```
static ssize_t show_bus_version(struct bus_type *bus, char *buf)
{
    return snprintf(buf, PAGE_SIZE, "%s\n", Version);
}

static BUS_ATTR(version, S_IRUGO, show_bus_version, NULL);
```

Creating the attribute file is done at module load time:

```
if (bus_create_file(&ldd_bus_type, &bus_attr_version))
    printk(KERN_NOTICE "Unable to create version attribute\n");
```

This call creates an attribute file (*/sys/bus/ldd/version*) containing the revision number for the *lddbus* code.

Devices

At the lowest level, every device in a Linux system is represented by an instance of struct device:

```
struct device {
    struct device *parent;
    struct kobject kobj;
    char bus_id[BUS_ID_SIZE];
    struct bus_type *bus;
    struct device_driver *driver;
    void *driver_data;
    void (*release)(struct device *dev);
    /* Several fields omitted */
};
```

There are many other struct device fields that are of interest only to the device core code. These fields, however, are worth knowing about:

struct device *parent
> The device's "parent" device—the device to which it is attached. In most cases, a parent device is some sort of bus or host controller. If parent is NULL, the device is a top-level device, which is not usually what you want.

struct kobject kobj;
> The kobject that represents this device and links it into the hierarchy. Note that, as a general rule, device->kobj->parent is equal to &device->parent->kobj.

```
char bus_id[BUS_ID_SIZE];
```
A string that uniquely identifies this device on the bus. PCI devices, for example, use the standard PCI ID format containing the domain, bus, device, and function numbers.

```
struct bus_type *bus;
```
Identifies which kind of bus the device sits on.

```
struct device_driver *driver;
```
The driver that manages this device; we examine struct device_driver in the next section.

```
void *driver_data;
```
A private data field that may be used by the device driver.

```
void (*release)(struct device *dev);
```
The method is called when the last reference to the device is removed; it is called from the embedded kobject's *release* method. All device structures registered with the core must have a *release* method, or the kernel prints out scary complaints.

At a minimum, the parent, bus_id, bus, and release fields must be set before the device structure can be registered.

Device registration

The usual set of registration and unregistration functions exists:

```
int device_register(struct device *dev);
void device_unregister(struct device *dev);
```

We have seen how the *lddbus* code registers its bus type. However, an actual bus is a device and must be registered separately. For simplicity, the *lddbus* module supports only a single virtual bus, so the driver sets up its device at compile time:

```
static void ldd_bus_release(struct device *dev)
{
    printk(KERN_DEBUG "lddbus release\n");
}

struct device ldd_bus = {
    .bus_id  = "ldd0",
    .release = ldd_bus_release
};
```

This is a top-level bus, so the parent and bus fields are left NULL. We have a simple, no-op *release* method, and, as the first (and only) bus, its name is ldd0. This bus device is registered with:

```
ret = device_register(&ldd_bus);
if (ret)
    printk(KERN_NOTICE "Unable to register ldd0\n");
```

Once that call is complete, the new bus can be seen under */sys/devices* in sysfs. Any devices added to this bus then shows up under */sys/devices/ldd0/*.

Device attributes

Device entries in sysfs can have attributes. The relevant structure is:

```
struct device_attribute {
    struct attribute attr;
    ssize_t (*show)(struct device *dev, char *buf);
    ssize_t (*store)(struct device *dev, const char *buf,
                     size_t count);
};
```

These attribute structures can be set up at compile time with this macro:

```
DEVICE_ATTR(name, mode, show, store);
```

The resulting structure is named by prepending dev_attr_ to the given name. The actual management of attribute files is handled with the usual pair of functions:

```
int device_create_file(struct device *device,
                       struct device_attribute *entry);
void device_remove_file(struct device *dev,
                        struct device_attribute *attr);
```

The dev_attrs field of struct bus_type points to a list of default attributes created for every device added to that bus.

Device structure embedding

The device structure contains the information that the device model core needs to model the system. Most subsystems, however, track additional information about the devices they host. As a result, it is rare for devices to be represented by bare device structures; instead, that structure, like kobject structures, is usually embedded within a higher-level representation of the device. If you look at the definitions of struct pci_dev or struct usb_device, you will find a struct device buried inside. Usually, low-level drivers are not even aware of that struct device, but there can be exceptions.

The *lddbus* driver creates its own device type (struct ldd_device) and expects individual device drivers to register their devices using that type. It is a simple structure:

```
struct ldd_device {
    char *name;
    struct ldd_driver *driver;
    struct device dev;
};

#define to_ldd_device(dev) container_of(dev, struct ldd_device, dev);
```

This structure allows the driver to provide an actual name for the device (which can be distinct from its bus ID, stored in the device structure) and a pointer to driver information. Structures for real devices usually also contain information about the vendor, device model, device configuration, resources used, and so on. Good examples can be found in struct pci_dev (*<linux/pci.h>*) or struct usb_device (*<linux/usb.h>*). A conve-nience macro (*to_ldd_device*) is also defined for struct ldd_device to make it easy to turn pointers to the embedded device structure into ldd_device pointers.

The registration interface exported by *lddbus* looks like this:

```
int register_ldd_device(struct ldd_device *ldddev)
{
    ldddev->dev.bus = &ldd_bus_type;
    ldddev->dev.parent = &ldd_bus;
    ldddev->dev.release = ldd_dev_release;
    strncpy(ldddev->dev.bus_id, ldddev->name, BUS_ID_SIZE);
    return device_register(&ldddev->dev);
}
EXPORT_SYMBOL(register_ldd_device);
```

Here, we simply fill in some of the embedded device structure fields (which individ-ual drivers should not need to know about), and register the device with the driver core. If we wanted to add bus-specific attributes to the device, we could do so here.

To show how this interface is used, let us introduce another sample driver, which we have called *sculld*. It is yet another variant on the *scullp* driver first introduced in Chapter 8. It implements the usual memory area device, but *sculld* also works with the Linux device model by way of the *lddbus* interface.

The *sculld* driver adds an attribute of its own to its device entry; this attribute, called dev, simply contains the associated device number. This attribute could be used by a module loading the script or the hotplug subsystem to automatically create device nodes when the device is added to the system. The setup for this attribute follows the usual patterns:

```
static ssize_t sculld_show_dev(struct device *ddev, char *buf)
{
    struct sculld_dev *dev = ddev->driver_data;

    return print_dev_t(buf, dev->cdev.dev);
}

static DEVICE_ATTR(dev, S_IRUGO, sculld_show_dev, NULL);
```

Then, at initialization time, the device is registered, and the dev attribute is created through the following function:

```
static void sculld_register_dev(struct sculld_dev *dev, int index)
{
    sprintf(dev->devname, "sculld%d", index);
    dev->ldev.name = dev->devname;
    dev->ldev.driver = &sculld_driver;
    dev->ldev.dev.driver_data = dev;
    register_ldd_device(&dev->ldev);
    device_create_file(&dev->ldev.dev, &dev_attr_dev);
}
```

Note that we make use of the driver_data field to store the pointer to our own, internal device structure.

Device Drivers

The device model tracks all of the drivers known to the system. The main reason for this tracking is to enable the driver core to match up drivers with new devices. Once drivers are known objects within the system, however, a number of other things become possible. Device drivers can export information and configuration variables that are independent of any specific device, for example.

Drivers are defined by the following structure:

```
struct device_driver {
    char *name;
    struct bus_type *bus;
    struct kobject kobj;
    struct list_head devices;
    int (*probe)(struct device *dev);
    int (*remove)(struct device *dev);
    void (*shutdown) (struct device *dev);
};
```

Once again, several of the structure's fields have been omitted (see *<linux/device.h>* for the full story). Here, name is the name of the driver (it shows up in sysfs), bus is the type of bus this driver works with, kobj is the inevitable kobject, devices is a list of all devices currently bound to this driver, *probe* is a function called to query the existence of a specific device (and whether this driver can work with it), remove is called when the device is removed from the system, and shutdown is called at shutdown time to quiesce the device.

The form of the functions for working with device_driver structures should be looking familiar by now (so we cover them very quickly). The registration functions are:

```
int driver_register(struct device_driver *drv);
void driver_unregister(struct device_driver *drv);
```

The usual attribute structure exists:

```
struct driver_attribute {
    struct attribute attr;
    ssize_t (*show)(struct device_driver *drv, char *buf);
    ssize_t (*store)(struct device_driver *drv, const char *buf,
                     size_t count);
};
DRIVER_ATTR(name, mode, show, store);
```

And attribute files are created in the usual way:

```
int driver_create_file(struct device_driver *drv,
                       struct driver_attribute *attr);
void driver_remove_file(struct device_driver *drv,
                        struct driver_attribute *attr);
```

The bus_type structure contains a field (drv_attrs) that points to a set of default attributes, which are created for all drivers associated with that bus.

Driver structure embedding

As is the case with most driver core structures, the device_driver structure is usually found embedded within a higher-level, bus-specific structure. The *lddbus* subsystem would never go against such a trend, so it has defined its own ldd_driver structure:

```
struct ldd_driver {
    char *version;
    struct module *module;
    struct device_driver driver;
    struct driver_attribute version_attr;
};

#define to_ldd_driver(drv) container_of(drv, struct ldd_driver, driver);
```

Here, we require each driver to provide its current software version, and *lddbus* exports that version string for every driver it knows about. The bus-specific driver registration function is:

```
int register_ldd_driver(struct ldd_driver *driver)
{
    int ret;

    driver->driver.bus = &ldd_bus_type;
    ret = driver_register(&driver->driver);
    if (ret)
        return ret;
    driver->version_attr.attr.name = "version";
    driver->version_attr.attr.owner = driver->module;
    driver->version_attr.attr.mode = S_IRUGO;
    driver->version_attr.show = show_version;
    driver->version_attr.store = NULL;
    return driver_create_file(&driver->driver, &driver->version_attr);
}
```

The first half of the function simply registers the low-level device_driver structure with the core; the rest sets up the version attribute. Since this attribute is created at runtime, we can't use the DRIVER_ATTR macro; instead, the driver_attribute structure must be filled in by hand. Note that we set the owner of the attribute to the driver module, rather than the *lddbus* module; the reason for this can be seen in the implementation of the *show* function for this attribute:

```
static ssize_t show_version(struct device_driver *driver, char *buf)
{
    struct ldd_driver *ldriver = to_ldd_driver(driver);

    sprintf(buf, "%s\n", ldriver->version);
    return strlen(buf);
}
```

One might think that the attribute owner should be the *lddbus* module, since the function that implements the attribute is defined there. This function, however, is working with the ldd_driver structure created (and owned) by the driver itself. If that structure were to go away while a user-space process tried to read the version number, things could get messy. Designating the driver module as the owner of the attribute prevents the module from being unloaded, while user-space holds the attribute file open. Since each driver module creates a reference to the *lddbus* module, we can be sure that *lddbus* will not be unloaded at an inopportune time.

For completeness, *sculld* creates its ldd_driver structure as follows:

```
static struct ldd_driver sculld_driver = {
    .version = "$Revision: 1.1 $",
    .module = THIS_MODULE,
    .driver = {
        .name = "sculld",
    },
};
```

A simple call to *register_ldd_driver* adds it to the system. Once initialization is complete, the driver information can be seen in sysfs:

```
$ tree /sys/bus/ldd/drivers
/sys/bus/ldd/drivers
`-- sculld
    |-- sculld0 -> ../../../../devices/ldd0/sculld0
    |-- sculld1 -> ../../../../devices/ldd0/sculld1
    |-- sculld2 -> ../../../../devices/ldd0/sculld2
    |-- sculld3 -> ../../../../devices/ldd0/sculld3
    `-- version
```

Classes

The final device model concept we examine in this chapter is the *class*. A class is a higher-level view of a device that abstracts out low-level implementation details. Drivers may see a SCSI disk or an ATA disk, but, at the class level, they are all simply disks. Classes allow user space to work with devices based on what they do, rather than how they are connected or how they work.

Almost all classes show up in sysfs under */sys/class*. Thus, for example, all network interfaces can be found under */sys/class/net*, regardless of the type of interface. Input devices can be found in */sys/class/input*, and serial devices are in */sys/class/tty*. The one exception is block devices, which can be found under */sys/block* for historical reasons.

Class membership is usually handled by high-level code without the need for explicit support from drivers. When the *sbull* driver (see Chapter 16) creates a virtual disk device, it automatically appears in */sys/block*. The *snull* network driver (see Chapter 17) does not have to do anything special for its interfaces to be represented in *sys/class/net*. There will be times, however, when drivers end up dealing with classes directly.

In many cases, the class subsystem is the best way of exporting information to user space. When a subsystem creates a class, it owns the class entirely, so there is no need to worry about which module owns the attributes found there. It also takes very little time wandering around in the more hardware-oriented parts of sysfs to realize that it can be an unfriendly place for direct browsing. Users more happily find information in */sys/class/some-widget* than under, say, */sys/devices/pci0000:00/0000:00:10.0/usb2/2-0:1.0*.

The driver core exports two distinct interfaces for managing classes. The *class_simple* routines are designed to make it as easy as possible to add new classes to the system; their main purpose, usually, is to expose attributes containing device numbers to enable the automatic creation of device nodes. The regular class interface is more complex but offers more features as well. We start with the simple version.

The class_simple Interface

The *class_simple* interface was intended to be so easy to use that nobody would have any excuse for not exporting, at a minimum, an attribute containing a device's assigned number. Using this interface is simply a matter of a couple of function calls, with little of the usual boilerplate associated with the Linux device model.

The first step is to create the class itself. That is accomplished with a call to *class_simple_create*:

```
struct class_simple *class_simple_create(struct module *owner, char *name);
```

This function creates a class with the given name. The operation can fail, of course, so the return value should always be checked (using *IS_ERR*, described in the section "Pointers and Error Values" in Chapter 1) before continuing.

A simple class can be destroyed with:

```
void class_simple_destroy(struct class_simple *cs);
```

The real purpose of creating a simple class is to add devices to it; that task is achieved with:

```
struct class_device *class_simple_device_add(struct class_simple *cs,
                                   dev_t devnum,
                                   struct device *device,
                                   const char *fmt, ...);
```

Here, cs is the previously created simple class, devnum is the assigned device number, device is the struct device representing this device, and the remaining parameters are a *printk*-style format string and arguments to create the device name. This call adds an entry to the class containing one attribute, dev, which holds the device number. If the device parameter is not NULL, a symbolic link (called device) points to the device's entry under */sys/devices*.

It is possible to add other attributes to a device entry. It is just a matter of using *class_device_create_file*, which we discuss in the next section with the rest of the full class subsystem.

Classes generate hotplug events when devices come and go. If your driver needs to add variables to the environment for the user-space event handler, it can set up a hotplug callback with:

```
int class_simple_set_hotplug(struct class_simple *cs,
                    int (*hotplug)(struct class_device *dev,
                            char **envp, int num_envp,
                            char *buffer, int buffer_size));
```

When your device goes away, the class entry should be removed with:

```
void class_simple_device_remove(dev_t dev);
```

Note that the class_device structure returned by *class_simple_device_add* is not needed here; the device number (which should certainly be unique) is sufficient.

The Full Class Interface

The *class_simple* interface suffices for many needs, but sometimes more flexibility is required. The following discussion describes how to use the full class mechanism, upon which *class_simple* is based. It is brief: the class functions and structures follow the same patterns as the rest of the device model, so there is little that is truly new here.

Managing classes

A class is defined by an instance of struct class:

```
struct class {
    char *name;
    struct class_attribute *class_attrs;
    struct class_device_attribute *class_dev_attrs;
    int (*hotplug)(struct class_device *dev, char **envp,
                int num_envp, char *buffer, int buffer_size);
    void (*release)(struct class_device *dev);
    void (*class_release)(struct class *class);
    /* Some fields omitted */
};
```

Each class needs a unique name, which is how this class appears under */sys/class*. When the class is registered, all of the attributes listed in the (NULL-terminated) array pointed to by class_attrs is created. There is also a set of default attributes for every device added to the class; class_dev_attrs points to those. There is the usual *hotplug* function for adding variables to the environment when events are generated. There are also two *release* methods: *release* is called whenever a device is removed from the class, while *class_release* is called when the class itself is released.

The registration functions are:

```
int class_register(struct class *cls);
void class_unregister(struct class *cls);
```

The interface for working with attributes should not surprise anybody at this point:

```
struct class_attribute {
    struct attribute attr;
    ssize_t (*show)(struct class *cls, char *buf);
    ssize_t (*store)(struct class *cls, const char *buf, size_t count);
};

CLASS_ATTR(name, mode, show, store);

int class_create_file(struct class *cls,
                        const struct class_attribute *attr);
void class_remove_file(struct class *cls,
                        const struct class_attribute *attr);
```

Class devices

The real purpose of a class is to serve as a container for the devices that are members of that class. A member is represented by struct class_device:

```
struct class_device {
    struct kobject kobj;
    struct class *class;
    struct device *dev;
    void *class_data;
    char class_id[BUS_ID_SIZE];
};
```

The class_id field holds the name of this device as it appears in sysfs. The class pointer should point to the class holding this device, and dev should point to the associated device structure. Setting dev is optional; if it is non-NULL, it is used to create a symbolic link from the class entry to the corresponding entry under /sys/devices, making it easy to find the device entry in user space. The class can use class_data to hold a private pointer.

The usual registration functions have been provided:

```
int class_device_register(struct class_device *cd);
void class_device_unregister(struct class_device *cd);
```

The class device interface also allows the renaming of an already registered entry:

```
int class_device_rename(struct class_device *cd, char *new_name);
```

Class device entries have attributes:

```
struct class_device_attribute {
    struct attribute attr;
    ssize_t (*show)(struct class_device *cls, char *buf);
    ssize_t (*store)(struct class_device *cls, const char *buf,
                    size_t count);
};
```

```
CLASS_DEVICE_ATTR(name, mode, show, store);

int class_device_create_file(struct class_device *cls,
                             const struct class_device_attribute *attr);
void class_device_remove_file(struct class_device *cls,
                             const struct class_device_attribute *attr);
```

A default set of attributes, in the class's class_dev_attrs field, is created when the class device is registered; *class_device_create_file* may be used to create additional attributes. Attributes may also be added to class devices created with the *class_simple* interface.

Class interfaces

The class subsystem has an additional concept not found in other parts of the Linux device model. This mechanism is called an *interface*, but it is, perhaps, best thought of as a sort of trigger mechanism that can be used to get notification when devices enter or leave the class.

An interface is represented by:

```
struct class_interface {
    struct class *class;
    int (*add) (struct class_device *cd);
    void (*remove) (struct class_device *cd);
};
```

Interfaces can be registered and unregistered with:

```
int class_interface_register(struct class_interface *intf);
void class_interface_unregister(struct class_interface *intf);
```

The functioning of an interface is straightforward. Whenever a class device is added to the class specified in the class_interface structure, the interface's *add* function is called. That function can perform any additional setup required for that device; this setup often takes the form of adding more attributes, but other applications are possible. When the device is removed from the class, the *remove* method is called to perform any required cleanup.

Multiple interfaces can be registered for a class.

Putting It All Together

To better understand what the driver model does, let us walk through the steps of a device's lifecycle within the kernel. We describe how the PCI subsystem interacts with the driver model, the basic concepts of how a driver is added and removed, and how a device is added and removed from the system. These details, while describing the PCI kernel code specifically, apply to all other subsystems that use the driver core to manage their drivers and devices.

The interaction between the PCI core, driver core, and the individual PCI drivers is quite complex, as Figure 14-3 shows.

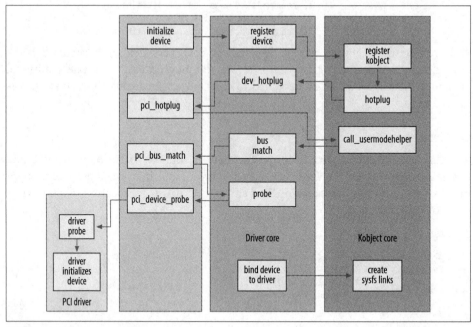

Figure 14-3. Device-creation process

Add a Device

The PCI subsystem declares a single struct bus_type called pci_bus_type, which is initialized with the following values:

```
struct bus_type pci_bus_type = {
    .name       = "pci",
    .match      = pci_bus_match,
    .hotplug    = pci_hotplug,
    .suspend    = pci_device_suspend,
    .resume     = pci_device_resume,
    .dev_attrs  = pci_dev_attrs,
};
```

This pci_bus_type variable is registered with the driver core when the PCI subsystem is loaded in the kernel with a call to *bus_register*. When that happens, the driver core creates a sysfs directory in */sys/bus/pci* that consists of two directories: *devices* and *drivers*.

All PCI drivers must define a struct pci_driver variable that defines the different functions that this PCI driver can do (for more information about the PCI subsystem and how to write a PCI driver, see Chapter 12). That structure contains a struct device_driver that is then initialized by the PCI core when the PCI driver is registered:

```
/* initialize common driver fields */
drv->driver.name = drv->name;
drv->driver.bus = &pci_bus_type;
drv->driver.probe = pci_device_probe;
drv->driver.remove = pci_device_remove;
drv->driver.kobj.ktype = &pci_driver_kobj_type;
```

This code sets up the bus for the driver to point to the pci_bus_type and points the *probe* and *remove* functions to point to functions within the PCI core. The ktype for the driver's kobject is set to the variable pci_driver_kobj_type, in order for the PCI driver's attribute files to work properly. Then the PCI core registers the PCI driver with the driver core:

```
/* register with core */
error = driver_register(&drv->driver);
```

The driver is now ready to be bound to any PCI devices it supports.

The PCI core, with help from the architecture-specific code that actually talks to the PCI bus, starts probing the PCI address space, looking for all PCI devices. When a PCI device is found, the PCI core creates a new variable in memory of type struct pci_dev. A portion of the struct pci_dev structure looks like the following:

```
struct pci_dev {
    /* ... */
    unsigned int    devfn;
    unsigned short vendor;
    unsigned short device;
    unsigned short subsystem_vendor;
    unsigned short subsystem_device;
    unsigned int    class;
    /* ... */
    struct pci_driver *driver;
    /* ... */
    struct device dev;
    /* ... */
};
```

The bus-specific fields of this PCI device are initialized by the PCI core (the devfn, vendor, device, and other fields), and the struct device variable's parent variable is set to the PCI bus device that this PCI device lives on. The bus variable is set to point at the pci_bus_type structure. Then the name and bus_id variables are set, depending on the name and ID that is read from the PCI device.

After the PCI device structure is initialized, the device is registered with the driver core with a call to:

```
device_register(&dev->dev);
```

Within the *device_register* function, the driver core initializes a number of the device's fields, registers the device's kobject with the kobject core (which causes a hotplug event to be generated, but we discuss that later in this chapter), and then adds the device to the list of devices that are held by the device's parent. This is done so that all devices can be walked in the proper order, always knowing where in the hierarchy of devices each one lives.

The device is then added to the bus-specific list of all devices, in this example, the pci_bus_type list. Then the list of all drivers that are registered with the bus is walked, and the *match* function of the bus is called for every driver, specifying this device. For the pci_bus_type bus, the *match* function was set to point to the *pci_bus_match* function by the PCI core before the device was submitted to the driver core.

The *pci_bus_match* function casts the struct device that was passed to it by the driver core, back into a struct pci_dev. It also casts the struct device_driver back into a struct pci_driver and then looks at the PCI device-specific information of the device and driver to see if the driver states that it can support this kind of device. If the match is not successful, the function returns 0 back to the driver core, and the driver core moves on to the next driver in its list.

If the match is successful, the function returns 1 back to the driver core. This causes the driver core to set the driver pointer in the struct device to point to this driver, and then it calls the *probe* function that is specified in the struct device_driver.

Earlier, before the PCI driver was registered with the driver core, the probe variable was set to point at the *pci_device_probe* function. This function casts (yet again) the struct device back into a struct pci_dev and the struct driver that is set in the device back into a struct pci_driver. It again verifies that this driver states that it can support this device (which seems to be a redundant extra check for some unknown reason), increments the reference count of the device, and then calls the PCI driver's *probe* function with a pointer to the struct pci_dev structure it should bind to.

If the PCI driver's *probe* function determines that it can not handle this device for some reason, it returns a negative error value, which is propagated back to the driver core and causes it to continue looking through the list of drivers to match one up with this device. If the *probe* function can claim the device, it does all the initialization that it needs to do to handle the device properly, and then it returns 0 back up to the driver core. This causes the driver core to add the device to the list of all devices currently bound by this specific driver and creates a symlink within the driver's directory in sysfs to the device that it is now controlling. This symlink allows users to see exactly which devices are bound to which devices. This can be seen as:

```
$ tree /sys/bus/pci
/sys/bus/pci/
|-- devices
|   |-- 0000:00:00.0 -> ../../../devices/pci0000:00/0000:00:00.0
|   |-- 0000:00:00.1 -> ../../../devices/pci0000:00/0000:00:00.1
|   |-- 0000:00:00.2 -> ../../../devices/pci0000:00/0000:00:00.2
```

```
  |    |-- 0000:00:02.0 -> ../../../devices/pci0000:00/0000:00:02.0
  |    |-- 0000:00:04.0 -> ../../../devices/pci0000:00/0000:00:04.0
  |    |-- 0000:00:06.0 -> ../../../devices/pci0000:00/0000:00:06.0
  |    |-- 0000:00:07.0 -> ../../../devices/pci0000:00/0000:00:07.0
  |    |-- 0000:00:09.0 -> ../../../devices/pci0000:00/0000:00:09.0
  |    |-- 0000:00:09.1 -> ../../../devices/pci0000:00/0000:00:09.1
  |    |-- 0000:00:09.2 -> ../../../devices/pci0000:00/0000:00:09.2
  |    |-- 0000:00:0c.0 -> ../../../devices/pci0000:00/0000:00:0c.0
  |    |-- 0000:00:0f.0 -> ../../../devices/pci0000:00/0000:00:0f.0
  |    |-- 0000:00:10.0 -> ../../../devices/pci0000:00/0000:00:10.0
  |    |-- 0000:00:12.0 -> ../../../devices/pci0000:00/0000:00:12.0
  |    |-- 0000:00:13.0 -> ../../../devices/pci0000:00/0000:00:13.0
  |    `-- 0000:00:14.0 -> ../../../devices/pci0000:00/0000:00:14.0
  `-- drivers
      |-- ALI15x3_IDE
      |    `-- 0000:00:0f.0 -> ../../../../devices/pci0000:00/0000:00:0f.0
      |-- ehci_hcd
      |    `-- 0000:00:09.2 -> ../../../../devices/pci0000:00/0000:00:09.2
      |-- ohci_hcd
      |    |-- 0000:00:02.0 -> ../../../../devices/pci0000:00/0000:00:02.0
      |    |-- 0000:00:09.0 -> ../../../../devices/pci0000:00/0000:00:09.0
      |    `-- 0000:00:09.1 -> ../../../../devices/pci0000:00/0000:00:09.1
      |-- orinoco_pci
      |    `-- 0000:00:12.0 -> ../../../../devices/pci0000:00/0000:00:12.0
      |-- radeonfb
      |    `-- 0000:00:14.0 -> ../../../../devices/pci0000:00/0000:00:14.0
      |-- serial
      `-- trident
           `-- 0000:00:04.0 -> ../../../../devices/pci0000:00/0000:00:04.0
```

Remove a Device

A PCI device can be removed from a system in a number of different ways. All Card-Bus devices are really PCI devices in a different physical form factor, and the kernel PCI core does not differenciate between them. Systems that allow the removal or addition of PCI devices while the machine is still running are becoming more popular, and Linux supports them. There is also a fake PCI Hotplug driver that allows developers to test to see if their PCI driver properly handles the removal of a device while the system is running. This module is called fakephp and causes the kernel to think the PCI device is gone, but it does not allow users to physically remove a PCI device from a system that does not have the proper hardware to do so. See the documentation with this driver for more information on how to use it to test your PCI drivers.

The PCI core exerts a lot less effort to remove a device than it does to add it. When a PCI device is to be removed, the *pci_remove_bus_device* function is called. This function does some PCI-specific cleanups and housekeeping, and then calls the *device_unregister* function with a pointer to the struct pci_dev's struct device member.

In the *device_unregister* function, the driver core merely unlinks the sysfs files from the driver bound to the device (if there was one), removes the device from its internal list of devices, and calls *kobject_del* with a pointer to the struct kobject that is contained in the struct device structure. That function makes a hotplug call to user space stating that the kobject is now removed from the system, and then it deletes all sysfs files associated with the kobject and the sysfs directory itself that the kobject had originally created.

The *kobject_del* function also removes the kobject reference of the device itself. If that reference was the last one (meaning no user-space files were open for the sysfs entry of the device), then the *release* function for the PCI device itself, *pci_release_dev*, is called. That function merely frees up the memory that the struct pci_dev took up.

After this, all sysfs entries associated with the device are removed, and the memory associated with the device is released. The PCI device is now totally removed from the system.

Add a Driver

A PCI driver is added to the PCI core when it calls the *pci_register_driver* function. This function merely initializes the struct device_driver structure that is contained within the struct pci_driver structure, as previously mentioned in the section about adding a device. Then the PCI core calls the *driver_register* function in the driver core with a pointer to the structdevice_driver structure contained in the struct pci_driver structure.

The *driver_register* function initializes a few locks in the struct device_driver structure, and then calls the *bus_add_driver* function. This function does the following steps:

- Looks up the bus that the driver is to be associated with. If this bus is not found, the function instantly returns.
- The driver's sysfs directory is created based on the name of the driver and the bus that it is associated with.
- The bus's internal lock is grabbed, and then all devices that have been registered with the bus are walked, and the match function is called for them, just like when a new device is added. If that match function succeeds, then the rest of the binding process occurs, as described in the previous section.

Remove a Driver

Removing a driver is a very simple action. For a PCI driver, the driver calls the *pci_unregister_driver* function. This function merely calls the driver core function *driver_unregister*, with a pointer to the struct device_driver portion of the struct pci_driver structure passed to it.

The *driver_unregister* function handles some basic housekeeping by cleaning up some sysfs attributes that were attached to the driver's entry in the sysfs tree. It then iterates over all devices that were attached to this driver and calls the *release* function for it. This happens exactly like the previously mentioned *release* function for when a device is removed from the system.

After all devices are unbound from the driver, the driver code does this unique bit of logic:

```
down(&drv->unload_sem);
up(&drv->unload_sem);
```

This is done right before returning to the caller of the function. This lock is grabbed because the code needs to wait for all reference counts on this driver to be dropped to 0 before it is safe to return. This is needed because the *driver_unregister* function is most commonly called as the exit path of a module that is being unloaded. The module needs to remain in memory for as long as the driver is being referenced by devices and by waiting for this lock to be freed, this allows the kernel to know when it is safe to remove the driver from memory.

Hotplug

There are two different ways to view hotplugging. The kernel views hotplugging as an interaction between the hardware, the kernel, and the kernel driver. Users view hotplugging as the interaction between the kernel and user space through the program called */sbin/hotplug*. This program is called by the kernel when it wants to notify user space that some type of hotplug event has just happened within the kernel.

Dynamic Devices

The most commonly used meaning of the term "hotplug" happens when discussing the fact that most all computer systems can now handle devices appearing or disappearing while the system is powered on. This is very different from the computer systems of only a few years ago, where the programmers knew that they needed to scan for all devices only at boot time, and they never had to worry about their devices disappearing until the power was turned off to the whole machine. Now, with the advent of USB, CardBus, PCMCIA, IEEE1394, and PCI Hotplug controllers, the Linux kernel needs to be able to reliably run no matter what hardware is added or removed from the system. This places an added burden on the device driver author, as they must now always handle a device being suddenly ripped out from underneath them without any notice.

Each different bus type handles the loss of a device in a different way. For example, when a PCI, CardBus, or PCMCIA device is removed from the system, it is usually a while before the driver is notified of this action through its *remove* function. Before that happens, all reads from the PCI bus return all bits set. This means that drivers need to always check the value of the data they read from the PCI bus and properly be able to handle a 0xff value.

An example of this can be seen in the *drivers/usb/host/ehci-hcd.c* driver, which is a PCI driver for a USB 2.0 (high-speed) controller card. It has the following code in its main handshake loop to detect if the controller card has been removed from the system:

```
result = readl(ptr);
if (result == ~(u32)0)     /* card removed */
    return -ENODEV;
```

For USB drivers, when the device that a USB driver is bound to is removed from the system, any pending urbs that were submitted to the device start failing with the error -ENODEV. The driver needs to recognize this error and properly clean up any pending I/O if it occurs.

Hotpluggable devices are not limited only to traditional devices such as mice, keyboards, and network cards. There are numerous systems that now support removal and addition of entire CPUs and memory sticks. Fortunately the Linux kernel properly handles the addition and removal of such core "system" devices so that individual device drivers do not need to pay attention to these things.

The /sbin/hotplug Utility

As alluded to earlier in this chapter, whenever a device is added or removed from the system, a "hotplug event" is generated. This means that the kernel calls the user-space program */sbin/hotplug*. This program is typically a very small bash script that merely passes execution on to a list of other programs that are placed in the */etc/hotplug.d/* directory tree. For most Linux distributions, this script looks like the following:

```
DIR="/etc/hotplug.d"
for I in "${DIR}/$1/"*.hotplug "${DIR}/"default/*.hotplug ; do
    if [ -f $I ]; then
        test -x $I && $I $1 ;
    fi
done
exit 1
```

In other words, the script searches for all programs bearing a *.hotplug* suffix that might be interested in this event and invokes them, passing to them a number of different environment variables that have been set by the kernel. More details about how the */sbin/hotplug* script works can be found in the comments in the program and in the *hotplug(8)* manpage.

As mentioned previously, /sbin/hotplug is called whenever a kobject is created or destroyed. The hotplug program is called with a single command-line argument providing a name for the event. The core kernel and specific subsystem involved also set a series of environment variables (described below) with information on what has just occurred. These variables are used by the hotplug programs to determine what has just happened in the kernel, and if there is any specific action that should take place.

The command-line argument passed to /sbin/hotplug is the name associated with this hotplug event, as determined by the kset assigned to the kobject. This name can be set by a call to the *name* function that is part of the kset's hotplug_ops structure described earlier in this chapter; if that function is not present or never called, the name is that of the kset itself.

The default environment variables that are always set for the /sbin/hotplug program are:

ACTION
> The string add or remove, depending on whether the object in question was just created or destroyed.

DEVPATH
> A directory path, within the sysfs filesystem, that points to the kobject that is being either created or destroyed. Note that the mount point of the sysfs filesystem is not added to this path, so it is up to the user-space program to determine that.

SEQNUM
> The sequence number for this hotplug event. The sequence number is a 64-bit number that is incremented for every hotplug event that is generated. This allows user space to sort the hotplug events in the order in which the kernel generates them, as it is possible for a user-space program to be run out of order.

SUBSYSTEM
> The same string passed as the command-line argument as described above.

A number of the different bus subsystems all add their own environment variables to the /sbin/hotplug call, when devices associated with the bus are added or removed from the system. They do this in their *hotplug* callback that is specified in the struct kset_hotplug_ops assigned to their bus (as described in the section "Hotplug Operations"). This allows user space to be able to automatically load any necessary module that might be needed to control the device that has been found by the bus. Here is a list of the different bus types and what environment variables they add to the /sbin/hotplug call.

IEEE1394 (FireWire)

Any devices on the IEEE1394 bus, also known as Firewire, have the */sbin/hotplug* parameter name and the SUBSYSTEM environment variable set to the value ieee1394. The ieee1394 subsystem also always adds the following four environment variables:

VENDOR_ID
> The 24-bit vendor ID for the IEEE1394 device

MODEL_ID
> The 24-bit model ID for the IEEE1394 device

GUID
> The 64-bit GUID for the device

SPECIFIER_ID
> The 24-bit value specifying the owner of the protocol spec for this device

VERSION
> The value that specifies the version of the protocol spec for this device

Networking

All network devices create a hotplug event when the device is registered or unregistered in the kernel. The */sbin/hotplug* call has the parameter name and the SUBSYSTEM environment variable set to the value net, and just adds the following environment variable:

INTERFACE
> The name of the interface that has been registered or unregistered from the kernel. Examples of this are lo and eth0.

PCI

Any devices on the PCI bus have the parameter name and the SUBSYSTEM environment variable set to the value pci. The PCI subsystem also always adds the following four environment variables:

PCI_CLASS
> The PCI class number for the device, in hex.

PCI_ID
> The PCI vendor and device IDs for the device, in hex, combined in the format vendor:device.

PCI_SUBSYS_ID
> The PCI subsystem vendor and subsystem device IDs, combined in the format subsys_vendor:subsys_device.

PCI_SLOT_NAME
> The PCI slot "name" that is given to the device by the kernel. It is in the format domain:bus:slot:function. An example might be 0000:00:0d.0.

Input

For all input devices (mice, keyboards, joysticks, etc.), a hotplug event is generated when the device is added and removed from the kernel. The */sbin/hotplug* parameter and the SUBSYSTEM environment variable are set to the value input. The input subsystem also always adds the following environment variable:

PRODUCT
A multivalue string listing values in hex with no leading zeros. It is in the format bustype:vendor:product:version.

The following environment variables may be present, if the device supports it:

NAME
The name of the input device as given by the device.

PHYS
The device's physical address that the input subsystem gave to this device. It is supposed to be stable, depending on the bus position into which the device was plugged.

EV
KEY
REL
ABS
MSC
LED
SND
FF
These all come from the input device descriptor and are set to the appropriate values if the specific input device supports it.

USB

Any devices on the USB bus have the parameter name and the SUBSYSTEM environment variable set to the value usb. The USB subsystem also always adds the following environment variables:

PRODUCT
A string in the format idVendor/idProduct/bcdDevice that specifies those USB device-specific fields

TYPE
A string in the format bDeviceClass/bDeviceSubClass/bDeviceProtocol that specifies those USB device-specific fields

If the bDeviceClass field is set to 0, the following environment variable is also set:

INTERFACE
A string in the format bInterfaceClass/bInterfaceSubClass/bInterfaceProtocol that specifies those USB device-specific fields.

If the kernel build option, CONFIG_USB_DEVICEFS, which selects the usbfs filesystem to be built in the kernel, is selected, the following environment variable is also set:

DEVICE

> A string that shows where in the usbfs filesystem the device is located. This string is in the format /proc/bus/usb/USB_BUS_NUMBER/USB_DEVICE_NUMBER, in which USB_BUS_NUMBER is the three-digit number of the USB bus that the device is on, and USB_DEVICE_NUMBER is the three-digit number that has been assigned by the kernel to that USB device.

SCSI

All SCSI devices create a hotplug event when the SCSI device is created or removed from the kernel. The */sbin/hotplug* call has the parameter name and the SUBSYSTEM environment variable set to the value scsi for every SCSI device that is added or removed from the system. There are no additional environment variables added by the SCSI system, but it is mentioned here because there is a SCSI-specific user-space script that can determine what SCSI drivers (disk, tape, generic, etc.) should be loaded for the specified SCSI device.

Laptop docking stations

If a Plug-and-Play-supported laptop docking station is added or removed from the running Linux system (by inserting the laptop into the station, or removing it), a hotplug event is created. The */sbin/hotplug* call has the parameter name and the SUBSYSTEM environment variable set to the value dock. No other environment variables are set.

S/390 and zSeries

On the S/390 architecture, the channel bus architecture supports a wide range of hardware, all of which generate */sbin/hotplug* events when they are added or removed from the Linux virtual system. These devices all have the */sbin/hotplug* parameter name and the SUBSYSTEM environment variable set to the value dasd. No other environment variables are set.

Using /sbin/hotplug

Now that the Linux kernel is calling */sbin/hotplug* for every device added and removed from the kernel, a number of very useful tools have been created in user space that take advantage of this. Two of the most popular tools are the Linux Hotplug scripts and *udev*.

Linux hotplug scripts

The Linux hotplug scripts started out as the very first user of the */sbin/hotplug* call. These scripts look at the different environment variables that the kernel sets to describe the device that was just discovered and then tries to find a kernel module that matches up with that device.

As has been described before, when a driver uses the MODULE_DEVICE_TABLE macro, the program, depmod, takes that information and creates the files located in */lib/module/ KERNEL_VERSION/modules.*map*. The * is different, depending on the bus type that the driver supports. Currently, the module map files are generated for drivers that work for devices that support the PCI, USB, IEEE1394, INPUT, ISAPNP, and CCW subsystems.

The hotplug scripts use these module map text files to determine what module to try to load to support the device that was recently discovered by the kernel. They load all modules and do not stop at the first match, in order to let the kernel work out what module works best. These scripts do not unload any modules when devices are removed. If they were to try to do that, they could accidentally shut down devices that were also controlled by the same driver of the device that was removed.

Note, now that the modprobe program can read the MODULE_DEVICE_TABLE information directly from the modules without the need of the module map files, the hotplug scripts might be reduced to a small wrapper around the modprobe program.

udev

One of the main reasons for creating the unified driver model in the kernel was to allow user space to manage the */dev* tree in a dynamic fashion. This had previously been done in user space with the implementation of devfs, but that code base has slowly rotted away, due to a lack of an active maintainer and some unfixable core bugs. A number of kernel developers realized that if all device information was exported to user space, it could perform all the necessary management of the */dev* tree.

devfs has some very fundamental flaws in its design. It requires every device driver to be modified to support it, and it requires that device driver to specify the name and location within the */dev* tree where it is placed. It also does not properly handle dynamic major and minor numbers, and it does not allow user space to override the naming of a device in a simple manner, forcing the device naming policy to reside within the kernel and not in user space. Linux kernel developers really hate having policy within the kernel, and since the devfs naming policy does not follow the Linux Standard Base specification, it really bothers them.

As the Linux kernel started to be installed on huge servers, a lot of users ran into the problem of how to manage very large numbers of devices. Disk drive arrays of over 10,000 unique devices presented the very difficult task of ensuring that a specific disk was always named with the same exact name, no matter where it was placed in the disk array or when it was discovered by the kernel. This same problem also plagued desktop users who tried to plug two USB printers into their system and then realized that they had no way of ensuring that the printer known as */dev/lpt0* would not change and be assigned to the other printer if the system was rebooted.

So, *udev* was created. It relies on all device information being exported to user space through sysfs and on being notified by */sbin/hotplug* that a device was added or removed. Policy decisions, such as what name to give a device, can be specified in user space, outside of the kernel. This ensures that the naming policy is removed from the kernel and allows a large amount of flexibility about the name of each device.

For more information on how to use *udev* and how to configure it, please see the documentation that comes included with the *udev* package in your distribution.

All that a device driver needs to do, for *udev* to work properly with it, is ensure that any major and minor numbers assigned to a device controlled by the driver are exported to user space through sysfs. For any driver that uses a subsystem to assign it a major and minor number, this is already done by the subsystem, and the driver doesn't have to do any work. Examples of subsystems that do this are the tty, misc, usb, input, scsi, block, i2c, network, and frame buffer subsystems. If your driver handles getting a major and minor number on its own, through a call to the *cdev_init* function or the older *register_chrdev* function, the driver needs to be modified in order for *udev* to work properly with it.

udev looks for a file called dev in the */class/* tree of sysfs, in order to determine what major and minor number is assigned to a specific device when it is called by the kernel through the */sbin/hotplug* interface. A device driver merely needs to create that file for every device it controls. The class_simple interface is usually the easiest way to do this.

As mentioned in the section "The class_simple Interface," the first step in using the class_simple interface is to create a struct class_simple with a call to the *class_simple_create* function:

```
static struct class_simple *foo_class;
...
foo_class = class_simple_create(THIS_MODULE, "foo");
if (IS_ERR(foo_class)) {
    printk(KERN_ERR "Error creating foo class.\n");
    goto error;
}
```

This code creates a directory in sysfs in */sys/class/foo*.

Whenever a new device is found by your driver, and you assign it a minor number as described in Chapter 3, the driver should call the *class_simple_device_add* function:

```
class_simple_device_add(foo_class, MKDEV(FOO_MAJOR, minor), NULL, "foo%d", minor);
```

This code causes a subdirectory under */sys/class/foo* to be created called *fooN*, where *N* is the minor number for this device. There is one file created in this directory, *dev*, which is exactly what *udev* needs in order to create a device node for your device.

When your driver is unbound from a device, and you give up the minor number that it was attached to, a call to *class_simple_device_remove* is needed to remove the sysfs entries for this device:

```
class_simple_device_remove(MKDEV(FOO_MAJOR, minor));
```

Later, when your entire driver is being shut down, a call to *class_simple_destroy* is needed to remove the class that you created originally with the call to *class_simple_create*:

```
class_simple_destroy(foo_class);
```

The *dev* file that is created by the call to *class_simple_device_add* consists of the major and minor numbers, separated by a : character. If your driver does not want to use the class_simple interface because you want to provide other files within the class directory for the subsystem, use the *print_dev_t* function to properly format the major and minor number for the specific device.

Dealing with Firmware

As a driver author, you may find yourself confronted with a device that must have firmware downloaded into it before it functions properly. The competition in many parts of the hardware market is so intense that even the cost of a bit of EEPROM for the device's controlling firmware is more than the manufacturer is willing to spend. So the firmware is distributed on a CD with the hardware, and the operating system is charged with conveying the firmware to the device itself.

You may be tempted to solve the firmware problem with a declaration like this:

```
static char my_firmware[ ] = { 0x34, 0x78, 0xa4, ... };
```

That approach is almost certainly a mistake, however. Coding firmware into a driver bloats the driver code, makes upgrading the firmware hard, and is very likely to run into licensing problems. It is highly unlikely that the vendor has released the firmware image under the GPL, so mixing it with GPL-licensed code is usually a mistake. For this reason, drivers containing wired-in firmware are unlikely to be accepted into the mainline kernel or included by Linux distributors.

The Kernel Firmware Interface

The proper solution is to obtain the firmware from user space when you need it. Please resist the temptation to try to open a file containing firmware directly from kernel space, however; that is an error-prone operation, and it puts policy (in the form of a file name) into the kernel. Instead, the correct approach is to use the firmware interface, which was created just for this purpose:

```
#include <linux/firmware.h>
int request_firmware(const struct firmware **fw, char *name,
                     struct device *device);
```

A call to *request_firmware* requests that user space locate and provide a firmware image to the kernel; we look at the details of how it works in a moment. The name should identify the firmware that is desired; the normal usage is the name of the firmware file as provided by the vendor. Something like *my_firmware.bin* is typical. If the firmware is successfully loaded, the return value is 0 (otherwise the usual error code is returned), and the fw argument is pointed to one of these structures:

```
struct firmware {
        size_t size;
        u8 *data;
};
```

That structure contains the actual firmware, which can now be downloaded to the device. Be aware that this firmware is unchecked data from user space; you should apply any and all tests you can think of to convince yourself that it is a proper firmware image before sending it to the hardware. Device firmware usually contains identification strings, checksums, and so on; check them all before trusting the data.

After you have sent the firmware to the device, you should release the in-kernel structure with:

```
void release_firmware(struct firmware *fw);
```

Since *request_firmware* asks user space to help, it is guaranteed to sleep before returning. If your driver is not in a position to sleep when it must ask for firmware, the asynchronous alternative may be used:

```
int request_firmware_nowait(struct module *module,
                     char *name, struct device *device, void *context,
                     void (*cont)(const struct firmware *fw, void *context));
```

The additional arguments here are module (which will almost always be THIS_MODULE), context (a private data pointer that is not used by the firmware subsystem), and cont. If all goes well, *request_firmware_nowait* begins the firmware load process and returns 0. At some future time, cont will be called with the result of the load. If the firmware load fails for some reason, fw is NULL.

How It Works

The firmware subsystem works with sysfs and the hotplug mechanism. When a call is made to *request_firmware*, a new directory is created under */sys/class/firmware* using your device's name. That directory contains three attributes:

loading

> This attribute should be set to one by the user-space process that is loading the firmware. When the load process is complete, it should be set to 0. Writing a value of -1 to loading aborts the firmware loading process.

data

> data is a binary attribute that receives the firmware data itself. After setting loading, the user-space process should write the firmware to this attribute.

device

> This attribute is a symbolic link to the associated entry under */sys/devices*.

Once the sysfs entries have been created, the kernel generates a hotplug event for your device. The environment passed to the hotplug handler includes a variable FIRMWARE, which is set to the name provided to *request_firmware*. The handler should locate the firmware file, and copy it into the kernel using the attributes provided. If the file cannot be found, the handler should set the *loading* attribute to -1.

If a firmware request is not serviced within 10 seconds, the kernel gives up and returns a failure status to the driver. That time-out period can be changed via the sysfs attribute */sys/class/firmware/timeout*.

Using the *request_firmware* interface allows you to distribute the device firmware with your driver. When properly integrated into the hotplug mechanism, the firmware loading subsystem allows devices to simply work "out of the box." It is clearly the best way of handling the problem.

Please indulge us as we pass on one more warning, however: device firmware should not be distributed without the permission of the manufacturer. Many manufacturers will agree to license their firmware under reasonable terms when asked politely; some others can be less cooperative. Either way, copying and distributing their firmware without permission is a violation of copyright law and an invitation for trouble.

Quick Reference

Many functions have been introduced in this chapter; here is a quick summary of them all.

Kobjects

```
#include <linux/kobject.h>
```
The include file containing definitions for kobjects, related structures, and functions.

```
void kobject_init(struct kobject *kobj);
int kobject_set_name(struct kobject *kobj, const char *format, ...);
```
Functions for kobject initialization.

```
struct kobject *kobject_get(struct kobject *kobj);
void kobject_put(struct kobject *kobj);
```
Functions that manage reference counts for kobjects.

```
struct kobj_type;
struct kobj_type *get_ktype(struct kobject *kobj);
```
Represents the type of structure within which a kobject is embedded. Use *get_ktype* to get the kobj_type associated with a given kobject.

```
int kobject_add(struct kobject *kobj);
extern int kobject_register(struct kobject *kobj);
void kobject_del(struct kobject *kobj);
void kobject_unregister(struct kobject *kobj);
```
kobject_add adds a kobject to the system, handling kset membership, sysfs representation, and hotplug event generation. *kobject_register* is a convenience function that combines *kobject_init* and *kobject_add*. Use *kobject_del* to remove a kobject or *kobject_unregister*, which combines *kobject_del* and *kobject_put*.

```
void kset_init(struct kset *kset);
int kset_add(struct kset *kset);
int kset_register(struct kset *kset);
void kset_unregister(struct kset *kset);
```
Initialization and registration functions for ksets.

```
decl_subsys(name, type, hotplug_ops);
```
A macro that makes it easier to declare subsystems.

```
void subsystem_init(struct subsystem *subsys);
int subsystem_register(struct subsystem *subsys);
void subsystem_unregister(struct subsystem *subsys);
struct subsystem *subsys_get(struct subsystem *subsys)
void subsys_put(struct subsystem *subsys);
```
Operations on subsystems.

Sysfs Operations

```
#include <linux/sysfs.h>
```
The include file containing declarations for sysfs.

```
int sysfs_create_file(struct kobject *kobj, struct attribute *attr);
int sysfs_remove_file(struct kobject *kobj, struct attribute *attr);
int sysfs_create_bin_file(struct kobject *kobj, struct bin_attribute *attr);
int sysfs_remove_bin_file(struct kobject *kobj, struct bin_attribute *attr);
int sysfs_create_link(struct kobject *kobj, struct kobject *target, char
                      *name);
void sysfs_remove_link(struct kobject *kobj, char *name);
```
Functions for creating and removing attribute files associated with a kobject.

Buses, Devices, and Drivers

```
int bus_register(struct bus_type *bus);
void bus_unregister(struct bus_type *bus);
```
Functions that perform registration and unregistration of buses in the device model.

```
int bus_for_each_dev(struct bus_type *bus, struct device *start, void *data,
                     int (*fn)(struct device *, void *));
int bus_for_each_drv(struct bus_type *bus, struct device_driver *start, void
                     *data, int (*fn)(struct device_driver *, void *));
```
Functions that iterate over each of the devices and drivers, respectively, that are attached to the given bus.

```
BUS_ATTR(name, mode, show, store);
int bus_create_file(struct bus_type *bus, struct bus_attribute *attr);
void bus_remove_file(struct bus_type *bus, struct bus_attribute *attr);
```
The *BUS_ATTR* macro may be used to declare a bus_attribute structure, which may then be added and removed with the above two functions.

```
int device_register(struct device *dev);
void device_unregister(struct device *dev);
```
Functions that handle device registration.

```
DEVICE_ATTR(name, mode, show, store);
int device_create_file(struct device *device, struct device_attribute *entry);
void device_remove_file(struct device *dev, struct device_attribute *attr);
```
Macros and functions that deal with device attributes.

```
int driver_register(struct device_driver *drv);
void driver_unregister(struct device_driver *drv);
```
Functions that register and unregister a device driver.

```
DRIVER_ATTR(name, mode, show, store);
int driver_create_file(struct device_driver *drv, struct driver_attribute
                        *attr);
void driver_remove_file(struct device_driver *drv, struct driver_attribute
                        *attr);
```
Macros and functions that manage driver attributes.

Classes

```
struct class_simple *class_simple_create(struct module *owner, char *name);
void class_simple_destroy(struct class_simple *cs);
struct class_device *class_simple_device_add(struct class_simple *cs, dev_t
  devnum, struct device *device, const char *fmt, ...);
void class_simple_device_remove(dev_t dev);
int class_simple_set_hotplug(struct class_simple *cs, int (*hotplug)(struct
  class_device *dev, char **envp, int num_envp, char *buffer, int
  buffer_size));
```
Functions that implement the class_simple interface; they manage simple class entries containing a dev attribute and little else.

```
int class_register(struct class *cls);
void class_unregister(struct class *cls);
```
Registration and unregistration of classes.

```
CLASS_ATTR(name, mode, show, store);
int class_create_file(struct class *cls, const struct class_attribute *attr);
void class_remove_file(struct class *cls, const struct class_attribute *attr);
```
The usual macros and functions for dealing with class attributes.

```
int class_device_register(struct class_device *cd);
void class_device_unregister(struct class_device *cd);
int class_device_rename(struct class_device *cd, char *new_name);
CLASS_DEVICE_ATTR(name, mode, show, store);
int class_device_create_file(struct class_device *cls, const struct
                            class_device_attribute *attr);
void class_device_remove_file(struct class_device *cls, const struct
                            class_device_attribute *attr);
```
Functions and macros that implement the class device interface.

```
int class_interface_register(struct class_interface *intf);
void class_interface_unregister(struct class_interface *intf);
```
Functions that add an interface to a class (or remove it).

Firmware

```
#include <linux/firmware.h>
int request_firmware(const struct firmware **fw, char *name, struct device
                     *device);
int request_firmware_nowait(struct module *module, char *name, struct device
  *device, void *context, void (*cont)(const struct firmware *fw, void
  *context));
void release_firmware(struct firmware *fw);
```

Functions that implement the kernel firmware-loading interface.

Memory Mapping and DMA

This chapter delves into the area of Linux memory management, with an emphasis on techniques that are useful to the device driver writer. Many types of driver programming require some understanding of how the virtual memory subsystem works; the material we cover in this chapter comes in handy more than once as we get into some of the more complex and performance-critical subsystems. The virtual memory subsystem is also a highly interesting part of the core Linux kernel and, therefore, it merits a look.

The material in this chapter is divided into three sections:

- The first covers the implementation of the *mmap* system call, which allows the mapping of device memory directly into a user process's address space. Not all devices require *mmap* support, but, for some, mapping device memory can yield significant performance improvements.

- We then look at crossing the boundary from the other direction with a discussion of direct access to user-space pages. Relatively few drivers need this capability; in many cases, the kernel performs this sort of mapping without the driver even being aware of it. But an awareness of how to map user-space memory into the kernel (with *get_user_pages*) can be useful.

- The final section covers direct memory access (DMA) I/O operations, which provide peripherals with direct access to system memory.

Of course, all of these techniques require an understanding of how Linux memory management works, so we start with an overview of that subsystem.

Memory Management in Linux

Rather than describing the theory of memory management in operating systems, this section tries to pinpoint the main features of the Linux implementation. Although you do not need to be a Linux virtual memory guru to implement *mmap*, a basic overview of how things work is useful. What follows is a fairly lengthy description of the data structures used by the kernel to manage memory. Once the necessary background has been covered, we can get into working with these structures.

Address Types

Linux is, of course, a virtual memory system, meaning that the addresses seen by user programs do not directly correspond to the physical addresses used by the hardware. Virtual memory introduces a layer of indirection that allows a number of nice things. With virtual memory, programs running on the system can allocate far more memory than is physically available; indeed, even a single process can have a virtual address space larger than the system's physical memory. Virtual memory also allows the program to play a number of tricks with the process's address space, including mapping the program's memory to device memory.

Thus far, we have talked about virtual and physical addresses, but a number of the details have been glossed over. The Linux system deals with several types of addresses, each with its own semantics. Unfortunately, the kernel code is not always very clear on exactly which type of address is being used in each situation, so the programmer must be careful.

The following is a list of address types used in Linux. Figure 15-1 shows how these address types relate to physical memory.

User virtual addresses
> These are the regular addresses seen by user-space programs. User addresses are either 32 or 64 bits in length, depending on the underlying hardware architecture, and each process has its own virtual address space.

Physical addresses
> The addresses used between the processor and the system's memory. Physical addresses are 32- or 64-bit quantities; even 32-bit systems can use larger physical addresses in some situations.

Bus addresses
> The addresses used between peripheral buses and memory. Often, they are the same as the physical addresses used by the processor, but that is not necessarily the case. Some architectures can provide an I/O memory management unit (IOMMU) that remaps addresses between a bus and main memory. An IOMMU can make life easier in a number of ways (making a buffer scattered in memory appear contiguous to the device, for example), but programming the IOMMU is an extra step that must be performed when setting up DMA operations. Bus addresses are highly architecture dependent, of course.

Kernel logical addresses
> These make up the normal address space of the kernel. These addresses map some portion (perhaps all) of main memory and are often treated as if they were physical addresses. On most architectures, logical addresses and their associated

physical addresses differ only by a constant offset. Logical addresses use the hardware's native pointer size and, therefore, may be unable to address all of physical memory on heavily equipped 32-bit systems. Logical addresses are usually stored in variables of type unsigned long or void *. Memory returned from *kmalloc* has a kernel logical address.

Kernel virtual addresses

Kernel virtual addresses are similar to logical addresses in that they are a mapping from a kernel-space address to a physical address. Kernel virtual addresses do not necessarily have the linear, one-to-one mapping to physical addresses that characterize the logical address space, however. All logical addresses *are* kernel virtual addresses, but many kernel virtual addresses are not logical addresses. For example, memory allocated by *vmalloc* has a virtual address (but no direct physical mapping). The *kmap* function (described later in this chapter) also returns virtual addresses. Virtual addresses are usually stored in pointer variables.

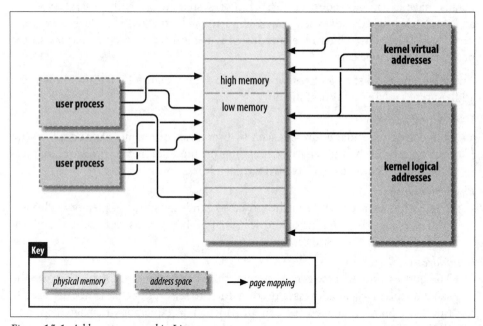

Figure 15-1. Address types used in Linux

If you have a logical address, the macro __pa() (defined in <asm/page.h>) returns its associated physical address. Physical addresses can be mapped back to logical addresses with __va(), but only for low-memory pages.

Different kernel functions require different types of addresses. It would be nice if there were different C types defined, so that the required address types were explicit, but we have no such luck. In this chapter, we try to be clear on which types of addresses are used where.

Physical Addresses and Pages

Physical memory is divided into discrete units called *pages*. Much of the system's internal handling of memory is done on a per-page basis. Page size varies from one architecture to the next, although most systems currently use 4096-byte pages. The constant PAGE_SIZE (defined in *<asm/page.h>*) gives the page size on any given architecture.

If you look at a memory address—virtual or physical—it is divisible into a page number and an offset within the page. If 4096-byte pages are being used, for example, the 12 least-significant bits are the offset, and the remaining, higher bits indicate the page number. If you discard the offset and shift the rest of an offset to the right, the result is called a *page frame number* (PFN). Shifting bits to convert between page frame numbers and addresses is a fairly common operation; the macro PAGE_SHIFT tells how many bits must be shifted to make this conversion.

High and Low Memory

The difference between logical and kernel virtual addresses is highlighted on 32-bit systems that are equipped with large amounts of memory. With 32 bits, it is possible to address 4 GB of memory. Linux on 32-bit systems has, until recently, been limited to substantially less memory than that, however, because of the way it sets up the virtual address space.

The kernel (on the x86 architecture, in the default configuration) splits the 4-GB virtual address space between user-space and the kernel; the same set of mappings is used in both contexts. A typical split dedicates 3 GB to user space, and 1 GB for kernel space.[*] The kernel's code and data structures must fit into that space, but the biggest consumer of kernel address space is virtual mappings for physical memory. The kernel cannot directly manipulate memory that is not mapped into the kernel's address space. The kernel, in other words, needs its own virtual address for any memory it must touch directly. Thus, for many years, the maximum amount of physical memory that could be handled by the kernel was the amount that could be mapped into the kernel's portion of the virtual address space, minus the space

---

[*] Many non-x86 architectures are able to efficiently do without the kernel/user-space split described here, so they can work with up to a 4-GB kernel address space on 32-bit systems. The constraints described in this section still apply to such systems when more than 4 GB of memory are installed, however.

needed for the kernel code itself. As a result, x86-based Linux systems could work with a maximum of a little under 1 GB of physical memory.

In response to commercial pressure to support more memory while not breaking 32-bit application and the system's compatibility, the processor manufacturers have added "address extension" features to their products. The result is that, in many cases, even 32-bit processors can address more than 4 GB of physical memory. The limitation on how much memory can be directly mapped with logical addresses remains, however. Only the lowest portion of memory (up to 1 or 2 GB, depending on the hardware and the kernel configuration) has logical addresses;* the rest (high memory) does not. Before accessing a specific high-memory page, the kernel must set up an explicit virtual mapping to make that page available in the kernel's address space. Thus, many kernel data structures must be placed in low memory; high memory tends to be reserved for user-space process pages.

The term "high memory" can be confusing to some, especially since it has other meanings in the PC world. So, to make things clear, we'll define the terms here:

Low memory
    Memory for which logical addresses exist in kernel space. On almost every system you will likely encounter, all memory is low memory.

High memory
    Memory for which logical addresses do not exist, because it is beyond the address range set aside for kernel virtual addresses.

On i386 systems, the boundary between low and high memory is usually set at just under 1 GB, although that boundary can be changed at kernel configuration time. This boundary is not related in any way to the old 640 KB limit found on the original PC, and its placement is not dictated by the hardware. It is, instead, a limit set by the kernel itself as it splits the 32-bit address space between kernel and user space.

We will point out limitations on the use of high memory as we come to them in this chapter.

The Memory Map and Struct Page

Historically, the kernel has used logical addresses to refer to pages of physical memory. The addition of high-memory support, however, has exposed an obvious problem—logical addresses are not available for high memory. Therefore, kernel functions that deal with memory are increasingly using pointers to struct page (defined in *<linux/mm.h>*) instead. This data structure is used to keep track of just about everything the kernel needs to know about physical memory;

---

* The 2.6 kernel (with an added patch) can support a "4G/4G" mode on x86 hardware, which enables larger kernel and user virtual address spaces at a mild performance cost.

there is one `struct page` for each physical page on the system. Some of the fields of this structure include the following:

`atomic_t count;`

The number of references there are to this page. When the count drops to 0, the page is returned to the free list.

`void *virtual;`

The kernel virtual address of the page, if it is mapped; `NULL`, otherwise. Low-memory pages are always mapped; high-memory pages usually are not. This field does not appear on all architectures; it generally is compiled only where the kernel virtual address of a page cannot be easily calculated. If you want to look at this field, the proper method is to use the *page_address* macro, described below.

`unsigned long flags;`

A set of bit flags describing the status of the page. These include `PG_locked`, which indicates that the page has been locked in memory, and `PG_reserved`, which prevents the memory management system from working with the page at all.

There is much more information within `struct page`, but it is part of the deeper black magic of memory management and is not of concern to driver writers.

The kernel maintains one or more arrays of `struct page` entries that track all of the physical memory on the system. On some systems, there is a single array called `mem_map`. On some systems, however, the situation is more complicated. Nonuniform memory access (NUMA) systems and those with widely discontiguous physical memory may have more than one memory map array, so code that is meant to be portable should avoid direct access to the array whenever possible. Fortunately, it is usually quite easy to just work with `struct page` pointers without worrying about where they come from.

Some functions and macros are defined for translating between `struct page` pointers and virtual addresses:

`struct page *virt_to_page(void *kaddr);`

This macro, defined in *<asm/page.h>*, takes a kernel logical address and returns its associated `struct page` pointer. Since it requires a logical address, it does not work with memory from *vmalloc* or high memory.

`struct page *pfn_to_page(int pfn);`

Returns the `struct page` pointer for the given page frame number. If necessary, it checks a page frame number for validity with *pfn_valid* before passing it to *pfn_to_page*.

`void *page_address(struct page *page);`

Returns the kernel virtual address of this page, if such an address exists. For high memory, that address exists only if the page has been mapped. This function is defined in *<linux/mm.h>*. In most situations, you want to use a version of *kmap* rather than *page_address*.

```
#include <linux/highmem.h>
void *kmap(struct page *page);
void kunmap(struct page *page);
```

> *kmap* returns a kernel virtual address for any page in the system. For low-memory pages, it just returns the logical address of the page; for high-memory pages, *kmap* creates a special mapping in a dedicated part of the kernel address space. Mappings created with *kmap* should always be freed with *kunmap*; a limited number of such mappings is available, so it is better not to hold on to them for too long. *kmap* calls maintain a counter, so if two or more functions both call *kmap* on the same page, the right thing happens. Note also that *kmap* can sleep if no mappings are available.

```
#include <linux/highmem.h>
#include <asm/kmap_types.h>
void *kmap_atomic(struct page *page, enum km_type type);
void kunmap_atomic(void *addr, enum km_type type);
```

> *kmap_atomic* is a high-performance form of *kmap*. Each architecture maintains a small list of slots (dedicated page table entries) for atomic kmaps; a caller of *kmap_atomic* must tell the system which of those slots to use in the type argument. The only slots that make sense for drivers are KM_USER0 and KM_USER1 (for code running directly from a call from user space), and KM_IRQ0 and KM_IRQ1 (for interrupt handlers). Note that atomic kmaps must be handled atomically; your code cannot sleep while holding one. Note also that nothing in the kernel keeps two functions from trying to use the same slot and interfering with each other (although there is a unique set of slots for each CPU). In practice, contention for atomic kmap slots seems to not be a problem.

We see some uses of these functions when we get into the example code, later in this chapter and in subsequent chapters.

Page Tables

On any modern system, the processor must have a mechanism for translating virtual addresses into its corresponding physical addresses. This mechanism is called a *page table*; it is essentially a multilevel tree-structured array containing virtual-to-physical mappings and a few associated flags. The Linux kernel maintains a set of page tables even on architectures that do not use such tables directly.

A number of operations commonly performed by device drivers can involve manipulating page tables. Fortunately for the driver author, the 2.6 kernel has eliminated any need to work with page tables directly. As a result, we do not describe them in any detail; curious readers may want to have a look at *Understanding The Linux Kernel* by Daniel P. Bovet and Marco Cesati (O'Reilly) for the full story.

Virtual Memory Areas

The virtual memory area (VMA) is the kernel data structure used to manage distinct regions of a process's address space. A VMA represents a homogeneous region in the virtual memory of a process: a contiguous range of virtual addresses that have the same permission flags and are backed up by the same object (a file, say, or swap space). It corresponds loosely to the concept of a "segment," although it is better described as "a memory object with its own properties." The memory map of a process is made up of (at least) the following areas:

- An area for the program's executable code (often called text)
- Multiple areas for data, including initialized data (that which has an explicitly assigned value at the beginning of execution), uninitialized data (BSS),[*] and the program stack
- One area for each active memory mapping

The memory areas of a process can be seen by looking in */proc/<pid/maps>* (in which *pid*, of course, is replaced by a process ID). */proc/self* is a special case of */proc/pid*, because it always refers to the current process. As an example, here are a couple of memory maps (to which we have added short comments in italics):

```
# cat /proc/1/maps    look at init
08048000-0804e000 r-xp 00000000 03:01 64652     /sbin/init   text
0804e000-0804f000 rw-p 00006000 03:01 64652     /sbin/init   data
0804f000-08053000 rwxp 00000000 00:00 0         zero-mapped BSS
40000000-40015000 r-xp 00000000 03:01 96278     /lib/ld-2.3.2.so  text
40015000-40016000 rw-p 00014000 03:01 96278     /lib/ld-2.3.2.so  data
40016000-40017000 rw-p 00000000 00:00 0         BSS for ld.so
42000000-4212e000 r-xp 00000000 03:01 80290     /lib/tls/libc-2.3.2.so  text
4212e000-42131000 rw-p 0012e000 03:01 80290     /lib/tls/libc-2.3.2.so  data
42131000-42133000 rw-p 00000000 00:00 0         BSS for libc
bffff000-c0000000 rwxp 00000000 00:00 0         Stack segment
ffffe000-fffff000 ---p 00000000 00:00 0         vsyscall page

# rsh wolf cat /proc/self/maps   #### x86-64 (trimmed)
00400000-00405000 r-xp 00000000 03:01 1596291    /bin/cat    text
00504000-00505000 rw-p 00004000 03:01 1596291    /bin/cat    data
00505000-00526000 rwxp 00505000 00:00 0                      bss
3252200000-3252214000 r-xp 00000000 03:01 1237890 /lib64/ld-2.3.3.so
3252300000-3252301000 r--p 00100000 03:01 1237890 /lib64/ld-2.3.3.so
3252301000-3252302000 rw-p 00101000 03:01 1237890 /lib64/ld-2.3.3.so
7fbfffe000-7fc0000000 rw-p 7fbfffe000 00:00 0                stack
ffffffffff600000-ffffffffffe00000 ---p 00000000 00:00 0     vsyscall
```

The fields in each line are:

```
start-end perm offset major:minor inode image
```

---

[*] The name *BSS* is a historical relic from an old assembly operator meaning "block started by symbol." The BSS segment of executable files isn't stored on disk, and the kernel maps the zero page to the BSS address range.

Each field in */proc/*/maps* (except the image name) corresponds to a field in struct vm_area_struct:

start
end
> The beginning and ending virtual addresses for this memory area.

perm
> A bit mask with the memory area's read, write, and execute permissions. This field describes what the process is allowed to do with pages belonging to the area. The last character in the field is either p for "private" or s for "shared."

offset
> Where the memory area begins in the file that it is mapped to. An offset of 0 means that the beginning of the memory area corresponds to the beginning of the file.

major
minor
> The major and minor numbers of the device holding the file that has been mapped. Confusingly, for device mappings, the major and minor numbers refer to the disk partition holding the device special file that was opened by the user, and not the device itself.

inode
> The inode number of the mapped file.

image
> The name of the file (usually an executable image) that has been mapped.

The vm_area_struct structure

When a user-space process calls *mmap* to map device memory into its address space, the system responds by creating a new VMA to represent that mapping. A driver that supports *mmap* (and, thus, that implements the *mmap* method) needs to help that process by completing the initialization of that VMA. The driver writer should, therefore, have at least a minimal understanding of VMAs in order to support *mmap*.

Let's look at the most important fields in struct vm_area_struct (defined in *<linux/mm.h>*). These fields may be used by device drivers in their *mmap* implementation. Note that the kernel maintains lists and trees of VMAs to optimize area lookup, and several fields of vm_area_struct are used to maintain this organization. Therefore, VMAs can't be created at will by a driver, or the structures break. The main fields of

VMAs are as follows (note the similarity between these fields and the */proc* output we just saw):

```
unsigned long vm_start;
unsigned long vm_end;
```
> The virtual address range covered by this VMA. These fields are the first two fields shown in */proc/*/maps*.

```
struct file *vm_file;
```
> A pointer to the struct file structure associated with this area (if any).

```
unsigned long vm_pgoff;
```
> The offset of the area in the file, in pages. When a file or device is mapped, this is the file position of the first page mapped in this area.

```
unsigned long vm_flags;
```
> A set of flags describing this area. The flags of the most interest to device driver writers are VM_IO and VM_RESERVED. VM_IO marks a VMA as being a memory-mapped I/O region. Among other things, the VM_IO flag prevents the region from being included in process core dumps. VM_RESERVED tells the memory management system not to attempt to swap out this VMA; it should be set in most device mappings.

```
struct vm_operations_struct *vm_ops;
```
> A set of functions that the kernel may invoke to operate on this memory area. Its presence indicates that the memory area is a kernel "object," like the struct file we have been using throughout the book.

```
void *vm_private_data;
```
> A field that may be used by the driver to store its own information.

Like struct vm_area_struct, the vm_operations_struct is defined in *<linux/mm.h>*; it includes the operations listed below. These operations are the only ones needed to handle the process's memory needs, and they are listed in the order they are declared. Later in this chapter, some of these functions are implemented.

```
void (*open)(struct vm_area_struct *vma);
```
> The *open* method is called by the kernel to allow the subsystem implementing the VMA to initialize the area. This method is invoked any time a new reference to the VMA is made (when a process forks, for example). The one exception happens when the VMA is first created by *mmap*; in this case, the driver's *mmap* method is called instead.

```
void (*close)(struct vm_area_struct *vma);
```
> When an area is destroyed, the kernel calls its *close* operation. Note that there's no usage count associated with VMAs; the area is opened and closed exactly once by each process that uses it.

```
struct page *(*nopage)(struct vm_area_struct *vma, unsigned long address, int
                        *type);
```
> When a process tries to access a page that belongs to a valid VMA, but that is
> currently not in memory, the *nopage* method is called (if it is defined) for the
> related area. The method returns the struct page pointer for the physical page
> after, perhaps, having read it in from secondary storage. If the *nopage* method
> isn't defined for the area, an empty page is allocated by the kernel.

```
int (*populate)(struct vm_area_struct *vm, unsigned long address, unsigned
   long len, pgprot_t prot, unsigned long pgoff, int nonblock);
```
> This method allows the kernel to "prefault" pages into memory before they are
> accessed by user space. There is generally no need for drivers to implement the
> *populate* method.

The Process Memory Map

The final piece of the memory management puzzle is the process memory map structure, which holds all of the other data structures together. Each process in the system (with the exception of a few kernel-space helper threads) has a struct mm_struct
(defined in *<linux/sched.h>*) that contains the process's list of virtual memory areas,
page tables, and various other bits of memory management housekeeping information, along with a semaphore (mmap_sem) and a spinlock (page_table_lock). The
pointer to this structure is found in the task structure; in the rare cases where a driver
needs to access it, the usual way is to use current->mm. Note that the memory management structure can be shared between processes; the Linux implementation of
threads works in this way, for example.

That concludes our overview of Linux memory management data structures. With
that out of the way, we can now proceed to the implementation of the *mmap* system
call.

The mmap Device Operation

Memory mapping is one of the most interesting features of modern Unix systems. As
far as drivers are concerned, memory mapping can be implemented to provide user
programs with direct access to device memory.

A definitive example of *mmap* usage can be seen by looking at a subset of the virtual
memory areas for the X Window System server:

```
cat /proc/731/maps
000a0000-000c0000 rwxs 000a0000 03:01 282652       /dev/mem
000f0000-00100000 r-xs 000f0000 03:01 282652       /dev/mem
00400000-005c0000 r-xp 00000000 03:01 1366927      /usr/X11R6/bin/Xorg
006bf000-006f7000 rw-p 001bf000 03:01 1366927      /usr/X11R6/bin/Xorg
2a95828000-2a958a8000 rw-s fcc00000 03:01 282652   /dev/mem
2a958a8000-2a9d8a8000 rw-s e8000000 03:01 282652   /dev/mem
...
```

The full list of the X server's VMAs is lengthy, but most of the entries are not of interest here. We do see, however, four separate mappings of /dev/mem, which give some insight into how the X server works with the video card. The first mapping is at a0000, which is the standard location for video RAM in the 640-KB ISA hole. Further down, we see a large mapping at e8000000, an address which is above the highest RAM address on the system. This is a direct mapping of the video memory on the adapter.

These regions can also be seen in /proc/iomem:

```
000a0000-000bffff : Video RAM area
000c0000-000ccfff : Video ROM
000d1000-000d1fff : Adapter ROM
000f0000-000fffff : System ROM
d7f00000-f7efffff : PCI Bus #01
  e8000000-efffffff : 0000:01:00.0
fc700000-fccfffff : PCI Bus #01
  fcc00000-fcc0ffff : 0000:01:00.0
```

Mapping a device means associating a range of user-space addresses to device memory. Whenever the program reads or writes in the assigned address range, it is actually accessing the device. In the X server example, using *mmap* allows quick and easy access to the video card's memory. For a performance-critical application like this, direct access makes a large difference.

As you might suspect, not every device lends itself to the *mmap* abstraction; it makes no sense, for instance, for serial ports and other stream-oriented devices. Another limitation of *mmap* is that mapping is PAGE_SIZE grained. The kernel can manage virtual addresses only at the level of page tables; therefore, the mapped area must be a multiple of PAGE_SIZE and must live in physical memory starting at an address that is a multiple of PAGE_SIZE. The kernel forces size granularity by making a region slightly bigger if its size isn't a multiple of the page size.

These limits are not a big constraint for drivers, because the program accessing the device is device dependent anyway. Since the program must know about how the device works, the programmer is not unduly bothered by the need to see to details like page alignment. A bigger constraint exists when ISA devices are used on some non-x86 platforms, because their hardware view of ISA may not be contiguous. For example, some Alpha computers see ISA memory as a scattered set of 8-bit, 16-bit, or 32-bit items, with no direct mapping. In such cases, you can't use *mmap* at all. The inability to perform direct mapping of ISA addresses to Alpha addresses is due to the incompatible data transfer specifications of the two systems. Whereas early Alpha processors could issue only 32-bit and 64-bit memory accesses, ISA can do only 8-bit and 16-bit transfers, and there's no way to transparently map one protocol onto the other.

There are sound advantages to using *mmap* when it's feasible to do so. For instance, we have already looked at the X server, which transfers a lot of data to and from video memory; mapping the graphic display to user space dramatically improves the throughput, as opposed to an *lseek/write* implementation. Another typical example is a program controlling a PCI device. Most PCI peripherals map their control registers to a memory address, and a high-performance application might prefer to have direct access to the registers instead of repeatedly having to call *ioctl* to get its work done.

The *mmap* method is part of the file_operations structure and is invoked when the *mmap* system call is issued. With *mmap*, the kernel performs a good deal of work before the actual method is invoked, and, therefore, the prototype of the method is quite different from that of the system call. This is unlike calls such as *ioctl* and *poll*, where the kernel does not do much before calling the method.

The system call is declared as follows (as described in the *mmap(2)* manual page):

```
mmap (caddr_t addr, size_t len, int prot, int flags, int fd, off_t offset)
```

On the other hand, the file operation is declared as:

```
int (*mmap) (struct file *filp, struct vm_area_struct *vma);
```

The filp argument in the method is the same as that introduced in Chapter 3, while vma contains the information about the virtual address range that is used to access the device. Therefore, much of the work has been done by the kernel; to implement *mmap*, the driver only has to build suitable page tables for the address range and, if necessary, replace vma->vm_ops with a new set of operations.

There are two ways of building the page tables: doing it all at once with a function called remap_pfn_range or doing it a page at a time via the *nopage* VMA method. Each method has its advantages and limitations. We start with the "all at once" approach, which is simpler. From there, we add the complications needed for a real-world implementation.

Using remap_pfn_range

The job of building new page tables to map a range of physical addresses is handled by *remap_pfn_range* and *io_remap_page_range*, which have the following prototypes:

```
int remap_pfn_range(struct vm_area_struct *vma,
                    unsigned long virt_addr, unsigned long pfn,
                    unsigned long size, pgprot_t prot);
int io_remap_page_range(struct vm_area_struct *vma,
                        unsigned long virt_addr, unsigned long phys_addr,
                        unsigned long size, pgprot_t prot);
```

The value returned by the function is the usual 0 or a negative error code. Let's look at the exact meaning of the function's arguments:

vma

The virtual memory area into which the page range is being mapped.

virt_addr

The user virtual address where remapping should begin. The function builds page tables for the virtual address range between virt_addr and virt_addr+size.

pfn

The page frame number corresponding to the physical address to which the virtual address should be mapped. The page frame number is simply the physical address right-shifted by PAGE_SHIFT bits. For most uses, the vm_pgoff field of the VMA structure contains exactly the value you need. The function affects physical addresses from (pfn<<PAGE_SHIFT) to (pfn<<PAGE_SHIFT)+size.

size

The dimension, in bytes, of the area being remapped.

prot

The "protection" requested for the new VMA. The driver can (and should) use the value found in vma->vm_page_prot.

The arguments to *remap_pfn_range* are fairly straightforward, and most of them are already provided to you in the VMA when your *mmap* method is called. You may be wondering why there are two functions, however. The first (*remap_pfn_range*) is intended for situations where pfn refers to actual system RAM, while *io_remap_page_range* should be used when phys_addr points to I/O memory. In practice, the two functions are identical on every architecture except the SPARC, and you see *remap_pfn_range* used in most situations. In the interest of writing portable drivers, however, you should use the variant of *remap_pfn_range* that is suited to your particular situation.

One other complication has to do with caching: usually, references to device memory should not be cached by the processor. Often the system BIOS sets things up properly, but it is also possible to disable caching of specific VMAs via the protection field. Unfortunately, disabling caching at this level is highly processor dependent. The curious reader may wish to look at the *pgprot_noncached* function from *drivers/char/mem.c* to see what's involved. We won't discuss the topic further here.

A Simple Implementation

If your driver needs to do a simple, linear mapping of device memory into a user address space, *remap_pfn_range* is almost all you really need to do the job. The following code is derived from *drivers/char/mem.c* and shows how this task is performed in a typical module called *simple* (Simple Implementation Mapping Pages with Little Enthusiasm):

```
static int simple_remap_mmap(struct file *filp, struct vm_area_struct *vma)
{
    if (remap_pfn_range(vma, vma->vm_start, vm->vm_pgoff,
                vma->vm_end - vma->vm_start,
                vma->vm_page_prot))
        return -EAGAIN;

    vma->vm_ops = &simple_remap_vm_ops;
    simple_vma_open(vma);
    return 0;
}
```

As you can see, remapping memory just a matter of calling *remap_pfn_range* to create the necessary page tables.

Adding VMA Operations

As we have seen, the vm_area_struct structure contains a set of operations that may be applied to the VMA. Now we look at providing those operations in a simple way. In particular, we provide *open* and *close* operations for our VMA. These operations are called whenever a process opens or closes the VMA; in particular, the *open* method is invoked anytime a process forks and creates a new reference to the VMA. The *open* and *close* VMA methods are called in addition to the processing performed by the kernel, so they need not reimplement any of the work done there. They exist as a way for drivers to do any additional processing that they may require.

As it turns out, a simple driver such as *simple* need not do any extra processing in particular. So we have created *open* and *close* methods, which print a message to the system log informing the world that they have been called. Not particularly useful, but it does allow us to show how these methods can be provided, and see when they are invoked.

To this end, we override the default vma->vm_ops with operations that call *printk*:

```
void simple_vma_open(struct vm_area_struct *vma)
{
    printk(KERN_NOTICE "Simple VMA open, virt %lx, phys %lx\n",
            vma->vm_start, vma->vm_pgoff << PAGE_SHIFT);
}

void simple_vma_close(struct vm_area_struct *vma)
{
    printk(KERN_NOTICE "Simple VMA close.\n");
}

static struct vm_operations_struct simple_remap_vm_ops = {
    .open =  simple_vma_open,
    .close = simple_vma_close,
};
```

To make these operations active for a specific mapping, it is necessary to store a pointer to simple_remap_vm_ops in the vm_ops field of the relevant VMA. This is usually done in the *mmap* method. If you turn back to the *simple_remap_mmap* example, you see these lines of code:

```
vma->vm_ops = &simple_remap_vm_ops;
simple_vma_open(vma);
```

Note the explicit call to *simple_vma_open*. Since the *open* method is not invoked on the initial *mmap*, we must call it explicitly if we want it to run.

Mapping Memory with nopage

Although *remap_pfn_range* works well for many, if not most, driver *mmap* implementations, sometimes it is necessary to be a little more flexible. In such situations, an implementation using the *nopage* VMA method may be called for.

One situation in which the *nopage* approach is useful can be brought about by the *mremap* system call, which is used by applications to change the bounding addresses of a mapped region. As it happens, the kernel does not notify drivers directly when a mapped VMA is changed by *mremap*. If the VMA is reduced in size, the kernel can quietly flush out the unwanted pages without telling the driver. If, instead, the VMA is expanded, the driver eventually finds out by way of calls to *nopage* when mappings must be set up for the new pages, so there is no need to perform a separate notification. The *nopage* method, therefore, must be implemented if you want to support the *mremap* system call. Here, we show a simple implementation of *nopage* for the *simple* device.

The *nopage* method, remember, has the following prototype:

```
struct page *(*nopage)(struct vm_area_struct *vma,
                       unsigned long address, int *type);
```

When a user process attempts to access a page in a VMA that is not present in memory, the associated *nopage* function is called. The address parameter contains the virtual address that caused the fault, rounded down to the beginning of the page. The *nopage* function must locate and return the struct page pointer that refers to the page the user wanted. This function must also take care to increment the usage count for the page it returns by calling the *get_page* macro:

```
get_page(struct page *pageptr);
```

This step is necessary to keep the reference counts correct on the mapped pages. The kernel maintains this count for every page; when the count goes to 0, the kernel knows that the page may be placed on the free list. When a VMA is unmapped, the kernel decrements the usage count for every page in the area. If your driver does not increment the count when adding a page to the area, the usage count becomes 0 prematurely, and the integrity of the system is compromised.

The *nopage* method should also store the type of fault in the location pointed to by the type argument—but only if that argument is not NULL. In device drivers, the proper value for type will invariably be VM_FAULT_MINOR.

If you are using *nopage*, there is usually very little work to be done when *mmap* is called; our version looks like this:

```
static int simple_nopage_mmap(struct file *filp, struct vm_area_struct *vma)
{
    unsigned long offset = vma->vm_pgoff << PAGE_SHIFT;

    if (offset >= __pa(high_memory) || (filp->f_flags & O_SYNC))
        vma->vm_flags |= VM_IO;
    vma->vm_flags |= VM_RESERVED;

    vma->vm_ops = &simple_nopage_vm_ops;
    simple_vma_open(vma);
    return 0;
}
```

The main thing *mmap* has to do is to replace the default (NULL) vm_ops pointer with our own operations. The *nopage* method then takes care of "remapping" one page at a time and returning the address of its struct page structure. Because we are just implementing a window onto physical memory here, the remapping step is simple: we only need to locate and return a pointer to the struct page for the desired address. Our *nopage* method looks like the following:

```
struct page *simple_vma_nopage(struct vm_area_struct *vma,
                unsigned long address, int *type)
{
    struct page *pageptr;
    unsigned long offset = vma->vm_pgoff << PAGE_SHIFT;
    unsigned long physaddr = address - vma->vm_start + offset;
    unsigned long pageframe = physaddr >> PAGE_SHIFT;

    if (!pfn_valid(pageframe))
        return NOPAGE_SIGBUS;
    pageptr = pfn_to_page(pageframe);
    get_page(pageptr);
    if (type)
        *type = VM_FAULT_MINOR;
    return pageptr;
}
```

Since, once again, we are simply mapping main memory here, the *nopage* function need only find the correct struct page for the faulting address and increment its reference count. Therefore, the required sequence of events is to calculate the desired physical address, and turn it into a page frame number by right-shifting it PAGE_SHIFT bits. Since user space can give us any address it likes, we must ensure that we have a valid page frame; the *pfn_valid* function does that for us. If the address is out of range, we return NOPAGE_SIGBUS, which causes a bus signal to be delivered to the calling process.

Otherwise, *pfn_to_page* gets the necessary struct page pointer; we can increment its reference count (with a call to *get_page*) and return it.

The *nopage* method normally returns a pointer to a struct page. If, for some reason, a normal page cannot be returned (e.g., the requested address is beyond the device's memory region), NOPAGE_SIGBUS can be returned to signal the error; that is what the *simple* code above does. *nopage* can also return NOPAGE_OOM to indicate failures caused by resource limitations.

Note that this implementation works for ISA memory regions but not for those on the PCI bus. PCI memory is mapped above the highest system memory, and there are no entries in the system memory map for those addresses. Because there is no struct page to return a pointer to, *nopage* cannot be used in these situations; you must use *remap_pfn_range* instead.

If the *nopage* method is left NULL, kernel code that handles page faults maps the zero page to the faulting virtual address. The *zero page* is a copy-on-write page that reads as 0 and that is used, for example, to map the BSS segment. Any process referencing the zero page sees exactly that: a page filled with zeroes. If the process writes to the page, it ends up modifying a private copy. Therefore, if a process extends a mapped region by calling *mremap*, and the driver hasn't implemented *nopage*, the process ends up with zero-filled memory instead of a segmentation fault.

Remapping Specific I/O Regions

All the examples we've seen so far are reimplementations of */dev/mem*; they remap physical addresses into user space. The typical driver, however, wants to map only the small address range that applies to its peripheral device, not all memory. In order to map to user space only a subset of the whole memory range, the driver needs only to play with the offsets. The following does the trick for a driver mapping a region of simple_region_size bytes, beginning at physical address simple_region_start (which should be page-aligned):

```
unsigned long off = vma->vm_pgoff << PAGE_SHIFT;
unsigned long physical = simple_region_start + off;
unsigned long vsize = vma->vm_end - vma->vm_start;
unsigned long psize = simple_region_size - off;

if (vsize > psize)
    return -EINVAL; /*  spans too high */
remap_pfn_range(vma, vma_>vm_start, physical, vsize, vma->vm_page_prot);
```

In addition to calculating the offsets, this code introduces a check that reports an error when the program tries to map more memory than is available in the I/O region of the target device. In this code, psize is the physical I/O size that is left after the offset has been specified, and vsize is the requested size of virtual memory; the function refuses to map addresses that extend beyond the allowed memory range.

Note that the user process can always use *mremap* to extend its mapping, possibly past the end of the physical device area. If your driver fails to define a *nopage* method, it is never notified of this extension, and the additional area maps to the zero page. As a driver writer, you may well want to prevent this sort of behavior; mapping the zero page onto the end of your region is not an explicitly bad thing to do, but it is highly unlikely that the programmer wanted that to happen.

The simplest way to prevent extension of the mapping is to implement a simple *nopage* method that always causes a bus signal to be sent to the faulting process. Such a method would look like this:

```
struct page *simple_nopage(struct vm_area_struct *vma,
                           unsigned long address, int *type);
{ return NOPAGE_SIGBUS; /* send a SIGBUS */}
```

As we have seen, the *nopage* method is called only when the process dereferences an address that is within a known VMA but for which there is currently no valid page table entry. If we have used *remap_pfn_range* to map the entire device region, the *nopage* method shown here is called only for references outside of that region. Thus, it can safely return NOPAGE_SIGBUS to signal an error. Of course, a more thorough implementation of *nopage* could check to see whether the faulting address is within the device area, and perform the remapping if that is the case. Once again, however, *nopage* does not work with PCI memory areas, so extension of PCI mappings is not possible.

Remapping RAM

An interesting limitation of *remap_pfn_range* is that it gives access only to reserved pages and physical addresses above the top of physical memory. In Linux, a page of physical addresses is marked as "reserved" in the memory map to indicate that it is not available for memory management. On the PC, for example, the range between 640 KB and 1 MB is marked as reserved, as are the pages that host the kernel code itself. Reserved pages are locked in memory and are the only ones that can be safely mapped to user space; this limitation is a basic requirement for system stability.

Therefore, *remap_pfn_range* won't allow you to remap conventional addresses, which include the ones you obtain by calling *get_free_page*. Instead, it maps in the zero page. Everything appears to work, with the exception that the process sees private, zero-filled pages rather than the remapped RAM that it was hoping for. Nonetheless, the function does everything that most hardware drivers need it to do, because it can remap high PCI buffers and ISA memory.

The limitations of *remap_pfn_range* can be seen by running *mapper*, one of the sample programs in *misc-progs* in the files provided on O'Reilly's FTP site. *mapper* is a simple tool that can be used to quickly test the *mmap* system call; it maps read-only parts of a file specified by command-line options and dumps the mapped region to standard output. The following session, for instance, shows that */dev/mem* doesn't map the physical page located at address 64 KB—instead, we see a page full of zeros (the host computer in this example is a PC, but the result would be the same on other platforms):

```
morgana.root# ./mapper /dev/mem 0x10000 0x1000 | od -Ax -t x1
mapped "/dev/mem" from 65536 to 69632
000000 00 00 00 00 00 00 00 00 00 00 00 00 00 00 00 00
*
001000
```

The inability of *remap_pfn_range* to deal with RAM suggests that memory-based devices like *scull* can't easily implement *mmap*, because its device memory is conventional RAM, not I/O memory. Fortunately, a relatively easy workaround is available to any driver that needs to map RAM into user space; it uses the *nopage* method that we have seen earlier.

Remapping RAM with the nopage method

The way to map real RAM to user space is to use vm_ops->nopage to deal with page faults one at a time. A sample implementation is part of the *scullp* module, introduced in Chapter 8.

scullp is a page-oriented char device. Because it is page oriented, it can implement *mmap* on its memory. The code implementing memory mapping uses some of the concepts introduced in the section "Memory Management in Linux."

Before examining the code, let's look at the design choices that affect the *mmap* implementation in *scullp*:

- *scullp* doesn't release device memory as long as the device is mapped. This is a matter of policy rather than a requirement, and it is different from the behavior of *scull* and similar devices, which are truncated to a length of 0 when opened for writing. Refusing to free a mapped *scullp* device allows a process to overwrite regions actively mapped by another process, so you can test and see how processes and device memory interact. To avoid releasing a mapped device, the driver must keep a count of active mappings; the vmas field in the device structure is used for this purpose.

- Memory mapping is performed only when the *scullp* order parameter (set at module load time) is 0. The parameter controls how __get_free_pages is invoked (see the section "get_free_page and Friends" in Chapter 8). The zero-order limitation (which forces pages to be allocated one at a time, rather than in larger groups) is dictated by the internals of __get_free_pages, the allocation function used by *scullp*. To maximize allocation performance, the Linux kernel maintains a list of free pages for each allocation order, and only the reference count of the first page in a cluster is incremented by get_free_pages and decremented by free_pages. The *mmap* method is disabled for a *scullp* device if the allocation order is greater than zero, because *nopage* deals with single pages rather than clusters of pages. *scullp* simply does not know how to properly manage reference counts for pages that are part of higher-order allocations. (Return to the section "A scull Using Whole Pages: scullp" in Chapter 8 if you need a refresher on *scullp* and the memory allocation order value.)

The zero-order limitation is mostly intended to keep the code simple. It *is* possible to correctly implement *mmap* for multipage allocations by playing with the usage count of the pages, but it would only add to the complexity of the example without introducing any interesting information.

Code that is intended to map RAM according to the rules just outlined needs to implement the *open*, *close*, and *nopage* VMA methods; it also needs to access the memory map to adjust the page usage counts.

This implementation of *scullp_mmap* is very short, because it relies on the *nopage* function to do all the interesting work:

```c
int scullp_mmap(struct file *filp, struct vm_area_struct *vma)
{
    struct inode *inode = filp->f_dentry->d_inode;

    /* refuse to map if order is not 0 */
    if (scullp_devices[iminor(inode)].order)
        return -ENODEV;

    /* don't do anything here: "nopage" will fill the holes */
    vma->vm_ops = &scullp_vm_ops;
    vma->vm_flags |= VM_RESERVED;
    vma->vm_private_data = filp->private_data;
    scullp_vma_open(vma);
    return 0;
}
```

The purpose of the if statement is to avoid mapping devices whose allocation order is not 0. *scullp*'s operations are stored in the vm_ops field, and a pointer to the device structure is stashed in the vm_private_data field. At the end, vm_ops->open is called to update the count of active mappings for the device.

open and *close* simply keep track of the mapping count and are defined as follows:

```c
void scullp_vma_open(struct vm_area_struct *vma)
{
    struct scullp_dev *dev = vma->vm_private_data;

    dev->vmas++;
}

void scullp_vma_close(struct vm_area_struct *vma)
{
    struct scullp_dev *dev = vma->vm_private_data;

    dev->vmas--;
}
```

Most of the work is then performed by *nopage*. In the *scullp* implementation, the address parameter to *nopage* is used to calculate an offset into the device; the offset is then used to look up the correct page in the *scullp* memory tree:

```
struct page *scullp_vma_nopage(struct vm_area_struct *vma,
                               unsigned long address, int *type)
{
    unsigned long offset;
    struct scullp_dev *ptr, *dev = vma->vm_private_data;
    struct page *page = NOPAGE_SIGBUS;
    void *pageptr = NULL; /* default to "missing" */

    down(&dev->sem);
    offset = (address - vma->vm_start) + (vma->vm_pgoff << PAGE_SHIFT);
    if (offset >= dev->size) goto out; /* out of range */

    /*
     * Now retrieve the scullp device from the list,then the page.
     * If the device has holes, the process receives a SIGBUS when
     * accessing the hole.
     */
    offset >>= PAGE_SHIFT; /* offset is a number of pages */
    for (ptr = dev; ptr && offset >= dev->qset;) {
        ptr = ptr->next;
        offset -= dev->qset;
    }
    if (ptr && ptr->data) pageptr = ptr->data[offset];
    if (!pageptr) goto out; /* hole or end-of-file */
    page = virt_to_page(pageptr);

    /* got it, now increment the count */
    get_page(page);
    if (type)
        *type = VM_FAULT_MINOR;
  out:
    up(&dev->sem);
    return page;
}
```

scullp uses memory obtained with *get_free_pages*. That memory is addressed using logical addresses, so all *scullp_nopage* has to do to get a struct page pointer is to call *virt_to_page*.

The *scullp* device now works as expected, as you can see in this sample output from the *mapper* utility. Here, we send a directory listing of */dev* (which is long) to the *scullp* device and then use the *mapper* utility to look at pieces of that listing with *mmap*:

```
morgana% ls -l /dev > /dev/scullp
morgana% ./mapper /dev/scullp 0 140
mapped "/dev/scullp" from 0 (0x00000000) to 140 (0x0000008c)
total 232
crw-------    1 root     root      10,  10 Sep 15 07:40 adbmouse
```

```
crw-r--r--    1 root     root       10, 175 Sep 15 07:40 agpgart
morgana% ./mapper /dev/scullp 8192 200
mapped "/dev/scullp" from 8192 (0x00002000) to 8392 (0x000020c8)
d0h1494
brw-rw----    1 root     floppy      2,  92 Sep 15 07:40 fd0h1660
brw-rw----    1 root     floppy      2,  20 Sep 15 07:40 fd0h360
brw-rw----    1 root     floppy      2,  12 Sep 15 07:40 fd0H360
```

Remapping Kernel Virtual Addresses

Although it's rarely necessary, it's interesting to see how a driver can map a kernel virtual address to user space using *mmap*. A true kernel virtual address, remember, is an address returned by a function such as *vmalloc*—that is, a virtual address mapped in the kernel page tables. The code in this section is taken from *scullv*, which is the module that works like *scullp* but allocates its storage through *vmalloc*.

Most of the *scullv* implementation is like the one we've just seen for *scullp*, except that there is no need to check the order parameter that controls memory allocation. The reason for this is that *vmalloc* allocates its pages one at a time, because single-page allocations are far more likely to succeed than multipage allocations. Therefore, the allocation order problem doesn't apply to *vmalloc*ed space.

Beyond that, there is only one difference between the *nopage* implementations used by *scullp* and *scullv*. Remember that *scullp*, once it found the page of interest, would obtain the corresponding struct page pointer with *virt_to_page*. That function does not work with kernel virtual addresses, however. Instead, you must use *vmalloc_to_page*. So the final part of the *scullv* version of *nopage* looks like:

```
    /*
     * After scullv lookup, "page" is now the address of the page
     * needed by the current process. Since it's a vmalloc address,
     * turn it into a struct page.
     */
    page = vmalloc_to_page(pageptr);

    /* got it, now increment the count */
    get_page(page);
    if (type)
        *type = VM_FAULT_MINOR;
out:
    up(&dev->sem);
    return page;
```

Based on this discussion, you might also want to map addresses returned by *ioremap* to user space. That would be a mistake, however; addresses from *ioremap* are special and cannot be treated like normal kernel virtual addresses. Instead, you should use *remap_pfn_range* to remap I/O memory areas into user space.

Performing Direct I/O

Most I/O operations are buffered through the kernel. The use of a kernel-space buffer allows a degree of separation between user space and the actual device; this separation can make programming easier and can also yield performance benefits in many situations. There are cases, however, where it can be beneficial to perform I/O directly to or from a user-space buffer. If the amount of data being transferred is large, transferring data directly without an extra copy through kernel space can speed things up.

One example of direct I/O use in the 2.6 kernel is the SCSI tape driver. Streaming tapes can pass a lot of data through the system, and tape transfers are usually record-oriented, so there is little benefit to buffering data in the kernel. So, when the conditions are right (the user-space buffer is page-aligned, for example), the SCSI tape driver performs its I/O without copying the data.

That said, it is important to recognize that direct I/O does not always provide the performance boost that one might expect. The overhead of setting up direct I/O (which involves faulting in and pinning down the relevant user pages) can be significant, and the benefits of buffered I/O are lost. For example, the use of direct I/O requires that the *write* system call operate synchronously; otherwise the application does not know when it can reuse its I/O buffer. Stopping the application until each write completes can slow things down, which is why applications that use direct I/O often use asynchronous I/O operations as well.

The real moral of the story, in any case, is that implementing direct I/O in a char driver is usually unnecessary and can be hurtful. You should take that step only if you are sure that the overhead of buffered I/O is truly slowing things down. Note also that block and network drivers need not worry about implementing direct I/O at all; in both cases, higher-level code in the kernel sets up and makes use of direct I/O when it is indicated, and driver-level code need not even know that direct I/O is being performed.

The key to implementing direct I/O in the 2.6 kernel is a function called *get_user_pages*, which is declared in *<linux/mm.h>* with the following prototype:

```
int get_user_pages(struct task_struct *tsk,
            struct mm_struct *mm,
            unsigned long start,
            int len,
            int write,
            int force,
            struct page **pages,
            struct vm_area_struct **vmas);
```

This function has several arguments:

tsk
> A pointer to the task performing the I/O; its main purpose is to tell the kernel who should be charged for any page faults incurred while setting up the buffer. This argument is almost always passed as current.

mm A pointer to the memory management structure describing the address space to be mapped. The mm_struct structure is the piece that ties together all of the parts (VMAs) of a process's virtual address space. For driver use, this argument should always be current->mm.

start
len
> start is the (page-aligned) address of the user-space buffer, and len is the length of the buffer in pages.

write
force
> If write is nonzero, the pages are mapped for write access (implying, of course, that user space is performing a read operation). The force flag tells *get_user_pages* to override the protections on the given pages to provide the requested access; drivers should always pass 0 here.

pages
vmas
> Output parameters. Upon successful completion, pages contain a list of pointers to the struct page structures describing the user-space buffer, and vmas contains pointers to the associated VMAs. The parameters should, obviously, point to arrays capable of holding at least len pointers. Either parameter can be NULL, but you need, at least, the struct page pointers to actually operate on the buffer.

get_user_pages is a low-level memory management function, with a suitably complex interface. It also requires that the mmap reader/writer semaphore for the address space be obtained in read mode before the call. As a result, calls to *get_user_pages* usually look something like:

```
down_read(&current->mm->mmap_sem);
result = get_user_pages(current, current->mm, ...);
up_read(&current->mm->mmap_sem);
```

The return value is the number of pages actually mapped, which could be fewer than the number requested (but greater than zero).

Upon successful completion, the caller has a pages array pointing to the user-space buffer, which is locked into memory. To operate on the buffer directly, the kernel-space code must turn each struct page pointer into a kernel virtual address with *kmap* or *kmap_atomic*. Usually, however, devices for which direct I/O is justified are using DMA operations, so your driver will probably want to create a scatter/gather list from the array of struct page pointers. We discuss how to do this in the section, "Scatter/gather mappings."

Once your direct I/O operation is complete, you must release the user pages. Before doing so, however, you must inform the kernel if you changed the contents of those pages. Otherwise, the kernel may think that the pages are "clean," meaning that they match a copy found on the swap device, and free them without writing them out to backing store. So, if you have changed the pages (in response to a user-space read request), you must mark each affected page dirty with a call to:

```
void SetPageDirty(struct page *page);
```

(This macro is defined in *<linux/page-flags.h>*). Most code that performs this operation checks first to ensure that the page is not in the reserved part of the memory map, which is never swapped out. Therefore, the code usually looks like:

```
if (! PageReserved(page))
    SetPageDirty(page);
```

Since user-space memory is not normally marked reserved, this check should not strictly be necessary, but when you are getting your hands dirty deep within the memory management subsystem, it is best to be thorough and careful.

Regardless of whether the pages have been changed, they must be freed from the page cache, or they stay there forever. The call to use is:

```
void page_cache_release(struct page *page);
```

This call should, of course, be made *after* the page has been marked dirty, if need be.

Asynchronous I/O

One of the new features added to the 2.6 kernel was the *asynchronous I/O* capability. Asynchronous I/O allows user space to initiate operations without waiting for their completion; thus, an application can do other processing while its I/O is in flight. A complex, high-performance application can also use asynchronous I/O to have multiple operations going at the same time.

The implementation of asynchronous I/O is optional, and very few driver authors bother; most devices do not benefit from this capability. As we will see in the coming chapters, block and network drivers are fully asynchronous at all times, so only char drivers are candidates for explicit asynchronous I/O support. A char device can benefit from this support if there are good reasons for having more than one I/O operation outstanding at any given time. One good example is streaming tape drives, where the drive can stall and slow down significantly if I/O operations do not arrive quickly enough. An application trying to get the best performance out of a streaming drive could use asynchronous I/O to have multiple operations ready to go at any given time.

For the rare driver author who needs to implement asynchronous I/O, we present a quick overview of how it works. We cover asynchronous I/O in this chapter, because its implementation almost always involves direct I/O operations as well (if you are buffering data in the kernel, you can usually implement asynchronous behavior without imposing the added complexity on user space).

Drivers supporting asynchronous I/O should include *<linux/aio.h>*. There are three *file_operations* methods for the implementation of asynchronous I/O:

```
ssize_t (*aio_read) (struct kiocb *iocb, char *buffer,
                     size_t count, loff_t offset);
ssize_t (*aio_write) (struct kiocb *iocb, const char *buffer,
                      size_t count, loff_t offset);
int (*aio_fsync) (struct kiocb *iocb, int datasync);
```

The *aio_fsync* operation is only of interest to filesystem code, so we do not discuss it further here. The other two, *aio_read* and *aio_write*, look very much like the regular *read* and *write* methods but with a couple of exceptions. One is that the offset parameter is passed by value; asynchronous operations never change the file position, so there is no reason to pass a pointer to it. These methods also take the iocb ("I/O control block") parameter, which we get to in a moment.

The purpose of the *aio_read* and *aio_write* methods is to initiate a read or write operation that may or may not be complete by the time they return. If it *is* possible to complete the operation immediately, the method should do so and return the usual status: the number of bytes transferred or a negative error code. Thus, if your driver has a *read* method called *my_read*, the following *aio_read* method is entirely correct (though rather pointless):

```
static ssize_t my_aio_read(struct kiocb *iocb, char *buffer,
                           ssize_t count, loff_t offset)
{
    return my_read(iocb->ki_filp, buffer, count, &offset);
}
```

Note that the struct file pointer is found in the ki_filp field of the kiocb structure.

If you support asynchronous I/O, you must be aware of the fact that the kernel can, on occasion, create "synchronous IOCBs." These are, essentially, asynchronous operations that must actually be executed synchronously. One may well wonder why things are done this way, but it's best to just do what the kernel asks. Synchronous operations are marked in the IOCB; your driver should query that status with:

```
int is_sync_kiocb(struct kiocb *iocb);
```

If this function returns a nonzero value, your driver must execute the operation synchronously.

In the end, however, the point of all this structure is to enable asynchronous operations. If your driver is able to initiate the operation (or, simply, to queue it until some future time when it can be executed), it must do two things: remember everything it needs to know about the operation, and return -EIOCBQUEUED to the caller. Remembering the operation information includes arranging access to the user-space buffer; once you return, you will not again have the opportunity to access that buffer while running in the context of the calling process. In general, that means you will likely have to set up a direct kernel mapping (with *get_user_pages*) or a DMA mapping. The -EIOCBQUEUED error code indicates that the operation is not yet complete, and its final status will be posted later.

When "later" comes, your driver must inform the kernel that the operation has completed. That is done with a call to *aio_complete*:

```
int aio_complete(struct kiocb *iocb, long res, long res2);
```

Here, iocb is the same IOCB that was initially passed to you, and res is the usual result status for the operation. res2 is a second result code that will be returned to user space; most asynchronous I/O implementations pass res2 as 0. Once you call *aio_complete*, you should not touch the IOCB or user buffer again.

An asynchronous I/O example

The page-oriented *scullp* driver in the example source implements asynchronous I/O. The implementation is simple, but it is enough to show how asynchronous operations should be structured.

The *aio_read* and *aio_write* methods don't actually do much:

```
static ssize_t scullp_aio_read(struct kiocb *iocb, char *buf, size_t count,
        loff_t pos)
{
    return scullp_defer_op(0, iocb, buf, count, pos);
}

static ssize_t scullp_aio_write(struct kiocb *iocb, const char *buf,
        size_t count, loff_t pos)
{
    return scullp_defer_op(1, iocb, (char *) buf, count, pos);
}
```

These methods simply call a common function:

```
struct async_work {
    struct kiocb *iocb;
    int result;
    struct work_struct work;
};

static int scullp_defer_op(int write, struct kiocb *iocb, char *buf,
        size_t count, loff_t pos)
{
    struct async_work *stuff;
    int result;
```

```
    /* Copy now while we can access the buffer */
    if (write)
        result = scullp_write(iocb->ki_filp, buf, count, &pos);
    else
        result = scullp_read(iocb->ki_filp, buf, count, &pos);

    /* If this is a synchronous IOCB, we return our status now. */
    if (is_sync_kiocb(iocb))
        return result;

    /* Otherwise defer the completion for a few milliseconds. */
    stuff = kmalloc (sizeof (*stuff), GFP_KERNEL);
    if (stuff == NULL)
        return result; /* No memory, just complete now */
    stuff->iocb = iocb;
    stuff->result = result;
    INIT_WORK(&stuff->work, scullp_do_deferred_op, stuff);
    schedule_delayed_work(&stuff->work, HZ/100);
    return -EIOCBQUEUED;
}
```

A more complete implementation would use *get_user_pages* to map the user buffer into kernel space. We chose to keep life simple by just copying over the data at the outset. Then a call is made to *is_sync_kiocb* to see if this operation must be completed synchronously; if so, the result status is returned, and we are done. Otherwise we remember the relevant information in a little structure, arrange for "completion" via a workqueue, and return -EIOCBQUEUED. At this point, control returns to user space.

Later on, the workqueue executes our completion function:

```
static void scullp_do_deferred_op(void *p)
{
    struct async_work *stuff = (struct async_work *) p;
    aio_complete(stuff->iocb, stuff->result, 0);
    kfree(stuff);
}
```

Here, it is simply a matter of calling *aio_complete* with our saved information. A real driver's asynchronous I/O implementation is somewhat more complicated, of course, but it follows this sort of structure.

Direct Memory Access

Direct memory access, or DMA, is the advanced topic that completes our overview of memory issues. DMA is the hardware mechanism that allows peripheral components to transfer their I/O data directly to and from main memory without the need to involve the system processor. Use of this mechanism can greatly increase throughput to and from a device, because a great deal of computational overhead is eliminated.

Overview of a DMA Data Transfer

Before introducing the programming details, let's review how a DMA transfer takes place, considering only input transfers to simplify the discussion.

Data transfer can be triggered in two ways: either the software asks for data (via a function such as *read*) or the hardware asynchronously pushes data to the system.

In the first case, the steps involved can be summarized as follows:

1. When a process calls *read*, the driver method allocates a DMA buffer and instructs the hardware to transfer its data into that buffer. The process is put to sleep.

2. The hardware writes data to the DMA buffer and raises an interrupt when it's done.

3. The interrupt handler gets the input data, acknowledges the interrupt, and awakens the process, which is now able to read data.

The second case comes about when DMA is used asynchronously. This happens, for example, with data acquisition devices that go on pushing data even if nobody is reading them. In this case, the driver should maintain a buffer so that a subsequent *read* call will return all the accumulated data to user space. The steps involved in this kind of transfer are slightly different:

1. The hardware raises an interrupt to announce that new data has arrived.

2. The interrupt handler allocates a buffer and tells the hardware where to transfer its data.

3. The peripheral device writes the data to the buffer and raises another interrupt when it's done.

4. The handler dispatches the new data, wakes any relevant process, and takes care of housekeeping.

A variant of the asynchronous approach is often seen with network cards. These cards often expect to see a circular buffer (often called a *DMA ring buffer*) established in memory shared with the processor; each incoming packet is placed in the next available buffer in the ring, and an interrupt is signaled. The driver then passes the network packets to the rest of the kernel and places a new DMA buffer in the ring.

The processing steps in all of these cases emphasize that efficient DMA handling relies on interrupt reporting. While it is possible to implement DMA with a polling driver, it wouldn't make sense, because a polling driver would waste the performance benefits that DMA offers over the easier processor-driven I/O.[*]

---

[*] There are, of course, exceptions to everything; see the section "Receive Interrupt Mitigation" in Chapter 17 for a demonstration of how high-performance network drivers are best implemented using polling.

Another relevant item introduced here is the DMA buffer. DMA requires device drivers to allocate one or more special buffers suited to DMA. Note that many drivers allocate their buffers at initialization time and use them until shutdown—the word *allocate* in the previous lists, therefore, means "get hold of a previously allocated buffer."

Allocating the DMA Buffer

This section covers the allocation of DMA buffers at a low level; we introduce a higher-level interface shortly, but it is still a good idea to understand the material presented here.

The main issue that arrises with DMA buffers is that, when they are bigger than one page, they must occupy contiguous pages in physical memory because the device transfers data using the ISA or PCI system bus, both of which carry physical addresses. It's interesting to note that this constraint doesn't apply to the SBus (see the section "SBus" in Chapter 12), which uses virtual addresses on the peripheral bus. Some architectures *can* also use virtual addresses on the PCI bus, but a portable driver cannot count on that capability.

Although DMA buffers can be allocated either at system boot or at runtime, modules can allocate their buffers only at runtime. (Chapter 8 introduced these techniques; the section "Obtaining Large Buffers" covered allocation at system boot, while "The Real Story of kmalloc" and "get_free_page and Friends" described allocation at runtime.) Driver writers must take care to allocate the right kind of memory when it is used for DMA operations; not all memory zones are suitable. In particular, high memory may not work for DMA on some systems and with some devices—the peripherals simply cannot work with addresses that high.

Most devices on modern buses can handle 32-bit addresses, meaning that normal memory allocations work just fine for them. Some PCI devices, however, fail to implement the full PCI standard and cannot work with 32-bit addresses. And ISA devices, of course, are limited to 24-bit addresses only.

For devices with this kind of limitation, memory should be allocated from the DMA zone by adding the GFP_DMA flag to the *kmalloc* or *get_free_pages* call. When this flag is present, only memory that can be addressed with 24 bits is allocated. Alternatively, you can use the generic DMA layer (which we discuss shortly) to allocate buffers that work around your device's limitations.

Do-it-yourself allocation

We have seen how *get_free_pages* can allocate up to a few megabytes (as order can range up to MAX_ORDER, currently 11), but high-order requests are prone to fail even when the requested buffer is far less than 128 KB, because system memory becomes fragmented over time.*

When the kernel cannot return the requested amount of memory or when you need more than 128 KB (a common requirement for PCI frame grabbers, for example), an alternative to returning -ENOMEM is to allocate memory at boot time or reserve the top of physical RAM for your buffer. We described allocation at boot time in the section "Obtaining Large Buffers" in Chapter 8, but it is not available to modules. Reserving the top of RAM is accomplished by passing a mem= argument to the kernel at boot time. For example, if you have 256 MB, the argument mem=255M keeps the kernel from using the top megabyte. Your module could later use the following code to gain access to such memory:

```
dmabuf = ioremap (0xFF00000 /* 255M */, 0x100000 /* 1M */);
```

The *allocator*, part of the sample code accompanying the book, offers a simple API to probe and manage such reserved RAM and has been used successfully on several architectures. However, this trick doesn't work when you have an high-memory system (i.e., one with more physical memory than could fit in the CPU address space).

Another option, of course, is to allocate your buffer with the GFP_NOFAIL allocation flag. This approach does, however, severely stress the memory management subsystem, and it runs the risk of locking up the system altogether; it is best avoided unless there is truly no other way.

If you are going to such lengths to allocate a large DMA buffer, however, it is worth putting some thought into alternatives. If your device can do scatter/gather I/O, you can allocate your buffer in smaller pieces and let the device do the rest. Scatter/gather I/O can also be used when performing direct I/O into user space, which may well be the best solution when a truly huge buffer is required.

Bus Addresses

A device driver using DMA has to talk to hardware connected to the interface bus, which uses physical addresses, whereas program code uses virtual addresses.

As a matter of fact, the situation is slightly more complicated than that. DMA-based hardware uses *bus*, rather than *physical*, addresses. Although ISA and PCI bus addresses are simply physical addresses on the PC, this is not true for every platform. Sometimes the interface bus is connected through bridge circuitry that maps I/O addresses to different physical addresses. Some systems even have a page-mapping scheme that can make arbitrary pages appear contiguous to the peripheral bus.

---

* The word *fragmentation* is usually applied to disks to express the idea that files are not stored consecutively on the magnetic medium. The same concept applies to memory, where each virtual address space gets scattered throughout physical RAM, and it becomes difficult to retrieve consecutive free pages when a DMA buffer is requested.

At the lowest level (again, we'll look at a higher-level solution shortly), the Linux kernel provides a portable solution by exporting the following functions, defined in *<asm/io.h>*. The use of these functions is strongly discouraged, because they work properly only on systems with a very simple I/O architecture; nonetheless, you may encounter them when working with kernel code.

```
unsigned long virt_to_bus(volatile void *address);
void *bus_to_virt(unsigned long address);
```

These functions perform a simple conversion between kernel logical addresses and bus addresses. They do not work in any situation where an I/O memory management unit must be programmed or where bounce buffers must be used. The right way of performing this conversion is with the generic DMA layer, so we now move on to that topic.

The Generic DMA Layer

DMA operations, in the end, come down to allocating a buffer and passing bus addresses to your device. However, the task of writing portable drivers that perform DMA safely and correctly on all architectures is harder than one might think. Different systems have different ideas of how cache coherency should work; if you do not handle this issue correctly, your driver may corrupt memory. Some systems have complicated bus hardware that can make the DMA task easier—or harder. And not all systems can perform DMA out of all parts of memory. Fortunately, the kernel provides a bus- and architecture-independent DMA layer that hides most of these issues from the driver author. We strongly encourage you to use this layer for DMA operations in any driver you write.

Many of the functions below require a pointer to a struct device. This structure is the low-level representation of a device within the Linux device model. It is not something that drivers often have to work with directly, but you do need it when using the generic DMA layer. Usually, you can find this structure buried inside the bus specific that describes your device. For example, it can be found as the dev field in struct pci_device or struct usb_device. The device structure is covered in detail in Chapter 14.

Drivers that use the following functions should include *<linux/dma-mapping.h>*.

Dealing with difficult hardware

The first question that must be answered before attempting DMA is whether the given device is capable of such an operation on the current host. Many devices are limited in the range of memory they can address, for a number of reasons. By default, the kernel assumes that your device can perform DMA to any 32-bit address. If this is not the case, you should inform the kernel of that fact with a call to:

```
int dma_set_mask(struct device *dev, u64 mask);
```

The mask should show the bits that your device can address; if it is limited to 24 bits, for example, you would pass mask as 0x0FFFFFF. The return value is nonzero if DMA is possible with the given mask; if *dma_set_mask* returns 0, you are not able to use DMA operations with this device. Thus, the initialization code in a driver for a device limited to 24-bit DMA operations might look like:

```
if (dma_set_mask (dev, 0xffffff))
    card->use_dma = 1;
else {
    card->use_dma = 0;    /* We'll have to live without DMA */
    printk (KERN_WARN, "mydev: DMA not supported\n");
}
```

Again, if your device supports normal, 32-bit DMA operations, there is no need to call *dma_set_mask*.

DMA mappings

A *DMA mapping* is a combination of allocating a DMA buffer and generating an address for that buffer that is accessible by the device. It is tempting to get that address with a simple call to *virt_to_bus*, but there are strong reasons for avoiding that approach. The first of those is that reasonable hardware comes with an IOMMU that provides a set of *mapping registers* for the bus. The IOMMU can arrange for any physical memory to appear within the address range accessible by the device, and it can cause physically scattered buffers to look contiguous to the device. Making use of the IOMMU requires using the generic DMA layer; *virt_to_bus* is not up to the task.

Note that not all architectures have an IOMMU; in particular, the popular x86 platform has no IOMMU support. A properly written driver need not be aware of the I/O support hardware it is running over, however.

Setting up a useful address for the device may also, in some cases, require the establishment of a *bounce buffer*. Bounce buffers are created when a driver attempts to perform DMA on an address that is not reachable by the peripheral device—a high-memory address, for example. Data is then copied to and from the bounce buffer as needed. Needless to say, use of bounce buffers can slow things down, but sometimes there is no alternative.

DMA mappings must also address the issue of cache coherency. Remember that modern processors keep copies of recently accessed memory areas in a fast, local cache; without this cache, reasonable performance is not possible. If your device changes an area of main memory, it is imperative that any processor caches covering that area be invalidated; otherwise the processor may work with an incorrect image of main memory, and data corruption results. Similarly, when your device uses DMA to read data from main memory, any changes to that memory residing in processor caches must be flushed out first. These *cache coherency* issues can create no end of obscure and difficult-to-find bugs if the programmer is not careful. Some architectures manage cache coherency in the hardware, but others require software support. The generic DMA layer goes to great lengths to ensure that things work correctly on all architectures, but, as we will see, proper behavior requires adherence to a small set of rules.

The DMA mapping sets up a new type, dma_addr_t, to represent bus addresses. Variables of type dma_addr_t should be treated as opaque by the driver; the only allowable operations are to pass them to the DMA support routines and to the device itself. As a bus address, dma_addr_t may lead to unexpected problems if used directly by the CPU.

The PCI code distinguishes between two types of DMA mappings, depending on how long the DMA buffer is expected to stay around:

Coherent DMA mappings

These mappings usually exist for the life of the driver. A coherent buffer must be simultaneously available to both the CPU and the peripheral (other types of mappings, as we will see later, can be available only to one or the other at any given time). As a result, coherent mappings must live in cache-coherent memory. Coherent mappings can be expensive to set up and use.

Streaming DMA mappings

Streaming mappings are usually set up for a single operation. Some architectures allow for significant optimizations when streaming mappings are used, as we see, but these mappings also are subject to a stricter set of rules in how they may be accessed. The kernel developers recommend the use of streaming mappings over coherent mappings whenever possible. There are two reasons for this recommendation. The first is that, on systems that support mapping registers, each DMA mapping uses one or more of them on the bus. Coherent mappings, which have a long lifetime, can monopolize these registers for a long time, even when they are not being used. The other reason is that, on some hardware, streaming mappings can be optimized in ways that are not available to coherent mappings.

The two mapping types must be manipulated in different ways; it's time to look at the details.

Setting up coherent DMA mappings

A driver can set up a coherent mapping with a call to *dma_alloc_coherent*:

```
void *dma_alloc_coherent(struct device *dev, size_t size,
                         dma_addr_t *dma_handle, int flag);
```

This function handles both the allocation and the mapping of the buffer. The first two arguments are the device structure and the size of the buffer needed. The function returns the result of the DMA mapping in two places. The return value from the function is a kernel virtual address for the buffer, which may be used by the driver; the associated bus address, meanwhile, is returned in dma_handle. Allocation is handled in this function so that the buffer is placed in a location that works with DMA; usually the memory is just allocated with *get_free_pages* (but note that the size is in bytes, rather than an order value). The flag argument is the usual GFP_ value describing how the memory is to be allocated; it should usually be GFP_KERNEL (usually) or GFP_ATOMIC (when running in atomic context).

When the buffer is no longer needed (usually at module unload time), it should be returned to the system with *dma_free_coherent*:

```
void dma_free_coherent(struct device *dev, size_t size,
                       void *vaddr, dma_addr_t dma_handle);
```

Note that this function, like many of the generic DMA functions, requires that all of the size, CPU address, and bus address arguments be provided.

DMA pools

A *DMA pool* is an allocation mechanism for small, coherent DMA mappings. Mappings obtained from *dma_alloc_coherent* may have a minimum size of one page. If your device needs smaller DMA areas than that, you should probably be using a DMA pool. DMA pools are also useful in situations where you may be tempted to perform DMA to small areas embedded within a larger structure. Some very obscure driver bugs have been traced down to cache coherency problems with structure fields adjacent to small DMA areas. To avoid this problem, you should always allocate areas for DMA operations explicitly, away from other, non-DMA data structures.

The DMA pool functions are defined in *<linux/dmapool.h>*.

A DMA pool must be created before use with a call to:

```
struct dma_pool *dma_pool_create(const char *name, struct device *dev,
                       size_t size, size_t align,
                       size_t allocation);
```

Here, name is a name for the pool, dev is your device structure, size is the size of the buffers to be allocated from this pool, align is the required hardware alignment for allocations from the pool (expressed in bytes), and allocation is, if nonzero, a memory boundary that allocations should not exceed. If allocation is passed as 4096, for example, the buffers allocated from this pool do not cross 4-KB boundaries.

When you are done with a pool, it can be freed with:

```
void dma_pool_destroy(struct dma_pool *pool);
```

You should return all allocations to the pool before destroying it.

Allocations are handled with *dma_pool_alloc*:

```
void *dma_pool_alloc(struct dma_pool *pool, int mem_flags,
                     dma_addr_t *handle);
```

For this call, mem_flags is the usual set of GFP_ allocation flags. If all goes well, a region of memory (of the size specified when the pool was created) is allocated and returned. As with *dma_alloc_coherent*, the address of the resulting DMA buffer is returned as a kernel virtual address and stored in handle as a bus address.

Unneeded buffers should be returned to the pool with:

```
void dma_pool_free(struct dma_pool *pool, void *vaddr, dma_addr_t addr);
```

Setting up streaming DMA mappings

Streaming mappings have a more complicated interface than the coherent variety, for a number of reasons. These mappings expect to work with a buffer that has already been allocated by the driver and, therefore, have to deal with addresses that they did not choose. On some architectures, streaming mappings can also have multiple, discontiguous pages and multipart "scatter/gather" buffers. For all of these reasons, streaming mappings have their own set of mapping functions.

When setting up a streaming mapping, you must tell the kernel in which direction the data is moving. Some symbols (of type enum dma_data_direction) have been defined for this purpose:

DMA_TO_DEVICE
DMA_FROM_DEVICE
> These two symbols should be reasonably self-explanatory. If data is being sent to the device (in response, perhaps, to a *write* system call), DMA_TO_DEVICE should be used; data going to the CPU, instead, is marked with DMA_FROM_DEVICE.

DMA_BIDIRECTIONAL
> If data can move in either direction, use DMA_BIDIRECTIONAL.

DMA_NONE
> This symbol is provided only as a debugging aid. Attempts to use buffers with this "direction" cause a kernel panic.

It may be tempting to just pick DMA_BIDIRECTIONAL at all times, but driver authors should resist that temptation. On some architectures, there is a performance penalty to pay for that choice.

When you have a single buffer to transfer, map it with *dma_map_single*:

```
dma_addr_t dma_map_single(struct device *dev, void *buffer, size_t size,
                          enum dma_data_direction direction);
```

The return value is the bus address that you can pass to the device or NULL if something goes wrong.

Once the transfer is complete, the mapping should be deleted with *dma_unmap_single*:

```
void dma_unmap_single(struct device *dev, dma_addr_t dma_addr, size_t size,
                      enum dma_data_direction direction);
```

Here, the size and direction arguments must match those used to map the buffer.

Some important rules apply to streaming DMA mappings:

- The buffer must be used only for a transfer that matches the direction value given when it was mapped.
- Once a buffer has been mapped, it belongs to the device, not the processor. Until the buffer has been unmapped, the driver should not touch its contents in any way. Only after *dma_unmap_single* has been called is it safe for the driver to access the contents of the buffer (with one exception that we see shortly). Among other things, this rule implies that a buffer being written to a device cannot be mapped until it contains all the data to write.
- The buffer must not be unmapped while DMA is still active, or serious system instability is guaranteed.

You may be wondering why the driver can no longer work with a buffer once it has been mapped. There are actually two reasons why this rule makes sense. First, when a buffer is mapped for DMA, the kernel must ensure that all of the data in that buffer has actually been written to memory. It is likely that some data is in the processor's cache when *dma_unmap_single* is issued, and must be explicitly flushed. Data written to the buffer by the processor after the flush may not be visible to the device.

Second, consider what happens if the buffer to be mapped is in a region of memory that is not accessible to the device. Some architectures simply fail in this case, but others create a bounce buffer. The bounce buffer is just a separate region of memory that *is* accessible to the device. If a buffer is mapped with a direction of DMA_TO_DEVICE, and a bounce buffer is required, the contents of the original buffer are copied as part of the mapping operation. Clearly, changes to the original buffer after the copy are not seen by the device. Similarly, DMA_FROM_DEVICE bounce buffers are copied back to the original buffer by *dma_unmap_single*; the data from the device is not present until that copy has been done.

Incidentally, bounce buffers are one reason why it is important to get the direction right. DMA_BIDIRECTIONAL bounce buffers are copied both before and after the operation, which is often an unnecessary waste of CPU cycles.

Occasionally a driver needs to access the contents of a streaming DMA buffer without unmapping it. A call has been provided to make this possible:

```
void dma_sync_single_for_cpu(struct device *dev, dma_handle_t bus_addr,
                 size_t size, enum dma_data_direction direction);
```

This function should be called before the processor accesses a streaming DMA buffer. Once the call has been made, the CPU "owns" the DMA buffer and can work with it as needed. Before the device accesses the buffer, however, ownership should be transferred back to it with:

```
void dma_sync_single_for_device(struct device *dev, dma_handle_t bus_addr,
                    size_t size, enum dma_data_direction direction);
```

The processor, once again, should not access the DMA buffer after this call has been made.

Single-page streaming mappings

Occasionally, you may want to set up a mapping on a buffer for which you have a struct page pointer; this can happen, for example, with user-space buffers mapped with *get_user_pages*. To set up and tear down streaming mappings using struct page pointers, use the following:

```
dma_addr_t dma_map_page(struct device *dev, struct page *page,
                        unsigned long offset, size_t size,
                        enum dma_data_direction direction);

void dma_unmap_page(struct device *dev, dma_addr_t dma_address,
                    size_t size, enum dma_data_direction direction);
```

The offset and size arguments can be used to map part of a page. It is recommended, however, that partial-page mappings be avoided unless you are really sure of what you are doing. Mapping part of a page can lead to cache coherency problems if the allocation covers only part of a cache line; that, in turn, can lead to memory corruption and extremely difficult-to-debug bugs.

Scatter/gather mappings

Scatter/gather mappings are a special type of streaming DMA mapping. Suppose you have several buffers, all of which need to be transferred to or from the device. This situation can come about in several ways, including from a *readv* or *writev* system call, a clustered disk I/O request, or a list of pages in a mapped kernel I/O buffer. You could simply map each buffer, in turn, and perform the required operation, but there are advantages to mapping the whole list at once.

Many devices can accept a *scatterlist* of array pointers and lengths, and transfer them all in one DMA operation; for example, "zero-copy" networking is easier if packets can be built in multiple pieces. Another reason to map scatterlists as a whole is to take advantage of systems that have mapping registers in the bus hardware. On such systems, physically discontiguous pages can be assembled into a single, contiguous array from the device's point of view. This technique works only when the entries in the scatterlist are equal to the page size in length (except the first and last), but when it does work, it can turn multiple operations into a single DMA, and speed things up accordingly.

Finally, if a bounce buffer must be used, it makes sense to coalesce the entire list into a single buffer (since it is being copied anyway).

So now you're convinced that mapping of scatterlists is worthwhile in some situations. The first step in mapping a scatterlist is to create and fill in an array of struct scatterlist describing the buffers to be transferred. This structure is architecture dependent, and is described in *<asm/scatterlist.h>*. However, it always contains three fields:

```
struct page *page;
```
   The struct page pointer corresponding to the buffer to be used in the scatter/gather operation.

```
unsigned int length;
unsigned int offset;
```
   The length of that buffer and its offset within the page

To map a scatter/gather DMA operation, your driver should set the page, offset, and length fields in a struct scatterlist entry for each buffer to be transferred. Then call:

```
int dma_map_sg(struct device *dev, struct scatterlist *sg, int nents,
               enum dma_data_direction direction)
```

where nents is the number of scatterlist entries passed in. The return value is the number of DMA buffers to transfer; it may be less than nents.

For each buffer in the input scatterlist, *dma_map_sg* determines the proper bus address to give to the device. As part of that task, it also coalesces buffers that are adjacent to each other in memory. If the system your driver is running on has an I/O memory management unit, *dma_map_sg* also programs that unit's mapping registers, with the possible result that, from your device's point of view, you are able to transfer a single, contiguous buffer. You will never know what the resulting transfer will look like, however, until after the call.

Your driver should transfer each buffer returned by *pci_map_sg*. The bus address and length of each buffer are stored in the struct scatterlist entries, but their location in the structure varies from one architecture to the next. Two macros have been defined to make it possible to write portable code:

```
dma_addr_t sg_dma_address(struct scatterlist *sg);
```
   Returns the bus (DMA) address from this scatterlist entry.

```
unsigned int sg_dma_len(struct scatterlist *sg);
```
   Returns the length of this buffer.

Again, remember that the address and length of the buffers to transfer may be different from what was passed in to *dma_map_sg*.

Once the transfer is complete, a scatter/gather mapping is unmapped with a call to *dma_unmap_sg*:

```
void dma_unmap_sg(struct device *dev, struct scatterlist *list,
                  int nents, enum dma_data_direction direction);
```

Note that nents must be the number of entries that you originally passed to *dma_map_sg* and not the number of DMA buffers the function returned to you.

Scatter/gather mappings are streaming DMA mappings, and the same access rules apply to them as to the single variety. If you must access a mapped scatter/gather list, you must synchronize it first:

```
void dma_sync_sg_for_cpu(struct device *dev, struct scatterlist *sg,
                         int nents, enum dma_data_direction direction);
void dma_sync_sg_for_device(struct device *dev, struct scatterlist *sg,
                            int nents, enum dma_data_direction direction);
```

PCI double-address cycle mappings

Normally, the DMA support layer works with 32-bit bus addresses, possibly restricted by a specific device's DMA mask. The PCI bus, however, also supports a 64-bit addressing mode, the *double-address cycle* (DAC). The generic DMA layer does not support this mode for a couple of reasons, the first of which being that it is a PCI-specific feature. Also, many implementations of DAC are buggy at best, and, because DAC is slower than a regular, 32-bit DMA, there can be a performance cost. Even so, there are applications where using DAC can be the right thing to do; if you have a device that is likely to be working with very large buffers placed in high memory, you may want to consider implementing DAC support. This support is available only for the PCI bus, so PCI-specific routines must be used.

To use DAC, your driver must include *<linux/pci.h>*. You must set a separate DMA mask:

```
int pci_dac_set_dma_mask(struct pci_dev *pdev, u64 mask);
```

You can use DAC addressing only if this call returns 0.

A special type (dma64_addr_t) is used for DAC mappings. To establish one of these mappings, call *pci_dac_page_to_dma*:

```
dma64_addr_t pci_dac_page_to_dma(struct pci_dev *pdev, struct page *page,
                                 unsigned long offset, int direction);
```

DAC mappings, you will notice, can be made only from struct page pointers (they should live in high memory, after all, or there is no point in using them); they must be created a single page at a time. The direction argument is the PCI equivalent of the enum dma_data_direction used in the generic DMA layer; it should be PCI_DMA_TODEVICE, PCI_DMA_FROMDEVICE, or PCI_DMA_BIDIRECTIONAL.

DAC mappings require no external resources, so there is no need to explicitly release them after use. It is necessary, however, to treat DAC mappings like other streaming mappings, and observe the rules regarding buffer ownership. There is a set of functions for synchronizing DMA buffers that is analogous to the generic variety:

```
void pci_dac_dma_sync_single_for_cpu(struct pci_dev *pdev,
                                     dma64_addr_t dma_addr,
                                     size_t len,
                                     int direction);
```

```
void pci_dac_dma_sync_single_for_device(struct pci_dev *pdev,
                                         dma64_addr_t dma_addr,
                                         size_t len,
                                         int direction);
```

A simple PCI DMA example

As an example of how the DMA mappings might be used, we present a simple example of DMA coding for a PCI device. The actual form of DMA operations on the PCI bus is very dependent on the device being driven. Thus, this example does not apply to any real device; instead, it is part of a hypothetical driver called *dad* (DMA Acquisition Device). A driver for this device might define a transfer function like this:

```
int dad_transfer(struct dad_dev *dev, int write, void *buffer,
                 size_t count)
{
    dma_addr_t bus_addr;

    /* Map the buffer for DMA */
    dev->dma_dir = (write ? DMA_TO_DEVICE : DMA_FROM_DEVICE);
    dev->dma_size = count;
    bus_addr = dma_map_single(&dev->pci_dev->dev, buffer, count,
                              dev->dma_dir);
    dev->dma_addr = bus_addr;

    /* Set up the device */

    writeb(dev->registers.command, DAD_CMD_DISABLEDMA);
    writeb(dev->registers.command, write ? DAD_CMD_WR : DAD_CMD_RD);
    writel(dev->registers.addr, cpu_to_le32(bus_addr));
    writel(dev->registers.len, cpu_to_le32(count));

    /* Start the operation */
    writeb(dev->registers.command, DAD_CMD_ENABLEDMA);
    return 0;
}
```

This function maps the buffer to be transferred and starts the device operation. The other half of the job must be done in the interrupt service routine, which looks something like this:

```
void dad_interrupt(int irq, void *dev_id, struct pt_regs *regs)
{
    struct dad_dev *dev = (struct dad_dev *) dev_id;

    /* Make sure it's really our device interrupting */

    /* Unmap the DMA buffer */
    dma_unmap_single(dev->pci_dev->dev, dev->dma_addr,
                     dev->dma_size, dev->dma_dir);

    /* Only now is it safe to access the buffer, copy to user, etc. */
    ...
}
```

Obviously, a great deal of detail has been left out of this example, including whatever steps may be required to prevent attempts to start multiple, simultaneous DMA operations.

DMA for ISA Devices

The ISA bus allows for two kinds of DMA transfers: native DMA and ISA bus master DMA. Native DMA uses standard DMA-controller circuitry on the motherboard to drive the signal lines on the ISA bus. ISA bus master DMA, on the other hand, is handled entirely by the peripheral device. The latter type of DMA is rarely used and doesn't require discussion here, because it is similar to DMA for PCI devices, at least from the driver's point of view. An example of an ISA bus master is the 1542 SCSI controller, whose driver is *drivers/scsi/aha1542.c* in the kernel sources.

As far as native DMA is concerned, there are three entities involved in a DMA data transfer on the ISA bus:

The 8237 DMA controller (DMAC)
> The controller holds information about the DMA transfer, such as the direction, the memory address, and the size of the transfer. It also contains a counter that tracks the status of ongoing transfers. When the controller receives a DMA request signal, it gains control of the bus and drives the signal lines so that the device can read or write its data.

The peripheral device
> The device must activate the DMA request signal when it's ready to transfer data. The actual transfer is managed by the DMAC; the hardware device sequentially reads or writes data onto the bus when the controller strobes the device. The device usually raises an interrupt when the transfer is over.

The device driver
> The driver has little to do; it provides the DMA controller with the direction, bus address, and size of the transfer. It also talks to its peripheral to prepare it for transferring the data and responds to the interrupt when the DMA is over.

The original DMA controller used in the PC could manage four "channels," each associated with one set of DMA registers. Four devices could store their DMA information in the controller at the same time. Newer PCs contain the equivalent of two DMAC devices:[*] the second controller (master) is connected to the system processor, and the first (slave) is connected to channel 0 of the second controller.[†]

---

[*] These circuits are now part of the motherboard's chipset, but a few years ago they were two separate 8237 chips.

[†] The original PCs had only one controller; the second was added in 286-based platforms. However, the second controller is connected as the master because it handles 16-bit transfers; the first transfers only eight bits at a time and is there for backward compatibility.

The channels are numbered from 0–7: channel 4 is not available to ISA peripherals, because it is used internally to cascade the slave controller onto the master. The available channels are, thus, 0–3 on the slave (the 8-bit channels) and 5–7 on the master (the 16-bit channels). The size of any DMA transfer, as stored in the controller, is a 16-bit number representing the number of bus cycles. The maximum transfer size is, therefore, 64 KB for the slave controller (because it transfers eight bits in one cycle) and 128 KB for the master (which does 16-bit transfers).

Because the DMA controller is a system-wide resource, the kernel helps deal with it. It uses a DMA registry to provide a request-and-free mechanism for the DMA channels and a set of functions to configure channel information in the DMA controller.

Registering DMA usage

You should be used to kernel registries—we've already seen them for I/O ports and interrupt lines. The DMA channel registry is similar to the others. After *<asm/dma.h>* has been included, the following functions can be used to obtain and release ownership of a DMA channel:

```
int request_dma(unsigned int channel, const char *name);
void free_dma(unsigned int channel);
```

The channel argument is a number between 0 and 7 or, more precisely, a positive number less than MAX_DMA_CHANNELS. On the PC, MAX_DMA_CHANNELS is defined as 8 to match the hardware. The name argument is a string identifying the device. The specified name appears in the file */proc/dma*, which can be read by user programs.

The return value from *request_dma* is 0 for success and -EINVAL or -EBUSY if there was an error. The former means that the requested channel is out of range, and the latter means that another device is holding the channel.

We recommend that you take the same care with DMA channels as with I/O ports and interrupt lines; requesting the channel at *open* time is much better than requesting it from the module initialization function. Delaying the request allows some sharing between drivers; for example, your sound card and your analog I/O interface can share the DMA channel as long as they are not used at the same time.

We also suggest that you request the DMA channel *after* you've requested the interrupt line and that you release it *before* the interrupt. This is the conventional order for requesting the two resources; following the convention avoids possible deadlocks. Note that every device using DMA needs an IRQ line as well; otherwise, it couldn't signal the completion of data transfer.

In a typical case, the code for *open* looks like the following, which refers to our hypothetical *dad* module. The *dad* device as shown uses a fast interrupt handler without support for shared IRQ lines.

```
int dad_open (struct inode *inode, struct file *filp)
{
    struct dad_device *my_device;
```

```
    /* ... */
    if ( (error = request_irq(my_device.irq, dad_interrupt,
                             SA_INTERRUPT, "dad", NULL)) )
        return error; /* or implement blocking open */

    if ( (error = request_dma(my_device.dma, "dad")) ) {
        free_irq(my_device.irq, NULL);
        return error; /* or implement blocking open */
    }
    /* ... */
    return 0;
}
```

The *close* implementation that matches the *open* just shown looks like this:

```
void dad_close (struct inode *inode, struct file *filp)
{
    struct dad_device *my_device;

    /* ... */
    free_dma(my_device.dma);
    free_irq(my_device.irq, NULL);
    /* ... */
}
```

Here's how the */proc/dma* file looks on a system with the sound card installed:

```
merlino% cat /proc/dma
 1: Sound Blaster8
 4: cascade
```

It's interesting to note that the default sound driver gets the DMA channel at system boot and never releases it. The cascade entry is a placeholder, indicating that channel 4 is not available to drivers, as explained earlier.

Talking to the DMA controller

After registration, the main part of the driver's job consists of configuring the DMA controller for proper operation. This task is not trivial, but fortunately, the kernel exports all the functions needed by the typical driver.

The driver needs to configure the DMA controller either when *read* or *write* is called, or when preparing for asynchronous transfers. This latter task is performed either at *open* time or in response to an *ioctl* command, depending on the driver and the policy it implements. The code shown here is the code that is typically called by the *read* or *write* device methods.

This subsection provides a quick overview of the internals of the DMA controller so you understand the code introduced here. If you want to learn more, we'd urge you to read *<asm/dma.h>* and some hardware manuals describing the PC architecture. In particular, we don't deal with the issue of 8-bit versus 16-bit data transfers. If you are writing device drivers for ISA device boards, you should find the relevant information in the hardware manuals for the devices.

The DMA controller is a shared resource, and confusion could arise if more than one processor attempts to program it simultaneously. For that reason, the controller is protected by a spinlock, called `dma_spin_lock`. Drivers should not manipulate the lock directly; however, two functions have been provided to do that for you:

`unsigned long claim_dma_lock( );`
> Acquires the DMA spinlock. This function also blocks interrupts on the local processor; therefore, the return value is a set of flags describing the previous interrupt state; it must be passed to the following function to restore the interrupt state when you are done with the lock.

`void release_dma_lock(unsigned long flags);`
> Returns the DMA spinlock and restores the previous interrupt status.

The spinlock should be held when using the functions described next. It should *not* be held during the actual I/O, however. A driver should never sleep when holding a spinlock.

The information that must be loaded into the controller consists of three items: the RAM address, the number of atomic items that must be transferred (in bytes or words), and the direction of the transfer. To this end, the following functions are exported by *<asm/dma.h>*:

`void set_dma_mode(unsigned int channel, char mode);`
> Indicates whether the channel must read from the device (`DMA_MODE_READ`) or write to it (`DMA_MODE_WRITE`). A third mode exists, `DMA_MODE_CASCADE`, which is used to release control of the bus. Cascading is the way the first controller is connected to the top of the second, but it can also be used by true ISA bus-master devices. We won't discuss bus mastering here.

`void set_dma_addr(unsigned int channel, unsigned int addr);`
> Assigns the address of the DMA buffer. The function stores the 24 least significant bits of addr in the controller. The addr argument must be a *bus* address (see the section "Bus Addresses" earlier in this chapter).

`void set_dma_count(unsigned int channel, unsigned int count);`
> Assigns the number of bytes to transfer. The count argument represents bytes for 16-bit channels as well; in this case, the number *must* be even.

In addition to these functions, there are a number of housekeeping facilities that must be used when dealing with DMA devices:

void disable_dma(unsigned int channel);
> A DMA channel can be disabled within the controller. The channel should be disabled before the controller is configured to prevent improper operation. (Otherwise, corruption can occur because the controller is programmed via 8-bit data transfers and, therefore, none of the previous functions is executed atomically).

void enable_dma(unsigned int channel);
> This function tells the controller that the DMA channel contains valid data.

int get_dma_residue(unsigned int channel);
> The driver sometimes needs to know whether a DMA transfer has been completed. This function returns the number of bytes that are still to be transferred. The return value is 0 after a successful transfer and is unpredictable (but not 0) while the controller is working. The unpredictability springs from the need to obtain the 16-bit residue through two 8-bit input operations.

void clear_dma_ff(unsigned int channel)
> This function clears the DMA flip-flop. The flip-flop is used to control access to 16-bit registers. The registers are accessed by two consecutive 8-bit operations, and the flip-flop is used to select the least significant byte (when it is clear) or the most significant byte (when it is set). The flip-flop automatically toggles when eight bits have been transferred; the programmer must clear the flip-flop (to set it to a known state) before accessing the DMA registers.

Using these functions, a driver can implement a function like the following to prepare for a DMA transfer:

```
int dad_dma_prepare(int channel, int mode, unsigned int buf,
                    unsigned int count)
{
    unsigned long flags;

    flags = claim_dma_lock( );
    disable_dma(channel);
    clear_dma_ff(channel);
    set_dma_mode(channel, mode);
    set_dma_addr(channel, virt_to_bus(buf));
    set_dma_count(channel, count);
    enable_dma(channel);
    release_dma_lock(flags);

    return 0;
}
```

Then, a function like the next one is used to check for successful completion of DMA:

```
int dad_dma_isdone(int channel)
{
```

```
    int residue;
    unsigned long flags = claim_dma_lock ( );
    residue = get_dma_residue(channel);
    release_dma_lock(flags);
    return (residue == 0);
}
```

The only thing that remains to be done is to configure the device board. This device-specific task usually consists of reading or writing a few I/O ports. Devices differ in significant ways. For example, some devices expect the programmer to tell the hardware how big the DMA buffer is, and sometimes the driver has to read a value that is hardwired into the device. For configuring the board, the hardware manual is your only friend.

Quick Reference

This chapter introduced the following symbols related to memory handling.

Introductory Material

```
#include <linux/mm.h>
#include <asm/page.h>
```
> Most of the functions and structures related to memory management are proto-typed and defined in these header files.

```
void *__va(unsigned long physaddr);
unsigned long __pa(void *kaddr);
```
> Macros that convert between kernel logical addresses and physical addresses.

```
PAGE_SIZE
PAGE_SHIFT
```
> Constants that give the size (in bytes) of a page on the underlying hardware and the number of bits that a page frame number must be shifted to turn it into a physical address.

```
struct page
```
> Structure that represents a hardware page in the system memory map.

```
struct page *virt_to_page(void *kaddr);
void *page_address(struct page *page);
struct page *pfn_to_page(int pfn);
```
> Macros that convert between kernel logical addresses and their associated memory map entries. *page_address* works only for low-memory pages or high-memory pages that have been explicitly mapped. *pfn_to_page* converts a page frame number to its associated struct page pointer.

```
unsigned long kmap(struct page *page);
void kunmap(struct page *page);
```
    kmap returns a kernel virtual address that is mapped to the given page, creating the mapping if need be. *kunmap* deletes the mapping for the given page.

```
#include <linux/highmem.h>
#include <asm/kmap_types.h>
void *kmap_atomic(struct page *page, enum km_type type);
void kunmap_atomic(void *addr, enum km_type type);
```
    The high-performance version of *kmap*; the resulting mappings can be held only by atomic code. For drivers, type should be KM_USER0, KM_USER1, KM_IRQ0, or KM_IRQ1.

```
struct vm_area_struct;
```
    Structure describing a VMA.

Implementing mmap

```
int remap_pfn_range(struct vm_area_struct *vma, unsigned long virt_add,
  unsigned long pfn, unsigned long size, pgprot_t prot);
int io_remap_page_range(struct vm_area_struct *vma, unsigned long virt_add,
  unsigned long phys_add, unsigned long size, pgprot_t prot);
```
    Functions that sit at the heart of *mmap*. They map size bytes of physical addresses, starting at the page number indicated by pfn to the virtual address virt_add. The protection bits associated with the virtual space are specified in prot. *io_remap_page_range* should be used when the target address is in I/O memory space.

```
struct page *vmalloc_to_page(void *vmaddr);
```
    Converts a kernel virtual address obtained from *vmalloc* to its corresponding struct page pointer.

Implementing Direct I/O

```
int get_user_pages(struct task_struct *tsk, struct mm_struct *mm, unsigned
  long start, int len, int write, int force, struct page **pages, struct
  vm_area_struct **vmas);
```
    Function that locks a user-space buffer into memory and returns the corresponding struct page pointers. The caller must hold mm->mmap_sem.

```
SetPageDirty(struct page *page);
```
    Macro that marks the given page as "dirty" (modified) and in need of writing to its backing store before it can be freed.

```
void page_cache_release(struct page *page);
```
    Frees the given page from the page cache.

```
int is_sync_kiocb(struct kiocb *iocb);
```
Macro that returns nonzero if the given IOCB requires synchronous execution.

```
int aio_complete(struct kiocb *iocb, long res, long res2);
```
Function that indicates completion of an asynchronous I/O operation.

Direct Memory Access

```
#include <asm/io.h>
unsigned long virt_to_bus(volatile void * address);
void * bus_to_virt(unsigned long address);
```
Obsolete and deprecated functions that convert between kernel, virtual, and bus addresses. Bus addresses must be used to talk to peripheral devices.

```
#include <linux/dma-mapping.h>
```
Header file required to define the generic DMA functions.

```
int dma_set_mask(struct device *dev, u64 mask);
```
For peripherals that cannot address the full 32-bit range, this function informs the kernel of the addressable range and returns nonzero if DMA is possible.

```
void *dma_alloc_coherent(struct device *dev, size_t size, dma_addr_t
  *bus_addr, int flag)
void dma_free_coherent(struct device *dev, size_t size, void *cpuaddr,
  dma_handle_t bus_addr);
```
Allocate and free coherent DMA mappings for a buffer that will last the lifetime of the driver.

```
#include <linux/dmapool.h>
struct dma_pool *dma_pool_create(const char *name, struct device *dev,
  size_t size, size_t align, size_t allocation);
void dma_pool_destroy(struct dma_pool *pool);
void *dma_pool_alloc(struct dma_pool *pool, int mem_flags, dma_addr_t
  *handle);
void dma_pool_free(struct dma_pool *pool, void *vaddr, dma_addr_t handle);
```
Functions that create, destroy, and use DMA pools to manage small DMA areas.

```
enum dma_data_direction;
DMA_TO_DEVICE
DMA_FROM_DEVICE
DMA_BIDIRECTIONAL
DMA_NONE
```
Symbols used to tell the streaming mapping functions the direction in which data is moving to or from the buffer.

```
dma_addr_t dma_map_single(struct device *dev, void *buffer, size_t size, enum
  dma_data_direction direction);
void dma_unmap_single(struct device *dev, dma_addr_t bus_addr, size_t size,
  enum dma_data_direction direction);
```
> Create and destroy a single-use, streaming DMA mapping.

```
void dma_sync_single_for_cpu(struct device *dev, dma_handle_t bus_addr, size_t
  size, enum dma_data_direction direction);
void dma_sync_single_for_device(struct device *dev, dma_handle_t bus_addr,
  size_t size, enum dma_data_direction direction);
```
> Synchronizes a buffer that has a streaming mapping. These functions must be used if the processor must access a buffer while the streaming mapping is in place (i.e., while the device owns the buffer).

```
#include <asm/scatterlist.h>
struct scatterlist { /* ... */ };
dma_addr_t sg_dma_address(struct scatterlist *sg);
unsigned int sg_dma_len(struct scatterlist *sg);
```
> The scatterlist structure describes an I/O operation that involves more than one buffer. The macros *sg_dma_address* and *sg_dma_len* may be used to extract bus addresses and buffer lengths to pass to the device when implementing scatter/gather operations.

```
dma_map_sg(struct device *dev, struct scatterlist *list, int nents,
  enum dma_data_direction direction);
dma_unmap_sg(struct device *dev, struct scatterlist *list, int nents, enum
  dma_data_direction direction);
void dma_sync_sg_for_cpu(struct device *dev, struct scatterlist *sg, int
  nents, enum dma_data_direction direction);
void dma_sync_sg_for_device(struct device *dev, struct scatterlist *sg, int
  nents, enum dma_data_direction direction);
```
> *dma_map_sg* maps a scatter/gather operation, and *dma_unmap_sg* undoes that mapping. If the buffers must be accessed while the mapping is active, *dma_sync_sg_** may be used to synchronize things.

```
/proc/dma
```
> File that contains a textual snapshot of the allocated channels in the DMA controllers. PCI-based DMA is not shown because each board works independently, without the need to allocate a channel in the DMA controller.

```
#include <asm/dma.h>
```
> Header that defines or prototypes all the functions and macros related to DMA. It must be included to use any of the following symbols.

```
int request_dma(unsigned int channel, const char *name);
void free_dma(unsigned int channel);
```
Access the DMA registry. Registration must be performed before using ISA DMA channels.

```
unsigned long claim_dma_lock( );
void release_dma_lock(unsigned long flags);
```
Acquire and release the DMA spinlock, which must be held prior to calling the other ISA DMA functions described later in this list. They also disable and reenable interrupts on the local processor.

```
void set_dma_mode(unsigned int channel, char mode);
void set_dma_addr(unsigned int channel, unsigned int addr);
void set_dma_count(unsigned int channel, unsigned int count);
```
Program DMA information in the DMA controller. addr is a bus address.

```
void disable_dma(unsigned int channel);
void enable_dma(unsigned int channel);
```
A DMA channel must be disabled during configuration. These functions change the status of the DMA channel.

```
int get_dma_residue(unsigned int channel);
```
If the driver needs to know how a DMA transfer is proceeding, it can call this function, which returns the number of data transfers that are yet to be completed. After successful completion of DMA, the function returns 0; the value is unpredictable while data is being transferred.

```
void clear_dma_ff(unsigned int channel)
```
The DMA flip-flop is used by the controller to transfer 16-bit values by means of two 8-bit operations. It must be cleared before sending any data to the controller.

CHAPTER 16
Block Drivers

So far, our discussion has been limited to char drivers. There are other types of drivers in Linux systems, however, and the time has come for us to widen our focus somewhat. Accordingly, this chapter discusses block drivers.

A block driver provides access to devices that transfer randomly accessible data in fixed-size blocks—disk drives, primarily. The Linux kernel sees block devices as being fundamentally different from char devices; as a result, block drivers have a distinct interface and their own particular challenges.

Efficient block drivers are critical for performance—and not just for explicit reads and writes in user applications. Modern systems with virtual memory work by shifting (hopefully) unneeded data to secondary storage, which is usually a disk drive. Block drivers are the conduit between core memory and secondary storage; therefore, they can be seen as making up part of the virtual memory subsystem. While it is possible to write a block driver without knowing about struct page and other important memory concepts, anybody needing to write a high-performance driver has to draw upon the material covered in Chapter 15.

Much of the design of the block layer is centered on performance. Many char devices can run below their maximum speed, and the performance of the system as a whole is not affected. The system cannot run well, however, if its block I/O subsystem is not well-tuned. The Linux block driver interface allows you to get the most out of a block device but imposes, necessarily, a degree of complexity that you must deal with. Happily, the 2.6 block interface is much improved over what was found in older kernels.

The discussion in this chapter is, as one would expect, centered on an example driver that implements a block-oriented, memory-based device. It is, essentially, a ramdisk. The kernel already contains a far superior ramdisk implementation, but our driver (called *sbull*) lets us demonstrate the creation of a block driver while minimizing unrelated complexity.

Before getting into the details, let's define a couple of terms precisely. A *block* is a fixed-size chunk of data, the size being determined by the kernel. Blocks are often 4096 bytes, but that value can vary depending on the architecture and the exact file-system being used. A *sector*, in contrast, is a small block whose size is usually determined by the underlying hardware. The kernel expects to be dealing with devices that implement 512-byte sectors. If your device uses a different size, the kernel adapts and avoids generating I/O requests that the hardware cannot handle. It is worth keeping in mind, however, that any time the kernel presents you with a sector number, it is working in a world of 512-byte sectors. If you are using a different hardware sector size, you have to scale the kernel's sector numbers accordingly. We see how that is done in the *sbull* driver.

Registration

Block drivers, like char drivers, must use a set of registration interfaces to make their devices available to the kernel. The concepts are similar, but the details of block device registration are all different. You have a whole new set of data structures and device operations to learn.

Block Driver Registration

The first step taken by most block drivers is to register themselves with the kernel. The function for this task is *register_blkdev* (which is declared in *<linux/fs.h>*):

```
int register_blkdev(unsigned int major, const char *name);
```

The arguments are the major number that your device will be using and the associated name (which the kernel will display in */proc/devices*). If major is passed as 0, the kernel allocates a new major number and returns it to the caller. As always, a negative return value from *register_blkdev* indicates that an error has occurred.

The corresponding function for canceling a block driver registration is:

```
int unregister_blkdev(unsigned int major, const char *name);
```

Here, the arguments must match those passed to *register_blkdev*, or the function returns -EINVAL and not unregister anything.

In the 2.6 kernel, the call to *register_blkdev* is entirely optional. The functions performed by *register_blkdev* have been decreasing over time; the only tasks performed by this call at this point are (1) allocating a dynamic major number if requested, and (2) creating an entry in */proc/devices*. In future kernels, *register_blkdev* may be removed altogether. Meanwhile, however, most drivers still call it; it's traditional.

Disk Registration

While *register_blkdev* can be used to obtain a major number, it does not make any disk drives available to the system. There is a separate registration interface that you must use to manage individual drives. Using this interface requires familiarity with a pair of new structures, so that is where we start.

Block device operations

Char devices make their operations available to the system by way of the file_ operations structure. A similar structure is used with block devices; it is struct block_device_operations, which is declared in *<linux/fs.h>*. The following is a brief overview of the fields found in this structure; we revisit them in more detail when we get into the details of the *sbull* driver:

```
int (*open)(struct inode *inode, struct file *filp);
int (*release)(struct inode *inode, struct file *filp);
```
> Functions that work just like their char driver equivalents; they are called whenever the device is opened and closed. A block driver might respond to an open call by spinning up the device, locking the door (for removable media), etc. If you lock media into the device, you should certainly unlock it in the *release* method.

```
int (*ioctl)(struct inode *inode, struct file *filp, unsigned int cmd,
  unsigned long arg);
```
> Method that implements the *ioctl* system call. The block layer first intercepts a large number of standard requests, however; so most block driver *ioctl* methods are fairly short.

```
int (*media_changed) (struct gendisk *gd);
```
> Method called by the kernel to check whether the user has changed the media in the drive, returning a nonzero value if so. Obviously, this method is only applicable to drives that support removable media (and that are smart enough to make a "media changed" flag available to the driver); it can be omitted in other cases.
>
> The struct gendisk argument is how the kernel represents a single disk; we will be looking at that structure in the next section.

```
int (*revalidate_disk) (struct gendisk *gd);
```
> The *revalidate_disk* method is called in response to a media change; it gives the driver a chance to perform whatever work is required to make the new media ready for use. The function returns an int value, but that value is ignored by the kernel.

```
struct module *owner;
```
> A pointer to the module that owns this structure; it should usually be initialized to THIS_MODULE.

Attentive readers may have noticed an interesting omission from this list: there are no functions that actually read or write data. In the block I/O subsystem, these operations are handled by the *request* function, which deserves a large section of its own and is discussed later in the chapter. Before we can talk about servicing requests, we must complete our discussion of disk registration.

The gendisk structure

struct gendisk (declared in *<linux/genhd.h>*) is the kernel's representation of an individual disk device. In fact, the kernel also uses gendisk structures to represent partitions, but driver authors need not be aware of that. There are several fields in struct gendisk that must be initialized by a block driver:

```
int major;
int first_minor;
int minors;
```
Fields that describe the device number(s) used by the disk. At a minimum, a drive must use at least one minor number. If your drive is to be partitionable, however (and most should be), you want to allocate one minor number for each possible partition as well. A common value for minors is 16, which allows for the "full disk" device and 15 partitions. Some disk drivers use 64 minor numbers for each device.

```
char disk_name[32];
```
Field that should be set to the name of the disk device. It shows up in */proc/partitions* and sysfs.

```
struct block_device_operations *fops;
```
Set of device operations from the previous section.

```
struct request_queue *queue;
```
Structure used by the kernel to manage I/O requests for this device; we examine it in the section "Request Processing."

```
int flags;
```
A (little-used) set of flags describing the state of the drive. If your device has removable media, you should set GENHD_FL_REMOVABLE. CD-ROM drives can set GENHD_FL_CD. If, for some reason, you do not want partition information to show up in */proc/partitions*, set GENHD_FL_SUPPRESS_PARTITION_INFO.

```
sector_t capacity;
```
The capacity of this drive, in 512-byte sectors. The sector_t type can be 64 bits wide. Drivers should not set this field directly; instead, pass the number of sectors to *set_capacity*.

```
void *private_data;
```
Block drivers may use this field for a pointer to their own internal data.

The kernel provides a small set of functions for working with gendisk structures. We introduce them here, then see how *sbull* uses them to make its disk devices available to the system.

struct gendisk is a dynamically allocated structure that requires special kernel manipulation to be initialized; drivers cannot allocate the structure on their own. Instead, you must call:

```
struct gendisk *alloc_disk(int minors);
```

The minors argument should be the number of minor numbers this disk uses; note that you cannot change the minors field later and expect things to work properly.

When a disk is no longer needed, it should be freed with:

```
void del_gendisk(struct gendisk *gd);
```

A gendisk is a reference-counted structure (it contains a kobject). There are *get_disk* and *put_disk* functions available to manipulate the reference count, but drivers should never need to do that. Normally, the call to *del_gendisk* removes the final reference to a gendisk, but there are no guarantees of that. Thus, it is possible that the structure could continue to exist (and your methods could be called) after a call to *del_gendisk*. If you delete the structure when there are no users (that is, after the final *release* or in your module *cleanup* function), however, you can be sure that you will not hear from it again.

Allocating a gendisk structure does not make the disk available to the system. To do that, you must initialize the structure and call *add_disk*:

```
void add_disk(struct gendisk *gd);
```

Keep one important thing in mind here: as soon as you call *add_disk*, the disk is "live" and its methods can be called at any time. In fact, the first such calls will probably happen even before *add_disk* returns; the kernel will read the first few blocks in an attempt to find a partition table. So you should not call *add_disk* until your driver is completely initialized and ready to respond to requests on that disk.

Initialization in sbull

It is time to get down to some examples. The *sbull* driver (available from O'Reilly's FTP site with the rest of the example source) implements a set of in-memory virtual disk drives. For each drive, *sbull* allocates (with *vmalloc*, for simplicity) an array of memory; it then makes that array available via block operations. The *sbull* driver can be tested by partitioning the virtual device, building filesystems on it, and mounting it in the system hierarchy.

Like our other example drivers, *sbull* allows a major number to be specified at compile or module load time. If no number is specified, one is allocated dynamically. Since a call to *register_blkdev* is required for dynamic allocation, *sbull* does so:

```
sbull_major = register_blkdev(sbull_major, "sbull");
if (sbull_major <= 0) {
```

```
        printk(KERN_WARNING "sbull: unable to get major number\n");
        return -EBUSY;
}
```

Also, like the other virtual devices we have presented in this book, the *sbull* device is described by an internal structure:

```
struct sbull_dev {
        int size;                        /* Device size in sectors */
        u8 *data;                        /* The data array */
        short users;                     /* How many users */
        short media_change;              /* Flag a media change? */
        spinlock_t lock;                 /* For mutual exclusion */
        struct request_queue *queue;     /* The device request queue */
        struct gendisk *gd;              /* The gendisk structure */
        struct timer_list timer;         /* For simulated media changes */
};
```

Several steps are required to initialize this structure and make the associated device available to the system. We start with basic initialization and allocation of the underlying memory:

```
memset (dev, 0, sizeof (struct sbull_dev));
dev->size = nsectors*hardsect_size;
dev->data = vmalloc(dev->size);
if (dev->data == NULL) {
    printk (KERN_NOTICE "vmalloc failure.\n");
    return;
}
spin_lock_init(&dev->lock);
```

It's important to allocate and initialize a spinlock before the next step, which is the allocation of the request queue. We look at this process in more detail when we get to request processing; for now, suffice it to say that the necessary call is:

```
dev->queue = blk_init_queue(sbull_request, &dev->lock);
```

Here, *sbull_request* is our *request* function—the function that actually performs block read and write requests. When we allocate a request queue, we must provide a spinlock that controls access to that queue. The lock is provided by the driver rather than the general parts of the kernel because, often, the request queue and other driver data structures fall within the same critical section; they tend to be accessed together. As with any function that allocates memory, *blk_init_queue* can fail, so you must check the return value before continuing.

Once we have our device memory and request queue in place, we can allocate, initialize, and install the corresponding gendisk structure. The code that does this work is:

```
dev->gd = alloc_disk(SBULL_MINORS);
if (! dev->gd) {
    printk (KERN_NOTICE "alloc_disk failure\n");
    goto out_vfree;
}
dev->gd->major = sbull_major;
```

```
dev->gd->first_minor = which*SBULL_MINORS;
dev->gd->fops = &sbull_ops;
dev->gd->queue = dev->queue;
dev->gd->private_data = dev;
snprintf (dev->gd->disk_name, 32, "sbull%c", which + 'a');
set_capacity(dev->gd, nsectors*(hardsect_size/KERNEL_SECTOR_SIZE));
add_disk(dev->gd);
```

Here, SBULL_MINORS is the number of minor numbers each *sbull* device supports. When we set the first minor number for each device, we must take into account all of the numbers taken by prior devices. The name of the disk is set such that the first one is *sbulla*, the second *sbullb*, and so on. User space can then add partition numbers so that the third partition on the second device might be */dev/sbullb3*.

Once everything is set up, we finish with a call to *add_disk*. Chances are that several of our methods will have been called for that disk by the time *add_disk* returns, so we take care to make that call the very last step in the initialization of our device.

A Note on Sector Sizes

As we have mentioned before, the kernel treats every disk as a linear array of 512-byte sectors. Not all hardware uses that sector size, however. Getting a device with a different sector size to work is not particularly hard; it is just a matter of taking care of a few details. The *sbull* device exports a hardsect_size parameter that can be used to change the "hardware" sector size of the device; by looking at its implementation, you can see how to add this sort of support to your own drivers.

The first of those details is to inform the kernel of the sector size your device supports. The hardware sector size is a parameter in the request queue, rather than in the gendisk structure. This size is set with a call to *blk_queue_hardsect_size* immediately after the queue is allocated:

```
blk_queue_hardsect_size(dev->queue, hardsect_size);
```

Once that is done, the kernel adheres to your device's hardware sector size. All I/O requests are properly aligned at the beginning of a hardware sector, and the length of each request is an integral number of sectors. You must remember, however, that the kernel always expresses itself in 512-byte sectors; thus, it is necessary to translate all sector numbers accordingly. So, for example, when *sbull* sets the capacity of the device in its gendisk structure, the call looks like:

```
set_capacity(dev->gd, nsectors*(hardsect_size/KERNEL_SECTOR_SIZE));
```

KERNEL_SECTOR_SIZE is a locally-defined constant that we use to scale between the kernel's 512-byte sectors and whatever size we have been told to use. This sort of calculation pops up frequently as we look at the *sbull* request processing logic.

The Block Device Operations

We had a brief introduction to the block_device_operations structure in the previous section. Now we take some time to look at these operations in a bit more detail before getting into request processing. To that end, it is time to mention one other feature of the *sbull* driver: it pretends to be a removable device. Whenever the last user closes the device, a 30-second timer is set; if the device is not opened during that time, the contents of the device are cleared, and the kernel will be told that the media has been changed. The 30-second delay gives the user time to, for example, mount an *sbull* device after creating a filesystem on it.

The open and release Methods

To implement the simulated media removal, *sbull* must know when the last user has closed the device. A count of users is maintained by the driver. It is the job of the *open* and *close* methods to keep that count current.

The *open* method looks very similar to its char-driver equivalent; it takes the relevant inode and file structure pointers as arguments. When an inode refers to a block device, the field i_bdev->bd_disk contains a pointer to the associated gendisk structure; this pointer can be used to get to a driver's internal data structures for the device. That is, in fact, the first thing that the *sbull open* method does:

```
static int sbull_open(struct inode *inode, struct file *filp)
{
    struct sbull_dev *dev = inode->i_bdev->bd_disk->private_data;

    del_timer_sync(&dev->timer);
    filp->private_data = dev;
    spin_lock(&dev->lock);
    if (! dev->users)
        check_disk_change(inode->i_bdev);
    dev->users++;
    spin_unlock(&dev->lock);
    return 0;
}
```

Once *sbull_open* has its device structure pointer, it calls *del_timer_sync* to remove the "media removal" timer, if any is active. Note that we do not lock the device spinlock until after the timer has been deleted; doing otherwise invites deadlock if the timer function runs before we can delete it. With the device locked, we call a kernel function called *check_disk_change* to check whether a media change has happened. One might argue that the kernel should make that call, but the standard pattern is for drivers to handle it at *open* time.

The last step is to increment the user count and return.

The task of the *release* method is, in contrast, to decrement the user count and, if indicated, start the media removal timer:

```
static int sbull_release(struct inode *inode, struct file *filp)
{
    struct sbull_dev *dev = inode->i_bdev->bd_disk->private_data;

    spin_lock(&dev->lock);
    dev->users--;

    if (!dev->users) {
        dev->timer.expires = jiffies + INVALIDATE_DELAY;
        add_timer(&dev->timer);
    }
    spin_unlock(&dev->lock);

    return 0;
}
```

In a driver that handles a real, hardware device, the *open* and *release* methods would set the state of the driver and hardware accordingly. This work could involve spinning the disk up or down, locking the door of a removable device, allocating DMA buffers, etc.

You may be wondering who actually opens a block device. There are some operations that cause a block device to be opened directly from user space; these include partitioning a disk, building a filesystem on a partition, or running a filesystem checker. A block driver also sees an *open* call when a partition is mounted. In this case, there is no user-space process holding an open file descriptor for the device; the open file is, instead, held by the kernel itself. A block driver cannot tell the difference between a *mount* operation (which opens the device from kernel space) and the invocation of a utility such as *mkfs* (which opens it from user space).

Supporting Removable Media

The block_device_operations structure includes two methods for supporting removable media. If you are writing a driver for a nonremovable device, you can safely omit these methods. Their implementation is relatively straightforward.

The *media_changed* method is called (from *check_disk_change*) to see whether the media has been changed; it should return a nonzero value if this has happened. The *sbull* implementation is simple; it queries a flag that has been set if the media removal timer has expired:

```
int sbull_media_changed(struct gendisk *gd)
{
    struct sbull_dev *dev = gd->private_data;

    return dev->media_change;
}
```

The *revalidate* method is called after a media change; its job is to do whatever is required to prepare the driver for operations on the new media, if any. After the call to *revalidate*, the kernel attempts to reread the partition table and start over with the device. The *sbull* implementation simply resets the media_change flag and zeroes out the device memory to simulate the insertion of a blank disk.

```
int sbull_revalidate(struct gendisk *gd)
{
    struct sbull_dev *dev = gd->private_data;

    if (dev->media_change) {
        dev->media_change = 0;
        memset (dev->data, 0, dev->size);
    }
    return 0;
}
```

The ioctl Method

Block devices can provide an *ioctl* method to perform device control functions. The higher-level block subsystem code intercepts a number of *ioctl* commands before your driver ever gets to see them, however (see *drivers/block/ioctl.c* in the kernel source for the full set). In fact, a modern block driver may not have to implement very many *ioctl* commands at all.

The *sbull ioctl* method handles only one command—a request for the device's geometry:

```
int sbull_ioctl (struct inode *inode, struct file *filp,
            unsigned int cmd, unsigned long arg)
{
    long size;
    struct hd_geometry geo;
    struct sbull_dev *dev = filp->private_data;

    switch(cmd) {
      case HDIO_GETGEO:
        /*
         * Get geometry: since we are a virtual device, we have to make
         * up something plausible.  So we claim 16 sectors, four heads,
         * and calculate the corresponding number of cylinders.  We set the
         * start of data at sector four.
         */
        size = dev->size*(hardsect_size/KERNEL_SECTOR_SIZE);
        geo.cylinders = (size & ~0x3f) >> 6;
        geo.heads = 4;
        geo.sectors = 16;
        geo.start = 4;
        if (copy_to_user((void __user *) arg, &geo, sizeof(geo)))
            return -EFAULT;
```

```
        return 0;
    }

    return -ENOTTY; /* unknown command */
}
```

Providing geometry information may seem like a curious task, since our device is purely virtual and has nothing to do with tracks and cylinders. Even most real-block hardware has been furnished with much more complicated structures for many years. The kernel is not concerned with a block device's geometry; it sees it simply as a linear array of sectors. There are certain user-space utilities that still expect to be able to query a disk's geometry, however. In particular, the *fdisk* tool, which edits partition tables, depends on cylinder information and does not function properly if that information is not available.

We would like the *sbull* device to be partitionable, even with older, simple-minded tools. So, we have provided an *ioctl* method that comes up with a credible fiction for a geometry that could match the capacity of our device. Most disk drivers do something similar. Note that, as usual, the sector count is translated, if need be, to match the 512-byte convention used by the kernel.

Request Processing

The core of every block driver is its *request* function. This function is where the real work gets done—or at least started; all the rest is overhead. Consequently, we spend a fair amount of time looking at request processing in block drivers.

A disk driver's performance can be a critical part of the performance of the system as a whole. Therefore, the kernel's block subsystem has been written with performance very much in mind; it does everything possible to enable your driver to get the most out of the devices it controls. This is a good thing, in that it enables blindingly fast I/O. On the other hand, the block subsystem unnecessarily exposes a great deal of complexity in the driver API. It is possible to write a very simple *request* function (we will see one shortly), but if your driver must perform at a high level on complex hardware, it will be anything but simple.

Introduction to the request Method

The block driver *request* method has the following prototype:

```
    void request(request_queue_t *queue);
```

This function is called whenever the kernel believes it is time for your driver to process some reads, writes, or other operations on the device. The *request* function does not need to actually complete all of the requests on the queue before it returns; indeed, it probably does not complete any of them for most real devices. It must, however, make a start on those requests and ensure that they are all, eventually, processed by the driver.

Every device has a request queue. This is because actual transfers to and from a disk can take place far away from the time the kernel requests them, and because the kernel needs the flexibility to schedule each transfer at the most propitious moment (grouping together, for instance, requests that affect sectors close together on the disk). And the *request* function, you may remember, is associated with a request queue when that queue is created. Let us look back at how *sbull* makes its queue:

```
dev->queue = blk_init_queue(sbull_request, &dev->lock);
```

Thus, when the queue is created, the *request* function is associated with it. We also provided a spinlock as part of the queue creation process. Whenever our *request* function is called, that lock is held by the kernel. As a result, the *request* function is running in an atomic context; it must follow all of the usual rules for atomic code discussed in Chapter 5.

The queue lock also prevents the kernel from queuing any other requests for your device while your *request* function holds the lock. Under some conditions, you may want to consider dropping that lock while the *request* function runs. If you do so, however, you must be sure not to access the request queue, or any other data structure protected by the lock, while the lock is not held. You must also reacquire the lock before the *request* function returns.

Finally, the invocation of the *request* function is (usually) entirely asynchronous with respect to the actions of any user-space process. You cannot assume that the kernel is running in the context of the process that initiated the current request. You do not know if the I/O buffer provided by the request is in kernel or user space. So any sort of operation that explicitly accesses user space is in error and will certainly lead to trouble. As you will see, everything your driver needs to know about the request is contained within the structures passed to you via the request queue.

A Simple request Method

The *sbull* example driver provides a few different methods for request processing. By default, *sbull* uses a method called *sbull_request*, which is meant to be an example of the simplest possible *request* method. Without further ado, here it is:

```
static void sbull_request(request_queue_t *q)
{
    struct request *req;

    while ((req = elv_next_request(q)) != NULL) {
        struct sbull_dev *dev = req->rq_disk->private_data;
        if (! blk_fs_request(req)) {
```

```
            printk (KERN_NOTICE "Skip non-fs request\n");
            end_request(req, 0);
            continue;
        }
        sbull_transfer(dev, req->sector, req->current_nr_sectors,
                req->buffer, rq_data_dir(req));
        end_request(req, 1);
    }
}
```

This function introduces the struct request structure. We will examine struct request in great detail later on; for now, suffice it to say that it represents a block I/O request for us to execute.

The kernel provides the function *elv_next_request* to obtain the first incomplete request on the queue; that function returns NULL when there are no requests to be processed. Note that *elv_next_request* does not remove the request from the queue. If you call it twice with no intervening operations, it returns the same request structure both times. In this simple mode of operation, requests are taken off the queue only when they are complete.

A block request queue can contain requests that do not actually move blocks to and from a disk. Such requests can include vendor-specific, low-level diagnostics operations or instructions relating to specialized device modes, such as the packet writing mode for recordable media. Most block drivers do not know how to handle such requests and simply fail them; *sbull* works in this way as well. The call to *block_fs_request* tells us whether we are looking at a filesystem request—one that moves blocks of data. If a request is not a filesystem request, we pass it to *end_request*:

```
    void end_request(struct request *req, int succeeded);
```

When we dispose of nonfilesystem requests, we pass succeeded as 0 to indicate that we did not successfully complete the request. Otherwise, we call *sbull_transfer* to actually move the data, using a set of fields provided in the request structure:

sector_t sector;
> The index of the beginning sector on our device. Remember that this sector number, like all such numbers passed between the kernel and the driver, is expressed in 512-byte sectors. If your hardware uses a different sector size, you need to scale sector accordingly. For example, if the hardware uses 2048-byte sectors, you need to divide the beginning sector number by four before putting it into a request for the hardware.

unsigned long nr_sectors;
> The number of (512-byte) sectors to be transferred.

```
char *buffer;
```
A pointer to the buffer to or from which the data should be transferred. This pointer is a kernel virtual address and can be dereferenced directly by the driver if need be.

```
rq_data_dir(struct request *req);
```
This macro extracts the direction of the transfer from the request; a zero return value denotes a read from the device, and a nonzero return value denotes a write to the device.

Given this information, the *sbull* driver can implement the actual data transfer with a simple *memcpy* call—our data is already in memory, after all. The function that performs this copy operation (*sbull_transfer*) also handles the scaling of sector sizes and ensures that we do not try to copy beyond the end of our virtual device:

```
static void sbull_transfer(struct sbull_dev *dev, unsigned long sector,
        unsigned long nsect, char *buffer, int write)
{
    unsigned long offset = sector*KERNEL_SECTOR_SIZE;
    unsigned long nbytes = nsect*KERNEL_SECTOR_SIZE;

    if ((offset + nbytes) > dev->size) {
        printk (KERN_NOTICE "Beyond-end write (%ld %ld)\n", offset, nbytes);
        return;
    }
    if (write)
        memcpy(dev->data + offset, buffer, nbytes);
    else
        memcpy(buffer, dev->data + offset, nbytes);
}
```

With the code, *sbull* implements a complete, simple RAM-based disk device. It is not, however, a realistic driver for many types of devices, for a couple of reasons.

The first of those reasons is that *sbull* executes requests synchronously, one at a time. High-performance disk devices are capable of having numerous requests outstanding at the same time; the disk's onboard controller can then choose to execute them in the optimal order (one hopes). As long as we process only the first request in the queue, we can never have multiple requests being fulfilled at a given time. Being able to work with more than one request requires a deeper understanding of request queues and the request structure; the next few sections help build that understanding.

There is another issue to consider, however. The best performance is obtained from disk devices when the system performs large transfers involving multiple sectors that are located together on the disk. The highest cost in a disk operation is always the positioning of the read and write heads; once that is done, the time required to actually read or write the data is almost insignificant. The developers who design and implement filesystems and virtual memory subsystems understand this, so they do their best to locate related data contiguously on the disk and to transfer as many sectors as possible in a single request. The block subsystem also helps in this regard;

request queues contain a great deal of logic aimed at finding adjacent requests and coalescing them into larger operations.

The *shull* driver, however, takes all that work and simply ignores it. Only one buffer is transferred at a time, meaning that the largest single transfer is almost never going to exceed the size of a single page. A block driver can do much better than that, but it requires a deeper understanding of request structures and the bio structures from which requests are built.

The next few sections delve more deeply into how the block layer does its job and the data structures that result from that work.

Request Queues

In the simplest sense, a block request queue is exactly that: a queue of block I/O requests. If you look under the hood, a request queue turns out to be a surprisingly complex data structure. Fortunately, drivers need not worry about most of that complexity.

Request queues keep track of outstanding block I/O requests. But they also play a crucial role in the creation of those requests. The request queue stores parameters that describe what kinds of requests the device is able to service: their maximum size, how many separate segments may go into a request, the hardware sector size, alignment requirements, etc. If your request queue is properly configured, it should never present you with a request that your device cannot handle.

Request queues also implement a plug-in interface that allows the use of multiple *I/O schedulers* (or *elevators*) to be used. An I/O scheduler's job is to present I/O requests to your driver in a way that maximizes performance. To this end, most I/O schedulers accumulate a batch of requests, sort them into increasing (or decreasing) block index order, and present the requests to the driver in that order. The disk head, when given a sorted list of requests, works its way from one end of the disk to the other, much like a full elevator moves in a single direction until all of its "requests" (people waiting to get off) have been satisfied. The 2.6 kernel includes a "deadline scheduler," which makes an effort to ensure that every request is satisfied within a preset maximum time, and an "anticipatory scheduler," which actually stalls a device briefly after a read request in anticipation that another, adjacent read will arrive almost immediately. As of this writing, the default scheduler is the anticipatory scheduler, which seems to give the best interactive system performance.

The I/O scheduler is also charged with merging adjacent requests. When a new I/O request is handed to the scheduler, it searches the queue for requests involving adjacent sectors; if one is found and if the resulting request would not be too large, the two requests are merged.

Request queues have a type of struct request_queue or request_queue_t. This type, and the many functions that operate on it, are defined in *<linux/blkdev.h>*. If you are interested in the implementation of request queues, you can find most of the code in *drivers/block/ll_rw_block.c* and *elevator.c*.

Queue creation and deletion

As we saw in our example code, a request queue is a dynamic data structure that must be created by the block I/O subsystem. The function to create and initialize a request queue is:

```
request_queue_t *blk_init_queue(request_fn_proc *request, spinlock_t *lock);
```

The arguments are, of course, the *request* function for this queue and a spinlock that controls access to the queue. This function allocates memory (quite a bit of memory, actually) and can fail because of this; you should always check the return value before attempting to use the queue.

As part of the initialization of a request queue, you can set the field queuedata (which is a void * pointer) to any value you like. This field is the request queue's equivalent to the private_data we have seen in other structures.

To return a request queue to the system (at module unload time, generally), call *blk_cleanup_queue*:

```
void blk_cleanup_queue(request_queue_t *);
```

After this call, your driver sees no more requests from the given queue and should not reference it again.

Queueing functions

There is a very small set of functions for the manipulation of requests on queues—at least, as far as drivers are concerned. You must hold the queue lock before you call these functions.

The function that returns the next request to process is *elv_next_request*:

```
struct request *elv_next_request(request_queue_t *queue);
```

We have already seen this function in the simple *sbull* example. It returns a pointer to the next request to process (as determined by the I/O scheduler) or NULL if no more requests remain to be processed. *elv_next_request* leaves the request on the queue but marks it as being active; this mark prevents the I/O scheduler from attempting to merge other requests with this one once you start to execute it.

To actually remove a request from a queue, use *blkdev_dequeue_request*:

```
void blkdev_dequeue_request(struct request *req);
```

If your driver operates on multiple requests from the same queue simultaneously, it must dequeue them in this manner.

Should you need to put a dequeued request back on the queue for some reason, you can call:

```
void elv_requeue_request(request_queue_t *queue, struct request *req);
```

Queue control functions

The block layer exports a set of functions that can be used by a driver to control how a request queue operates. These functions include:

```
void blk_stop_queue(request_queue_t *queue);
void blk_start_queue(request_queue_t *queue);
```
> If your device has reached a state where it can handle no more outstanding commands, you can call *blk_stop_queue* to tell the block layer. After this call, your *request* function will not be called until you call *blk_start_queue*. Needless to say, you should not forget to restart the queue when your device can handle more requests. The queue lock must be held when calling either of these functions.

```
void blk_queue_bounce_limit(request_queue_t *queue, u64 dma_addr);
```
> Function that tells the kernel the highest physical address to which your device can perform DMA. If a request comes in containing a reference to memory above the limit, a bounce buffer will be used for the operation; this is, of course, an expensive way to perform block I/O and should be avoided whenever possible. You can provide any reasonable physical address in this argument, or make use of the predefined symbols BLK_BOUNCE_HIGH (use bounce buffers for high-memory pages), BLK_BOUNCE_ISA (the driver can DMA only into the 16-MB ISA zone), or BLK_BOUNCE_ANY (the driver can perform DMA to any address). The default value is BLK_BOUNCE_HIGH.

```
void blk_queue_max_sectors(request_queue_t *queue, unsigned short max);
void blk_queue_max_phys_segments(request_queue_t *queue, unsigned short max);
void blk_queue_max_hw_segments(request_queue_t *queue, unsigned short max);
void blk_queue_max_segment_size(request_queue_t *queue, unsigned int max);
```
> Functions that set parameters describing the requests that can be satisfied by this device. *blk_queue_max_sectors* can be used to set the maximum size of any request in (512-byte) sectors; the default is 255. *blk_queue_max_phys_segments* and *blk_queue_max_hw_segments* both control how many physical segments (nonadjacent areas in system memory) may be contained within a single request. Use *blk_queue_max_phys_segments* to say how many segments your driver is prepared to cope with; this may be the size of a staticly allocated scatterlist, for example. *blk_queue_max_hw_segments*, in contrast, is the maximum number of segments that the device itself can handle. Both of these parameters default to 128. Finally, *blk_queue_max_segment_size* tells the kernel how large any individual segment of a request can be in bytes; the default is 65,536 bytes.

```
blk_queue_segment_boundary(request_queue_t *queue, unsigned long mask);
```
Some devices cannot handle requests that cross a particular size memory boundary; if your device is one of those, use this function to tell the kernel about that boundary. For example, if your device has trouble with requests that cross a 4-MB boundary, pass in a mask of 0x3fffff. The default mask is 0xffffffff.

```
void blk_queue_dma_alignment(request_queue_t *queue, int mask);
```
Function that tells the kernel about the memory alignment constraints your device imposes on DMA transfers. All requests are created with the given alignment, and the length of the request also matches the alignment. The default mask is 0x1ff, which causes all requests to be aligned on 512-byte boundaries.

```
void blk_queue_hardsect_size(request_queue_t *queue, unsigned short max);
```
Tells the kernel about your device's hardware sector size. All requests generated by the kernel are a multiple of this size and are properly aligned. All communications between the block layer and the driver continues to be expressed in 512-byte sectors, however.

The Anatomy of a Request

In our simple example, we encountered the request structure. However, we have barely scratched the surface of that complicated data structure. In this section, we look, in some detail, at how block I/O requests are represented in the Linux kernel.

Each request structure represents one block I/O request, although it may have been formed through a merger of several independent requests at a higher level. The sectors to be transferred for any particular request may be distributed throughout main memory, although they always correspond to a set of consecutive sectors on the block device. The request is represented as a set of segments, each of which corresponds to one in-memory buffer. The kernel may join multiple requests that involve adjacent sectors on the disk, but it never combines read and write operations within a single request structure. The kernel also makes sure not to combine requests if the result would violate any of the request queue limits described in the previous section.

A request structure is implemented, essentially, as a linked list of bio structures combined with some housekeeping information to enable the driver to keep track of its position as it works through the request. The bio structure is a low-level description of a portion of a block I/O request; we take a look at it now.

The bio structure

When the kernel, in the form of a filesystem, the virtual memory subsystem, or a system call, decides that a set of blocks must be transferred to or from a block I/O device; it puts together a bio structure to describe that operation. That structure is then handed to the block I/O code, which merges it into an existing request structure or, if need be, creates a new one. The bio structure contains everything that a block driver needs to carry out the request without reference to the user-space process that caused that request to be initiated.

The bio structure, which is defined in *<linux/bio.h>*, contains a number of fields that may be of use to driver authors:

sector_t bi_sector;
> The first (512-byte) sector to be transferred for this bio.

unsigned int bi_size;
> The size of the data to be transferred, in bytes. Instead, it is often easier to use bio_sectors(bio), a macro that gives the size in sectors.

unsigned long bi_flags;
> A set of flags describing the bio; the least significant bit is set if this is a write request (although the macro bio_data_dir(bio) should be used instead of looking at the flags directly).

unsigned short bio_phys_segments;
unsigned short bio_hw_segments;
> The number of physical segments contained within this BIO and the number of segments seen by the hardware after DMA mapping is done, respectively.

The core of a bio, however, is an array called bi_io_vec, which is made up of the following structure:

```
struct bio_vec {
        struct page     *bv_page;
        unsigned int    bv_len;
        unsigned int    bv_offset;
};
```

Figure 16-1 shows how these structures all tie together. As you can see, by the time a block I/O request is turned into a bio structure, it has been broken down into individual pages of physical memory. All a driver needs to do is to step through this array of structures (there are bi_vcnt of them), and transfer data within each page (but only len bytes starting at offset).

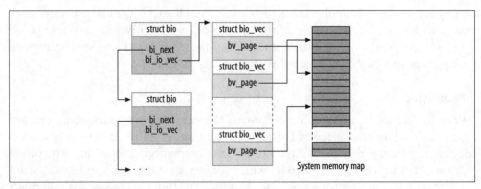

Figure 16-1. The bio structure

Working directly with the `bi_io_vec` array is discouraged in the interest of kernel developers being able to change the bio structure in the future without breaking things. To that end, a set of macros has been provided to ease the process of working with the bio structure. The place to start is with `bio_for_each_segment`, which simply loops through every unprocessed entry in the `bi_io_vec` array. This macro should be used as follows:

```
int segno;
struct bio_vec *bvec;

bio_for_each_segment(bvec, bio, segno) {
    /* Do something with this segment
}
```

Within this loop, bvec points to the current `bio_vec` entry, and segno is the current segment number. These values can be used to set up DMA transfers (an alternative way using *blk_rq_map_sg* is described in the section "Block requests and DMA"). If you need to access the pages directly, you should first ensure that a proper kernel virtual address exists; to that end, you can use:

```
char *__bio_kmap_atomic(struct bio *bio, int i, enum km_type type);
void __bio_kunmap_atomic(char *buffer, enum km_type type);
```

This low-level function allows you to directly map the buffer found in a given `bio_vec`, as indicated by the index i. An atomic kmap is created; the caller must provide the appropriate slot to use (as described in the section "The Memory Map and Struct Page" in Chapter 15).

The block layer also maintains a set of pointers within the bio structure to keep track of the current state of request processing. Several macros exist to provide access to that state:

`struct page *bio_page(struct bio *bio);`
Returns a pointer to the page structure representing the page to be transferred next.

`int bio_offset(struct bio *bio);`
Returns the offset within the page for the data to be transferred.

`int bio_cur_sectors(struct bio *bio);`
Returns the number of sectors to be transferred out of the current page.

`char *bio_data(struct bio *bio);`
Returns a kernel logical address pointing to the data to be transferred. Note that this address is available only if the page in question is not located in high memory; calling it in other situations is a bug. By default, the block subsystem does not pass high-memory buffers to your driver, but if you have changed that setting with *blk_queue_bounce_limit*, you probably should not be using bio_data.

```
char *bio_kmap_irq(struct bio *bio, unsigned long *flags);
void bio_kunmap_irq(char *buffer, unsigned long *flags);
```
> *bio_kmap_irq* returns a kernel virtual address for any buffer, regardless of whether it resides in high or low memory. An atomic kmap is used, so your driver cannot sleep while this mapping is active. Use *bio_kunmap_irq* to unmap the buffer. Note that the flags argument is passed by pointer here. Note also that since an atomic kmap is used, you cannot map more than one segment at a time.

All of the functions just described access the "current" buffer—the first buffer that, as far as the kernel knows, has not been transferred. Drivers often want to work through several buffers in the bio before signaling completion on any of them (with *end_that_request_first*, to be described shortly), so these functions are often not useful. Several other macros exist for working with the internals of the bio structure (see *<linux/bio.h>* for details).

Request structure fields

Now that we have an idea of how the bio structure works, we can get deep into struct request and see how request processing works. The fields of this structure include:

```
sector_t hard_sector;
unsigned long hard_nr_sectors;
unsigned int hard_cur_sectors;
```
> Fields that track the sectors that the driver has yet to complete. The first sector that has *not* been transferred is stored in hard_sector, the total number of sectors yet to transfer is in hard_nr_sectors, and the number of sectors remaining in the current bio is hard_cur_sectors. These fields are intended for use only within the block subsystem; drivers should not make use of them.

```
struct bio *bio;
```
> bio is the linked list of bio structures for this request. You should not access this field directly; use *rq_for_each_bio* (described later) instead.

```
char *buffer;
```
> The simple driver example earlier in this chapter used this field to find the buffer for the transfer. With our deeper understanding, we can now see that this field is simply the result of calling *bio_data* on the current bio.

```
unsigned short nr_phys_segments;
```
> The number of distinct segments occupied by this request in physical memory after adjacent pages have been merged.

```
struct list_head queuelist;
```
> The linked-list structure (as described in the section "Linked Lists" in Chapter 11) that links the request into the request queue. If (and only if) you

```
```

remove the request from the queue with *blkdev_dequeue_request*, you may use this list head to track the request in an internal list maintained by your driver.

Figure 16-2 shows how the request structure and its component bio structures fit together. In the figure, the request has been partially satisfied; the cbio and buffer fields point to the first bio that has not yet been transferred.

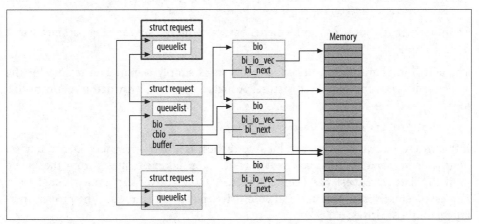

Figure 16-2. A request queue with a partially processed request

There are many other fields inside the request structure, but the list in this section should be enough for most driver writers.

Barrier requests

The block layer reorders requests before your driver sees them to improve I/O performance. Your driver, too, can reorder requests if there is a reason to do so. Often, this reordering happens by passing multiple requests to the drive and letting the hardware figure out the optimal ordering. There is a problem with unrestricted reordering of requests, however: some applications require guarantees that certain operations will complete before others are started. Relational database managers, for example, must be absolutely sure that their journaling information has been flushed to the drive before executing a transaction on the database contents. Journaling filesystems, which are now in use on most Linux systems, have very similar ordering constraints. If the wrong operations are reordered, the result can be severe, undetected data corruption.

The 2.6 block layer addresses this problem with the concept of a *barrier request*. If a request is marked with the REQ_HARDBARRER flag, it must be written to the drive before any following request is initiated. By "written to the drive," we mean that the data must actually reside and be persistent on the physical media. Many drives perform caching of write requests; this caching improves performance, but it can defeat the purpose of barrier requests. If a power failure occurs when the critical data is still sitting in the drive's cache, that data is still lost even if the drive has reported completion. So a driver that implements barrier requests must take steps to force the drive to actually write the data to the media.

If your driver honors barrier requests, the first step is to inform the block layer of this fact. Barrier handling is another of the request queues; it is set with:

```
void blk_queue_ordered(request_queue_t *queue, int flag);
```

To indicate that your driver implements barrier requests, set the flag parameter to a nonzero value.

The actual implementation of barrier requests is simply a matter of testing for the associated flag in the request structure. A macro has been provided to perform this test:

```
int blk_barrier_rq(struct request *req);
```

If this macro returns a nonzero value, the request is a barrier request. Depending on how your hardware works, you may have to stop taking requests from the queue until the barrier request has been completed. Other drives can understand barrier requests themselves; in this case, all your driver has to do is to issue the proper operations for those drives.

Nonretryable requests

Block drivers often attempt to retry requests that fail the first time. This behavior can lead to a more reliable system and help to avoid data loss. The kernel, however, sometimes marks requests as not being retryable. Such requests should simply fail as quickly as possible if they cannot be executed on the first try.

If your driver is considering retrying a failed request, it should first make a call to:

```
int blk_noretry_request(struct request *req);
```

If this macro returns a nonzero value, your driver should simply abort the request with an error code instead of retrying it.

Request Completion Functions

There are, as we will see, several different ways of working through a request structure. All of them make use of a couple of common functions, however, which handle the completion of an I/O request or parts of a request. Both of these functions are atomic and can be safely called from an atomic context.

When your device has completed transferring some or all of the sectors in an I/O request, it must inform the block subsystem with:

```
int end_that_request_first(struct request *req, int success, int count);
```

This function tells the block code that your driver has finished with the transfer of count sectors starting where you last left off. If the I/O was successful, pass success as 1; otherwise pass 0. Note that you must signal completion in order from the first sector to the last; if your driver and device somehow conspire to complete requests out of order, you have to store the out-of-order completion status until the intervening sectors have been transferred.

The return value from *end_that_request_first* is an indication of whether all sectors in this request have been transferred or not. A return value of 0 means that all sectors have been transferred and that the request is complete. At that point, you must dequeue the request with *blkdev_dequeue_request* (if you have not already done so) and pass it to:

```
void end_that_request_last(struct request *req);
```

end_that_request_last informs whoever is waiting for the request that it has completed and recycles the request structure; it must be called with the queue lock held.

In our simple *sbull* example, we didn't use any of the above functions. That example, instead, is called *end_request*. To show the effects of this call, here is the entire *end_request* function as seen in the 2.6.10 kernel:

```
void end_request(struct request *req, int uptodate)
{
    if (!end_that_request_first(req, uptodate, req->hard_cur_sectors)) {
        add_disk_randomness(req->rq_disk);
        blkdev_dequeue_request(req);
        end_that_request_last(req);
    }
}
```

The function *add_disk_randomness* uses the timing of block I/O requests to contribute entropy to the system's random number pool; it should be called only if the disk's timing is truly random. That is true for most mechanical devices, but it is not true for a memory-based virtual device, such as *sbull*. For this reason, the more complicated version of *sbull* shown in the next section does not call *add_disk_randomness*.

Working with bios

You now know enough to write a block driver that works directly with the bio structures that make up a request. An example might help, however. If the *sbull* driver is loaded with the request_mode parameter set to 1, it registers a bio-aware *request* function instead of the simple function we saw above. That function looks like this:

```
static void sbull_full_request(request_queue_t *q)
{
    struct request *req;
    int sectors_xferred;
    struct sbull_dev *dev = q->queuedata;

    while ((req = elv_next_request(q)) != NULL) {
        if (! blk_fs_request(req)) {
            printk (KERN_NOTICE "Skip non-fs request\n");
```

```
                end_request(req, 0);
                continue;
            }
            sectors_xferred = sbull_xfer_request(dev, req);
            if (! end_that_request_first(req, 1, sectors_xferred)) {
                blkdev_dequeue_request(req);
                end_that_request_last(req);
            }
        }
    }
```

This function simply takes each request, passes it to *sbull_xfer_request*, then completes it with *end_that_request_first* and, if necessary, *end_that_request_last*. Thus, this function is handling the high-level queue and request management parts of the problem. The job of actually executing a request, however, falls to *sbull_xfer_request*:

```
static int sbull_xfer_request(struct sbull_dev *dev, struct request *req)
{
    struct bio *bio;
    int nsect = 0;

    rq_for_each_bio(bio, req) {
        sbull_xfer_bio(dev, bio);
        nsect += bio->bi_size/KERNEL_SECTOR_SIZE;
    }
    return nsect;
}
```

Here we introduce another macro: *rq_for_each_bio*. As you might expect, this macro simply steps through each bio structure in the request, giving us a pointer that we can pass to *sbull_xfer_bio* for the transfer. That function looks like:

```
static int sbull_xfer_bio(struct sbull_dev *dev, struct bio *bio)
{
    int i;
    struct bio_vec *bvec;
    sector_t sector = bio->bi_sector;

    /* Do each segment independently. */
    bio_for_each_segment(bvec, bio, i) {
        char *buffer = __bio_kmap_atomic(bio, i, KM_USER0);
        sbull_transfer(dev, sector, bio_cur_sectors(bio),
                buffer, bio_data_dir(bio) == WRITE);
        sector += bio_cur_sectors(bio);
        __bio_kunmap_atomic(bio, KM_USER0);
    }
    return 0; /* Always "succeed" */
}
```

This function simply steps through each segment in the bio structure, gets a kernel virtual address to access the buffer, then calls the same *sbull_transfer* function we saw earlier to copy the data over.

Each device has its own needs, but, as a general rule, the code just shown should serve as a model for many situations where digging through the bio structures is needed.

Block requests and DMA

If you are working on a high-performance block driver, chances are you will be using DMA for the actual data transfers. A block driver can certainly step through the bio structures, as described above, create a DMA mapping for each one, and pass the result to the device. There is an easier way, however, if your device can do scatter/gather I/O. The function:

```
int blk_rq_map_sg(request_queue_t *queue, struct request *req,
                  struct scatterlist *list);
```

fills in the given list with the full set of segments from the given request. Segments that are adjacent in memory are coalesced prior to insertion into the scatterlist, so you need not try to detect them yourself. The return value is the number of entries in the list. The function also passes back, in its third argument, a scatterlist suitable for passing to *dma_map_sg*. (See the section "Scatter-gather mappings" in Chapter 15 for more information on *dma_map_sg*.)

Your driver must allocate the storage for the scatterlist before calling *blk_rq_map_sg*. The list must be able to hold at least as many entries as the request has physical segments; the struct request field nr_phys_segments holds that count, which will not exceed the maximum number of physical segments specified with *blk_queue_max_phys_segments*.

If you do not want *blk_rq_map_sg* to coalesce adjacent segments, you can change the default behavior with a call such as:

```
clear_bit(QUEUE_FLAG_CLUSTER, &queue->queue_flags);
```

Some SCSI disk drivers mark their request queue in this way, since they do not benefit from the coalescing of requests.

Doing without a request queue

Previously, we have discussed the work the kernel does to optimize the order of requests in the queue; this work involves sorting requests and, perhaps, even stalling the queue to allow an anticipated request to arrive. These techniques help the system's performance when dealing with a real, spinning disk drive. They are completely wasted, however, with a device like *sbull*. Many block-oriented devices, such as flash memory arrays, readers for media cards used in digital cameras, and RAM disks have truly random-access performance and do not benefit from advanced-request queueing logic. Other devices, such as software RAID arrays or virtual disks created by logical volume managers, do not have the performance characteristics for which the block layer's request queues are optimized. For this kind of device, it would be better to accept requests directly from the block layer and not bother with the request queue at all.

For these situations, the block layer supports a "no queue" mode of operation. To make use of this mode, your driver must provide a "make request" function, rather than a *request* function. The *make_request* function has this prototype:

```
typedef int (make_request_fn) (request_queue_t *q, struct bio *bio);
```

Note that a request queue is still present, even though it will never actually hold any requests. The *make_request* function takes as its main parameter a bio structure, which represents one or more buffers to be transferred. The *make_request* function can do one of two things: it can either perform the transfer directly, or it can redirect the request to another device.

Performing the transfer directly is just a matter of working through the bio with the accessor methods we described earlier. Since there is no request structure to work with, however, your function should signal completion directly to the creator of the bio structure with a call to *bio_endio*:

```
void bio_endio(struct bio *bio, unsigned int bytes, int error);
```

Here, bytes is the number of bytes you have transferred so far. It can be less than the number of bytes represented by the bio as a whole; in this way, you can signal partial completion, and update the internal "current buffer" pointers within the bio. You should either call *bio_endio* again as your device makes further process, or signal an error if you are unable to complete the request. Errors are indicated by providing a nonzero value for the error parameter; this value is normally an error code such as -EIO. The *make_request* should return 0, regardless of whether the I/O is successful.

If *sbull* is loaded with request_mode=2, it operates with a *make_request* function. Since *sbull* already has a function that can transfer a single bio, the *make_request* function is simple:

```
static int sbull_make_request(request_queue_t *q, struct bio *bio)
{
    struct sbull_dev *dev = q->queuedata;
    int status;

    status = sbull_xfer_bio(dev, bio);
    bio_endio(bio, bio->bi_size, status);
    return 0;
}
```

Please note that you should never call *bio_endio* from a regular *request* function; that job is handled by *end_that_request_first* instead.

Some block drivers, such as those implementing volume managers and software RAID arrays, really need to redirect the request to another device that handles the actual I/O. Writing such a driver is beyond the scope of this book. We note, however, that if the *make_request* function returns a nonzero value, the bio is submitted again. A "stacking" driver can, therefore, modify the bi_bdev field to point to a different device, change the starting sector value, then return; the block system then passes the bio to the new device. There is also a *bio_split* call that can be used to split a bio into multiple chunks for submission to more than one device. Although if the queue parameters are set up correctly, splitting a bio in this way should almost never be necessary.

Either way, you must tell the block subsystem that your driver is using a custom *make_request* function. To do so, you must allocate a request queue with:

```
request_queue_t *blk_alloc_queue(int flags);
```

This function differs from *blk_init_queue* in that it does not actually set up the queue to hold requests. The flags argument is a set of allocation flags to be used in allocating memory for the queue; usually the right value is GFP_KERNEL. Once you have a queue, pass it and your *make_request* function to *blk_queue_make_request*:

```
void blk_queue_make_request(request_queue_t *queue, make_request_fn *func);
```

The *sbull* code to set up the *make_request* function looks like:

```
dev->queue = blk_alloc_queue(GFP_KERNEL);
if (dev->queue == NULL)
    goto out_vfree;
blk_queue_make_request(dev->queue, sbull_make_request);
```

For the curious, some time spent digging through *drivers/block/ll_rw_block.c* shows that all queues have a *make_request* function. The default version, *generic_make_request*, handles the incorporation of the bio into a request structure. By providing a *make_request* function of its own, a driver is really just overriding a specific *request queue* method and sorting out much of the work.

Some Other Details

This section covers a few other aspects of the block layer that may be of interest for advanced drivers. None of the following facilities need to be used to write a correct driver, but they may be helpful in some situations.

Command Pre-Preparation

The block layer provides a mechanism for drivers to examine and preprocess requests before they are returned from *elv_next_request*. This mechanism allows drivers to set up the actual drive commands ahead of time, decide whether the request can be handled at all, or perform other sorts of housekeeping.

If you want to use this feature, create a command preparation function that fits this prototype:

```
typedef int (prep_rq_fn) (request_queue_t *queue, struct request *req);
```

The request structure includes a field called cmd, which is an array of BLK_MAX_CDB bytes; this array may be used by the preparation function to store the actual hardware command (or any other useful information). This function should return one of the following values:

BLKPREP_OK

> Command preparation went normally, and the request can be handed to your driver's *request* function.

BLKPREP_KILL

> This request cannot be completed; it is failed with an error code.

BLKPREP_DEFER

> This request cannot be completed at this time. It stays at the front of the queue but is not handed to the *request* function.

The preparation function is called by *elv_next_request* immediately before the request is returned to your driver. If this function returns BLKPREP_DEFER, the return value from *elv_next_request* to your driver is NULL. This mode of operation can be useful if, for example, your device has reached the maximum number of requests it can have outstanding.

To have the block layer call your preparation function, pass it to:

```
void blk_queue_prep_rq(request_queue_t *queue, prep_rq_fn *func);
```

By default, request queues have no preparation function.

Tagged Command Queueing

Hardware that can have multiple requests active at once usually supports some form of *tagged command queueing* (TCQ). TCQ is simply the technique of attaching an integer "tag" to each request so that when the drive completes one of those requests, it can tell the driver which one. In previous versions of the kernel, block drivers that implemented TCQ had to do all of the work themselves; in 2.6, a TCQ support infrastructure has been added to the block layer for all drivers to use.

If your drive performs tagged command queueing, you should inform the kernel of that fact at initialization time with a call to:

```
int blk_queue_init_tags(request_queue_t *queue, int depth,
                        struct blk_queue_tag *tags);
```

Here, queue is your request queue, and depth is the number of tagged requests your device can have outstanding at any given time. tags is an optional pointer to an array of struct blk_queue_tag structures; there must be depth of them. Normally, tags can be passed as NULL, and *blk_queue_init_tags* allocates the array. If, however, you need to share the same tags between multiple devices, you can pass the tags array pointer (stored in the queue_tags field) from another request queue. You should never actually allocate the `tags` array yourself; the block layer needs to initialize the array and does not export the initialization function to modules.

Since *blk_queue_init_tags* allocates memory, it can fail; it returns a negative error code to the caller in that case.

If the number of tags your device can handle changes, you can inform the kernel with:

```
int blk_queue_resize_tags(request_queue_t *queue, int new_depth);
```

The queue lock must be held during the call. This call can fail, returning a negative error code in that case.

The association of a tag with a request structure is done with *blk_queue_start_tag*, which must be called with the queue lock held:

```
int blk_queue_start_tag(request_queue_t *queue, struct request *req);
```

If a tag is available, this function allocates it for this request, stores the tag number in req->tag, and returns 0. It also dequeues the request from the queue and links it into its own tag-tracking structure, so your driver should take care not to dequeue the request itself if it's using tags. If no more tags are available, *blk_queue_start_tag* leaves the request on the queue and returns a nonzero value.

When all transfers for a given request have been completed, your driver should return the tag with:

```
void blk_queue_end_tag(request_queue_t *queue, struct request *req);
```

Once again, you must hold the queue lock before calling this function. The call should be made after *end_that_request_first* returns 0 (meaning that the request is complete) but before calling *end_that_request_last*. Remember that the request is already dequeued, so it would be a mistake for your driver to do so at this point.

If you need to find the request associated with a given tag (when the drive reports completion, for example), use *blk_queue_find_tag*:

```
struct request *blk_queue_find_tag(request_queue_t *qeue, int tag);
```

The return value is the associated request structure, unless something has gone truly wrong.

If things really do go wrong, your driver may find itself having to reset or perform some other act of violence against one of its devices. In that case, any outstanding tagged commands will not be completed. The block layer provides a function that can help with the recovery effort in such situations:

```
void blk_queue_invalidate_tags(request_queue_t *queue);
```

This function returns all outstanding tags to the pool and puts the associated requests back into the request queue. The queue lock must be held when you call this function.

Quick Reference

```
#include <linux/fs.h>
int register_blkdev(unsigned int major, const char *name);
int unregister_blkdev(unsigned int major, const char *name);
```
> *register_blkdev* registers a block driver with the kernel and, optionally, obtains a major number. A driver can be unregistered with *unregister_blkdev*.

```
struct block_device_operations
```
> Structure that holds most of the methods for block drivers.

```
#include <linux/genhd.h>
struct gendisk;
```
> Structure that describes a single block device within the kernel.

```
struct gendisk *alloc_disk(int minors);
void add_disk(struct gendisk *gd);
```
> Functions that allocate gendisk structures and return them to the system.

```
void set_capacity(struct gendisk *gd, sector_t sectors);
```
> Stores the capacity of the device (in 512-byte sectors) within the gendisk structure.

```
void add_disk(struct gendisk *gd);
```
> Adds a disk to the kernel. As soon as this function is called, your disk's methods can be invoked by the kernel.

```
int check_disk_change(struct block_device *bdev);
```
> A kernel function that checks for a media change in the given disk drive and takes the required cleanup action when such a change is detected.

```
#include <linux/blkdev.h>
request_queue_t blk_init_queue(request_fn_proc *request, spinlock_t *lock);
void blk_cleanup_queue(request_queue_t *);
```
> Functions that handle the creation and deletion of block request queues.

```
struct request *elv_next_request(request_queue_t *queue);
void end_request(struct request *req, int success);
```
> *elv_next_request* obtains the next request from a request queue; *end_request* may be used in very simple drivers to mark the completion of (or part of) a request.

```
void blkdev_dequeue_request(struct request *req);
void elv_requeue_request(request_queue_t *queue, struct request *req);
```
> Functions that remove a request from a queue and put it back on if necessary.

```
void blk_stop_queue(request_queue_t *queue);
void blk_start_queue(request_queue_t *queue);
```
> If you need to prevent further calls to your *request* method, a call to *blk_stop_queue* does the trick. A call to *blk_start_queue* is necessary to cause your *request* method to be invoked again.

```
void blk_queue_bounce_limit(request_queue_t *queue, u64 dma_addr);
void blk_queue_max_sectors(request_queue_t *queue, unsigned short max);
void blk_queue_max_phys_segments(request_queue_t *queue, unsigned short max);
void blk_queue_max_hw_segments(request_queue_t *queue, unsigned short max);
void blk_queue_max_segment_size(request_queue_t *queue, unsigned int max);
blk_queue_segment_boundary(request_queue_t *queue, unsigned long mask);
void blk_queue_dma_alignment(request_queue_t *queue, int mask);
void blk_queue_hardsect_size(request_queue_t *queue, unsigned short max);
```
> Functions that set various queue parameters that control how requests are created for a particular device; the parameters are described in the section "Queue control functions."

```
#include <linux/bio.h>
struct bio;
```
> Low-level structure representing a portion of a block I/O request.

```
bio_sectors(struct bio *bio);
bio_data_dir(struct bio *bio);
```
> Two macros that yield the size and direction of a transfer described by a bio structure.

```
bio_for_each_segment(bvec, bio, segno);
```
> A pseudocontrol structure used to loop through the segments that make up a bio structure.

```
char *__bio_kmap_atomic(struct bio *bio, int i, enum km_type type);
void __bio_kunmap_atomic(char *buffer, enum km_type type);
```
> *__bio_kmap_atomic* may be used to create a kernel virtual address for a given segment within a bio structure. The mapping must be undone with *__bio_kunmap_atomic*.

```
struct page *bio_page(struct bio *bio);
int bio_offset(struct bio *bio);
int bio_cur_sectors(struct bio *bio);
char *bio_data(struct bio *bio);
char *bio_kmap_irq(struct bio *bio, unsigned long *flags);
void bio_kunmap_irq(char *buffer, unsigned long *flags);
```
> A set of accessor macros that provide access to the "current" segment within a bio structure.

```
void blk_queue_ordered(request_queue_t *queue, int flag);
int blk_barrier_rq(struct request *req);
```
> Call *blk_queue_ordered* if your driver implements barrier requests—as it should. The macro *blk_barrier_rq* returns a nonzero value if the current request is a barrier request.

```
int blk_noretry_request(struct request *req);
```
This macro returns a nonzero value if the given request should not be retried on errors.

```
int end_that_request_first(struct request *req, int success, int count);
void end_that_request_last(struct request *req);
```
Use *end_that_request_first* to indicate completion of a portion of a block I/O request. When that function returns 0, the request is complete and should be passed to *end_that_request_last*.

```
rq_for_each_bio(bio, request)
```
Another macro-implemented control structure; it steps through each bio that makes up a request.

```
int blk_rq_map_sg(request_queue_t *queue, struct request *req, struct
  scatterlist *list);
```
Fills the given scatterlist with the information needed to map the buffers in the given request for a DMA transfer.

```
typedef int (make_request_fn) (request_queue_t *q, struct bio *bio);
```
The prototype for the *make_request* function.

```
void bio_endio(struct bio *bio, unsigned int bytes, int error);
```
Signal completion for a given bio. This function should be used only if your driver obtained the bio directly from the block layer via the *make_request* function.

```
request_queue_t *blk_alloc_queue(int flags);
void blk_queue_make_request(request_queue_t *queue, make_request_fn *func);
```
Use *blk_alloc_queue* to allocate a request queue that is used with a custom *make_request* function. That function should be set with *blk_queue_make_request*.

```
typedef int (prep_rq_fn) (request_queue_t *queue, struct request *req);
void blk_queue_prep_rq(request_queue_t *queue, prep_rq_fn *func);
```
The prototype and setup functions for a command preparation function, which can be used to prepare the necessary hardware command before the request is passed to your *request* function.

```
int blk_queue_init_tags(request_queue_t *queue, int depth, struct
  blk_queue_tag *tags);
int blk_queue_resize_tags(request_queue_t *queue, int new_depth);
int blk_queue_start_tag(request_queue_t *queue, struct request *req);
void blk_queue_end_tag(request_queue_t *queue, struct request *req);
struct request *blk_queue_find_tag(request_queue_t *qeue, int tag);
void blk_queue_invalidate_tags(request_queue_t *queue);
```
Support functions for drivers using tagged command queueing.

## CHAPTER 17

Network Drivers

Having discussed char and block drivers, we are now ready to move on to the world of networking. Network interfaces are the third standard class of Linux devices, and this chapter describes how they interact with the rest of the kernel.

The role of a network interface within the system is similar to that of a mounted block device. A block device registers its disks and methods with the kernel, and then "transmits" and "receives" blocks on request, by means of its *request* function. Similarly, a network interface must register itself within specific kernel data structures in order to be invoked when packets are exchanged with the outside world.

There are a few important differences between mounted disks and packet-delivery interfaces. To begin with, a disk exists as a special file in the */dev* directory, whereas a network interface has no such entry point. The normal file operations (read, write, and so on) do not make sense when applied to network interfaces, so it is not possible to apply the Unix "everything is a file" approach to them. Thus, network interfaces exist in their own namespace and export a different set of operations.

Although you may object that applications use the *read* and *write* system calls when using sockets, those calls act on a software object that is distinct from the interface. Several hundred sockets can be multiplexed on the same physical interface.

But the most important difference between the two is that block drivers operate only in response to requests from the kernel, whereas network drivers receive packets asynchronously from the outside. Thus, while a block driver is *asked* to send a buffer toward the kernel, the network device *asks* to push incoming packets toward the kernel. The kernel interface for network drivers is designed for this different mode of operation.

Network drivers also have to be prepared to support a number of administrative tasks, such as setting addresses, modifying transmission parameters, and maintaining traffic and error statistics. The API for network drivers reflects this need and, therefore, looks somewhat different from the interfaces we have seen so far.

The network subsystem of the Linux kernel is designed to be completely protocol-independent. This applies to both networking protocols (Internet protocol [IP] versus IPX or other protocols) and hardware protocols (Ethernet versus token ring, etc.). Interaction between a network driver and the kernel properly deals with one network packet at a time; this allows protocol issues to be hidden neatly from the driver and the physical transmission to be hidden from the protocol.

This chapter describes how the network interfaces fit in with the rest of the Linux kernel and provides examples in the form of a memory-based modularized network interface, which is called (you guessed it) *snull*. To simplify the discussion, the interface uses the Ethernet hardware protocol and transmits IP packets. The knowledge you acquire from examining *snull* can be readily applied to protocols other than IP, and writing a non-Ethernet driver is different only in tiny details related to the actual network protocol.

This chapter doesn't talk about IP numbering schemes, network protocols, or other general networking concepts. Such topics are not (usually) of concern to the driver writer, and it's impossible to offer a satisfactory overview of networking technology in less than a few hundred pages. The interested reader is urged to refer to other books describing networking issues.

One note on terminology is called for before getting into network devices. The networking world uses the term *octet* to refer to a group of eight bits, which is generally the smallest unit understood by networking devices and protocols. The term byte is almost never encountered in this context. In keeping with standard usage, we will use octet when talking about networking devices.

The term "header" also merits a quick mention. A header is a set of bytes (err, octets) prepended to a packet as it is passed through the various layers of the networking subsystem. When an application sends a block of data through a TCP socket, the networking subsystem breaks that data up into packets and puts a TCP header, describing where each packet fits within the stream, at the beginning. The lower levels then put an IP header, used to route the packet to its destination, in front of the TCP header. If the packet moves over an Ethernet-like medium, an Ethernet header, interpreted by the hardware, goes in front of the rest. Network drivers need not concern themselves with higher-level headers (usually), but they often must be involved in the creation of the hardware-level header.

How snull Is Designed

This section discusses the design concepts that led to the *snull* network interface. Although this information might appear to be of marginal use, failing to understand it might lead to problems when you play with the sample code.

The first, and most important, design decision was that the sample interfaces should remain independent of real hardware, just like most of the sample code used in this book. This constraint led to something that resembles the loopback interface. *snull* is not a loopback interface; however, it simulates conversations with real remote hosts in order to better demonstrate the task of writing a network driver. The Linux loopback driver is actually quite simple; it can be found in *drivers/net/loopback.c.*

Another feature of *snull* is that it supports only IP traffic. This is a consequence of the internal workings of the interface—*snull* has to look inside and interpret the packets to properly emulate a pair of hardware interfaces. Real interfaces don't depend on the protocol being transmitted, and this limitation of *snull* doesn't affect the fragments of code shown in this chapter.

Assigning IP Numbers

The *snull* module creates two interfaces. These interfaces are different from a simple loopback, in that whatever you transmit through one of the interfaces loops back to the other one, not to itself. It looks like you have two external links, but actually your computer is replying to itself.

Unfortunately, this effect can't be accomplished through IP number assignments alone, because the kernel wouldn't send out a packet through interface A that was directed to its own interface B. Instead, it would use the loopback channel without passing through *snull*. To be able to establish a communication through the *snull* interfaces, the source and destination addresses need to be modified during data transmission. In other words, packets sent through one of the interfaces should be received by the other, but the receiver of the outgoing packet shouldn't be recognized as the local host. The same applies to the source address of received packets.

To achieve this kind of "hidden loopback," the *snull* interface toggles the least significant bit of the third octet of both the source and destination addresses; that is, it changes both the network number and the host number of class C IP numbers. The net effect is that packets sent to network A (connected to sn0, the first interface) appear on the sn1 interface as packets belonging to network B.

To avoid dealing with too many numbers, let's assign symbolic names to the IP numbers involved:

- snullnet0 is the network that is connected to the sn0 interface. Similarly, snullnet1 is the network connected to sn1. The addresses of these networks should differ only in the least significant bit of the third octet. These networks must have 24-bit netmasks.

- local0 is the IP address assigned to the sn0 interface; it belongs to snullnet0. The address associated with sn1 is local1. local0 and local1 must differ in the least significant bit of their third octet and in the fourth octet.

- remote0 is a host in snullnet0, and its fourth octet is the same as that of local1. Any packet sent to remote0 reaches local1 after its network address has been modified by the interface code. The host `remote1` belongs to `snullnet1`, and its fourth octet is the same as that of `local0`.

The operation of the *snull* interfaces is depicted in Figure 17-1, in which the hostname associated with each interface is printed near the interface name.

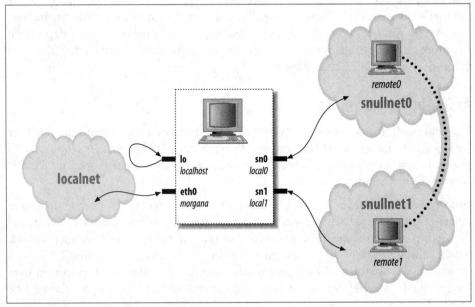

Figure 17-1. How a host sees its interfaces

Here are possible values for the network numbers. Once you put these lines in */etc/networks*, you can call your networks by name. The values were chosen from the range of numbers reserved for private use.

```
snullnet0      192.168.0.0
snullnet1      192.168.1.0
```

The following are possible host numbers to put into */etc/hosts*:

```
192.168.0.1    local0
192.168.0.2    remote0
192.168.1.2    local1
192.168.1.1    remote1
```

The important feature of these numbers is that the host portion of `local0` is the same as that of `remote1`, and the host portion of `local1` is the same as that of `remote0`. You can use completely different numbers as long as this relationship applies.

Be careful, however, if your computer is already connected to a network. The numbers you choose might be real Internet or intranet numbers, and assigning them to your interfaces prevents communication with the real hosts. For example, although the numbers just shown are not routable Internet numbers, they could already be used by your private network.

Whatever numbers you choose, you can correctly set up the interfaces for operation by issuing the following commands:

```
ifconfig sn0 local0
ifconfig sn1 local1
```

You may need to add the netmask 255.255.255.0 parameter if the address range chosen is not a class C range.

At this point, the "remote" end of the interface can be reached. The following screendump shows how a host reaches remote0 and remote1 through the *snull* interface:

```
morgana% ping -c 2 remote0
64 bytes from 192.168.0.99: icmp_seq=0 ttl=64 time=1.6 ms
64 bytes from 192.168.0.99: icmp_seq=1 ttl=64 time=0.9 ms
2 packets transmitted, 2 packets received, 0% packet loss

morgana% ping -c 2 remote1
64 bytes from 192.168.1.88: icmp_seq=0 ttl=64 time=1.8 ms
64 bytes from 192.168.1.88: icmp_seq=1 ttl=64 time=0.9 ms
2 packets transmitted, 2 packets received, 0% packet loss
```

Note that you won't be able to reach any other "host" belonging to the two networks, because the packets are discarded by your computer after the address has been modified and the packet has been received. For example, a packet aimed at 192.168.0.32 will leave through sn0 and reappear at sn1 with a destination address of 192.168.1.32, which is not a local address for the host computer.

The Physical Transport of Packets

As far as data transport is concerned, the *snull* interfaces belong to the Ethernet class.

snull emulates Ethernet because the vast majority of existing networks—at least the segments that a workstation connects to—are based on Ethernet technology, be it 10base-T, 100base-T, or Gigabit. Additionally, the kernel offers some generalized support for Ethernet devices, and there's no reason not to use it. The advantage of being an Ethernet device is so strong that even the *plip* interface (the interface that uses the printer ports) declares itself as an Ethernet device.

The last advantage of using the Ethernet setup for *snull* is that you can run *tcpdump* on the interface to see the packets go by. Watching the interfaces with *tcpdump* can be a useful way to see how the two interfaces work.

As was mentioned previously, *snull* works only with IP packets. This limitation is a result of the fact that *snull* snoops in the packets and even modifies them, in order for the code to work. The code modifies the source, destination, and checksum in the IP header of each packet without checking whether it actually conveys IP information.

This quick-and-dirty data modification destroys non-IP packets. If you want to deliver other protocols through *snull*, you must modify the module's source code.

Connecting to the Kernel

We start looking at the structure of network drivers by dissecting the *snull* source. Keeping the source code for several drivers handy might help you follow the discussion and to see how real-world Linux network drivers operate. As a place to start, we suggest *loopback.c*, *plip.c*, and *e100.c*, in order of increasing complexity. All these files live in *drivers/net*, within the kernel source tree.

Device Registration

When a driver module is loaded into a running kernel, it requests resources and offers facilities; there's nothing new in that. And there's also nothing new in the way resources are requested. The driver should probe for its device and its hardware location (I/O ports and IRQ line)—but not register them—as described in "Installing an Interrupt Handler" in Chapter 10. The way a network driver is registered by its module initialization function is different from char and block drivers. Since there is no equivalent of major and minor numbers for network interfaces, a network driver does not request such a number. Instead, the driver inserts a data structure for each newly detected interface into a global list of network devices.

Each interface is described by a struct net_device item, which is defined in <*linux/netdevice.h*>. The *snull* driver keeps pointers to two of these structures (for sn0 and sn1) in a simple array:

```
struct net_device *snull_devs[2];
```

The net_device structure, like many other kernel structures, contains a kobject and is, therefore, reference-counted and exported via sysfs. As with other such structures, it must be allocated dynamically. The kernel function provided to perform this allocation is *alloc_netdev*, which has the following prototype:

```
struct net_device *alloc_netdev(int sizeof_priv,
                        const char *name,
                        void (*setup)(struct net_device *));
```

Here, sizeof_priv is the size of the driver's "private data" area; with network devices, that area is allocated along with the net_device structure. In fact, the two are allocated together in one large chunk of memory, but driver authors should pretend that they don't know that. name is the name of this interface, as is seen by user space; this name can have a *printf*-style %d in it. The kernel replaces the %d with the next available interface number. Finally, setup is a pointer to an initialization function that is called to set up the rest of the net_device structure. We get to the initialization function shortly, but, for now, suffice it to say that *snull* allocates its two device structures in this way:

```
snull_devs[0] = alloc_netdev(sizeof(struct snull_priv), "sn%d",
        snull_init);
snull_devs[1] = alloc_netdev(sizeof(struct snull_priv), "sn%d",
        snull_init);
if (snull_devs[0] == NULL || snull_devs[1] == NULL)
    goto out;
```

As always, we must check the return value to ensure that the allocation succeeded.

The networking subsystem provides a number of helper functions wrapped around *alloc_netdev* for various types of interfaces. The most common is *alloc_etherdev*, which is defined in *<linux/etherdevice.h>*:

```
struct net_device *alloc_etherdev(int sizeof_priv);
```

This function allocates a network device using eth%d for the name argument. It provides its own initialization function (*ether_setup*) that sets several net_device fields with appropriate values for Ethernet devices. Thus, there is no driver-supplied initialization function for *alloc_etherdev*; the driver should simply do its required initialization directly after a successful allocation. Writers of drivers for other types of devices may want to take advantage of one of the other helper functions, such as *alloc_fcdev* (defined in *<linux/fcdevice.h>*) for fiber-channel devices, *alloc_fddidev* (*<linux/fddidevice.h>*) for FDDI devices, or *alloc_trdev* (*<linux/trdevice.h>*) for token ring devices.

snull could use *alloc_etherdev* without trouble; we chose to use *alloc_netdev* instead, as a way of demonstrating the lower-level interface and to give us control over the name assigned to the interface.

Once the net_device structure has been initialized, completing the process is just a matter of passing the structure to *register_netdev*. In *snull*, the call looks as follows:

```
for (i = 0; i < 2;  i++)
    if ((result = register_netdev(snull_devs[i])))
        printk("snull: error %i registering device \"%s\"\n",
                result, snull_devs[i]->name);
```

The usual cautions apply here: as soon as you call *register_netdev*, your driver may be called to operate on the device. Thus, you should not register the device until everything has been completely initialized.

Initializing Each Device

We have looked at the allocation and registration of net_device structures, but we passed over the intermediate step of completely initializing that structure. Note that struct net_device is always put together at runtime; it cannot be set up at compile time in the same manner as a file_operations or block_device_operations structure. This initialization must be complete before calling *register_netdev*. The net_device structure is large and complicated; fortunately, the kernel takes care of some Ethernet-wide defaults through the *ether_setup* function (which is called by *alloc_etherdev*).

Since *snull* uses *alloc_netdev*, it has a separate initialization function. The core of this function (*snull_init*) is as follows:

```
ether_setup(dev); /* assign some of the fields */

dev->open            = snull_open;
dev->stop            = snull_release;
dev->set_config      = snull_config;
dev->hard_start_xmit = snull_tx;
dev->do_ioctl        = snull_ioctl;
dev->get_stats       = snull_stats;
dev->rebuild_header  = snull_rebuild_header;
dev->hard_header     = snull_header;
dev->tx_timeout      = snull_tx_timeout;
dev->watchdog_timeo  = timeout;
/* keep the default flags, just add NOARP */
dev->flags           |= IFF_NOARP;
dev->features        |= NETIF_F_NO_CSUM;
dev->hard_header_cache = NULL;      /* Disable caching */
```

The above code is a fairly routine initialization of the net_device structure; it is mostly a matter of storing pointers to our various driver functions. The single unusual feature of the code is setting IFF_NOARP in the flags. This specifies that the interface cannot use the Address Resolution Protocol (ARP). ARP is a low-level Ethernet protocol; its job is to turn IP addresses into Ethernet medium access control (MAC) addresses. Since the "remote" systems simulated by *snull* do not really exist, there is nobody available to answer ARP requests for them. Rather than complicate *snull* with the addition of an ARP implementation, we chose to mark the interface as being unable to handle that protocol. The assignment to hard_header_cache is there for a similar reason: it disables the caching of the (nonexistent) ARP replies on this interface. This topic is discussed in detail in the section "MAC Address Resolution" later in this chapter.

The initialization code also sets a couple of fields (tx_timeout and watchdog_timeo) that relate to the handling of transmission timeouts. We cover this topic thoroughly in the section "Transmission Timeouts."

We look now at one more struct net_device field, priv. Its role is similar to that of the private_data pointer that we used for char drivers. Unlike fops->private_data, this priv pointer is allocated along with the net_device structure. Direct access to the priv field is also discouraged, for performance and flexibility reasons. When a driver needs to get access to the private data pointer, it should use the *netdev_priv* function. Thus, the *snull* driver is full of declarations such as:

```
struct snull_priv *priv = netdev_priv(dev);
```

The *snull* module declares a snull_priv data structure to be used for priv:

```
struct snull_priv {
    struct net_device_stats stats;
    int status;
    struct snull_packet *ppool;
    struct snull_packet *rx_queue;  /* List of incoming packets */
    int rx_int_enabled;
    int tx_packetlen;
    u8 *tx_packetdata;
    struct sk_buff *skb;
    spinlock_t lock;
};
```

The structure includes, among other things, an instance of struct net_device_stats, which is the standard place to hold interface statistics. The following lines in *snull_init* allocate and initialize dev->priv:

```
priv = netdev_priv(dev);
memset(priv, 0, sizeof(struct snull_priv));
spin_lock_init(&priv->lock);
snull_rx_ints(dev, 1);      /* enable receive interrupts */
```

Module Unloading

Nothing special happens when the module is unloaded. The module cleanup function simply unregisters the interfaces, performs whatever internal cleanup is required, and releases the net_device structure back to the system:

```
void snull_cleanup(void)
{
    int i;

    for (i = 0; i < 2;  i++) {
        if (snull_devs[i]) {
            unregister_netdev(snull_devs[i]);
            snull_teardown_pool(snull_devs[i]);
            free_netdev(snull_devs[i]);
        }
    }
    return;
}
```

The call to *unregister_netdev* removes the interface from the system; *free_netdev* returns the net_device structure to the kernel. If a reference to that structure exists somewhere, it may continue to exist, but your driver need not care about that. Once you have unregistered the interface, the kernel no longer calls its methods.

Note that our internal cleanup (done in *snull_teardown_pool*) cannot happen until the device has been unregistered. It must, however, happen before we return the net_device structure to the system; once we have called *free_netdev*, we cannot make any further references to the device or our private area.

The net_device Structure in Detail

The net_device structure is at the very core of the network driver layer and deserves a complete description. This list describes all the fields, but more to provide a reference than to be memorized. The rest of this chapter briefly describes each field as soon as it is used in the sample code, so you don't need to keep referring back to this section.

Global Information

The first part of struct net_device is composed of the following fields:

char name[IFNAMSIZ];
> The name of the device. If the name set by the driver contains a %d format string, *register_netdev* replaces it with a number to make a unique name; assigned numbers start at 0.

unsigned long state;
> Device state. The field includes several flags. Drivers do not normally manipulate these flags directly; instead, a set of utility functions has been provided. These functions are discussed shortly when we get into driver operations.

struct net_device *next;
> Pointer to the next device in the global linked list. This field shouldn't be touched by the driver.

int (*init)(struct net_device *dev);
> An initialization function. If this pointer is set, the function is called by *register_netdev* to complete the initialization of the net_device structure. Most modern network drivers do not use this function any longer; instead, initialization is performed before registering the interface.

Hardware Information

The following fields contain low-level hardware information for relatively simple devices. They are a holdover from the earlier days of Linux networking; most modern drivers do make use of them (with the possible exception of if_port). We list them here for completeness.

unsigned long rmem_end;
unsigned long rmem_start;
unsigned long mem_end;
unsigned long mem_start;
> Device memory information. These fields hold the beginning and ending addresses of the shared memory used by the device. If the device has different receive and transmit memories, the mem fields are used for transmit memory and the rmem fields for receive memory. The rmem fields are never referenced outside

of the driver itself. By convention, the end fields are set so that end - start is the amount of available onboard memory.

unsigned long base_addr;
> The I/O base address of the network interface. This field, like the previous ones, is assigned by the driver during the device probe. The *ifconfig* command can be used to display or modify the current value. The base_addr can be explicitly assigned on the kernel command line at system boot (via the netdev= parameter) or at module load time. The field, like the memory fields described above, is not used by the kernel.

unsigned char irq;
> The assigned interrupt number. The value of dev->irq is printed by *ifconfig* when interfaces are listed. This value can usually be set at boot or load time and modified later using *ifconfig*.

unsigned char if_port;
> The port in use on multiport devices. This field is used, for example, with devices that support both coaxial (IF_PORT_10BASE2) and twisted-pair (IF_PORT_100BASET) Ethernet connections. The full set of known port types is defined in <*linux/netdevice.h*>.

unsigned char dma;
> The DMA channel allocated by the device. The field makes sense only with some peripheral buses, such as ISA. It is not used outside of the device driver itself but for informational purposes (in *ifconfig*).

Interface Information

Most of the information about the interface is correctly set up by the *ether_setup* function (or whatever other setup function is appropriate for the given hardware type). Ethernet cards can rely on this general-purpose function for most of these fields, but the flags and dev_addr fields are device specific and must be explicitly assigned at initialization time.

Some non-Ethernet interfaces can use helper functions similar to *ether_setup*. *drivers/ net/net_init.c* exports a number of such functions, including the following:

void ltalk_setup(struct net_device *dev);
> Sets up the fields for a LocalTalk device

void fc_setup(struct net_device *dev);
> Initializes fields for fiber-channel devices

void fddi_setup(struct net_device *dev);
> Configures an interface for a Fiber Distributed Data Interface (FDDI) network

```
void hippi_setup(struct net_device *dev);
```
Prepares fields for a High-Performance Parallel Interface (HIPPI) high-speed interconnect driver

```
void tr_setup(struct net_device *dev);
```
Handles setup for token ring network interfaces

Most devices are covered by one of these classes. If yours is something radically new and different, however, you need to assign the following fields by hand:

```
unsigned short hard_header_len;
```
The hardware header length, that is, the number of octets that lead the transmitted packet before the IP header, or other protocol information. The value of hard_header_len is 14 (ETH_HLEN) for Ethernet interfaces.

```
unsigned mtu;
```
The maximum transfer unit (MTU). This field is used by the network layer to drive packet transmission. Ethernet has an MTU of 1500 octets (ETH_DATA_LEN). This value can be changed with *ifconfig*.

```
unsigned long tx_queue_len;
```
The maximum number of frames that can be queued on the device's transmission queue. This value is set to 1000 by *ether_setup*, but you can change it. For example, *plip* uses 10 to avoid wasting system memory (*plip* has a lower throughput than a real Ethernet interface).

```
unsigned short type;
```
The hardware type of the interface. The type field is used by ARP to determine what kind of hardware address the interface supports. The proper value for Ethernet interfaces is ARPHRD_ETHER, and that is the value set by *ether_setup*. The recognized types are defined in *<linux/if_arp.h>*.

```
unsigned char addr_len;
unsigned char broadcast[MAX_ADDR_LEN];
unsigned char dev_addr[MAX_ADDR_LEN];
```
Hardware (MAC) address length and device hardware addresses. The Ethernet address length is six octets (we are referring to the hardware ID of the interface board), and the broadcast address is made up of six 0xff octets; *ether_setup* arranges for these values to be correct. The device address, on the other hand, must be read from the interface board in a device-specific way, and the driver should copy it to dev_addr. The hardware address is used to generate correct Ethernet headers before the packet is handed over to the driver for transmission. The *snull* device doesn't use a physical interface, and it invents its own hardware address.

```
unsigned short flags;
int features;
```
Interface flags (detailed next).

The flags field is a bit mask including the following bit values. The IFF_ prefix stands for "interface flags." Some flags are managed by the kernel, and some are set by the interface at initialization time to assert various capabilities and other features of the interface. The valid flags, which are defined in *<linux/if.h>*, are:

IFF_UP
> This flag is read-only for the driver. The kernel turns it on when the interface is active and ready to transfer packets.

IFF_BROADCAST
> This flag (maintained by the networking code) states that the interface allows broadcasting. Ethernet boards do.

IFF_DEBUG
> This marks debug mode. The flag can be used to control the verbosity of your *printk* calls or for other debugging purposes. Although no in-tree driver currently uses this flag, it can be set and reset by user programs via *ioctl*, and your driver can use it. The *misc-progs/netifdebug* program can be used to turn the flag on and off.

IFF_LOOPBACK
> This flag should be set only in the loopback interface. The kernel checks for IFF_LOOPBACK instead of hardwiring the lo name as a special interface.

IFF_POINTOPOINT
> This flag signals that the interface is connected to a point-to-point link. It is set by the driver or, sometimes, by *ifconfig*. For example, *plip* and the PPP driver have it set.

IFF_NOARP
> This means that the interface can't perform ARP. For example, point-to-point interfaces don't need to run ARP, which would only impose additional traffic without retrieving useful information. *snull* runs without ARP capabilities, so it sets the flag.

IFF_PROMISC
> This flag is set (by the networking code) to activate promiscuous operation. By default, Ethernet interfaces use a hardware filter to ensure that they receive broadcast packets and packets directed to that interface's hardware address only. Packet sniffers such as *tcpdump* set promiscuous mode on the interface in order to retrieve all packets that travel on the interface's transmission medium.

IFF_MULTICAST
> This flag is set by drivers to mark interfaces that are capable of multicast transmission. *ether_setup* sets IFF_MULTICAST by default, so if your driver does not support multicast, it must clear the flag at initialization time.

IFF_ALLMULTI
> This flag tells the interface to receive all multicast packets. The kernel sets it when the host performs multicast routing, only if IFF_MULTICAST is set. IFF_ALLMULTI is

read-only for the driver. Multicast flags are used in the section "Multicast," later in this chapter.

IFF_MASTER
IFF_SLAVE
> These flags are used by the load equalization code. The interface driver doesn't need to know about them.

IFF_PORTSEL
IFF_AUTOMEDIA
> These flags signal that the device is capable of switching between multiple media types; for example, unshielded twisted pair (UTP) versus coaxial Ethernet cables. If IFF_AUTOMEDIA is set, the device selects the proper medium automatically. In practice, the kernel makes no use of either flag.

IFF_DYNAMIC
> This flag, set by the driver, indicates that the address of this interface can change. It is not currently used by the kernel.

IFF_RUNNING
> This flag indicates that the interface is up and running. It is mostly present for BSD compatibility; the kernel makes little use of it. Most network drivers need not worry about IFF_RUNNING.

IFF_NOTRAILERS
> This flag is unused in Linux, but it exists for BSD compatibility.

When a program changes IFF_UP, the *open* or *stop* device method is called. Furthermore, when IFF_UP or any other flag is modified, the *set_multicast_list* method is invoked. If the driver needs to perform some action in response to a modification of the flags, it must take that action in *set_multicast_list*. For example, when IFF_PROMISC is set or reset, *set_multicast_list* must notify the onboard hardware filter. The responsibilities of this device method are outlined in the section "Multicast."

The features field of the net_device structure is set by the driver to tell the kernel about any special hardware capabilities that this interface has. We will discuss some of these features; others are beyond the scope of this book. The full set is:

NETIF_F_SG
NETIF_F_FRAGLIST
> Both of these flags control the use of scatter/gather I/O. If your interface can transmit a packet that has been split into several distinct memory segments, you should set NETIF_F_SG. Of course, you have to actually implement the scatter/gather I/O (we describe how that is done in the section "Scatter/Gather I/O"). NETIF_F_FRAGLIST states that your interface can cope with packets that have been fragmented; only the loopback driver does this in 2.6.

> Note that the kernel does not perform scatter/gather I/O to your device if it does not also provide some form of checksumming as well. The reason is that, if the

kernel has to make a pass over a fragmented ("nonlinear") packet to calculate the checksum, it might as well copy the data and coalesce the packet at the same time.

NETIF_F_IP_CSUM
NETIF_F_NO_CSUM
NETIF_F_HW_CSUM

These flags are all ways of telling the kernel that it need not apply checksums to some or all packets leaving the system by this interface. Set NETIF_F_IP_CSUM if your interface can checksum IP packets but not others. If no checksums are ever required for this interface, set NETIF_F_NO_CSUM. The loopback driver sets this flag, and *snull* does, too; since packets are only transferred through system memory, there is (one hopes!) no opportunity for them to be corrupted, and no need to check them. If your hardware does checksumming itself, set NETIF_F_HW_CSUM.

NETIF_F_HIGHDMA

Set this flag if your device can perform DMA to high memory. In the absence of this flag, all packet buffers provided to your driver are allocated in low memory.

NETIF_F_HW_VLAN_TX
NETIF_F_HW_VLAN_RX
NETIF_F_HW_VLAN_FILTER
NETIF_F_VLAN_CHALLENGED

These options describe your hardware's support for 802.1q VLAN packets. VLAN support is beyond what we can cover in this chapter. If VLAN packets confuse your device (which they really shouldn't), set the NETIF_F_VLAN_CHALLENGED flag.

NETIF_F_TSO

Set this flag if your device can perform TCP segmentation offloading. TSO is an advanced feature that we cannot cover here.

The Device Methods

As happens with the char and block drivers, each network device declares the functions that act on it. Operations that can be performed on network interfaces are listed in this section. Some of the operations can be left NULL, and others are usually untouched because *ether_setup* assigns suitable methods to them.

Device methods for a network interface can be divided into two groups: fundamental and optional. Fundamental methods include those that are needed to be able to use the interface; optional methods implement more advanced functionalities that are not strictly required. The following are the fundamental methods:

int (*open)(struct net_device *dev);

Opens the interface. The interface is opened whenever *ifconfig* activates it. The *open* method should register any system resource it needs (I/O ports, IRQ,

DMA, etc.), turn on the hardware, and perform any other setup your device requires.

`int (*stop)(struct net_device *dev);`
Stops the interface. The interface is stopped when it is brought down. This function should reverse operations performed at open time.

`int (*hard_start_xmit) (struct sk_buff *skb, struct net_device *dev);`
Method that initiates the transmission of a packet. The full packet (protocol headers and all) is contained in a socket buffer (sk_buff) structure. Socket buffers are introduced later in this chapter.

`int (*hard_header) (struct sk_buff *skb, struct net_device *dev, unsigned`
`short type, void *daddr, void *saddr, unsigned len);`
Function (called before *hard_start_xmit*) that builds the hardware header from the source and destination hardware addresses that were previously retrieved; its job is to organize the information passed to it as arguments into an appropriate, device-specific hardware header. *eth_header* is the default function for Ethernet-like interfaces, and *ether_setup* assigns this field accordingly.

`int (*rebuild_header)(struct sk_buff *skb);`
Function used to rebuild the hardware header after ARP resolution completes but before a packet is transmitted. The default function used by Ethernet devices uses the ARP support code to fill the packet with missing information.

`void (*tx_timeout)(struct net_device *dev);`
Method called by the networking code when a packet transmission fails to complete within a reasonable period, on the assumption that an interrupt has been missed or the interface has locked up. It should handle the problem and resume packet transmission.

`struct net_device_stats *(*get_stats)(struct net_device *dev);`
Whenever an application needs to get statistics for the interface, this method is called. This happens, for example, when *ifconfig* or *netstat -i* is run. A sample implementation for *snull* is introduced in the section "Statistical Information."

`int (*set_config)(struct net_device *dev, struct ifmap *map);`
Changes the interface configuration. This method is the entry point for configuring the driver. The I/O address for the device and its interrupt number can be changed at runtime using *set_config*. This capability can be used by the system administrator if the interface cannot be probed for. Drivers for modern hardware normally do not need to implement this method.

The remaining device operations are optional:

```
int weight;
int (*poll)(struct net_device *dev; int *quota);
```
Method provided by NAPI-compliant drivers to operate the interface in a polled mode, with interrupts disabled. NAPI (and the weight field) are covered in the section "Receive Interrupt Mitigation."

```
void (*poll_controller)(struct net_device *dev);
```
Function that asks the driver to check for events on the interface in situations where interrupts are disabled. It is used for specific in-kernel networking tasks, such as remote consoles and kernel debugging over the network.

```
int (*do_ioctl)(struct net_device *dev, struct ifreq *ifr, int cmd);
```
Performs interface-specific *ioctl* commands. (Implementation of those commands is described in the section "Custom ioctl Commands.") The corresponding field in struct net_device can be left as NULL if the interface doesn't need any interface-specific commands.

```
void (*set_multicast_list)(struct net_device *dev);
```
Method called when the multicast list for the device changes and when the flags change. See the section "Multicast" for further details and a sample implementation.

```
int (*set_mac_address)(struct net_device *dev, void *addr);
```
Function that can be implemented if the interface supports the ability to change its hardware address. Many interfaces don't support this ability at all. Others use the default *eth_mac_addr* implementation (from *drivers/net/net_init.c*). *eth_mac_addr* only copies the new address into dev->dev_addr, and it does so only if the interface is not running. Drivers that use *eth_mac_addr* should set the hardware MAC address from dev->dev_addr in their *open* method.

```
int (*change_mtu)(struct net_device *dev, int new_mtu);
```
Function that takes action if there is a change in the maximum transfer unit (MTU) for the interface. If the driver needs to do anything particular when the MTU is changed by the user, it should declare its own function; otherwise, the default does the right thing. *snull* has a template for the function if you are interested.

```
int (*header_cache) (struct neighbour *neigh, struct hh_cache *hh);
```
header_cache is called to fill in the hh_cache structure with the results of an ARP query. Almost all Ethernet-like drivers can use the default *eth_header_cache* implementation.

```
int (*header_cache_update) (struct hh_cache *hh, struct net_device *dev,
    unsigned char *haddr);
```
Method that updates the destination address in the hh_cache structure in response to a change. Ethernet devices use *eth_header_cache_update*.

```
int (*hard_header_parse) (struct sk_buff *skb, unsigned char *haddr);
```
The *hard_header_parse* method extracts the source address from the packet contained in skb, copying it into the buffer at haddr. The return value from the function is the length of that address. Ethernet devices normally use *eth_header_parse*.

Utility Fields

The remaining struct net_device data fields are used by the interface to hold useful status information. Some of the fields are used by *ifconfig* and *netstat* to provide the user with information about the current configuration. Therefore, an interface should assign values to these fields:

```
unsigned long trans_start;
unsigned long last_rx;
```
Fields that hold a jiffies value. The driver is responsible for updating these values when transmission begins and when a packet is received, respectively. The trans_start value is used by the networking subsystem to detect transmitter lockups. last_rx is currently unused, but the driver should maintain this field anyway to be prepared for future use.

```
int watchdog_timeo;
```
The minimum time (in jiffies) that should pass before the networking layer decides that a transmission timeout has occurred and calls the driver's *tx_timeout* function.

```
void *priv;
```
The equivalent of filp->private_data. In modern drivers, this field is set by *alloc_netdev* and should not be accessed directly; use *netdev_priv* instead.

```
struct dev_mc_list *mc_list;
int mc_count;
```
Fields that handle multicast transmission. mc_count is the count of items in mc_list. See the section "Multicast" for further details.

```
spinlock_t xmit_lock;
int xmit_lock_owner;
```
The xmit_lock is used to avoid multiple simultaneous calls to the driver's *hard_start_xmit* function. xmit_lock_owner is the number of the CPU that has obtained xmit_lock. The driver should make no changes to these fields.

There are other fields in struct net_device, but they are not used by network drivers.

Opening and Closing

Our driver can probe for the interface at module load time or at kernel boot. Before the interface can carry packets, however, the kernel must open it and assign an address to it. The kernel opens or closes an interface in response to the *ifconfig* command.

When *ifconfig* is used to assign an address to the interface, it performs two tasks. First, it assigns the address by means of ioctl(SIOCSIFADDR) (Socket I/O Control Set Interface Address). Then it sets the IFF_UP bit in dev->flag by means of ioctl(SIOCSIFFLAGS) (Socket I/O Control Set Interface Flags) to turn the interface on.

As far as the device is concerned, ioctl(SIOCSIFADDR) does nothing. No driver function is invoked—the task is device independent, and the kernel performs it. The latter command (ioctl(SIOCSIFFLAGS)), however, calls the *open* method for the device.

Similarly, when the interface is shut down, *ifconfig* uses ioctl(SIOCSIFFLAGS) to clear IFF_UP, and the *stop* method is called.

Both device methods return 0 in case of success and the usual negative value in case of error.

As far as the actual code is concerned, the driver has to perform many of the same tasks as the char and block drivers do. *open* requests any system resources it needs and tells the interface to come up; *stop* shuts down the interface and releases system resources. Network drivers must perform some additional steps at *open* time, however.

First, the hardware (MAC) address needs to be copied from the hardware device to dev->dev_addr before the interface can communicate with the outside world. The hardware address can then be copied to the device at open time. The *snull* software interface assigns it from within *open*; it just fakes a hardware number using an ASCII string of length ETH_ALEN, the length of Ethernet hardware addresses.

The *open* method should also start the interface's transmit queue (allowing it to accept packets for transmission) once it is ready to start sending data. The kernel provides a function to start the queue:

```
void netif_start_queue(struct net_device *dev);
```

The *open* code for *snull* looks like the following:

```
int snull_open(struct net_device *dev)
{
    /* request_region( ), request_irq( ), ....  (like fops->open) */

    /*
     * Assign the hardware address of the board: use "\0SNULx", where
     * x is 0 or 1. The first byte is '\0' to avoid being a multicast
     * address (the first byte of multicast addrs is odd).
     */
    memcpy(dev->dev_addr, "\0SNUL0", ETH_ALEN);
    if (dev == snull_devs[1])
```

```
        dev->dev_addr[ETH_ALEN-1]++; /* \0SNUL1 */
    netif_start_queue(dev);
    return 0;
}
```

As you can see, in the absence of real hardware, there is little to do in the *open* method. The same is true of the *stop* method; it just reverses the operations of *open*. For this reason, the function implementing *stop* is often called *close* or *release*.

```
int snull_release(struct net_device *dev)
{
    /* release ports, irq and such -- like fops->close */

    netif_stop_queue(dev); /* can't transmit any more */
    return 0;
}
```

The function:

```
void netif_stop_queue(struct net_device *dev);
```

is the opposite of *netif_start_queue*; it marks the device as being unable to transmit any more packets. The function must be called when the interface is closed (in the *stop* method) but can also be used to temporarily stop transmission, as explained in the next section.

Packet Transmission

The most important tasks performed by network interfaces are data transmission and reception. We start with transmission because it is slightly easier to understand.

Transmission refers to the act of sending a packet over a network link. Whenever the kernel needs to transmit a data packet, it calls the driver's *hard_start_transmit* method to put the data on an outgoing queue. Each packet handled by the kernel is contained in a socket buffer structure (struct sk_buff), whose definition is found in *<linux/skbuff.h>*. The structure gets its name from the Unix abstraction used to represent a network connection, the *socket*. Even if the interface has nothing to do with sockets, each network packet belongs to a socket in the higher network layers, and the input/output buffers of any socket are lists of struct sk_buff structures. The same sk_buff structure is used to host network data throughout all the Linux network subsystems, but a socket buffer is just a packet as far as the interface is concerned.

A pointer to sk_buff is usually called skb, and we follow this practice both in the sample code and in the text.

The socket buffer is a complex structure, and the kernel offers a number of functions to act on it. The functions are described later in the section "The Socket Buffers"; for now, a few basic facts about sk_buff are enough for us to write a working driver.

The socket buffer passed to *hard_start_xmit* contains the physical packet as it should appear on the media, complete with the transmission-level headers. The interface doesn't need to modify the data being transmitted. skb->data points to the packet being transmitted, and skb->len is its length in octets. This situation gets a little more complicated if your driver can handle scatter/gather I/O; we get to that in the section "Scatter/Gather I/O."

The *snull* packet transmission code follows; the physical transmission machinery has been isolated in another function, because every interface driver must implement it according to the specific hardware being driven:

```
int snull_tx(struct sk_buff *skb, struct net_device *dev)
{
    int len;
    char *data, shortpkt[ETH_ZLEN];
    struct snull_priv *priv = netdev_priv(dev);

    data = skb->data;
    len = skb->len;
    if (len < ETH_ZLEN) {
        memset(shortpkt, 0, ETH_ZLEN);
        memcpy(shortpkt, skb->data, skb->len);
        len = ETH_ZLEN;
        data = shortpkt;
    }
    dev->trans_start = jiffies; /* save the timestamp */

    /* Remember the skb, so we can free it at interrupt time */
    priv->skb = skb;

    /* actual deliver of data is device-specific, and not shown here */
    snull_hw_tx(data, len, dev);

    return 0; /* Our simple device can not fail */
}
```

The transmission function, thus, just performs some sanity checks on the packet and transmits the data through the hardware-related function. Do note, however, the care that is taken when the packet to be transmitted is shorter than the minimum length supported by the underlying media (which, for *snull*, is our virtual "Ethernet"). Many Linux network drivers (and those for other operating systems as well) have been found to leak data in such situations. Rather than create that sort of security vulnerability, we copy short packets into a separate array that we can explicitly zero-pad out to the full length required by the media. (We can safely put that data on the stack, since the minimum length—60 bytes—is quite small).

The return value from *hard_start_xmit* should be 0 on success; at that point, your driver has taken responsibility for the packet, should make its best effort to ensure that transmission succeeds, and must free the skb at the end. A nonzero return value indicates that the packet could not be transmitted at this time; the kernel will retry later. In this situation, your driver should stop the queue until whatever situation caused the failure has been resolved.

The "hardware-related" transmission function (*snull_hw_tx*) is omitted here since it is entirely occupied with implementing the trickery of the *snull* device, including manipulating the source and destination addresses, and has little of interest to authors of real network drivers. It is present, of course, in the sample source for those who want to go in and see how it works.

Controlling Transmission Concurrency

The *hard_start_xmit* function is protected from concurrent calls by a spinlock (xmit_lock) in the net_device structure. As soon as the function returns, however, it may be called again. The function returns when the software is done instructing the hardware about packet transmission, but hardware transmission will likely not have been completed. This is not an issue with *snull*, which does all of its work using the CPU, so packet transmission is complete before the transmission function returns.

Real hardware interfaces, on the other hand, transmit packets asynchronously and have a limited amount of memory available to store outgoing packets. When that memory is exhausted (which, for some hardware, happens with a single outstanding packet to transmit), the driver needs to tell the networking system not to start any more transmissions until the hardware is ready to accept new data.

This notification is accomplished by calling *netif_stop_queue*, the function introduced earlier to stop the queue. Once your driver has stopped its queue, it *must* arrange to restart the queue at some point in the future, when it is again able to accept packets for transmission. To do so, it should call:

```
void netif_wake_queue(struct net_device *dev);
```

This function is just like *netif_start_queue*, except that it also pokes the networking system to make it start transmitting packets again.

Most modern network hardware maintains an internal queue with multiple packets to transmit; in this way it can get the best performance from the network. Network drivers for these devices must support having multiple transmisions outstanding at any given time, but device memory can fill up whether or not the hardware supports multiple outstanding transmissions. Whenever device memory fills to the point that there is no room for the largest possible packet, the driver should stop the queue until space becomes available again.

If you must disable packet transmission from anywhere other than your *hard_start_xmit* function (in response to a reconfiguration request, perhaps), the function you want to use is:

```
void netif_tx_disable(struct net_device *dev);
```

This function behaves much like *netif_stop_queue*, but it also ensures that, when it returns, your *hard_start_xmit* method is not running on another CPU. The queue can be restarted with *netif_wake_queue*, as usual.

Transmission Timeouts

Most drivers that deal with real hardware have to be prepared for that hardware to fail to respond occasionally. Interfaces can forget what they are doing, or the system can lose an interrupt. This sort of problem is common with some devices designed to run on personal computers.

Many drivers handle this problem by setting timers; if the operation has not completed by the time the timer expires, something is wrong. The network system, as it happens, is essentially a complicated assembly of state machines controlled by a mass of timers. As such, the networking code is in a good position to detect transmission timeouts as part of its regular operation.

Thus, network drivers need not worry about detecting such problems themselves. Instead, they need only set a timeout period, which goes in the watchdog_timeo field of the net_device structure. This period, which is in jiffies, should be long enough to account for normal transmission delays (such as collisions caused by congestion on the network media).

If the current system time exceeds the device's trans_start time by at least the timeout period, the networking layer eventually calls the driver's *tx_timeout* method. That method's job is to do whatever is needed to clear up the problem and to ensure the proper completion of any transmissions that were already in progress. It is important, in particular, that the driver not lose track of any socket buffers that have been entrusted to it by the networking code.

snull has the ability to simulate transmitter lockups, which is controlled by two load-time parameters:

```
static int lockup = 0;
module_param(lockup, int, 0);

static int timeout = SNULL_TIMEOUT;
module_param(timeout, int, 0);
```

If the driver is loaded with the parameter lockup=n, a lockup is simulated once every n packets transmitted, and the watchdog_timeo field is set to the given timeout value. When simulating lockups, *snull* also calls *netif_stop_queue* to prevent other transmission attempts from occurring.

The *snull* transmission timeout handler looks like this:

```
void snull_tx_timeout (struct net_device *dev)
{
    struct snull_priv *priv = netdev_priv(dev);
```

```
PDEBUG("Transmit timeout at %ld, latency %ld\n", jiffies,
        jiffies - dev->trans_start);
    /* Simulate a transmission interrupt to get things moving */
priv->status = SNULL_TX_INTR;
snull_interrupt(0, dev, NULL);
priv->stats.tx_errors++;
netif_wake_queue(dev);
return;
}
```

When a transmission timeout happens, the driver must mark the error in the interface statistics and arrange for the device to be reset to a sane state so that new packets can be transmitted. When a timeout happens in *snull*, the driver calls *snull_interrupt* to fill in the "missing" interrupt and restarts the transmit queue with *netif_wake_queue*.

Scatter/Gather I/O

The process of creating a packet for transmission on the network involves assembling multiple pieces. Packet data must often be copied in from user space, and the headers used by various levels of the network stack must be added as well. This assembly can require a fair amount of data copying. If, however, the network interface that is destined to transmit the packet can perform scatter/gather I/O, the packet need not be assembled into a single chunk, and much of that copying can be avoided. Scatter/gather I/O also enables "zero-copy" transmission of network data directly from user-space buffers.

The kernel does not pass scattered packets to your *hard_start_xmit* method unless the NETIF_F_SG bit has been set in the features field of your device structure. If you have set that flag, you need to look at a special "shared info" field within the skb to see whether the packet is made up of a single fragment or many and to find the scattered fragments if need be. A special macro exists to access this information; it is called *skb_shinfo*. The first step when transmitting potentially fragmented packets usually looks something like this:

```
if (skb_shinfo(skb)->nr_frags == 0) {
    /* Just use skb->data and skb->len as usual */
}
```

The nr_frags field tells how many fragments have been used to build the packet. If it is 0, the packet exists in a single piece and can be accessed via the data field as usual. If, however, it is nonzero, your driver must pass through and arrange to transfer each individual fragment. The data field of the skb structure points conveniently to the first fragment (as compared to the full packet, as in the unfragmented case). The length of the fragment must be calculated by subtracting skb->data_len from skb->len (which still contains the length of the full packet). The remaining fragments are to be found in an array called frags in the shared information structure; each entry in frags is an skb_frag_struct structure:

```
struct skb_frag_struct {
    struct page *page;
```

```
    __u16 page_offset;
    __u16 size;
};
```

As you can see, we are once again dealing with page structures, rather than kernel virtual addresses. Your driver should loop through the fragments, mapping each for a
DMA transfer and not forgetting the first fragment, which is pointed to by the skb
directly. Your hardware, of course, must assemble the fragments and transmit them
as a single packet. Note that, if you have set the NETIF_F_HIGHDMA feature flag, some
or all of the fragments may be located in high memory.

Packet Reception

Receiving data from the network is trickier than transmitting it, because an sk_buff
must be allocated and handed off to the upper layers from within an atomic context.
There are two modes of packet reception that may be implemented by network drivers: interrupt driven and polled. Most drivers implement the interrupt-driven technique, and that is the one we cover first. Some drivers for high-bandwidth adapters
may also implement the polled technique; we look at this approach in the section
"Receive Interrupt Mitigation."

The implementation of *snull* separates the "hardware" details from the device-independent housekeeping. Therefore, the function *snull_rx* is called from the *snull*
"interrupt" handler after the hardware has received the packet, and it is already in
the computer's memory. *snull_rx* receives a pointer to the data and the length of the
packet; its sole responsibility is to send the packet and some additional information
to the upper layers of networking code. This code is independent of the way the data
pointer and length are obtained.

```
void snull_rx(struct net_device *dev, struct snull_packet *pkt)
{
    struct sk_buff *skb;
    struct snull_priv *priv = netdev_priv(dev);

    /*
     * The packet has been retrieved from the transmission
     * medium. Build an skb around it, so upper layers can handle it
     */
    skb = dev_alloc_skb(pkt->datalen + 2);
    if (!skb) {
        if (printk_ratelimit())
            printk(KERN_NOTICE "snull rx: low on mem - packet dropped\n");
        priv->stats.rx_dropped++;
        goto out;
    }
    memcpy(skb_put(skb, pkt->datalen), pkt->data, pkt->datalen);

    /* Write metadata, and then pass to the receive level */
    skb->dev = dev;
```

```
    skb->protocol = eth_type_trans(skb, dev);
    skb->ip_summed = CHECKSUM_UNNECESSARY; /* don't check it */
    priv->stats.rx_packets++;
    priv->stats.rx_bytes += pkt->datalen;
    netif_rx(skb);
  out:
    return;
}
```

The function is sufficiently general to act as a template for any network driver, but some explanation is necessary before you can reuse this code fragment with confidence.

The first step is to allocate a buffer to hold the packet. Note that the buffer allocation function (*dev_alloc_skb*) needs to know the data length. The information is used by the function to allocate space for the buffer. *dev_alloc_skb* calls *kmalloc* with atomic priority, so it can be used safely at interrupt time. The kernel offers other interfaces to socket-buffer allocation, but they are not worth introducing here; socket buffers are explained in detail in the section "The Socket Buffers."

Of course, the return value from *dev_alloc_skb* must be checked, and *snull* does so. We call *printk_ratelimit* before complaining about failures, however. Generating hundreds or thousands of console messages per second is a good way to bog down the system entirely and hide the real source of problems; *printk_ratelimit* helps prevent that problem by returning 0 when too much output has gone to the console, and things need to be slowed down a bit.

Once there is a valid skb pointer, the packet data is copied into the buffer by calling *memcpy*; the *skb_put* function updates the end-of-data pointer in the buffer and returns a pointer to the newly created space.

If you are writing a high-performance driver for an interface that can do full bus-mastering I/O, there is a possible optimization that is worth considering here. Some drivers allocate socket buffers for incoming packets prior to their reception, then instruct the interface to place the packet data directly into the socket buffer's space. The networking layer cooperates with this strategy by allocating all socket buffers in DMA-capable space (which may be in high memory if your device has the NETIF_F_HIGHDMA feature flag set). Doing things this way avoids the need for a separate copy operation to fill the socket buffer, but requires being careful with buffer sizes because you won't know in advance how big the incoming packet is. The implementation of a *change_mtu* method is also important in this situation, since it allows the driver to respond to a change in the maximum packet size.

The network layer needs to have some information spelled out before it can make sense of the packet. To this end, the dev and protocol fields must be assigned before the buffer is passed upstairs. The Ethernet support code exports a helper function (*eth_type_trans*), which finds an appropriate value to put into protocol. Then we need to specify how checksumming is to be performed or has been performed on the

packet (*snull* does not need to perform any checksums). The possible policies for
skb->ip_summed are:

CHECKSUM_HW

The device has already performed checksums in hardware. An example of a
hardware checksum is the SPARC HME interface.

CHECKSUM_NONE

Checksums have not yet been verified, and the task must be accomplished by
system software. This is the default in newly allocated buffers.

CHECKSUM_UNNECESSARY

Don't do any checksums. This is the policy in *snull* and in the loopback interface.

You may be wondering why the checksum status must be specified here when we
have already set a flag in the features field of our net_device structure. The answer is
that the features flag tells the kernel about how our device treats outgoing packets.
It is not used for incoming packets, which must, instead, be marked individually.

Finally, the driver updates its statistics counter to record that a packet has been
received. The statistics structure is made up of several fields; the most important are
rx_packets, rx_bytes, tx_packets, and tx_bytes, which contain the number of packets received and transmitted and the total number of octets transferred. All the fields
are thoroughly described in the section "Statistical Information."

The last step in packet reception is performed by *netif_rx*, which hands off the socket
buffer to the upper layers. *netif_rx* actually returns an integer value; NET_RX_SUCCESS
(0) means that the packet was successfully received; any other value indicates trouble.
There are three return values (NET_RX_CN_LOW, NET_RX_CN_MOD, and NET_RX_CN_HIGH) that
indicate increasing levels of congestion in the networking subsystem; NET_RX_DROP
means the packet was dropped. A driver could use these values to stop feeding packets into the kernel when congestion gets high, but, in practice, most drivers ignore the
return value from *netif_rx*. If you are writing a driver for a high-bandwidth device and
wish to do the right thing in response to congestion, the best approach is to implement NAPI, which we get to after a quick discussion of interrupt handlers.

The Interrupt Handler

Most hardware interfaces are controlled by means of an interrupt handler. The hardware interrupts the processor to signal one of two possible events: a new packet has
arrived or transmission of an outgoing packet is complete. Network interfaces can
also generate interrupts to signal errors, link status changes, and so on.

The usual interrupt routine can tell the difference between a new-packet-arrived interrupt and a done-transmitting notification by checking a status register found on the
physical device. The *snull* interface works similarly, but its status word is implemented

in software and lives in dev->priv. The interrupt handler for a network interface looks like this:

```
static void snull_regular_interrupt(int irq, void *dev_id, struct pt_regs *regs)
{
    int statusword;
    struct snull_priv *priv;
    struct snull_packet *pkt = NULL;
    /*
     * As usual, check the "device" pointer to be sure it is
     * really interrupting.
     * Then assign "struct device *dev"
     */
    struct net_device *dev = (struct net_device *)dev_id;
    /* ... and check with hw if it's really ours */

    /* paranoid */
    if (!dev)
        return;

    /* Lock the device */
    priv = netdev_priv(dev);
    spin_lock(&priv->lock);

    /* retrieve statusword: real netdevices use I/O instructions */
    statusword = priv->status;
    priv->status = 0;
    if (statusword & SNULL_RX_INTR) {
        /* send it to snull_rx for handling */
        pkt = priv->rx_queue;
        if (pkt) {
            priv->rx_queue = pkt->next;
            snull_rx(dev, pkt);
        }
    }
    if (statusword & SNULL_TX_INTR) {
        /* a transmission is over: free the skb */
        priv->stats.tx_packets++;
        priv->stats.tx_bytes += priv->tx_packetlen;
        dev_kfree_skb(priv->skb);
    }

    /* Unlock the device and we are done */
    spin_unlock(&priv->lock);
    if (pkt) snull_release_buffer(pkt); /* Do this outside the lock! */
    return;
}
```

The handler's first task is to retrieve a pointer to the correct struct net_device. This pointer usually comes from the dev_id pointer received as an argument.

The interesting part of this handler deals with the "transmission done" situation. In this case, the statistics are updated, and *dev_kfree_skb* is called to return the (no longer needed) socket buffer to the system. There are, actually, three variants of this function that may be called:

dev_kfree_skb(struct sk_buff *skb);
> This version should be called when you know that your code will not be running in interrupt context. Since *snull* has no actual hardware interrupts, this is the version we use.

dev_kfree_skb_irq(struct sk_buff *skb);
> If you know that you will be freeing the buffer in an interrupt handler, use this version, which is optimized for that case.

dev_kfree_skb_any(struct sk_buff *skb);
> This is the version to use if the relevant code could be running in either interrupt or noninterrupt context.

Finally, if your driver has temporarily stopped the transmission queue, this is usually the place to restart it with *netif_wake_queue*.

Packet reception, in contrast to transmission, doesn't need any special interrupt handling. Calling *snull_rx* (which we have already seen) is all that's required.

Receive Interrupt Mitigation

When a network driver is written as we have described above, the processor is interrupted for every packet received by your interface. In many cases, that is the desired mode of operation, and it is not a problem. High-bandwidth interfaces, however, can receive thousands of packets per second. With that sort of interrupt load, the overall performance of the system can suffer.

As a way of improving the performance of Linux on high-end systems, the networking subsystem developers have created an alternative interface (called NAPI)[*] based on polling. "Polling" can be a dirty word among driver developers, who often see polling techniques as inelegant and inefficient. Polling is inefficient, however, only if the interface is polled when there is no work to do. When the system has a high-speed interface handling heavy traffic, there is *always* more packets to process. There is no need to interrupt the processor in such situations; it is enough that the new packets be collected from the interface every so often.

Stopping receive interrupts can take a substantial amount of load off the processor. NAPI-compliant drivers can also be told not to feed packets into the kernel if those packets are just dropped in the networking code due to congestion, which can also help performance when that help is needed most. For various reasons, NAPI drivers are also less likely to reorder packets.

---

[*] NAPI stands for "new API"; the networking hackers are better at creating interfaces than naming them.

Not all devices can operate in the NAPI mode, however. A NAPI-capable interface must be able to store several packets (either on the card itself, or in an in-memory DMA ring). The interface should be capable of disabling interrupts for received packets, while continuing to interrupt for successful transmissions and other events. There are other subtle issues that can make writing a NAPI-compliant driver harder; see *Documentation/networking/NAPI_HOWTO.txt* in the kernel source tree for the details.

Relatively few drivers implement the NAPI interface. If you are writing a driver for an interface that may generate a huge number of interrupts, however, taking the time to implement NAPI may well prove worthwhile.

The *snull* driver, when loaded with the use_napi parameter set to a nonzero value, operates in the NAPI mode. At initialization time, we have to set up a couple of extra struct net_device fields:

```
if (use_napi) {
    dev->poll       = snull_poll;
    dev->weight     = 2;
}
```

The poll field must be set to your driver's polling function; we look at *snull_poll* shortly. The weight field describes the relative importance of the interface: how much traffic should be accepted from the interface when resources are tight. There are no strict rules for how the weight parameter should be set; by convention, 10 MBps Ethernet interfaces set weight to 16, while faster interfaces use 64. You should not set weight to a value greater than the number of packets your interface can store. In *snull*, we set the weight to two as a way of demonstrating deferred packet reception.

The next step in the creation of a NAPI-compliant driver is to change the interrupt handler. When your interface (which should start with receive interrupts enabled) signals that a packet has arrived, the interrupt handler should *not* process that packet. Instead, it should disable further receive interrupts and tell the kernel that it is time to start polling the interface. In the *snull* "interrupt" handler, the code that responds to packet reception interrupts has been changed to the following:

```
if (statusword & SNULL_RX_INTR) {
    snull_rx_ints(dev, 0);  /* Disable further interrupts */
    netif_rx_schedule(dev);
}
```

When the interface tells us that a packet is available, the interrupt handler leaves it in the interface; all that needs to happen at this point is a call to *netif_rx_schedule*, which causes our *poll* method to be called at some future point.

The *poll* method has this prototype:

```
int (*poll)(struct net_device *dev, int *budget);
```

The *snull* implementation of the *poll* method looks like this:

```
static int snull_poll(struct net_device *dev, int *budget)
{
    int npackets = 0, quota = min(dev->quota, *budget);
    struct sk_buff *skb;
    struct snull_priv *priv = netdev_priv(dev);
    struct snull_packet *pkt;

    while (npackets < quota && priv->rx_queue) {
        pkt = snull_dequeue_buf(dev);
        skb = dev_alloc_skb(pkt->datalen + 2);
        if (! skb) {
            if (printk_ratelimit())
                printk(KERN_NOTICE "snull: packet dropped\n");
            priv->stats.rx_dropped++;
            snull_release_buffer(pkt);
            continue;
        }
        memcpy(skb_put(skb, pkt->datalen), pkt->data, pkt->datalen);
        skb->dev = dev;
        skb->protocol = eth_type_trans(skb, dev);
        skb->ip_summed = CHECKSUM_UNNECESSARY; /* don't check it */
        netif_receive_skb(skb);

            /* Maintain stats */
        npackets++;
        priv->stats.rx_packets++;
        priv->stats.rx_bytes += pkt->datalen;
        snull_release_buffer(pkt);
    }
    /* If we processed all packets, we're done; tell the kernel and reenable ints */
    *budget -= npackets;
    dev->quota -= npackets;
    if (! priv->rx_queue) {
        netif_rx_complete(dev);
        snull_rx_ints(dev, 1);
        return 0;
    }
    /* We couldn't process everything. */
    return 1;
}
```

The central part of the function is concerned with the creation of an skb holding the packet; this code is the same as what we saw in *snull_rx* before. A number of things are different, however:

- The budget parameter provides a maximum number of packets that we are allowed to pass into the kernel. Within the device structure, the quota field gives another maximum; the *poll* method must respect the lower of the two limits. It should also decrement both dev->quota and *budget by the number of packets actually received. The budget value is a maximum number of packets that the current CPU can receive from all interfaces, while quota is a per-interface value that usually starts out as the weight assigned to the interface at initialization time.

- Packets should be fed to the kernel with *netif_receive_skb*, rather than *netif_rx*.
- If the *poll* method is able to process all of the available packets within the limits given to it, it should re-enable receive interrupts, call *netif_rx_complete* to turn off polling, and return 0. A return value of 1 indicates that there are packets remaining to be processed.

The networking subsystem guarantees that any given device's *poll* method will not be called concurrently on more than one processor. Calls to *poll* can still happen concurrently with calls to your other device methods, however.

Changes in Link State

Network connections, by definition, deal with the world outside the local system. Therefore, they are often affected by outside events, and they can be transient things. The networking subsystem needs to know when network links go up or down, and it provides a few functions that the driver may use to convey that information.

Most networking technologies involving an actual, physical connection provide a *carrier* state; the presence of the carrier means that the hardware is present and ready to function. Ethernet adapters, for example, sense the carrier signal on the wire; when a user trips over the cable, that carrier vanishes, and the link goes down. By default, network devices are assumed to have a carrier signal present. The driver can change that state explicitly, however, with these functions:

```
void netif_carrier_off(struct net_device *dev);
void netif_carrier_on(struct net_device *dev);
```

If your driver detects a lack of carrier on one of its devices, it should call *netif_carrier_off* to inform the kernel of this change. When the carrier returns, *netif_carrier_on* should be called. Some drivers also call *netif_carrier_off* when making major configuration changes (such as media type); once the adapter has finished resetting itself, the new carrier is detected and traffic can resume.

An integer function also exists:

```
int netif_carrier_ok(struct net_device *dev);
```

This can be used to test the current carrier state (as reflected in the device structure).

The Socket Buffers

We've now covered most of the issues related to network interfaces. What's still missing is some more detailed discussion of the sk_buff structure. The structure is at the core of the network subsystem of the Linux kernel, and we now introduce both the main fields of the structure and the functions used to act on it.

Although there is no strict need to understand the internals of sk_buff, the ability to look at its contents can be helpful when you are tracking down problems and when you are trying to optimize your code. For example, if you look in *loopback.c*, you'll find an optimization based on knowledge of the sk_buff internals. The usual warning applies here: if you write code that takes advantage of knowledge of the sk_buff structure, you should be prepared to see it break with future kernel releases. Still, sometimes the performance advantages justify the additional maintenance cost.

We are not going to describe the whole structure here, just the fields that might be used from within a driver. If you want to see more, you can look at *<linux/skbuff.h>*, where the structure is defined and the functions are prototyped. Additional details about how the fields and functions are used can be easily retrieved by grepping in the kernel sources.

The Important Fields

The fields introduced here are the ones a driver might need to access. They are listed in no particular order.

`struct net_device *dev;`

> The device receiving or sending this buffer.

`union { /* ... */ } h;`
`union { /* ... */ } nh;`
`union { /*... */} mac;`

> Pointers to the various levels of headers contained within the packet. Each field of the union is a pointer to a different type of data structure. h hosts pointers to transport layer headers (for example, `struct tcphdr *th`); nh includes network layer headers (such as `struct iphdr *iph`); and mac collects pointers to link-layer headers (such as `struct ethdr *ethernet`).
>
> If your driver needs to look at the source and destination addresses of a TCP packet, it can find them in skb->h.th. See the header file for the full set of header types that can be accessed in this way.
>
> Note that network drivers are responsible for setting the mac pointer for incoming packets. This task is normally handled by *eth_type_trans*, but non-Ethernet drivers have to set skb->mac.raw directly, as shown in the section "Non-Ethernet Headers."

`unsigned char *head;`
`unsigned char *data;`
`unsigned char *tail;`
`unsigned char *end;`

> Pointers used to address the data in the packet. head points to the beginning of the allocated space, data is the beginning of the valid octets (and is usually slightly greater than head), tail is the end of the valid octets, and end points to

the maximum address `tail` can reach. Another way to look at it is that the *available* buffer space is `skb->end - skb->head`, and the *currently used* data space is `skb->tail - skb->data`.

`unsigned int len;`
`unsigned int data_len;`

len is the full length of the data in the packet, while `data_len` is the length of the portion of the packet stored in separate fragments. The `data_len` field is 0 unless scatter/gather I/O is being used.

`unsigned char ip_summed;`

The checksum policy for this packet. The field is set by the driver on incoming packets, as described in the section "Packet Reception."

`unsigned char pkt_type;`

Packet classification used in its delivery. The driver is responsible for setting it to `PACKET_HOST` (this packet is for me), `PACKET_OTHERHOST` (no, this packet is not for me), `PACKET_BROADCAST`, or `PACKET_MULTICAST`. Ethernet drivers don't modify pkt_type explicitly because *eth_type_trans* does it for them.

`shinfo(struct sk_buff *skb);`
`unsigned int shinfo(skb)->nr_frags;`
`skb_frag_t shinfo(skb)->frags;`

For performance reasons, some skb information is stored in a separate structure that appears immediately after the skb in memory. This "shared info" (so called because it can be shared among copies of the skb within the networking code) must be accessed via the *shinfo* macro. There are several fields in this structure, but most of them are beyond the scope of this book. We saw `nr_frags` and `frags` in the section "Scatter/Gather I/O."

The remaining fields in the structure are not particularly interesting. They are used to maintain lists of buffers, to account for memory belonging to the socket that owns the buffer, and so on.

Functions Acting on Socket Buffers

Network devices that use an `sk_buff` structure act on it by means of the official interface functions. Many functions operate on socket buffers; here are the most interesting ones:

`struct sk_buff *alloc_skb(unsigned int len, int priority);`
`struct sk_buff *dev_alloc_skb(unsigned int len);`

Allocate a buffer. The *alloc_skb* function allocates a buffer and initializes both skb->data and skb->tail to skb->head. The *dev_alloc_skb* function is a shortcut that calls *alloc_skb* with `GFP_ATOMIC` priority and reserves some space between skb->head and skb->data. This data space is used for optimizations within the network layer and should not be touched by the driver.

```
void kfree_skb(struct sk_buff *skb);
void dev_kfree_skb(struct sk_buff *skb);
void dev_kfree_skb_irq(struct sk_buff *skb);
void dev_kfree_skb_any(struct sk_buff *skb);
```
Free a buffer. The *kfree_skb* call is used internally by the kernel. A driver should use one of the forms of *dev_kfree_skb* instead: *dev_kfree_skb* for noninterrupt context, *dev_kfree_skb_irq* for interrupt context, or *dev_kfree_skb_any* for code that can run in either context.

```
unsigned char *skb_put(struct sk_buff *skb, int len);
unsigned char *__skb_put(struct sk_buff *skb, int len);
```
Update the tail and len fields of the sk_buff structure; they are used to add data to the end of the buffer. Each function's return value is the previous value of skb->tail (in other words, it points to the data space just created). Drivers can use the return value to copy data by invoking memcpy(skb_put(...), data, len) or an equivalent. The difference between the two functions is that *skb_put* checks to be sure that the data fits in the buffer, whereas *__skb_put* omits the check.

```
unsigned char *skb_push(struct sk_buff *skb, int len);
unsigned char *__skb_push(struct sk_buff *skb, int len);
```
Functions to decrement skb->data and increment skb->len. They are similar to *skb_put*, except that data is added to the beginning of the packet instead of the end. The return value points to the data space just created. The functions are used to add a hardware header before transmitting a packet. Once again, *__skb_push* differs in that it does not check for adequate available space.

```
int skb_tailroom(struct sk_buff *skb);
```
Returns the amount of space available for putting data in the buffer. If a driver puts more data into the buffer than it can hold, the system panics. Although you might object that a *printk* would be sufficient to tag the error, memory corruption is so harmful to the system that the developers decided to take definitive action. In practice, you shouldn't need to check the available space if the buffer has been correctly allocated. Since drivers usually get the packet size before allocating a buffer, only a severely broken driver puts too much data in the buffer, and a panic might be seen as due punishment.

```
int skb_headroom(struct sk_buff *skb);
```
Returns the amount of space available in front of data, that is, how many octets one can "push" to the buffer.

```
void skb_reserve(struct sk_buff *skb, int len);
```
Increments both data and tail. The function can be used to reserve headroom before filling the buffer. Most Ethernet interfaces reserve two bytes in front of the packet; thus, the IP header is aligned on a 16-byte boundary, after a 14-byte Ethernet header. *snull* does this as well, although the instruction was not shown in "Packet Reception" to avoid introducing extra concepts at that point.

```
unsigned char *skb_pull(struct sk_buff *skb, int len);
```
Removes data from the head of the packet. The driver won't need to use this function, but it is included here for completeness. It decrements skb->len and increments skb->data; this is how the hardware header (Ethernet or equivalent) is stripped from the beginning of incoming packets.

```
int skb_is_nonlinear(struct sk_buff *skb);
```
Returns a true value if this skb is separated into multiple fragments for scatter/gather I/O.

```
int skb_headlen(struct sk_buff *skb);
```
Returns the length of the first segment of the skb (that part pointed to by skb->data).

```
void *kmap_skb_frag(skb_frag_t *frag);
void kunmap_skb_frag(void *vaddr);
```
If you must directly access fragments in a nonlinear skb from within the kernel, these functions map and unmap them for you. An atomic kmap is used, so you cannot have more than one fragment mapped at a time.

The kernel defines several other functions that act on socket buffers, but they are meant to be used in higher layers of networking code, and the driver doesn't need them.

MAC Address Resolution

An interesting issue with Ethernet communication is how to associate the MAC addresses (the interface's unique hardware ID) with the IP number. Most protocols have a similar problem, but we concentrate on the Ethernet-like case here. We try to offer a complete description of the issue, so we show three situations: ARP, Ethernet headers without ARP (such as *plip*), and non-Ethernet headers.

Using ARP with Ethernet

The usual way to deal with address resolution is by using the Address Resolution Protocol (ARP). Fortunately, ARP is managed by the kernel, and an Ethernet interface doesn't need to do anything special to support ARP. As long as dev->addr and dev->addr_len are correctly assigned at open time, the driver doesn't need to worry about resolving IP numbers to MAC addresses; *ether_setup* assigns the correct device methods to dev->hard_header and dev->rebuild_header.

Although the kernel normally handles the details of address resolution (and caching of the results), it calls upon the interface driver to help in the building of the packet. After all, the driver knows about the details of the physical layer header, while the authors of the networking code have tried to insulate the rest of the kernel from that knowledge. To this end, the kernel calls the driver's *hard_header* method to lay out the packet with the results of the ARP query. Normally, Ethernet driver writers need not know about this process—the common Ethernet code takes care of everything.

Overriding ARP

Simple point-to-point network interfaces, such as *plip*, might benefit from using Ethernet headers, while avoiding the overhead of sending ARP packets back and forth. The sample code in *snull* also falls into this class of network devices. *snull* cannot use ARP because the driver changes IP addresses in packets being transmitted, and ARP packets exchange IP addresses as well. Although we could have implemented a simple ARP reply generator with little trouble, it is more illustrative to show how to handle physical-layer headers directly.

If your device wants to use the usual hardware header without running ARP, you need to override the default *dev->hard_header* method. This is how *snull* implements it, as a very short function:

```
int snull_header(struct sk_buff *skb, struct net_device *dev,
                 unsigned short type, void *daddr, void *saddr,
                 unsigned int len)
{
    struct ethhdr *eth = (struct ethhdr *)skb_push(skb,ETH_HLEN);

    eth->h_proto = htons(type);
    memcpy(eth->h_source, saddr ? saddr : dev->dev_addr, dev->addr_len);
    memcpy(eth->h_dest,   daddr ? daddr : dev->dev_addr, dev->addr_len);
    eth->h_dest[ETH_ALEN-1]   ^= 0x01;   /* dest is us xor 1 */
    return (dev->hard_header_len);
}
```

The function simply takes the information provided by the kernel and formats it into a standard Ethernet header. It also toggles a bit in the destination Ethernet address, for reasons described later.

When a packet is received by the interface, the hardware header is used in a couple of ways by *eth_type_trans*. We have already seen this call in *snull_rx*:

```
skb->protocol = eth_type_trans(skb, dev);
```

The function extracts the protocol identifier (ETH_P_IP, in this case) from the Ethernet header; it also assigns skb->mac.raw, removes the hardware header from packet data (with *skb_pull*), and sets skb->pkt_type. This last item defaults to PACKET_HOST at skb allocation (which indicates that the packet is directed to this host), and *eth_type_trans* changes it to reflect the Ethernet destination address: if that address does not match the address of the interface that received it, the pkt_type field is set to PACKET_OTHERHOST. Subsequently, unless the interface is in promiscuous mode or packet forwarding is enabled in the kernel, *netif_rx* drops any packet of type PACKET_OTHERHOST. For this reason, *snull_header* is careful to make the destination hardware address match that of the "receiving" interface.

If your interface is a point-to-point link, you won't want to receive unexpected multi-cast packets. To avoid this problem, remember that a destination address whose first octet has 0 as the least significant bit (LSB) is directed to a single host (i.e., it is either PACKET_HOST or PACKET_OTHERHOST). The *plip* driver uses 0xfc as the first octet of its hardware address, while *snull* uses 0x00. Both addresses result in a working Ethernet-like point-to-point link.

Non-Ethernet Headers

We have just seen that the hardware header contains some information in addition to the destination address, the most important being the communication protocol. We now describe how hardware headers can be used to encapsulate relevant information. If you need to know the details, you can extract them from the kernel sources or the technical documentation for the particular transmission medium. Most driver writers are able to ignore this discussion and just use the Ethernet implementation.

It's worth noting that not all information has to be provided by every protocol. A point-to-point link such as *plip* or *snull* could avoid transferring the whole Ethernet header without losing generality. The *hard_header* device method, shown earlier as implemented by *snull_header*, receives the delivery information—both protocol-level and hardware addresses—from the kernel. It also receives the 16-bit protocol number in the type argument; IP, for example, is identified by ETH_P_IP. The driver is expected to correctly deliver both the packet data and the protocol number to the receiving host. A point-to-point link could omit addresses from its hardware header, transferring only the protocol number, because delivery is guaranteed independent of the source and destination addresses. An IP-only link could even avoid transmitting any hardware header whatsoever.

When the packet is picked up at the other end of the link, the receiving function in the driver should correctly set the fields skb->protocol, skb->pkt_type, and skb->mac.raw.

skb->mac.raw is a char pointer used by the address-resolution mechanism imple-mented in higher layers of the networking code (for instance, *net/ipv4/arp.c*). It must point to a machine address that matches dev->type. The possible values for the device type are defined in *<linux/if_arp.h>*; Ethernet interfaces use ARPHRD_ETHER. For example, here is how *eth_type_trans* deals with the Ethernet header for received packets:

```
skb->mac.raw = skb->data;
skb_pull(skb, dev->hard_header_len);
```

In the simplest case (a point-to-point link with no headers), skb->mac.raw can point to a static buffer containing the hardware address of this interface, protocol can be set to ETH_P_IP, and packet_type can be left with its default value of PACKET_HOST.

Because every hardware type is unique, it is hard to give more specific advice than already discussed. The kernel is full of examples, however. See, for example, the

AppleTalk driver (*drivers/net/appletalk/cops.c*), the infrared drivers (such as *drivers/net/irda/smc_ircc.c*), or the PPP driver (*drivers/net/ppp_generic.c*).

Custom ioctl Commands

We have seen that the *ioctl* system call is implemented for sockets; SIOCSIFADDR and SIOCSIFMAP are examples of "socket *ioctls*." Now let's see how the third argument of the system call is used by networking code.

When the *ioctl* system call is invoked on a socket, the command number is one of the symbols defined in *<linux/sockios.h>*, and the *sock_ioctl* function directly invokes a protocol-specific function (where "protocol" refers to the main network protocol being used, for example, IP or AppleTalk).

Any *ioctl* command that is not recognized by the protocol layer is passed to the device layer. These device-related *ioctl* commands accept a third argument from user space, a struct ifreq *. This structure is defined in *<linux/if.h>*. The SIOCSIFADDR and SIOCSIFMAP commands actually work on the ifreq structure. The extra argument to SIOCSIFMAP, although defined as ifmap, is just a field of ifreq.

In addition to using the standardized calls, each interface can define its own *ioctl* commands. The *plip* interface, for example, allows the interface to modify its internal timeout values via *ioctl*. The *ioctl* implementation for sockets recognizes 16 commands as private to the interface: SIOCDEVPRIVATE through SIOCDEVPRIVATE+15.[*]

When one of these commands is recognized, dev->do_ioctl is called in the relevant interface driver. The function receives the same struct ifreq * pointer that the general-purpose *ioctl* function uses:

```
int (*do_ioctl)(struct net_device *dev, struct ifreq *ifr, int cmd);
```

The ifr pointer points to a kernel-space address that holds a copy of the structure passed by the user. After *do_ioctl* returns, the structure is copied back to user space; Therefore, the driver can use the private commands to both receive and return data.

The device-specific commands can choose to use the fields in struct ifreq, but they already convey a standardized meaning, and it's unlikely that the driver can adapt the structure to its needs. The field ifr_data is a caddr_t item (a pointer) that is meant to be used for device-specific needs. The driver and the program used to invoke its *ioctl* commands should agree about the use of ifr_data. For example, *ppp-stats* uses device-specific commands to retrieve information from the *ppp* interface driver.

---

[*] Note that, according to *<linux/sockios.h>*, the SIOCDEVPRIVATE commands are deprecated. What should replace them is not clear, however, and numerous in-tree drivers still use them.

It's not worth showing an implementation of *do_ioctl* here, but with the information in this chapter and the kernel examples, you should be able to write one when you need it. Note, however, that the *plip* implementation uses `ifr_data` incorrectly and should not be used as an example for an *ioctl* implementation.

Statistical Information

The last method a driver needs is *get_stats*. This method returns a pointer to the statistics for the device. Its implementation is pretty easy; the one shown works even when several interfaces are managed by the same driver, because the statistics are hosted within the device data structure.

```
struct net_device_stats *snull_stats(struct net_device *dev)
{
    struct snull_priv *priv = netdev_priv(dev);
    return &priv->stats;
}
```

The real work needed to return meaningful statistics is distributed throughout the driver, where the various fields are updated. The following list shows the most interesting fields in `struct net_device_stats`:

`unsigned long rx_packets;`
`unsigned long tx_packets;`
> The total number of incoming and outgoing packets successfully transferred by the interface.

`unsigned long rx_bytes;`
`unsigned long tx_bytes;`
> The number of bytes received and transmitted by the interface.

`unsigned long rx_errors;`
`unsigned long tx_errors;`
> The number of erroneous receptions and transmissions. There's no end of things that can go wrong with packet transmission, and the `net_device_stats` structure includes six counters for specific receive errors and five for transmit errors. See *<linux/netdevice.h>* for the full list. If possible, your driver should maintain detailed error statistics, because they can be most helpful to system administrators trying to track down a problem.

`unsigned long rx_dropped;`
`unsigned long tx_dropped;`
> The number of packets dropped during reception and transmission. Packets are dropped when there's no memory available for packet data. `tx_dropped` is rarely used.

```
unsigned long collisions;
```
The number of collisions due to congestion on the medium.

```
unsigned long multicast;
```
The number of multicast packets received.

It is worth repeating that the *get_stats* method can be called at any time—even when the interface is down—so the driver must retain statistical information for as long as the net_device structure exists.

Multicast

A *multicast* packet is a network packet meant to be received by more than one host, but not by all hosts. This functionality is obtained by assigning special hardware addresses to groups of hosts. Packets directed to one of the special addresses should be received by all the hosts in that group. In the case of Ethernet, a multicast address has the least significant bit of the first address octet set in the destination address, while every device board has that bit clear in its own hardware address.

The tricky part of dealing with host groups and hardware addresses is performed by applications and the kernel, and the interface driver doesn't need to deal with these problems.

Transmission of multicast packets is a simple problem because they look exactly like any other packets. The interface transmits them over the communication medium without looking at the destination address. It's the kernel that has to assign a correct hardware destination address; the *hard_header* device method, if defined, doesn't need to look in the data it arranges.

The kernel handles the job of tracking which multicast addresses are of interest at any given time. The list can change frequently, since it is a function of the applications that are running at any given time and the users' interest. It is the driver's job to accept the list of interesting multicast addresses and deliver to the kernel any packets sent to those addresses. How the driver implements the multicast list is somewhat dependent on how the underlying hardware works. Typically, hardware belongs to one of three classes, as far as multicast is concerned:

- Interfaces that cannot deal with multicast. These interfaces either receive packets directed specifically to their hardware address (plus broadcast packets) or receive every packet. They can receive multicast packets only by receiving every packet, thus, potentially overwhelming the operating system with a huge number of "uninteresting" packets. You don't usually count these interfaces as multicast capable, and the driver won't set IFF_MULTICAST in dev->flags.

  Point-to-point interfaces are a special case because they always receive every packet without performing any hardware filtering.

- Interfaces that can tell multicast packets from other packets (host-to-host or broadcast). These interfaces can be instructed to receive every multicast packet and let the software determine if the address is interesting for this host. The overhead introduced in this case is acceptable, because the number of multicast packets on a typical network is low.

- Interfaces that can perform hardware detection of multicast addresses. These interfaces can be passed a list of multicast addresses for which packets are to be received, and ignore other multicast packets. This is the optimal case for the kernel, because it doesn't waste processor time dropping "uninteresting" packets received by the interface.

The kernel tries to exploit the capabilities of high-level interfaces by supporting the third device class, which is the most versatile, at its best. Therefore, the kernel notifies the driver whenever the list of valid multicast addresses is changed, and it passes the new list to the driver so it can update the hardware filter according to the new information.

Kernel Support for Multicasting

Support for multicast packets is made up of several items: a device method, a data structure, and device flags:

`void (*dev->set_multicast_list)(struct net_device *dev);`
> Device method called whenever the list of machine addresses associated with the device changes. It is also called when dev->flags is modified, because some flags (e.g., IFF_PROMISC) may also require you to reprogram the hardware filter. The method receives a pointer to struct net_device as an argument and returns void. A driver not interested in implementing this method can leave the field set to NULL.

`struct dev_mc_list *dev->mc_list;`
> A linked list of all the multicast addresses associated with the device. The actual definition of the structure is introduced at the end of this section.

`int dev->mc_count;`
> The number of items in the linked list. This information is somewhat redundant, but checking mc_count against 0 is a useful shortcut for checking the list.

`IFF_MULTICAST`
> Unless the driver sets this flag in dev->flags, the interface won't be asked to handle multicast packets. Nonetheless, the kernel calls the driver's *set_multicast_list* method when dev->flags changes, because the multicast list may have changed while the interface was not active.

IFF_ALLMULTI

Flag set in dev->flags by the networking software to tell the driver to retrieve all multicast packets from the network. This happens when multicast routing is enabled. If the flag is set, dev->mc_list shouldn't be used to filter multicast packets.

IFF_PROMISC

Flag set in dev->flags when the interface is put into promiscuous mode. Every packet should be received by the interface, independent of dev->mc_list.

The last bit of information needed by the driver developer is the definition of struct dev_mc_list, which lives in *<linux/netdevice.h>*:

```
struct dev_mc_list {
    struct dev_mc_list  *next;          /* Next address in list */
    __u8                dmi_addr[MAX_ADDR_LEN]; /* Hardware address */
    unsigned char       dmi_addrlen;    /* Address length */
    int                 dmi_users;      /* Number of users */
    int                 dmi_gusers;     /* Number of groups */
};
```

Because multicasting and hardware addresses are independent of the actual transmission of packets, this structure is portable across network implementations, and each address is identified by a string of octets and a length, just like dev->dev_addr.

A Typical Implementation

The best way to describe the design of *set_multicast_list* is to show you some pseudocode.

The following function is a typical implementation of the function in a full-featured (ff) driver. The driver is full featured in that the interface it controls has a complex hardware packet filter, which can hold a table of multicast addresses to be received by this host. The maximum size of the table is FF_TABLE_SIZE.

All the functions prefixed with ff_ are placeholders for hardware-specific operations:

```
void ff_set_multicast_list(struct net_device *dev)
{
    struct dev_mc_list *mcptr;

    if (dev->flags & IFF_PROMISC) {
        ff_get_all_packets();
        return;
    }
    /* If there's more addresses than we handle, get all multicast
    packets and sort them out in software. */
    if (dev->flags & IFF_ALLMULTI || dev->mc_count > FF_TABLE_SIZE) {
        ff_get_all_multicast_packets();
        return;
    }
    /* No multicast? Just get our own stuff */
    if (dev->mc_count == 0) {
```

```
        ff_get_only_own_packets( );
        return;
    }
    /* Store all of the multicast addresses in the hardware filter */
    ff_clear_mc_list( );
    for (mc_ptr = dev->mc_list; mc_ptr; mc_ptr = mc_ptr->next)
        ff_store_mc_address(mc_ptr->dmi_addr);
    ff_get_packets_in_multicast_list( );
}
```

This implementation can be simplified if the interface cannot store a multicast table in the hardware filter for incoming packets. In that case, FF_TABLE_SIZE reduces to 0, and the last four lines of code are not needed.

As was mentioned earlier, even interfaces that can't deal with multicast packets need to implement the *set_multicast_list* method to be notified about changes in dev->flags. This approach could be called a "nonfeatured" (nf) implementation. The implementation is very simple, as shown by the following code:

```
    void nf_set_multicast_list(struct net_device *dev)
    {
        if (dev->flags & IFF_PROMISC)
            nf_get_all_packets( );
        else
            nf_get_only_own_packets( );
    }
```

Implementing IFF_PROMISC is important, because otherwise the user won't be able to run *tcpdump* or any other network analyzers. If the interface runs a point-to-point link, on the other hand, there's no need to implement *set_multicast_list* at all, because users receive every packet anyway.

A Few Other Details

This section covers a few other topics that may be of interest to network driver authors. In each case, we simply try to point you in the right direction. Obtaining a complete picture of the subject probably requires spending some time digging through the kernel source as well.

Media Independent Interface Support

Media Independent Interface (or MII) is an IEEE 802.3 standard describing how Ethernet transceivers can interface with network controllers; many products on the market conform with this interface. If you are writing a driver for an MII-compliant controller, the kernel exports a generic MII support layer that may make your life easier.

To use the generic MII layer, you should include *<linux/mii.h>*. You need to fill out an mii_if_info structure with information on the physical ID of the transceiver, whether full duplex is in effect, etc. Also required are two methods for the mii_if_info structure:

```
int (*mdio_read) (struct net_device *dev, int phy_id, int location);
void (*mdio_write) (struct net_device *dev, int phy_id, int location, int val);
```

As you might expect, these methods should implement communications with your specific MII interface.

The generic MII code provides a set of functions for querying and changing the operating mode of the transceiver; many of these are designed to work with the *ethtool* utility (described in the next section). Look in *<linux/mii.h>* and *drivers/net/mii.c* for the details.

Ethtool Support

Ethtool is a utility designed to give system administrators a great deal of control over the operation of network interfaces. With *ethtool*, it is possible to control various interface parameters including speed, media type, duplex operation, DMA ring setup, hardware checksumming, wake-on-LAN operation, etc., but only if *ethtool* is supported by the driver. *Ethtool* may be downloaded from *http://sf.net/projects/gkernel/*.

The relevant declarations for *ethtool* support may be found in *<linux/ethtool.h>*. At the core of it is a structure of type ethtool_ops, which contains a full 24 different methods for *ethtool* support. Most of these methods are relatively straightforward; see *<linux/ethtool.h>* for the details. If your driver is using the MII layer, you can use *mii_ethtool_gset* and *mii_ethtool_sset* to implement the *get_settings* and *set_settings* methods, respectively.

For *ethtool* to work with your device, you must place a pointer to your ethtool_ops structure in the net_device structure. The macro SET_ETHTOOL_OPS (defined in *<linux/netdevice.h>*) should be used for this purpose. Do note that your *ethtool* methods can be called even when the interface is down.

Netpoll

"Netpoll" is a relatively late (2.6.5) addition to the network stack; its purpose is to enable the kernel to send and receive packets in situations where the full network and I/O subsystems may not be available. It is used for features like remote network consoles and remote kernel debugging. Supporting netpoll in your driver is not, by any means, necessary, but it may make your device more useful in some situations. Supporting netpoll is also relatively easy in most cases.

Drivers implementing netpoll should implement the *poll_controller* method. Its job is to keep up with anything that may be happening on the controller in the absence of device interrupts. Almost all *poll_controller* methods take the following form:

```
void my_poll_controller(struct net_device *dev)
{
    disable_device_interrupts(dev);
    call_interrupt_handler(dev->irq, dev, NULL);
    reenable_device_interrupts(dev);
}
```

The *poll_controller* method, in essence, is simply simulating interrupts from the given device.

Quick Reference

This section provides a reference for the concepts introduced in this chapter. It also explains the role of each header file that a driver needs to include. The lists of fields in the net_device and sk_buff structures, however, are not repeated here.

```
#include <linux/netdevice.h>
```
> Header that hosts the definitions of struct net_device and struct net_device_stats, and includes a few other headers that are needed by network drivers.

```
struct net_device *alloc_netdev(int sizeof_priv, char *name, void
    (*setup)(struct net_device *));
struct net_device *alloc_etherdev(int sizeof_priv);
void free_netdev(struct net_device *dev);
```
> Functions for allocating and freeing net_device structures.

```
int register_netdev(struct net_device *dev);
void unregister_netdev(struct net_device *dev);
```
> Registers and unregisters a network device.

```
void *netdev_priv(struct net_device *dev);
```
> A function that retrieves the pointer to the driver-private area of a network device structure.

```
struct net_device_stats;
```
> A structure that holds device statistics.

```
netif_start_queue(struct net_device *dev);
netif_stop_queue(struct net_device *dev);
netif_wake_queue(struct net_device *dev);
```
> Functions that control the passing of packets to the driver for transmission. No packets are transmitted until *netif_start_queue* has been called. *netif_stop_queue* suspends transmission, and *netif_wake_queue* restarts the queue and pokes the network layer to restart transmitting packets.

skb_shinfo(struct sk_buff *skb);
> A macro that provides access to the "shared info" portion of a packet buffer.

void netif_rx(struct sk_buff *skb);
> Function that can be called (including at interrupt time) to notify the kernel that a packet has been received and encapsulated into a socket buffer.

void netif_rx_schedule(dev);
> Function that informs the kernel that packets are available and that polling should be started on the interface; it is used only by NAPI-compliant drivers.

int netif_receive_skb(struct sk_buff *skb);
void netif_rx_complete(struct net_device *dev);
> Functions that should be used only by NAPI-compliant drivers. *netif_receive_skb* is the NAPI equivalent to *netif_rx*; it feeds a packet into the kernel. When a NAPI-compliant driver has exhausted the supply of received packets, it should reenable interrupts, and call *netif_rx_complete* to stop polling.

#include <linux/if.h>
> Included by *netdevice.h*, this file declares the interface flags (IFF_ macros) and struct ifmap, which has a major role in the *ioctl* implementation for network drivers.

void netif_carrier_off(struct net_device *dev);
void netif_carrier_on(struct net_device *dev);
int netif_carrier_ok(struct net_device *dev);
> The first two functions may be used to tell the kernel whether a carrier signal is currently present on the given interface. *netif_carrier_ok* tests the carrier state as reflected in the device structure.

#include <linux/if_ether.h>
ETH_ALEN
ETH_P_IP
struct ethhdr;
> Included by *netdevice.h*, *if_ether.h* defines all the ETH_ macros used to represent octet lengths (such as the address length) and network protocols (such as IP). It also defines the ethhdr structure.

#include <linux/skbuff.h>
> The definition of struct sk_buff and related structures, as well as several inline functions to act on the buffers. This header is included by *netdevice.h*.

```
struct sk_buff *alloc_skb(unsigned int len, int priority);
struct sk_buff *dev_alloc_skb(unsigned int len);
void kfree_skb(struct sk_buff *skb);
void dev_kfree_skb(struct sk_buff *skb);
void dev_kfree_skb_irq(struct sk_buff *skb);
void dev_kfree_skb_any(struct sk_buff *skb);
```
Functions that handle the allocation and freeing of socket buffers. Drivers should normally use the dev_ variants, which are intended for that purpose.

```
unsigned char *skb_put(struct sk_buff *skb, int len);
unsigned char *__skb_put(struct sk_buff *skb, int len);
unsigned char *skb_push(struct sk_buff *skb, int len);
unsigned char *__skb_push(struct sk_buff *skb, int len);
```
Functions that add data to an skb; *skb_put* puts the data at the end of the skb, while *skb_push* puts it at the beginning. The regular versions perform checking to ensure that adequate space is available; double-underscore versions leave those tests out.

```
int skb_headroom(struct sk_buff *skb);
int skb_tailroom(struct sk_buff *skb);
void skb_reserve(struct sk_buff *skb, int len);
```
Functions that perform management of space within an skb. *skb_headroom* and *skb_tailroom* tell how much space is available at the beginning and end, respectively, of an skb. *skb_reserve* may be used to reserve space at the beginning of an skb, which must be empty.

```
unsigned char *skb_pull(struct sk_buff *skb, int len);
```
skb_pull "removes" data from an skb by adjusting the internal pointers.

```
int skb_is_nonlinear(struct sk_buff *skb);
```
Function that returns a true value if this skb is separated into multiple fragments for scatter/gather I/O.

```
int skb_headlen(struct sk_buff *skb);
```
Returns the length of the first segment of the skb—that part pointed to by skb-> data.

```
void *kmap_skb_frag(skb_frag_t *frag);
void kunmap_skb_frag(void *vaddr);
```
Functions that provide direct access to fragments within a nonlinear skb.

```
#include <linux/etherdevice.h>
void ether_setup(struct net_device *dev);
```
Function that sets most device methods to the general-purpose implementation for Ethernet drivers. It also sets dev->flags and assigns the next available ethx name to dev->name if the first character in the name is a blank space or the NULL character.

unsigned short eth_type_trans(struct sk_buff *skb, struct net_device *dev);

When an Ethernet interface receives a packet, this function can be called to set skb->pkt_type. The return value is a protocol number that is usually stored in skb->protocol.

#include <linux/sockios.h>

SIOCDEVPRIVATE

The first of 16 *ioctl* commands that can be implemented by each driver for its own private use. All the network *ioctl* commands are defined in *sockios.h*.

#include <linux/mii.h>

struct mii_if_info;

Declarations and a structure supporting drivers of devices that implement the MII standard.

#include <linux/ethtool.h>

struct ethtool_ops;

Declarations and structures that let devices work with the *ethtool* utility.

CHAPTER 18

TTY Drivers

A tty device gets its name from the very old abbreviation of teletypewriter and was originally associated only with the physical or virtual terminal connection to a Unix machine. Over time, the name also came to mean any serial port style device, as terminal connections could also be created over such a connection. Some examples of physical tty devices are serial ports, USB-to-serial-port converters, and some types of modems that need special processing to work properly (such as the traditional Win-Modem style devices). tty virtual devices support virtual consoles that are used to log into a computer, from either the keyboard, over a network connection, or through a xterm session.

The Linux tty driver core lives right below the standard character driver level and provides a range of features focused on providing an interface for terminal style devices to use. The core is responsible for controlling both the flow of data across a tty device and the format of the data. This allows tty drivers to focus on handling the data to and from the hardware, instead of worrying about how to control the interaction with user space in a consistent way. To control the flow of data, there are a number of different line disciplines that can be virtually "plugged" into any tty device. This is done by different tty line discipline drivers.

As Figure 18-1 shows, the tty core takes data from a user that is to be sent to a tty device. It then passes it to a tty line discipline driver, which then passes it to the tty driver. The tty driver converts the data into a format that can be sent to the hardware. Data being received from the tty hardware flows back up through the tty driver, into the tty line discipline driver, and into the tty core, where it can be retrieved by a user. Sometimes the tty driver communicates directly to the tty core, and the tty core sends data directly to the tty driver, but usually the tty line discipline has a chance to modify the data that is sent between the two.

The tty driver never sees the tty line discipline. The driver cannot communicate directly with the line discipline, nor does it realize it is even present. The driver's job is to format data that is sent to it in a manner that the hardware can understand, and receive data from the hardware. The tty line discipline's job is to format the data

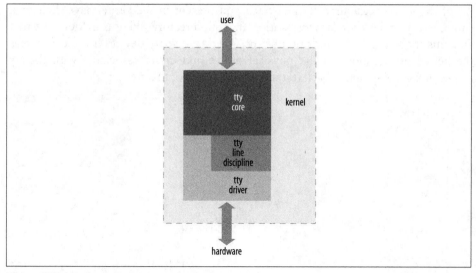

Figure 18-1. tty core overview

received from a user, or the hardware, in a specific manner. This formatting usually takes the form of a protocol conversion, such as PPP or Bluetooth.

There are three different types of tty drivers: console, serial port, and pty. The console and pty drivers have already been written and probably are the only ones needed of these types of tty drivers. This leaves any new drivers using the tty core to interact with the user and the system as serial port drivers.

To determine what kind of tty drivers are currently loaded in the kernel and what tty devices are currently present, look at the */proc/tty/drivers* file. This file consists of a list of the different tty drivers currently present, showing the name of the driver, the default node name, the major number for the driver, the range of minors used by the driver, and the type of the tty driver. The following is an example of this file:

```
/dev/tty        /dev/tty        5      0 system:/dev/tty
/dev/console    /dev/console    5      1 system:console
/dev/ptmx       /dev/ptmx       5      2 system
/dev/vc/0       /dev/vc/0       4      0 system:vtmaster
usbserial       /dev/ttyUSB     188  0-254 serial
serial          /dev/ttyS       4    64-67 serial
pty_slave       /dev/pts        136  0-255 pty:slave
pty_master      /dev/ptm        128  0-255 pty:master
pty_slave       /dev/ttyp       3    0-255 pty:slave
pty_master      /dev/pty        2    0-255 pty:master
unknown         /dev/tty        4     1-63 console
```

The */proc/tty/driver/* directory contains individual files for some of the tty drivers, if they implement that functionality. The default serial driver creates a file in this directory that shows a lot of serial-port-specific information about the hardware. Information on how to create a file in this directory is described later.

All of the tty devices currently registered and present in the kernel have their own subdirectory under */sys/class/tty*. Within that subdirectory, there is a "dev" file that contains the major and minor number assigned to that tty device. If the driver tells the kernel the locations of the physical device and driver associated with the tty device, it creates symlinks back to them. An example of this tree is:

```
/sys/class/tty/
|-- console
|   `-- dev
|-- ptmx
|   `-- dev
|-- tty
|   `-- dev
|-- tty0
|   `-- dev
    ...
|-- ttyS1
|   `-- dev
|-- ttyS2
|   `-- dev
|-- ttyS3
|   `-- dev
    ...
|-- ttyUSB0
|   |-- dev
|   |-- device -> ../../../devices/pci0000:00/0000:00:09.0/usb3/3-1/3-1:1.0/ttyUSB0
|   `-- driver -> ../../../bus/usb-serial/drivers/keyspan_4
|-- ttyUSB1
|   |-- dev
|   |-- device -> ../../../devices/pci0000:00/0000:00:09.0/usb3/3-1/3-1:1.0/ttyUSB1
|   `-- driver -> ../../../bus/usb-serial/drivers/keyspan_4
|-- ttyUSB2
|   |-- dev
|   |-- device -> ../../../devices/pci0000:00/0000:00:09.0/usb3/3-1/3-1:1.0/ttyUSB2
|   `-- driver -> ../../../bus/usb-serial/drivers/keyspan_4
`-- ttyUSB3
    |-- dev
    |-- device -> ../../../devices/pci0000:00/0000:00:09.0/usb3/3-1/3-1:1.0/ttyUSB3
    `-- driver -> ../../../bus/usb-serial/drivers/keyspan_4
```

A Small TTY Driver

To explain how the tty core works, we create a small tty driver that can be loaded, written to and read from, and unloaded. The main data structure of any tty driver is the struct tty_driver. It it used to register and unregister a tty driver with the tty core and is described in the kernel header file *<linux/tty_driver.h>*.

To create a struct tty_driver, the function *alloc_tty_driver* must be called with the number of tty devices this driver supports as the paramater. This can be done with the following brief code:

```
/* allocate the tty driver */
tiny_tty_driver = alloc_tty_driver(TINY_TTY_MINORS);
if (!tiny_tty_driver)
    return -ENOMEM;
```

After the *alloc_tty_driver* function is successfully called, the struct tty_driver should be initialized with the proper information based on the needs of the tty driver. This structure contains a lot of different fields, but not all of them have to be initialized in order to have a working tty driver. Here is an example that shows how to initialize the structure and sets up enough of the fields to create a working tty driver. It uses the *tty_set_operations* function to help copy over the set of function operations that is defined in the driver:

```
static struct tty_operations serial_ops = {
    .open = tiny_open,
    .close = tiny_close,
    .write = tiny_write,
    .write_room = tiny_write_room,
    .set_termios = tiny_set_termios,
};

...

    /* initialize the tty driver */
    tiny_tty_driver->owner = THIS_MODULE;
    tiny_tty_driver->driver_name = "tiny_tty";
    tiny_tty_driver->name = "ttty";
    tiny_tty_driver->devfs_name = "tts/ttty%d";
    tiny_tty_driver->major = TINY_TTY_MAJOR,
    tiny_tty_driver->type = TTY_DRIVER_TYPE_SERIAL,
    tiny_tty_driver->subtype = SERIAL_TYPE_NORMAL,
    tiny_tty_driver->flags = TTY_DRIVER_REAL_RAW | TTY_DRIVER_NO_DEVFS,
    tiny_tty_driver->init_termios = tty_std_termios;
    tiny_tty_driver->init_termios.c_cflag = B9600 | CS8 | CREAD | HUPCL | CLOCAL;
    tty_set_operations(tiny_tty_driver, &serial_ops);
```

The variables and functions listed above, and how this structure is used, are explained in the rest of the chapter.

To register this driver with the tty core, the struct tty_driver must be passed to the *tty_register_driver* function:

```
/* register the tty driver */
retval = tty_register_driver(tiny_tty_driver);
if (retval) {
    printk(KERN_ERR "failed to register tiny tty driver");
    put_tty_driver(tiny_tty_driver);
    return retval;
}
```

When *tty_register_driver* is called, the kernel creates all of the different sysfs tty files for the whole range of minor devices that this tty driver can have. If you use *devfs* (not covered in this book) and unless the TTY_DRIVER_NO_DEVFS flag is specified, *devfs* files are created, too. The flag may be specified if you want to call *tty_register_device* only for the devices that actually exist on the system, so the user always has an up-to-date view of the devices present in the kernel, which is what *devfs* users expect.

After registering itself, the driver registers the devices it controls through the *tty_register_device* function. This function has three arguments:

- A pointer to the struct tty_driver that the device belongs to.
- The minor number of the device.
- A pointer to the struct device that this tty device is bound to. If the tty device is not bound to any struct device, this argument can be set to NULL.

Our driver registers all of the tty devices at once, as they are virtual and not bound to any physical devices:

```
for (i = 0; i < TINY_TTY_MINORS; ++i)
    tty_register_device(tiny_tty_driver, i, NULL);
```

To unregister the driver with the tty core, all tty devices that were registered by calling *tty_register_device* need to be cleaned up with a call to *tty_unregister_device*. Then the struct tty_driver must be unregistered with a call to *tty_unregister_driver*:

```
for (i = 0; i < TINY_TTY_MINORS; ++i)
    tty_unregister_device(tiny_tty_driver, i);
tty_unregister_driver(tiny_tty_driver);
```

struct termios

The init_termios variable in the struct tty_driver is a struct termios. This variable is used to provide a sane set of line settings if the port is used before it is initialized by a user. The driver initializes the variable with a standard set of values, which is copied from the tty_std_termios variable. tty_std_termios is defined in the tty core as:

```
struct termios tty_std_termios = {
    .c_iflag = ICRNL | IXON,
    .c_oflag = OPOST | ONLCR,
    .c_cflag = B38400 | CS8 | CREAD | HUPCL,
    .c_lflag = ISIG | ICANON | ECHO | ECHOE | ECHOK |
               ECHOCTL | ECHOKE | IEXTEN,
    .c_cc = INIT_C_CC
};
```

The struct termios structure is used to hold all of the current line settings for a specific port on the tty device. These line settings control the current baud rate, data size, data flow settings, and many other values. The different fields of this structure are:

`tcflag_t c_iflag;`
> The input mode flags

`tcflag_t c_oflag;`
> The output mode flags

`tcflag_t c_cflag;`
> The control mode flags

`tcflag_t c_lflag;`
> The local mode flags

`cc_t c_line;`
> The line discipline type

`cc_t c_cc[NCCS];`
> An array of control characters

All of the mode flags are defined as a large bitfield. The different values of the modes, and what they are used for, can be seen in the termios manpages available in any Linux distribution. The kernel provides a set of useful macros to get at the different bits. These macros are defined in the header file *include/linux/tty.h*.

All the fields that were defined in the `tiny_tty_driver` variable are necessary to have a working tty driver. The `owner` field is necessary in order to prevent the tty driver from being unloaded while the tty port is open. In previous kernel versions, it was up to the tty driver itself to handle the module reference counting logic. But kernel programmers determined that it would to be difficult to solve all of the different possible race conditions, and so the tty core now handles all of this control for the tty drivers.

The `driver_name` and `name` fields look very similar, yet are used for different purposes. The `driver_name` variable should be set to something short, descriptive, and unique among all tty drivers in the kernel. This is because it shows up in the */proc/tty/drivers* file to describe the driver to the user and in the sysfs tty class directory of tty drivers currently loaded. The `name` field is used to define a name for the individual tty nodes assigned to this tty driver in the */dev* tree. This string is used to create a tty device by appending the number of the tty device being used at the end of the string. It is also used to create the device name in the sysfs */sys/class/tty/* directory. If devfs is enabled in the kernel, this name should include any subdirectory that the tty driver wants to be placed into. As an example, the serial driver in the kernel sets the name field to `tts/` if devfs is enabled and `ttyS` if it is not. This string is also displayed in the */proc/tty/drivers* file.

As we mentioned, the */proc/tty/drivers* file shows all of the currently registered tty drivers. With the *tiny_tty* driver registered in the kernel and no *devfs*, this file looks something like the following:

```
$ cat /proc/tty/drivers
tiny_tty             /dev/ttty      240       0-3 serial
usbserial            /dev/ttyUSB    188     0-254 serial
serial               /dev/ttyS        4    64-107 serial
pty_slave            /dev/pts       136     0-255 pty:slave
pty_master           /dev/ptm       128     0-255 pty:master
pty_slave            /dev/ttyp        3     0-255 pty:slave
pty_master           /dev/pty         2     0-255 pty:master
unknown              /dev/vc/         4      1-63 console
/dev/vc/0            /dev/vc/0        4         0 system:vtmaster
/dev/ptmx            /dev/ptmx        5         2 system
/dev/console         /dev/console     5         1 system:console
/dev/tty             /dev/tty         5         0 system:/dev/tty
```

Also, the sysfs directory */sys/class/tty* looks something like the following when the tiny_tty driver is registered with the tty core:

```
$ tree /sys/class/tty/ttty*
/sys/class/tty/ttty0
`-- dev
/sys/class/tty/ttty1
`-- dev
/sys/class/tty/ttty2
`-- dev
/sys/class/tty/ttty3
`-- dev

$ cat /sys/class/tty/ttty0/dev
240:0
```

The major variable describes what the major number for this driver is. The type and subtype variables declare what type of tty driver this driver is. For our example, we are a serial driver of a "normal" type. The only other subtype for a tty driver would be a "callout" type. Callout devices were traditionally used to control the line settings of a device. The data would be sent and received through one device node, and any line setting changes would be sent to a different device node, which was the callout device. This required the use of two minor numbers for every single tty device. Thankfully, almost all drivers handle both the data and line settings on the same device node, and the callout type is rarely used for new drivers.

The flags variable is used by both the tty driver and the tty core to indicate the current state of the driver and what kind of tty driver it is. Several bitmask macros are defined that you must use when testing or manipulating the flags. Three bits in the flags variable can be set by the driver:

TTY_DRIVER_RESET_TERMIOS
    This flag states that the tty core resets the termios setting whenever the last process has closed the device. This is useful for the console and pty drivers. For

instance, suppose the user leaves a terminal in a weird state. With this flag set, the terminal is reset to a normal value when the user logs out or the process that controlled the session is "killed."

`TTY_DRIVER_REAL_RAW`

This flag states that the tty driver guarantees to send notifications of parity or break characters up-to-the-line discipline. This allows the line discipline to process received characters in a much quicker manner, as it does not have to inspect every character received from the tty driver. Because of the speed benefits, this value is usually set for all tty drivers.

`TTY_DRIVER_NO_DEVFS`

This flag states that when the call to *tty_register_driver* is made, the tty core does not create any devfs entries for the tty devices. This is useful for any driver that dynamically creates and destroys the minor devices. Examples of drivers that set this are the USB-to-serial drivers, the USB modem driver, the USB Bluetooth tty driver, and a number of the standard serial port drivers.

When the tty driver later wants to register a specific tty device with the tty core, it must call *tty_register_device*, with a pointer to the tty driver, and the minor number of the device that has been created. If this is not done, the tty core still passes all calls to the tty driver, but some of the internal tty-related functionality might not be present. This includes */sbin/hotplug* notification of new tty devices and sysfs representation of the tty device. When the registered tty device is removed from the machine, the tty driver must call *tty_unregister_device*.

The one remaining bit in this variable is controlled by the tty core and is called `TTY_DRIVER_INSTALLED`. This flag is set by the tty core after the driver has been registered and should never be set by a tty driver.

tty_driver Function Pointers

Finally, the *tiny_tty* driver declares four function pointers.

open and close

The *open* function is called by the tty core when a user calls open on the device node the tty driver is assigned to. The tty core calls this with a pointer to the `tty_struct` structure assigned to this device, and a file pointer. The open field must be set by a tty driver for it to work properly; otherwise, `-ENODEV` is returned to the user when open is called.

When this *open* function is called, the tty driver is expected to either save some data within the `tty_struct` variable that is passed to it, or save the data within a static array that can be referenced based on the minor number of the port. This is necessary so the tty driver knows which device is being referenced when the later close, write, and other functions are called.

The *tiny_tty* driver saves a pointer within the tty structure, as can be seen with the following code:

```
static int tiny_open(struct tty_struct *tty, struct file *file)
{
    struct tiny_serial *tiny;
    struct timer_list *timer;
    int index;

    /* initialize the pointer in case something fails */
    tty->driver_data = NULL;

    /* get the serial object associated with this tty pointer */
    index = tty->index;
    tiny = tiny_table[index];
    if (tiny == NULL) {
        /* first time accessing this device, let's create it */
        tiny = kmalloc(sizeof(*tiny), GFP_KERNEL);
        if (!tiny)
            return -ENOMEM;

        init_MUTEX(&tiny->sem);
        tiny->open_count = 0;
        tiny->timer = NULL;

        tiny_table[index] = tiny;
    }

    down(&tiny->sem);

    /* save our structure within the tty structure */
    tty->driver_data = tiny;
    tiny->tty = tty;
```

In this code, the tiny_serial structure is saved within the tty structure. This allows the *tiny_write*, *tiny_write_room*, and *tiny_close* functions to retrieve the tiny_serial structure and manipulate it properly.

The tiny_serial structure is defined as:

```
struct tiny_serial {
    struct tty_struct    *tty;       /* pointer to the tty for this device */
    int          open_count; /* number of times this port has been opened */
    struct semaphore    sem;        /* locks this structure */
    struct timer_list   *timer;

};
```

As we've seen, the open_count variable is initialized to 0 in the open call the first time the port is opened. This is a typical reference counter, needed because the *open* and *close* functions of a tty driver can be called multiple times for the same device in order to allow multiple processes to read and write data. To handle everything correctly, a count of how many times the port has been opened or closed must be kept; the driver increments and decrements the count as the port is used. When the port is opened for the first time, any needed hardware initialization and memory allocation can be done. When the port is closed for the last time, any needed hardware shutdown and memory cleanup can be done.

The rest of the *tiny_open* function shows how to keep track of the number of times the device has been opened:

```
++tiny->open_count;
if (tiny->open_count == 1) {
    /* this is the first time this port is opened */
    /* do any hardware initialization needed here */
```

The *open* function must return either a negative error number if something has happened to prevent the open from being successful, or a 0 to indicate success.

The *close* function pointer is called by the tty core when *close* is called by a user on the file handle that was previously created with a call to *open*. This indicates that the device should be closed at this time. However, since the *open* function can be called more than once, the *close* function also can be called more than once. So this function should keep track of how many times it has been called to determine if the hardware should really be shut down at this time. The *tiny_tty* driver does this with the following code:

```
static void do_close(struct tiny_serial *tiny)
{
    down(&tiny->sem);

    if (!tiny->open_count) {
        /* port was never opened */
        goto exit;
    }

    --tiny->open_count;
    if (tiny->open_count <= 0) {
        /* The port is being closed by the last user. */
        /* Do any hardware specific stuff here */

        /* shut down our timer */
        del_timer(tiny->timer);
    }
exit:
    up(&tiny->sem);
}

static void tiny_close(struct tty_struct *tty, struct file *file)
{
    struct tiny_serial *tiny = tty->driver_data;
```

```
    if (tiny)
        do_close(tiny);
}
```

The *tiny_close* function just calls the *do_close* function to do the real work of closing the device. This is done so that the shutdown logic does not have to be duplicated here and when the driver is unloaded and a port is open. The *close* function has no return value, as it is not supposed to be able to fail.

Flow of Data

The *write* function call is called by the user when there is data to be sent to the hardware. First the tty core receives the call, and then it passes the data on to the tty driver's *write* function. The tty core also tells the tty driver the size of the data being sent.

Sometimes, because of the speed and buffer capacity of the tty hardware, not all characters requested by the writing program can be sent at the moment the *write* function is called. The *write* function should return the number of characters that was able to be sent to the hardware (or queued to be sent at a later time), so that the user program can check if all of the data really was written. It is much easier for this check to be done in user space than it is for a kernel driver to sit and sleep until all of the requested data is able to be sent out. If any errors happen during the *write* call, a negative error value should be returned instead of the number of characters that were written.

The *write* function can be called from both interrupt context and user context. This is important to know, as the tty driver should not call any functions that might sleep when it is in interrupt context. These include any function that might possibly call *schedule*, such as the common functions *copy_from_user*, *kmalloc*, and *printk*. If you really want to sleep, make sure to check first whether the driver is in interrupt context by calling *in_interrupt*.

This sample tiny tty driver does not connect to any real hardware, so its write function simply records in the kernel debug log what data was supposed to be written. It does this with the following code:

```
static int tiny_write(struct tty_struct *tty,
            const unsigned char *buffer, int count)
{
    struct tiny_serial *tiny = tty->driver_data;
    int i;
    int retval = -EINVAL;

    if (!tiny)
        return -ENODEV;

    down(&tiny->sem);
```

```
    if (!tiny->open_count)
        /* port was not opened */
        goto exit;

    /* fake sending the data out a hardware port by
     * writing it to the kernel debug log.
     */
    printk(KERN_DEBUG "%s - ", __FUNCTION__);
    for (i = 0; i < count; ++i)
        printk("%02x ", buffer[i]);
    printk("\n");

exit:
    up(&tiny->sem);
    return retval;
}
```

The *write* function can be called when the tty subsystem itself needs to send some data out the tty device. This can happen if the tty driver does not implement the *put_char* function in the tty_struct. In that case, the tty core uses the *write* function callback with a data size of 1. This commonly happens when the tty core wants to convert a newline character to a line feed plus a newline character. The biggest problem that can occur here is that the tty driver's *write* function must not return 0 for this kind of call. This means that the driver must write that byte of data to the device, as the caller (the tty core) does not buffer the data and try again at a later time. As the *write* function can not determine if it is being called in the place of *put_char*, even if only one byte of data is being sent, try to implement the *write* function so it always writes at least one byte before returning. A number of the current USB-to-serial tty drivers do not follow this rule, and because of this, some terminals types do not work properly when connected to them.

The *write_room* function is called when the tty core wants to know how much room in the write buffer the tty driver has available. This number changes over time as characters empty out of the write buffers and as the *write* function is called, adding characters to the buffer.

```
static int tiny_write_room(struct tty_struct *tty)
{
    struct tiny_serial *tiny = tty->driver_data;
    int room = -EINVAL;

    if (!tiny)
        return -ENODEV;

    down(&tiny->sem);

    if (!tiny->open_count) {
        /* port was not opened */
        goto exit;
    }
```

```
    /* calculate how much room is left in the device */
    room = 255;

exit:
    up(&tiny->sem);
    return room;
}
```

Other Buffering Functions

The *chars_in_buffer* function in the `tty_driver` structure is not required in order to have a working tty driver, but it is recommended. This function is called when the tty core wants to know how many characters are still remaining in the tty driver's write buffer to be sent out. If the driver can store characters before it sends them out to the hardware, it should implement this function in order for the tty core to be able to determine if all of the data in the driver has drained out.

Three functions callbacks in the `tty_driver` structure can be used to flush any remaining data that the driver is holding on to. These are not required to be implemented, but are recommended if the tty driver can buffer data before it sends it to the hardware. The first two function callbacks are called *flush_chars* and *wait_until_sent*. These functions are called when the tty core has sent a number of characters to the tty driver using the *put_char* function callback. The *flush_chars* function callback is called when the tty core wants the tty driver to start sending these characters out to the hardware, if it hasn't already started. This function is allowed to return before all of the data is sent out to the hardware. The *wait_until_sent* function callback works much the same way; but it must wait until all of the characters are sent before returning to the tty core or until the passed in *timeout* value has expired, whichever occurrence happens first. The tty driver is allowed to sleep within this function in order to complete it. If the timeout value passed to the *wait_until_sent* function callback is set to 0, the function should wait until it is finished with the operation.

The remaining data flushing function callback is *flush_buffer*. It is called by the tty core when the tty driver is to flush all of the data still in its write buffers out of memory. Any data remaining in the buffer is lost and not sent to the device.

No read Function?

With only these functions, the *tiny_tty* driver can be registered, a device node opened, data written to the device, the device node closed, and the driver unregistered and unloaded from the kernel. But the tty core and `tty_driver` structure do not provide a read function; in other words; no function callback exists to get data from the driver to the tty core.

Instead of a conventional read function, the tty driver is responsible for sending any data received from the hardware to the tty core when it is received. The tty core buffers the data until it is asked for by the user. Because of the buffering logic the tty core provides, it is not necessary for every tty driver to implement its own buffering logic. The tty core notifies the tty driver when a user wants the driver to stop and start sending data, but if the internal tty buffers are full, no such notification occurs.

The tty core buffers the data received by the tty drivers in a structure called struct tty_flip_buffer. A flip buffer is a structure that contains two main data arrays. Data being received from the tty device is stored in the first array. When that array is full, any user waiting on the data is notified that data is available to be read. While the user is reading the data from this array, any new incoming data is being stored in the second array. When that array is finished, the data is again flushed to the user, and the driver starts to fill up the first array. Essentially, the data being received "flips" from one buffer to the other, hopefully not overflowing both of them. To try to prevent data from being lost, a tty driver can monitor how big the incoming array is, and, if it fills up, tell the tty driver to flush the buffer at this moment in time, instead of waiting for the next available chance.

The details of the struct tty_flip_buffer structure do not really matter to the tty driver, with one exception, the variable count. This variable contains how many bytes are currently left in the buffer that are being used for receiving data. If this value is equal to the value TTY_FLIPBUF_SIZE, the flip buffer needs to be flushed out to the user with a call to *tty_flip_buffer_push*. This is shown in the following bit of code:

```
for (i = 0; i < data_size; ++i) {
    if (tty->flip.count >= TTY_FLIPBUF_SIZE)
        tty_flip_buffer_push(tty);
    tty_insert_flip_char(tty, data[i], TTY_NORMAL);
}
tty_flip_buffer_push(tty);
```

Characters that are received from the tty driver to be sent to the user are added to the flip buffer with a call to *tty_insert_flip_char*. The first parameter of this function is the struct tty_struct the data should be saved in, the second parameter is the character to be saved, and the third parameter is any flags that should be set for this character. The flags value should be set to TTY_NORMAL if this is a normal character being received. If this is a special type of character indicating an error receiving data, it should be set to TTY_BREAK, TTY_FRAME, TTY_PARITY, or TTY_OVERRUN, depending on the error.

In order to "push" the data to the user, a call to *tty_flip_buffer_push* is made. This function should also be called if the flip buffer is about to overflow, as is shown in this example. So whenever data is added to the flip buffer, or when the flip buffer is full, the tty driver must call *tty_flip_buffer_push*. If the tty driver can accept data at very high rates, the tty->low_latency flag should be set, which causes the call to *tty_flip_buffer_push* to be immediately executed when called. Otherwise, the *tty_flip_buffer_push* call schedules itself to push the data out of the buffer at some later point in the near future.

TTY Line Settings

When a user wants to change the line settings of a tty device or retrieve the current line settings, he makes one of the many different termios user-space library function calls or directly makes an *ioctl* call on the tty device node. The tty core converts both of these interfaces into a number of different tty driver function callbacks and *ioctl* calls.

set_termios

The majority of the termios user-space functions are translated by the library into an *ioctl* call to the driver node. A large number of the different tty *ioctl* calls are then translated by the tty core into a single *set_termios* function call to the tty driver. The *set_termios* callback needs to determine which line settings it is being asked to change, and then make those changes in the tty device. The tty driver must be able to decode all of the different settings in the termios structure and react to any needed changes. This is a complicated task, as all of the line settings are packed into the termios structure in a wide variety of ways.

The first thing that a *set_termios* function should do is determine whether anything actually has to be changed. This can be done with the following code:

```
unsigned int cflag;

cflag = tty->termios->c_cflag;

/* check that they really want us to change something */
if (old_termios) {
    if ((cflag == old_termios->c_cflag) &&
        (RELEVANT_IFLAG(tty->termios->c_iflag) ==
         RELEVANT_IFLAG(old_termios->c_iflag))) {
        printk(KERN_DEBUG " - nothing to change...\n");
        return;
    }
}
```

The RELEVANT_IFLAG macro is defined as:

```
#define RELEVANT_IFLAG(iflag) ((iflag) & (IGNBRK|BRKINT|IGNPAR|PARMRK|INPCK))
```

and is used to mask off the important bits of the cflags variable. This is then compared to the old value, and see if they differ. If not, nothing needs to be changed, so we return. Note that the old_termios variable is first checked to see if it points to a valid structure first, before it is accessed. This is required, as sometimes this variable is set to NULL. Trying to access a field off of a NULL pointer causes the kernel to panic.

To look at the requested byte size, the CSIZE bitmask can be used to separate out the proper bits from the cflag variable. If the size can not be determined, it is customary to default to eight data bits. This can be implemented as follows:

```
/* get the byte size */
switch (cflag & CSIZE) {
    case CS5:
        printk(KERN_DEBUG " - data bits = 5\n");
        break;
    case CS6:
        printk(KERN_DEBUG " - data bits = 6\n");
        break;
    case CS7:
        printk(KERN_DEBUG " - data bits = 7\n");
        break;
    default:
    case CS8:
        printk(KERN_DEBUG " - data bits = 8\n");
        break;
}
```

To determine the requested parity value, the PARENB bitmask can be checked against the cflag variable to tell if any parity is to be set at all. If so, the PARODD bitmask can be used to determine if the parity should be odd or even. An implementation of this is:

```
/* determine the parity */
if (cflag & PARENB)
    if (cflag & PARODD)
        printk(KERN_DEBUG " - parity = odd\n");
    else
        printk(KERN_DEBUG " - parity = even\n");
else
    printk(KERN_DEBUG " - parity = none\n");
```

The stop bits that are requested can also be determined from the cflag variable using the CSTOPB bitmask. An implemention of this is:

```
/* figure out the stop bits requested */
if (cflag & CSTOPB)
    printk(KERN_DEBUG " - stop bits = 2\n");
else
    printk(KERN_DEBUG " - stop bits = 1\n");
```

There are a two basic types of flow control: hardware and software. To determine if the user is asking for hardware flow control, the CRTSCTS bitmask can be checked against the cflag variable. An exmple of this is:

```
/* figure out the hardware flow control settings */
if (cflag & CRTSCTS)
    printk(KERN_DEBUG " - RTS/CTS is enabled\n");
else
    printk(KERN_DEBUG " - RTS/CTS is disabled\n");
```

Determining the different modes of software flow control and the different stop and start characters is a bit more involved:

```
/* determine software flow control */
/* if we are implementing XON/XOFF, set the start and
 * stop character in the device */
if (I_IXOFF(tty) || I_IXON(tty)) {
    unsigned char stop_char  = STOP_CHAR(tty);
    unsigned char start_char = START_CHAR(tty);

    /* if we are implementing INBOUND XON/XOFF */
    if (I_IXOFF(tty))
        printk(KERN_DEBUG " - INBOUND XON/XOFF is enabled, "
            "XON = %2x, XOFF = %2x", start_char, stop_char);
    else
        printk(KERN_DEBUG" - INBOUND XON/XOFF is disabled");

    /* if we are implementing OUTBOUND XON/XOFF */
    if (I_IXON(tty))
        printk(KERN_DEBUG" - OUTBOUND XON/XOFF is enabled, "
            "XON = %2x, XOFF = %2x", start_char, stop_char);
    else
        printk(KERN_DEBUG" - OUTBOUND XON/XOFF is disabled");
}
```

Finally, the baud rate needs to be determined. The tty core provides a function, *tty_get_baud_rate*, to help do this. The function returns an integer indicating the requested baud rate for the specific tty device:

```
/* get the baud rate wanted */
printk(KERN_DEBUG " - baud rate = %d", tty_get_baud_rate(tty));
```

Now that the tty driver has determined all of the different line settings, it can set the hardware up properly based on these values.

tiocmget and tiocmset

In the 2.4 and older kernels, there used to be a number of tty *ioctl* calls to get and set the different control line settings. These were denoted by the constants TIOCMGET, TIOCMBIS, TIOCMBIC, and TIOCMSET. TIOCMGET was used to get the line setting values of the kernel, and as of the 2.6 kernel, this *ioctl* call has been turned into a tty driver callback function called *tiocmget*. The other three *ioctls* have been simplified and are now represented with a single tty driver callback function called *tiocmset*.

The *tiocmget* function in the tty driver is called by the tty core when the core wants to know the current physical values of the control lines of a specific tty device. This is usually done to retrieve the values of the DTR and RTS lines of a serial port. If the tty driver cannot directly read the MSR or MCR registers of the serial port, because the hardware does not allow this, a copy of them should be kept locally. A number of the

USB-to-serial drivers must implement this kind of "shadow" variable. Here is how this function could be implemented if a local copy of these values are kept:

```
static int tiny_tiocmget(struct tty_struct *tty, struct file *file)
{
    struct tiny_serial *tiny = tty->driver_data;

    unsigned int result = 0;
    unsigned int msr = tiny->msr;
    unsigned int mcr = tiny->mcr;

    result = ((mcr & MCR_DTR)  ? TIOCM_DTR  : 0) |  /* DTR is set */
             ((mcr & MCR_RTS)  ? TIOCM_RTS  : 0) |  /* RTS is set */
             ((mcr & MCR_LOOP) ? TIOCM_LOOP : 0) |  /* LOOP is set */
             ((msr & MSR_CTS)  ? TIOCM_CTS  : 0) |  /* CTS is set */
             ((msr & MSR_CD)   ? TIOCM_CAR  : 0) |  /* Carrier detect is set*/
             ((msr & MSR_RI)   ? TIOCM_RI   : 0) |  /* Ring Indicator is set */
             ((msr & MSR_DSR)  ? TIOCM_DSR  : 0);   /* DSR is set */

    return result;
}
```

The *tiocmset* function in the tty driver is called by the tty core when the core wants to set the values of the control lines of a specific tty device. The tty core tells the tty driver what values to set and what to clear, by passing them in two variables: set and clear. These variables contain a bitmask of the lines settings that should be changed. An *ioctl* call never asks the driver to both set and clear a particular bit at the same time, so it does not matter which operation occurs first. Here is an example of how this function could be implemented by a tty driver:

```
static int tiny_tiocmset(struct tty_struct *tty, struct file *file,
                         unsigned int set, unsigned int clear)
{
    struct tiny_serial *tiny = tty->driver_data;
    unsigned int mcr = tiny->mcr;

    if (set & TIOCM_RTS)
        mcr |= MCR_RTS;
    if (set & TIOCM_DTR)
        mcr |= MCR_RTS;

    if (clear & TIOCM_RTS)
        mcr &= ~MCR_RTS;
    if (clear & TIOCM_DTR)
        mcr &= ~MCR_RTS;

    /* set the new MCR value in the device */
    tiny->mcr = mcr;
    return 0;
}
```

ioctls

The *ioctl* function callback in the struct `tty_driver` is called by the tty core when *ioctl*(2) is called on the device node. If the tty driver does not know how to handle the *ioctl* value passed to it, it should return `-ENOIOCTLCMD` to try to let the tty core implement a generic version of the call.

The 2.6 kernel defines about 70 different tty *ioctls* that can be be sent to a tty driver. Most tty drivers do not handle all of these, but only a small subset of the more common ones. Here is a list of the more popular tty *ioctls*, what they mean, and how to implement them:

TIOCSERGETLSR

Gets the value of this tty device's line status register (LSR).

TIOCGSERIAL

Gets the serial line information. A caller can potentially get a lot of serial line information from the tty device all at once in this call. Some programs (such as *setserial* and *dip*) call this function to make sure that the baud rate was properly set and to get general information on what type of device the tty driver controls. The caller passes in a pointer to a large struct of type `serial_struct`, which the tty driver should fill up with the proper values. Here is an example of how this can be implemented:

```
static int tiny_ioctl(struct tty_struct *tty, struct file *file,
                      unsigned int cmd, unsigned long arg)
{
    struct tiny_serial *tiny = tty->driver_data;
    if (cmd == TIOCGSERIAL) {
        struct serial_struct tmp;
        if (!arg)
            return -EFAULT;
        memset(&tmp, 0, sizeof(tmp));
        tmp.type            = tiny->serial.type;
        tmp.line            = tiny->serial.line;
        tmp.port            = tiny->serial.port;
        tmp.irq             = tiny->serial.irq;
        tmp.flags           = ASYNC_SKIP_TEST | ASYNC_AUTO_IRQ;
        tmp.xmit_fifo_size  = tiny->serial.xmit_fifo_size;
        tmp.baud_base       = tiny->serial.baud_base;
        tmp.close_delay     = 5*HZ;
        tmp.closing_wait    = 30*HZ;
        tmp.custom_divisor  = tiny->serial.custom_divisor;
        tmp.hub6            = tiny->serial.hub6;
        tmp.io_type         = tiny->serial.io_type;
        if (copy_to_user((void __user *)arg, &tmp, sizeof(tmp)))
            return -EFAULT;
        return 0;
    }
    return -ENOIOCTLCMD;
}
```

TIOCSSERIAL

Sets the serial line information. This is the opposite of `TIOCGSERIAL` and allows the user to set the serial line status of the tty device all at once. A pointer to a struct `serial_struct` is passed to this call, full of data that the tty device should now be set to. If the tty driver does not implement this call, most programs still works properly.

TIOCMIWAIT

Waits for MSR change. The user asks for this *ioctl* in the unusual circumstances that it wants to sleep within the kernel until something happens to the MSR register of the tty device. The arg parameter contains the type of event that the user is waiting for. This is commonly used to wait until a status line changes, signaling that more data is ready to be sent to the device.

Be careful when implementing this *ioctl*, and do not use the *interruptible_sleep_on* call, as it is unsafe (there are lots of nasty race conditions involved with it). Instead, a *wait_queue* should be used to avoid these problems. Here's an example of how to implement this ioctl:

```
static int tiny_ioctl(struct tty_struct *tty, struct file *file,
                 unsigned int cmd, unsigned long arg)
{
    struct tiny_serial *tiny = tty->driver_data;
    if (cmd == TIOCMIWAIT) {
        DECLARE_WAITQUEUE(wait, current);
        struct async_icount cnow;
        struct async_icount cprev;
        cprev = tiny->icount;
        while (1) {
            add_wait_queue(&tiny->wait, &wait);
            set_current_state(TASK_INTERRUPTIBLE);
            schedule( );
            remove_wait_queue(&tiny->wait, &wait);
            /* see if a signal woke us up */
            if (signal_pending(current))
                return -ERESTARTSYS;
            cnow = tiny->icount;
            if (cnow.rng == cprev.rng && cnow.dsr == cprev.dsr &&
                cnow.dcd == cprev.dcd && cnow.cts == cprev.cts)
                return -EIO; /* no change => error */
            if (((arg & TIOCM_RNG) && (cnow.rng != cprev.rng)) ||
                ((arg & TIOCM_DSR) && (cnow.dsr != cprev.dsr)) ||
                ((arg & TIOCM_CD)  && (cnow.dcd != cprev.dcd)) ||
                ((arg & TIOCM_CTS) && (cnow.cts != cprev.cts)) ) {
                return 0;
            }
            cprev = cnow;
        }
    }
    return -ENOIOCTLCMD;
}
```

Somewhere in the tty driver's code that recognizes that the MSR register changes, the following line must be called for this code to work properly:

```
wake_up_interruptible(&tp->wait);
```

TIOCGICOUNT

Gets interrupt counts. This is called when the user wants to know how many serial line interrupts have happened. If the driver has an interrupt handler, it should define an internal structure of counters to keep track of these statistics and increment the proper counter every time the function is run by the kernel.

This *ioctl* call passes the kernel a pointer to a structure serial_icounter_struct, which should be filled by the tty driver. This call is often made in conjunction with the previous TIOCMIWAIT *ioctl* call. If the tty driver keeps track of all of these interrupts while the driver is operating, the code to implement this call can be very simple:

```
static int tiny_ioctl(struct tty_struct *tty, struct file *file,
                      unsigned int cmd, unsigned long arg)
{
    struct tiny_serial *tiny = tty->driver_data;
    if (cmd == TIOCGICOUNT) {
        struct async_icount cnow = tiny->icount;
        struct serial_icounter_struct icount;
        icount.cts  = cnow.cts;
        icount.dsr  = cnow.dsr;
        icount.rng  = cnow.rng;
        icount.dcd  = cnow.dcd;
        icount.rx   = cnow.rx;
        icount.tx   = cnow.tx;
        icount.frame    = cnow.frame;
        icount.overrun  = cnow.overrun;
        icount.parity   = cnow.parity;
        icount.brk  = cnow.brk;
        icount.buf_overrun = cnow.buf_overrun;
        if (copy_to_user((void __user *)arg, &icount, sizeof(icount)))
            return -EFAULT;
        return 0;
    }
    return -ENOIOCTLCMD;
}
```

proc and sysfs Handling of TTY Devices

The tty core provides a very easy way for any tty driver to maintain a file in the */proc/tty/driver* directory. If the driver defines the *read_proc* or *write_proc* functions, this file is created. Then, any read or write call on this file is sent to the driver. The formats of these functions are just like the standard */proc* file-handling functions.

As an example, here is a simple implementation of the *read_proc tty* callback that merely prints out the number of the currently registered ports:

```
static int tiny_read_proc(char *page, char **start, off_t off, int count,
                          int *eof, void *data)
{
    struct tiny_serial *tiny;
    off_t begin = 0;
    int length = 0;
    int i;

    length += sprintf(page, "tinyserinfo:1.0 driver:%s\n", DRIVER_VERSION);
    for (i = 0; i < TINY_TTY_MINORS && length < PAGE_SIZE; ++i) {
        tiny = tiny_table[i];
        if (tiny == NULL)
            continue;

        length += sprintf(page+length, "%d\n", i);
        if ((length + begin) > (off + count))
            goto done;
        if ((length + begin) < off) {
            begin += length;
            length = 0;
        }
    }
    *eof = 1;
done:
    if (off >= (length + begin))
        return 0;
    *start = page + (off-begin);
    return (count < begin+length-off) ? count : begin + length-off;
}
```

The tty core handles all of the sysfs directory and device creation when the tty driver is registered, or when the individual tty devices are created, depending on the TTY_DRIVER_NO_DEVFS flag in the struct tty_driver. The individual directory always contains the *dev* file, which allows user-space tools to determine the major and minor number assigned to the device. It also contains a *device* and *driver* symlink, if a pointer to a valid struct device is passed in the call to *tty_register_device*. Other than these three files, it is not possible for individual tty drivers to create new sysfs files in this location. This will probably change in future kernel releases.

The tty_driver Structure in Detail

The tty_driver structure is used to register a tty driver with the tty core. Here is a list of all of the different fields in the structure and how they are used by the tty core:

struct module *owner;
    The module owner for this driver.

`int magic;`

The "magic" value for this structure. Should always be set to `TTY_DRIVER_MAGIC`. Is initialized in the *alloc_tty_driver* function.

`const char *driver_name;`

Name of the driver, used in */proc/tty* and sysfs.

`const char *name;`

Node name of the driver.

`int name_base;`

Starting number to use when creating names for devices. This is used when the kernel creates a string representation of a specific tty device assigned to the tty driver.

`short major;`

Major number for the driver.

`short minor_start;`

Starting minor number for the driver. This is usually set to the same value as name_base. Typically, this value is set to 0.

`short num;`

Number of minor numbers assigned to the driver. If an entire major number range is used by the driver, this value should be set to 255. This variable is initialized in the *alloc_tty_driver* function.

`short type;`
`short subtype;`

Describe what kind of tty driver is being registered with the tty core. The value of subtype depends on the type. The type field can be:

`TTY_DRIVER_TYPE_SYSTEM`

Used internally by the tty subsystem to remember that it is dealing with an internal tty driver. subtype should be set to `SYSTEM_TYPE_TTY`, `SYSTEM_TYPE_CONSOLE`, `SYSTEM_TYPE_SYSCONS`, or `SYSTEM_TYPE_SYSPTMX`. This type should not be used by any "normal" tty driver.

`TTY_DRIVER_TYPE_CONSOLE`

Used only by the console driver.

`TTY_DRIVER_TYPE_SERIAL`

Used by any serial type driver. subtype should be set to `SERIAL_TYPE_NORMAL` or `SERIAL_TYPE_CALLOUT`, depending on which type your driver is. This is one of the most common settings for the type field.

`TTY_DRIVER_TYPE_PTY`

Used by the pseudo terminal interface (pty). subtype needs to be set to either `PTY_TYPE_MASTER` or `PTY_TYPE_SLAVE`.

`struct termios init_termios;`

Initial struct termios values for the device when it is created.

```
int flags;
```
Driver flags, as described earlier in this chapter.

```
struct proc_dir_entry *proc_entry;
```
This driver's *proc* entry structure. It is created by the tty core if the driver implements the *write_proc* or *read_proc* functions. This field should not be set by the tty driver itself.

```
struct tty_driver *other;
```
Pointer to a tty slave driver. This is used only by the pty driver and should not be used by any other tty driver.

```
void *driver_state;
```
Internal state of the tty driver. Should be used only by the pty driver.

```
struct tty_driver *next;
struct tty_driver *prev;
```
Linking variables. These variables are used by the tty core to chain all of the different tty drivers together, and should not be touched by any tty driver.

The tty_operations Structure in Detail

The tty_operations structure contains all of the function callbacks that can be set by a tty driver and called by the tty core. Currently, all of the function pointers contained in this structure are also in the tty_driver structure, but that will be replaced soon with only an instance of this structure.

```
int (*open)(struct tty_struct * tty, struct file * filp);
```
The *open* function.

```
void (*close)(struct tty_struct * tty, struct file * filp);
```
The *close* function.

```
int (*write)(struct tty_struct * tty, const unsigned char *buf, int count);
```
The *write* function.

```
void (*put_char)(struct tty_struct *tty, unsigned char ch);
```
The single-character *write* function. This function is called by the tty core when a single character is to be written to the device. If a tty driver does not define this function, the *write* function is called instead when the tty core wants to send a single character.

```
void (*flush_chars)(struct tty_struct *tty);
void (*wait_until_sent)(struct tty_struct *tty, int timeout);
```
The function that flushes data to the hardware.

```
int (*write_room)(struct tty_struct *tty);
```
The function that indicates how much of the buffer is free.

```
int (*chars_in_buffer)(struct tty_struct *tty);
```
The function that indicates how much of the buffer is full of data.

```
int (*ioctl)(struct tty_struct *tty, struct file * file, unsigned int cmd,
             unsigned long arg);
```
The *ioctl* function. This function is called by the tty core when *ioctl(2)* is called on the device node.

```
void (*set_termios)(struct tty_struct *tty, struct termios * old);
```
The *set_termios* function. This function is called by the tty core when the device's termios settings have been changed.

```
void (*throttle)(struct tty_struct * tty);
void (*unthrottle)(struct tty_struct * tty);
void (*stop)(struct tty_struct *tty);
void (*start)(struct tty_struct *tty);
```
Data-throttling functions. These functions are used to help control overruns of the tty core's input buffers. The *throttle* function is called when the tty core's input buffers are getting full. The tty driver should try to signal to the device that no more characters should be sent to it. The *unthrottle* function is called when the tty core's input buffers have been emptied out, and it can now accept more data. The tty driver should then signal to the device that data can be received. The *stop* and *start* functions are much like the *throttle* and *unthrottle* functions, but they signify that the tty driver should stop sending data to the device and then later resume sending data.

```
void (*hangup)(struct tty_struct *tty);
```
The *hangup* function. This function is called when the tty driver should hang up the tty device. Any special hardware manipulation needed to do this should occur at this time.

```
void (*break_ctl)(struct tty_struct *tty, int state);
```
The *line break* control function. This function is called when the tty driver is to turn on or off the line BREAK status on the RS-232 port. If state is set to -1, the BREAK status should be turned on. If state is set to 0, the BREAK status should be turned off. If this function is implemented by the tty driver, the tty core will handle the TCSBRK, TCSBRKP, TIOCSBRK, and TIOCCBRK *ioctls*. Otherwise, these *ioctls* are sent to the driver to the *ioctl* function.

```
void (*flush_buffer)(struct tty_struct *tty);
```
Flush buffer and lose any remaining data.

```
void (*set_ldisc)(struct tty_struct *tty);
```
The *set line discipline* function. This function is called when the tty core has changed the line discipline of the tty driver. This function is generally not used and should not be defined by a driver.

```
void (*send_xchar)(struct tty_struct *tty, char ch);
```
Send *X-type char* function. This function is used to send a high-priority XON or XOFF character to the tty device. The character to be sent is specified in the ch variable.

```
int (*read_proc)(char *page, char **start, off_t off, int count, int *eof,
                void *data);
int (*write_proc)(struct file *file, const char *buffer, unsigned long count,
                void *data);
```
    /proc read and write functions.

```
int (*tiocmget)(struct tty_struct *tty, struct file *file);
```
    Gets the current line settings of the specific tty device. If retrieved successfully
    from the tty device, the value should be returned to the caller.

```
int (*tiocmset)(struct tty_struct *tty, struct file *file, unsigned int set,
                unsigned int clear);
```
    Sets the current line settings of the specific tty device. set and clear contain the
    different line settings that should either be set or cleared.

The tty_struct Structure in Detail

The tty_struct variable is used by the tty core to keep the current state of a specific
tty port. Almost all of its fields are to be used only by the tty core, with a few exceptions. The fields that a tty driver can use are described here:

```
unsigned long flags;
```
    The current state of the tty device. This is a bitfield variable and is accessed
    through the following macros:

    TTY_THROTTLED
        Set when the driver has had the *throttle* function called. Should not be set by
        a tty driver, only the tty core.

    TTY_IO_ERROR
        Set by the driver when it does not want any data to be read from or written
        to the driver. If a user program attempts to do this, it receives an -EIO error
        from the kernel. This is usually set as the device is shutting down.

    TTY_OTHER_CLOSED
        Used only by the pty driver to notify when the port has been closed.

    TTY_EXCLUSIVE
        Set by the tty core to indicate that a port is in exclusive mode and can only
        be accessed by one user at a time.

    TTY_DEBUG
        Not used anywhere in the kernel.

    TTY_DO_WRITE_WAKEUP
        If this is set, the line discipline's *write_wakeup* function is allowed to be
        called. This is usually called at the same time the *wake_up_interruptible*
        function is called by the tty driver.

```
```

TTY_PUSH

Used only internally by the default tty line discipline.

TTY_CLOSING

Used by the tty core to keep track if a port is in the process of closing at that moment in time or not.

TTY_DONT_FLIP

Used by the default tty line discipline to notify the tty core that it should not change the flip buffer when it is set.

TTY_HW_COOK_OUT

If set by a tty driver, it notifies the line discipline that it will "cook" the output sent to it. If it is not set, the line discipline copies output of the driver in chunks; otherwise, it has to evaluate every byte sent individually for line changes. This flag should generally not be set by a tty driver.

TTY_HW_COOK_IN

Almost identical to setting the TTY_DRIVER_REAL_RAW flag in the driver flags variable. This flag should generally not be set by a tty driver.

TTY_PTY_LOCK

Used by the pty driver to lock and unlock a port.

TTY_NO_WRITE_SPLIT

If set, the tty core does not split up writes to the tty driver into normal-sized chunks. This value should not be used to prevent denial-of-service attacks on tty ports by sending large amounts of data to a port.

`struct tty_flip_buffer flip;`

The flip buffer for the tty device.

`struct tty_ldisc ldisc;`

The line discipline for the tty device.

`wait_queue_head_t write_wait;`

The *wait_queue* for the tty writing function. A tty driver should wake this up to signal when it can receive more data.

`struct termios *termios;`

Pointer to the current termios settings for the tty device.

`unsigned char stopped:1;`

Indicates whether the tty device is stopped. The tty driver can set this value.

`unsigned char hw_stopped:1;`

Indicates whether or not the tty device's hardware is stopped. The tty driver can set this value.

`unsigned char low_latency:1;`

Indicates whether the tty device is a low-latency device, capable of receiving data at a very high rate of speed. The tty driver can set this value.

`unsigned char closing:1;`
> Indicates whether the tty device is in the middle of closing the port. The tty driver can set this value.

`struct tty_driver driver;`
> The current `tty_driver` structure that controls this tty device.

`void *driver_data;`
> A pointer that the `tty_driver` can use to store data local to the tty driver. This variable is not modified by the tty core.

Quick Reference

This section provides a reference for the concepts introduced in this chapter. It also explains the role of each header file that a tty driver needs to include. The lists of fields in the `tty_driver` and `tty_device` structures, however, are not repeated here.

`#include <linux/tty_driver.h>`
> Header file that contains the definition of struct `tty_driver` and declares some of the different flags used in this structure.

`#include <linux/tty.h>`
> Header file that contains the definition of struct `tty_struct` and a number of different macros to access the individual values of the struct `termios` fields easily. It also contains the function declarations of the tty driver core.

`#include <linux/tty_flip.h>`
> Header file that contains some tty flip buffer inline functions that make it easier to manipulate the flip buffer structures.

`#include <asm/termios.h>`
> Header file that contains the definition of struct `termio` for the specific hardware platform the kernel is built for.

`struct tty_driver *alloc_tty_driver(int lines);`
> Function that creates a struct `tty_driver` that can be later passed to the *tty_register_driver* and *tty_unregister_driver* functions.

`void put_tty_driver(struct tty_driver *driver);`
> Function that cleans up a struct `tty_driver` structure that has not been successfully registered with the tty core.

`void tty_set_operations(struct tty_driver *driver, struct tty_operations *op);`
> Function that initializes the function callbacks of a struct `tty_driver`. This is necessary to call before *tty_register_driver* can be called.

`int tty_register_driver(struct tty_driver *driver);`
`int tty_unregister_driver(struct tty_driver *driver);`
> Functions that register and unregister a tty driver from the tty core.

```
void tty_register_device(struct tty_driver *driver, unsigned minor, struct
                         device *device);
void tty_unregister_device(struct tty_driver *driver, unsigned minor);
```
Functions that register and unregister a single tty device with the tty core.

```
void tty_insert_flip_char(struct tty_struct *tty, unsigned char ch,
                          char flag);
```
Function that inserts characters into the tty device's flip buffer to be read by a user.

TTY_NORMAL
TTY_BREAK
TTY_FRAME
TTY_PARITY
TTY_OVERRUN

Different values for the flag paramater used in the *tty_insert_flip_char* function.

```
int tty_get_baud_rate(struct tty_struct *tty);
```
Function that gets the baud rate currently set for the specific tty device.

```
void tty_flip_buffer_push(struct tty_struct *tty);
```
Function that pushes the data in the current flip buffer to the user.

tty_std_termios

Variable that initializes a termios structure with a common set of default line settings.

Bibliography

Most of the information in this book has been extracted from the kernel sources, which are the best documentation about the Linux kernel.

Kernel sources can be retrieved from hundreds of FTP sites around the world, so we won't list them here.

Version dependencies are best checked by looking at the patches, which are available from the same places where you get the whole source. The program called *repatch* might help you in checking how a single file has been modified throughout the different kernel patches; it is available in the source files provided on the O'Reilly FTP site.

Books

While the bookstores are full of technical books, there are surprisingly few that are directly relevant to Linux kernel programming. Here is a selection of books found on our shelves.

Linux Kernel

Bovet, Daniel P. and Marco Cesate. *Understanding the Linux Kernel,* Second Edition. Sebastopol, CA: O'Reilly & Associates, Inc. 2003. This book covers the design and implementation of the Linux kernel in great detail. It is more oriented toward providing an understanding of the algorithms used than documenting the kernel API. This book covers the 2.4 kernel but still contains a great deal of useful information.

Gorman, Mel. *Understanding the Linux Virtual Memory Manager.* Upper Saddle River, NJ: Prentice Hall PTR, 2004. Developers wanting to know more about the Linux virtual memory subsystem may wish to have a look at this book. It is centered around the 2.4 kernel but contains 2.6 information as well.

Love, Robert. *Linux Kernel Development.* Indianapolis: Sams Publishing, 2004. This book covers Linux kernel programming with a broad scope. It is a reference that should be on every Linux hacker's bookshelf.

Yaghmour, Karim. *Building Embedded Systems.* Sebastopol, CA: O'Reilly & Associates, Inc. 2003. This book will be useful to those writing Linux code for embedded systems.

Unix Design and Internals

Bach, Maurice. *The Design of the Unix Operating System.* Upper Saddle River, NJ: Prentice Hall, 1987. Though quite old, this book covers all the issues related to Unix implementations. It was the main source of inspiration for Linus in the first Linux version.

Stevens, Richard. *Advanced Programming in the UNIX Environment.* Boston: Addison-Wesley, 1992. Every detail of Unix system calls is described herein, which is a good companion when implementing advanced features in the device methods.

Stevens, Richard. *Unix Network Programming.* Upper Saddle River, NJ: Prentice Hall PTR, 1990. Perhaps the definitive book on the Unix network programming API.

Web Sites

In the fast-moving world of Linux kernel development, the most current information is often found online. The following is our selection of the best web sites as of this writing:

http://www.kernel.org
ftp://ftp.kernel.org
This site is the home of Linux kernel development. You'll find the latest kernel release and related information. Note that the FTP site is mirrored throughout the world, so you'll most likely find a mirror near you.

http://www.bkbits.net
This site hosts the source repositories used by a number of prominent kernel developers. In particular, the project called "linus" contains the mainline kernel as maintained by Linus Torvalds. If you are curious about the very latest patches which have been applied to the kernel, this is the place to look.

http://www.tldp.org
The Linux Documentation Project carries a lot of interesting documents called "HOWTOs"; some of them are pretty technical and cover kernel-related topics.

http://www.linux.it/kerneldocs
This page contains many kernel-oriented magazine articles written by Alessandro Rubini. Some of them date back a few years, but they usually still apply;

some of them are in Italian, but usually an English translation is available as well.

http://lwn.net

At the risk of seeming self-serving, we point out this news site that, among other things, offers regular kernel development coverage and API change information.

http://www.kerneltraffic.org

Kernel Traffic is a popular site that provides weekly summaries of discussions on the Linux kernel development mailing list.

http://www.kerneltrap.org/

This site picks up occasional interesting developments in the Linux and BSD kernel communities.

http://www.kernelnewbies.org

This site is oriented toward new kernel developers. There is beginning information, a FAQ, and an associated IRC channel for those looking for immediate assistance.

http://janitor.kernelnewbies.org/

The Linux Kernel Janitor project is the place where new kernel programmers can learn how to join in the development effort. A wide range of small, generally simple tasks that need to be done all over the kernel are described here. There is a mailing list that helps new developers get these changes into the main kernel tree. This is a great place for anyone wanting to start doing Linux kernel development but not knowing where to begin.

Index

We'd like to hear your suggestions for improving our indexes. Send email to *index@oreilly.com*.

B

back-casting kobject pointers, 365
barriers
  memory, 237, 238, 255
  requests, 485
base module parameter, 247
baud rates (tty drivers), 562
BCD (binary-coded decimal) forms, 346
bEndpointAddress field (USB), 330
bibliography, 575
big-endian byte order, 293
bi_io_vec array, 482
binary attributes (kobjects), 374
binary-coded decimal (BCD) forms, 346
bin_attribute structure, 374
bInterval field (USB), 331
bio structure, 482, 487
bitfields (ioctl commands), 137, 180
bits
  clearing, 269
  operations, 126
  specifications, 246
BLK_BOUNCE_HIGH symbol, 480
blk_cleanup_queue function, 479
blkdev_dequeue_request function, 479
blk_queue_hardsect_size function, 470
blk_queue_segment_boundary function, 481
block devices, 7
block drivers
  command pre-preparation, 491
  functions, 494–496
  operations, 471–474
  registration, 465–470
  request processing, 474–491
  TCQ, 492–493
block_fsync method, 167
blocking
  I/O, 147–162, 176
  open method, 176
  operations, 151
  release method, 176
bmAttributes field (USB), 330
BogoMips value, 195
boot time (memory allocation), 230, 234
booting (PCI), 306
bottom halves
  interrupt handlers, 275–278
  tasklets and, 276
bounce buffers, 445
  block drivers, 480
  streaming DMA mappings and, 449
bridges, 303

BSS segments, 419
buffers
  allocation of, 530
  bounce, 445
    block drivers, 480
    streaming DMA mappings and, 449
  circular, 78, 123
  DMA (unmapping), 449
  freeing, 531
  I/O, 151
  large (obtaining), 230, 234
  output, 152
  overrun errors, 9, 95
  for printk function, 78
  ring (DMA), 441
  socket (see socket buffers)
  sockets, 522, 528–532
  synchronization, 452
  transfers, 448
  tty drivers, 558
  USB, 338
  user space (direct I/O), 436
  write-buffering example, 282
bugs (see debugging; troubleshooting)
BULK endpoints (USB), 330
bulk urbs (USB), 343
bus_add_driver function, 396
BUS_ATTR macro, 380
bus_attribute type, 380
buses
  addresses, 413, 443
  attributes, 380
  functions, 409
  IEEE1394 (Firewire), 400
  iteration, 379
  Linux device model, 377–381
  match function, 379
  methods, 379
  PCI (see PCI)
  registers, 445
  registration, 378
  USB (see USB)
bus_for_each_dev function, 380
bus_register function, 378
bus_type structure, 378
busy loops, 191
busy-waiting implementation, 190
bytes
  CSIZE bitmask, 561
  order, 293
  orders, 300

About the Authors

Jonathan Corbet got his first look at the BSD Unix source back in 1981, when an instructor at the University of Colorado let him "fix" the paging algorithm. He has been digging around inside every system he could get his hands on ever since, working on drivers for VAX, Sun, Ardent, and x86 systems. He got his first Linux system in 1993 and has never looked back. Jonathan is currently the cofounder and executive editor of *Linux Weekly News* (*http://www.LWN.net*). He lives in Boulder, Colorado with his wife and two children.

Alessandro Rubini installed Linux 0.99.14 soon after getting his degree as an electronic engineer. He then received a Ph.D. in computer science at the University of Pavia despite his aversion toward modern technology. He left the University after getting his Ph.D. because he didn't want to write articles. He now works as a freelancer, writing device drivers and articles. He used to be a young hacker before his babies were born; now he's an old advocate of free software who developed a bias for non-PC computer platforms.

Greg Kroah-Hartman has been writing Linux kernel drivers since 1999 and is currently the maintainer for the USB, PCI, I2C, driver core, and sysfs kernel subsystems. He is also the maintainer of the udev and hotplug userspace programs, as well as a Gentoo kernel maintainer, ensuring that his inbox is never empty. He is a contributing editor to *Linux Journal* magazine.

Colophon

Our look is the result of reader comments, our own experimentation, and feedback from distribution channels. Distinctive covers complement our distinctive approach to technical topics, breathing personality and life into potentially dry subjects.

The image on the cover of *Linux Device Drivers*, Third Edition is a bucking bronco. A colorful description of this animal appears in *Marvels of the New West: A Vivid Portrayal of the Stupendous Marvels in the Vast Wonderland West of the Missouri River*, by William Thayer (The Henry Bill Publishing Co., Norwich, CT, 1888). Thayer quotes a stockman, who gives this description of a bucking horse: "When a horse bucks he puts his head down between his legs, arches his back like an angry cat, and springs into the air with all his legs at once, coming down again with a frightful jar, and he sometimes keeps on repeating the performance until he is completely worn out with the excursion. The rider is apt to feel rather worn out too by that time, if he has kept his seat, which is not a very easy matter, especially if the horse is a real scientific bucker, and puts a kind of side action into every jump. The double girth commonly attached to these Mexican saddles is useful for keeping the saddle in its place during one of those bouts, but there is no doubt that they frequently make a horse buck who would not do so with a single girth. With some animals you can never draw up the flank girth without setting them bucking."

Matt Hutchinson was the production editor for *Linux Device Drivers*, Third Edition. Octal Publishing, Inc. provided production services. Genevieve d'Entremont, Sanders Kleinfeld, and Claire Cloutier provided quality control.

Edie Freedman designed the cover of this book, based on a series design by herself and Hanna Dyer. The cover image is a 19th-century engraving from the Dover Pictorial Archive. Emma Colby produced the cover layout with Adobe InDesign CS using Adobe's ITC Garamond font.

Melanie Wang designed the interior layout, based on a series design by David Futato. The chapter opening images are from the Dover Pictorial Archive, *Marvels of the New West*, and *The Pioneer History of America: A Popular Account of the Heroes and Adventures*, by Augustus Lynch Mason, A.M. (The Jones Brothers Publishing Company, 1884). This book was converted by Julie Hawks to FrameMaker 5.5.6 with a format conversion tool created by Erik Ray, Jason McIntosh, Neil Walls, and Mike Sierra that uses Perl and XML technologies. The text font is Linotype Birka; the heading font is Adobe Myriad Condensed; and the code font is LucasFont's TheSans Mono Condensed. The illustrations that appear in the book were produced by Robert Romano, Jessamyn Read, and Lesley Borash using Macromedia FreeHand MX and Adobe Photoshop CS. The tip and warning icons were drawn by Christopher Bing.

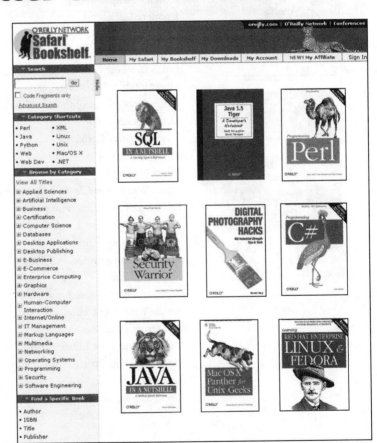

Related Titles Available from O'Reilly

Linux

Building Embedded Linux Systems
Building Secure Servers with Linux
The Complete FreeBSD, *4th Edition*
Even Grues Get Full
Exploring the JDS Linux Desktop
Extreme Programming Pocket Guide
Knoppix Hacks
Learning Red Hat Enterprise Linux and Fedora, *4th Edition*
Linux Cookbook
Linux in a Nutshell, *4th Edition*
Linux iptables Pocket Reference
Linux Network Administrator's Guide, *3rd Edition*
Linux Pocket Guide
Linux Security Cookbook
Linux Server Hacks
Linux Unwired
Linux Web Server CD Bookshelf, *Version 2.0*
LPI Linux Certification in a Nutshell, *2nd Edition*
Managing RAID on Linux
OpenOffice.org Writer
Programming with Qt, *2nd Edition*
Root of all Evil
Running Linux, *4th Edition*
Samba Pocket Reference, *2nd Edition*
Test Driving Linux
Understanding the Linux Kernel, *2nd Edition*
Understanding Open Source & Free Software Licensing
User Friendly
Using Samba, *3rd Edition*

Keep in touch with O'Reilly

1. Download examples from our books

To find example files for a book, go to:

www.oreilly.com/catalog

select the book, and follow the "Examples" link.

2. Register your O'Reilly books

Register your book at *register.oreilly.com*

Why register your books?
Once you've registered your O'Reilly books you can:

- Win O'Reilly books, T-shirts or discount coupons in our monthly drawing.
- Get special offers available only to registered O'Reilly customers.
- Get catalogs announcing new books (US and UK only).
- Get email notification of new editions of the O'Reilly books you own.

3. Join our email lists

Sign up to get topic-specific email announcements of new books and conferences, special offers, and O'Reilly Network technology newsletters at:

elists.oreilly.com

It's easy to customize your free elists subscription so you'll get exactly the O'Reilly news you want.

4. Get the latest news, tips, and tools

www.oreilly.com

- "Top 100 Sites on the Web"—PC Magazine
- CIO Magazine's Web Business 50 Awards

Our web site contains a library of comprehensive product information (including book excerpts and tables of contents), downloadable software, background articles, interviews with technology leaders, links to relevant sites, book cover art, and more.

5. Work for O'Reilly

Check out our web site for current employment opportunities:

jobs.oreilly.com

6. Contact us

O'Reilly & Associates
1005 Gravenstein Hwy North
Sebastopol, CA 95472 USA

TEL: 707-827-7000 or 800-998-9938
(6am to 5pm PST)

FAX: 707-829-0104

order@oreilly.com
For answers to problems regarding your order or our products. To place a book order online, visit:

www.oreilly.com/order_new

catalog@oreilly.com
To request a copy of our latest catalog.

booktech@oreilly.com
For book content technical questions or corrections.

corporate@oreilly.com
For educational, library, government, and corporate sales.

proposals@oreilly.com
To submit new book proposals to our editors and product managers.

international@oreilly.com
For information about our international distributors or translation queries. For a list of our distributors outside of North America check out:

international.oreilly.com/distributors.html

adoption@oreilly.com
For information about academic use of O'Reilly books, visit:

academic.oreilly.com

O'REILLY®

Our books are available at most retail and online bookstores.
To order direct: 1-800-998-9938 • order@oreilly.com • www.oreilly.com
Online editions of most O'Reilly titles are available by subscription at safari.oreilly.com